W9-CMR-946

HISTORICAL DICTIONARIES OF SPORTS
Jon Woronoff, Series Editor

1. *Competitive Swimming*, by John Lohn, 2010.
2. *Basketball*, by John Grasso, 2011.
3. *Golf*, by Bill Mallon and Randon Jerris, 2011.

Historical Dictionary of Golf

Bill Mallon
Randon Jerris

Historical Dictionaries of Sports, No. 3

The Scarecrow Press, Inc.
Lanham • Toronto • Plymouth, UK
2011

Published by Scarecrow Press, Inc.
A wholly owned subsidiary of The Rowman & Littlefield Publishing Group, Inc.
4501 Forbes Boulevard, Suite 200, Lanham, Maryland 20706
http://www.scarecrowpress.com

Estover Road, Plymouth PL6 7PY, United Kingdom

British Library Cataloguing in Publication Information Available

Library of Congress Cataloging-in-Publication Data

Mallon, Bill.
Historical dictionary of golf / Bill Mallon, Randon Jerris.
p. cm. — (Historical dictionaries of sports ; no. 3)
Includes bibliographical references.
ISBN 978-0-8108-7197-7 (cloth : alk. paper) — ISBN 978-0-8108-7465-7 (ebook)
1. Golf—History—Dictionaries. I. Jerris, Randon Matthew Newman, 1969–. II. Title.
GV963.M25 2011
796.35203—dc22 2010030030

∞™ The paper used in this publication meets the minimum requirements of American National Standard for Information Sciences—Permanence of Paper for Printed Library Materials, ANSI/NISO Z39.48-1992.

Printed in the United States of America

All photos in this book courtesy of the USGA

Contents

Editor's Foreword *Jon Woronoff* vii

Preface ix

Acronyms and Abbreviations xi

Chronology xiii

Introduction 1

The Dictionary 25

Appendixes

1. World Golf Hall of Fame 346
2. Men's Major Professional Champions 350
3. Women's Major Professional Champions 380
4. Other Professional Champions 402
5. International Team Events 493
6. Men's Major Amateur Champions 527
7. Women's Major Amateur Champions 583
8. Other USGA Champions 636
9. Other International Champions 658
10. Professional Tour Awards 668
11. Other Awards 694

Bibliography 725

About the Authors 797

Editor's Foreword

There will eventually be many more books in this series, as there are a multitude of sports practiced around the world. Yet none of them is quite like golf. It is hardly unique in its characteristics, but there is something special about it. Since there are variations for the handicapped, it can be played by nearly everyone. It is played by an enormous number of amateurs—more than almost any other sport. And that number is increasing around the world—not only in Europe and the United States, but the rest of the Americas, Africa, and parts of Asia. Although golfers are part of a social nexus playing both with and/or against others, golf is not a team sport. It leaves room for individuals to compete not only against others but also (and this is particularly significant) against themselves. Most strikingly, it is a sport one can begin playing at a young age and continue playing when most other sports have been forgotten or can no longer be played; therefore, it is a large part of the lifestyles of many retired people. It is hardly surprising that golf has become one of the most popular sports in the world.

The *Historical Dictionary of Golf* details this sport and its history through the use of a chronology, an introduction, and hundreds of dictionary entries that do more than just relate facts and figures, accomplishments and records. They show what golf is like to practitioners and spectators by providing extensive information on rules and regulations, gear and equipment, more notable golf courses and competitions, and, above all, many of the world's top golfers over the 20th and into the 21st centuries. While the vast majority of golfers do this mainly for recreation or fun, there is usually a competitive angle; thus it is helpful to have handy lists of winners of the major tournaments in the appendixes. Finally, there is a substantial bibliography containing a variety of books—some of a do-it-yourself nature, others providing tips from the pros, a large number of more scholarly works, and, to top it all off, books by and about leading golfers.

This volume was written by Bill Mallon and Randon Jerris. Dr. Mallon is an orthopedic surgeon who has written extensively on medicine and is presently the editor in chief of the *Journal of Shoulder and Elbow Surgery*. His other career was in golf, both as an amateur and a professional, culminating in his playing on the U.S. PGA tour from 1975 to 1979. He has also written on sports history, in particular, the Olympics. This includes several books on the earliest Olympic Games and three editions of the *Historical Dictionary of the Olympic Movement*, which have since become part of this new series, Historical Dictionaries of Sports. Randon Jerris, who holds a Ph.D. in art and archaeology, also has special insight into golf, having worked for the U.S. Golf Association since 1988 in various capacities. These include historian, librarian, and, in particular, since 2002, director of the USGA Museum. He has also written extensively on golf, including the award-winning *Golf's Golden Age*. Between them, Drs. Mallon and Jerris have produced an exceptional compendium to be treasured by any golfer who takes a serious interest in the sport.

Jon Woronoff
Series Editor

Preface

Golf has been described as the game of a lifetime, played by both young toddlers and older adults—often into their 80s and 90s. Just as the game often has a long history in a person's lifetime, the game of golf has a long history as well. Its origins can be traced at least as far back as the 15th century in Scotland, and there is evidence that golf-like games existed for a few centuries prior to that in the Low Countries of Europe. Thus, writing a historical dictionary of the game seemed a daunting task. But it has been an enjoyable, educational experience.

This is my second project for Scarecrow Press in the Historical Dictionary series, following three editions of the *Historical Dictionary of the Olympic Movement*, the first two of which I wrote with the late British Olympic historian Ian Buchanan. When Jon Woronoff approached me about writing a *Historical Dictionary of Golf*, it was easy to agree to the project, given my own personal history with the game, which is much deeper than any active competitive experience I have had in Olympic sports.

While I briefly competed as a cyclist in the early 1960s, in the mid-1960s I turned to golf and later played the game at Duke University. For four years, from 1975 to 1979, I was a professional on the PGA Tour. During that time, I assembled a large collection of books on golf, so I could do much of the research for this book from my home library. The Internet, and its vast resources, also makes such projects easier these days. Despite my background in golf, and what I thought was a pretty good grasp on its history, I was surprised by how much I learned while completing the book.

I have been aided by Dr. Randon Jerris, whose assistance has greatly improved the book. Rand and I share an affiliation with Duke, where he did graduate work in geology, followed by master's degrees and a Ph.D. in art and archaeology from Princeton. But since 1988, he has worked for the U.S. Golf Association, first as an intern and curatorial assistant, then as historian and librarian of the USGA Library, and, since 2002, as the director of the USGA Museum. I cannot overstate my thanks to him.

Other people have also been very helpful. Hilary Evans, my Welsh e-mail pal, who works on the genealogy of seemingly every Olympic athlete ever, provided a huge amount of new information on obscure facts about older golfers, often from the nineteenth century. As always, he answered all my queries quickly and willingly.

I owe special thanks to Rhonda Glenn, Nancy Stulack, and David Fay, all of whom are with the USGA, who, by mining the USGA Archives, found and provided material we requested. In addition to the USGA, archivists at the Royal and Ancient, the Ladies Golf Union of Great Britain, the Royal Canadian Golf Association, and various national golf federations were especially helpful. David Fay was also very kind in allowing us to use photographs from the USGA collection in return for some earlier work done for the USGA.

Many of the golfers, architects, and other golf luminaries whose bios can be found in this volume contributed by personally answering my somewhat inane questions about obscure facets of their lives. I thank them all, though they are too numerous to mention by name.

Finally, my wife, Karen, continues to allow me hours at the computer, working on various projects that bring me joy but sometimes keep me away from her more than they should—and for her patience I am ever appreciative. There are five dogs who share such a fate as well, so to Kaci, Murphy, Maggie, Marty, and Barney I promise that in 2010 we'll take more hikes up the Piper Trail.

* * *

I hope you like it.

Bill Mallon, M.D.

Acronyms and Abbreviations

AIAW	Association for Intercollegiate Athletics for Women
AJGA	American Junior Golf Association
ASGCA	American Society of Golf Course Architects
CC	Country Club
DGWS	Division for Girls' and Women's Sports
DQ	Disqualification
EIGCA	European Institute of Golf Course Architects
G&CC	Golf and Country Club
GC	Golf Club/Golf Course
GCSAA	Golf Course Superintendents' Association of America
GIR	Green in regulation
GWAA	Golf Writers Association of America
IGF	International Golf Federation
IOC	International Olympic Committee
JGTO	Japan Golf Tour Organization
LET	Ladies' European Tour
LGU	Ladies' Golf Union
LPGA	Ladies' Professional Golf Association
NAGA	National Amputee Golf Association
NCAA	National Collegiate Athletic Association
NGF	National Golf Foundation
OB	Out-of-bounds
PGA	Professional Golfers' Association
PPA	Professional Putters' Association
Q School	Qualifying School
R&A	Royal and Ancient Golf Club of St. Andrews, Scotland
RCGA	Royal Canadian Golf Association
TPC	Tournament Player's Championship/Club
UGA	United Golfers Association

USBGA	United States Blind Golfers Association
USGA	United States Golf Association
WGA	Western Golf Association
WGF	World Golf Foundation
WPGA	Women's Professional Golf Association

Chronology

1297 A golf-like game, *kolven*, is first recorded as being played on 26 February in Loenen aan de Vecht, in the Netherlands.

1353 The first reference to *chole*, the probable antecedent of golf, is recorded cross-country in Flanders (Belgium). It is a derivative of hockey played by hitting balls with clubs toward a fixed mark.

1421 A Scottish regiment assisting the French at the Siege of Bauge against the English is introduced to the game of chole. Hugh Kennedy, Robert Stewart, and John Smale, three of the known players, are credited with introducing the game to Scotland.

1457 The Scottish Parliament, under King James II of Scotland, bans golf and futball (soccer) and encourages the practice of archery. This was the first of three times that the Scottish Parliament banned *gowf*.

1471 Golf is again banned in Scotland, this time by King James III.

1491 The golf ban is affirmed again by parliament, this time by King James IV.

1502 With the signing of the Treaty of Glasgow between England and Scotland, the ban on golf is lifted. King James IV makes the first recorded purchase of golf equipment, a set of clubs from a bow maker in Perth, Scotland.

1504 King James IV displays his own affinity for the game by playing golf with the Earl of Bothwell.

1513 Queen Catherine of Aragon, in a letter to Cardinal Wolsey, refers to the growing popularity of golf in England.

1527 The obituary of Sir Robert Maule references his playing golf on Barry Links, Angus (near the modern-day town of Carnoustie), this being the first reference to golf played on "links."

1552 The first evidence of golf being played at St. Andrews, Scotland, is recorded, indicating, however, that golf had been played there for many years prior.

1553 The archbishop of St. Andrews confirms the right of the local populace to play golf on the links at St. Andrews.

1554 The record books of the Town Council of Edinburgh reference the golf ball makers of Leith, with indications that these early golf balls were made of leather.

1567 Mary, Queen of Scots, is criticized for playing golf at Seton shortly after the death of her husband, Lord Darnley. Although the tale could be apocryphal, many historians regard her as the first known female golfer.

1589 Golf is banned in the Blackfriars Yard, Glasgow. This is the earliest reference to golf in the west of Scotland.

1592 The City of Edinburgh Town Council bans golfing at Leith on Sunday "in tyme of sermonis." It is the first documented ban of golf on the Sabbath issued by a government body.

1593 The Edinburgh Town Council amends its Sunday golfing ban to apply only "during divine services."

1603 King James VI (James I of England) appoints William Mayne his personal clubmaker.

1608 Legendary founding of the Royal Blackheath Golf Club, marking the migration of golf to England. However, the earliest documentary evidence for the club dates from 1783.

1618 King James VI appoints James Melvill, William Berwick, and associates golf ball makers, with a monopoly granted to make and sell golf balls at four pence apiece. King James VI (James I of England) confirms the right of the populace to play golf on Sundays, provided that citizens first attend church services.

1621 The first reference to golf on the links of Dornoch (later Royal Dornoch), in the far north of Scotland, is recorded.

1627 Record books of James Graham, a student at St. Andrews University, include the first mention of a player employing a porter (caddie) to carry his clubs.

1633 King Charles I rules that people should not be molested during lawful recreations, such as golf, provided they have done their divine services first.

1636 The first documented reference to iron clubs, as well as clubs designed specifically for playing from a bunker, appears in a Latin grammar written in Aberdeen, Scotland. This document also contains the earliest known reference to teeing a ball as well as the first direct reference to a "hole."

1641 Charles I is playing golf at Leith when he learns of the Irish Rebellion, marking the beginning of the English Civil War. He finishes his round.

1642 John Dickson receives a license as ball maker for Aberdeen, Scotland.

1658 Golf in London is mentioned for the first time, at "Tuttlefields."

1672 Earliest documentary evidence of golf at Musselburgh, Scotland is recorded.

1682 In the first recorded international golf match, the Duke of York and John Paterson of Scotland defeat two English noblemen in a match played on the links of Leith. Andrew Dickson, carrying clubs for the Duke of York, is the first recorded caddie.

1687 The diary of Thomas Kincaid, a doctor from Edinburgh, contains the first references on how golf clubs are made as well as the earliest known practical golf instruction, providing the earliest comprehensive insight into the game.

1690 The earliest documented reference to "putting" is recorded in a letter written by James Ogilvie of Banffshire.

1691 A letter written by Professor Alexander Munro, a regent at the University of St. Andrews, contains the reference to a "set" of golf clubs comprising a "play club, scraper, and tin faced club."

1717 James Brownhill constructs a tavern on the Bruntsfield Links in Edinburgh; known as "Golfhall," the tavern serves as the first clubhouse in the history of the game.

1718 Records of the Edinburgh Town Council refer to the "first hole" at Bruntsfield Links, indicating that golf courses were laid out on a permanent basis with a predetermined route for players to follow.

1721 A poem written by Allan Ramsay introduces the word "driving" into the lexicon of the game.

1724 "A solemn match of golf" between Alexander Elphinston and Captain John Porteous becomes the first match reported in a newspaper (*Caledonian Mercury*). Elphinston fights and wins a duel on the same ground in 1729.

1729 An inventory of the estate of William Burnet, governor of Massachusetts, includes a reference to golf clubs and may be the earliest mention of golf in America.

1735 This is traditionally considered the year of the formation of the Edinburgh Burgess Golfing Society, often cited as the first golf club in the history of the game.

1743 Thomas Mathison's epic *The Goff, an Heroi-Comical Poem in Three Cantos* is the first publication devoted solely to golf. It contains the first detailed description of the manufacture of a featherie ball as well as the first use of the word "green" to describe the putting area around the hole. Customs accounts document a shipment of 96 golf clubs and 432 golf balls from Leith, Scotland, to Charleston, South Carolina.

1744 The Town Council of Edinburgh formally recognizes the formation of "The Gentlemen Golfers" (later called the Honourable Company of Edinburgh Golfers), playing at Leith Links. It is the first documented formation of a golf club. They write the earliest known set of rules, which are often called "Thirteen Articles" or "Articles and Laws in Playing at Golf." The City of Edinburgh purchases a Silver Club to be awarded to the annual champion inan open competition played at Leith Links. John Rattray is the first champion of the oldest documented golf trophy.

1748 Documentary evidence is recorded of a shipment of golf clubs and golf balls from Scotland to Russia.

1750 Customs accounts document shipments of golf clubs and golf balls from Greenock, Scotland, to Virginia.

1754 The St. Andrews Society (forerunner of the Royal and Ancient Golf Club of St. Andrews), comprising 22 members, is formed. The Society adopts a code of rules that largely follows the "Thirteen Articles" of The Gentlemen Golfers. Golfers at St. Andrews purchase a silver club for a competition played over the 22 holes of the Old Course. Bailie William Landale is the first champion.

1758 The first formal amendment to the "Thirteen Articles" is adopted, asserting the obligation of the golfer to "play the ball where it lies."

1759 Earliest documentary evidence of a stroke-play competition at St. Andrews is recorded. Previously, most competitions were conducted at match play, although there is evidence that the competitions for the Leith Silver Club may have been stroke-play events.

1762 A notice printed in *Faulkners Dublin Journal* provides the earliest reference to the formation of a golf club in Ireland.

1764 The competition for the Silver Club at Leith is restricted to members of the Honourable Company of Edinburgh Golfers. The first four holes at St. Andrews are combined into two, reducing the round from 22 holes (11 out and in) to 18 (nine out and in). St. Andrews becomes the first 18-hole golf course and sets the standard for future courses.

1765 The customs acounts of Glasgow and West Lothian document shipping golf clubs and golf balls to Maryland and North Carolina.

1766 The Blackheath Club, near London, becomes the first golf club formed outside of Scotland, with a silver club donated for a competition on its links. Golf was known to be played there as early as 1608. The earliest reference to the existence of a "Golf House" at St. Andrews documents the increasing social aspects of the game.

1767 James Durham returns a score of 94 in winning the Silver Club at St. Andrews, setting a course record that remained unbroken for 86 years. The account book of a wine merchant from Bordeaux contains the first documented reference to golf in France.

1768 The Golf House at Leith is erected. It is the first known custom-built golf clubhouse.

1771 The minute book of The Gentlemen Golfers contains the earliest recorded usage of the term "cadie."

1772 The publication of *Sermons to Gentlemen upon Temperance and Exercise* by Benjamin Rush marks the first reference to golf in an American publication, extolling golf as a healthy recreation. Thomas McMillan offers a silver cup for competition at Musselburgh. He wins the first competition. The Edinburgh Burgess Society hires a "green-keeper," whose functions are to tend the green, maintain the holes, serve as caddie for the captain of the club, and serve as a waiter at dinner.

1779 *Rivington's Royal Gazette*, published in New York, contains an advertisement for the sale of golf clubs and golf balls.

1780 The Society of Aberdeen Golfers (later Royal Aberdeen Golf Club) is formed.

1783 A Silver Club is offered for competition at Glasgow.

1786 The South Carolina Golf Club, the first golf club outside of the United Kingdom, is formed in Charleston. The Crail Golfing Society is formed.

1787 The Glasgow Golf Club is created.

1795 This is the possible date for the formation of a golf club in Savannah, Georgia, the second known golf club in America.

1797 The town of St. Andrews sells the land containing the Old Course (known then as Pilmor Links) to Thomas Erskine for 805 pounds. Erskine was required to preserve the course for golf.

1803 A record book from the Honourable Company of Edinburgh Golfers contains the first known reference to an iron club designed specifically for putting; earlier references to putters all describe wooden-headed clubs.

1806 The St. Andrews Club chooses to elect its captains rather than award captaincy to the winner of the Silver Club. Thus begins the tradition of the captain "playing himself into office" by hitting a single shot before the start of the annual competition.

1810 The earliest reference to a women's competition at Musselburgh, held for the fishwives of Musselburgh, is recorded.

1812 Hugh Philp, sometimes known as the "Stradivarius of Golf," opens a club repair and refurbishing business in St. Andrews. The St. Andrews Golfing Society introduces the words "bunker" and "putting green" into a revision of the Rules of Golf.

1817 The Edinburgh Burgess Golfing Society sanctions the establishment of a golfing society in Barbados in the West Indies.

1820 The Bangalore Club, the first club in India, is formed. A notice in the *Montréal Herald* marks the first documented reference to golf in Canada.

1827 The *Colonial Times* (Tasmania) publishes the earliest known report of golf in Australia.

1828 Hickory imported from America to England is used to make golf shafts. The earliest known reference to a hole cutter, purchased for use by the Musselburgh Golf Club, is recorded.

1830 The Dum Dum Golfing Club, later called the Calcutta Golf Club, and still later, the Royal Calcutta Golf Club, is formed.

1831 The St. Andrews Golf Society announces a handicap competition; it is the earliest documented record of a competition played with handicaps.

1832 The North Berwick Club is founded: it is the first to include women in its activities, although they are not permitted to play in competitions.

1833 King William IV confers the distinction of "Royal" on the Perth Golfing Society; as Royal Perth, it is the first club to hold the distinction. The St. Andrews' Golfers ban the stymie, but rescind the ban one year later.

1834 William IV confers the title "Royal and Ancient" on the Golf Club at St. Andrews.

1836 The Honourable Company of Edinburgh Golfers abandons the deteriorating Leith Links and moves to Musselburgh. The longest drive ever recorded with a featherie ball, 361 yards, is achieved by Samuel Messieux on the Elysian Fields on the Old Course at St. Andrews.

1837 St. Andrews holds the first annual autumn competition for the King William Medal (Royal Medal).

1839 Carnoustie Golf Club is formed.

1842 The Bombay Golfing Society (later Royal Bombay) is founded.

1844 Blackheath follows Leith in expanding its course from five to seven holes. North Berwick also had seven holes at the time, although the trend toward a standard 18 had begun.

1848 The "guttie," the gutta-percha ball, is invented. It flies farther than the featherie, is much less expensive, and contributes greatly to the expansion of the game.

1849 The first well-known head-to-head match is held; two St. Andrews professionals, Allan Robertson and Old Tom Morris, defeat the Dunn brothers, Jamie and Willie, in a £400 challenge match contested over "three greens" or courses.

1851 The Prestwick Golf Club is founded.

1854 St. Andrews adopts the formal name "The Royal and Ancient Golf Club of St. Andrews." The famed clubhouse is completed.

1855 George Glennie records an 88 to win the Royal Medal at St. Andrews; it is the first time that 90 was broken in this event. His record stood for 29 years.

1856 The Royal Curragh Golf Club, the first golf club in Ireland, is founded at Kildare. Pau Golf Club, the first on the Continent, is founded in France. A rule change, stipulating that, in match play, the ball must be played as it lies or the hole must be conceded, is enacted. It is the last recorded toughening of the rules structure.

1857 The first book on golf instruction, *The Golfer's Manual*, written by H. B. Farnie under the pseudonym of "A Keen Hand," is published. The Prestwick Club institutes the first Championship Meeting, a foursomes competition at St. Andrews attended by 11 golf clubs. George Glennie and J. C. Stewart win for Blackheath. The first club match is played at St. Andrews. Eleven clubs enter, with Blackheath winning.

1858 The Royal and Ancient holds the first Grand National Amateur Championship; W. R. Chambers wins to become known as the first amateur champion. Allan Robertson becomes the first player to break 80 at St. Andrews, recording a 79. The King James VI Golf Club is founded in Perth, Scotland.

1859 The first Amateur Championship is won by George Condie of Perth. Allan Robertson, considered the first great professional golfer, dies.

1860 True championship golf dates to this year with the first Open Championship (British), contested entirely by professionals, held at Prestwick. Willie Park Sr. wins the first Championship Belt.

1861 The Open Championship (British) is opened to all players; Old Tom Morris wins.

1863 Willie Park wins his fourth consecutive Open Championship (British).

1864 The (Royal) North Devon Club is founded at Westward Ho!, which becomes the first seaside course in England.

1867 The Ladies' Putting Club is formed at St. Andrews; they play on the Himalayas putting course.

1869 The Liverpool (later Royal Liverpool) Golf Club is founded at Hoylake. Young Tom Morris, at only 17 years of age, wins the first of four consecutive Open Championships (British).

1870 (Royal) Adelaide Golf Club, the first in Australia, is opened in Adelaide. Young Tom Morris wins his third consecutive Open

Championship (British), retiring the Challenge Belt. The Open Championship will not be held in 1871 as a result.

1871 Dunedin Golf Club is opened in New Zealand, followed, in 1872, by the Christchurch Golf Club. Both clubs soon fold and golf will not reappear in New Zealand until 1891.

1872 After a year's hiatus, the Open Championship (British) returns, and Young Tom Morris wins his fourth consecutive title. It is decided to rotate the championship among three clubs—Prestwick, Musselburgh, and St. Andrews. A new trophy, the Claret Jug, is offered, however, it is not ready to be given to Young Tom this year and is awarded for the first time to the 1873 champion, Tom Kidd.

1873 The Royal Montréal Golf Club, the first club in North America, is founded. The Open Championship (British) is held for the first time at the Old Course in St. Andrews.

1875 Cambridge and Oxford universities form the first collegiate golf clubs. Young Tom Morris dies on Christmas Day, presumably from heartbreak due to the recent death of his young wife during childbirth. Vesper Country Club is formed in Tyngsboro, Massachusetts, in the United States. One hundred years later, it is the site of the New England Amateur Championship, won by the author of this book.

1878 First intercollegiate golf match is played between Cambridge and Oxford universities.

1881 The (Royal) Belfast Golf Club, the first in Ireland, is founded. A mold is used for cover patterns on gutta-perchas. Golfers had found that the guttie flew much truer after it had been hit several times and scuffed up slightly.

1885 The inaugural Amateur Championship (British) is won by A. F. MacFie over a field of 44 players. He defeated Horace Hutchinson in the final. The Royal Cape Golf Club, the first club in Africa, is founded at Wynberg, South Africa.

1887 The Foxburg Country Club, the oldest golf course in the United States in continuous use in one place, is founded in Foxburg, Pennsylvania. A. J. Balfour is appointed chief secretary (cabinet minister) of Ireland; his rise to political and social prominence has an incalculable positive effect on the popularity of golf, because he is an indefatigable player and catalyzes great interest in the game through his writing and public speaking. The first instruction book with photographs—Walter Simpson's *The Art of Golf*—is published.

1888 The St. Andrew's Golf Club, the oldest continuously existing golf club in the United States, is formed in Yonkers, New York. Belgium's first golf course, Royal Antwerp, is founded.

1889 Hong Kong Golf Club, later the Royal Hong Kong Golf Club, is founded.

1890 Royal Bangkok Golf Club, the first in Southeast Asia, is founded in Thailand. John Ball of England becomes the first non-Scotsman and first amateur to win the Open Championship (British). Hugh Rotherham invents the "bogey," considered the score of a golfer playing perfectly on each hole. Dr. Thomas Brown, honorary secretary of the Great Yarmouth Club, christens this hypothetical man a "Bogey Man," after a popular song of the day. The Hotel Champlain in Bluff Point, New York, opens the first resort course in the United States.

1891 Göteborg (Gothenburg) Golf Club in Sweden becomes the first course in Scandanavia. The Honourable Company of Edinburgh Golfers, the oldest golf club in existence, moves from Musselburgh to Muirfield. The Golfing Union of Ireland is founded on 12 October 1891; it is the oldest golfing union in the world.

1892 Lomas Golf Club, the first golf course in South America, is founded in Argentina. The first Indian Amateur Championship, often considered the first international championship event, is contested. The Irish Amateur Championship is contested for the first time. In a match between Douglas Rollard and Jack White at Cambridge, gate money is charged for the first time. Shinnecock Hills Golf Club in Southampton, New York, opens the first clubhouse in America; it is designed by noted architect Stanford White.

1893 The (British) Ladies' Golf Union is formed and sponsors the first British Ladies Amateur Championship, which is won by Lady Margaret Scott. The first New Zealand Amateur Championship is held. The Chicago Golf Club, the United States' first 18-hole golf course, opens on the site of the present-day Downers Grove Golf Course. The Chicago Golf Club moved to its current location in 1895.

1894 The Open Championship (British) is contested in England for the first time, at Sandwich. The United States Golf Association (USGA) is formed by representatives of five clubs: Shinnecock Hills Golf Club; The Country Club (Brookline); Chicago Golf Club; St. Andrew's Golf Club; and Newport Golf Club. The Tacoma Golf Club, the first golf club on the Pacific Coast of the United States, is founded. A. G. Spalding offers for sale the first golf clubs made in America. Morris County Golf Club, the first golf club for women only, opens in Morristown, New Jersey.

1895 The USGA holds its first three championships—the U.S. Open, won by Horace Rawlins; the U.S. Amateur, won by Charles Blair Macdonald; and the U.S. Women's Amateur, won by Lucy Barnes Brown. The first Canadian Amateur Championship is contested. The first public golf course in the United States, Van Cortlandt Park Golf Course, is founded. The first two courses in Germany, one at Bad Homburg and one at Baden-Baden, are built. The pool cue is banned as a putter by the USGA.

1896 The Royal Canadian Golf Association is formed. Harry Vardon wins the Open Championship (British), his first of six titles in the event; it is still a record.

1897 The R&A forms its first Rules of Golf Committee. The first U.S. Intercollegiate Golf Championship is won by Yale University, with Louis Bayard of Princeton earning individual honors. The Metropolitan Golf Association (New York) is formed. The first golf course, a nine-hole course at Pueblo, opens in Mexico. The first golf magazine in America, *Golf*, is published.

1898 The Western Golf Association is created in Chicago. The Haskell ball is designed and patented by Coburn Haskell. It is the first rubber-cored ball. The term "birdie" is used for the first time. First noted at the Atlantic City Country Club, it referred to "a bird of a hole."

1899 The first Western Open, played at Glenview Golf Club, is contested. The Pacific Northwest Golf Association is formed and contests its first men's and women's amateur championships. Dr. George Grant, one of the first African Americans to graduate from Harvard College, receives the first patent for a wooden golf tee, but he never markets the product commercially.

1900 Harry Vardon conducts an exhibition tour in the United States to promote the Spalding Vardon Flyer golf ball and wins the U.S. Open during the tour. Golf is played at the Olympic Games in Paris, one of only two times (through 2012) that golf has been on the Olympic Program. Americans Charles Sands and Margaret Abbott win the gold medals. John Gammeter develops a thread-winding machine that allows for the mass production of the new rubber-core golf ball. Three years after taking up the game, 38-year-old Walter Travis wins the U.S. Amateur.

1901 The Trans-Mississippi Golf Association is formed. Donald Ross completes the first course at the Carolina Hotel; later it becomes the Pinehurst Resort and Country Club in Pinehurst, North Carolina. Ross will eventually design more than 600 courses. The Professional Golfers' Association (PGA) of Great Britain and Ireland is formed. Walter Travis wins his second U.S. Amateur and becomes the first golfer to win a major title with a rubber-cored golf ball.

1902 The first international match is played at the Royal Liverpool Golf Club in Hoylake between Scotland and England. The Southern Golf Association is formed. E. Burr of England receives a patent for "rib-faced" irons with exaggerated grooves to impart additional spin on the golf ball. Laurie Auchterlonie becomes the first golfer to break 80 in all four rounds of the U.S. Open, held at Garden City Golf Club on Long Island. Willie Anderson shoots 299 in the Western Open at the Euclid Club in Cleveland, Ohio, thereby becoming the first golfer in America to break 300 for 72 holes.

1903 The Oxford and Cambridge (Oxbridge) Golfing Society tours the United States, playing several intercollegiate matches. The first international professional match is played between Scotland and England at Prestwick, with Scotland winning. The first golf course, a nine-hole course laid out by Arthur Hasketh Groom on the slopes of Mount Rokkō, opens in Japan, near Kobe. William and Henry Fownes open Oakmont Country Club in Pittsburgh, Pennsylvania. With its famous "Church Pews" bunker, Oakmont soon earns a reputation as the most difficult golf course in the country. Arthur Franklin Knight patents the controversial "Schenectady" center-shafted mallet putter. The famed No. 2 course at Pinehurst is completed by Donald Ross and opened for play.

1904 Walter Travis wins the British Amateur Championship, the first victory by an American. He wins using a controversial center-shafted putter. The inaugural French Amateur Championship is held. John H. Oke wins the inaugural Canadian Open at Royal Montréal Golf Club. Michael Scott, an English amateur, wins the inaugural Australian Open at Kensington Golf Club. Golf makes its second Olympic appearance at the 1904 Olympic Games in St. Louis. The golf competitions are held at the Glen Echo Country Club.

1905 William Taylor patents the first dimple pattern for golf balls in England. Former U.S. Open champion James Foulis patents the first concave-faced golf club. The first international match between Great Britain and the United States is held between teams of female amateurs. The British defeat the Americans, 6-1, at Cromer, England. Willie Anderson wins a record third-consecutive, and fourth overall, U.S. Open title at Myopia Hunt Club in Hamilton, Massachusetts. Leighton Caulkins develops a new handicapping system that is employed by the USGA to establish eligibility for the U.S. Amateur. The Goodyear Tire and Rubber Company introduces a golf ball with a rubber core filled with compressed air. The "Pneumatic" proves quite lively, but is prone to explode in warm weather.

1906 French professional Arnaud Massy wins the inaugural French Open at his home club, La Boulie.

1907 Arnaud Massy of France becomes the first non-British winner of the Open Championship (British), with a two-stroke victory over J. H. Taylor at Hoylake. It is the last victory by a Continental European player in a major championship until 1979.

1908 The United States defeats Canada, 27-7, in their first international amateur match, held at Toronto. Mrs. Gordon Robertson, at Princes Ladies Golf Club, becomes the first female golf professional. Arnold Haultain publishes *The Mystery of Golf*, a metaphysical approach to the game. It is considered one of the early classics of golf literature. Walter Travis establishes *The American Golfer*, which will become the most popular golf magazine in the United States until it ceases publication in 1936. Golf is on the program of the 1908 Olympic Games in London, but disputes over the rules of amateur status and the format of the competition, as well as sparse entry from outside Great Britain, lead to its cancellation.

1909 The USGA rules that caddies, caddiemasters, and greenkeepers over the age of 16 are professional golfers. The ruling is later modified and eventually rescinded in 1963. Dorothy Campbell becomes the first player to win the U.S. Women's Amateur and British Ladies' Open Amateur in the same year. The R&A bans the center-shafted putter while the USGA keeps it legal, marking the beginning of a 42-year period with two official versions of the Rules of Golf. President William Howard Taft, America's first golf-loving president, is elected to office.

1910 The first patent for a steel shaft is issued to Arthur F. Knight of Schenectady, New York. Scotsman James Braid wins his fifth and final Open Championship (British), beating Alexander Herd by four strokes on the Old Course at St. Andrews.

1911 Seventeen-year-old John McDermott becomes the first native-born American to win the U.S. Open; he remains the youngest champion ever. The first German Open Championship is held at Baden-Baden. England's Harold Hilton wins the U.S. Amateur at the Apawamis Club in Rye, New York, to become the first non-American to claim the title as well as the first player to win the U.S. Amateur and British Amateur in the same year. The Canadian Professional Golfers Association is organized. Chicagoan Charles Blair Macdonald opens the National Golf Links of America in Southampton, New York, establishing a new era in American golf course design.

1912 England's John Ball wins his eighth British Amateur championship, defeating Abe Mitchell on the 38th hole of the final match at Royal North Devon Golf Club in Westward Ho!, England.

1913 Francis Ouimet, an amateur and caddie from Boston, wins the U.S. Open Championship at The Country Club in Brookline, Massachusetts, defeating Britain's Harry Vardon and Ted Ray in a play-off. His victory is credited with popularizing golf in the United States. The first professional international match is played between France and the United States at La Boulie Golf Club, France. English professional J. H. Taylor wins the Open Championship (British) for a fifth and final time, recording an eight-stroke victory at Hoylake.

1914 Formation of The Tokyo Club at Komozawa kicks off the Japanese golf boom. Harry Vardon, at 44, wins the Open Championship (British) for a record sixth time, defeating rival J. H. Taylor by seven strokes at Prestwick, Scotland.

1915 The Open and Amateur Championships (British) are cancelled due to the onset of World War I and will not resume until 1920. The Canadian championships are also suspended until 1919.

1916 The PGA of America is formed; Jim Barnes wins the inaugural PGA Championship, defeating Jock Hutchison at Siwanoy Country Club in Bronxville, New York. James Barber opens the world's first miniature golf course near the Carolina Hotel in Pinehurst, North Carolina. At the age of only 14, Bob Jones makes his first appearance in a national championship, advancing to the quarterfinal round of the U.S. Amateur at Merion Cricket Club before losing 5 & 3 to Robert Gardner.

1917 The USGA and PGA of America cancel championships due to World War I.

1919 The R&A assumes management authority over the Open and Amateur Championships (British). The famed Gleneagles Hotel, with the King's and Queen's courses, opens in Perthshire, Scotland. Two-time PGA champion Jim Barnes publishes *Picture Analysis of Golf Strokes*, the first instructional book to take advantage of stop-action photography. Pebble Beach Golf Links opens as the Del Monte Golf Links in Pebble Beach, California, on the Monterey Peninsula. J. Douglas Edgar wins the Canadian Open at Hamilton Golf Club in Ontario by a record 16 strokes over Bob Jones.

1920 Scotland's Alister MacKenzie publishes *Golf Course Architecture*, the seminal treatise on the subject of golf design. The USGA Green Section is established.

1921 The R&A and the USGA place the first limits on the size and weight of a golf ball—1.62 inches in diameter and 1.62 ounces. The first men's international amateur match between Britain and the United States takes place at Hoylake, with the U.S. winning 9-3. The event is a forerunner of the Walker Cup, first contested the next year. Jock Hutchison wins the Open Championship (British); he is the first U.S. citizen to win the title; he was, however, a naturalized U.S. citizen, having been born at St. Andrews, Scotland, and becoming an American citizen in 1917.

1922 The first U.S. Amateur Public Links Championship, open only to players from public golf courses, is conducted by the USGA and won by Edmund Held. Walter Hagen wins the Open Championship (British), the first native-born American citizen to win the title. Later in the year, he becomes the first golf professional to establish a golf equipment company using his own name. The Walker Cup Match, an amateur team event between the United States and Great Britain–Ireland, begins at the National Golf Links of America on Long Island; it is won by the United States. The Prince of Wales is elected captain of the R&A. The first Texas Open, the second-oldest surviving PGA Tour event, is held. Pine Valley Golf Club, for many years considered the hardest golf course in the world, opens in New Jersey. At the age of 20, Gene Sarazen wins the U.S. Open and PGA Championship to become the first golfer to win both titles in the same year. For the first time, spectators pay for admission to the U.S. Open.

1923 Winged Foot Golf Club, and its famed West Course designed by A. W. Tillinghast, opens in Mamaroneck, New York. Bob Jones finally breaks through, winning the U.S. Open at Inwood on Long Island for his first national championship title.

1924 Joyce Wethered wins her record fifth consecutive English Ladies' Championship. Bob Jones wins his first of five U.S. Amateur titles, defeating George Von Elm, 9 & 8, in the final at Merion. The USGA legalizes steel-shafted golf clubs. The R&A will not do so until 1929.

1925 The first fairway irrigation system is installed at Brook Hollow Country Club in Dallas, Texas. The USGA and R&A agree to ban deep-grooved irons. William Lowell receives a patent for a wooden golf tee, which he calls the Reddy Tee. It is the prototype of the modern tee.

1926 Jess Sweetser becomes the first native-born American to win the British Amateur. Gate money is instituted at the Open Championship (British). Walter Hagen defeats Bob Jones, 12 & 11, in a privately sponsored 72-hole match in Florida. The Los Angeles Open, the third-oldest surviving PGA Tour event and the first tournament to offer a $10,000 purse, is inaugurated. With victories at Royal Lytham and St. Annes and Scioto Country Club, Bob Jones becomes the first golfer to win the U.S. Open and Open Championship (British) in the same year.

1927 The first Ryder Cup matches, played at Worcester Country Club in Massachusetts, are won by the United States. Bent grass is developed for putting greens by the U.S. Department of Agriculture. Herb and Joe Graffis launch *Golfdom*, the first magazine devoted to the business of the game. Walter Hagen wins his fourth consecutive PGA Championship title, defeating Joe Turnesa, 1 up, in the final at Cedar Crest Country Club in Dallas, Texas.

1928 Archie Compston defeats Walter Hagen, 18 & 17, in a challenge match at Moor Park in London. Cypress Point Club, designed by Alister MacKenzie, opens for play on the Monterey Peninsula.

1929 The R&A joins the USGA in legalizing steel shafts. Bob Harlow is hired as manager of the PGA's Tournament Bureau, and he first proposes the idea of expanding "The Circuit," as the tour is then known, from a series of winter events leading up to the season-ending North and South Open in spring, into a year-round tour.

1930 Bob Jones wins the Grand Slam, encompassing the U.S. Amateur, U.S. Open, British Amateur, and British Open and, at the time, called "The Impregnable Quadrilateral" by sportswriter George Trevor. Since Jones is an amateur, however, the financial windfall belongs to professional Bobby Cruickshank, who bets on Jones to complete the Slam, at 120-1 odds, and pockets $60,000. Soon after he completes his Grand Slam, Bob Jones retires from competitive golf and announces his plans to make a series of instructional films for Warner Brothers. The Duke of York, later King George VI, is elected captain of the R&A.

1931 The USGA increases the minimum size of the ball from 1.62 inches to 1.68 inches and decreases the maximum weight from 1.62 ounces to 1.55. The R&A does not follow suit. The lighter, larger "balloon ball" is universally despised, and, eventually, the USGA raises the weight back to 1.62 ounces. The USGA bans the concave-faced sand wedge, concerned that it strikes the ball twice during a swing. With his victory at Inverness Club in Toledo, Ohio, Billy Burke becomes the first player to win the U.S. Open using steel-shafted clubs. He defeats George Von Elm by a single stroke in their epic 72-hole play-off.

1932 The Curtis Cup, held at Wentworth, England, is played for the first time. It is a match between amateur teams of women from the United States and Great Britain–Ireland. Gene Sarazen is credited with the popularization of the sand wedge, which he uses to win the British Open at Prince's Golf Club in England.

1933 The Hershey Chocolate Company becomes the first corporate sponsor on the PGA Tour, with the Hershey Open. Augusta National Golf Club, designed by Alister MacKenzie with advice from Bob Jones, opens for play. Johnny Goodman wins the U.S. Open at the North Shore Country Club in Glenview, Illinois; through 2009, he is the last amateur to win the U.S. Open.

1934 The Masters Tournament is held for the first time, starting on 22 March, and is won by Horton Smith. It is originally known as the Augusta National Invitation Tournament. The U.S. PGA Tour, built around events like the major championships, the Western Open, the North and South Open, and the Los Angeles Open, is created. Paul Runyan leads the first official money list. Henry Cotton becomes the first British professional to win the Open Championship (British) since 1923, claiming the title at Royal St. George's Golf Club. He ties the championship record with a 67 in the first round, then breaks it with a 65 in the second round. Cotton used a Dunlop ball, and Dunlop popularizes his victory by producing the well-known Dunlop 65 ball.

1935 Gene Sarazen wins the second Masters Tournament. His victory is highlighted by a rare double-eagle on the 15th hole, while trailing by three shots. The shot enables him to tie Craig Wood, whom he defeats in a play-off the next day. The victory also gives him titles in the U.S. Open, Open Championship (British), PGA Championship, and what would become the Masters, making him the first player to win the career professional Grand Slam of golf, although it would not be known as such for over 25 years. With a victory over Patty Berg in the final at Interlachen Country Club, Glenna Collett Vare wins her sixth U.S. Women's Amateur, still a record. Pinehurst No. 2 is completed by Donald Ross; it is generally described as his masterpiece. Bethpage Black, designed by A. W. Tillinghast and constructed by President Roosevelt's Works Progress Administration (WPA), opens for play on Long Island. Lawson Little completes the "Little Slam," winning both the U.S. and British Amateurs in 1934 and 1935.

1936 Johnny Fisher wins the U.S. Amateur and becomes the last golfer to win a major championship with hickory-shafted clubs.

1937 Harry Vardon, the first superstar of golf, six-time winner of the Open Championship (British), dies on 20 March 1937, at the age of 66. Sam Snead wins the Oakland Open in California, his first of a record 82 PGA Tour victories. The Bing Crosby Pro-Am is inaugurated in San Diego. A few years later it moves to the Monterey Peninsula, where the tournament, now renamed the AT&T Pebble Beach National Pro-Am, remains to this day.

1938 The USGA begins a two-year trial of the first major modification to the stymie. An obstructing ball within six inches (15 cm) of the hole could be marked and moved regardless of the distance between the balls. The USGA made this rule permanent in 1941, but the R&A never made this change until the stymie was outlawed by both ruling bodies in 1952. The USGA institutes the 14-club rule; two years later, the R&A follows suit. The Palm Beach Invitational becomes the first tournament to make a contribution to charity—$10,000. With his victory at Cherry Hills Country Club in Denver, Ralph Guldahl becomes just the fourth player to win back-to-back U.S. Open titles. Babe Didrikson competes in the Los Angeles Open, thus becoming the first woman to play in a PGA Tour event. Ben Hogan partners with Vic Ghezzi to win the Hershey Four-Ball tournament; it is Hogan's first victory as a professional.

1940 The R&A cancels the Open and Amateur Championships (British) for the duration of World War II. The USGA and R&A agree to cancel the Walker Cup.

1941 The USGA develops a machine for measuring the initial velocity of a golf ball at impact, but plans to implement a new rule limiting initial velocity are put on hold until after the war.

1942 The USGA cancels its national championships for the duration of World War II. The U.S. government halts the manufacturing of golf equipment. Ben Hogan wins the Hale America National Open Tournament. Throughout his life, he insisted it was a fifth victory in the U.S. Open, although the USGA does not recognize it.

1943 Augusta National Golf Club is closed and the Masters is cancelled for the duration of World War II. The PGA Tour schedule is reduced to three tournaments due to the war. The PGA Championship is cancelled.

1945 Byron Nelson wins the Canadian Open for his 11th consecutive victory on the PGA Tour in 11 tournament starts. During the year, he wins seven other official events and one unofficial event for a total of 19 in the year; records that have not been approached to this day. Babe Zaharias, who dominated the 1932 Olympic track and field competition for women, plays in the Los Angeles Open.

1946 The USGA, R&A, and Augusta National Golf Club resume their championships following the conclusion of World War II. The U.S. Women's Open, conducted by the Women's Professional Golf Association (WPGA), is held for the first time. Contested at match play for the only time ever, it is held at the Spokane Country Club and is won by Patty Berg. Sam Snead wins the Open Championship (British) on the Old Course at St. Andrews, but loses money because his travel expenses exceed his championship winnings. Byron Nelson retires from competitive golf at age 34 to establish his ranch in Texas. Ben Hogan wins 13 PGA Tour events, including the PGA Championship; he loses the Masters and U.S. Open, each by a single stroke.

1947 The first golf event on television, the U.S. Open, is televised live in the St. Louis area. The U.S. Open is televised nationally for the first time in 1954. Babe Zaharias becomes the first American to win the British Ladies' Amateur Golf Championship. Jim Ferrier becomes the first Australian to win a major championship, the PGA Championship. South Africa's Bobby Locke joins the PGA Tour and wins six times in his rookie year. The first issue of *Golf World*, a weekly newsmagazine, is published in Pinehurst, North Carolina.

1948 The U.S. Junior Amateur Championship is played for the first time and won by Dean Lind, who defeats Ken Venturi in the final. Ben

Hogan claims his first of four U.S. Open titles with a victory at Riviera. Bobby Locke wins the Chicago Victory Open by a PGA Tour record 16 strokes at Midlothian Country Club. At the age of 41, Henry Cotton wins his third Open Championship (British), at Muirfield in Scotland. African American professionals Ted Rhodes and Bill Spiller finish in the top-25 at the Los Angeles Open, one of the few events they are allowed to play.

1949 While dominating the Tour in 1948 and January 1949, Ben Hogan and his wife decide to drive back to Texas for a holiday. Outside El Paso, driving in a thick fog, his car is struck by a Greyhound Bus. To save his wife's life, Hogan throws himself across her lap, and is almost killed in the accident. He spends months in the hospital and further months in rehab. Considered fortunate to even walk again, against all odds he returns to play in 1950 and wins six of the nine major championships in which he plays from 1950 to 1953. The U.S. Girls' Junior Championship is played for the first time and is won by Marlene Bauer (later Hagge). Bobby Locke wins the Open Championship (British), thereby becoming the first South African to win a major golf championship.

1950 The LPGA (Ladies' Professional Golf Association) is formed; it replaces the struggling WPGA. Ben Hogan wins the U.S. Open at Merion Golf Club in a play-off, formalizing his dramatic comeback from a horrific automobile accident in early February 1949.

1951 Francis Ouimet, winner of the dramatic 1913 U.S. Open, becomes the first American to be named the captain of the Royal and Ancient Golf Club of St. Andrews, Scotland. The USGA and the R&A, in a conference, complete a newly revised Rules of Golf. Although in 1951 the R&A and the USGA continue to differ over the size of the golf ball, all other conflicts are resolved in this momentous conference. The center-shafted putter is legalized worldwide. The out-of-bounds penalty is standardized at stroke-and-distance, and the stymie is finally and forever abolished. The first issue of *Golf Digest* is published.

1952 Dwight David Eisenhower, a renowned former general during World War II, is elected U.S. president. Eisenhower is an avid golfer and is credited with increasing the popularity of the game. Ted Rhodes, Bill Spiller, and Eural Clark play in the Phoenix Open after the PGA

Tour adopts a rule that allows African Americans to enter a tournament if the sponsor agrees.

1953 The Tam O'Shanter World Championship becomes the first tournament to be nationally televised. Lew Worsham holes a 104-yard (95 meters) wedge shot on the final hole for eagle and victory in one of the most dramatic finishes ever. The first PGA Merchandise Show is held in a parking lot in Dunedin, Florida, outside the PGA National Golf Club. Salesmen work the show out of the trunks of their cars. The current yardage guides for par are adopted by the USGA. Lifting, cleaning, and repairing ball marks is allowed on the putting green for the first time. Ben Hogan wins the Masters, U.S. Open, and Open Championship (British) and becomes the first player to win three of the four current major championships in the same calendar year. The first Canada Cup is contested, in Montréal, Québec, Canada, and is won by Argentina, represented by Roberto De Vicenzo and António Cerda. Babe Zaharias is stricken with colon cancer and undergoes radical surgery, but returns to play later in the year.

1954 The U.S. Open is televised nationally for the first time. It is won by Ed Furgol, and it is his only major championship. The Tam O'Shanter World Golf Championship becomes the first golf tournament with a total purse of $100,000. Babe Zaharias wins the U.S. Women's Open by a then-record 12 strokes, completing her heroic comeback from cancer. Arnold Palmer wins the U.S. Amateur at Detroit Country Club, an event he calls "the turning point" in his career. He turns pro later in the year. Billy Joe Patton threatens to become the first amateur to win The Masters, until he makes a costly double-bogey on the 13th hole in the final round.

1955 Mike Souchak wins the Texas Open, shooting a 28-under-par 256, a four-round record for the PGA Tour that will stand until 2003. The first USGA Senior Amateur Championship, open to players aged 55 and older, is contested and won by J. Wood Platt. The first LPGA Championship is won by Beverly Hanson at Orchard Ridge Country Club in Fort Wayne, Indiana. Jack Fleck, the professional at a municipal course, stuns Ben Hogan in a play-off for the U.S. Open at the Olympic Club in San Francisco, California. Arnold Palmer wins his first professional tournament, the Canadian Open.

1956 Ken Venturi, a 24-year-old amateur from San Francisco, leads the Masters by four strokes after three rounds but falters with six bogeys on the back nine and loses to Jackie Burke. Ann Gregory, playing in the U.S. Women's Amateur at Meridian Hills Country Club in Indianapolis, Indiana, becomes the first African American woman to compete in a USGA championship. Three-time Olympic medalist and three-time U.S. Women's Open champion Babe Zaharias loses her battle with colon cancer at the age of 42. Australia's Peter Thomson wins his third consecutive Open Championship (British).

1957 Hawaiian professional Jackie Pung appears to win the U.S. Women's Open but is disqualified after signing an incorrect scorecard. On the Old Course at St. Andrews, South Africa's Bobby Locke wins his fourth Open Championship (British). JoAnne Gunderson wins her first of five U.S. Women's Amateur titles by defeating Ann Casey Johnstone, 8 & 6. Charlie Sifford becomes the first African American to win a PGA Tour event with his victory in the Long Beach Open.

1958 The first World Amateur Team Championship is contested. Four-man teams from countries around the world compete for the Eisenhower Trophy, which is won by Australia on the Old Course in St. Andrews. Bob Jones is named a freeman of the City of St. Andrews, Scotland; he is only the second American so named since Benjamin Franklin in 1759. Despite being crippled by syringomyelia, Jones travels to the ceremony in St. Andrews. In an emotional ceremony, he walks to the podium, rare for him at that point in his life, telling the people that if his life consisted of only his experiences in St. Andrews, it would have been a long, full life. As the ceremony ends, the audience spontaneously and poignantly breaks into singing "Will Ye' No Come Back Again?" knowing that it could never happen. Arnold Palmer wins his first major, claiming the Masters by one stroke over Doug Ford and Fred Hawkins. Mickey Wright claims her first professional title by winning the LPGA Championship at Churchill Valley Country Club in Penn Hills, Pennsylvania, by six strokes over Fay Crocker. Patty Berg wins the Women's Western Open at age 40; it is the last of her record 15 major titles. South Africa's Gary Player wins the Kentucky Derby Open to claim his first victory on the PGA Tour. The PGA Championship changes format, from match play to stroke play; Dow Finsterwald wins the title at Llanerch Country Club in Havertown, Pennsylvania.

1959 Betsy Rawls wins 10 times on the LPGA Tour, setting a new money record and capturing the Vare Trophy. Bill Wright wins the U.S. Amateur Public Links, thereby becoming the first African American to win a USGA national championship. The first issue of *Golf* magazine is published.

1960 Arnold Palmer wins the Masters and U.S. Open and then travels to Britain to play in the Open Championship (British) on the Old Course at St. Andrews, attempting to win what he terms the modern Grand Slam of golf, a name that will stick. Palmer's attempt fails, but just barely, as he finishes second by one shot to Australia's Kel Nagle. Repairing ball marks on the putting green is allowed by the Rules of Golf for the first time.

1961 The PGA Tour is legally integrated when the Caucasian-only clause is stricken from the PGA of America Constitution. Mickey Wright completes one of the greatest years in women's professional golf, winning three majors (Titleholders Championship, U.S. Women's Open, and Women's Western Open) as well as seven other LPGA tournaments.

1962 Jack Nicklaus wins his first professional title, the U.S. Open, in a play-off at Oakmont over hometown hero Arnold Palmer. Arnold Palmer wins his second consecutive Open Championship (British) after placing second in 1960 in an attempt to win the modern professional Grand Slam of golf. Palmer's travels to Britain to play in the Open Championship popularize the event and reestablish it as one of the great championships in golf after several years in which its position had slipped somewhat. The first USGA Women's Senior Amateur Championship, open to players 55 and older, is contested and won by Maureen Orcutt. Chick Evans, at age 72, plays in the U.S. Amateur for the 50th time.

1963 Bob Charles wins the Open Championship (British) and becomes the first left-hander to win a major championship. Arnold Palmer becomes the first professional to win more than $100,000 in official money in a single season. Mickey Wright wins 13 tournaments on the LPGA Tour, a record that stands through 2010.

1964 Pete Brown wins the Waco Turner Open, thus becoming the first African American to win a PGA Tour event. The first Women's

World Amateur Team Championship is contested in France with the women competing for the Espirito Santo Trophy. Ken Venturi wins the U.S. Open at Congressional Country Club despite suffering from heat prostration during the 36-hole final day. Mickey Wright shoots a then–LPGA Tour record 62 in the final round and comes from 10 strokes behind to win the Tall City Open, her 10th of 11 victories for the year.

1965 Gary Player wins the U.S. Open to become the third player, after Gene Sarazen and Ben Hogan, to win the career professional Grand Slam, which consists of the U.S. Open, the Open Championship (British), the Masters, and the PGA Championship. Sam Snead earns his final PGA Tour victory at the Greater Greensboro Open. At age 52 years 10 months, he is the oldest winner of a PGA Tour event through 2009. Peter Thomson wins the Open Championship (British) for the fifth time.

1966 Jack Nicklaus wins the Open Championship (British) at Muirfield by one stroke over Doug Sanders and Dave Thomas; he joins Gene Sarazen, Ben Hogan, and Gary Player as winners of the career professional Grand Slam. Arnold Palmer loses seven strokes over the final nine holes of the U.S. Open to finish in a tie with Billy Casper at the Olympic Club. Palmer loses the play-off the next day.

1967 The Canada Cup, the international two-man professional team competition, changes its name to the World Cup. The event, held in Mexico City, is won by the U.S. team of Arnold Palmer and Jack Nicklaus. Charles Sifford wins the Greater Hartford Open and becomes the second African American to win a PGA Tour event. He is not invited to the Masters Tournament despite the victory. With her victory at Virginia Hot Springs Golf and Tennis Club, Catherine Lacoste becomes the first and, through 2009, the only amateur to win the U.S. Women's Open. Ram introduces the first golf ball with a cover made of Surlyn, a synthetic material made by Dupont that is far more resistant than the traditional balata cover. Jack Nicklaus wins the U.S. Open at Baltusrol. Ben Hogan plays in the national championship for the final time, but it is the fifth-place finish by Lee Trevino in his major championship debut that catches the attention of the media and galleries. Roberto De Vicenzo wins the Open Championship (British) at Hoylake, thereby becoming the first player from South America to capture a major championship title.

1968 The Tournament Players' Division of the PGA of America is established. Bob Goalby wins the Masters when Argentina's Roberto De Vicenzo signs an incorrect scorecard, which prevents him from participating in a play-off against Goalby. Forty-eight-year-old Julius Boros, with his victory in the PGA Championship, becomes the oldest player through 2009 to win a major championship. Arnold Palmer becomes the first player to top $1 million in career earnings. Spalding introduces the first two-piece ball under the brand name Top-Flite. Lee Trevino becomes the first golfer to break 70 in all four rounds of the U.S. Open en route to victory at Oak Hill Country Club in Rochester, New York. It is also Trevino's first professional victory.

1969 In the Ryder Cup, Jack Nicklaus performs one of the great acts of sportsmanship in golf history. On the final green, playing Britain's Tony Jacklin with the match tied, he concedes a two-foot putt to Jacklin, which allows the match to remain tied. Nicklaus tells Jacklin, "I don't think you would have missed that putt, but in these circumstances, I would never give you the opportunity." Hollis Stacy wins the U.S. Girls' Junior Championship, the first of her three consecutive championships in the event, at only 15 years of age. At the time, she is the youngest ever to win the title. With her victory at the Burdine's Invitational, JoAnne Gunderson becomes the last amateur through 2009 to win an LPGA event. Joseph C. Dey, executive director of the USGA, is named the first commissioner of the newly formed Tournament Players Division of the PGA of America.

1970 Pete Brown wins the Andy Williams San Diego Invitational; it is his second victory on the PGA Tour and the fourth victory ever by an African American on the PGA Tour. Despite this, he is not invited to the Masters Tournament. Mickey Wright retires from full-time competition at the age of 34; she plays only occasionally in the years that follow.

1971 The official birth of the PGA European Tour. U.S. astronaut Alan Shepard plays golf on the moon using a soil-sampling tool that has been modified with a Wilson Staff 6-iron clubhead. A cable was sent from the R&A to Alan Shepard: "Please refer to rules of golf on etiquette, paragraph 6. Before leaving a bunker, a player should carefully fill up all holes made by him therein." Jack Nicklaus becomes the first player to win all four professional major championships twice by winning the PGA Championship at PGA National. Bob Jones, considered the greatest amateur player ever and one of the greatest professional players ever, dies on 18 December at the age of 69 after a long debilitating illness caused by syringomyelia. Lee Trevino wins the U.S. Open, Canadian Open, and Open Championship (British) within a span of 21 days. JoAnne Carner, earning her first major title as a professional, wins the U.S. Women's Open at the Kahkwa Club in Erie, Pennsylvania.

1972 The Colgate–Dinah Shore Winners Circle debuts on the LPGA Tour with the first six-figure purse in women's golf. Title IX of the Education Amendments of 1972, better known simply as Title IX, is passed, which forces universities to provide equal opportunities for female athletes, including golfers. Jack Nicklaus wins the first two major championships of the year—the Masters and U.S. Open—but his bid for a Grand Slam ends when he misses out by one stroke to Lee Trevino in the Open Championship (British).

1973 The graphite shaft is invented. Ben Crenshaw wins the NCAA Championship for his third consecutive victory in the event; a feat that would later be matched by Phil Mickelson. The classic golf novel *Golf in the Kingdom*, which would achieve cult status with its story of Shivas Irons, the mystical Scottish pro, is published. Mickey Wright wins the last of her 82 LPGA titles—the Colgate–Dinah Shore Winners Circle. Johnny Millers shoots a U.S. Open record 63 in the final round at Oakmont to win the championship.

1974 The Tournament Players' Championship, later to be called the "Players' Championship," now often shortened simply to "The Players" is contested for the first time; it is held initially at the Atlanta Country Club. Deane Beman, at age 35, is named commissioner of the PGA Tour. The World Golf Hall of Fame opens in Pinehurst, North Carolina. It would later move to St. Augustine, Florida. Victor Regalado wins the Pleasant Valley Classic by one stroke over Tom Weiskopf and becomes the first Mexican national to win a PGA Tour event.

1975 Lee Elder becomes the first black golfer to play in the Masters. Lee Trevino, Jerry Heard, and Bobby Nichols are struck by lightning during the Western Open. The incident prompts new safety standards in weather preparedness at PGA Tour events, but one spectator is killed when struck by lightning during the 1991 U.S. Open at Hazeltine National, and one is struck at the PGA Championship at Crooked Stick later that summer. Ray Volpe is named the first commissioner of the LPGA Tour.

1976 The USGA institutes the Overall Distance Standard. Balls that fly more than 280 yards during a standard test are banned. Judy Rankin becomes the first LPGA Tour player to win more than $100,000 in a single season. Clifford Roberts, at age 82, steps down as chairman of the Masters after 42 years. He is replaced by Bill Lane.

1977 Al Geiberger records the first sub-60 round in PGA Tour history on 10 June with a 59 in the Danny Thomas Memphis Classic at Colonial Country Club. The Ryder Cup expands the British side, to include players from the Republic of Ireland, now opening the event to all players from the British Isles. A "sudden-death" play-off is used for the first time in a major championship when Lanny Wadkins defeats Gene Littler for the PGA Championship played at Pebble Beach. The first U.S. Women's Amateur Public Links Championships, open only to players from public golf courses, is contested by the USGA and won by Kelly Fuiks. Tom Watson and Jack Nicklaus battle for the Open Championship (British) in an epic final round at Turnberry. Watson wins the "Duel in the Sun" by one stroke with a birdie on the final hole, breaking the championship scoring record by eight strokes. Chako Higuchi wins the LPGA Championship to become the first Japanese and the first Asian player to claim a women's major championship title. Despite a death threat, Hubert Green remains focused to win the U.S. Open at Southern Hills in Tulsa, Oklahoma.

1978 The Legends of Golf Tournament, open to professionals over 50 years of age, is held for the first time in Austin, Texas. Its popularity will lead to the Senior PGA Tour, later to be called the Champions Tour. LPGA Tour rookie Nancy Lopez wins nine tournaments, including five consecutively.

1979 Seve Ballesteros wins the Open Championship (British), thereby becoming the first Spaniard to win a major championship and making him the first Continental European to win a major championship since Frenchman Arnaud Massy's victory in the Open Championship in 1907. TaylorMade introduces its first metal wood, revolutionizing the golf club industry. The Ryder Cup expands the non-U.S. team from a British Isles team to one made up of any player from Europe, but the U.S Team still emerges victorious at the Greenbrier in White Sulphur Springs, West Virginia.

1980 Roberto De Vicenzo wins the inaugural U.S. Senior Open at Winged Foot Golf Club. The Tournament Players Club at Sawgrass, designed by Pete Dye, opens for play. It is the first course of the PGA Tour's TPC network. Coming off his worst season since joining the PGA Tour in 1962, 40-year-old Jack Nicklaus returns to form and wins the U.S. Open, setting a new 72-hole scoring record; he also wins the PGA Championship. *Caddyshack*, widely considered the funniest and best golf film ever made, debuts on the silver screen. At age 23 years and 4 days, Seve Ballesteros becomes the youngest Masters champion to date with his four-stroke victory at Augusta National.

1981 The first U.S. Mid-Amateur Championship, open to players age 25 and older, is contested and is won by Jim Holtgrieve. Kathy Whitworth becomes the first woman to surpass $1 million in career earnings. Patty Sheehan wins her first LPGA Tour event at the Mazda Japan Classic and celebrates with a somersault on the final green.

1982 Tom Watson wins the U.S. Open with a miraculous chip-in on the 71st hole at Pebble Beach. At the Hawaiian Open, Wayne Levi becomes the first golfer to win a tour event using an orange ball. Jerry Pate wins the first Tournament Players Championship, played on the TPC at Sawgrass, and celebrates by tossing PGA Tour Commissioner Deane Beman and course architect Pete Dye into the water by the 18th green and then jumping in himself. John Laupheimer replaces Ray Volpe as commissioner of the LPGA Tour. Juli Inkster wins her third consecutive U.S. Women's Amateur title, becoming the first player to do so since Virginia Van Wie in 1932–1934.

1983 Tom Watson wins his fifth Open Championship (British), edging Andy Bean at Royal Birkdale.

1984 Greg Norman holes a 45-foot par putt on the final hole at Winged Foot and ties Fuzzy Zoeller, but loses the U.S. Open title in a play-off the following day. In her first full year as a professional, Juli Inkster grabs two major titles with victories in the Nabisco Dinah Shore and Du Maurier Classic. Ben Crenshaw captures his first major championship title with a victory in the Masters.

1985 The USGA introduces the Slope System to allow golfers to adjust their handicaps to allow for the relative difficulty of a course compared to players of their own ability. For the first time since 1957, Europe wins the Ryder Cup with a 16½-11½ victory at The Belfry in Sutton Coldfield, England. At age 46, JoAnne Carner becomes the oldest player to win an LPGA Tour event with her victory in the Safeco Classic.

1986 The Panasonic Las Vegas Invitational offers the first $1 million purse. Jack Nicklaus wins the Masters at age 46, his sixth Masters and 18th professional major title. Bob Tway holes out from a bunker to defeat Greg Norman in the PGA Championship at Inverness. Pat Bradley wins three major titles in one year with victories in the Nabisco Dinah Shore, LPGA Championship, and Du Maurier Classic. Forty-three-year-old Ray Floyd wins the U.S. Open title at Shinnecock Hills and becomes the oldest champion to date. Arnold Palmer records holes-in-one on consecutive days at the Senior Tour's Chrysler Cup played at the TPC at Avenel.

1987 The first U.S. Women's Mid-Amateur Championship, open to players age 25 and older, is contested. Larry Mize stuns Greg Norman by holing a 100-foot pitch on the second hole of a sudden-death playoff for the Masters. Judy Bell becomes the first woman elected to the USGA Executive Committee.

1988 Curtis Strange claims the U.S. Open title en route to becoming the first PGA Tour player to win official money of more than $1 million (U.S.) in a single year. Square-grooved clubs such as the PING Eye2 irons are banned by the USGA, which claims that the clubs give an unfair competitive advantage to PING customers. Karsten Manufacturing, maker of the clubs, fights both the USGA and the PGA Tour to have the ban rescinded, and eventually both organizations drop the ban.

1989 With his victory at Oak Hill Country Club in Rochester, New York, Curtis Strange becomes the first player since Ben Hogan in 1950–1951 to win consecutive U.S. Open titles.

1990 The Ben Hogan Tour comes into existence as a developmental circuit. In 1993, it was renamed the "Nike Tour," followed by the

"Buy.com tour," and then the "Nationwide Tour." The R&A, after 38 years, adopts the 1.68 inch diameter ball, and, for the first time since 1910, the Rules of Golf are fully standardized throughout the world. Great controversy envelops the PGA Championship, to be held at Shoal Creek Country Club in Alabama, when it is discovered that the club's bylaws do not allow black members. The rule is soon changed and a black member admitted shortly before the event begins. The PGA Tour and PGA of America later change their rules to require clubs that host their events to have open membership policies. The Solheim Cup, a professional women's team competition that is contested by a team from the United States and an international team from Europe, is held for the first time. It is first held at Lake Nona Golf & Country Club in Orlando, Florida. Hale Irwin, defeating Mike Donald in a sudden-death play-off at Medinah Country Club at the age of 45, becomes the oldest U.S. Open champion through 2009.

1991 Oversized metal woods are introduced, with Callaway's Big Bertha quickly establishing itself as the dominant brand; the Big Bertha driver becomes one of the biggest-selling clubs of all time. Fifteen-year-old Tiger Woods wins his first of three consecutive U.S. Junior Championships and becomes the youngest player ever to win it. John Daly, who makes it into the field as an alternate, wins the PGA Championship at Crooked Stick and awes the fans with his long drives. Phil Mickelson, then a 20-year-old amateur, wins the Northern Telecom Open.

1992 Ray Floyd wins the Doral Ryder Open 29 years after his first PGA Tour victory, tying the record for the longest span between victories, which was first set by Sam Snead. Betsy King wins the LPGA Championship with rounds of 68-66-67-66 to become the first player to post four sub-par rounds in a women's major. Patty Sheehan becomes the first player to win the U.S. Women's Open and British Women's Open in the same year, though the latter is not yet considered a major.

1993 An ownership group led by Joe Gibbs and Arnold Palmer announces plans for the Golf Channel, a 24/7 cable channel. SoftSpikes are introduced in an effort to combat the damage to putting greens caused by traditional metal golf spikes. Tiger Woods becomes the only player to win three consecutive U.S. Junior Amateur Championships.

Phil Mickelson, playing in his first professional event, wins the Buick Invitational. Bernhard Langer wins the Masters using a persimmon driver and becomes the last player to win a major with a wooden-headed driver.

1994 The President's Cup is held for the first time, at the Robert Trent Jones Golf Club in Gainesville, Virginia. The competition matches teams of professionals from the United States with those from outside of Europe. Tiger Woods, at age 18, wins the U.S. Amateur Championship following his three consecutive victories in the U.S. Junior and becomes the youngest champion to date. Arnold Palmer plays in his last U.S. Open before a hometown crowd at Oakmont Country Club.

1995 The first major international tournament is played in China—the World Cup of Golf at Mission Hills. Annika Sörenstam's first official professional victory comes at the U.S. Women's Open.

1996 Tiger Woods wins his third consecutive U.S. Amateur Championship, which follows three consecutive U.S. Junior Championships, giving him a USGA Championship in six consecutive years. Later in the year, Woods turns professional and wins two events on the PGA Tour. Karrie Webb leads the LPGA money list, winning $1,002,000 and becoming the first woman to win more than $1 million (U.S.) in official money in a single season. Greg Norman leads the Masters by six strokes entering the final round but loses by five strokes to Nick Faldo in suffering the worst final-round collapse in Masters history. Judy Bell becomes the first female president of the U.S. Golf Association. The major professional tours come together to form the International Federation of PGA Tours, leading to the creation of the World Golf Championships and the first widely accepted world ranking system. Spalding introduces the Strata golf ball, the first multilayer non-wound golf ball. Precept introduces the MC Tour ball, the first three-piece, non-wound ball with a urethane cover.

1997 Tiger Woods storms onto the scene winning five events, including the Masters by 12 strokes, and accumulates 13 top-ten finishes in his rookie year. Ben Hogan, considered the greatest golfer ever by some golf historians, dies on 25 July 1997, at the age of 84. Europe wins the Ryder Cup at Valderrama in Spain, the first time the match is held outside the United States and Great Britain. John Daly becomes the first player on record to finish the PGA Tour season with an average driving distance that exceeds 300 yards.

1998 Casey Martin becomes the first and, through 2009, the only player to use a golf cart at the U.S. Open. Pak Se-Ri, at age 19, wins the U.S. Women's Open and LPGA Championship, igniting a surge of interest in women's golf in Korea.

1999 Aree Wongluekiet (later Aree Song) wins the U.S. Girls Junior at age 13 to become the youngest player to date to win a USGA national Championship. In a dramatic final-day comeback, the U.S. wins the Ryder Cup at The Country Club in Brookline, Massachusetts. The USGA begins testing metal-headed drivers for springlike effect. The first three World Golf Championships are held with Jeff Maggert winning the inaugural WGC event, the Accenture Match Play Championship.

2000 Tiger Woods wins the 100th U.S. Open by a record 15 strokes at Pebble Beach. He later adds the Open Championship (British Open) and PGA Championship and becomes the first player since Ben Hogan in 1953 to win three majors in one year. Woods also joins Lee Trevino as the only players in history to win the U.S., British, and Canadian opens in the same year. Shigeki Maruyama shoots 58 in U.S. Open qualifying. Titleist introduces the solid-core, urethane-covered Pro V1 golf ball, leading to the rapid demise of the wound ball. Ten-year-old Michelle Wie qualifies for the U.S. Women's Amateur Public Links Championship. Meg Mallon wins the last Du Maurier Classic, which had been a women's major since 1979.

2001 Tiger Woods wins the Masters Tournament, making him holder of the four major golf championships—the U.S. Open (2000), British Open (2000), PGA (2000), and Masters (2001). Considered a Grand Slam by many, purists demur that the Slam has to be won in one calendar year, and his feat is often called the "Tiger Slam." The Ryder Cup is postponed until 2002 due to the 9/11 attacks on the World Trade Center and the Pentagon, and the crash in Pennsylvania. Bob Estes becomes the last player on the PGA Tour to play with a persimmon driver when he finally switches to a metal-headed club. Annika Sörenstam becomes the first player in LPGA history to shoot 59 in the Standard Register PING. The British Women's Open replaces the Du Maurier Classic as one of the women's majors. Pak Se-Ri is the first to win the event as a major.

2002 Sam Snead, one of the greatest players in golf history, dies on 23 May 2002, at the age of 90. Tiger Woods wins the U.S. Open at Bethpage State Park's Black Course, the first time the U.S. Open is held at a truly public golf course.

2003 Mike Weir becomes the first Canadian, and the first left-handed golfer, to win the Masters, defeating Len Mattiace on the first play-off hole. Annika Sörenstam is invited to, and plays in, the Colonial Invitational Tournament at Fort Worth. Sörenstam's appearance makes her the first woman to play in a PGA Tour event since Babe Zaharias played in the 1945 Los Angeles Open. Shortly after Sörenstam's appearance in the Colonial, Suzy Whaley plays in the Greater Hartford Open (GHO), having qualified for that event by winning the 2002 Connecticut PGA Section Championship. She won that championship playing from the ladies' tees while the men played the full course. At the GHO she plays the full course. The PGA rule was later changed; termed the "Whaley Rule," it requires all players in Section Championships to play from the same tees. Tommy Armour III wins the Valero Texas Open by shooting 254 (26-under-par) and breaking the long-standing PGA Tour record of 256 set by Mike Souchak, also in winning the Texas Open (1955). At age 13, Michelle Wie wins the U.S. Women's Amateur Public Links to become the youngest ever winner of an adult USGA championhip. Tiger Woods wins his fourth consecutive Bay Hill Invitational and joins Walter Hagen and Gene Sarazen as the only players to win the same event in four straight years.

2004 At the age of 14, golf prodigy Michelle Wie becomes the youngest woman (and only the fourth overall) to play in a PGA Tour event, shooting 72-68 (even par) at the Sony Open at Waialae Country Club in her hometown of Honolulu and missing the cut by only one stroke. Vijay Singh wins nine events on the PGA Tour, including the PGA Championship, thus becoming the first golfer to win more than $10 million in one season.

2006 Byron Nelson, "Lord Byron," one of the game's greatest players and perhaps its greatest gentleman and ambassador, dies on 26 September 2006, at the age of 94. Arnold Palmer plays his final competitive round at the Champions Tour Administaff Small Business Classic. Kimberly Kim, at only 14 years of age, becomes the youngest champion to date in the U.S. Women's Amateur. Europe, winning for the third consecutive time, continues to dominate the Ryder Cup. The 9-point margin (18½-9½) ties the European record for largest margin of victory in the event.

2007 Tiger Woods wins the first tournament of the year, the Buick Invitational, and extends his consecutive winning streak to seven, second best to Byron Nelson's 11 in 1945. Morgan Pressel, at age 18 years, 10 months, 9 days, becomes the youngest winner of a women's major with her victory at the Kraft Nabisco Championship. Alexis Thompson, at age 12 years, 4 months, 1 day, becomes the youngest player ever to qualify for the U.S. Women's Open. Ariya Jutanugarn of Thailand, at age 11 years, 11 months, 2 days, becomes the youngest player ever to compete in an LPGA Tour event—the Honda Thailand Classic. Spain's Pablo Martin wins the Estoril Open and thus becomes the first amateur to win a European Tour event. Fifteen-year-old Ryo Ishikawa wins the Munsingwear Open KSB Cup to become the youngest winner ever on the Japan Tour. Bob Charles, at age 71, makes the cut and finishes 23rd at the New Zealand Open, cosponsored by the European and Australasian Tours. He is the oldest player to make the cut in a tournament on any of the world's major professional tours.

2008 Annika Sörenstam announces her retirement from competitive golf and finishes her final round at the U.S Women's Open with a remarkable eagle on the 18th hole at Interlachen. At age 10 years, 3 months, Allisen Corpuz of Hawaii plays in the U.S. Women's Amateur Public Links Championship, thereby becoming the youngest player in history to play in a USGA national championship.

2009 Ángel Cabrera defeats Loren Roberts and Chad Campbell in a play-off to become the first player from South America to win the Masters. Yang Yong-Eun of Korea outduels Tiger Woods in the final round of the PGA Championship and becomes the first Asian to win a men's major championship title. It is also the first time Woods fails to win a major championship when leading after three rounds. Having struggled for several years since turning professional, Michelle Wie leads the U.S. to victory in the Solheim Cup and then claims her first

LPGA victory at the Lorena Ochoa Invitational. In the British Open at Turnberry, 59-year-old Tom Watson bids to become the oldest player to win a major until he bogeys the 72nd hole; he then loses the subsequent play-off to Stewart Cink. The USGA and R&A announce the first rule that rolls back equipment in 72 years, it limits the volume of grooves as well as the sharpness of groove edges on irons and wedges; the change takes effect 1 January 2010. After a letter from LPGA players requests her resignation, LPGA Commissioner Carolyn Bivens steps down after a short and very tumultuous term. Michael Whan becomes the new LPGA commissioner in October 2009. Golf feels the impact of the global recession as rounds played, equipment sales, course openings, and club membership levels drop. Professional tours lose sponsors and reduce prize money. Tiger Woods announces his "indefinite leave" from professional golf following a car accident and revelations of marital infidelity.

Introduction

Golf has been called the greatest of all games, and it has been derided by none other than Mark Twain as nothing more than a "good walk spoiled." It has been called the most human of games and a reflection of life by one of its greatest players. That player, Bob Jones, noted, "One reason we enjoy it and that it challenges us is it enables us to run the entire gamut of human emotions not only in a brief space of time, but likewise without measurable damage to ourselves or others."

Two prime ministers of Great Britain have tried to define the game, with Winston Churchill noting, "Golf is a game whose aim is to hit a very small ball into an even smaller hole, with weapons singularly ill designed for that purpose." But the Earl of Balfour was less sanguine, stating, "A tolerable day, a tolerable green, a tolerable opponent—they supply, or ought to supply, all that any reasonably constituted human should require in the way of entertainment." And the sportswriter Paul Gallico one described the game as "a mystery—as much a one as the universe, solar system, electricity, or ironic affinities."

Golf has been called a sport and has been derided as not being a sport since it requires minimal athletic ability. It is a game that can be played by toddlers, witnessed by the feats of three-year-old Tiger Woods, perhaps the greatest of all champions, and it is a game that can be played into one's 80s and 90s, which makes it truly a game of a lifetime. But it is also a game for gentlemen, perhaps unlike any other.

In 1925, Bob Jones was in a play-off for the U.S. Open title when he saw his ball move in the rough while he was addressing it and called the penalty on himself, although no one else saw the ball's motion. He was lauded for this in the press, but Jones would not hear of this, noting, "You may as well praise a man for not robbing a bank." It highlighted one of the tenets of the game of golf, even at the highest professional levels, which is sportsmanship. It is unlike other sports, where the athletes attempt to get away with whatever they can to win, and in which, if referees fail to notice an infraction, nothing is done about it (at least in the days before televised replay). But in golf, there are no strict outside referees. Players police themselves and frequently call penalties on themselves. In fact, among professional players, there is no greater opprobrium for a player than to be known as someone who has not policed him- or herself when the situation called for it. This has happened a few times, but only rarely, as such players are all but ostracized. Because of the sportsmanship inherent in the game, golf is often termed a gentlemen's game, and it is almost unique in today's sports world by its emphasis on sportsmanship.

ORIGINS

Golf consists of using a series of various clubs to strike a small ball and eventually place that ball into a small hole in the ground, over a series of holes termed a "golf course." It has been around as a game, a sport, an activity—what have you—since at least the 15th century, with the traditional teaching being that the game originated in Scotland. But there is historical evidence of games similar to golf being played as far back as the 13th century, mostly in the Low Countries of Europe. Over the many centuries of its evolution, the balls used have changed greatly, as have the clubs and the holes and the courses and the entire game itself.

Although the game likely did not originate in Scotland, that nation provided the game its early impetus, with many of the current rules deriving from an early set of rules established by the Honourable Company of Edinburgh Golfers. These were later supplanted by a set of rules instituted by the Royal and Ancient Golf Club of St. Andrews. As one might expect, the original rules were brief, but the Rules of Golf greatly expanded in the ensuing centuries such that now we have not only a booklet defining the rules but a substantial book detailing the decisions on the Rules of Golf. But the basic essence of the game has not changed over the years. One still strikes a ball with a club in an effort to place it into a hole with the fewest number of strokes. And all of the Rules of Golf can be summarized by three basic principles: 1) play the ball as it lies, 2) play the course as you find it, and 3) when "1" or "2" is not possible, do what is fair.

In addition to the rules, Scotland provided many of the modern features of the game of golf. Scotland was the home of the first true golf championship—the Open Championship, often called the British Open in the United States, which began in 1860. Prior to that time, professionals measured themselves in money matches against one another. The greatest match player of the 1850s was Allan Robertson, and when Robertson died in 1859, the decision was made to hold a tournament to find his worthy successor as the champion golfer, and thus was born the Open Championship.

Scotland was where the vocation of golf professional became a reality, and this evolved into two variants—club professionals, who made their living serving their clubs and their memberships; and professional golfers, who made their living playing in tournaments for prize money. Scotland is the true home of modern golf courses, often designed by course designers or architects who eventually established this as a profession. Prior to the designing of golf courses, the game was played in open fields, often trimmed by sheep that kept the "fairways" short as they grazed upon them, with teeing areas and holes simply chosen at random. But in Scotland, certain golf courses were laid out and specifically designated for play. Many of these were on land near the sea, bringing to the fore the term "links golf"—the land on which the courses were built being considered to "link" the mainland to the ocean, thus the term.

In addition to its domestic promotion of the game, due to which eventually nearly all small towns would have their own courses, in the late 19th century, Scotland sent its emissaries abroad, thereby spreading the gospel of the game to other countries, notably the United States and Canada. Most of the first golf professionals in the United States were Scottish émigrés who were in search of a better living. They designed, built, and taught at some of the new courses in America. One of these was Donald Ross, who was born and grew up in Dornoch, Scotland. He became a golf professional near Boston and distinguished himself as a player, winning several tournaments, notably the North and South Open and the Massachusetts Open, but Ross earned most of his fame from designing golf courses. At first, he designed and helped build many of the early courses around Boston and New England. As his fame grew, he was sought after around the country and built courses in over 30 states—his greatest effort likely being Pinehurst No. 2 in North Carolina.

THE EARLY 20TH CENTURY

As golf spread to America at the turn of the 20th century, golf tournaments began to be contested in the United States and Canada, and this would eventually lead to a professional golf tour. Originally, golf tournaments in the United States consisted of the national championships—the U.S. Open and U.S. Amateur, with many state and association championships contested as well. This led to events such as the PGA Championship for professional golfers only; the Western Open, conducted by the Western Golf Association; and the North and South Open, contested over the Pinehurst No. 2 course. But through the 1920s, there was no defined golf tour, only a series of itinerant golf tournaments. Most golf professionals considered themselves club professionals and usually had summer jobs at a club, often in the Northeast or Midwest. In the winter, spring, and late fall, they would often travel to play these few tournaments. Very few professionals were able to make a living from tournament winnings alone.

But in the late 1920s and early 1930s, the tournaments coalesced into a defined pro golf tour in the United States, which was really the first one in the world. There is no exact year in which this occurred, but by the mid-1930s, it was possible for pro golfers to play in tournaments almost year-round and make their livings from doing so. Beginning in the 1930s and 1940s with the triumvirate of Ben Hogan, Byron Nelson, and Sam Snead, many touring pros became quite famous. Until the 1930s, most of the great players of the world were either British or Scottish professionals, or, in the United States, mostly amateur players. The greatest player at the turn of the 20th century had been Harry Vardon, an Englishman who, with two of his contemporaries, James Braid and J. H. Taylor, made up the first "Great Triumvirate of Golf."

Scottish professionals had been the top players in the game since the mid-19th century, led first by Allan Robertson and followed by Tom Morris, who would later be called "Old Tom Morris" as his playing ability and record were surpassed by his son, known as Young Tom Morris. After Robertson and the Morrises, Vardon was the next player acknowledged as the best in the world. But there the British dominance of the game ended, and through the beginning of the 21st century, they have never reclaimed that mantle.

From 1905 to 1920, no golfer was really considered preeminent. But in the 1920s, an American amateur, Bob Jones, was the outstanding player, and he is still considered among the greatest golfers of all time. Jones won four U.S. Open Championships, five U.S. Amateur Championships, three Open Championships (British), and one British Amateur. He effectively ended his competitive career after 1930, a year in which he won all four of what were then considered the major championships—the Open and Amateur championships of the United States and Great Britain. Termed by sportswriter George Trevor (*New York Sun*) the "Impregnable Quadrilateral," the feat has since become known as the Grand Slam of golf. Golfers to this day continue to reach for this Holy Grail, but the feat has not been duplicated, neither in its original set of titles nor in the modern professional equivalent of winning the Masters, the U.S. Open, the British Open, and the PGA title—all in a single year. Jones himself was responsible for this change in Grand Slam tournaments. In the early 1930s, he designed, with golf course architect Alister MacKenzie, the Augusta National Golf Club, where, in 1934, he started a tournament that soon became known as the Masters.

FROM BRITAIN TO AMERICA AND BEYOND

But after British and Scottish dominance ended around 1910 and Jones' meteoric career passed, the mantle of golf greatness was passed to American professional golfers, at least into the 1980s, when the game became more international. The PGA Tour was responsible for this in a number of ways. First, the large continental mass of the United States allowed golf to be played almost year-round, as golfers "followed the sun" to play in tournaments. Second, the PGA Tour was supported almost from the beginning by civic and charitable organizations, which allowed U.S. tournaments to offer the largest purses and the most money. Because of this, the best players eventually flocked to the United States in an effort to get their hands on some of this money.

It was not until the early 1970s that the Europeans would establish a similar tour, the European PGA Tour. Third, until the late 1980s, there were two sets of Rules of Golf, one established by the Royal and Ancient Golf Club of St. Andrews (R&A) and one by the United States Golf Association (USGA). The rules were very similar with only minor differences (except for one), which were completely resolved in 1990 when golf, for the first time, had a single, uniform set of rules. But there was that one very important difference that had to be resolved. Until 1990, U.S. golfers played with a golf ball that was 1.68 inches in diameter, and British and international players used one that was 1.62 inches in diameter. The smaller ball went farther and was easier to play in the wind—important in the windy British Isles. But using the larger golf ball, which was more difficult to master, gave a great advantage to American players, who had to learn to control it. It is no coincidence that when the rules were standardized in 1990 and the American 1.68-inch ball was chosen as the standard, the international players improved greatly and began to approach, and in some cases, even surpass their American counterparts.

The second Great Triumvirate of Golf, the American one of Ben Hogan, Byron Nelson, and Sam Snead, dominated the game into the mid-1950s. Snead even won PGA tournaments through 1965 and was competitive into the early 1970s, when he was in his 60s. In the late 1950s, however, the game of golf's popularity increased almost exponentially, shepherded by another triumvirate, this one comprising the American president, television, and Arnold Palmer.

In 1952, Dwight David Eisenhower, heroic general of World War II, was elected U.S. president and served through 1960. An avid golfer, he was a member of the Augusta National, and his frequent forays to Augusta and the golf course were well documented by the American press. As the First Golfer, he helped popularize the sport. Almost concurrent with this, television came into American homes, and in 1953 a golf tournament was shown on national television for the first time. It was George May's World Championship at the Tam O'Shanter Country Club near Chicago. If the televised sport needed drama to give it impetus, it got it on the final hole when Lew Worsham holed a full-wedge shot for an eagle to win the tournament by one shot over Chandler Harper.

The U.S. Open was first televised nationally in 1954, and over the next decade many of the PGA Tour events found their way onto the tube. But if more was needed to popularize golf on television, the game found it in the person of Arnold Palmer. Movie-star handsome with a ballerina-like waist and forearms of a stevedore, Palmer lit up the tube with his charisma and his heroic winning ways. Famed for coming from behind in the last round (known as "Arnie's charges"), he became the most popular golfer in the world since Bob Jones. He was followed by an ever-increasing crowd known as "Arnie's Army." But it was not just his attractiveness to the televised audience that made him so popular, Palmer was truly one of the greatest players ever, eventually winning four Masters, two Open Championships, and one U.S. Open. As the popularity of golf, and especially golf on television, increased, purses on the PGA Tour greatly escalated as well. One pro golfer, Frank Beard, remarked in the mid-1970s that pro golfers owed at least 25 cents of every dollar they made to Arnold Palmer. While Palmer was important in increasing the popularity of the game, Eisenhower's influence and television were equally responsible. But Palmer did become the first multimillionaire in the game due to the marketing opportunities that his fame engendered.

After Palmer, the next great player was Jack Nicklaus, who won the U.S. Amateur title in 1959 and 1961 and then turned professional. He won his first pro tournament at the 1962 U.S. Open when he defeated Palmer in a play-off. The championship was held near Palmer's hometown at Oakmont Country Club in Pittsburgh, and when Nicklaus triumphed, all Pennsylvania mourned, heralding the changing of the guard. Palmer won the 1962 Open Championship (British) and the 1964 Masters, but from 1963 through the late 1970s, Nicklaus was the greatest player in the world. He eventually won 18 major professional championships and is usually mentioned with Bob Jones and Ben Hogan as the greatest player ever, later joined by Tiger Woods. But Nicklaus never captured the public's imagination like Palmer and he suffered in comparison to the charismatic Arnie. He overcame this by the sheer force of his golfing brilliance.

INTERNATIONALISM OF THE GAME

From the beginning of the 1930s through the middle of the 1970s, there were only a few exceptions to American golf dominance. Briton Henry

Cotton won three Open Championships in 1934, 1937, and 1948, but he rarely crossed the Atlantic to challenge the Americans. He played in the Masters only three times and the U.S. Open only twice, and he never finished in the top 10 in either event. In the late 1940s, South African Bobby Locke became the first non-American to win consistently in the United States—he won 15 tournaments on the PGA Tour including six in 1947 alone, and he also won four Open Championships (British). Portly and somewhat rotund, he looked nothing like an athlete and hooked every shot he hit including his putts, but he is still considered among the greatest putters ever. In the 1950s, Australian Peter Thomson became the first player to play internationally. He won five Open Championships (1954–1956, 1958, 1965), one other event on the PGA Tour, 33 Australasian professional tournaments, and 26 pro tournaments in Europe.

But it was left to another South African, Gary Player, to fully internationalize the game of golf. Player played his first major event in 1956, placing fourth at the Open Championship (British), an event he would win in 1958. He traveled widely to compete against the best and won on almost every continent. In 1965, following his 1958 Open Championship and victories in 1961 at the Masters and 1962 at the PGA, Player won the U.S. Open to complete the career Grand Slam. He eventually won over 160 professional tournaments worldwide and established records with seven wins at the Australian Open and 13 at the South African Open. Smaller than most great golfers, Player developed his body with an arduous exercise and weight-lifting regimen, and a health-food diet. Often wearing all black, purportedly to bring him strength, he was called the "Black Knight." In the 1960s, the next Great Triumvirate of Golf was considered to be Palmer, Nicklaus, and Player.

But through the late 1970s, only a few international players challenged the Americans, notably Tony Jacklin, who won the Open Championship (British) in 1969 and the U.S. Open in 1970. In 1977, however, a young player from Spain, a nation with no prior great international golfers, placed second at the Open Championship behind Johnny Miller. And thus was born the legend of Severiano Ballesteros—"Seve."

Seve won the Open Championship in 1979 and would go on to win that title a total of three times, adding victories in 1984 and 1988. He became the first European to win the Masters in 1980 and won it again in 1983. But it was more the way he won that was so remarkable. Blessed with a simple, solid-appearing golf swing, Ballesteros was nevertheless a very wild driver. But it mattered little to him, since he was a magician at getting out of trouble. Like Palmer in the early 1960s, with his charges and his escapes from seeming disaster, Ballesteros won over the galleries with his mystical recoveries and winning ways. His swarthy good looks and his simple background as a former caddie in rural Spain, made him attractive to the masses in Europe, and his prominence began a resurgence of the game in Europe that continues into the 21st century. Ballesteros played in the United States, but he preferred the European Tour, and his support of that tour and his many victories there brought the European Tour to greater prominence.

And after Ballesteros popularized the game in Europe, other great players began to develop and rival the best players in America. These include Sandy Lyle, who won the Open Championship (British) in 1985 and the Masters in 1988; Nick Faldo, who won six major championships between 1987 and 1996; Bernhard Langer, who twice won the Masters in 1985 and 1993; Ian Woosnam, winner of the Masters in 1991; and José María Olazabal, who won the Masters in 1994 and 1999. Together with Ballesteros, this fivesome made Europe a formidable golfing region and transformed team events.

International team events had been around since the 1920s—the Ryder Cup, which matched teams of professionals from the United States with those from Great Britain (and later Great Britain and Ireland), and the Walker Cup, which matched teams of amateurs from the United States with those of Great Britain and Ireland. But the events had been one-sided, with the U.S. players almost always winning easily—so easily, in fact, that in 1973, the Ryder Cup was expanded, allowing Irish players on the British team, but to little effect. In 1979, to bring more drama to the competition, the Ryder Cup was changed to a competition between U.S. and European players, and, with the prominence of the Big Five of European golf, Europe won 8 of 11 matches beginning in 1985. The Walker Cup remained a contest between U.S. and British Isles players, but even there Britain improved, winning five of eight matches beginning in 1989.

Several of the Ryder Cup matches were the stuff of high drama, notably the 1991 match at Kiawah Island in South Carolina—"The War on the Shore." They became so popular that American players, who formerly often had little interest in playing, now lobbied to be on the team. And the popularity engendered other copycat competitions, notably the President's Cup, a team event started in 1994 that matched an American team against an international team composed of players from outside of Europe. The women also began a team competition. While women amateurs had competed in the Curtis Cup since 1932, beginning in 1990 women professionals contested the Solheim Cup, which matched American and European players.

FROM CHAMPION TO CHAMPION

Australian professionals had been prominent since Peter Thomson began winning Open Championships in the early 1950s. Several other top Aussies include Bruce Devlin and Bruce Crampton over the next decades. But in the 1980s, Australia produced its greatest champion, one who would follow in the footsteps of Walter Hagen, Arnold Palmer, and Seve Ballesteros by capturing public acclaim with his charisma. This was Greg Norman. Tall, with a wispy waist, a shock of golden hair reaching down to his aquiline nose, and known as the "Great White Shark," Norman hit the ball prodigious distances and with great accuracy, which led Nicklaus to proclaim him the straightest long driver of a golf ball ever.

Norman seemed set to take over the mantle of world's greatest player in the early 1980s, a title held since the late 1970s by Tom Watson. But Norman was ill-fated and became a somewhat controversial figure in the game. Playing in Europe, Australia, and the United States, he finished fourth in the Masters and PGA in 1981 and seemed set to start winning major championships. In 1986, he completed what some have termed the "Saturday Slam"—leading all four major championships after the third round, which ended on Saturday. Yet he won only one of those, the Open Championship (British). At Augusta, he fell victim to a late charge from 46-year-old Jack Nicklaus, who won his sixth green jacket and 18th major championship. At the PGA Championship at Inverness Club, tied for the lead as he approached the 72nd hole, Norman had to watch as Bob Tway holed an improbable bunker shot on the final hole to deprive him again. And at the next major, the 1987 Masters, Norman was tied with Larry Mize after 72 holes. The play-off began on the 10th hole, and on the 11th hole, Mize missed the green far right, resulting in a very difficult chip shot. To Norman's consternation, Mize holed that almost impossible shot, and when Norman's long putt missed, he was shut out again. Norman won one other major, the 1993 Open Championship, but in 1996 at Augusta, he suffered his most difficult loss. Leading by six shots after three rounds, he shot 78 in the final round, losing 11 shots to Nick Faldo and losing the tournament by five shots. Norman's career legacy seemed to be one of unfulfilled promise, someone who could not finish the deal at majors.

Norman's controversial side came when he fought with the PGA Tour over plans to start a worldwide golf tour in the early 1990s. Norman promoted the idea and was willing to fund and support it, but the U.S. PGA Tour showed little interest, causing him to abandon the idea. A few years later, the idea resurfaced in the form of World Golf Tour events, now sponsored and supported by the PGA Tour, which gave Norman no credit for the idea, greatly rankling him. After Norman and Faldo began their descent from golf's Mount Olympus in the late 1990s, the golf world looked for somebody to become the next great player. They did not need to look far, as he had been around for several years.

In 1991, Eldrick "Tiger" Woods won the U.S. Junior Amateur Championship when he was only 15 years old, the youngest player to win it at that time. Woods had been around and known in the golf world for over a decade. He had appeared on "The Mike Douglas Show" at the age of three, where he demonstrated his golf swing. He had won almost 100 junior tournaments by 1991, and had tried to qualify for the Los Angeles Open when he was only 14. He won the U.S. Junior again in 1992 and 1993, and followed that by winning the U.S. Amateur in 1994–1996, which gave him six consecutive national titles. Woods was the NCAA Champion in 1996 while a sophomore at Stanford when he turned professional in the fall of that year. That fall, after turning pro, Woods needed to win enough money to avoid having to attend Q School. He easily solved that problem by winning two tournaments and ranking 24th on the year-end money list despite having played a very short schedule.

Although Woods had played several major championships prior to the 1997 Masters, he had never challenged in any of them. At that Masters, he started poorly, shooting 40 on the front nine of the first round but recovered with a 30 on the back nine for a first round 70, and he eventually won the title by 12 shots over Tom Kite. The players already knew they were dealing with a new force. After Woods had taken the third-round lead, Colin Montgomerie, who was close behind, was asked, considering the collapse of Norman in the final round only the year before, if he might be able to catch Woods. Montgomerie replied, "Tiger Woods is not Greg Norman," implying both the problems Norman had had finishing the deal, and the steely resolve that would mark Woods' career.

For many years, the Masters had not allowed black players to compete, and when he won in 1997, it was also a sociological victory for Woods, who is part black. Since that victory he has become the greatest player in the world, bar none, and possibly the greatest of all time. His sights are set on bettering Nicklaus' record of 18 major championships, and through 2009, he had won 14 majors and over 70 PGA Tour championships. It can be argued that nobody has ever dominated the PGA Tour like Woods has. An extremely long hitter, his only weakness is some wild driving, but this is usually saved by putting skill that is nothing short of remarkable. And thus stands the world of men's professional golf as we enter the second decade of the 21st century—dominated by Woods, with no peer to truly challenge him, though several have tried in vain, among them Phil Mickelson, Vijay Singh, Ernie Els, and Retief Goosen.

Woods' victories and ascendance in golf have highlighted one of the bad marks against the game and one of its continuing problems. The game is not very popular among ethnic minorities, and in its early days, the PGA Tour (then run by the PGA of America) practiced outright discrimination by including in its bylaws a Caucasian-only clause that was not deleted until 1962. Some of the problems with bringing the game to minorities have dealt with the expense of playing the game. Further, in the past, minorities often entered the game via the caddie yard, but that vehicle is rarely open to them now. More evidence of this can be seen on the PGA Tour. In the 1970s, after the Caucasian-only clause had been removed and a few years had allowed blacks the opportunity to progress, although not without difficulty, there were up to 10 black golfers on the tour. But in the 21st century, Woods is the only black golfer on the tour. And because many minorities started as caddies, many of the former professional caddies in the 1970s were African Americans, but most of the current professional caddie yard is lily white.

AMATEUR GOLF

But the game of golf is more than just the world of professional golf, although that is its most visible portion. While many other sports have abandoned the difference between amateurs and professionals, blurring the distinction, golf continues to revel in having robust amateur tournaments. Many of these are now dominated by younger, college-age players or, among the women, often high schoolers, and this has led the USGA and R&A to institute Mid-Amateur Championships, open to players 25 years or older.

The golf world wants to continue support of the amateur game because that is where the future of golf must lie, in terms of participant numbers. In a golf world without caddie programs as a means of ingress to the game, increasing participant numbers are critically important in order for the golf industry to maintain its customer base. While the professional game is the publicized side of the sport that helps promote the game, the golf industry realizes that amateur golf and golf played at clubs, both public and private, are what will continue to increase its revenues. Without that support, for a number of sociological reasons, golf participant numbers may continue to decrease, at least in the United States. Golf businesses know this and know that a viable option for them is to look overseas, especially to China.

SPREADING THE GAME WORLDWIDE

Golf has been a worldwide sport, but in name only for most of its existence. The game began in Scotland, spread to the United States, and by 2000, was immensely popular in Japan, Korea, and Australia. But many countries, particularly those formerly called "Third World," barely know of the game. Part of that relates to the fact that golf has not been in the Olympics since 1904, and most of the world's nations concentrate their sporting efforts on sports that are played in the Olympics. But golf was recently placed back on the Olympic program, and will be featured at the 2016 Olympic Games.

With golf back in the Olympics, it is expected that many nations, including many where golf was virtually unknown in 2000, will now increase their support of the game. This occurred in tennis, which returned to the Olympic program only in 1988. The pro tennis tours are now an international conglomerate rather than being dominated by American and Australian players, as they had once been. It is expected that a similar worldwide interest will develop with respect to golf, and this has already been proven in China. Prior to 2004, there were only six golf courses and fewer than 50,000 golfers in China, a country of one billion plus people. But China has been building courses at a furious rate, and the largest resort in the world is now Mission Hills in Shenzhen, which has 12 golf courses and now hosts the annual World Cup of Golf.

The golf industry is looking to China, and other countries around the world, with high hopes for the explosion of interest that will be needed to increase growth. In fact, the golf industry has been looking in vain for this since 1996. In that year, golf was expected to begin a boom, based on the popularity of Tiger Woods, but the vaunted "Tiger Effect" has not occurred. The golf industry started pouring money into the game, expecting that its popularity would explode because of Tiger. Golf courses were built in abundance in preparation for the influx of new golfers that would surely soon populate them. But they often sat fallow because the influx never occurred, and many of these courses soon declared bankruptcy or simply closed altogether. In fact, since the early 1990s, the number of golfers in the United States has decreased slightly.

Why is this? Analysts point to several reasons, but among them, the sociological factors are emphasized the most. In the 1950s and 1960s, it was common for men to leave their families and spend a "day at the club" on weekends—playing golf in the morning, having a few drinks and playing cards in the afternoon, and often being away from home most of the weekend. That no longer flies in the 21st century because men now have difficulty justifying that much time away from their families, and, therefore, country club usage has declined. Country clubs have noted this and have had to become much more innovative. Now, they attempt to entice whole families to their clubs in order to keep their membership roles at a level necessary to maintain their clubs.

Where is it going? No one can predict precisely. If they could, everyone would be betting on winners. But it is safe to say that in 2050 the world of golf will look different from how it looks today. Because China and the Pacific Rim are starting to emphasize the sport and because of the possibility that the Olympics will open up the game to many other countries, the pro golf tours may very well begin to look more like the pro tennis tours, that is, have much more of an international quality. It is likely that there will be golf courses in parts of the world where the game is unknown today, and golf course architects will likely be the first beneficiaries of this, as they will be called upon to design these courses, often by large conglomerates or possibly even governments. One interesting course building project will soon occur in or near Rio de Janeiro, which has been chosen to host the 2016 Olympic Games. With golf now on the Olympic program for that year, a golf course for the tournaments will be necessary, and no suitable championship-level golf course exists near Rio. Every major golf course architect would like to be known as the one who built the Olympic course, and they are all champing at the bit in anticipation.

WOMEN AND GOLF

Women's golf also continues to figure prominently because the sport is one that allows women to compete almost on an equal footing with men. Women began playing a professional golf tour, the Women's Professional Golf Association (WPGA), in 1944. In 1950, the LPGA was established with a group of 13 prominent women as the founding players. The LPGA Tour has never been as popular as the men's tour and has struggled in a number of ways despite the presence of great players such as Babe Didrikson Zaharias in the 1950s, Mickey Wright in the 1960s, Nancy Lopez in the 1970s and 1980s, Kathy Whitworth from the 1960s into the 1980s, and Annika Sörenstam in the 1990s and the 2000s. Although some LPGA events are televised, and Golf Channel recently made an agreement to televise most of the women's events, women's golf has never drawn the audience that the men's game has. Thus purses have been smaller, and endorsement opportunities for women professionals have been far fewer.

In the 1990s, women's golf began to see the internationalism that men's golf had first found in Gary Player and Seve Ballesteros. The first influx came from Sweden with Liselotte Neumann winning the U.S. Women's Open in 1988, followed by Helen Alfredsson and then Annika Sörenstam. Sörenstam turned professional in 1992, after two years at the University of Arizona, and soon became the greatest player on the LPGA Tour and possibly the greatest ever. She won 72 tournaments and 10 major titles before retiring at the end of the 2008 season to start a family.

In addition to the Swedes, a number of prominent Korean players began playing the LPGA in the 2000s, and this has caused some problems. Although they are brilliant players, many of the Koreans do not speak English well. This led LPGA Commissioner Carolyn Bivens to institute a rule in 2008 requiring them to learn English—a rule that was greeted with great controversy and that Bivens, who had only a short, tumultuous term as commissioner, quickly rescinded. But part of the appeal of the pro tours is pro-am events, in which the professionals interact with usually well-heeled amateur partners, often funded by corporations that support the tournaments in return for this opportunity. The Korean players are unable to do this well because of their difficulty with English. Also, their problems with media interviews have led to some drop off in the popularity of the women's game.

In 2007–2008, another international player arose who has none of these problems, and she has taken over from Sörenstam as the best player in the women's game—Lorena Ochoa of Mexico. Fluent in English and extremely popular in Latin America, Ochoa overcomes some of the American audience problems that the Korean players are unable to overcome. But the LPGA's problem is not simply an influx of international players but the fact that the American players are no longer the best in the world, and the American public, media, and television audience has had trouble identifying with the international players.

When the worldwide recession hit in 2008, the LPGA experienced further difficulty. Carolyn Bivens had taken over as LPGA commissioner in 2005, and she immediately attempted to improve the LPGA by instituting several policies similar to those of the PGA Tour, but things did not work out well for her. There was her rule about learning English, which went nowhere. Bivens also tried to limit LPGA photography so that the LPGA had the rights to all photos, which started a media boycott, and that rule had to be reversed. She also tried to improve television rights and the pension and insurance plans for the players. But to do that, she had to increase sponsors' contributions, but they balked at that. The 2008 recession made it even more difficult for the sponsors, and several of them dropped off the tour citing difficulties in dealing with Bivens and in being able to meet the increased financial requirements. Midway through the 2009 LPGA season, the tour was well below its high of over 35 in the mid-1970s. At the time of the 2009 U.S. Women's Open, the leading players wrote Bivens a letter asking her to resign, and she did so shortly after the open. But her legacy remains and the LPGA is currently in some trouble trying to obtain sufficient sponsorship to contest a full-year tour. There has even been some concern that, for numerous reasons, the LPGA may survive only if absorbed by the men's PGA Tour, similar to the WNBA. In late 2009, the LPGA hired a new commissioner, Michael Whan, who faces a daunting task. When he announced the LPGA schedule for 2010, it had only 24 events, with just 14 of those in the United States.

GOLF'S CURRENT PROBLEM LIST

Internationally, golf continues to thrive, led by the early 1980s European ascension and the influx of Swedish and Korean female players. Professional tours exist in Europe, Japan, Southeast Asia, Australasia, and South Africa, and there are multiple minor tours available for those players who are not qualified for the main events in many regions as well. But many national golf federations are looking for a boost from the addition of golf to the Olympic program for the 2016 Olympic Games. Government sports funding is very important in smaller countries because of a problem inherent in golf itself: the game is expensive and requires a certain amount of resources to play competitively. Belonging to a golf or country club, or playing frequently at a public course, is not cheap. Equipment is also expensive, with a top-line full set of clubs now costing over $1,000. To play in sufficient tournaments to get to the top levels requires extensive travel and lodging, tournament fees, caddie fees, and meal expenses; and a top amateur player can easily spend $50,000 in a single season. So for players who are not from wealthy families, this is usually prohibitive, and golf has historically been a game played predominantly by the rich. Those who have overcome this have often come from the caddie yard, which provided them with the opportunities to play at the courses where they caddied. In poorer countries, government support of players will be necessary to grow the game, but this support will likely be possible only because of golf's addition to the Olympic program.

At the top levels, the game is often played with a caddie, but caddies themselves are a disappearing breed. While caddies are still prominent on the major tours, it used to be that many country clubs had an established caddie program, and most players walked the course using a caddie to carry the clubs and bag. This was beneficial to the game of golf in several ways. First, the use of caddies usually exposed a number of boys and teenagers to the game. They often developed an interest in golf and became lifelong players. Second, walking the golf course was beneficial to the players as it gave the golfers more cardiovascular exercise in a game/sport often derided for its lack of physical conditioning. Finally, caddie usage enabled clubs to not have to build cart paths for cart usage.

But in the 1950s, gasoline-powered and electric-powered golf carts began to appear on American golf courses, and their use has sadly become ubiquitous in the United States. The carts are a source of income for the clubs and the golf professionals, who often share in the profits they generate. But they have led to a decline in the use of caddies, thus depriving the game of a source of future players and giving club players almost no chance to derive exercise from the game. They have also led to the creation of paved cart paths, which many people believe are an eyesore. But at many U.S. courses, especially resort courses, golf cart usage is actually mandatory. Fortunately, the blight has not affected the game to the same degree in Europe or internationally. One former USGA president, Sandy Tatum, has cynically referred to the two different games as "golf" and "cartball."

The expense of playing golf and the current dearth of caddies in the United States has led to the formation of some programs to encourage the young, especially those who aren't rich, to play the game. Both the USGA and PGA of America have had such programs. In the 1990s, Tiger Woods lent his support to the First Tee Program, which has now become the best known program of its kind and which holds clinics and camps for inner city kids, encouraging them to learn to play golf. It is one solution to the problem that golf has had in keeping up its participant numbers.

Golf tours have had a long history of working with both charities and the business world. The PGA Tour, and to a lesser extent, the LPGA Tour and the Senior Tour, has always been noted for its significant emphasis on charitable giving. Virtually all of the major tournaments contribute to charities. The most well-known of these is the Memphis professional tournament, which has had various names, through which millions of dollars have been contributed to St. Jude's Children's Hospital. In 2008, the PGA Tour passed a milestone when it was announced that its total charitable giving passed $1 billion (U.S.). In addition to the corporate giving by the PGA and its tournaments, many of the players, male and female, have started their own charitable foundations. They are often supported through pro-am tournaments held near the end of the year.

In the past, golf has frequently been used as a vehicle for businessmen to meet potential partners or associates. Many well-heeled businessmen are golfers, and they often play a round with a potential business associate or prospective employee. They use the social interaction on the golf course as a way to better learn about the person with whom they might work. It has been said that more business deals have been made on the golf course than any other single place. Though that is surely an exaggeration, there is some truth to it, because golf courses have always been an easy place for the business world to network.

But with the decline in country club usage and membership in the 21st century, it is not certain if this trend will continue. It is not always a given that a potential employee or associate will be a golfer, so corporate bigwigs cannot count on deals on the golf course. That may be another detriment to golf clubs since it may diminish their use for that particular function.

The corporate world has long embraced golf in other ways, not simply for business rounds with potential clients. Corporate outings, sometimes in the form of pro-ams, have been an important part of marketing companies to their customers, either actual or imagined. If golf continues to decline among the business and corporate world, such outings may become less important and may decrease in number.

The effect of golf on the environment has become a big issue over the past decade as environmental groups have decried the use of land for golf courses. They claim that it not only takes away precious land that could be used, to their thinking, for better purposes but that golf courses may adversely affect the environment through the excessive use of water and the use of chemical pesticides and fertilizers for maintenance. These groups are also concerned about possible deleterious effects on birds and other wildlife by the loss of wetlands due to course construction. They also claim that golf courses obstruct corridors used by migrating animals and reduce the number of wildlife sanctuary areas.

In some areas, these concerns have led to protests, vandalism, and violence. Golf is perceived by the protesters as elitist, which makes golf courses a popular target for protests and opposition. In the Philippines and Indonesia, resisting golf tourism has become an objective of land-reform movements. Opposition to golf developments has also become an issue for the residents of Great Guana Cay and Bimini, who have started legal and political opposition to golf course developments on their islands on the grounds that the golf courses will destroy the ecosystem on which their coral reef and mangrove systems depend.

Another concern for today's golf course architects is that players now hit the ball much farther due to better technology, which necessitates longer and wider golf courses thus increasing the amount of land needed to build modern golf courses. Courses built in the past 20 years have required 10 percent more land than those built in the 1960s. An 18-hole course will now use about 150 acres of land, but golf course superintendents point out that only about 75 acres of that will be manicured land. Adding to the problem is that many courses are now built as part of golf course communities, and the communities themselves often place water restrictions on the residents and on the golf course superintendents.

But like many other political issues, these environmental concerns have actually led to better use of land for golf course development. Superintendents have used recent research in agronomy and turfgrasses to significantly reduce the amount of water needed on courses and to use more environmentally friendly pesticides and fertilizers. In actuality, the turf on golf courses is an excellent water filter that communities have used to cleanse gray water, such as in bioswales. Many golf courses in the world are irrigated with non-potable water and/or rainwater.

Further, golf course design has changed to reflect the concern for the environment. In the 1960s and 1970s, courses saw an "Augusta National Effect." Augusta National appears on television screens each April with a pristine, perfectly manicured course in brilliant green, often seen by northern golfers who pine for the winter to end. It led to many members wanting their own courses to look like Augusta National and insisting that their superintendents aim for this highly manicured look. But modern courses try to use the land in a more natural way, leaving much more of the land on which a course is built as wild areas and not manicuring these areas to any degree. This decreases the amount of water that is needed on the wild areas, and the areas are rarely fertilized.

These developments have led to significant changes in the way newer golf courses look. While the work of many architects in the 1960s and 1970s, especially Robert Trent Jones, often had a highly maintained, parkland-like look, modern courses are starting to trend back toward their roots on linksland in Scotland. There, the original courses were "laid out" by nature, and the bunkers were formed in places that sheep huddled to protect themselves from inclement weather. Pete Dye began this trend in the 1970s. He even used railroad ties on bunker walls, a trick he had learned in Scotland. Contemporary architects, such as Tom Doak, Bill Coore and Ben Crenshaw, and Brian Silva, are noted for the natural look of their courses, with areas off the fairway having a much more wild appearance. Among newer courses, Sand Hills Golf Course in Nebraska, Whistling Straits in Wisconsin, and Bandon Dunes in Oregon all have this very natural, somewhat native look.

GOLF TECHNOLOGY—ANOTHER PROBLEM?

Technology also became a hot topic in the golf world by the turn of the 21st century. Through the 1920s, golf club shafts were made of wood, but by the 1930s, metal shafts had begun to dominate the world of golf. They were stronger, more consistent, stiffer, and eventually could be made more cheaply. Through the 1960s, steel-shafted clubs were the standard, and there was very little change in club technology until that time. In the 1960s, however, fiberglass shafts appeared, followed in the early 1970s by graphite-shafted clubs, which eventually became an improvement over steel and metal shafts, although not initially because of problems with torque control in graphite.

In the 1980s and 1990s, golf club and golf ball technology literally exploded, completely changing the game of golf and engendering multiple other problems. First, graphite and titanium, and hybrids, became commonly used for golf club shafts. These were lighter, stronger, could be made more consistently, and had less torque than steel. And then, woods no longer remained woods. The driver and lesser wood clubs began to be made with metal heads, and eventually these heads were greatly increased in size. Because the metal heads were hollow, there was almost no limit to the size the head could become, and metal wood heads at the turn of the century were often three or four times the size of a traditional wood head from the 1970s. This eventually led the USGA to put a limit on their size.

The metal heads were larger, which gave them a much higher moment of inertia, and it actually made it harder to hit the ball off-line, which was a great advantage to players. And because they were lighter, greatly increased driving distance became possible. At about the same time, significant improvements in golf ball technology also added to the increase in driving distance.

From about 1905 through the 1960s, almost all golf balls were basically of the same design—usually a 3-piece ball with a core, sometimes solid, sometimes liquid filled, wrapped by elastic bands, and covered with a rubberized compound, most often balata. Then around 1970, multiple changes began appearing in golf balls with manufacturers changing dimple patterns, changing weight distributions, and even moving away from balata to longer-lasting synthetic covers, usually either Surlyn or urethane.

All the various changes in golf ball technology led to a series of golf balls in the 1990s that were harder to cut, easier to control, and went much farther. When combined with the new metal woods and other changes in golf club design, greatly increased driving distance occurred. When the PGA Tour began compiling driving distance stats in 1980, the leader for the year was Dan Pohl, who averaged 274.3 yards. By 2008, that average drive would rank a player 187th on the PGA Tour for the year, and the leader that year, Bubba Watson, averaged 315.1 yards, an increase of over 40 yards over Pohl. While players by 2008 were larger and more physically fit, the increase in driving distance was so dramatic that many of the Senior PGA players actually saw their driving distance increase as they got older, which defies any other explanation but technology.

This increase in distance was realized also by average golfers, who loved it. But the problem was that the pros were now hitting golf balls so far that most courses were becoming somewhat obsolete as they were too short to mount a challenge for the professionals. They simply overpowered the courses, and even increased amounts of hazards, rough, and faster greens could not prevent the onslaught of lower scores. This problem is ongoing, though even Jack Nicklaus, by now a golf course architect who has seen the increased distance affect his courses, has said it is a major problem and has called for a scaling back of the golf ball and even for the use of a standard golf ball in professional events.

The USGA has looked at ways to limit the increase in driving distance and has enacted rules to limit the size of clubs. It has also developed what is called the "overall distance standard." If a ball goes farther than a predetermined limit, it will not be considered legal. The problems are not resolved as of 2010.

So golf has several problems as it begins its seventh century of existence, but it also has a lot to offer. Most prominent among these to the public is what Tiger Woods has meant to the game. Televised events with Tiger usually garner huge ratings, while those he skips suffer in comparison. His appeal alone has increased PGA Tour purses multiple times. And the game of golf itself endures. It is truly a game of a lifetime, played by toddlers and nonagenarians. It is played in beautiful, wooded, park-like settings, or open fields, allowing players to be in the out-of-doors for several hours each day obtaining some exercise, especially if they eschew golf carts.

The game of golf will endure and prosper. It has been with us for at least five centuries, perhaps as long as any sport or game, and it is not going away despite any problems it may be having. The principles on which it has been built, mainly the sportsmanship inherent in the game, will provide a base on which it can and will grow. For it is, as it has been called by Ben Hogan, perhaps its best player ever, "the greatest game of all."

The Dictionary

– A –

ABBOTT (-DUNNE), MARGARET IVES. B. 15 June 1878, Calcutta (Kolkata), West Bengal, India; D. 10 June 1955, Greenwich, Connecticut, United States. With a nine-hole score of 47, Margaret Abbott gained a measure of renown by becoming the first American woman, and second overall, to win an Olympic gold medal. She won the 1900 Olympic golf event for **women** and remains, through 2010, the only female Olympic golf champion. Miss Abbott was from Chicago but traveled to France with her mother to study art and music. While there, she learned of the Olympic golf event and, already an accomplished golfer, entered. Her mother also played, finishing eighth. Margaret Abbott learned golf at the Chicago Golf Club, schooled by **Charles Blair Macdonald** and H. J. Whigham, two of the top American **amateurs**. Although she never played in a major tournament in this country, she was probably Chicago's top woman player in 1900, winning many of the local events. While in Paris, Margaret Abbott studied art under Edgar Degas and Auguste Rodin. She then met Finley Peter Dunne, who would later become a noted American humorist. She and Dunne were married in 1902 and lived in New York for many years.

ACE. *See* HOLE-IN-ONE.

ADAIR (-CUTHELL), RHONA KATHLEEN. B. 1882, Cookstown, County Tyrone, Ireland; D. 1961. Rhona Adair was an Irish **amateur** player who was born to Hugh and Augusta Adair in Cookstown, **Ireland**. Her father owned a linen firm, which was the county's largest employer, and his means gave Rhona the time and finances to support her amateur career. She won the **British Ladies' Open Amateur Championship** in 1900 and 1903 and won the Irish Ladies' Closed Championship for four consecutive years, from 1900 to 1903. In 1904, Adair traveled to the **United States** and gave an exhibition tour. She married Major Algernon Cuthell, who was killed in action in World War I at Suvla Bay, Turkey, during the Gallipoli campaign in August 1915. Rhona Adair-Cuthell remained active in **women**'s golf circles and was president of the Irish Ladies' Golf Union for many years, holding that position until her death in 1961.

AGRONOMY. Agronomy is the study of turfgrasses and soils, and it is quite important in developing **grasses** for **golf courses** and preventing erosion and environmental problems on courses. The science has attempted to develop sturdy, stable grasses that grow in various climates, while withstanding the foot traffic of a golf course, especially on greens. Many colleges offer degrees in agronomy or landscape architecture, which help students become proficient in the science. *See also* TURFGRASS RESEARCH AND MANAGEMENT.

ALBATROSS. An albatross is a three-under-**par** score on any hole, also more commonly known as a **double eagle**. It is extremely rare and usually occurs by scoring a two on a par-five, although a **hole-in-one** on a par-four is also considered a double eagle or an albatross. The most famous albatross in golf history occurred in the final round of the 1935 **Masters** when **Gene Sarazen** holed his second shot on the par-five 15th for a deuce, to make up three shots and enable him to tie for the lead. He won the title in a play-off the next day.

ALCOTT, AMY. B. 22 February 1956, Kansas City, Missouri, United States. Amy Alcott first came to national attention when she won the **U.S. Girls' Junior** in 1973. She turned **professional** shortly after taking that title, one of the first junior golfers to skip college in order to turn professional, won in only her third professional start (at the 1975 Orange Blossom Classic), and was named **LPGA** Rookie of the Year in 1975. Alcott won 29 LPGA tournaments in her career, including five majors: the 1980 **U.S. Women's Open**, the 1979 **Du Maurier Classic**, and the **Kraft Nabisco (Dinah Shore)** Championship in 1983, 1988, and 1991. At the 1991 Dinah Shore, Alcott started the tradition of the winner jumping into the lake alongside the 18th green. In three years she won four tournaments on the LPGA (1979, 1980, and 1984), also winning the **Vare Trophy** in 1980 for the lowest scoring average for the year. Alcott was inducted into the **World Golf Hall of Fame** in 1999 and is also a member of the National Jewish Museum Sports Hall of Fame.

ALFREDSSON (-NILSSON), HELEN. B. 9 April 1965, Göteborg, Sweden. Helen Alfredsson grew up playing junior golf in Sweden. She represented Sweden in both the European Junior and Senior Team championships, later playing for Sweden at the **Women's World Amateur Team Championship** in 1986 and 1988. She attended college in the **United States** at U.S. International University, graduating in 1988 with a degree in international business. She then briefly tried modeling in Paris and flew with the Blue Angels, but she continued playing tournaments in Sweden. Alfredsson began her **professional** career in 1989 in Europe, winning Rookie of the Year honors on the **Ladies European Tour**. She won the 1993 **Kraft Nabisco (Dinah Shore)**, her only major championship, although she won the 1990 **Women's British Open** before it was considered a major. She won 11 tournaments on the Ladies European Tour and seven on the **LPGA** through 2009. She played seven times for the European Team at the **Solheim Cup**, in 1990, 1992, 1994, 1996, 1998, 2000, and 2002. Alfredsson is married to former NHL player Kent Nilsson.

ALISON, CHARLES HUGH. B. 1883, Preston, Lancashire, England; D. 20 October 1952, Rondebosch, Cape Province, South Africa. Charles Alison was a British **golf course architect** who worked for many years with **Harry Colt**, with whom he formed the firm of Colt, Alison, Morrison, Ltd, which also included John Morrison. The two also collaborated with **Alister MacKenzie** on several courses and were heavily influenced by him. Although both Alison and Colt were British they worked on many American courses, among them Milwaukee Country Club, designed in 1929, and Century Country Club in Purchase, New York, built in 1927. Alison is also responsible for **Hirono Golf Club**, often considered the best course in **Japan**.

Alison served in both World War I and II as a code breaker, helping to decipher codes.

ALLISS, PERCY. B. 8 January 1897, Sheffield, England; D. 31 March 1975, Bournemouth, England. Percy Alliss was an English **professional** golfer who played in the era before there was a true European tour. Alliss' first professional win was the 1920 Welsh PGA Championship. He later lived in Germany, working as a club professional, and won the German Open five times, four times consecutively from 1926 to 1929. His biggest European wins were the 1933 and 1937 News of the World Match Play Tournaments. His best finish at the Open Championship (**British Open**) was equal third in 1932, and he was three times equal fourth, in 1928, 1929, and 1933. Alliss settled back in **England** and was club pro at Ferndown Golf Club in Dorset for 28 years, before his retirement at age 70. Alliss played in the **Ryder Cup** in 1929, 1931, 1933, 1935, and 1937. His son, **Peter Alliss**, a top professional and golf announcer, also played in the Ryder Cup. They were the first father-son duo to play in that team match.

ALLISS, PETER. B. 28 February 1931, Berlin, Germany. Peter Alliss is best known as a golf announcer, both on European and American television. He is the son of **Percy Alliss**, a top British **professional** from the 1920s and 1930s. Peter Alliss left school at 14 years of age and turned professional when he was only 16. He won three British PGA championships and played on eight **Ryder Cup** teams, he and his father being the first father-son duo to play in that team match. He also represented **England** 10 times in the World Cup. Alliss won at least 23 professional tournaments even though he played before there was a structured **European Tour**. These include wins at the Spanish Open (twice), Portuguese Open, Italian Open, and Brazilian Open, winning national titles in 1958 in Italy, Spain, and Portugal. After his playing career ended, Alliss began announcing European golf tournaments and later, after the death of **Henry Longhurst**, was hired to announce for ABC Television in the **United States**. He has also announced in **Australia** and **Canada**. He is also a well-known **golf course** designer in Europe, with over 20 courses in his portfolio, and has written over 20 books. Peter Alliss has received two honorary doctorates, in 2002 from Bournemouth University, and in July 2005, an honorary doctor of laws from **St. Andrews** University.

ALTERNATE BALL. An alternate ball is played when players are not certain of a particular rule or ruling. It may be played only in **stroke play**. Players playing an alternate ball must announce in advance to their marker which ball they wish to play for their score if the ruling is in their favor. When the ruling is made, players must use the score shot with the ball that they stated they wished to use for their score, even if they made a higher score with that ball. If players do not announce which ball they prefer to use, the score with the original ball counts. Play with an alternate ball is defined in the **Rules of Golf** under Rule 3-3 "Doubt as to Procedure," although the term "alternate ball" is not used in that rule. However, the term is common in tournament golf.

AMATEUR. "Amateur" is generally defined as someone who does not play a sport for money. There are separate events in golf for amateurs and **professionals** as well as events open to both. The concept of amateurism in golf is somewhat complex and the precise definitions have varied over the years. The **Rules of Golf** have a large section defining the current definiton of "amateur," as well as what constitutes violations of amateurism. *See also* AMATEUR STATUS.

AMATEUR STATUS. "**Amateur**" is a term derived originally from the Greek word for lover, and originally referred to someone who played or did something only for the love of it and not, specifically, for any financial reimbursement. The original concept was actually unknown to the ancient Greeks, however, although many people have claimed that the ancient Olympic Games were open to amateurs only. The concept began in the mid-19th century, when rowing was a very popular sport in Great Britain. The elite class originally dominated rowing races but soon found themselves unable to compete against people who worked as manual laborers and had developed their muscles through hard work. To the British, the word "amateur" originally denoted a class distinction and excluded anyone who made a living via manual labor. A person who made a living via manual labor was labeled "**professional**," a term denoting someone who was not a gentleman. Over the next century, the definition evolved until it meant someone who doesn't receive money or financial gain from playing a particular sport.

In golf, many of the original events were played among amateurs or, basically, club members. The **U.S. Golf Association (USGA)** first held a **U.S. Amateur** Championship in 1895, the same year the **U.S. Open** began. However, in Britain, the **British Amateur (The Amateur Championship)** was first held in 1885, 25 years after the **Open Championship (British Open)**. Over the years, the USGA and the **R&A** defined strict rules of amateur status. Originally quite restrictive, even prohibiting expense money for playing in tournaments or announcing that one was planning to eventually turn professional, the rules have been progressively loosened. The current USGA rules note that "An 'amateur golfer' is one who plays the game as a non-remunerative and non-profit-making sport and who does not receive remuneration for teaching golf or for other activities because of golf skill or reputation, except as provided in the Rules." The amateur status rules then list several definitions and define the restrictions at various levels of competition. Notably, however, the rules state that an amateur may not play for prize money and that "an amateur golfer must not accept a prize (other than a symbolic prize) or prize voucher of retail value in excess of $750 or the equivalent, or such a lesser figure as may be decided by the USGA." The rules on expenses are rather lengthy and deal with various categories of play (from juniors to college play, and team and international play) and from whom an amateur may accept expenses for play in golf tournaments.

A known violation of the rules of amateur status will cause the ruling bodies to declare the golfer a professional. One notable time this may occur is when a prize is given for making a **hole-in-one** in an amateur tournament. Accepting the prize, which has been as high as $1 million, causes the player to lose amateur status. If amateur status is lost, the golfer may be able to return to play as an amateur, which is not true in many other sports. This is termed "reinstatement of amateur status." The golfer must apply for reinstatement to the governing body. If reinstated, the golfer must serve a probationary period, usually from two to five years, after which the golfer may play in amateur tournaments again. During the probationary period, the golfer may play in open tournaments listed as an "Applicant for Reinstatement (AR)." Golfers who have reached a high level of professional play will usually not be allowed reinstatement. It is possible for a golfer to be reinstated to amateur status more than one time.

AMEN CORNER. "Amen Corner" is a term that refers to the 11th, 12th, and 13th holes at **Augusta National Golf Club**, home of the **Masters**. The term was coined by **Herbert Warren Wind** in an article in *Sports Illustrated* about the 1958 Masters. There are **water hazards** on all three holes, but the 12th is a short par-three that can be **birdied** and the 13th is a very reachable par-five. Therefore, Amen Corner often decides the Masters because players can go through the holes 1- or 2-under-par or they can find disaster due to the **hazards** that guard all three greens. Wind later described the origin of the phrase. He was looking for something catchy and remembered a jazz record from the 1930s, which he stated was by Chicago's Mezz Mezzrow, called "Shouting in That Amen Corner." Later research by *Golf World*'s Bill Fields found that the song was actually written by Andy Razaf and recorded by the Dorsey Brothers Orchestra, with vocals by Mildred Bailey.

AMERICAN JUNIOR GOLF ASSOCIATION (AJGA). The American Junior Golf Association is a nonprofit organization that conducts junior golf tournaments for boys and girls 12–18 years of age throughout the **United States**. The idea started with Mike Bentley, a Georgia sportswriter who formed the DeKalb Junior Golf Association in 1974, which became the Atlanta Junior Golf Association. He realized that there was no national group organizing tournaments for juniors and started the AJGA in 1978. In 1984, the group hired Stephen Hamblin as executive director. He has now served in that role for 25 years. The AJGA is headquartered at Chateau Elan Resort in Braselton, Georgia, and now conducts over 75 tournaments a year for junior golfers. It has many corporate sponsors and each year names its Rolex Junior All-America team and the Rolex Junior Player of the Year winners. AJGA players have gone on to great college and **professional** success, with previous Rolex Junior Players of the year including **Tiger Woods**, **Phil Mickelson**, Cristie Kerr, and Paula Creamer.

AMERICAN SOCIETY OF GOLF COURSE ARCHITECTS (ASGCA). The American Society of Golf Course Architects was founded in 1946 to represent the interests of **golf course architects** in the **United States** and **Canada**. Membership requires that a golf course architect or designer has completed a minimum of five major golf course projects, and all members are peer-reviewed by the organization. One major current thrust of the organization is to promote environmentally responsible golf course design. The ASGCA has recently published three editions of *An Environmental Approach to Golf Course Development* to help educate permitting boards, town councils, developers, media, and the general public as to how golf courses may positively impact the environment. The third edition, released in 2008, highlights 18 case studies that showcase how to deal successfully with sensitive habitats.

ANDERSON, JAMES "JAMIE." B. 1842, St. Andrews, Scotland; D. 1905, Thornton, Fife, Scotland. Jamie Anderson was a Scottish golf **professional** who became the second player, after **Old Tom Morris**, to win the **Open Championship (British Open)** three times. Anderson won his titles consecutively, in 1877–1879, then did not play in 1880 because the date of the tournament was given out so late that he forgot to enter. He was the son of a golf pioneer called "Old Daw" who also ran a ginger beer stall and whose name was used for the 4th hole of the **Old Course** in **St. Andrews**. Anderson was known for his approach shot accuracy and his consistency in money matches. He simply waited for his opponents to make mistakes. Despite his skill in money games, he died penniless. He was living at the time of his death in Dysart Combination Poorhouse in Thornton, Fife. He is buried in a graveyard overlooking St. Andrews Cathedral in a grave with his son, who died in infancy. Jamie Anderson's name is not listed on the gravestone.

ANDERSON, WILLIAM LAW "WILLIE." B. 21 October 1879, North Berwick, East Lothian, Scotland; D. 25 October 1910, Chestnut Hill, Pennsylvania, United States. Willie Anderson's fame in golf rests on his winning four **U.S. Open** championships, the first player to do so and a mark that has not been bettered through 2010. He won his first title in 1901 and then won three consecutively from

1903 to 1905. He is still the only player to win the title for three straight years. Anderson grew up in **Scotland**, but immigrated to the **United States** with his family in 1896. He played in the 1897 U.S. Open, placing second, and his first major win in the United States was the 1899 Southern California Open. Anderson also won the **Western Open** four times, at the time considered the second most important tournament in the United States, in 1902, 1904, 1908, and 1909. He played with a flat swing that was characteristic of the Scots and was known as the **St. Andrews** swing. Off the **golf course**, Anderson had a difficult life. He was a **club professional** but had a drinking problem and worked at 10 clubs in 14 years. He was one of the best clubmakers among professionals and started his club career at Misquamicut Golf Club in Rhode Island. He later worked at **Baltusrol Golf Club** and Montclair Country Club (then Apawamis Country Club) in New Jersey (1903–1906), Onwentsia Country Club (1906–1909), St. Louis Country Club (1909–1910), and, finally, at Philadelphia Cricket Club (1910) until his death. The official cause of death was epilepsy, but it was written that he died from chronic alcoholism.

AOKI, ISAO. B. 31 August 1941, Abiko, Chiba, Japan. Isao Aoki was a Japanese **professional** golfer who was inducted into the **World Golf Hall of Fame** in 2004. He played mostly on the **Japanese PGA Tour**, winning 51 events there from 1972 to 1990 and leading their money list five times—1976 and 1978–1981. But Aoki also played worldwide, including fairly steady play on the U.S. **PGA Tour** from 1981 to 1990, during which time he won one tournament, the 1983 Hawaiian Open. He also won nine times on the U.S. **Champions Tour** from 1992 to 2003, won one event on the Australasian Tour, and won the 1978 **World Match Play Championship** at Wentworth, **England**. Aoki never won a major championship but placed second at the 1980 **U.S. Open**, at **Baltusrol Golf Club** in a storied duel with **Jack Nicklaus**.

APPROACH. An approach shot is the shot played into the green on a par-four or par-five. It is usually the second shot on a par-four and the third shot on a par-five, although the second shot on a par-five may be considered an approach shot if the player is going for the green.

APRON. *See* COLLAR.

ARMOUR, THOMAS DICKSON "TOMMY," "THE SILVER SCOT." B. 24 September 1894, Edinburgh, Scotland; D. 11 September 1968, Larchmont, New York, United States. Tommy Armour grew up in **Scotland** and served in World War I, where he lost the sight in his right eye after a mustard gas explosion, although it later returned somewhat. In 1920, Armour won the French Amateur Championship, and shortly thereafter, immigrated to the **United States.** He eventually became a U.S. citizen, although he would always be known as the "Silver Scot" because of his silvery gray hair. Armour turned **professional** in 1924, mentored by his idol, **Walter Hagen**. At the time, there was no real **PGA Tour**, but he won at least 25 professional titles in the 1920s and early 1930s beginning with the 1925 Florida West Coast Open. Armour won three major titles, the 1927 **U.S. Open**, the 1930 **PGA Championship**, and the 1931 **Open Championship (British Open).** He also won the **Canadian Open** in 1927, 1930, and 1934, and the **Western Open** in 1929, when those two events were essentially of major status. Armour retired from competition in 1935 and settled in Boca Raton, Florida, as a teaching professional. He became the best-known teacher of his era, and his book *How to Play Your Best Golf All the Time* was for many years the best-selling golf book of all-time. Armour was inducted into the **World Golf Hall of Fame** in 1976.

ARMY GOLF. "Army golf" is a derogatory term for one's play often heard among tournament players. It refers to a player who is hitting the ball all over the **golf course**, or in Army terms, "Left, right, left, right, . . ."

AUGUSTA NATIONAL GOLF CLUB. Augusta National Golf Club is the home of the annual Masters Tournament and may be the best-known golf club in the world. The club was founded by **Bob Jones** and **Clifford Roberts** in the early 1930s and opened for play in January 1933. The **golf course** was designed by **Alister MacKenzie**. Roberts was a wealthy New York investor who counseled Jones and chose Augusta, Georgia, because wealthy northeasterners frequently wintered there for the mild climate, often staying at the

Bon Air Vanderbilt Hotel. They bought a rolling site of land that had been a nursery. Opened in 1857 by a Belgian family led by Baron Prosper Jules Alphonse Berckmans, it was called "Fruitlands." Jones and Roberts envisioned Augusta National as a winter club for their wealthy friends, and it became so. To this day, the membership, which is kept strictly secret by the club, consists primarily of very wealthy, mostly white, men.

In 1934, Jones and Roberts decided to hold a golf tournament for many of Jones' friends, who often spent the winter at clubs in Florida and were traveling north in early April, preparing to work at their summer clubs. The 1934 tournament was not called the **Masters** but rather the Augusta National Invitation Tournament and was won by **Horton Smith**. In 1935, **Gene Sarazen** made golf history when he scored a **double eagle** two on the 15th hole of the final round, which enabled him to tie for the lead. He won the next day in a play-off. By 1936, the tournament had become known as the Masters. Over the next decades, because of the magisterial presence of Jones, it became one of the most popular tournaments in the world and, by the 1950s, was considered one of the four major championships.

The membership of Augusta National has been a source of controversy over the years. Originally a lily-white club, it first accepted a black member, Ron Townsend, in 1990, at the time the president of Gannett Television. The biggest controversy over its membership occurred in 2002 when **women**'s groups, notably the National Council of Women's Organizations, led by their chairperson, Martha Burk, demanded that women be admitted to the club as long as the club continued to host the Masters. Burk demanded a boycott of sponsors' products being advertised on television during the tournament. Augusta National responded by broadcasting the 2003 and 2004 tournaments with no commercials and no sponsors. Through 2009, Augusta National still has no female members.

Augusta National members are given a green jacket upon becoming members. The jacket is symbolic of the club, with the club's logo over the left breast pocket, and is not supposed to be worn off the club grounds. Many of the members wear it while dining at the club. The green jacket is given each year to the winner of the Masters (first given out in 1949), who becomes an honorary member of the club. The membership is led by a chairman, and there have only been a few over the years. The Augusta National chairmen have been Clifford Roberts (1934–1976), William Lane (1976–1980), Hord Hardin (1980–1991), Jack Stephens (1991–1998), William "Hootie" Johnson (1998–2006), and Billy Payne (2006–present).

AUSTRALIA. The first **golf course** in Australia is considered to be the Bothwell Golf Club in the Tasmanian midlands, which was originally founded in 1839. On the mainland, the Royal Adelaide Golf Club was founded in 1870, while the Australian Golf Club in Sydney was formed in 1882, followed by the Royal Melbourne Golf Club in 1891. The first major Australian tournament was the Australian Amateur, first held in 1894, followed by the Australian Open in 1904 and the Australian PGA in 1905. The Women's Australian Open premiered in 1974. The first great Australian **professional** was **Norman Von Nida**, who won the Queensland Amateur in 1932 and later won the Australian Open and Australian PGA three times each. He was followed by **Peter Thomson**, who won five Open championships (British Open). In the late 1950s and 1960s, the top Australian professionals were **Kel Nagle**, **Bruce Crampton**, and **Bruce Devlin**. The Australian star of the 1970s was Graham Marsh and he was followed by the greatest Australian player to date, **Greg Norman**, who was ranked number one in the world for 331 weeks in the 1980s and 1990s. Among women, the first great Australian player was **Jan Stephenson** in the 1970s. She was surpassed in the 1990s by **Karrie Webb**, who became the first Australian woman to be considered the best player in the world. The **Australian PGA Tour**, technically known as the PGA Tour of Australasia, was founded in 1973 and is one of the six tours recognized by the International Federation of PGA Tours. It is estimated that 500,000 Australians play golf more than 25 times per year, and as many as 1,000,000 Australians play some golf. Australia trails only **Scotland** and New Zealand in "most golf courses per capita" of any country.

AUSTRALIAN OPEN. The Australian Open, first played in 1904, is one of the major national open championships. The winner receives the Stonehaven Cup. The championship is rotated among various courses in **Australia**. **Gary Player** won the title seven times—1958, 1962, 1963, 1965, 1969, 1970, and 1974. He is followed by **Jack**

Nicklaus, who won six times between 1964 and 1978; **Greg Norman**, who won five times between 1980 and 1996; and Ivo Whitton, an **amateur** who won the championship in 1912, 1913, 1926, 1929, and 1931. There is also an Australian Women's Open, first held in 1994, and won that year by **Annika Sörenstam**. It has been won four times by **Karrie Webb**. Appendix 4 includes a list of champions of the men's Australian Open.

AUSTRALIAN PGA TOUR. Although there have been **professional** tournaments in **Australia** and Oceania since the beginning of the **Australian Open** in 1904, the PGA Tour of Australia was formed in 1973. In 1991, the name was changed to the PGA Tour of Australasia, although it is usually known as the Australian PGA Tour. The major tournaments are the Australian Open, New Zealand Open, Australian Masters, and Australian PGA Championship. Leading players who have played on this tour include Graham Marsh, **Greg Norman**, **Steve Elkington**, and Adam Scott. Many of the top Australian players often move on to either the **European PGA Tour** or the **PGA Tour** in the **United States**. There was a developmental tour to the Australian PGA Tour, originally termed the "Von Nida Tour" (after **Norman Von Nida**), but it has been absorbed by the main tour.

In January 2009, the Australian PGA Tour announced plans to begin a series of tournaments in concert with the China Golf Association, the **Japan** Golf Tour, the Korean Golf Association, and the Korean PGA. Termed the "OneAsia Tour," the plan was to consolidate a professional tour in the Pacific Rim and compete against the European PGA Tour and the U.S. PGA Tour. Some of the events in the OneAsia Tour were already sanctioned events on the Asian tours, and this idea has not been embraced by other leading golf administrators.

AZINGER, PAUL WILLIAM. B. 6 January 1960, Holyoke, Massachusetts, United States. Paul Azinger is a U.S. golfer who attended Florida State University and turned **professional** in 1981. He won 12 events on the **PGA Tour**, including the 1993 **PGA Championship**, his only major title. Shortly after that victory, Azinger was diagnosed with non-Hodgkin's lymphoma, which was found in his shoulder blade (scapula). He underwent chemotherapy and radiation therapy and recovered from that cancer. In 1995, he received the **Ben Hogan**

Award, given for golf accomplishments in the face of serious handicap, injury, or illness. Azinger's most notable recent accomplishment was serving as captain of the U.S. **Ryder Cup** team in 2008, which regained the Cup from Europe, and his motivational tactics were given credit for the team's victory. Azinger was a very close friend of **Payne Stewart** and gave the eulogy at his funeral.

– B –

BACK NINE. The "back nine" refers to the final nine holes of an 18-hole course. *See also* INWARD NINE.

BACK SIDE. *See* BACK NINE.

BACKSPIN. Backspin is the spin placed on almost all golf shots by the angled clubface striking the ball. The ball stays on the clubface during impact, actually rising up on the clubface during the milliseconds of impact and making the ball spin in a direction away from the target. Such backspin helps give the ball lift in the early parts of its flight, and on landing, backspin keeps a ball from rolling uncontrollably and may even make the ball spin backward toward the player upon landing on the green.

BACKSWING. The backswing is the early part of the golf swing, which begins with a **takeaway** as the player starts the swing of the clubhead away from the ball, and it ends with the club and hands over the player's right shoulder (for a right-handed player). From that position, the club is swung down toward the ball, usually called the **downswing**.

BALFOUR, ARTHUR JAMES "A. J.," FIRST EARL OF BALFOUR, KG, OM, PC, DL. B. 25 July 1848, Whittingehame, East Lothian, Scotland; D. 19 March 1930, Fisher's Hill, Woking, Surrey, England. A. J. Balfour was a Conservative British politician and statesman, mostly known for having served as British prime minister from 1902 to 1905. He was educated at Trinity College, Cambridge, graduating in 1869, and was known for his enthusiastic support of golf, the first such politician to espouse the game, predating **Dwight Eisenhower** by some 50 years. Balfour served as captain of the **Royal and Ancient Golf Club of St. Andrews** in 1894–1895 and wrote "The Humours of Golf," a chapter in the Badminton Library book on golf (edited by **Horace Hutchinson**), in 1890.

BALL IN PLAY. The **Rules of Golf** have a very specific definition for when a ball becomes "in play," specifically noting as follows: "A ball is in play as soon as the player has made a stroke on the teeing ground. It remains in play until it is holed, except when it is lost, **out-of-bounds** or lifted, or another ball has been substituted whether or not the substitution is permitted; a ball so substituted becomes the ball in play." The term is not used much in club matches or tournaments. In **professional** or major **amateur** tournaments, however, when a player seeks a ruling, the official will usually arrive and assist the player in defining the proper rule. The official then shows where a drop should be made. After the drop is properly made, the official will announce, "Ball is in play," and the player will play the ball from that position.

BALL MARK. A ball mark is the impact mark made on **putting greens** by a ball upon its landing. Ball marks cause damage to greens and should be repaired by all players after they arrive at the green. Repair is often done with a tee, but small ball mark repair tools are also available. Players may repair damage to the green from a ball mark prior to putting, even if the mark is not their own.

BALL MARKER. A ball marker is a small marker placed behind a ball, usually on the **putting green**, to allow the ball to be cleaned prior to play, or to move a ball to allow another player to have an unobstructed line to the hole. The item used as a ball marker is not specified in the rules, but some **local rules** make it mandatory that it be a small coin or similar small, round marker. In tournaments, ball markers are virtually always small, round coins or similar markers. In casual play, players may occasionally place a tee behind the ball as a marker, even on the putting green. Tees are often used to mark balls **through the green**, when taking a lift or drop in accordance with the rules.

BALL RETRIEVER. A ball retriever is an accessory item that some club players carry in their golf bags. The retriever has a long, extendable shaft with a semi-spherical socket at one end that allows a player to retrieve a ball from a water hazard, providing it can be seen and reached by the ball retriever.

BALL STRIKER. Golfers win golf tournaments by shooting the lowest scores, but among top golfers, the ability to be a good ball striker is highly prized. Putting or an excellent short game is often considered less of an achievement, though **professionals** usually understand the importance of putting and the short game to scoring. Among professionals, great ball strikers are often spoken of with some reverence for their abilities. Among the top ball strikers in golf history were **Ben Hogan**, **Moe Norman**, **Lee Trevino**, and in earlier years, Dick Metz and **Jim Barnes**.

BALL WASHER. Ball washers are items found on many **golf courses** near the tee for each hole. Balls may be placed in the ball washers to clean them. These are more common on public golf courses. On private courses, at least in the era of **caddies**, keeping the ball clean is one of the caddie's jobs, and ball washers are not as commonly seen.

BALL, JOHN, JR. B. 24 December 1861, Hoylake, Merseyside, England; D. 2 December 1940, Holywell, Wales. John Ball was the first great **amateur** player, winning the **Amateur Championship (British Amateur)** a record eight times—1888, 1890, 1892, 1894, 1899, 1907, 1910, and 1912. His eight victories is a record for any of the tournaments that have ever been considered major championships. Ball also won the **Open Championship (British Open)** in 1890, and he and **Bob Jones** are the only two players to have won the British Amateur and Open in the same year, Jones doing so in his **Grand Slam** year of 1930. Ball also had two runner-up finishes in the Amateur Championship and was runner-up at the 1892 Open Championship. Ball had a very long career as a top amateur, advancing to the fifth round of the Amateur Championship in 1921 at the age of 60. He grew up playing at **Royal Liverpool Golf Club** and was noted for his low trajectory, achieved by using a closed clubface to keep the flight beneath the wind. Ball's swing is regarded as one the best in the history of the game.

BALLESTEROS SOTA, SEVERIANO "SEVE." B. 9 April 1957, Pedreña, Cantabria, Spain. Seve Ballesteros was the first great continental European player. He grew up as a caddie and mainly learned to play on beaches near his home, often playing by himself with a single club, a 3-iron. He turned **professional** at age 16, and in 1976, at 19, he became well known when he finished second, behind **Johnny Miller,** in the **Open Championship** (**British Open**) at **Royal Birkdale**. He led the European Tour Order of Merit in 1976 and would win that award six times in his career, a record at the time, since surpassed by **Colin Montgomerie**. Ballesteros eventually won five major championships—the Open in 1979, 1984, and 1988 and **the Masters** in 1980 and 1983—and 91 professional tournaments worldwide, including 45 on the European Tour, and nine on the **PGA Tour**. He was ranked number one in the world for 61 weeks from 1986 to 1989. He also was feted in Europe for his play in the **Ryder Cup**, leading the European Team to five wins as a player and captain. Well-known for his **match play** skills, he won the **World Match Play Championship** five times.

Ballesteros was known for his swarthy good looks and his swashbuckling, wild style of play, somewhat reminiscent of **Arnold Palmer**. He was a very wild **driver**, although fairly long, but was a master at recovery play and the short game, and he was considered by **Ben Crenshaw** to be "a genius" with a golf club for his recovery efforts. Later in his career, Ballesteros struggled with back injuries and fell off his game dramatically in the 1990s. He planned to play some senior tournaments, but in July 2007, he announced his retirement from competitive golf. In October 2008, he was found to be gravely ill and was hospitalized, eventually being diagnosed with a brain tumor, specifically an oligoastrocytoma. He has had several surgeries as well as chemotherapy and radiation therapy, and he has recovered to make a few public appearances. Ballesteros was inducted into the **World Golf Hall of Fame** in 1999.

BALLYBUNION GOLF CLUB. Ballybunion Golf Club is one of the great links courses in the world. Located in County Kerry, **Ireland**, it was opened in 1893 and shortly after a nine-hole course was built, the club suffered grave financial problems. In 1906, it was saved by an investment from Colonel Bartholomew and the second nine holes were built in 1927. In 1937, the current course was developed after a remodeling. Its remote location has kept Ballybunion from being used for many major tournaments, but many great players, notably **Tom Watson**, have made their way to the west coast of Ireland to play the course and have spread its reputation. In 2005, Ballybunion was ranked by *Golf Digest* the seventh best course in the world outside the **United States**.

BALTUSROL GOLF CLUB. Baltusrol Golf Club, located in Springfield, New Jersey, is one of the great championship **golf courses** in the **United States.** It has hosted the **U.S. Open** seven times, the **U.S. Women's Open**, the **U.S. Amateur**, the **PGA Championship**, and the **U.S. Women's Amateur**. Through 2009, it has hosted 16 major championships. Baltusrol Golf Club consists of 36 holes (two courses). Known as the Upper Course and Lower Course, both are high-quality courses. They were designed and built in 1922 by **A. W. Tillinghast**, one of the best-known early golf course designers. The men's championships are usually held on the Lower Course, but the 1936 U.S. Open, 1985 U.S. Women's Open, and 2000 U.S. Amateur were held on the Upper Course. The Lower Course is a **par** 72 for members, but plays as a par 70 for major championships.

The course originally opened in 1895. It was built on land that had been owned by Baltus Roll, hence the club's name. Louis Keller, the publisher of the *New York Social Register,* purchased the land in the early 1890s. It was designed at the time to be a country course for many wealthy New Yorkers. There was originally only one course, which hosted five major championships—the 1903 and 1915 U.S. Open, the 1904 U.S. Amateur, and the 1901 and 1911 U.S. Women's Amateur. After the construction of the second course in 1922, the Lower Course was redesigned in 1952 by **Robert Trent Jones** in preparation for the 1954 U.S. Open. The most famous hole on the course is the fourth, a long par-three over water, and the members complained to Trent Jones about the difficulty of the hole. He went out to the hole with several members to play it with them and address their complaints. On Trent Jones' first shot on the hole, he scored a **hole-in-one**, and announced to the members, "As you can see, gentlemen, this hole is not too difficult!" The Lower Course was redesigned again in 1992 by his son, **Rees Jones**, in preparation for the 1993 U.S. Open.

BANFF SPRINGS GOLF CLUB. Banff Springs Golf Club is located in Banff, Alberta, **Canada**, and is considered by many the most scenic **golf course** in the world. It is set in the Canadian Rockies, with many panoramic vistas of the mountains, and has several mountain lakes. It has been described by some as akin to "a religious experience." The course, designed by **Stanley Thompson**, opened in 1928 and is now operated by the Fairmont Banff Springs Hotel. The course winds along the Bow River near Sulphur Mountain and Mount Rundle, which are snow capped most of the year. In 1989, the club added an additional nine holes, giving the resort 27.

BARBER, CARL JEROME "JERRY." B. 25 April 1916, Woodson, Illinois, United States; D. 23 September 1994, Glendale, California, United States. Jerry Barber was a U.S. **professional** and a top player despite his small size (five feet five inches [165 cm]) and short driving distance. His short game and putting were outstanding, enabling him to overcome his lack of distance. Barber won seven times on the **PGA Tour**, including one major, the 1961 **PGA Championship**. His skills were highlighted in the final round, when he holed a 20-footer for **birdie** on the 16th hole, a 40-footer for **par** on the 17th, and a 60-foot birdie putt on the final hole. This tied him with Don January, whom he defeated the next day in a play-off. Barber played on two **Ryder Cup** teams, 1955 and 1961, captaining the 1961 team. He also holds the rather esoteric record of being the oldest player to play in a PGA Tour event, playing at the 1994 Buick Invitational when he was 77 years, 313 days old.

BARNES, JAMES MARTIN "JIM" "LONG JIM." B. 8 April 1886, Lelant, Cornwall, England; D. 24 May 1966, East Orange, New Jersey, United States. Jim Barnes was best known as the first player to win the **PGA Championship**, which he did in 1916. Barnes repeated that victory in 1919 and won the 1921 **U.S. Open** and the 1924 **Open Championship (British)**. Since the 1917–1918 PGA Championship was not held, Barnes actually won the first two titles in that major championship. Barnes won the **North and South Open** in 1916 and 1919, which was virtually a major in that era. His best year was 1919, when he won the North and South, PGA, **Western Open**, and Shawnee Open. Born in **England**, Barnes came to the **United States** in 1906 and became a U.S. citizen. Very tall for his era at six foot three (190 cm), he was called "Long Jim Barnes" and was a premier ball striker. He won a total of 21 **professional** tournaments even though, in that era, there was not a true **PGA Tour**. Barnes was a charter member of the PGA Hall of Fame.

BARTON, PAMELA ESPEUT "PAM." B. 4 March 1917, Barnes, Greater London, England; D. 13 November 1943, Detling, Kent, England. Pam Barton was a British **amateur** player whose first major title was the 1934 French International Ladies Golf Championship. In 1936, she won the **British Ladies' Amateur** title and then came to the **United States**, where she won the **U.S. Women's Amateur**. This made her the first foreign winner of the U.S. Women's Amateur in 23 years, and this was the first time in 27 years that a player held both titles in the same year. She competed in the 1934 and 1936 **Curtis Cup** competition and won a second British title in 1939. When World War II broke out, Barton signed up and worked as an ambulance driver in London during the Battle of Britain. She was killed in November 1943 in a plane crash while serving in the military and was buried with full military honors in Margate Cemetery, Margate, Kent. The winner of the Ladies' British Open Amateur (British Ladies' Amateur) now receives the Pam Barton Memorial Salver (a flat silver tray) in her honor.

BAUER-HAGGE (-VOSSLER), MARLENE. B. 16 February 1934, Eureka, South Dakota, United States. Marlene Bauer-Hagge was one of the 13 founders of the **LPGA** in 1950. She first became known nationally when she won the 1949 **U.S. Girls' Junior** (as Marlene Bauer) in the first year that championship was held. She was a true prodigy, winning the Long Beach City Boys title when she was only 10, and in 1947, she made the cut at the **U.S. Women's Open** when she was only 13. She is still the youngest player ever to make the cut at that championship. During her LPGA career, Bauer-Hagge won

26 tournaments, including the 1956 **LPGA Championship**, which came in her greatest year, when she won eight events and led the money list. Bauer-Hagge was also known for her good looks, which marketed well and helped her in being one of the most popular LPGA players. Originally married to Bob Hagge, she later married former **PGA Tour** player Ernie Vossler. Marlene Bauer-Hagge's older sister, Alice Bauer, was also a top junior player who played for a time on the LPGA but with less success.

BAUGH, LAURA ZONETTA. B. 31 May 1955, Gainesville, Florida, United States. Laura Baugh was a prodigious golf champion who used her model-like looks to become one of the best-known female golfers of the 1970s, but she had a difficult life after that decade. Baugh was born to Hale Baugh, a former U.S. Olympic modern pentathlon athlete, and as a child was a five-time champion in the National PeeWee Championships. In 1971, she won the **U.S. Women's Amateur** Championship when she was only 16 years old. Early in 1972, she was named *Golf Digest*'s "Most Beautiful Golfer," and played that year for the **United States** on the **Curtis Cup** team and the **Women's World Amateur Team Championship**. She turned **professional** in 1973, had several runner-up finishes, and was named Rookie of the Year on the **LPGA.** Although Baugh played on the LPGA through the 1980s and sporadically through 1997, she never won an LPGA event.

She was married several times, most notably twice to **South African** touring professional Bobby Cole, by whom she had seven children. By the late 1980s, she was known to have a significant problem with alcohol. In the mid-1990s, she came close to dying when liver problems, caused by her drinking, resulted in major bleeding problems. She spent rehabilitation time at the Betty Ford Clinic in 1996 and overcame this problem. She now works as a television announcer on golf broadcasts and runs workshops for **women** golfers.

BAYER, GEORGE. B. 15 September 1925, Bremerton, Washington, United States; D. 16 March 2003, Palm Springs, California, United States. George Bayer was a U.S. **professional** who was known for his long driving ability. He was the longest **driver** on the **PGA Tour** when he played from the late 1950s through the 1960s. Bayer started out as a football player, playing at the University of Washington from 1946–1949, and was drafted by the Washington Redskins in the 20th round of the 1949 NFL draft. He played one year of minor league professional football with the Brooklyn Brooks and Richmond Arrows of the American Football League. He began playing golf in 1954 at the age of 29, starting out as a **caddie** in Washington state. Bayer won three events on the PGA Tour—the 1957 **Canadian Open**, the 1958 Mayfair Inn Open, and the 1960 St. Petersburg Open Invitational. His long driving was due to his size, six feet five inches (196 cm), 250 lbs. (114 kg.), which was huge for the PGA Tour at that time. Bayer also played sporadically on the Champions (Senior) Tour, winning the 1996 Legend of Golf Demaret Division with Jim Ferree.

BEARD, JOSEPH FRANKLIN "FRANK." B. 1 May 1939, Dallas, Texas, United States. Frank Beard was a U.S. **professional** golfer who came from an athletic family. His brother, Ralph Beard, an All-American basketball player at the University of Kentucky, won a gold medal with the 1948 U.S. Olympic team and played briefly in the NBA. Frank Beard grew up in Kentucky, was state high school champion his senior year, and then attended the University of Florida. Beard won 11 tournaments on the **PGA Tour**, with his best year being 1969, when he was the leading money winner, but he never managed to win a major championship. He played on the **Ryder Cup** team in 1969 and 1971 and won one tournament on the Senior PGA Tour. Beard is possibly better known as the coauthor (with Dick Schaap) of the book *Pro: Frank Beard on the Golf Tour*, which chronicled his year on the tour in 1969. He also did some golf commentary on television. Beard overcame a serious illness when young, coming close to dying in his twenties from encephalitis, an infection of the brain, and, in later life, he had difficulty with alcohol use. He was married twice, the second time to **LPGA** player Susan O'Connor, and he credits O'Connor with helping him overcome his alcoholism.

BELL, JUDY. B. 23 September 1936, Wichita, Kansas, United States. Judy Bell was a solid **amateur** golfer. She played on the U.S. **Curtis Cup** team in 1960 and 1962 and in several **USGA** events. But she is best known as a golf administrator. In 1961, Bell became a volunteer with the USGA, serving first on the Girls' Junior Committee. Over the next 25 years, she continually increased her presence within the USGA and in 1987, became the first woman to be named to the Executive Committee of the USGA. In 1996, she was named president of the USGA, the first woman to hold that role or any role that high in any major golf organization. In 2001, she was named to the **World Golf Hall of Fame** in the Lifetime Achievement category.

BELLY PUTTER. "Belly putter" refers to the longer **putters** that have become popular since the late 1980s, often used by players on the Champions (Senior) Tour. The putters are often the longest club in the bag, and, when putting, they rest against a player's belly or even chest and are usually held with a split grip. The top hand stabilizes the club, which is then swung in a pendulum-like manner with the bottom hand. Players usually resort to a longer, or belly, putter when their putting with a conventional-style putter fails them. In addition, players with back problems may benefit from the belly putter because one can stand very upright when using it, which doesn't place the back in the often painful position of being bent over from the waist.

BEMAN, DEANE R. B. 22 April 1938, Washington, D.C., United States. Deane Beman was a top **amateur** golfer in the late 1950s and early 1960s, while he had a career in insurance in the Washington area. He graduated from the University of Maryland. He won the 1959 **British Amateur**, was **U.S. Amateur** Champion in 1960 and 1963, and won the prestigious Eastern Amateur four times (1960–1961, 1963–1964). Beman seemed to be a career amateur, but in 1967, he surprisingly turned **professional** and played for seven years on the **PGA Tour**. He was a very short hitter, which he overcame with a superb short game and putting, and he won four PGA Tour events in addition to finishing second at the 1969 **U.S. Open**. In 1974, Beman left the competitive world of golf and was named the second commissioner of the PGA Tour. He served in that post from 1974 to 1994. During his tenure as commissioner, he significantly increased purses and was responsible for the concept of the PGA Tour building its own courses and holding tournaments on them, notably **The Players Championship**, held at the **TPC at Sawgrass**.

BEN HOGAN AWARD. There are actually two Ben Hogan Awards. The first, and better known, is presented by the **Golf Writers Association of America** (GWAA) to a golfer who has continued to be active in golf while having a physical handicap or serious illness or injury. It is named for renowned golfer **Ben Hogan** in recognition of his comeback from the life-threatening accident in 1949, when his car was struck by an oncoming bus. The other award is presented to a college golfer. First announced in 1990, it was originally given to a top collegiate player who also demonstrated outstanding work in academics. Since 2002, the criteria have changed, and it is now given to the player considered the top male college golfer. Appendix 11 includes a list of recipients of both awards.

BEN HOGAN TOUR. *See* NATIONWIDE TOUR.

BENDELOW, THOMAS "TOM." B. 2 September 1868, Aberdeen, Scotland; D. 24 March 1936, River Forest, Illinois, United States. Tom Bendelow was born in **Scotland** and immigrated to the **United States** in 1892. He first worked in the United States as a newspaperman but soon began giving golf lessons, having learned the game in Scotland, notably to the Pratt family of Standard Oil fame. He became friendly with sporting goods pioneer Albert G. Spalding, and his connections with Spalding and the Pratts led him to become involved in **golf course architecture**. Bendelow is probably the most prolific American golf course architect, credited with over 800 designs. He was called "The Johnny Appleseed of American Golf" (also the subtitle of a biography of Bendelow) because he laid the seeds of **golf courses** in so many places in the United States. His best known course designs are **Medinah** No. 3 near Chicago, which was the site of the **U.S. Open** three times and the **PGA Championship** twice, and the East Lake Golf Club in Atlanta, now the site of the Tour Championship on the **PGA Tour**. Bendelow's design approach has been termed a naturalist approach and has also been called "Olmstedian," having been influenced by noted landscape architects Frederick Law Olmsted Jr. and Sr. Bendelow was inducted into the Illinois Golf Hall of Fame in 2005.

BENT GRASS. Bent grass is a **grass** commonly found on **golf courses**, especially in northern climates. However, more recent types of bent grass have been developed that survive in southern climes. Bent grass is from the genus *Agrostis*, which has over 100 species in the grass family *Poaceae*. Bent grass has several advantages for golf courses—it can be mowed to a very short length without damage, it can handle a great amount of foot traffic, and it has a shallow root system that is thick and dense. Bent grass was originally used on **putting greens**, where the ability to cut it closely made for very fast putting surfaces. Many different varieties of bent grass have been developed for golf courses. The original varieties were creeping bent, common bent, or velvet bent.

BERG, PATRICIA JANE "PATTY." B. 13 February 1918, Minneapolis, Minnesota, United States; D. 10 September 2006, Fort Myers, Florida, United States. Patty Berg was one of the first female **professional** golfers and still merits consideration among the greatest **women** players of all time. She grew up in Minnesota and first came to national attention in 1935 when she lost in the final of the **U.S. Women's Amateur**. Berg won that title in 1938. In 1948, she became one of the founding members of the **LPGA** and eventually won 57 LPGA events, including a record 15 major championships. These include a record seven wins at the **Titleholders** and **Western Open**, and one **U.S. Women's Open**, but she never managed to win the **LPGA Championship**. Berg was Associated Press Woman Athlete of the Year three times, in 1938, 1942, and 1955. In 1963, she was presented with the **Bob Jones Award** by the **USGA**, for distinguished sportsmanship in golf. In 1979, the LPGA established the Patty Berg Award, which is presented to someone who "exemplifies diplomacy, sportsmanship, goodwill and contributions to the game of golf." Berg is a member of the **World Golf Hall of Fame**.

BERMUDA GRASS. Bermuda grass, or technically *Cynodon dactylon*, is a popular type of **grass** used on **golf courses**, primarily in the southern **United States** and in hot climates. Bermuda grass is a stoloniferous grass that spreads by creeping along the ground and putting down roots at intervals. Although it is found in Bermuda, the grass is not native to that island. Bermuda grass grows best in hot weather and becomes dormant in the winter and in cooler climates. It is a very tough grass that is resistant to heavy foot traffic. However, on **putting greens** it cannot be cut as short as **bent grass** or **ryegrass**

or grasses native to cooler or more northern climates. Because of this, many hybrid grasses of bermuda and other grasses have been developed, many of them in Tifton, Georgia, and often using part or all of "Tifton" in the name of the grass, such as "Tifton 328," "Tifdwarf," or "Tifeagle."

BERNING, SUSIE. *See* MAXWELL-BERNING, SUZANNE, "SUSIE."

BEST-BALL. *See* FOUR-BALL.

BETHPAGE BLACK. Bethpage Black is one of five **municipal courses** at the Bethpage State Park on Long Island. It is the most difficult of the Bethpage courses and was the site of the 2002 and 2009 **U.S. Open** Championships, making it the first publicly owned and operated course to host a U.S. Open. The course opened in 1936, designed by **A. W. Tillinghast**. It is extremely difficult, measuring over 7,365 yards at a **par** 71, and a sign near the first tee warns players that the course is too difficult for all but the best players.

BETTER-BALL. *See* FOUR-BALL.

BILL STRAUSBAUGH AWARD. The Bill Strausbaugh Award, presented by the **PGA of America**, was established in 1979 in honor of Bill Strausbaugh, longtime **professional** at Columbia Country Club in Chevy Chase, Maryland, and a two-time PGA Professional of the Year in the 1960s. Strausbaugh was known for his work supporting fellow professionals and improving their employment opportunities and situations. The PGA of America notes that "the Bill Strausbaugh Award is presented to a PGA Professsional who by their day-to-day efforts have distinguished themselves by mentoring their fellow PGA Professionals in improving their employment situations and through service to the community. The award reflects the characteristics and qualities of Strausbaugh, a Middle Atlantic PGA Master Professional who died in 1999. Award candidates should demonstrate a record of service to their Section or Association; leadership ability, involvement in civic activities and local charitable causes within their community and be recognized as someone of outstanding character."

The most recent recipient, in 2009, was Dennis Satyshur, who was formerly an assistant professional working under Strausbaugh at Columbia and is now the director of golf at Caves Valley Country Club in Owings Mills, Maryland. Each PGA Section gives out a Sectional Bill Strausbaugh Award each year. Appendix 11 includes a list of recipients.

BINGO-BANGO-BONGO. Bingo-bango-bongo, also called "bingle-bangle-bungle," is a popular betting game played in club golf. It gives lesser players a chance to win because it is not based on scores made on holes. Rather, all players compete for three points on each hole—one point to the first player to get a ball on the green (bingo/bingle), one point to the player with the ball closest to the hole once all players have reached the green (bango/bangle), and one point to the first to hole out (bongo/bungle). Points are accumulated on every hole, and the winner is the player with the most points at the end of the round.

BIRDIE. A birdie is a score of one-under-**par** on any golf hole. The term was coined in 1899 at the Atlantic City Country Club in a group containing four players—George Crump (later the designer of **Pine Valley**), noted **golf course architect A. W. Tillinghast**, William Smith (a founding member of Pine Valley), and his brother, Ab Smith. Crump hit a shot that finished only a few inches from the hole. The Smith brothers noted that his shot was a "bird." The expression stuck, was spread to other nearby courses, and eventually became commonplace as a term for one-under-par on a hole.

BLACKWELL, EDWARD BAIRD HAY "TED." B. 21 July 1866, St. Andrews, Fife, Scotland; D. 22 June 1945, St. Andrews, Fife, Scotland. At six foot one (185 cm) and sturdily built, Ted Blackwell was known for his long driving and is usually considered the first player termed the "**longest driver**" in golf. In 1892, Blackwell drove a **gutta percha** ball on the 17th hole of the Old Course, to a spot near the first green, which was measured at 366 yards, a record for the guttie. He built his strength as a cricketeer and football player at Trinity College in Glenalmond. A solid player as well as a long hitter, he was runner-up to **Walter Travis** at the 1904 **Amateur Championship**

(British Amateur) and also went to the sixth round in 1905. In 1912, during the George Glennie Medal, he set an amateur record of 73 for the Old Course at **St. Andrews**. Blackwell served as the first president of the Midland Counties Golf Association from 1906 to 1914 and became captain of the **Royal and Ancient Golf Club of St. Andrews** in 1925–1926. His brother, Ernley, also became captain of the Royal and Ancient, and two family relatives became captains in the 1960s. The entire family was descended from Thomas Blackwell, who in 1830 cofounded Crosse & Blackwell, a specialty foods company that still operates today.

BLALOCK, JANE. B. 19 September 1945, Portsmouth, New Hampshire, United States. Jane Blalock was a U.S. **professional** golfer from New Hampshire. She attended Rollins College, was a four-time New Hampshire Women's Amateur Champion, and won the New England Women's Amateur in 1968. Blalock turned professional in 1969 and was **LPGA** Rookie of the Year in that year. She eventually won 27 events on the LPGA, including the 1972 **Dinah Shore**, now considered a major championship. Blalock's greatest accomplishment may be that she made 299 consecutive cuts on the LPGA, from 1969 to 1980, a record that still stands. In 1972, Blalock was accused of cheating, and a ruling by the LPGA Executive Board stated that she was moving her ball on the greens after marking it. She was suspended for one year but fought the ruling and won, and she was allowed to continue playing. Due to her legal challenge, the LPGA was found guilty of antitrust violations, and this led to the establishment of the first LPGA commissioner.

Blalock became involved in the corporate world and golf management since her retirement as a player, and she helped establish the Legends Tour. Her company started as Jane Blalock Co., but was renamed "JBC Golf." It has under its umbrella LPGA Golf Clinics, Jane Blalock Golf Academies, the Legends Tour, and corporate golf event management. Blalock is a member of the New England Sports Hall of Fame.

BLIND GOLF. Blind golf is a sport played by the visually impaired. The game is usually played with a blind golfer and a coach. The coach lines up the shot for the player, giving instructions about course conditions and distances. This is done on the **putting green** as well. In competitive golf, there are now several classes of competition for blind golfers at the national level, although, through 2003, there was only one class of competition. The only rules difference for the visually impaired is that they are allowed to ground their clubs in **hazards**, specifically sand bunkers. National championships have been contested in the **United States** since 1946. The three best-known champions have been **Charley Boswell**, 16-time national champion (1947, 1949–1953, 1955–1961, 1965–1966, 1970); **Joe Lazaro**, eight-time national champion (1962, 1964, 1967–1969, 1971, 1973–1974) and senior champion in 2007; and **Pat Browne**, 23-time national champion (1975, 1978–1997, 1999, 2005). *See also* UNITED STATES BLIND GOLFERS ASSOCIATION.

BOATWRIGHT, PURVIS JAMES "P. J.," JR. B. 1928, Spartanburg, South Carolina, United States; D. 5 April 1991, Morristown, New Jersey, United States. P. J. Boatwright was a top amateur golfer growing up in South Carolina, where he won the Carolina Open in 1957 and 1959. He qualified for four **U.S. Amateur** Championships and made the cut at the 1950 **U.S. Open**. Boatwright played college golf at Georgia Tech and Wofford College. In 1959, Boatwright joined the **USGA** as assistant director, and in 1969, he succeeded **Joe Dey** as executive director of the USGA. Boatwright was the world's leading authority on the **Rules of Golf**. He was inducted into the Carolinas Golf Hall of Fame, the South Carolina Athletic Hall of Fame, and the Wofford College Hall of Fame

BOB JONES AWARD. The Bob Jones Award is presented annually by the **USGA** in recognition of distinguished sportsmanship in golf. It has been awarded since 1955, and is named for **Robert T. Jones Jr.**, the great amateur player of the 1920s. Appendix 11 includes a list of recipients.

BOGEY. "Bogey" is the term used for scoring one-over-**par** on any golf hole. Originally, the term had a different meaning—in 19th-century Britain, "going round in bogey" meant playing the course in par. This was based on a popular song called "Here Comes the Bogey Man," and players would often say that they were matching themselves against "Colonel Bogey." In the early 20th century, the standard of expert play became par golf, and "bogey" usually referred to one-over-par. However, for a number of years, golf holes had both a par and bogey standard. While bogey was usually one more than par, there were times when they were the same number; it related to the difficulty of the hole. By the 1920s, however, par and bogey had their current meanings. Higher scores on a hole are usually referred to in terms of "bogey," such as "double bogey"—two-over-par, "triple bogey"—three-over-par, and the dreaded "quadruple bogey"—four-over-par.

BOLT, THOMAS HENRY "TOMMY." B. 31 March 1916, Haworth, Oklahoma, United States; D. 30 August 2008, Batesville, Arkansas, United States. Tommy Bolt was a U.S. **professional** golfer known for his superb golf swing and for a violent temper, which led to nicknames such as "Terrible Tempered Tommy" Bolt, or "Thunder" Bolt. On the **PGA Tour**, numerous stories abound about Bolt's temper tantrums and club-throwing antics. But he also had one of the greatest swings in golf history and was a top player as well. Bolt won 15 times on the PGA Tour, including the 1958 **U.S. Open**, and was a member of the **Ryder Cup** team in 1955 and 1957. He also won the 1969 PGA Senior Championship, and in 1980, he and Art Wall won the Legends of Golf Event in a thrilling multi-hole play-off, an event that many consider to have provided the stimulus for the **Senior PGA Tour**. Bolt was inducted into the **World Golf Hall of Fame** in 2002.

BONALLACK, SIR MICHAEL F. B. 31 December 1934, Chigwell, Essex, England. Sir Michael Bonallack was a British amateur player and later a top golf administrator. He first became known when he won the 1952 **British Boys** title. He later went on to win the **Amateur Championship (British Amateur)** five times (1961, 1965, 1968–1970) and the English Amateur five times (1962–1963, 1965, 1967–68). Bonallack played on nine **Walker Cup** teams, and he played in the **World Amateur Team Championship** seven times. He was twice low amateur at the **Open Championship (British Open)**, in 1968 and 1971. Bonallack was unusual for his era because he was a top amateur who never turned **professional**. From 1984–1999, he was the secretary or executive director of the **R&A**, the governing body of the sport outside the **United States**. In 2000, he was named captain of the **Royal and Ancient Golf Club of St. Andrews**. He has served in administration in multiple other ways—as president of the Golf Club Managers' Association (1974–1984), chairman of the Golf Foundation of Great Britain (1977–1982), chairman of the PGA of Great Britain and **Ireland** (1976–1981), president of the English Golf Union (1982), and president of the **European PGA Tour**. In 1971, Bonallack was honored with the Order of the British Empire (OBE) for his services to golf, and in 1998, he was made a Knight Bachelor. In 1972, the **USGA** named him the recipient of the **Bob Jones Award**. He was inducted into the **World Golf Hall of Fame** in 2000.

BOOMER, PERCY HUGH. B. 1885, Islington, London, England; D. 29 April 1949, Sunningdale, Berkshire, England. Percy Boomer was a well-known golf teacher of the early 20th century and wrote one of the most popular instructional books of the era, *On Learning Golf*, published in 1942. He grew up on the Isle of Jersey, where his father was a schoolteacher in Grouville. He learned to play golf through the writings of **Harry Vardon** and **Ted Ray**. He was a solid player, winning the Belgian Open (1923), Swiss Open (1924), and Dutch Open (1927), but he was overshadowed as a player by his brother, Aubrey Boomer, a four-time winner of the **French Open**. Percy Boomer, one of the top teachers in Europe, spent most of his **professional** career at St. Cloud Country Club in the Paris suburbs. He emphasized muscle memory, tried to eliminate negative thoughts in favor of accentuating the positive, and was one of the first teachers to use stop-action photography. *On Learning Golf* is among the best golf instructional books ever written.

BOROS, JULIUS NICHOLAS. B. 3 March 1920, Bridgeport, Connecticut, United States; D. 28 May 1994, Fort Lauderdale, Florida, United States. A U.S. **professional**, Julius Boros is a member of the **World Golf Hall of Fame**, having been inducted in 1982. He turned professional rather late, working in his twenties as an accountant. But in 1952, he won his first professional event, the **U.S. Open**, and followed up by winning the World Championship of Golf that year. Boros won 18 tournaments on the **PGA Tour**, including three major championships. He won the U.S. Open again in 1963 and the **PGA**

Championship in 1968. Boros was 48 when he won the PGA, to date the oldest winner of a major championship. He also played on four **Ryder Cup** teams, in 1959, 1963, 1965, and 1967. Boros was known for his relaxed, nonchalant manner on the course and his rhythmic, almost syrupy swing. He described his playing style as "swing easy, hit hard." Boros' son, Guy Boros, also became a professional and, in 1996, won the PGA Tour's Greater Vancouver Open.

BOSWELL, CHARLES ALBERT "CHARLEY." B. 22 December 1916, Birmingham, Alabama, United States; D. 22 October 1995, Birmingham, Alabama, United States. Charley Boswell was one of the greatest **blind golfers** in history and is really the pioneering player in that sport for the visually impaired. Boswell was a top athlete in high school in Alabama, played football at the University of Alabama, and then played minor league baseball with the Atlanta Crackers in 1941. Serving in the U.S. Army in World War II, Captain Boswell was commanding the Third Battalion, 335th Infantry Regiment, 84th Infantry Division in Lindern, Germany, when he attempted to pull a wounded soldier from a burning tank. The tank exploded, permanently blinding Boswell despite several surgical attempts to restore his sight.

During his rehabilitation in the **United States**, he was introduced to golf, a sport he had never played. His athletic ability allowed him to improve rapidly, and he placed second in 1946 at the National Blind Golf Championship. He won the title in 1947, the first of his 16 national championships, and he won the International Blind Championship 11 times. Boswell was president of the **United States Blind Golfers Association (USBGA)** from 1956 to 1976. Boswell served as the first chairman of the board for the Helen Keller Eye Research Foundation from 1990 to 1995. He also founded the Charley Boswell Celebrity Golf Classic, which he chaired for 15 years and which raised some $1.5 million for Birmingham's Eye Foundation Hospital. Boswell's career was in insurance. He ran the Boswell Insurance Agency for 40 years, and from 1971 to 1979, he served as revenue commissioner for the state of Alabama. In 1982, the Veterans Administration's Charley Boswell Southeastern Blind Rehabilitation Center in Birmingham was dedicated in his name. Boswell received the 1958 **Ben Hogan Award** for overcoming disabilities in golf.

BRADLEY, PAT. B. 24 March 1951, Westford, Massachusetts, United States. Pat Bradley is one of the greatest-ever female players, having won 31 **LPGA** events and six major championships in her playing career. Bradley grew up in southern New Hampshire, where she won the New Hampshire Women's Amateur in 1967 and 1969 and the New England Women's Amateur in 1972–1973. She joined the LPGA in 1974 and won her first tournament in 1976. Her first big year was 1978, when she won three tournaments. Her greatest year was 1986, when she won five tournaments, including three of the year's four majors, won the **Vare Trophy** for low scoring average, and was the leading money winner. Bradley became only the third woman, after **Louise Suggs** and **Mickey Wright**, to have won all four major championships available to her during her career, which included three **Du Maurier Classics**, one **LPGA Championship**, one **U.S. Women's Open**, and one victory at the **Kraft Nabisco (Dinah Shore)**. Her other top years were 1983 and 1991, when she won four LPGA events in each year. She was LPGA Player of the Year in 1986 and 1991, and was later inducted into the **World Golf Hall of Fame**.

BRADSHAW, HARRY. B. 9 October 1913, Delgany, County Wicklow, Ireland; D. December 1990. Harry Bradshaw was one of the first great Irish **professional** golfers. He was the son of Ned Bradshaw, a professional in their native Delgany, and Harry and his three brothers, Jimmy, Eddie, and Hughie, all became professionals as well. Harry Bradshaw was Irish Professional Champion 10 times between 1941 and 1957 and was Irish Open Champion in 1947 and 1949. In 1958, he paired with Christy O'Connor to lead **Ireland** to victory in the **Canada Cup**. Bradshaw was on the **Ryder Cup** team in 1953, 1955, and 1957, and he won the British Masters in 1953 and 1955. At the 1949 **Open Championship (British Open)**, he tied **Bobby Locke** after 72 holes but lost the play-off.

BRAID, JAMES. B. 6 February 1870, Earlsferry, Fife, Scotland; D. 27 November 1950, Walton Heath, Surrey, England. A Scottish **professional**, James Braid won the **Open Championship (British Open)** five times (1901, 1905–1906, 1908, 1910). Braid, along with **Harry Vardon** and **J. H. Taylor,** was part of the original Great Triumvirate of professional golf. The trio won 16 of 22 Open championships from 1893 to 1914. His other significant titles include four wins at the News of the World Match Play Championship (1903, 1905, 1907, 1911) and the 1910 **French Open** Championship. Braid retired from competitive play in 1912 and became the club professional at Walton Heath. He later became a well-known **golf course architect** and is sometimes credited with inventing the concept of the dogleg. He designed the King's and Queen's courses at **Gleneagles**, and in 1926, he remodeled **Carnoustie** in preparation for the Open Championship.

BRASSIE. A brassie was a two-wood in the era when clubs were known by names and not numbers. The two-wood, or brassie, is almost never used anymore. It was last used frequently in the 1940s and 1950s.

BREWER, GAY ROBERT. B. 19 March 1932, Middletown, Ohio, United States; D. 31 August 2007, Lexington, Kentucky, United States. Gay Brewer was a U.S. **professional** who won 10 events on the **PGA Tour**, including one major, the 1967 **Masters**, which he won after losing in a play-off at the 1966 Masters. Growing up in Kentucky, Brewer was state junior champion from 1949 to 1951, and in 1949, he won the second **U.S. Junior Amateur** title. At the 1967 Pensacola Open, Brewer won the tournament after standing 25-under-**par** for the first three rounds, the lowest score for 54 holes on the PGA Tour and a record that stood through 2009. Brewer played on the 1967 and 1973 **Ryder Cup** teams. He attended the University of Kentucky and is a member of the UK Hall of Fame.

BRITISH AMATEUR (THE AMATEUR CHAMPIONSHIP). The Amateur Championship, which began in 1885 and is known throughout much of the world as the British Amateur, was the first major amateur championship. It is organized by the **R&A**. Prior to World War II, the British Amateur was considered one of the major championships and was one of the championships won by **Bob Jones** in his **Grand Slam** year of 1930. The event has always been contested at **match play** and has had varying numbers in the field over the years. In recent years, qualifying has consisted of **stroke play**, with 18-hole matches until a 36-hole final, for 64 match play spots. **John Ball** won the most titles, eight, followed by **Michael Bonallack** with five and **Harold Hilton** with four. Five courses have hosted the event 10 or more times through 2009—**Royal Liverpool Golf Club** (18), the Old Course (**St. Andrews**) (16), **Royal St. George's** (13), **Prestwick** (11), and **Muirfield** (10). Appendix 6 includes a list of champions.

BRITISH BOYS' AMATEUR. The British Boys' Amateur Championship, first played in 1921, is an **R&A** Championship. It was originally for boys 15 year of age or younger, but in 1923, the age limit was raised to 17. The event was originally hosted and conducted by the Royal Ascot Golf Club , but in 1948, it was taken over by the R&A. Appendix 9 includes a list of champions.

BRITISH JUNIOR OPEN. The British Junior Open was inaugurated in 1994 and came under control of the **R&A** in 2000. It is a championship held biennially for boys and girls, 15 years of age or younger but is intended to be an international event. Therefore all of golf's national governing bodies are invited to send one boy and one girl.

BRITISH LADIES' AMATEUR (LADIES' BRITISH OPEN AMATEUR CHAMPIONSHIP). The Ladies' British Open Amateur Championship (British Ladies' Amateur), founded in 1893 by the **Ladies' Golf Union** of Great Britain, was the first major amateur championship for **women**. The event has always been contested at **match play**. The first three championships were won by Lady Margaret Scott. The first foreign winner was **Simone Thion de la Chaume** of France in 1924, while the first American to win the title was **Babe Zaharias** in 1947. The champion receives the Pam Barton Memorial Salver, named for **Pam Barton**, who won the title in 1936 and 1939 and lost her life in service to her country during World War II. Appendix 7 includes a list of champions.

BRITISH OPEN. *See* THE OPEN CHAMPIONSHIP (BRITISH OPEN).

BRITISH SENIOR OPEN. The British Senior Open began in 1987 as a part of the European Seniors Tour and since 2003 has been considered one of the five Champions (Senior) Tour major championships.

It is held at 72-holes **stroke play** on a rotation of courses in the British Isles. Unlike the **Open Championship**, which visited **Ireland** only once, the British Senior Open was held in Northern Ireland for eight consecutive years—1995–2002, first at **Royal Portrush** for five years and then three years at **Royal County Down**. **Tom Watson** and **Gary Player** have won the event three times each, while Brian Barnes, **Bob Charles**, and **Christy O'Connor Jr.** have each won twice.

BRITISH SENIORS OPEN AMATEUR. The British Seniors Open Amateur, or British Senior Amateur Championship, was started by the **R&A** in 1969 to help Great Britain and Ireland select a senior team to play in the World Senior Amateur Team Championship. It is limited to players age 55 or older and is conducted over 54 holes **stroke play**. Charlie Green won the event six times, winning six of seven competitions beginning in 1988.

BRITISH WOMEN'S OPEN. *See* WOMEN'S BRITISH OPEN.

BROWN, PETE. B. 2 February 1935, Port Gibson, Mississippi, United States. Pete Brown was a U.S. **professional** who grew up playing the **United Golfers Association** (UGA) tour in the late 1950s and early 1960s. Since he was African American, he was not allowed to play on the **PGA Tour** at that time due to discrimination. The PGA Tour later prevented him from finding sponsorship to play on the tour. Brown won the National Negro Open four times, finally earning a PGA Tour Card in 1963. In 1964, Brown won the Waco Turner Open, becoming the first African American to win a PGA Tour event. He won the 1970 Andy Williams-San Diego Open for his second tour victory, but neither win earned him admission to the **Masters** tournament. He later became a club professional at Madden Golf Club in Dayton, Ohio.

BROWNE, PAT. B. 1932, New Orleans, Louisiana, United States. Pat Browne is a **blind golfer** who has won the championship for the visually impaired more often than has any other player. Browne grew up in Louisiana where he was an outstanding athlete, lettering in golf and basketball three times at Tulane. He later received a law degree from Tulane and practiced law for 18 years before going into banking. In 1966, he lost his sight after an automobile accident. Still an avid golfer at the time, he continued to play, aided by a golf coach for the blind, and has won the national title 23 times (1975, 1978–1997, 1999, 2005), including 20 titles in a row. He has won 65 blind golf tournaments worldwide. Browne recorded the lowest 72-hole score ever by a blind player, a 303 (75-74-79-75) at Mission Hills Golf Club in Palm Springs, California, and is a member of the U.S. Blind Golf Association Hall of Fame.

BUMP-AND-RUN. *See* CHIP-AND-RUN or PITCH-AND-RUN.

BUNKERS. A bunker is one of the **hazards** in the game of golf. Bunkers usually consist of depressions in the land that are filled with sand. The precise definition in the rules is "a hazard consisting of a prepared area of ground, often a hollow, from which turf or soil has been removed and replaced with sand or the like. **Grass**-covered ground bordering or within a bunker is not part of the bunker. The margin of a bunker extends vertically downwards, but not upwards." The **Rules of Golf** contain separate rules for play in a hazard (and thus a bunker): A player may not ground his club in a hazard, and he may not move a loose impediment in a hazard. If a ball in a hazard is completely covered over by sand, he is allowed to clear enough sand to see the top of the ball. He is not allowed to clear enough sand to identify his ball, and because of this, there is no penalty for playing a **wrong ball** in a hazard.

There are three basic types of bunkers—greenside bunkers, which guard **putting greens**; **fairway** bunkers, usually placed at the distance of well-struck drives; and **waste bunkers**, which are also usually around fairways and serve as large, unkempt areas providing difficult recoveries for players. *See also* POT BUNKER.

BURKE, JOHN JOSEPH "JACK," JR. B. 29 January 1923, Fort Worth, Texas, United States. Jack Burke is a **U.S. professional** who turned pro in 1940 and won 16 **PGA Tour** events during his career, including two major championships in 1956, the **Masters** and PGA. In that year, he was selected PGA Player of the Year. Burke played on the 1951, 1953, 1955, 1957, and 1959 **Ryder Cup** teams, and captained the team in 1973. After his competitive career wound down, he founded Champions Golf Club in Houston along with **Jimmy Demaret**. Burke became a member of the **World Golf Hall of Fame** in 2000 and received the PGA Tour Lifetime Achievement Award in 2003.

BUY.COM TOUR. *See* NATIONWIDE TOUR.

BYRON NELSON AWARD. *See* VARDON TROPHY.

– C –

CABRERA, ÁNGEL "EL PATO" ("THE DUCK"). B. 12 September 1969, Villa Allende, Córdoba, Argentina. Ángel Cabrera was only three years old when his parents split and left him to the care of his paternal grandmother. He began **to caddie** at age 10 at the Córdoba Country Club, and learned the game. He turned **professional** at age 20, but it took him until 1996 to qualify for the **European PGA Tour**, where he played primarily. He won over 40 professional tournaments, including five wins (through 2009) on the European Tour. He played sparingly in the **United States**, mostly visiting for the major championships and winning two majors, the 2007 **U.S. Open** at **Oakmont** and the 2009 Masters. A large, stocky man, who drives the ball a long way, Cabrera cuts an unusual figure on the course in this era with his incessant smoking, although in late 2009, he stopped the habit.

CADDIE. A caddie is the person who carries a player's bag and offers advice and information such as distances to the holes, suggestions as to club selection, and assistance with reading the greens. The caddie also replaces divots and rakes **bunkers** for the player. The term is derived from the French *cadet*. Another type of caddie is a **forecaddie,** who either follows a group or stays some distance ahead of it and identifies the position of balls. The forecaddie may be employed by the club or tournament. In the 19th and early 20th century, most clubs had large numbers of caddies, often young boys who did the job as a way to make money in the summer. With the advent of golf carts, the number of caddies available at clubs shrank dramatically, and except for some northern clubs, caddie programs and caddie yards are now exceptionally rare in the United States. Many top players originally began playing golf because of the exposure to the game as a caddie, but this is now much less common because of the dearth of opportunities to caddie. On **professional** tours, nearly every top player has a private caddie who travels along with the tour and caddies exclusively for the player, such as Steve Williams for **Tiger Woods**, or Jim McKay for **Phil Mickelson**. Professional tour caddies are usually paid a salary as well as a percentage of a player's winnings, with bonuses usually given for tournament victories.

CADDYSHACK. "Caddyshack" is the term for a small enclosure on some **golf courses** with **caddie** programs, where the caddiemaster works, and many of the caddies wait during the day while trying to get out on the course. But the term is better known as the title of the most famous golf movie ever, *Caddyshack*. The movie was a comedy that came out in 1980 starring Bill Murray, Chevy Chase, Rodney Dangerfield, Ted Knight, and Michael O'Keefe. On many lists of funny movies, it is considered one of the funniest ever made. The movie concerns several days in the life of Danny Noonan (O'Keefe), who is trying to earn the caddie scholarship at Bushwood Country Club (a fictitious club—the movie was filmed at the Rolling Hills Golf Club in Florida). Danny seems to have the scholarship when he wins the club caddie tournament. Judge Smailes (Knight) is the leader of the club, and an obnoxious guest, Al Czervik (Dangerfield), a nouveau riche real estate developer, irritates him. Czervik enlists young Ty Webb (Chase), the best player at the club, to play a match against Smailes and Dr. Beeper, another top player at the club. Smailes and Dr. Beeper are beating Czervik and Webb handily when Czervik fakes an injury to get out of the match. But Smailes insists they continue to play, so Czervik enlists Danny Noonan to play in his stead, although he had been Smailes' caddie. Assistant greenkeeper Carl Spackler (Murray) has been on a mission to kill gophers on the course. He does this with plastic explosives that go off as the big match winds down to its denouement. One of the blasts knocks Danny's final putt into the hole, winning him the match with a dramatic putt on the final hole, which probably loses him the caddie scholarship, although the movie ends without divulging this. The movie is known for having many famous lines that are frequently quoted by golfers and sportscasters—"so it's got that going for it, which is nice" (a line paraphrased from the movie).

CALCUTTA. A Calcutta is a type of golf tournament betting pool that usually occurs at private club tournaments. They are often conducted in conjunction with **member-guest** tournaments. In a Calcutta, an auction is held in which players and members of the club may bid on any team. The winning bidder, or bidders, then "owns" that team in the tournament. The money raised in the bidding process is placed into a pool. An owner wins money, a proportion of the pool, if that owner's team wins the tournament or finishes with a high placement. There are many variations, from only the winning team collecting the entire pot, to various levels of placement being paid off. The players on a team may buy their own team. If the team was bought by another bidder or group, most Calcuttas allow the team players the option of buying back half of their own team. Calcuttas are a form of **gambling** that technically skirt the rules of **amateur status** and even the laws against gambling in some states. The most famous Calcutta occurred in 1955 at Deepdale Golf Club on Long Island, where the total pool was $45,000, with a $16,000 first prize, huge amounts of money for that era. The tournament was won by two players (who had grossly padded their **handicaps**), and the buyers of their team were aware of their true playing ability. The **USGA** became involved and made its first pronouncement against high-stakes gambling at clubs. *See also* NASSAU, SANDBAGGER.

CALLAWAY HANDICAP SYSTEM. The Callaway Handicap System is an ad hoc system of handicapping that is useful for a one-day event in which not all players may have a **handicap**. The player's **stroke play** scores are used. Each score allows a deduction of worst hole(s) from the final score, in a predetermined manner. Thus a player shooting 78 subtracts her worst score on a hole, while a player shooting 88 subtracts her worst two holes. There is also another final adjustment of strokes, ranging from +2 to -2 and based on the original gross score, after the worst hole(s) are deducted.

CAMPBELL (-HURD-HOWE), DOROTHY IONA. B. 24 March 1883, North Berwick, Scotland; D. 20 March 1945, Yemassee, South Carolina, United States. Dorothy Campbell was born in **Scotland** but moved to **Canada** in 1910 and to the **United States** in 1913. She is the only woman who was **amateur** champion of Great Britain, Canada, and the United States. Her first significant titles were the Scottish Ladies' Championships in 1906 and 1908–1909. She was **U.S. Women's Amateur** Champion in 1909–1910 and 1924 and **British Ladies' Amateur** Champion in 1909 and 1911. She won Canadian titles in the Ladies' Open in 1910–1911 and the Women's Amateur in 1912. Her wins in the United States and Britain in 1909 made her the first woman to win both titles, and she is still the only player to win both in the same year. Campbell also won three titles in the **North and South Women's Amateur** in 1918 and 1920–1921. As a senior, she won the U.S. Senior Women's Championship in 1938 (although not the **USGA** title, which was not established until 1961). Campbell is a member of the Canadian Golf Hall of Fame and was inducted into the **World Golf Hall of Fame** in 1978.

CAMPBELL, MICHAEL SHANE. B. 23 February 1969, Hawera, Taranaki, New Zealand. Michael Campbell is a New Zealand **professional** who has played primarily on the **European PGA Tour**. However, in 2005, he won the **U.S. Open** Championship at **Pinehurst**, edging out **Tiger Woods** and becoming the first player from Australasia to win the U.S. Open. In the same year, he won the £1,000,000 HSBC **World Match Play Championship**, the richest prize in golf to that time. Campbell is predominantly of Maori ethnicity, with some Scottish ancestry. Since his U.S. Open win, he has struggled on the world tours and has not regained the form he showed in 2005. The U.S. Open remains his only win on the **PGA Tour**. He posted eight wins on the European PGA Tour from 1999 to 2005, and Campbell helped New Zealand win the **Eisenhower Trophy** title in 1992. In 1995 at the **Open Championship** (**British Open**), Campbell led after three rounds but faded to third place after a final-round 76.

CAMPBELL, WILLIAM CAMMACK "BILL." B. 5 May 1923, Huntingdon, West Virginia, United States. Bill Campbell is known as a gentleman and as one of America's top amateur golfers and golfing ambassadors. A West Virginia native, he has always lived in his home state. He attended Princeton and became an insurance broker in Huntingdon. He also served in his state's legislature. His greatest victory came when he won the 1964 **U.S. Amateur**. But he was also West Virginia Amateur Champion 15 times and won the West Virginia Open three times. At the **North and South Amateur**, he was a four-time champion, in 1950, 1953, 1957, and 1967. Campbell played for the **United States** in eight **Walker Cup** matches between 1951 and 1975, never losing a singles match. He served as president of the **USGA** in 1982–1983 and in 1987 became only the third American to serve as captain of the **Royal and Ancient Golf Club of St. Andrews**. Campbell received the 1956 **Bob Jones Award** from the USGA in recognition of distinguished sportsmanship in golf.

CANADA. The first **golf course** in North America was founded in 1873, when eight former Scots gathered together and formed the **Royal Montréal Golf Club**. But golf had been played sporadically in Canada for many years by that time, as there were notices in the *Montréal Herald* in 1826 asking for interested Scots to gather together to play some golf at Priest's Farm. Canada was also progressive in **women**'s golf as women's clubs were quickly formed in Montréal, Ottawa, and Toronto in the early 1890s.

The Royal Canadian Golf Association was formed in 1894 and governs the game in Canada. In 1895, the group organized the first Canadian Amateur Championship; in 1901, they held the first Canadian Ladies' Amateur Championship; and in 1904, they added the **Canadian Open**. The Canadian Women's Open (formerly the **Du Maurier Classic**) was held for the first time in 1973. Canada ranks sixth in the world in terms of number of golf courses per capita.

CANADA CUP. *See* WORLD CUP OF GOLF.

CANADIAN OPEN. The Canadian Open, which has been played since 1904, is one of the world's top national open championships. Many of the game's greatest players have won the title, notably **Walter Hagen**, **Tommy Armour**, **Sam Snead**, **Byron Nelson**, **Bobby Locke**, **Lee Trevino**, **Greg Norman**, and **Tiger Woods**. **Arnold Palmer**

won the Canadian Open for his first PGA Tour victory in 1955. Most unusual, the Canadian Open is the most significant tournament that **Jack Nicklaus** never managed to win, although he did place second seven times. The record for most victories in the event is held by **Leo Diegel** with four in 1924–1925 and 1928–1929. Historically, the tournament rotated around the country, being held on many of the top Canadian courses. But in 1977, **Glen Abbey Golf Course**, just west of Toronto, was designated as the permanent home for the event, and 19 of the next 20 championships were held on that **Jack Nicklaus** designed course. In 1996, the championship again began rotating to various courses in **Canada**, although it is still held at Glen Abbey every few years. **Royal Montréal Golf Club** has hosted the tournament nine times. Ontario or Québec has held all but eight Canadian Opens. Those other eight championships have been held in New Brunswick (1939), Manitoba (1952, 1961), Alberta (1958), and British Columbia (1948, 1954, 1966, and 2005). The last Canadian to win the tournament was Pat Fletcher in 1954. In the past decade, Canadian hopes have rested on the shoulders of their greatest player, **Mike Weir**, but he has not been able to break through. Although it has been a PGA Tour event since the 1950s, a limited number of entries are allocated to players on the Canadian Tour. Appendix 4 contains a list of champions.

CANADIAN WOMEN'S OPEN. *See* DU MAURIER CLASSIC.

CAPONI (-YOUNG-BYRNES), DONNA. B. 29 January 1945, Detroit, Michigan, United States. Donna Caponi is an American female **professional** golfer who was inducted into the **World Golf Hall of Fame** in 2001. Caponi, who played for many years as Donna Caponi-Young, started on the **LPGA** in 1965 and won 24 events on that tour, including four major championships. She had back-to-back **U.S. Women's Open** titles in 1969–1970 and two **LPGA championships** in 1979 and 1981. Her 1969 U.S. Women's Open title was her first LPGA victory. Caponi also won the **Dinah Shore** and the **Du Maurier Classic** before they were designated major championships by the LPGA. She later became a golf announcer on television, originally on network television, but more recently, on the **Golf Channel**.

CARNER, JOANNE GUNDERSON "THE GREAT GUNDY." B. 4 April 1939, Kirkland, Washington, United States. JoAnne Gunderson Carner is one of the greatest female players in the history of the game. She won the **U.S. Girls' Junior** in 1956 and five **U.S. Women's Amateur** titles between 1956 and 1968. In 1971, she won the **U.S. Women's Open**, becoming the first person to have won three different **USGA** titles, a mark since tied by **Arnold Palmer**, **Jack Nicklaus**, **Tiger Woods**, and **Carol Semple-Thompson**. Carner remained an amateur until she was 30, playing most years as JoAnne Gunderson before her marriage to Don Carner. But in 1969, she won the Burdine's Invitational in Miami as an amateur and turned **professional** later that year. She won 43 **LPGA** titles, adding another major championship in 1976 with her second U.S. Women's Open victory. In 1981, Carner received the **Bob Jones Award** from the USGA in recognition of distinguished sportsmanship in golf. She was the captain of the 1994 U.S. **Solheim Cup** team.

CARNOUSTIE GOLF LINKS. Carnoustie Golf Links is one of the courses on the rotation of the **Open Championship** (**British Open**) and is one of the great **golf courses** in the world. Many people consider it the most difficult course in the British Isles. It is located in Carnoustie, Angus, on the east Scottish coast. Golf has been played in this location since the 16th century. The current course was laid out in 1867 by **Old Tom Morris**. The course was modified in 1926 by **James Braid**, after which the Open was first held there in 1931. The course is traversed by a creek, the Barry Burn, which influences play on several holes, notably the 17th and 18th. Carnoustie hosted the Open Championship in 1931, 1937, 1953, 1968, 1975, 1999, and 2007. In 1953, **Ben Hogan** made his only appearance in the Open, winning the title at Carnoustie and completing his Triple Crown year of winning the **Masters**, **U.S. Open**, and **British Open**. In 1999, the event was won by Paul Lawrie of **Scotland**, but only after one of the most monumental collapses in golf history. Jean Van de Velde came to the 18th hole with a three-shot lead and needed only a double **bogey** to win the title. But he made a seven, falling into a tie with Lawrie and Justin Leonard. Lawrie won the play-off.

CARR, JOSEPH BENEDICT "JOE." B. 22 February 1922, Inchicore, County Dublin, Ireland; D. 3 June 2004, Dublin, County Dublin, Ireland. Joe Carr is considered by many the greatest ever Irish **amateur** player. He was a three-time winner of the **Amateur Championship (British Amateur)** in 1953, 1958, and 1960 and won 37 regional or national Irish titles. He was twice low amateur at the **Open Championship (British Open)** (1956, 1958) and in 1967 became the first Irish player to compete at the **Masters**. In 1961, Carr received the **Bob Jones Award** from the **USGA**, the first non-American to win the award. He played on a record 11 **Walker Cup** teams. In 1991, Carr became the first Irishman to be named captain of the **Royal and Ancient Golf Club of St. Andrews**. He was elected to the **World Golf Hall of Fame** in 2007 in the Lifetime Achievement category.

CASA DE CAMPO, TEETH OF THE DOG COURSE. The Teeth of the Dog Course at Casa de Campo Resort in the Dominican Republic is one of the most spectacular **golf courses** in the world. The course opened in 1971, designed by **Pete Dye**, and is a 6,888 yard, **par** 72 course, with a **course rating** of 75.9 and slope of 145. The course is built along the ocean, with several carries over ocean inlets. Dye later said of the course that he designed 11 holes and God created seven. There are three courses at the Casa de Campo Resort, including Dye Fore and the Links, but the resort is known for the Teeth of the Dog Course.

CASEY MARTIN RULING. Casey Martin is a U.S. **professional** golfer who played briefly on the **PGA Tour** and is now a golf coach at the University of Oregon. Martin was a college teammate of **Tiger Woods** at Stanford. He became a top player despite a congenital disability, Klippel-Trenaunay-Weber Syndrome, a circulatory disorder which affected his right leg. It has put his leg at risk for multiple fractures and even amputation. Martin has always played with a golf cart because of his disability. As his game improved and he envisioned playing on the PGA Tour, he sued the PGA Tour in 2001 for the right to use a **golf cart**, based on the Americans with Disabilities Act. Martin was successful. He won the suit and received the right to use a golf cart, which allowed other players to successfully petition golf organizations to use a golf cart in competition, which is normally prohibited by the **Rules of Golf**. But the case eventually went to the U.S. Supreme Court. The decision in PGA Tour, Inc. *v*. Martin, 532 U.S. 661 (2001) ruled in Martin's favor by a seven to two margin, with the dissenting opinion written by Judge Antonin Scalia. Martin played on the PGA Tour and the **Nationwide/Nike Tour** from 1998 to 2004, but his PGA Tour career was not overly successful and he retired from high-level competition in 2005 and became golf coach at Oregon in 2006.

CASPER, WILLIAM EARL "BILLY," JR. B. 24 June 1931, San Diego, California, United States. Billy Casper is one of the great players in golf history but also one of the most underrated. He turned **professional** in 1954 and played on the **PGA Tour** through the 1970s. During that time, he won 51 PGA Tour events, ranking him seventh all-time for most victories on the PGA Tour. His best years were 1964–1970 when he won 27 times, the most of any player during that period, despite the presence of **Jack Nicklaus** and **Arnold Palmer** as competitors. Casper was the leading money winner in 1966 and 1968 and won the **Vardon Trophy** five times (1960, 1963, 1965–1966, 1968). He played on eight **Ryder Cup** teams and was a nonplaying captain in 1979. Casper won three major championships, the 1959 and 1966 **U.S. Opens**, and the 1970 **Masters**. He was inducted into the **World Golf Hall of Fame** in 1978.

CASUAL WATER. "Casual water" is defined as any temporary accumulation of water on the course that is visible before or after the player takes his stance, but which is not in a water hazard. A player is entitled to relief from casual water via a free drop. The drop may be made no nearer the hole and within one club length of the point at which complete relief can be taken from the casual water. Snow and natural ice, other than frost, are considered either casual water or **loose impediments**, at the player's option. Dew and frost are not considered casual water. A ball is in casual water when it lies in or any part of it touches the casual water, but a player is also entitled to relief if the casual water interferes with the player's stance. Rule 25 of the **Rules of Golf** covers relief from casual water.

CHAMPIONS TOUR. The Champions Tour is a U.S. tour for senior male **professionals** age 50 or older. The tour was known as the Senior PGA Tour until late in 2002. The idea for the Senior Tour grew out of the Legends of Golf Event, a senior **four-ball** tournament that started in 1978 and was highly successful. The PGA Senior Championship has been held since 1937, with the **U.S. Senior Open** starting in 1980. The full U.S. Senior PGA Tour was established in 1980. Most of the tournaments are 54 holes, but the senior major championships are still played over 72 holes.

CHARLES, SIR ROBERT JAMES "BOB," KNZM, CBE. B. 14 March 1936, Cartertown, Wairarapa, North Island, New Zealand. Bob Charles is a New Zealand **professional** golfer who was the first left-hander to win a major golf championship, winning the **Open Championship (British Open)** in 1963 in a play-off with Phil Rodgers. Charles first came to notice Down Under when he won the New Zealand Open as an 18-year-old amateur in 1954. He turned professional in 1960 and in 1963 won the Houston Classic on the **PGA Tour**, only two months before his Open Championship. He eventually won six titles on the PGA Tour and remained a top player as a senior, winning 23 times on the PGA Senior/ **Champions Tour**. Best known for his putting prowess, Charles was one of the greatest putters in the history of the game. Charles was made a Member of the Order of the British Empire (MBE) by Queen Elizabeth in 1972 and was named Commander in the same Order in 1992 (CBE). He became Sir Bob Charles in 1999 when he was made a Knight Companion of the New Zealand Order of Merit (KNZM).

CHIP SHOT. A chip shot is a short shot around the green played when the ball lies within a few feet of the putting surface. The player selects a club and hits the ball a short distance in the air landing it on the green (ideally) and allowing it to run toward the hole from there. It is also called a chip-and-run. A chip shot (chip-and-run) is differentiated from a pitch shot (pitch-and-run) by being hit with a lower lofted club and allowing the ball to run farther after landing.

CHIP-AND-RUN. *See* CHIP SHOT.

CLARET JUG. The Claret Jug is the trophy given to the winner of the **Open Championship (British Open)**. It was first awarded in 1873. The original prize for the Open was a championship belt, with the proviso that any player winning the event in three consecutive years would retire the belt. That was not expected to occur, but in 1868–1870, **Young Tom Morris** did exactly that to retire the belt. The Open was not contested in 1871 as a result, and the **R&A** came up with the Claret Jug as the replacement. The original Claret Jug was made by Mackay Cunningham & Company of Edinburgh for a cost of £30. It was not ready in time for the 1872 championship, again won by Young Tom, but was first presented to the 1873 champion, Tom Kidd. A newer model trophy, similar to the original, was awarded beginning in 1928, first to **Walter Hagen**. Winners of the Open Championship receive possession of the Claret Jug for one year and must return it prior to the next event. They also receive a smaller replica for their permanent possession.

CLEEK. In the days when golf clubs were named, and specifically in the wooden shaft era, a cleek was a very low-lofted iron, most comparable to the later 1-iron. There was also a wooden cleek, which approximated the current 4-wood. Alternately, the term was used in the late 19th and early 20th centuries to refer to any iron club.

CLOSEST TO THE PIN/CLOSEST TO THE HOLE. In many tournaments, especially club tournaments, a prize is offered on a par-three hole for the player who hits the ball closest to the pin with the tee shot. Prizes can vary greatly, from a dozen balls up to a new car in some **professional** tournaments.

CLUB DE GOLF VALDERRAMA. Club de Golf Valderrama, or Valderrama Golf Club, located in Sotogrande, in Andalucia, only a few miles north of Gibraltar, is the best-known Spanish course. The course was designed in 1974 by **Robert Trent Jones** and was originally known as Sotogrande New and later Las Aves. The course hosted the 1997 **Ryder Cup** and the Volvo Masters in 1988–1996 and 2002–2010. The signature hole is the par-five fourth, which requires a carry over a pond fronting a green that is severely sloped and two-tiered.

COE, CHARLES ROBERT "CHARLIE." B. 26 October 1923, Ardmore, Oklahoma, United States; D. 16 May 2001, Oklahoma City, Oklahoma, United States. Charlie Coe was one of the last great career **amateurs**. After serving as a pilot in World War II, he played at the University of Oklahoma (1948), winning three conference golf championships. Coe won the 1949 **U.S. Amateur** and repeated that feat in 1958. He lost the 1959 final to **Jack Nicklaus**. His other major amateur titles include the 1950 **Western Amateur** and four wins at the **Trans-Miss** (1947, 1949, 1952, 1956). He was also runner-up at the 1951 **British Amateur**. Coe played in 18 **Masters** tournaments placing second in 1961, the best finish ever by an amateur, and he was sixth in 1959 and ninth in 1962. He played on six **Walker Cup** teams, captaining the 1957 and 1959 teams. In 1964, Coe received the **Bob Jones Award** from the **USGA** in recognition of distinguished sportsmanship in golf. The Charlie Coe Golf Center at the University of Oklahoma is named in his honor.

COEFFICIENT OF RESTITUTION. "Coefficient of restitution" is a physics, or engineering, term that entered the golf vocabulary with the newer metal woods. Some newer metal woods produce a springlike effect when the ball impacts on the clubface, increasing the rebound from the club and as a result, the distance the ball will travel. "Coefficient of restitution" technically refers to the ratio of the velocity of an object striking a surface relative to the velocity of the object rebounding from the surface. A higher coefficient of restitution means that more energy is transferred to the ball in the rebound off the clubface, resulting in greater distance. The **Rules of Golf** now limit the coefficient of restitution of clubs, which may not be greater than 0.830.

COLES, NEIL CHAPMAN, MBE. B. 26 September 1934, Marylebone, Greater London, England. Neil Coles was one of the great British **professionals** of the 1960s and 1970s. His career came along before the official start of the **European PGA Tour**, but he won 31 professional tournaments in Europe and Great Britain, including seven on the European PGA Tour after it was established in 1972. Five times he finished in the top ten at the **Open Championship (British Open)**, with best placements of second in 1973 and third in 1961. Because of a fear of flying he rarely played in the **United States**. He was an eight-time member of the **Ryder Cup** team—1961, 1963, 1965, 1967, 1969, 1971, 1973, and 1977. In 2000, Coles was inducted into the **World Golf Hall of Fame**.

COLLAR. The collar refers to the shortly mown **grass** surrounding the edge of a **putting green**. It is typically mowed slightly shorter than **fairway** grass, but longer than the putting green grass, allowing a player to putt from it in many cases. Golf synonyms for the collar are "apron," "fringe," and "frog hair."

COLLETT, GLENNA. *See* VARE, GLENNA COLLETT.

COLONIAL NATIONAL INVITATIONAL. The Colonial National Invitational is a **PGA Tour** event held at the Colonial Country Club in Fort Worth, Texas. First contested in 1946, it was originally dominated by **Ben Hogan**, a native of Fort Worth, who won the tournament five times, and, for that reason, the course is often termed **Hogan's Alley**. Although originally called only the "Colonial National Invitational," it has had several corporate sponsors, among them Southwestern Bell, MasterCard, Bank of America, and most recently, Crowne Plaza. As of 2009, it is the longest running PGA Tour event still held on the same course. Known colloquially as "The Colonial," it is one of the few invitational events on the PGA Tour. It has a unique feature called the "Champion's Choice" by which previous champions vote and offer invitations to two players not otherwise eligible. The event created a media furor in 2003 when **Annika Sörenstam** was invited to play, the first woman to play in a PGA Tour event since **Babe Zaharias** played in the **Los Angeles Open** in 1945.

COLT, HENRY SHAPLAND "HARRY." B. 4 August 1869, Highgate, England; D. 21 November 1951, East Hendred, Berkshire, England. Harry Colt was a British **golf course architect** who worked with **Charles Alison** and John Morrison in the firm of Colt, Alison, & Morrison, Ltd. Colt studied at Cambridge, where he captained the university's golf team, eventually earning a law degree from Clare College. Colt designed over 300 courses, the best known being the East and West courses at **Wentworth Club** and Stoke Poges, the setting for the golf scenes in the movie *Goldfinger*. Colt was also a founding member of the Rules of Golf Committee for the **R&A**.

COMPOSITE SHAFTS. Composite shafts are golf shafts that are made of several dissimilar materials. The advantage is that composite shafts often incorporate the good features of both or all materials. Many golf shafts are now composite, often including graphite fiber with fiberglass, aramid fiber (best known for Kevlar), or carbon fiber.

COMPSTON, ARCHIBALD EDWARD WONES "ARCHIE." B. 1892, Penn, Wolverhampton, England; D. 8 August 1962, London, England. Archie Compston was an English **professional** of the 1920s who is regarded as one of the best match players of the era—a time when many professionals made more money from challenge matches against fellow pros than they did in tournament play. In his most famous match in 1928, Compston, who was the 1925 and 1927 British Match Play Champion, played **Walter Hagen**, U.S. **PGA** Champion from 1924 to 1927, and defeated him 18 & 17 in a 72-hole challenge match. Compston played on the **Ryder Cup** team in 1927, 1929, and 1931. Compston never won the **Open Championship (British Open)**; his best finishes were equal second in 1925 and third in 1928.

CONCEDED PUTT. In **match play**, a player or side may concede the opponent's next shot, usually a putt, at any time during the play of a hole. If a shot is conceded, the player does not have the right to play the ball, even in a **four-ball** match—the rule, expressed by the match play phrase "the player away controls the ball," is the determining factor.

COOPER, HARRY "LIGHTHORSE." B. 4 August 1904, Leatherhead, England; D. 17 October 2000, White Plains, New York, United States. Harry "Lighthorse" Cooper is among the greatest players never to have won a major championship. He played for over 20 years in the larger **professional** events beginning in 1922, before the real inception of the **PGA Tour**. During that time, he won 31 events that are now PGA Tour events. His greatest year was 1937 when he won seven tournaments, won the first **Vardon Trophy**, and led the money list. His biggest wins were the 1934 **Western Open** and the 1937 **Los Angeles** and **Canadian Opens**. His 1934 Western Open victory was considered a major championship at the time, but Cooper never managed a victory at the current four majors. He did, however, place second three times, at the 1927 and 1936 **U.S. Open**, and at the 1936 **Masters**. Cooper was inducted into the **World Golf Hall of Fame** in 1992. After his playing career, he was a club professional at Metropolis Country Club near New York, and after his retirement there, he became a teaching pro at Westchester Country Club.

COORE, WILLIAM ERNEST "BILL." B. 19 December 1945, Richmond, Virginia, United States. Bill Coore is a **golf course architect** who is best known for his work with **Ben Crenshaw**. Coore graduated in 1968 from Wake Forest University and then joined the U.S. Army for two-and-one-half years. After being discharged, he worked for various **golf course** design companies, starting with **Pete Dye** in 1972 and working with him through 1975. He worked as a superintendent from 1975 to 1982 at Waterwood National in East Texas, a course he helped Dye build, then opened his own golf course design firm in 1982. The firm of Coore & Crenshaw, which designed or rebuilt many of the top courses in the **United States,** was formed in December 1985. They are best known for their work on Sand Hills Golf Club in rural Nebraska, which opened in 1995 and is considered by many the best course built since the 1960s. They have also designed Bandon Trails in Bandon, Oregon (2005); Old Sandwich Golf Club in Plymouth, Massachusetts (2004); and East Hampton Golf Club in East Hampton, New York (2000), which are among their many outstanding designs.

CORCORAN, FREDERICK J. "FRED." B. 4 April 1905, Cambridge, Massachusetts, United States; D. 23 June 1977, White Plains, New York, United States. Fred Corcoran was among the first sports agents and one of the first to work with **professional** golfers. He was introduced to the game as a boy in Massachusetts, where he **caddied** at Belmont Country Club. He later worked for the Massachusetts Golf Association, the **USGA**, and for **Donald Ross** at **Pinehurst**. In 1936, Corcoran became tournament manager for the **PGA Tour** and became business manager for **Sam Snead**, probably the first golfer-agent association. He later worked with golfers **Babe Zaharias**, **Jimmy Demaret**, **Marlene Bauer-Hagge** and her sister, Alice Bauer, **Tony Lema**, **Ken Venturi**, and **Tom Weiskopf**. But Corcoran did not limit himself to golfers; he was probably best known for representing Ted Williams. He was also an agent for Stan Musial and NFL kicker Pete Gogolak. Corcoran was given the **William D. Richardson Award** by the **Golf Writers Association of America** in 1960 for outstanding contributions to golf. In 1975, he was inducted into the **World Golf Hall of Fame**.

CORNISH, GEOFFREY. B. 6 August 1914, Winnipeg, Manitoba, Canada. Geoffrey Cornish grew up in **Canada**, earning his college degree at the University of British Columbia and a master's degree in **agronomy** at the University of Massachusetts. He settled in New England, where he made his reputation as a **golf course architect**. In the late 1940s, he began a five-year association with Lawrence Dickinson, a turfgrass scientist at the University of Massachusetts. He worked for many years as a designer with William Robinson in the firm of Cornish and Robinson. Cornish designed over 200 courses, but was best known as a promoter of the profession. He was one of the charter members of the **American Society of Golf Course Architects (ASGCA)** in the 1960s and served as president in 1975. He taught courses around the country on **golf course** design, in affiliation with the Harvard Graduate School of Design and the University of Massachusetts at Stockbridge Winter School for Turf Management. In 1981, he and golf writer Ron Whitten wrote the definitive history of the profession, *The Golf Course* (later edition called *The Architects of Golf*). Cornish received the **Donald Ross** Award from the ASGCA in 1982, and in 1984, he was given the Outstanding Service Award by the **National Golf Foundation**. He was inducted into the Canadian Golf Hall of Fame in 1996.

COTTON, SIR HENRY THOMAS, MBE. B. 26 January 1907, Cheshire, England; D. 22 December 1987, Algarve, Portugal. Henry Cotton won the **Open Championship (British Open)** three times, in 1934, 1937, and 1948. He was the greatest British player of the later 20th century up until the resurrection of European golf in the 1970s. Cotton started out as a cricketer but turned to golf, turning

professional at age 17. He was a very hard worker, often practicing until his hands bled. He emphasized the importance of strong hands in the golf swing and did many exercises to build up his hands, notably, swinging a club into a tire laid on the ground. Known to like high style and with somewhat extravagant spending habits, Cotton did well after his first two British Open championships, but his lifestyle left him close to broke at the end of World War II. However, he did restore his fortune after his 1948 victory. Cotton earned his MBE for playing exhibition matches to raise money for the war effort during World War II. He was captain of the British **Ryder Cup** team in 1947 and 1953 and played in the match in 1937. Cotton was inducted into the **World Golf Hall of Fame** in 1980.

THE COUNTRY CLUB. The Country Club in Brookline, Massachusetts, is the oldest country club in the **United States** that is still in existence. The proper name of the course is "The Country Club," and not "Brookline Country Club," as one occasionally hears. The club was founded in 1881 and was one of the five charter clubs that formed the **USGA** in 1894. The club is most famous for hosting the 1913 **U.S. Open**, won by **Francis Ouimet**, a young American **amateur**, in a major upset. The club hosted the 1963 and 1988 U.S. Open, celebrating the 50th and 75th anniversaries of Ouimet's victory. The Country Club also hosted the **U.S. Amateur** in 1910, 1922, 1934, 1957, 1982 and is scheduled to be the host in 2013. It was the site of the **U.S. Women's Amateur** in 1902, 1941, and 1995, and in 1999, it hosted the **Ryder Cup**. The club has 27 holes, including the Clyde and Squirrel nines, which comprise the Main Course, and the Primrose nine. The championship layout is a composite of the 27 holes—the entire Squirrel nine, six holes from the Clyde nine, and 3½ holes (making up three holes) from the Primrose nine. The original six holes were laid out in 1893 by three club members, and the course was enlarged to 18 holes by Scot Willie Campbell between 1893 and 1899. The Primrose nine was built by William Flynn in 1927. The championship layout was redesigned in the 1980s by **Rees Jones** in preparation for the 1988 U.S. Open.

COUNTRY CLUBS. A country club is a club, usually private, organized for sporting activities. Most country clubs are now centered around **golf courses**, and these may also be termed "golf clubs." However, clubs may also offer tennis courts, swimming facilities, croquet fields, skeet or trap ranges, paddle tennis courts, and some indoor workout facilities. Nowadays, clubs are often family oriented and offer dining facilities. Most membership is by annual subscription, and clubs with restaurants and bars often have minimum food and beverage dues in addition to club dues.

COUPLES, FREDERICK STEPHEN "FRED" "BOOM-BOOM." B. 3 October 1959, Seattle, Washington, United States. Fred Couples, one of the most popular pros, is a U.S. **professional** who was one of the world's top players in the 1990s. He attended the University of Houston, where one of his roommates was future sportscaster **Jim Nantz**. He has won 15 times on the **PGA Tour**, with one major title, the 1992 **Masters**, and he won the **Players Championship** twice (1984 and 1996). Couples was PGA Player of the Year in both 1991 and 1992, and he won the **Vardon Trophy** both of those years. He played on five **Ryder Cup** teams—1989, 1991, 1993, 1995, and 1997. Couples is perhaps best known for his play, after the end of the regular PGA Tour season, in what many call the "Silly Season." He has won the **Skins Game** numerous times and has won many made-for-TV events later in the year, which has earned him the nickname of "King of the Silly Season." He was also known as "Boom-Boom" early in his career for his long drives.

COURSE RATING. Course rating is used in the **United States** to rate the difficulty of **golf courses**. Two numbers are now used, the course rating and the slope. The course rating measures the difficulty for an expert golfer and is a number somewhat similar to the course's **par**. A course rating several points above par indicates a very difficult course. The slope measures how difficult a course is for an average golfer.

CRAMPTON, BRUCE. B. 28 September 1935, Sydney, New South Wales, Australia. Bruce Crampton followed in the line of **Norman Von Nida** and **Peter Thomson** as one of the great **professionals** produced in Australia. He turned professional in 1953 and played in Australia for several years, winning the 1956 **Australian Open.**

He joined the U.S. **PGA Tour** in 1961. He won his first tournament in the **United States** that year and eventually won 14 events on the PGA Tour. Crampton never managed a major title but was second four times, most notably to **Jack Nicklaus** at the 1972 **Masters** and **U.S. Open** and at the 1973 and 1975 **PGA Championship**. He later starred on the **Champions (Senior) Tour**, winning 20 tournaments. His greatest year was 1973, when he won four times on the PGA Tour and claimed the **Vardon Trophy** for lowest scoring average. He also won that award in 1975.

CRAWLEY, LEONARD GEORGE. B. 26 July 1903, Nocton, England; D. 9 July 1981, Worlington, Suffolk, England. Leonard Crawley was one of the first well-known golf writers. A top player, he was the 1931 English Amateur champion and played for Great Britain and Ireland in the **Walker Cup** in 1932, 1934, 1938, and 1947. Crawley became the golf correspondent for the *Daily Telegraph* after World War II and held that position into the 1970s. Crawley was also an accomplished cricketer, playing for Cambridge while at university, then with the Marylebone Cricket Club, and later with Essex. He played only a few games each summer but recorded several centuries, including 176 not out in 1927 to beat Sussex and his high score of 222 in 1928 against Glamorgan.

CRENSHAW, BENJAMIN DANIEL "BEN." B. 11 January 1952, Austin, Texas, United States. Ben Crenshaw was a junior and **amateur** phenom growing up in Texas. He won the International Jaycee Junior title in 1968 and was a three-time **NCAA** champion while at the University of Texas. He was so dominant as an amateur that it was thought by many that he would be the next **Nicklaus** when he turned **professional** in 1973. He gave hints that this might be true when he won the Q School in the fall of 1973 by 13 shots and then won the first tournament of his **PGA Tour** career. Crenshaw became one of the top professionals on the tour, but he never quite became the game's next great player. He had difficulty with a thyroid disorder in the early 1980s, which hampered his career. He won 19 PGA Tour events, including two majors, the **Masters** in 1984 and 1995, and was the leading money winner in 1976. Crenshaw played in the **Ryder Cup** in 1981, 1983, 1987, and 1995, and captained the team in 1999. He was one of the greatest putters ever and possibly the nicest superstar ever in sports. Crenshaw was also very interested in the history of the game and **golf course architecture**. He later joined with **Bill Coore** to form Coore & Crenshaw, a renowned **golf course** design firm. In 1991, Crenshaw received the **Bob Jones Award** from the **USGA**, which is given for distinguished sportsmanship in golf. He was inducted into the **World Golf Hall of Fame** in 2002.

CROCKER, FAY. B. 2 August 1914, Montevideo, Uruguay. Fay Crocker was the first non-American woman to win a major ladies' golf championship when she triumphed at the 1955 **U.S. Women's Open**. She won the 1960 **Titleholders**, setting a record that still stands—oldest winner (45 years, 332 days) of an **LPGA** major. Crocker, whose father won the Uruguayan men's golf championship 27 times and whose mother was a Uruguayan champion in both golf and tennis, began playing golf at the age of six. Fay Crocker won the Uruguay **women**'s championship 20 times and the Argentine women's title 14 times. She first played in the **U.S. Women's Amateur** in 1939 but did not turn pro until 1954, at the age of 39. Crocker eventually won 12 tournaments on the LPGA. In Argentina, South American teams of junior golfers compete annually for the Fay Crocker Cup.

CROSBY, HARRY LILLIS "BING." B. 3 May 1903, Tacoma, Washington, United States; D. 14 October 1977, Madrid, Spain. Bing Crosby was an American singer and movie star who was known for his interest in golf and for promoting the game. He started the best-known **pro-am** in golf, the Bing Crosby Pro-Am, held on Monterey Peninsula, It was often called the "Crosby Clambake" because it brought many movie stars together with the golf pros. His entertainment career is well documented as one of America's best-known singers. He is especially known for his rendition of "White Christmas" and made multiple movies, many with **Bob Hope** in the "Road to . . ." series. As a golfer, he was quite skilled—he carried a best **handicap** of 2, and he played in both the **U.S. and British Amateur** championships. For his promotion and support of golf, the **Golf Writers' Association of America** awarded Crosby the **William D. Richardson Award** in 1950, and for distinguished sportsmanship in golf, the **USGA** honored him with the **Bob Jones Award** in 1978. He died in the manner that he probably wished he would—shortly after playing a round of golf—in Madrid, Spain.

CURTIS CUP. The Curtis Cup is a biennial **amateur** team match for **women** representing the **United States** and Great Britain–Ireland. It was first held in 1932 with a silver bowl trophy donated by the Curtis sisters—Harriot, who was 1906 **U.S. Women's Amateur** champion, and Margaret, who won that title in 1907, and 1911–1912. The competition consists of singles, **foursomes**, and **four-ball match play**. The event has been dominated by the **United States**, which has won 27 of the 35 matches through 2008. Appendix 5 includes a list of champions and captains.

CURTIS, MARGARET. B. 8 October 1883, Boston, Massachusetts, United States; D. 24 December 1965, Boston, Massachusetts, United States. Margaret Curtis was the youngest of 10 children born into a prominent North Shore, Massachusetts, family. Her father served as assistant secretary of the treasury to President William Taft. Her cousin, Laurence Curtis, was the second president of the **USGA** in 1897–1898. Margaret began playing golf and tennis at a young age alongside her sister Harriot, who also became a prominent player. In 1906, Harriot won the **U.S. Women's Amateur** title, and in 1907, Margaret won the event, defeating Harriot in the final match. Margaret Curtis also won the event in 1911–1912, which gave her three national golf titles in her career. Margaret also won the U.S. Women's doubles tennis title in 1908 alongside Eleanor Sears, making her the only woman to win national titles in both golf and tennis. Curtis later became prominent in social work, serving with the Red Cross as head of its Bureau of Refugees in Paris for three years at the end of World War I. In 1932, Margaret and Harriot donated a trophy for a team competition between **amateurs** representing the **United States** and Great Britain, an event that became known as the **Curtis Cup**. In 1958, Margaret Curtis received the **Bob Jones Award** from the **USGA**, in recognition of outstanding sportsmanship in golf.

THE CUT. In most **professional** tournaments and many major **amateur** tournaments, the competition is held over 72 holes. Usually, after 36 holes, the field is "cut" to a smaller field. The size of the cut varies between tournaments. On the **PGA Tour**, the field is cut to the low 70 players and ties at most tournaments, while at the **U.S. Open** the cut is for the low 60 players and ties, and any player within 10 shots of the lead after two rounds. At the **Masters**, the cut is to the low 44 players and ties, and all players within 10 shots of the leader. At the **Bing Crosby** Pro-Am/AT&T National Pro-Am, the cut occurs after the third round, and at the **Bob Hope** Desert Classic, the cut occurs after the fourth round.

CYPRESS POINT CLUB. Cypress Point Club is a very exclusive **golf club** on the Monterey Peninsula in Monterey, California. The course was designed by **Alister MacKenzie** in 1928. The course is set along the Pacific Ocean but winds inland among the redwood forests of the peninsula. The 15th–18th holes border the ocean and are some of the most spectacular holes in golf, especially the 16th, a 230-yard par-three with the green set on a peninsula out in the ocean, which requires the player to carry an inlet of the ocean for virtually the entire length of the hole. Cypress Point is a men's club and was one of the courses used for the **Bing Crosby Pro-Am** until 1991, when it was excluded because the **PGA Tour** ruled that all their courses had to be nondiscriminatory and open to both men and **women**. Cypress Point was the site of one of the most famous private matches in golf history. In 1956, **Ben Hogan** and **Byron Nelson** played a **four-ball** match against top California **amateurs**, **Ken Venturi** and **Harvie Ward**. Hogan and Nelson won 1 up, with Hogan shooting a course record 63 as he and Nelson recorded a **better-ball** score of 57, while Ward and Venturi shot a 58.

– D –

DALY, FREDERICK "FRED." B. 11 October 1911, Portrush, County Antrim, Ireland; D. 18 November 1990, Belfast, Northern Ireland. Fred Daly was the first Irishman to win the **Open Championship (British Open)** when he won at **Royal Liverpool** in 1947. Daly was best known as a match player, winning the News of the World Match Play event in 1947–1948 and 1952. He won the Irish

Open in 1946 and the Irish PGA in 1940, 1946, and 1952. Daly played for Great Britain and Ireland in the **Ryder Cup** matches in 1947, 1949, 1951, and 1953.

DALY, JOHN PATRICK. B. 28 April 1966, Carmichael, California, United States. John Daly was one of the most popular American **professionals** of the 1990s, but he was also a controversial one. He became well-known in 1991 when he won the **PGA Championship** after getting into the event as an alternate. For years the longest **driver** on the tour, he was known as "Long John Daly" and attracted fans for his casual attitude and long drives. His career went up and down several times, which was probably related to his profligate lifestyle, but produced five wins on the **PGA Tour**. After a few lean years, he came back in 1995 to win the **Open Championship (British Open)** at **St. Andrews**. But after that, Daly's career spiraled downward, fueled by drinking, gambling, several failed marriages, and arrests for drunkenness and assaulting **women**. Grossly out of shape, a heavy smoker and drinker, Daly made and lost several fortunes, making them from many sponsorship deals due to his popularity, and then losing them to his gambling and drinking.

DANIEL, BETH. B. 14 October 1956, Charleston, South Carolina, United States. As an **amateur**, Beth Daniel played at Furman University, won the **U.S. Women's Amateur** in 1975 and 1977, and played on the **Curtis Cup** team in 1976 and 1978. She then turned **professional** and joined the **LPGA** in 1979, earning Rookie of the Year honors. During her career, Daniel won 33 LPGA events. Her best year was 1990, when she won seven tournaments, including the **LPGA Championship**, her only major championship and for which she was named Associated Press Female Athlete of the Year. She was also LPGA Player of the Year in 1980, when she won four tournaments. Daniel led the LPGA in wins in 1982, 1990, and 1994, and she won the **Vare Trophy** three times, awarded for the lowest scoring average for an entire season.

DARWIN, BERNARD RICHARD MEIRION, CBE, JP. B. 7 September 1876, Downe, Kent, England; D. 18 October 1961, South Heighton, Sussex, England. A grandson of Charles Darwin, Bernard Darwin is considered by some the best golf writer of all time. He was educated at Eton College and graduated with a law degree from Trinity College, Cambridge, where he earned his Blue in golf in 1895–1897. He was a solid player, reaching the semifinal of the **British Amateur** in 1909 and 1921 and playing in the first **Walker Cup** match for Great Britain in 1922. After school, Darwin started as a barrister but disliked the job and became a journalist. He covered golf for the *Times* (London) from 1907–1952, and for *Country Life* from 1907 to 1961. He also occasionally wrote on cricket. Darwin was an authority on Charles Dickens and wrote several articles on him. Darwin served as Captain of the **Royal and Ancient Golf Club of St. Andrews** in 1934. He was elected to the **World Golf Hall of Fame** in 2005.

DAVIES, LAURA JANE, CBE, MBE. B. 5 October 1963, Coventry, England. Laura Davies is the greatest-ever female English **professional** golfer. She has played on both the **LPGA** and the **Ladies' European Tour (LET)**. On the LET, she led the Order of Merit in 1985–1986, 1992, 1996, 1999, 2004, and 2006. On the LPGA, she has won 20 tournaments, including four majors—1987 **U.S. Women's Open**, 1994 and 1996 **LPGA Championship**, and the 1996 **Du Maurier Classic**. Worldwide she has won over 70 professional tournaments. In 1994, Davies became the first professional, male or female, to win tournaments in five different tours in one year, winning in the **United States**, Europe, Asia, **Japan**, and **Australia**. Davies has been, for most of her career, the longest hitter in **women**'s professional golf, which has provided an advantage over her peers. She was awarded an MBE in 1988 and a CBE in 2000.

DE LA CHAUME (-LACOSTE), SIMONE THION. B. 24 November 1908, Saint-Jean-de-Luz, Pyrénées-Atlantiques, France; D. 4 September 2001, Saint-Jean-de-Luz, Pyrénées-Atlantiques, France. Simone de la Chaume was a French female **amateur** who in 1924 became the first non-British player to win the British Girls' Amateur. She followed that in 1927 with a victory at the **British Ladies' Amateur**. That year she also entered the **U.S. Women's Amateur** for the only time, losing in the third round to **Alexa Stirling-Fraser**. De la Chaume was a seven-time French champion. She married French tennis star René Lacoste, one of the "Four Musketeers," and together they started the Lacoste Company, a sportswear conglomerate. In 1967, their daughter, **Catherine Lacoste**, became the first and to date the only amateur golfer to win the **U.S. Women's Open**.

DE VICENZO, ROBERTO. B. 14 April 1923, Villa Ballester, Buenos Aires, Argentina. Roberto De Vicenzo was the first great South American golfer and probably won more golf tournaments than any golfer in history. The list is difficult to define precisely, but he definitely won more than 200 tournaments, and some put the number at over 230. He had over 60 wins in South America, including most of the national opens, most of which he won several times. A big man for his era and a very long hitter, he won seven tournaments on the U.S. **PGA Tour** between 1951 and 1968, including one major championship, the 1967 **Open Championship (British Open)**. Unfortunately, he is best known for an incident that may have prevented him from winning another major championship. At the 1968 **Masters**, De Vicenzo shot 65 on the final day to apparently tie Bob Goalby for first place. But it turned out that his score was recorded incorrectly on the scorecard—a 4 was recorded on the 17th hole when he had actually made a **birdie** 3. The score had to stand, giving him a 66 and placing him second. Unfortunately, Goalby also suffered because he was considered by many an unworthy champion, which was not true, and he still may well have won a play-off the next day. De Vicenzo's comment was a classic—he commented in his somewhat broken English, "What a stupid I am." De Vicenzo was one of the great gentlemen and ambassadors of the game of golf. A legendary story on the PGA Tour concerns a time that a **caddie** asked to borrow money from him to help pay for medical treatment for his son. When De Vicenzo was admonished by another player that the caddie may have been lying, he replied, "I pray you are correct."

DECKER, ANNE. *See* QUAST (-DECKER-WELT-SANDER), ANNE.

DEMARET, JAMES NEWTON "JIMMY." B. 24 May 1910, Houston, Texas, United States; D. 28 December 1983, Houston, Texas, United States. Jimmy Demaret was a U.S. **professional** and one of the great ambassadors of the game of golf. He was also a top player, best known as the first player to win the **Masters** three times (1940, 1947, 1950). Playing on the **PGA Tour** from 1935 to 1957, he won 31 PGA Tour events. He then spent many years as a golf commentator, most notably on the popular U.S. program in the 1960s, **Shell's Wonderful World of Golf**. He helped found the Champions Golf Club in Houston and for many years served as its codirector of golf with **Jack Burke**.

DEVLIN, BRUCE WILLIAM. B. 10 October 1937, Armidale, New South Wales, Australia. Bruce Devlin followed Peter Thomson and **Kel Nagle** as the next great player from **Australia**. After winning the **Australian Open** as an **amateur** in 1960, he turned pro in 1961 and joined the U.S. **PGA Tour**. He won eight tournaments on the PGA Tour. He later became best known in the **United States** as an announcer on televised golf events. Now settled in the United States, he has become a **golf course architect**, based out of Scottsdale, Arizona.

DEW SWEEPER. "Dew sweepers" is a derogatory term for players in tournaments, usually on the pro tours, who are very low in the standings after several rounds and therefore have to tee off at the beginning of the day when there is still dew on the ground. These players are also sometimes called the "dawn patrol." In the early rounds of the **professional** tournaments, there is a hierarchy in which the better players are given the preferred tee times, and the players first off the tee in those rounds may also be referred to as "dew sweepers."

DEY, JOSEPH C. "JOE," JR. B. 17 November 1907, Norfolk, Virginia, United States; D. 3 March 1991, Locust Valley, Long Island, New York, United States. Joe Dey is considered by many the most important administrator in golf history. After a brief career as a sportswriter (primarily a golf writer) in New Orleans and Philadelphia, he served as executive director of the **USGA** for 34 years, from 1934 to 1968. He then served as the first commissioner of the **PGA Tour** from 1969 to 1974. He was one of the foremost experts on the **Rules of Golf**. In 1975, Dey was named captain of the **Royal and Ancient Golf Club of St. Andrews**, one of the few Americans to hold that honorary position. He won multiple awards during his career in golf, including the 1961 **William D. Richardson Trophy**, given by the **Golf Writers Association of America** for distinguished service to golf, and the 1977 **Bob Jones Award**, given by the USGA for sportsmanship in golf. In 1975, he was inducted into the **World Golf Hall of Fame**.

DIEGEL, LEO HARVEY. B. 27 April 1899, Detroit, Michigan, United States; D. 8 May 1951, North Hollywood, California, United States. Leo Diegel was a U.S. **professional** who played the top events from 1920 through the mid-1930s. He spent much of his career barnstorming in the era before a true **PGA Tour** existed, but he is credited with 29 wins in PGA Tour events. These include back-to-back **PGA championship**s in 1928–1929 and the **Canadian Open** in 1924–1925 and 1928–1929. Diegel was a top ball striker but struggled with his putting and invented an unusual posture in which he had a wide stance with stiff wrists and with his elbows bent out wide, far from his body, which became known as "Diegeling." Diegel played on the **Ryder Cup** team in 1927, 1929, 1931, and 1933, and was inducted into the **World Golf Hall of Fame** in 2003.

DIMPLES. Dimples are the multiple small recessed areas on golf balls. Balls most commonly have between 300 to 400 dimples. In the 19th century, when golf balls were first made from **gutta percha (gutties)**, they were originally smooth. But golfers found that the balls flew better after they were played a few holes or rounds and became scratched or dented. Eventually, mesh-like patterns were molded onto the surface of gutta percha balls. By the end of the 19th century, golf balls were made with bramble markings, that is, multiple small elevations on the surface. In the early 20th century, these gave way to dimples. The first patent for a dimpled golf ball was given to William Taylor, an Englishman, in 1908. Dimples work by smoothing out the aerodynamics of air turbulence around a golf ball as it spins, providing lift and a truer flight.

DINAH SHORE. *See* KRAFT NABISCO (DINAH SHORE).

DIVOT. A divot is the scar on the ground left after a small piece of turf is scraped from the ground by a player after striking the ball. The term "divot" may refer to the scar itself or to the piece of turf that has been removed from the ground. They are usually made with iron shots, although occasionally a **fairway wood**/metal will make a small divot. Divots are thicker and deeper when taken with short irons and especially wedges. Among good players, most have a characteristic divot style, with some players taking only small strips or even just brushing the **grass**, while other players will gouge out large hunks of turf. Golf etiquette requires that divots be replaced after they are taken out of the turf, and this is usually the job of the **caddie**, when one is used.

DOGLEG. A dogleg is a bend in the **fairway** of either a par-four or par-five hole. A dogleg may bend to either the left or right, and it is so called because of its resemblance to the bend in a dog's leg. Par-fives may actually have two doglegs, termed a "double dogleg." Many credit top British **professional James Braid** with popularizing the use of doglegs in **golf course** design.

DORAL GOLF RESORT AND SPA. Doral is one of the best-known golf resorts in the **United States** and has hosted a **PGA Tour** event regularly since the resort was opened in 1962. The resort has five **golf courses**—the Red, Gold, Silver, Great White, and Blue Monster. The Doral PGA Tour event has always been held on the Blue Monster course, famous for its very difficult 18th hole, which is a long par-four with a lake on the left that must be carried on the drive. The lake again borders the green and requires a carry over water on the second shot. The resort was founded by real estate developer Alfred Kaskel, who named it for the first names of he and his wife—Dor(is)-Al. The club also has a tennis resort, and for many years, the tennis **professional** representing the club was the esteemed American professional Arthur Ashe. Since the early 1990s, the director of golf has been the American teaching professional **Jim McLean**.

DORMIE. "Dormie" is a **match play** term that means that a player or side is in the lead by the same number of holes as there are holes remaining to be played. Thus, if a player is 3 up after the 15th, that player is dormie. When a player is dormie, especially with several holes remaining, victory is all but assured, because that player must only halve any of the remaining holes. "Dormie" is used incorrectly when it is used to refer to the trailing player. The exact origin of the term is unknown, but it may have originated in **Scotland**, where dormice, or dormies, are small rodents that inhabit the heaths. They are quite reclusive, and a dormice sighting is said to be good luck, hence the term. Another theory is that the term comes from the French *dormir*, "to sleep," indicating that a player who is dormie may now relax, having the match well in hand.

DOUBLE EAGLE. A double eagle is a score of three-under-par on any hole, sometimes called an "**albatross**." It is extremely rare and usually occurs by scoring a two on a par-five, although a **hole-in-one** on a par-four is also considered a double eagle. The most famous double eagle in golf history occurred in the final round of the 1935 Masters when **Gene Sarazen** holed his second shot on the par-five 15th for a deuce, to make up three shots and enable him to tie for the lead. He won the title in a play-off the next day.

DOWNSWING. The downswing is the forward movement of the club from the top of the **backswing** down into the impact zone and is followed by the follow-thru. The movement is also called the "forward swing," although "downswing" is the more common term.

DQ. "DQ" is golfer's lingo for a disqualification, which may occur from one or more various violations of the **Rules of Golf**. On **professional** tours, it is sometimes called a "Dairy Queen," as in, "I got Dairy Queened for . . ."

DRAW. A draw is a golf shot that bends slightly from right to left for a right-handed player or from left to right for a left-handed player. A draw is the milder, more controlled form of a **hook**. "Draw" may also refer to the selection of competitors (who plays whom) in a **match play** tournament, but that term is more commonly used in tennis.

DRIVER. The driver is the **golf club** that players usually use off the tee, except on par-three holes, and it will hit a **golf ball** farther than any of the other clubs in the bag—well over 300 yards by top players and long drivers in many cases. Until the onset of **belly putters**, drivers were also the longest club in length in the bag as well. Since wood heads have been supplanted by hollow metal heads, termed "metal woods," drivers and other "woods" can be made much lighter, which has allowed clubs to become much longer. This has greatly increased driving distance, leading the **USGA** to recently restrict the maximum length of clubs to 48 inches, except for **putters**. In addition to length, because of the increased size of metal wood clubheads, the USGA also recently restricted clubhead size, which primarily affects drivers, to no more than 460 cc (28.06 cu. in.).

A driver is also the least-lofted club, with lofts ranging from 5 to 10 degrees. This is usually a personal preference, at least in the case of better players. The driver was at one time also called a "one-wood," but this term is now rarely used. The ability to drive long and accurately is critical to top-quality play. *See also* LONGEST DRIVERS.

DRIVING RANGE. A driving range is a practice area where players may hit golf shots. Most courses have a **practice range** or practice area where players may practice, honing their games or simply warming up before a round. But the term "driving range" is usually reserved for ranges that are lone practice areas, often found away from **golf courses**. On most driving ranges, golfers hit balls off rubber tees, or off rubber mats. A few have places where players may practice off **grass** or hit iron shots, but usually golfers hit only **drivers** at driving ranges.

DU MAURIER CLASSIC. The Du Maurier Classic is actually the Canadian Women's Open, managed by the **Royal Canadian Golf Association**. It has been **Canada**'s national championship since its founding in 1973 and has featured on the **LPGA.** From 1979 to 2000, it was one of the major championships for **women professionals.** It was best known as the Du Maurier Classic when Du Maurier Tobacco Company sponsored it. Its sponsors also inlude Peter Jackson (a brand of Imperial Cigarettes), the Bank of Montréal, and the Canadian National Railway. The championship has been contested on various courses. **Pat Bradley** is the only player to have won the title three times—1980, 1985, and 1986. Appendix 3 includes a list of champions.

DUCK HOOK. A duck hook is a golf shot that turns sharply from right to left for a right-handed player. It is always a very poor shot and often finds the rough, the trees, or **a hazard** on the left side of the **fairway**. A duck hook usually results when a stronger player releases the club too early or too violently. It is sometimes combined with a slightly outside-in clubhead path, resulting in a pull hook, which may go even more viciously to the left. Duck hooks and pull hooks are often called "shrimps" by touring pros, because the shape of the shot resembles the sharp curve of a shrimp.

DUFFER. *See* HACKER.

DUNN, SEYMOUR GOURLAY. B. 11 March 1882, North Berwick, Scotland; D. January 1959, Lake Placid, New York, United States. Seymour Dunn was one of the early great teachers of golf. Born in northern **Scotland**, he was named pro at the Société Golf de Paris when he was only 17. He designed and built several courses in continental Europe, specifically in France, Belgium, and Italy. In 1904, Dunn became pro at **Royal County Down** in Northern Ireland, but he summered in Lake Placid, New York, and was associated with that area for the remainder of his life. In 1907, he immigrated to the **United States** to live permanently and became pro at Wykagyl Golf Club in New Rochelle, New York. In 1909, he designed the Lake Placid Resort Golf Club and moved to Lake Placid full-time, serving as the pro at the resort. He worked as a teaching pro with many top **professionals**, including **Jim Barnes**, **Walter Hagen**, and **Gene Sarazen**. He also wrote many articles for golf magazines, but Dunn is best known for his pioneering instructional book *Golf Fundamentals—Orthodoxy of Style*, which is still one of the classic golf instructional books.

DUNN, WILLIAM "WILLIE," JR. B. 1865, Blackheath, Greater London, England; D. 1917, London, Greater London, England. Willie Dunn Jr. was the son of **Willie Dunn Sr.,** a Scottish golf **professional** from North Berwick, who had three famous golfing sons: **Seymour Dunn**, who was a well-known teaching professional, Tom Dunn, who was a top Scottish club professional, and Willie Dunn Jr., who was a clubmaker and course architect. Willie Jr. was a top player, competing in the **Open Championship** (**British Open**) in 1883, 1884, and 1886, with a best finish of ninth in 1883. In 1886, Dunn laid out the North Devon Golf Course at Westward Ho! and stayed there as professional until 1888, when he moved to Biarritz, France, where brother Tom had laid out the course. In 1891, Dunn moved to the **United States**, where he designed the original 12 holes at **Shinnecock Hills**, and began playing competitively again, placing second in the inaugural **U.S. Open** in 1895. Sponsored by the Vanderbilts, who he met at Biarritz, Dunn started as a teaching professional at Newport Country Club in Rhode Island, then became head pro at the Ardsley Country Club in suburban New York. There he started a club design company, importing clubs from **Scotland**, and later, worked for Spalding, MacGregor, and Wright & Ditson. He continued designing **golf courses** and is one of the most important early influences on American golf because of his clubmaking, teaching, and architecture. Some of his other top designs include Algona Country Club, Algona, New York; Apawamis Club, Rye, New York; Ocean City Golf Course, Ocean City, New Jersey; and Saranac Inn Golf and Country Club, Saranac Lake, New York.

DUTRA, OLIN ANTHONY. B. 17 January 1901, Monterey, California, United States; D. 5 May 1983, Newman, California, United States. Olin Dutra was a U.S. **professional** who played the **PGA Tour** in the 1920s and 1930s. It was the early years of the PGA Tour when records of wins are uncertain, but it is quite well known that Dutra won two major championships. He triumphed at the 1932 **PGA Championship** in **match play** and then won the 1934 **U.S. Open** at **Merion**, coming from eight shots back after two rounds despite being quite ill with dysentery on the final day. Dutra played on the 1933 and 1935 **Ryder Cup** teams.

DUVAL, DAVID ROBERT. B. 9 November 1971, Jacksonville, Florida, United States. After a top junior and college career, which included winning the 1989 **U.S. Junior Amateur** and being named a four-time All-American at Georgia Tech, David Duval turned **professional**, earning his **PGA Tour** card in 1995. He immediately became one of the top players in the world, but he had difficulty winning tournaments in his first few years. Then in late 1997, something sparked in his game, and he won 13 PGA Tour events from 1997 to 2001, which include his only major, the 2001 **Open Championship** (**British Open**). And then he lost his game. After the 2001 Open title, Duval, who was world-ranked number one for parts of 1999, dropped into the 1,000s in the **World Golf Ranking**. His career seemed to be over by 2005, but he gradually returned to the tour and had better results, highlighted by a tie for second at the 2009 **U.S. Open**. Attributed to various sources—health problems, injuries, personal difficulties—the precise reason for Duval's decline is not known. One of Duval's most dramatic victories came at the 1999 **Bob Hope** Chrysler Classic, when he shot 59 in the final round to win the tournament by one shot, eagling the final hole. Duval played on the 1999 and 2002 **Ryder Cup** teams.

DYE, PAUL B. "PETE." B. 29 December 1925, Urbana, Ohio, United States. Although he was a top **amateur** player in the state of Indiana, Pete Dye's first career was in insurance. But in his mid-30s, he transitioned to a career designing **golf courses** and became one of the most famous golf course architects. Early in his career, Dye visited **Scotland** to learn the secrets of the original Scottish courses, incorporating many of their features into his courses. His first well-known course was Crooked Stick in Carmel, Indiana, built in 1964–1965, which hosted the 1991 **PGA Championship** and about which one golf announcer, **David Feherty**, famously proclaimed, "The course is so long you have to take the curvature of the earth into effect." In 1967, he began work on The Golf Club near Columbus and asked **Jack Nicklaus** to assist him. This led to several years in which the two collaborated on several courses and jump-started Nicklaus' later career as a golf course architect. Their most famous work together is **Harbour Town Golf Links** in Hilton Head, South Carolina, site of the Heritage Classic (known by various names), an annual **PGA Tour** event.

Dye is probably most famous for his design of **TPC Sawgrass** in Ponte Vedra, Florida, home of the annual Players Championship and best known for its frightening 17th hole, a short par-three to an island green. Dye also designed the Ocean Course at **Kiawah Island**, one of the world's most difficult courses and site of the "War on the Shore," the 1991 **Ryder Cup**. Internationally, his best-known course is the Teeth of the Dog at **Casa de Campo Resort** in the Dominican Republic. Dye has received multiple honors, including the 2003 **Old Tom Morris** Award from the **Golf Course Superintendents Association of America**, its highest honor, and the 2005 PGA Tour Lifetime Achievement Award. In 2008, he was inducted into the **World Golf Hall of Fame**.

– E –

EAGLE. An eagle is a score of two-under-par on a single golf hole. An eagle usually occurs in one of four ways: 1) a player reaches a par-five green in two shots and sinks the putt for a three, 2) a player drives a par-four green with the tee shot and sinks the putt for a two, 3) a player holes the second shot on a par-four, or 4) a player makes a **hole-in-one** on a par-three.

EGAN, HENRY CHANDLER. B. 21 August 1884, Chicago, Illinois, United States; D. 5 April 1936, Everett, Washington, United States. Chandler Egan was a top American **amateur** in the early years of the 20th century but was better known for his contributions as a **golf course architect**. Egan was a member of the Harvard golf team and led them to the NCAA team championship in 1902–1904. He won the individual title in 1902. Egan later won two consecutive **U.S. Amateur** Championships in 1904 and 1905, making him the first person to win both the **NCAA** and U.S. Amateur titles. In 1904, Egan also lost to **George Lyon** in the final of the Olympic golf tournament. His tournament victories include four titles at the **Western Amateur** (1902, 1904, 1905, 1907) and five at the Pacific Northwest Amateur (1915, 1920, 1923, 1925, 1932). In 1911, Egan purchased land in Oregon and settled in the Pacific Northwest. He started golf course design in the 1920s, mostly in Oregon and Washington.

EIGHTEEN (18) HOLES. The earliest **golf courses** did not always have 18 holes. In fact, most of the early courses in **Scotland** had various numbers of holes. **Prestwick Golf Club**, the original site of the **Open Championship (British Open)**, consisted of only 12 holes, and the first 13 British Opens were held over 36 holes, with players going round the course three times. A few courses had more than 18 holes, and some had as many as 23. In the later 19th century, 18 holes became the standard for a full round of golf. There is an apocryphal, legendary story, too good not to tell, of how this came to be. The major clubs in Scotland decided that they needed to choose a standard for the number of holes on a course. A committee, with representatives from the top clubs in Scotland, met, but they had difficulty coming to a consensus. Each club promoted its own cause so it would not have to change its course. They were then visited by one golfer, who told the story of why he always played 18 holes. The reason was that he carried a small tin with him, with some Scotch in it to refresh him, and he made it a habit to take a wee bit of a nip on each tee. It so happened that his tin held exactly 18 nips, so he would play 18 holes and when the tin was emptied, he stopped playing. It seemed as good a reason as any to the committee, so we now have 18 holes as a standard round of golf. However, more realistically, the 18-hole standard came about because there were then 18 holes at **St. Andrews** (although it originally had 22), and other clubs deferred to St. Andrews as the rule-making authority of the game.

EISENHOWER TROPHY. *See* WORLD AMATEUR TEAM CHAMPIONSHIP.

EISENHOWER, DWIGHT DAVID "IKE." B. 14 October 1890, Denison, Texas; D. 28 March 1969, Washington, D.C., United States. Dwight Eisenhower was a U.S. military hero who served as the 34th president of the **United States** from 1952 to 1960. Eisenhower attended West Point, where he played football. He served in World War I and rose to brigadier general in 1941. In 1942, he was promoted to full general status and named commanding general of the European Theater of Operations, overseeing the Allied efforts in Europe. He was eventually given a rare fifth star as general of the army. Eisenhower was elected president in 1952 on the Republican ticket and served two terms.

His golf contributions, which contributed to his being named to the **World Golf Hall of Fame** in 2009, were in popularizing the sport as president. He played frequently, often at **Augusta National**, where he became a member, with 210 recorded rounds there during his presidential terms. Many people attribute the explosion of golf's popularity in the later 1950s and early 1960 to three factors: televised golf tournaments, **Arnold Palmer**'s charisma while winning many tournaments, and Ike's support and promotion of the game. Eisenhower had a **putting green** installed on the South Lawn of the White House. At Augusta National, he is remembered for his tee shots often getting caught by the loblolly pine tree in the left-center of the 17th **fairway**. He actually petitioned the club, unsuccessfully, to have the tree, which is now called the "Eisenhower Pine," taken down. In 1958, the **World Amateur Team Championship** for men took place for the first time, with teams competing for the **Eisenhower Trophy**.

ELDER, ROBERT LEE. B. 14 July 1934, Dallas, Texas, United States. Lee Elder was the first African American to play in the **Masters** tournament. Elder began playing golf at 16 and progressed after he enlisted in the Army in 1959 due in large part to having a commanding colonel who was an avid golfer. In 1961, after his discharge, he joined the **United Golfers Association** (UGA) Tour for black players, and he was dominant on that tour, at one time winning 18 of 22 tournaments. He qualified for the **PGA Tour** in 1967, and in his 1968 rookie year, he placed 40th on the money list. Elder was invited by **Gary Player** to play in the 1971 South African PGA Championship in Johannesburg, which was a momentous sporting occasion during the era of **South African** apartheid. Elder played several tournaments in Africa that year, among them the Nigerian Open, which he won. In 1974, Elder won the Monsanto Open, which qualified him for the Masters. He played at **Augusta National** in April 1975 despite receiving numerous pieces of hate mail, and he was well protected during the tournament, enlisting personal security for fears of his own safety. In 1979, Elder became the first African American to play in the **Ryder Cup**. He won four PGA Tour events between 1974 and 1978. Elder and his wife, Rose, have been very active in charitable causes, supporting the United Negro College Fund and forming the Lee Elder Foundation, which provides money for low-income students to help them attend college. Aside from being a great player, he is a fine, fine gentleman.

ELKINGTON, STEPHEN JOHN "STEVE." B. 8 December 1962, Inverell, New South Wales, Australia. Steve Elkington is an **Australian professional** who is primarily known for his play on the U.S. **PGA Tour**, where he won 10 tournaments, including the 1995 **PGA Championship**, his only major title. Elkington also won the 1991 and 1997 **Players Championships**, all but major titles to most tour pros. He played on the **Presidents Cup** teams in 1994, 1996, 1998, and 2000. In 1995, he led the PGA Tour in scoring average, winning the **Vardon Trophy**. He has one of the simplest, smoothest swings in golf. After his top years in the 1990s, Elkington was hampered by health problems, various allergies and sinus infections, one of which threatened his life for a time.

ELS, THEODORE ERNEST "ERNIE" "THE BIG EASY." B. 17 October 1969, Johannesburg, South Africa. Ernie Els has been one of the world's top **professionals** since the early 1990s. One of the largest great golfers ever, at over 6 feet 3 inches (191 cm), he is a long hitter but does it with an effortless swing, which earned him the nickname the "Big Easy." Els holds three major titles, the 1994 and 1997 **U.S. Open** and the 2002 **Open Championship (British Open)**. He has 16 tournament wins on the **PGA Tour** and 24 on the **European PGA Tour**, and he has won his national championship, the **South African Open**, four times. Els spreads his play between the U.S. and European tours and was European PGA Order of Merit winner in 2003 and 2004. Notably, he has won the **World Match Play Championship** in Wentworth, England, seven times, breaking the record of his countryman **Gary Player**, who won five times, as did **Seve Ballesteros**. After his European Tour wins in 2005, Els struggled somewhat, attributable to his undergoing knee surgery and to dealing with his young child being diagnosed with autism.

ENGLAND. The home of golf is considered to be **Scotland**, even though its **origins** are not well defined. But the game quickly spread from Scotland to England. When King James VI succeeded to the thrones of **England** and **Ireland** in 1603, he took a number of his court to London with him. There is some evidence that members of his court brought the game to England, playing golf first at Blackheath, on the hill behind Greenwich Palace.

The **Open Championship (British Open)** was held in Scotland from 1860 to 1893, but in 1894, it was held for the first time in England, at **Royal St. George's Golf Club**. Since that time, the championship has frequently been held in England, and the current rota of the Open Championship includes five Scottish clubs and four English ones. In the late 19th and early 20th centuries, England also contributed several of the great players in the game, notably **John Ball** and **Harold Hilton** among the **amateurs**. **Harry Vardon** was the greatest player in the game until the advent of Bob Jones and is usually considered English, although technically, he was from the Isle of Jersey. In the 1920s, **Joyce Wethered**, later Lady Heathcoat-Amory, was the best player in the **women**'s game and is still considered among the finest ever. The best English **professional** ever is probably recent player **Nick Faldo**, winner of six major championships.

England has a number of **golf courses**, but ranks 10th worldwide in number of courses per capita, trailing Scotland, Wales, Ireland, and Northern Ireland in the United Kingdom, and behind **Australia**, **Canada**, New Zealand, and the **United States**. Golf in England is governed by the **R&A**, formerly the **Royal and Ancient Golf Club of St. Andrews**, founded in 1754. The **Ladies' Golf Union**, founded in 1893, oversees the women's game in England.

ESPIRITO SANTO TROPHY. *See* WOMEN'S WORLD AMATEUR TEAM CHAMPIONSHIP.

EUROPEAN INSTITUTE OF GOLF COURSE ARCHITECTS (EIGCA). In July 1971, eight British **golf course architects**, among them C. K. Cotton (1887–1974), J. Hamilton Stutt (1924–2008), and Fred Hawtree (1916–2000), met at the Great Western Hotel in Paddington to discuss the formation of a society of British golf course architects. They formed the British Association of Golf Course Architects. (The name changed to the British Institute in the early 1990s.) In 1983, Robert Berthet helped form the Association Française des Architectes de Golf, initially with 20 members. In 1989, The European Society of Golf Course Architects (ESGA) was founded by the Austrian Gerold Hauser, who became the first president of ESGA from 1989 to 1994. Throughout the 1990s, the three groups discussed a merger. In 2000, the three groups combined to form the European

Institute of Golf Course Architects. The goals of the EIGCA are to enhance the status of the **golf course** design profession, increase the opportunities for members to practice throughout the world, and educate future golf course architects. The French designer, Alain Prat, noted that the group "becomes a gathering place for our shared experience, information, training and promotion for the common goal, and that our knowledge in the fields of design, construction, landscaping and the environment, becomes the basis to enhance the quality of European golf architecture."

EUROPEAN PGA TOUR. The European PGA Tour is the organization responsible for conducting major European **professional** events, including the regular tour, the **Senior Tour,** and a developmental, or challenge, tour. Its headquarters is at the **Wentworth Club** in Surrey, **England**. There have been multiple European professional events, both in Great Britain and on the continent, since the early 20th century. But the European PGA Tour was organized as a distinct entity just in 1972. Although most of the European Tour events are in Europe, several of the tournaments have been in Asia, notably Dubai. The European PGA Tour contests an Order of Merit, essentially given to the leading money winner on the tour, which is a high honor to European professionals. In 2009, this was re-titled the "Race to Dubai," because the leading money winners will play in a season-ending tournament in Dubai. The Order of Merit has been led eight times by **Colin Montgomerie** and six times by **Seve Ballesteros**.

EVANS SCHOLARS FOUNDATION. In 1916, after winning the **U.S. Open** and **U.S. Amateur**, **Chick Evans** recorded a series of golf instructions for the Brunswick Record Company. He received several thousand dollars for this, which cost him his **amateur status**. His mother suggested he use the money to start a scholarship fund for **caddies,** and the Evans Scholars Foundation was eventually born. Evans always gave credit for the idea to his mother. He approached the Western Golf Association, which at first was reluctant to participate, but in 1929, they formed the Evans Scholars Foundation. In that year, Harold Fink and Jim McGinnis were the first two Evans scholars provided scholarship money to attend college. To date, over 8,000 caddies have received scholarship money from the foundation. The

Western Open, as part of its charitable programs, provided money to the Evans Scholars Foundation until its demise in 2006. There are Evans Scholarship Houses at several universities in the Midwest, including, notably, the University of Colorado, the University of Illinois, Northwestern University, Marquette University, the University of Wisconsin, Purdue University, Ohio State University, Northern Illinois University, the University of Missouri, Indiana University, the University of Michigan, Michigan State University, Miami University, and the University of Minnesota. However, Evans scholars may use the money to attend any university to which they are accepted.

EVANS, CHARLES E. "CHICK," JR. B. 18 July 1890, Indianapolis, Indiana, United States; D. 6 November 1979, Chicago, Illinois, United States. Chick Evans was one of the top **amateurs** of the early 20th century but is best known for the **caddie** scholarship he established, which carries his name. In 1916, Evans became the first player to win the **U.S. Open** and **U.S. Amateur** in the same year. He won a second U.S. Amateur title in 1920 and was runner-up three times. He competed in 50 U.S. Amateurs in a very long career, and he played on the **Walker Cup** teams of 1922, 1924, and 1928. Evans was also the first amateur to win the **Western Open**, in 1910, and he was an eight-time champion at the **Western Amateur**. After his banner year of 1916, he recorded a series of golf instructional records. Preferring to remain an amateur, in 1929, he used the money he received to establish a scholarship fund for caddies, which enabled him to maintain his **amateur status**. The Chick Evans Scholarship Fund has since been maintained by the Western Golf Association, and over 8,000 caddies have received scholarship help to attend college. It is the largest scholarship program in sports and the largest privately funded scholarship program in the **United States**. In 1960, Evans received the **Bob Jones Award**, given by the **USGA** in recognition of distinguished sportsmanship in golf.

EXECUTIVE COURSES. Executive **golf courses** are shorter courses, often built where land is tight. They are also popular among beginners and older players who cannot manage to play modern championship courses because of their length. Executive courses are not strictly par-three courses, although they usually contain an abundance of those holes, since they often include several, relatively short par-fours.

– F –

FADE. A fade is a golf shot that bends slightly from left-to-right for a right-handed player or from right-to-left for a left-handed player. A fade is the milder, more controlled form of a **slice**.

FAIRWAY. The fairway is the area between the **teeing grounds** and the **putting green** that is cut short. The term is not defined in the **Rules of Golf**, which only recognize four areas of a **golf course**—teeing grounds, **hazards**, putting greens, and **through the green**. Through the green encompasses both the fairway and the **rough**, which is the longer **grass** off the fairway that is more difficult to play from. On par-fours and par-fives, the purpose of the tee shot is to place the ball in the fairway, which gives an easier **approach shot** to the green.

FAIRWAY WOODS. Fairway woods are a series of clubs, more lofted than a **driver**, that are usually played off the **fairway**. In the early 20th century, the standard series of fairway woods was a 2-wood (or brassie), 3-wood (also called a "spoon"), and 4-wood. By the 1960s, the 2-wood was rarely used, and many players started using a 5-wood. In the 1970s, it was not uncommon to see players with more lofted woods in the bag, such as 7-woods, 9-woods, and as high as a 17-woods. Like drivers, fairway "woods" are now always made with a hollow metal head. In addition to playing fairway woods off the fairway, they are often used for the tee shot on tighter or shorter holes, sacrificing some distance for greater control.

FALDO, SIR NICHOLAS ALEXANDER, "NICK," MBE. B. 18 July 1957, Welwyn Garden City, England. Nick Faldo is an English **professional**, probably the greatest English player since **Harry Vardon**. In 1975, Faldo won the English Amateur and British Youths championships and then enrolled at the University of Houston, but he lasted there less than a semester and turned professional in 1976.

He won tournaments on the European Tour in 1977 and 1978 and was third on the Order of Merit in 1978. He led the Order of Merit in 1983, although by then he was playing primarily on the U.S. **PGA Tour**. Faldo was the best player in the world in the late 1980s and early 1990s, rivaled only by **Curtis Strange** for a few years, and was ranked number one in the world for 98 weeks. He won nine times on the U.S. PGA Tour and 30 times on the European Tour, including six major titles—the **Open Championship** (**British Open**) in 1987, 1990, and 1997, and the **Masters** in 1989, 1990, and 1996. Faldo lost a play-off to Strange for the 1988 **U.S. Open**. He was inducted into the **World Golf Hall of Fame** in 1997. Rather than play on a **Senior Tour**, he is now a golf commentator for CBS Sports in the **United States**. Faldo was knighted in 2009 for services to golf.

FALSE FRONT. A false front describes one particular shape of **putting green**. In a green with a false front, the front of the green will be elevated, usually fairly sharply. A ball landing on the false front will usually simply roll back off the green, therefore the illusion that hitting that part of the green will keep the ball on the putting surface is false.

FARRELL, JOHN JOSEPH "JOHNNY." B. 1 April 1901, White Plains, New York, United States; D. 14 June 1988, Boynton Beach, Florida, United States. Johnny Farrell was a golfing great of the 1920s but is little remembered today. In the days before an official **PGA Tour**, he won 22 **professional** tournaments that are now tour events. He won one major, the 1928 **U.S. Open**, defeating **Bob Jones** in a play-off. Farrell played in the first three **Ryder Cups** in 1927, 1929, and 1931. He spent many years as the head professional at **Baltusrol Golf Club** in New Jersey. In addition to the prize money he collected for his fine play, Farrell also collected considerable sums from clothing and department stores as the "Best Dressed Golfer" at numerous tour events.

FAT. Fat refers to a shot in which the player strikes the turf before striking the ball, taking a divot that starts behind the ball. Fat shots usually are considered flubs in their extreme form, and often will end up many yards short of their intended target. A shot that is hit slightly fat, usually by striking the ball and turf together, will often be a slight **flyer**, and the flyer effect will offset the fat effect. Such a shot, termed a fat flyer by the pros, will usually travel approximately the intended distance, but it is not a well-controlled shot.

FAULKNER, HERBERT GUSTAVUS MAX, OBE. B. 29 July 1916, Bexhill, England; D. 26 February 2005, Chichester, England. Max Faulkner was an English **professional** who was the son of a golf professional. He started in sports as a boxer, winning the British Services title. Playing mostly in the late 1940s and 1950s, he won 16 European professional events that are now on the **European PGA Tour**. His greatest win was the 1951 **Open Championship (British Open)**, although he was a three-time champion of the Spanish Open and won the 1951 British Masters and the 1953 News of the World Match Play event. He was well known for his colorful outfits while playing.

FAY, DAVID BRIAN. B. 12 October 1950, New York, New York, United States. David Fay is a golf administrator who has been the executive director of the **USGA** since 1990. Fay came to know the game as a **caddie** in the New York area, and later attended Colgate University. After graduating in 1972, he worked for the Metropolitan Golf Association until he joined the USGA in 1978. After working in various positions with the USGA he moved up to executive director in July 1989 after serving for a few months as interim executive director and has served in that capacity through 2009.

FAZIO, GEORGE. B. 12 November 1912, Philadelphia, Pennsylvania, United States; D. 6 June 1986, Jupiter, Florida, United States. George Fazio was a solid American player on the **PGA Tour**, winning two events, the 1946 **Canadian Open** and the 1947 **Bing Crosby Pro-Am**, but he was best known as a **golf course architect**. Fazio never won a major title but came close in 1950 when he tied for first at the **U.S. Open** at **Merion** with **Ben Hogan** and **Lloyd Mangrum**, losing the play-off to Hogan. He spent many years as the head **professional** at Hillcrest **Country Club** in Los Angeles and taught many Hollywood celebrities. Fazio began a golf course architectural firm in the 1960s. He was later assisted by his nephew, **Tom Fazio**, who became a renowned course designer and designed many well-known courses, most notably, Jupiter Hills in Florida and Butler National in Oak Brook, Illinois, longtime home of the **Western Open**.

FAZIO, THOMAS "TOM." B. 10 February 1945. Tom Fazio was the nephew of **George Fazio**, a top **professional** player who became a **golf course architect** later in his career. Tom followed in his uncle's footsteps but not as a player. In the late 1960s, he joined his uncle's golf course design firm but stayed only a few years. He formed his own golf course architectural firm in 1972, based in Jupiter, Florida. He has become one of the most highly respected architects, with many of his courses appearing on *Golf Digest*'s and *Golfweek*'s lists of top American courses. In 1995, Tom Fazio received the Old Tom Morris Award from the **American Society of Golf Course Architects**.

FEATHERIE. Although no examples survive, it is believed that the earliest **golf balls** were round, wooden balls. In the early 17th century, the first major advance occurred in golf balls, with a ball termed the "featherie." Featheries were made by stitching together a cowhide sphere, leaving a small opening in it. A top hat was then filled with feathers that were soaked in water to shrink them. After a thorough soaking, the feathers were stuffed into the hole in the cowhide, and it was stitched over. As the feathers dried, they expanded to create a firm, round golf ball. Featheries were the standard golf ball until the mid-19th century when they were replaced by **gutta percha** balls. Featheries worked reasonably well in dry weather, although they did not fly nearly as far as gutties or, especially, more modern wound balls. But in wet weather, they became soft and almost useless. Featheries were made by golf **professionals,** and it was a primary source of their income. The Scottish professionals of the 1800s resisted the move to gutta percha because it would cost them the money they made from the manufacture and sale of golf balls.

FEHERTY, DAVID. B. 13 August 1958, Bangor, County Down, Northern Ireland. David Feherty was an Irish **professional** golfer who was a solid player on the **European PGA Tour**, making the 1991 **Ryder Cup** team. But he has become much better known as a broadcaster on U.S. television and a humorous writer on golf. He won five tournaments on the European Tour, and was twice in the Order of Merit Top 10—1989 (10th) and 1990 (8th). Feherty played in the **United States** in 1994–1995, with his best finish being a second place at the 1994 New England Classic. In 1997, he retired from competition and joined CBS Sports as an announcer. He has also written several books and is a contributor to *Golf Magazine*. Feherty has had difficulty with alcoholism and depression but has overcome that through rehab and therapy. Formerly somewhat heavy, he has lost the weight through vigorous exercise, mainly cycling. In 2008, he was injured in a cycling accident that left him with some permanent nerve damage in his left hand.

FERGUSON, ROBERT "BOB." B. 1848, Musselburgh, East Lothian, Scotland; D. 1915. Bob Ferguson was a Scottish **professional** who first became known when he won the 1866 Leith Tournament with a score of 131 over four rounds of Leith's seven-hole **links**. He competed in the **Open Championship** for over a dozen years before breaking through with a best early finish of third in 1869. But he then won three consecutively, from 1880 to 1882. Attempting to tie **Young Tom Morris**' streak of four consecutive, he tied for first in 1883 but lost the play-off to Willie Fernie. He led the play-off by one shot standing on the 36th tee and parred the hole but lost when Fernie **eagled** the drivable par-four. Shortly thereafter, Ferguson contracted typhoid fever and retired from competitive golf. He later became custodian of the Links at **Musselburgh**, and taught golf to the boys of Loretto School.

FESCUE. "Fescue," or technically, *festuca*, refers to a genus of perennial **grasses**, which are often used on **golf courses**. In the **United States**, fescue is found mostly in the rough, while in the United Kingdom, fescue grasses are commonly used in the **fairway**, where the sandy links soil allows them to grow more easily. On linksland, fescue may be cut very short, allowing the fairways to be tight, which lets the ball run a lot.

FINCHEM, TIMOTHY W. "TIM." B. 19 April 1947, Ottawa, Illinois, United States. Tim Finchem has been commissioner of the **PGA Tour** since 1994, succeeding **Deane Beman**. Finchem graduated from the University of Richmond and then attended the University of Virginia School of Law. He practiced law in Virginia Beach for three years before serving in the Carter administration as a deputy advisor to the president in the Office of Economic Affairs. He joined the PGA Tour in administration, serving in various positions, among them deputy commissioner and chief operating officer under Beman, before succeeding to the commissioner's position in 1994.

THE FIRST TEE. The First Tee is a program, created by The **World Golf Foundation** in November 1997, whose purpose is to expose children, and especially disadvantaged children, to the game of golf and its positive values. The mission of the First Tee is "to impact the lives of young people by providing learning facilities and educational programs that promote character-development and life-enhancing values through the game of golf." The program is run by a committee comprised of members representing the **Masters Tournament**, the **Ladies Professional Golf Association**, **PGA of America**, **PGA Tour**, and the **USGA**, with former president George H. W. Bush serving as honorary chairman. The First Tee sets up golf facilities around the country that allow children to learn the game. Their goal is to have facilities and a chapter in every state.

FIVE FOUNDING CLUBS. The **United States Golf Association** (USGA) was established in 1894 when five of the oldest golf clubs in the United States gathered together and formed the organization as the governing body of golf in America. The five original **USGA** clubs were **The Country Club**, Brookline, Massachusetts; **Shinnecock Hills Golf Club**, Southampton, New York; Newport Country Club, Newport, Rhode Island; St. Andrew's Golf Club, Hastings-on-Hudson, New York; and Chicago Golf Club in Chicago.

FLAGSTICK. The flagstick is a stick that usually has a flag and is placed in the hole on each **putting green** to mark the location of the hole for players in the **fairway** or on the tee. The flagstick is often termed a "pin," but the **Rules of Golf** do not recognize that term and instead use "flagstick." While virtually all clubs have flags atop the flagstick, the **Merion Golf Club** in Philadelphia has famously always had wicker baskets at the top of its "flagsticks."

FLECK, JACK. B. 7 November 1921, Bettendorf, Iowa, United States. Jack Fleck was a U.S. **professional** golfer who played the **PGA Tour** in the 1950s and 1960s. He is best known for a huge upset victory, winning the 1955 **U.S. Open** at the **Olympic Club**, in which he defeated the formidable **Ben Hogan** in a play-off, preventing Hogan from winning his fifth U.S. Open. Fleck won two other PGA Tour events, in 1960 and 1961, and won the 1979 PGA Seniors title. He was inducted into the Iowa Golf Hall of Fame in 1989.

FLICK, JAMES MYRON "JIM." B. 17 November 1929, Bedford, Indiana, United States. Jim Flick is a golf teacher who was one of the best-known teachers in the 1970s, 1980s, and 1990s. He attended Wake Forest University, where he played on the golf team briefly with **Arnold Palmer**. Flick then became a golf **professional** in 1954, serving at Losantiville Country Club in Cincinnati in the 1960s and early 1970s. In 1970, Flick was involved with a revolutionary golf instructional book, *The Square to Square Golf Swing: Model Method for the Modern Player*. He became well known as a teacher due to this book and taught at PGA instructional courses. This led him to work with *Golf Digest* in their golf schools from 1972 to 1990, where the teaching methods of **Bob Toski** heavily influenced him. In the late 1980s, he began to work with both **Jack Nicklaus** and Tom Lehman, which led to the formation of the Nicklaus/Flick Golf Schools. They operated from 1991 to 2001 and have since been replaced by Jim Flick Premier Schools. Later, he helped develop ESPN Golf Schools. Flick was named PGA Teacher of the Year in 1988, and in 2002, he was inducted into the World Golf Teachers Hall of Fame. He is also a member of the Wake Forest University Athletic Hall of Fame.

FLOP SHOT. A flop shot is a type of short pitch shot played around the greens. It has become more widely used since the advent of highly lofted **lob wedges** or X-wedges. In a flop shot, the players uses a lob wedge to loft the pitch shot well up into the air, landing on the green and stopping with minimal run. Both **Phil Mickelson** and **Tiger Woods** are particularly known for playing flop shots around the green.

FLOYD, RAYMOND LORAN "RAY." B. 4 September 1942, Fort Bragg, North Carolina, United States. Ray Floyd grew up in North Carolina and briefly attended the University of North Carolina, leaving after his freshman year to turn **professional**. He won his first **PGA Tour** event in 1963, before he turned 21. Floyd eventually won 22 times on the PGA Tour, winning four major championships—the 1969 and 1982 **PGA Championship**, the 1976 **Masters**, and the 1986 **U.S. Open**. He won 14 times on the PGA **Senior Tour**. During his career, he played on eight **Ryder Cup** Teams (1969, 1975, 1977, 1981, 1983, 1985, 1991, 1993) and was team captain in 1989. Floyd won the **Vardon Trophy** in 1983 and was inducted into the **World Golf Hall of Fame** in 1989. In addition to his tournament record, Floyd was a top money player in private matches among golf pros.

FLYER. A flyer is a shot in which **grass** gets between the clubface and the golf ball, preventing the grooves on the club from applying the normal amount of backspin. A flyer will often fly erratically toward the target and on landing, with minimal spin, will often run off the green, sometimes into trouble. **Professionals** hate flyers, preferring to fully control the ball. Flyers usually occur when hitting out of the rough, the longer grass in the rough getting between the clubface and the ball, but they may occur on poorer shots hit from the **fairway** (a fat flyer) or on fairways that have longer grass. Since newer club technology has changed the style of groove from V-shaped to square, flyers have had less impact on better players. But the **USGA** is mandating a change in groove specifications, which will reduce the overall volume of grooves as well as edge sharpness beginning in 2010.

FLYNN, WILLIAM STEPHEN "BILL." B. 25 December 1890, Milton, Massachusetts, United States; D. 24 January 1944, Philadelphia, Pennsylvania, United States. Bill Flynn was an American **golf course architect** who began his career near his native Boston but eventually designed courses throughout the **United States**. A close childhood friend of **Francis Ouimet**, Flynn's first course design was at Heartwellville, Vermont in 1909. He was shortly thereafter hired by **Hugh Wilson** to finish the design of **Merion Golf Club**'s East Course in Philaldelphia, a well-known **U.S. Open** course. Flynn stayed in Philadelphia as the superintendent at the course and assisted in changing several holes over the next 25 years. Flynn's most prominent designs also include the Cascades Course at The Homestead in Virginia; Cherry Hills Country Club near Denver; and the addition of the Primrose nine to **The Country Club** in Brookline, Massachusetts. After World War I, Flynn formed a design firm with Howard Toomey. The firm of Toomey & Flynn was then hired to rebuild **Shinnecock Hills**, finishing the work in 1931 and keeping only two of the original holes. Other prominent courses that Toomey and Flynn worked on together include Concord Country Club, West Chester, Pennsylvania; The Kittanset Club, Marion, Massachusetts; Huntingdon Valley Country Club, Huntingdon Valley, Pennsylvania; Philadelphia Country Club, Gladwyne, Pennsylvania; and Manor Country Club, Rockville, Maryland.

FORD, DOUGLAS MICHAEL "DOUG," SR. (NÉ DOUGLAS FORTUNATO). B. 6 August 1922, West Haven, Connecticut, United States. Doug Ford turned **professional** in 1949 and played through the 1960s, winning 19 **PGA Tour** events between 1952 and 1963, including two major championships, the 1955 **PGA Championship** and the 1957 **Masters**. He played on four **Ryder Cup** teams—1955, 1957, 1959, and 1961. Ford was not a long hitter but had a superb short game, especially his wedge play, which overcame his lack of driving length. Ford was inducted into the Connecticut Golf Hall of Fame in 1972 and the National Italian-American Sports Hall of Fame in 1992.

FORECADDIE. A forecaddie is a **caddie** employed by the tournament committee to indicate to players the position of balls during play. A forecaddie is an **outside agency** and is not employed by any specific competitor or competitors.

FORWARD PRESS. A forward press is a motion of the hands made by a player prior to initiating the golf swing. In a forward press, the hands are pressed forward slightly toward the target, and this slight motion then triggers the takeaway, or backswing. A forward press follows a waggle, and both motions are ways for a player to stay moving, rather than starting the swing from a purely static position.

Some players have exaggerated forward presses, although this is less common nowadays. Forward presses are also used on putting strokes.

FOUR-BALL. Four-ball is a type of golf match that is sometimes called a "best-ball," although it is more accurately called "better-ball." In such a competition, two teams of two players play **match play** against each other, with the better-ball of each pair used as the score for a hole. Holes are won by the team with the lowest better-ball score on each hole. Although there are some four-ball stroke play events (notably, the **PGA Tour** has one in many years), most four-ball competition is contested at match play. Four-ball is one of the formats used at most major team events, including the **Ryder Cup**, **Walker Cup**, **President's Cup**, **Curtis Cup**, and **Solheim Cup**. *See also* HAM-AND-EGG.

FOURSOMES. Foursomes is a competition format that originated in **Scotland** but is rarely played anymore, except in team match competition. In foursomes play, two-man teams play alternate shots until their ball is holed, virtually always playing **match play** against another pair. There are some variations. In pure foursomes play, one player on each team tees off on odd-numbered holes, while the other player on each team tees off on even-numbered holes. In another variation, both players on each team hit tee shots, and each team selects one to play alternately from there into the hole. Foursomes is contested at the **Ryder Cup**, **President's Cup**, **Solheim Cup**, **Walker Cup**, and **Curtis Cup**, but it is rarely seen in club competition. It is also called "alternate shot format" by some, but the preferred term is "foursomes." *See also* SCOTCH FOURSOMES.

FOWNES, WILLIAM CLARK, "W. C." B. 22 October 1878, Chicago, Illinois, United States; D. 4 July 1950. W. C. Fownes is known in golf primarily as the original architect of the famed **Oakmont Country Club** near Pittsburgh. He was an MIT student, earning a degree in metallurgical engineering. He then made a fortune building industrial plants in the Pittsburgh area. He was also an accomplished golfer, winning the Pennsylvania State Amateur four times and playing in the first and second **Walker Cup** matches. Fownes was president of the **USGA** in 1926–1927.

FRALEY, OSCAR. B. 2 August 1914, Philadelphia, Pennsylvania, United States; D. 6 January 1994, Fort Lauderdale, Florida, United States. Oscar Fraley was a journalist and golf writer whose greatest fame was not in golf but as the coauthor (with Eliot Ness) of the famous book *The Untouchables*. The book was a memoir of Ness and his quest to take down Chicago mobster Al Capone. It was later made into an American television series and a movie starring Kevin Costner and Sean Connery. Fraley wrote 31 books and was the ghostwriter for a number of golf books. He also served as a sports reporter for United Press International from 1940 to 1965, mostly covering golf tournaments. He also wrote a book on another well-known mobster, Jimmy Hoffa, entitled *Hoffa: The Real Story* (1975).

FRENCH OPEN (OPEN DE FRANCE). The French Open (Open de France) began in 1906 and is the oldest Continental European Open Championship. It has been a part of the **European PGA Tour** since that tour's inception in 1972. The championship was of only minor worldwide importance for much of its existence, since golf has never been a popular sport in France. But in the 21st century, the Fédération Française de Golf has tried to upgrade its status by discontinuing a named sponsor and instituting regional qualifying events, similar to the **U.S. Open** and the **Open Championship (British Open)**. The French Open does enjoy the distinction of being the last golf tournament ever won by golf legend **Byron Nelson**, in 1955. Appendix 4 includes a list of champions.

FRINGE. *See* COLLAR.

FROG HAIR. *See* COLLAR.

FRONT NINE. The "front nine" refers to the first nine holes of an 18-hole course. *See also* OUTWARD NINE.

FRONT SIDE. *See* FRONT NINE.

FURYK, JAMES MICHAEL "JIM." B. 12 May 1970, West Chester, Pennsylvania, United States. Jim Furyk is a U.S. **professional** who has been in the World Top 10 for over half of the weeks between

1999 and 2009, a testament to his consistent play. Furyk is known for his unusual swing. It starts with a double-overlap grip, then a backswing with a sharply upright move halfway through, then a loop, bringing the club back down onto a more normal plane. The swing was described by **David Feherty** as "an octopus falling out of a tree," but the swing is quite repeatable. Although not a long hitter, Furyk is a very accurate **driver** and is rarely out of contention in major professional tournaments. Except for a wrist injury he sustained in 2004–2005, necessitating surgery, Furyk has rarely been out of the World Top 10 in the 21st century. Furyk attended the University of Arizona, turning professional in 1992. Through 2009, he has won 13 tournaments on the **PGA Tour**, highlighted by his victory at the 2003 **U.S. Open** at Olympia Fields when he shot 272 to tie the record for the lowest score ever at the U.S. Open. Furyk also won the Grand Slam of Golf, contested between winners of the four major tournaments, in 2003 and 2008. Furyk has played on the **Ryder Cup** team six times—1997, 1999, 2002, 2004, 2006, and 2008—and the **President's Cup** team six times—1998, 2000, 2003, 2005, 2007, and 2009.

FUTURES GOLF TOUR. The Futures Golf Tour is a developmental tour for female **professionals**, now affiliated with the **LPGA.** The Futures Golf Tour began in the early 1990s and started its association with the LPGA in 1999, being formally acquired by the LPGA in July 2007. Each year, the top money winners of the Futures Golf Tour earn LPGA cards for the coming year. From 1999 to 2002, three players advanced to the LPGA, while from 2003 to 2007, five players earned LPGA cards. Since 2008, the top 10 Futures money winners have advanced to the LPGA in the following year. In 2006, Duramed Pharmaceuticals became the title sponsor of the Futures Tour, now called the Duramed Futures Golf Tour. Through 2009, over 350 LPGA tournaments have been won by alums of the Futures Golf Tour, including more than 35 major titles. In 2008, Futures Tour graduates won 17 of the 34 LPGA tournaments and two of the four major championships. Graduates of the Futures Golf Tour include **Lorena Ochoa**, Beth Bauer, Grace Park, Mina Harigae, Kim Song-Hee, Park In-Bee, Virada Nirapathpongporn, and Stacy Prammanasudh.

– G –

GAMBLING. Gambling is a part of the game of golf. Most club players have some sort of friendly wager going on during their matches. The **USGA** understands this and does not condemn it, but they do have some guidelines on gambling, and the **Rules of Golf** contain an appendix that lists their policies on gambling. It states, in essence, that they have no objection to informal gambling and defines this as 1) the players know each other, 2) the gambling is optional and limited only to the players, 3) the money is not excessive, and 4) the sole source of the money is the players themselves. Many club tournaments, however, have more extensive gambling, known as **Calcutta** pools, associated with them. These are not permitted in general, but the determining factor is if the money involved is excessive. In 1955, a major scandal erupted at Deepdale Country Club on Long Island related to a Calcutta for significant amounts of money. *See also* NASSAU; THOMPSON, ALVIN CLARENCE "TITANIC."

GEIBERGER, ALLEN LEE "AL." B. 1 September 1937, Red Bluff, California, United States. Al Geiberger is a U.S. **professional** who played on the U.S. **PGA Tour** primarily in the 1960s and 1970s, winning 11 times, including the 1966 **PGA Championship**, his only major title. He was on the 1967 and 1975 **Ryder Cup** teams. He is best known for being the first PGA Tour player to have scored 59 in competition on the tour, achieving this in the second round of the Danny Thomas Memphis Classic in 1977. Geiberger's later career was hampered by health problems with inflammatory bowel disease, which eventually required a permanent colostomy. His son, Brent Geiberger, later played on the PGA Tour and won two events, while another son, John, is a college golf coach, most recently at Pepperdine University.

GIBSON, ALTHEA. B. 25 August 1927, Silver, South Carolina, United States; D. 28 September 2003, East Orange, New Jersey, United States. Although never one of the greatest female golf **professionals**, Althea Gibson is one of the greatest female athletes of all time and a pioneer for African Americans in two sports. Gibson grew up in Harlem, New York, and began playing tennis at the Harlem

River Tennis Courts. She attended Florida A&M University on a tennis and basketball scholarship, graduating in 1953. Despite segregation that prevented her from playing many tournaments, Gibson played on the tennis circuit, at that time an **amateur** circuit. In 1955, she won the Italian title, followed by a win at the French Championship in 1956. In 1956, she also won doubles titles at the French Open and Wimbledon, partnered with Jewish Englishwoman Angela Buxton. They were called the "Minority Pair" by the British press. In 1957–1958, Althea Gibson became the greatest player in the world, winning singles titles at the U.S. Championship and Wimbledon both years and making it to the final at the Australian Championship in 1957.

Because of financial constraints, Gibson then stopped playing major amateur tournaments. She took up golf and in 1963 joined the **LPGA**, the first black woman to play on that tour. She was never as good at golf as she was at tennis, never winning an LPGA title, although she placed second at the 1970 Buick Open and played through the 1978 season. Gibson had a difficult life as she grew older. She was burdened with financial difficulties and health issues, and she suffered numerous small strokes that eventually incapacitated her. It was a sad end for one of the greatest female athletes ever, one who carried herself with grace and class at all times, while being denied opportunities solely because of the color of her skin. In 1971, she was inducted into the International Tennis Hall of Fame.

GIMME. A gimme usually refers to a short putt conceded by an opponent in **match play**. In casual club rounds, many short putts are gimmes, and in fact, there are some casual matches in which all putts "**inside the leather**" are conceded automatically.

GLEN ABBEY GOLF COURSE. Glen Abbey is a course in Oakville, Ontario, **Canada**, just west of Toronto, which was designed by **Jack Nicklaus** and opened in 1976. The course is the home of the **Royal Canadian Golf Association** and the Canadian Golf Hall of Fame. For many years, Glen Abbey was the home of the **Canadian Open**, hosting the championship all but two years from 1977 to 2000, but the event now rotates among various Canadian courses. However, Glen Abbey did host the Canadian Open in 2004, 2008, and

2009. The course is marked by the "Valley Holes," a stretch of five holes—11 through 15—that run through a deep valley surrounded by large granite walls, with Sixteen Mile Creek meandering among the Valley Holes.

GLENEAGLES. Gleneagles is a Scottish resort with three **golf courses**, notably the King's Course, which is a top Scottish course. Gleneagles is located in the Perthshire Hills of **Scotland**, equidistant from Edinburgh and Glasgow. It is set on 850 acres, highlighted by the Gleneagles Hotel, a five-star resort hotel, which opened in 1924. The King's Course was designed in 1919 by **James Braid**, who won multiple Open championships (**British Open**). The Queen's golf course, also designed by Braid, is a shorter, easier layout, while the third course is the PGA Centenary Course, designed by **Jack Nicklaus** and set to host the 2014 **Ryder Cup**. Gleneagles also has the Wee Course, a short, executive-type course for beginners and children; an 11-acre championship practice ground; a nine-hole pitch-and-putt course; and several **putting greens**.

GOLF 20/20. Golf 20/20 was formed in 2000 to bring together most of the major players within the golf industry in a collaborative effort to help with strategic initiatives and grassroots activism to ensure the future vitality of the game. Golf 20/20 is managed by the **World Golf Foundation** and **The First Tee**. The group is led by a large executive board that comprises most of the leaders of the various groups within the golf industry.

GOLF BAG. The golf bag is the implement that holds a player's clubs. Golf bags range from very large, heavy satchels used by **professionals**, with multiple pockets for extra balls, tees, gloves, sweaters, rain jackets, and food, to smaller carrying bags used by club players that are very light and easily carried by the player. Professional golf bags may weigh, without clubs or other necessities, up to 45 pounds (20 kg). Many club players now use professional-type bags, preferring their appearance, but never carry them, instead, they have them driven about on motorized golf carts. In the 19th century, players used only a few clubs, and they often had no golf bags. They simply carried their clubs in their hands as they walked the course.

GOLF BALLS. The golf ball is the small round ball that is struck with a golf club in an effort to move it from the tee into the hole on the **putting green**. As the game became more formalized in the 15th century, the first golf balls were wooden spheres. These were replaced in the 17th century by the **featherie**, which was a cowhide sphere stitched together and stuffed with feathers. The featherie was the standard ball for two centuries. It performed well in dry weather but became soft in wet weather, and the stitches often came apart, making it useless when wet.

In 1848, the Reverend Dr. Robert Adams Paterson invented a new ball made from **gutta percha**, the dried sap of a Sapodilla tree, found mostly in Indonesia. The sap was rubberlike and could be shaped into a sphere when it was hot. The guttie flew farther than the featherie, was much more durable, and quickly replaced the old featheries, much to the chagrin of golf **professionals**, who made much of their income by making featheries. It was soon discovered that gutta percha balls, termed "gutties," flew better after they were used a bit and scuffed up some. The irregularities gave the ball better spin and a truer flight. Golf ball manufacturers soon added multiple raised nipples, or "brambles," on the surface of the ball to make this truer flight more regular. These were soon replaced by indentations, or **dimples**.

In 1898, Coburn Haskell of Cleveland developed a golf ball with a solid core wrapped by tightly wound rubber thread, and a thin outer shell made for many years from balata. This was termed the **"Haskell ball"** and was a big improvement over the guttie. By 1905, the Haskell ball had virtually replaced the guttie among top players. The basic design of the Haskell ball is similar to modern golf balls of the 21st century, but with some modifications.

Over the years, the solid core was replaced at times by a liquid core. In the 1970s, balata, which cut very easily, began to be replaced by synthetic materials, usually surlyn or urethane blends, and today virtually all balls have synthetic covers. The ball actually did not change much from about 1910 until the 1970s. Then around 1970, Spalding pioneered the Top-Flite golf ball, which was a two-piece ball with much of its weight around the perimeter, rather than the center. This gave it an increased moment of inertia and caused it to spin much more slowly. Professionals did not like it because they could not control the ball well, and since it spun slowly, it ran and ran, rather than stopping, when it hit the green. But to **amateurs**, it was a boon, because the slow spin rate caused it to be less affected by air resistance, and they were able to generate extra distance with the ball. The Top-Flite was also one of the first balls with a surlyn, or synthetic cover.

Almost concurrently, Royal, which no longer makes golf balls, pioneered an unusual ball called the Royal Plus 6, which had deeper hexagonal dimples. It allowed the ball to stay in the air longer, but it was useless to the pros, who already had this ability. In fact, pros hated it because it flew so high that it was hard to control in the wind and actually cost them distance. But it also had some advantages to average players, since it helped them keep the ball in the air longer and gave them added length. But the idea of changing the dimple patterns sparked the "dimple wars" of the 1970s. Previously, most balls were built with 336 dimples in a pattern of two bands around the ball, which crossed each other at perpendiculars, with dimples filling in the triangular gaps between the bands. While it worked fairly well, the ball was not symmetric when spinning, leading to problems with perturbation effects.

Spurred on by the Royal Plus 6, most ball manufacturers began altering their dimple patterns, looking for a better golf ball. Acushnet, which made the most popular ball, **Titleist**, came out with a symmetric, deeper dimple design, which was supposed to be an improvement but again was scorned by the tour players. Acushnet responded with the Low Trajectory, with shallower dimples, which was better for the pros but not great, and they countered again with the Pro Trajectory, which eventually was used by many pros. The joke among the tour players was that the next design by Acushnet would be the No Trajectory.

Another innovative ball design in the 1970s was the Polara golf ball. This ball was not symmetric at all in terms of dimple design nor was it intended to be. In fact, the Polara was designed to be a self-correcting golf ball, so that as it spun off-line, the dimples and an asymmetric weight distribution would align such that the ball would not turn off-line as much. A nice idea, but it was quickly banned by golf's ruling authorities, who made a rule that the ball must be spherically symmetrical, and the Polara was not around long. But all the various changes in golf ball technology led to a series of golf balls in the 1990s that were harder to cut, easier to control, and went much farther.

The **Rules of Golf** currently specify that a golf ball must weigh no more than 1.620 oz. (45.93 grams), have a diameter not less than 1.680 inches (42.67 mm), and perform within specified velocity, distance, and symmetry limits. Like golf clubs, golf balls are subject to testing and approval by the **R&A** and the **USGA**, and those that do not conform to regulations cannot be used in competitions. The maximum velocity of the ball may not exceed 250 feet-per-second (76 m/s) under test conditions. At one time, non-American golf balls were smaller. Until 1990, the R&A version of the rules specified that balls could not have a diameter less than 1.620 inches (41.15 mm). This actually hampered the development of British and European players, because the ball was much easier to play in the wind. In the early 1980s, the R&A converted to the American-sized ball for professional competition, and in 1990, they converted all golf play to the 1.68 inch ball.

GOLF CARTS. Golf carts are motorized vehicles that transport golfers around a **golf course**. The original carts were electric powered, but gasoline carts later came into use. With green concepts now popular, most of the carts are again electric powered. Golf carts came into use in the early 1950s, with the Marketeer Company starting production of them in 1951. Several different companies manufacture golf carts, notably, E-Z-Go, Cushman, Club Car, and Harley-Davidson. Golf carts are mostly common in the **United States**. They provide a source of revenue for **country clubs** and golf **professionals**, who often share in the revenue from the carts. Golf carts have also necessitated the building of paved golf paths, on most American courses, to help the carts get from hole to hole and even tee to green. While golf carts are a source of revenue for the golf industry, they have several detrimental factors that have changed the game of golf. They lessen the need for **caddies**, which deprives the game of many young golf recruits who would have been introduced to the game through caddieing. They all but eliminate any benefit of walking a golf course for exercise. And the cart paths as well as the exhausts from the carts themselves (electric or gasoline) have been roundly criticized by environmental groups. *See also* CASEY MARTIN RULING.

GOLF CHANNEL. Golf Channel, formerly known as "The Golf Channel," is a cable television channel that broadcasts golf-related programs 24 hours a day. The channel started in January 1995, launched by the media mogul Joseph Gibbs of Birmingham, Alabama, with financial support from **Arnold Palmer**. The major program focus of the channel is Golf Central, a golf news program that airs several times per day, similar to Sports Center on ESPN. Golf Channel also now covers numerous tournaments on the Champions (Senior) Tour, the European Tour, the **Nationwide Tour**, and the **LPGA.** Other shows include golf talk shows, various instructional shows, and a golf reality show, the Big Break, in which contestants attempt to earn exemptions to **PGA Tour** and LPGA events by a series of competitions. In 2007, Golf Channel became the official cable channel for the PGA Tour, and it now shows early round coverage of at least 30 PGA Tour events.

GOLF CLUB TECHNOLOGY. Golf clubs are the implements a player uses to hit the golf ball. There have been significant changes in the design of clubs since the early 19th century. At that time, all clubs had wooden shafts, usually hickory. Wooden clubs in that era had very wide (heel to toe) and shallow heads. Iron clubs often had very heavy heads, allowing the player to power the ball from the many poor lies that resulted from the lack of more modern methods of greenkeeping. These were standards through the 19th century. In the early 20th century, the heads of both woods and irons began to approach their more modern appearances. The biggest change in golf club technology probably occurred in the 1930s when steel shafts replaced hickory shafts. Steel shafts were much stiffer, much more durable, and much more consistent than their hickory counterparts. There were few changes in golf clubs from then until the 1960s.

In the early 1960s, club manufacturers began to experiment with fiberglass shafts. Fiberglass was supposed to have a softer feel and provide a higher ball flight. But the shafts had great variability, and it was difficult to get an entire set of clubs with a consistent feel. **Gary Player** won the 1965 **U.S. Open** with fiberglass shafts and later called this his greatest victory, for overcoming the difficulties with fiberglass. In the early 1970s, shafts made of graphite were introduced. These could be made very stiff, but they also had very poor torque resistance, and after a brief popularity, they fell from the scene. But graphite returned in the 1980s as the problems with torque were solved.

In the late 1970s, steel shafts changed when manufacturers introduced lightweight steel, which actually was not of lighter density. It was, however, much stronger than traditional steel alloys, and thus the shaft could be built with a thinner wall thickness, which resulted in the overall weight of the shaft being lighter. Another short-lived innovation of the late 1960s and early 1970s was aluminum shafts.

Golf shaft technology greatly changed in the 1980s when graphite became a more consistent material for shafts. Graphite was much lighter than steel and could be built very stiff. At about this time, many different materials began to appear in shafts. Titanium became popular for a while, as did carbon fiber shafts. Finally, shafts were built as a composite of different types of materials, often graphite, carbon, aramid fiber (Kevlar), and/or titanium. These shafts had several advantages; notably, they were much lighter than steel, even lightweight steel, while retaining great stiffness and torque resistance. As club shafts became lighter, clubs were able to be made longer. Traditional **driver** lengths in the 1960s–1970s were about 43 inches. But by the late 1980s, many pros were using drivers of 45 inches and even longer, up to 48 inches. In fact, club shafts could be made so long that long driving competitions had to limit the length of the clubs used to 48 inches, and the **USGA**, as well, has now adopted that limit.

In the early 1980s, a huge revolution occurred when metal-headed "woods" were first built. Gradually, these have replaced wood-headed woods. The metal woods are hollow structures that are lighter than traditional wooden heads. Because of their lightness, they can be made much larger. The size of metal wood heads has increased dramatically over the past 25 years, and the USGA found it necessary to limit the size of metal wood heads. The heel-to-toe dimension can be no more than 5 inches (127 mm), the height (sole-to-crown) must be no more than 2.8 inches (71.12 mm), and the clubhead size must not exceed 28.06 cu. in. (460 cc).

The new, larger clubheads provide much greater torque resistance when a ball is struck, which limits the amount of sidespin delivered to the ball. This has allowed modern clubhead technology to provide straighter shots in general. In addition, the increased length and decreased weight of the club allow it to be swung faster, increasing clubhead speeds and ball distance. All of these changes to clubs since the early 1980s have increased driving distance among the pros dramatically. While this seems like a good thing, the problem is that the improved golf club technology now puts many courses at risk of being obsolete, because they are too short to challenge modern **professionals**.

There may be more to come. Since the early 1990s, the USGA and the **R&A** have resisted these changes in golf club (and golf ball) technology because of their fear that they will make courses too short. Several changes to the **Rules of Golf** have been made (some described above), and many more have been proposed. But many of the proposed rules have been opposed by golf club and golf ball manufacturers, who want to increase technology, which enables them to sell newer, better, and more expensive clubs and balls. The battle goes on, and several of the proposed rule changes have been challenged in court by the manufacturers.

One battle that will soon be won by the USGA relates to the grooves on the clubface of irons. In the mid-1980s, the previous V-shaped grooves were gradually replaced with square grooves. The increased overall volumetric depth of square grooves allowed players to put much more spin on a golf ball. This negated the disadvantage of missing a **fairway**, because players could now spin the ball well enough from the rough so that they could usually hold the green. This has caused the game of golf at the professional level to somewhat devolve into players simply driving the ball as far as they can, with little concern for being in the rough, and completely negating the previous big advantage that accrued to an accurate driver. But starting in 2010, the USGA has changed the rules for competition, and the **PGA Tour** will follow, decreasing the volume of grooves and reducing edge sharpness.

There have been other golf club changes over the past few decades. Iron heads have also changed significantly. They are now much larger than they were from 1900 to 1980. The increased head size is also usually accompanied by perimeter weighting. This increases the moment of inertia of the clubhead, decreasing torque on any off-center hits, which limits sidespin and off-line shots.

Putters also began to change in the 1980s. Many of the senior players started this change when they increased the length of their putters and began using a split grip. Putters are now exempt from the length restriction of 48 inches. *See also* BELLY PUTTER.

GOLF CLUBS. Golf clubs are the implements with which a player strikes the ball. There are three main types of golf clubs: woods, irons, and putters. Wood clubs are the longest clubs and allow the player to hit the ball the longest distance. The longest of these is the **driver**, with the other "woods" now simply numbered—3-wood, 4-wood, etc. In the early days, the woods had names—"**spoon**," "**brassie**," and "**cleek**." "Woods" is now a misnomer—in the mid-1980s wooden headed clubs began to be replaced by hollowed-out metal clubheads, and these are now often termed "metal woods." Almost no clubs are made with actual wood heads anymore.

Irons constitute the bulk of a golfer's bag of clubs. These are numbered now also, although again in the 19th century and into the early 20th century, many of these had names, such as "**mashie**" or "**niblick**." Irons are numbered from 1 through 9, and occasionally 10. The lower numbers allow a player to hit the ball lower and farther. **Long irons** are usually designated as the 1–4 irons, although, in truth, with the revolution in golf club technology that has occurred since the 1980s, most players never use, or now even know about, 1- or 2-irons. **Mid-irons** are usually considered the 5–7 irons. **Short irons** are considered the 8–9 irons and the **wedges**. Wedges come in various forms, and many players now carry three or four wedges in their bags, including a pitching wedge, a **sand wedge**, a **lob wedge**, and occasionally, an extremely lofted variant of the lob wedge, sometimes called an "X-wedge." **Putters** are shorter clubs (usually) with relatively flat faces that allow a player to roll the ball on the **putting green**. In the 1980s, some players began using longer putters, such that the putter is sometimes the longest club in the bag, and putting with a more upright, pendulum-like stroke.

The **Rules of Golf** place a limit on the number of clubs players may carry in their bags, with the limit now 14, since 1938. Prior to that time, there was no limit, and one top player, **Lawson Little**, was known for carrying multiple extra clubs, often as many as 26, in his bag. The rules also place numerous restrictions on the design of golf clubs. Much of this is discussed in **golf club technology**.

A golf club has certain characteristic parts or sections. All of them have a clubhead, which strikes the ball, and a shaft, which connects the clubhead to the grip, which is the top of the club that a player holds while making a stroke. The grip must be plain and basically circular in cross-section, per the rules. Grips were originally made of leather, but were later made of rubber and other composite materials. In addition, many of them now have small stringlike ridges in them, often called "cord grips," that allow for better gripping. Other parts of a club are the hosel, which connects the shaft to the clubhead, although some more modern clubs have almost no hosel. A ferrule is a small cover that smooths the transition from club shaft to hosel and is mostly for decorative purposes. *See also* FAIRWAY WOODS; GRAPHITE SHAFTS; HOSEL; HYBRID CLUB; JIGGER; LEAD TAPE; LONG IRONS; OFFSET; ONE (1)-IRON; PUTTER; SHAFT STIFFNESS; SWEET SPOT; SWINGWEIGHT; TEXAS WEDGE; WEDGES.

GOLF COURSE. A golf course is the land on which the game of golf is played. It usually consists of 18 holes, although in areas where land is more limited, it may have only nine holes, with players going around the course twice for a full 18-hole round. There are many types of golf courses, such as **public courses**, private courses, **municipal courses**, **resort courses**, **par-three courses**, and **executive courses**. *See also* GOLF COURSE ARCHITECTURE AND DESIGN.

GOLF COURSE ARCHITECTURE AND DESIGN. Golf course architecture is a specialty of people who become designers and builders of **golf courses**. Many of them become quite well known, witness **Donald Ross**, **Pete Dye**, **Robert Trent Jones.** Several players have gone on to design golf courses as their playing careers wound down, notably, **Jack Nicklaus** and **Ben Crenshaw**. The field has its own organizations, including the **American Society of Golf Course Architects**, the **European Institute of Golf Course Architects**, and the Society of Australian Golf Course Architects. The first well-known golf course architect was **Willie Park Jr.**, who won the **Open Championship** (**British Open**) twice, best known for his design of

Sunningdale Old near London. In the early 20th century, the best-known architect in the **United States** was **Donald Ross**, who designed hundreds of courses, his best-known course being **Pinehurst** No. 2, which is considered his masterpiece.

Golf course architects must consider several things in their design of a golf course. Primarily, they are hired by a group of people who will own the course or club and will have their own thoughts about what they want. Should it be a championship level course or a relatively easy one for club play? If a championship course, do they prefer a penal-type layout or one with more strategic holes? The next consideration is the landscape on which they are to design the course. This limits every architect to some degree, with some pieces of land giving an architect multiple options for a course, while others have little appeal for a golf course. While land can be altered to suit the architect's needs, this brings into play the budget. Each group of owners will have a budget, and the architect will need to follow that. While large amounts of earth can be moved for design purposes, and lakes and **water hazards** can be built artificially, this is expensive and may not be within the budget.

More recently, the environment has become a concern for golf course architects. Many environmental groups decry the use of land for golf courses, considering it a waste of land and injurious to the environment, often endangering wildlife. Other issues include the significant amount of water needed on a golf course and the use of pesticides and fertilizers. But golf course architects have responded and are now very attuned to these problems. In addition, turfgrass research has allowed golf course designers to use much less water and chemicals on the courses. *See also* AMERICAN SOCIETY OF GOLF COURSE ARCHITECTS (ASGCA); BENDELOW, THOMAS "TOM"; COLT, HENRY SHAPLAND "HARRY"; COORE, WILLIAM ERNEST "BILL"; CORNISH, GEOFFREY; CRENSHAW, BENJAMIN DANIEL "BEN"; DYE, PAUL B. "PETE"; EGAN, HENRY CHANDLER; EUROPEAN INSTITUTE OF GOLF COURSE ARCHITECTS (EIGCA); FAZIO, GEORGE; FAZIO, THOMAS "TOM"; FLYNN, WILLIAM STEPHEN "BILL"; FOWNES, WILLIAM CLARK, "W. C."; HOLLINS, MARION; JONES, REES; JONES, ROBERT TRENT "BOBBY," JR.; JONES, ROBERT TRENT, SR.; MACDONALD, CHARLES

BLAIR; MacKENZIE, ALISTER; NICKLAUS, JACK WILLIAM "THE GOLDEN BEAR"; RAYNOR, SETH JAGGER; REDAN/REDAN HOLE; ROSS, DONALD JAMES; THOMAS, GEORGE CLIFFORD, JR.; THOMPSON, STANLEY; TILLINGHAST, ALBERT WARREN "A. W."; WILSON, HUGH IRVINE.

GOLF COURSE SUPERINTENDENT. "Golf course superintendent" is the current title for the person responsible for maintaining and grooming a **golf course** and the grounds around a club. The earlier title for this position was "**greenkeeper**." *See also* GOLF COURSE SUPERINTENDENTS ASSOCIATION OF AMERICA (GCSAA).

GOLF COURSE SUPERINTENDENTS ASSOCIATION OF AMERICA (GCSAA). The Golf Course Superintendents Association of America was founded in 1926 when 60 superintendents met at the Sylvania Country Club in Toledo, Ohio, forming what was originally known as the National Association of Greenkeepers of America (NAGA). The organization serves as the voice of **golf course superintendents** and **greenkeepers** and is now located in Lawrence, Kansas. As of 2009, the group has 21,000 members in more than 72 nations. The GCSAA has a philanthropic organization, the Environmental Institute for Golf, which serves to strengthen the nexus between golf and the natural environment by providing research grants and supporting educational programs.

GOLF GLOVES. Most competitive players, although not all, use a golf glove to aid in gripping the club, usually on the target-side hand (left hand for a right-handed player). A few players wear gloves on both hands. Gloves have been around since the 1890s, and originally, many of them were half gloves with open-ended fingers. By the 1960s, virtually all gloves had full fingers. Notable players who have not worn a glove include **Ben Hogan** and **Fred Couples**. Many players who wear a glove will remove the glove for putting and even occasional chip or pitch shots around the green, preferring the feel given by the fingers on the grip for more delicate shots.

GOLF GRIP. There are two things in golf termed "golf grip." One is the type of grip players use in placing their hands on the club. The classic grip is the overlap grip, often termed the "Vardon grip" in honor of **Harry Vardon**, who popularized it. In this grip, for right-handers, the small finger of the right hand overlaps the knuckles of the index finger of the left hand. More recently, many golfers have turned to the interlocking grip. This was popularized in the 1960s when **Jack Nicklaus** used it, and **Tiger Woods** also uses this grip. In the interlock, the right-hand small finger is held between the index and long fingers of the left hand. A third variant is the baseball, or 10-finger grip, with no definite connection between the hands. This is rarely used now, the last well-known **professional** to use it was Art Wall in the 1950s and 1960s. There are also numerous variant grips used in putting. For many years, the most popular was a reverse overlap, with the left-hand index finger overlapping the small and ring fingers of the right hand. But now, with the onset of long putters, putting strokes have numerous variants. These include split grips, claw grips, and numerous combinations.

"Golf grip" may also refer to the thickened end of a **golf club** that a player holds while making a stroke. The grip is a softer, thicker material that covers the shaft and gives a gripping surface for the player. Most golf grips were originally made of leather, but in the 1950s, rubber grips and other composite grips became popular. In the 1960s, stringlike ribs were added to rubber or composite grips. Often called "cord grips," they have a better gripping surface but are also harder on a player's hands. There are other numerous varieties of grips available to players. For top players, grips wear out relatively quickly, and most professionals will change the grips on their clubs at least one or two times per year.

GOLF PROFESSIONAL. A golf professional is someone who makes a living working as a professional at a club serving the membership or daily fee players and is usually contrasted with a professional golfer. Golf professionals in the **United States** are usually members of the **PGA of America**. They make their living through a salary provided by the club but also earn income from giving lessons. Some receive a percentage of sales in the golf shop, or pro shop, and some receive income from a percentage of golf cart sales. In addition to these activities, golf pros are responsible for running tournaments and clinics at courses. Most golf professionals start out as assistant pros in the hope of working their way up to become head professionals. Playing at a high tournament level is not a mandatory requirement for a golf professional, although most play near a scratch level or lower. The PGA of America does have a mandatory Playing Ability Test for club professionals who hope to earn full membership, termed "Class A status."

GOLF SHOES. Most players use golf shoes, which are specially designed shoes to provide traction during the golf swing, especially on uneven terrain. For many years, golf shoes were made with metal spikes that made marks on greens and could significantly damage greens. However, more recently, spikes have been made of plastic, and instead of a single long metal spike, the plastic spikes have small nubs around a central core. Most golf clubs now mandate that plastic spikes be used, to prevent green damage from metal spikes. On the professional tours, the pros continue to use mostly metal spikes. Golf shoes first became popular in the 1890s.

GOLF SHOP. *See* PRO SHOP.

GOLF TEES. There are two meanings to the term "golf tee." The first refers to the small wooden post with a concave, wider top, on which a golfer places his ball before teeing off. Golf tees, which elevate the ball several inches off the ground, are used most commonly when playing a **driver**. They enable the driver to hit the ball with an ascending blow, giving greater distance. In fact, because golfers have recently started using longer and longer tees and bigger driver heads, in 2000, the **USGA** limited the length of a tee to 4 inches. The current **Rules of Golf** necessitate that the tee "not be longer than 4 inches (101.6 mm) and it must not be designed or manufactured in such a way that it could indicate the line of play or influence the movement of the ball." Golf tees first appeared in the 1890s. Prior to that time, players often raised a small mound of dirt, sand, or turf and placed their ball on that.

"Golf tee" also refers to the area from which a golfer begins play of each hole, or tees off. This is a closely mown area, now cut almost as short as a **putting green**, and is usually rectangular, or roughly rectangular, in design. Virtually all courses and golf holes have several sets of golf tees. The championship tees, or back tees, play the course at its full length, and are frequently used in competition, especially **professional** play. The middle tees, often called the "members tees," are those usually used by club members for recreational play. There is also usually a set of shorter tees, originally called "ladies' tees," from which female club members often play. Some clubs will have a fourth set of tees, usually between the middle and ladies' tees, designed for male seniors who can no longer hit the ball long enough to play from the regular members tees. On courses with the standard three sets of tees, the tee markers, which label the area from which one tees off, are painted different colors, and the standard is as follows: blue tees—championship/back tees, white tees—middle/member tees, red tees—ladies/senior tees. This is no longer universally followed, and many courses now call their longest tee markers "gold tees" or "black tees."

GOLF WRITERS ASSOCIATION OF AMERICA (GWAA). The Golf Writers Association of America is an organization of golf writers that was formed in 1946 at the **PGA Championship** in Portland, Oregon. At the end of the tournament, the golf writers covering the tournament met in an abandoned ice cream concession stand and formed the GWAA. The first president was Russ Newland of the Associated Press, with Charles Bartlett of the *Chicago Tribune* serving as the first secretary. As of 2009, the group has 950 members. It publishes a monthly newsletter and a yearly directory, and maintains a members-only Web site. The GWAA annually presents the **William D. Richardson Award**, named for a former *New York Times* golf writer, which is given in honor of outstanding contributions to golf. The first winner was Robert Hudson, who built the press headquarters that were used at the 1946 PGA. They also give out the **Ben Hogan Award** to a player who has overcome serious illness, injury, or disability to contribute to the game. The Board of Directors of the GWAA meets annually with officials from various golf organizations to review policies and working conditions at events, and to discuss ways in which the groups can work together more efficiently. The GWAA also has a scholarship program, begun in 1988, which helps prospective journalism students at universities around the country by providing scholarships and internships.

GOODMAN, JOHNNY G. B. 28 December 1909, South Omaha, Nebraska, United States; D. 8 August 1970. In 1933, Johnny Goodman won the **U.S. Open** Championship as an **amateur** in a major upset, and this remains the last victory for an amateur in the U.S. Open (through 2009). Goodman, who was from Nebraska, also won the **U.S. Amateur** in 1937. Orphaned as a young child, Goodman grew up in the slaughterhouse district of Omaha, learned the game as a **caddie**, and in his early years, often traveled to tournaments by hitching rides on cattle cars. He was a three-time winner of the Nebraska Amateur (1929, 1930, 1931) and the **Trans-Mississippi Amateur** (1927, 1931, 1935), and twice won the Mexican Amateur (1936, 1937). Goodman's career was insurance sales, although he became a **professional** golfer after he was 50 years old.

GOOSEN, RETIEF. B. 3 February 1969, Pietersburg (Polokwane), Limpopo, South Africa. Retief Goosen is a **South African professional** who has been in the World Top 10 for most of the 21st century and was, for a time, among the top five players in the world—with **Tiger Woods**, **Phil Mickelson**, **Ernie Els**, and **Vijay Singh**. Goosen won the South African Amateur in 1990 and turned professional a few weeks later. He played most of his early career in Europe, leading the Order of Merit in 2001–2002. Through 2009, he has recorded over 40 professional wins worldwide, including 12 in Europe, nine in South Africa on the Sunshine Tour, and five on the U.S. **PGA Tour**. These include two major championships, the 2001 and 2004 **U.S. Open** titles. His other titles include the 2000 and 2003 **Lancome Trophy**, the 1997 and 1999 **French Open**, the 2002 Johnnie Walker Classic, and the 2004 European Open. After 2005, Goosen went into a relative slump, dropping from the World Top 10 in 2007 but came back in 2009 to win again on the U.S. PGA Tour.

GRAFFIS, HERB. B. 31 May 1893, Logansport, Indiana, United States; D. 13 February 1989, Fort Myers, Florida, United States.

Herb Graffis was an American golf writer who was named to the **World Golf Hall of Fame** in 1977 for his contributions to the game. Graffis was a longtime sports and golf writer at the *Chicago Sun-Times*. He founded *Golfdom* magazine in 1919, the *Chicago Golfer* in 1927, and *Golfing* magazine in 1933. In 1951, he cofounded the **Golf Writers Association of America** and was named the group's first president. Along with his brother, Joe, Herb Graffis founded the **National Golf Foundation** and the **Golf Course Superintendents Association of America**. Graffis is perhaps best known as coauthor of one of the best-selling golf instruction books, *How to Play Your Best Golf All the Time*, written with **Tommy Armour**. Graffis' administrative contributions to the game are legion and, besides the above, include serving as president of National Golf Day, working as a member of the PGA's Advisory Board and Public Relations Committee, and serving on the **USGA**'s Green Section and Museum committees. Also, at one time, he was president of the Chicago Press Club, the Headline Club of Chicago, the Indiana Club of Chicago, and the Illinois Senior Golf Association.

GRAHAM, ANTHONY DAVID. B. 23 May 1946, Windsor, Queensland, Australia. David Graham is an **Australian** golfer who turned **professional** at age 16 in 1962 despite the protestations of his father, who never again spoke to him. He won over 35 professional tournaments worldwide, starting in Australia. By 1976, he was a member of the U.S. **PGA Tour**, where he won eight times, including the 1979 **PGA Championship** and 1981 **U.S. Open**. His other worldwide victories include the 1976 **World Match Play Championship** at Wentworth, the 1977 **Australian Open**, and the 1981–1982 **Lancome Trophy**. During his playing days in the **United States**, Graham was known for working on his clubs assiduously and for writing a column in *Golf World* magazine. A taciturn, hard man, possibly spurred by his difficult early years, he was not always well liked by other players. He won five times on the **Champions Tour** in the United States, but he collapsed at a tournament in 2004 and was diagnosed with congestive heart failure, which ended his career.

GRAND SLAM. "Grand Slam" means the winning of all of golf's major championships in one calendar year. The original Grand Slam consisted of the **U.S. and British opens and amateurs**, won in 1930 by **Bob Jones**. Although golf writer George Trevor of the *New York Sun* originally called it the "Impregnable Quadrilateral," the term "Grand Slam" is attributable to Jones' Boswell, **O. B. Keeler**. In 1960, **Arnold Palmer** won the **Masters** and U.S. Open and made known his intention to travel to Great Britain and compete in the **Open Championship (British Open)**. Palmer was attempting a modern **professional** Grand Slam, which he considered the Masters, U.S. Open, Open Championship, and **PGA Championship**, basically, coining the modern definition. The modern professional Grand Slam has never been technically accomplished, although **Tiger Woods** came very close. He won the U.S. Open, Open Championship, and PGA Championship in 2000, and the Masters in 2001, and he held all four trophies at one time. This has been termed the "Tiger Slam," and Tiger said he considers it a Grand Slam, but purists demur.

In 1953, **Ben Hogan** won the Masters, U.S. Open, and Open Championship. Hogan was unable to play in the PGA Championship that year because its final rounds overlapped with the qualifying rounds of the British Open. In addition, Hogan never again played in the PGA Championship at **match play** after his car accident in 1949 because the consecutive days of 36-hole play were too much for his injured legs. Two other players have won the Masters and U.S. Open in the same year—**Jack Nicklaus** in 1972 and **Craig Wood** in 1941. Wood did it before the modern term existed. In 1960 and 1972, Palmer and Nicklaus, respectively, placed second at the Open Championship, ending their quest. Five players have won the career Grand Slam—**Gene Sarazen**, Hogan, **Gary Player**, Nicklaus, and Woods.

The renowned golf writer **Dan Jenkins** wrote cogently in *Golf Digest* about redefining the Grand Slam in more accurate historical terms. Jenkins argues correctly that the British Open was not truly a major in the early years after World War II and probably in the 1930s. At that time, the best players were American and rarely traveled to Great Britain for the tournament. He has also noted that at various times, other tournaments were considered majors to the touring professionals, among them the **Western Open**, the **North and South Open**, and the **Metropolitan Open**. In a 1949 issue of *Current Biography*, Jenkins' thesis is supported by the article on Hogan, which states that in 1948 he won the three major professional tournaments—the U.S. Open, PGA Championship, and Western Open.

There are some who argue that there should be five major tournaments, since some American touring professionals certainly consider **The Players Championship** a major. First held in 1974, the tournament originally rotated among various clubs, but, like the Masters, it is now held every year at an iconic course, the **TPC Sawgrass**, which has the well-known par-three 17th hole island green. The Players Championship annually has the strongest field in golf, with almost all of the players in the top 150 of the **World Golf Ranking**.

Women's golf also recognizes a set of tournaments for their Grand Slam, although this has been more variable over the history of the **LPGA.** The current four major championships constituting the Grand Slam are the **U.S. Women's Open**, the **LPGA Championship**, the **Kraft Nabisco (Dinah Shore)**, and the **Women's British Open**. In the early years of the LPGA (1951–1970), the Grand Slam consisted of the U.S. Women's Open, LPGA, **Titleholders** (1937–1966, 1972), and **Women's Western Open** (1930–1967). But the Titleholders was discontinued after 1966 except for one brief resurrection in 1972, while the Women's Western Open has not been held since 1967. The **Du Maurier Classic**, or, effectively, the **Canadian Women's Open**, was considered a major championship from 1979 to 2000, with the Women's British Open replacing it in 2001. As with the men, nobody has won all four in a single year, but in 1950, **Babe Zaharias** won all three majors contested that year, and in 1974, **Sandra Haynie** won both the U.S. Women's Open and LPGA, the only two majors contested that year. Six **women** have won all the major championships available to them: **Mickey Wright**, **Louise Suggs**, **Pat Bradley**, **Juli Inkster**, **Annika Sörenstam**, and **Karrie Webb**.

GRAPHITE SHAFTS. Graphite shafts first appeared in the early 1970s, but early shafts were hampered by very poor torque resistance, which made them quite variable, and ball flight was difficult to control. This problem was solved by the early 1980s, and many shafts are now made with graphite, either in whole or as a composite with other materials. Graphite shafts are made by winding carbon or graphite fiber around a central core. Composite shafts often have several layers of fiber winding to increase stiffness and rigidity. The advantage of graphite shafts is that they are much lighter than metal shafts. Therefore, clubs can be made lighter, which enables them to be made longer.

GRASS. Grass is integral to the game of golf, which is played mostly on grass. Grass covers **putting greens**, **teeing grounds**, **rough**, and **fairways**. Many different varieties of grass are used on **golf courses**, usually depending on the local climate. Certain grasses tolerate warm weather better, while some flourish in cooler climes. One of the responsibilities of the **golf course architect** is to choose the appropriate grasses for the course, depending on the playing characteristics desired and the local weather. Maintaining the grass in all areas of the course is the responsibility of the **golf course superintendent**. Grasses are often developed specifically for use on golf courses. They must be able to be cut very closely, for use on putting greens and teeing grounds. Also, they must be able to withstand the trauma inflicted by the **golf carts** and golf spikes of the hundreds of rounds played on them daily. *See also* AGRONOMY; BENT GRASS; BERMUDA GRASS; FESCUE; KIKUYU; POA ANNUA; RYEGRASS; TURFGRASS RESEARCH AND MANAGEMENT; ZOYSIA.

GREATEST PUTTERS. Over the years, many players have been known for their putting ability. Because putting is such an important part of scoring in golf, many of the best putters have been among the top players. Interestingly, great putters have become better known since World War II because **golf course** grooming has made greens much smoother and faster, which allows better putters to excel. The first **professional** known for his putting ability was **South African Bobby Locke**. An unlikely athlete, with a paunch and several chins, Locke hooked every shot he hit, including his putts. Nevertheless, his putting enabled him to win the **Open Championship (British Open)** four times. The first American professional renowned for his putting was **Billy Casper**, who won the **U.S. Open** in 1959 and 1966. At about the same time, New Zealander **Bob Charles** used a silky-smooth putting stroke to win the 1963 Open Championship (British). Later, **Ben Crenshaw,** with an old Wilson 8802 putter and his superb putting, won the **Masters** twice, on the very fast and rolling greens of Augusta National. More recently, Brad Faxon and Loren Roberts have starred on the greens of the **PGA Tour**, with Roberts earning the nickname "Boss of the Moss."

GREEN. *See* PUTTING GREEN.

GREEN FEE. A green fee is a payment made to golf on a public, or municipal, course. Most green fees allow a player to play all day for only one fee. Some courses have a nine-hole fee after a certain hour in the afternoon, which is a lesser fee because it is likely only nine holes can be played before dark or closing.

GREEN IN REGULATION (GIR). "Green in regulation" means reaching the **putting green** within a certain number of shots. The number is always the **par** on the hole minus two shots which leaves two putts to attain par. Tournament players consider the number of greens in regulation during a round a measure of their ball striking. Thus, reaching a green in regulation is tantamount to par status for ball striking on a hole. On par-five holes, or shorter par-fours, a player may reach the green in one shot less than regulation, setting up a two-putt **birdie** or a one-putt **eagle**. It is rare for even the best pros to hit all 18 greens in regulation. **Professional** tours keep statistics on greens in regulation hit by a player during the year. Hitting 70 percent or more greens in regulation over the year indicates top-quality ball striking ability.

GREEN, HUBERT MYATT. B. 28 December 1946, Birmingham, Alabama, United States. Hubert Green graduated from Florida State in 1968 and turned **professional** the next year. He played for over 20 years on the **PGA Tour**, winning 19 events, including the 1977 **U.S. Open** and 1985 **PGA Championship**. His 1977 U.S. Open victory came under particular duress. On the day of the final round, Green received a death threat stating that he would be taken out on the 15th green. **USGA** officials notified Green on the 15th tee, giving him the option of what to do. He elected to continue playing and bravely won the title. At the 1978 Masters, Green missed a three-foot putt on the final green that would have tied **Gary Player**. The miss came when he was disrupted by the voice of one of the announcers, but Green refused to make an excuse of it. Green had a quick, short, somewhat unusual swing and an even odder putting style, with a split-hand grip on an old hickory-shafted putter, but he used both well to become one of the most respected professionals on the PGA Tour. He later won four events on the **Champions Tour**. Green played on the **Ryder Cup** team in 1977, 1979, and 1985, and he was inducted into the **World Golf Hall of Fame** in 2007. In 2003, Green was diagnosed with throat cancer but fought it off with surgery and chemotherapy. He now does some work as a **golf course** designer and plays occasional senior events.

GREENKEEPER. Originally, a greenkeeper was the person responsible for maintaining and grooming a **golf course** and the grounds around a club. However, now the title is more often "golf course superintendent."

GREGORY (MOORE-), ANN. B. 25 July 1912, Aberdeen, Mississippi, United States; D. 5 February 1990, Gary, Indiana. Little known today, Ann Gregory was a pioneer for female African American golfers, preceding **Althea Gibson** and **Renée Powell** by several years. In September 1956, Gregory played in the **U.S. Women's Amateur** Championship at Meridian Hills Country Club in Indianapolis, becoming the first black woman to play in a **USGA** National Championship. A good natural athlete, Gregory started out playing tennis and won the Gary, Indiana, city tennis championship in 1937. In 1943, she joined the Chicago Women's Golf Association (CWGA), an organization for African Americans. She soon began winning at golf, including victories in the CWGA championship, the **Joe Louis** Invitational in Detroit, and the championship of the **United Golfers Association** (UGA), a national organization for black players. Black-oriented papers hailed her as the "Queen of Negro Women's Golf," and in 1947, George S. May invited her to play in his open invitational tournament, the Tam O'Shanter, as the only black woman in the field.

Prejudice followed her everywhere, typified by the 1959 U.S. Women's Amateur, when Congressional Country Club in suburban Washington banned her from the clubhouse for the players' dinner. In 1971, Gregory made it to the final of the **USGA Senior Women's**

Amateur, where she played Carolyn Cudone, an old friend (they had played in the first round at the 1956 U.S. Women's Amateur) who had supported her against several episodes of prejudice. Cudone won on the final hole but noted "Ann was a lady and she could play. She was a fine competitor, a good winner and a good loser, who played the game as you wanted to see it played." Gregory competed in the USGA Senior Women's Amateur through 1988. She always lived near Chicago or Gary, Indiana, and in 1954 became the first black appointed to the Gary Public Library Board.

GRIFFIN, ELLEN JEAN. B. 19 December 1918; D. October 1986, Randleman, North Carolina, United States. Ellen Griffin was one of the pioneers of **women**'s **professional golf** in the **United States**. She graduated in 1940 from North Carolina Women's College (now the University of North Carolina at Greensboro [UNCG]), and then, after earning a master's degree at UNC (Chapel Hill), she joined the physical education faculty at UNCG, where she began teaching golf until 1968. In 1944, with **Betty Hicks** and **Hope Seignious**, Griffin formed the **Women's Professional Golf Association** (WPGA), the first women's professional golf tour. It did not last long, but it was soon followed by the **LPGA**, in 1950. Griffin continued to teach golf and in 1962 was named Teacher of the Year by the LPGA, the same year in which she opened her own private teaching facility, The Farm, near Greensboro. In that year, she also became the educational director of the **National Golf Foundation**. Ellen Griffin was made an honorary member of the LPGA and was given the only honorary master classification by the LPGA Teaching Division. Since 1989, the LPGA has given out the Ellen Griffin Rolex Award to teachers who "demonstrate in their teaching, the same spirit, love, and dedication to golf that Ellen did . . . and make a major contribution to the teaching of golf." In 1999, the University of North Carolina at Greensboro dedicated the Ellen Griffin Golf Practice Facility on their campus, with funds donated by one of Griffin's former students, Sue Rice.

GROUND UNDER REPAIR. Ground under repair is any part of the course marked as such by the tournament committee. While it often refers to an area of the course that is under repair, it sometimes refers to an area of the course that is in such poor condition that the tournament committee feels that playing from it could be unfair to the competitors. A ball is in ground under repair when it lies in or any part of it touches the ground under repair. A player is entitled to relief if the ball lies within the margin of the ground under repair, if the player's stance occurs within the area, or if the ground under repair interferes with the area of the player's intended swing. Under those circumstances, **through the green**, a player is entitled to a free drop no nearer the hole, within one club length of the nearest point of relief.

GULDAHL, RALPH J., "GOLDIE." B. 22 November 1911, Dallas, Texas, United States; D. 11 June 1987, Sherman Oaks, California, United States. Ralph Guldahl was a U.S. **professional** golfer who, for a brief time, was the greatest player in the sport. Guldahl turned pro in 1931 and won an event in his rookie year. He tied for second at the 1933 **U.S. Open** but then quit the sport in 1935 and worked, for a time, as a car salesman. He returned to the tour in 1936, winning the **Western Open** late in that year. He won that tournament again in 1937–1938, then considered a major title. In 1937–1938, Guldahl doubled by winning the U.S. Open, and in 1939, he won the **Masters**. In his U.S. Open win, he stopped before approaching the final green and took out a comb to clean up his thick black hair. He said that he knew he was going to win and wanted to look good for the photographers, noting that he was always proud of his thick head of hair. From 1937 to 1939, Guldahl was definitely the top player in the world. And that was it. Like **David Duval** 65 years later, he completely lost his game. He managed to win two events in 1940 and never won another tournament after that. He returned to work as a club professional, teaching at Braemar Country Club in Tarzana, California, from 1959 until his death. Guldahl was inducted into the **World Golf Hall of Fame** in 1981.

GUTTIES (GUTTA PERCHA). Gutties, or golf balls made out of gutta percha, were discovered in 1848 by the Reverend Dr. Robert Adams Paterson. Gutties were made from the dried sap of the sapodilla tree. The sap was formed into a spherical mold while it was hot. The ball was a significant improvement over the **featherie** and soon made that ball obsolete. Gutties were the dominant ball for the second half of the 19th century. It was soon discovered that new gutties, which were quite smooth, flew somewhat erratically, but after a few holes, with a few nicks on them, they seemed to fly better. This led to the addition of small raised edges all over the ball, termed the "bramble pattern." This led to the use of dimples on a golf ball, which made possible a more aerodynamic flight.

– H –

HACKER. Hacker is a derogatory term for a poor golfer. Such players are also called "duffers."

HAGEN, WALTER CHARLES. B. 21 December 1892, Rochester, New York, United States; D. 6 October 1969, Traverse City, Michigan, United States. Walter Hagen was one of the great showmen of golf and one of its greatest champions. Playing primarily in the 1910s and 1920s, he won 11 major championships, including the **PGA Championship** a record five times (1921, 1924–1927), the **U.S. Open** twice (1914, 1919), and the **Open Championship (British Open)** four times (1922, 1924, 1928, and 1929). Hagen's mark of 11 major championships trails only **Jack Nicklaus** (18), **Tiger Woods** (14 through 2009), and **Bob Jones** (13). But Hagen also won the **Western Open** five times (1916, 1921, 1926, 1927, 1932), at a time when it was the third most important tournament on tour, after the U.S. Open and PGA, and, therefore, some golf historians consider him to have won 16 major titles. Further, he also won the **North and South Open** in 1918, 1923, and 1924 and the **Metropolitan Open** in 1916, 1919, and 1920, when those were among the major tournaments on the tour.

Hagen was a great match player, as witnessed by his four consecutive victories in the PGA, then held at **match play**. In 1925, Hagen played **Bob Jones**, the greatest **amateur** ever and considered by many the greatest player of the era, in a 72-hole exhibition match and defeated him 12 & 11. Hagen was a dashing, flamboyant player, known for the way he dressed and his millionaire-like lifestyle. He raised the status of golf **professionals**, who were often shunned in his era, refusing to dress in the car like they were often required to do. **Gene Sarazen** said of him, "All the professionals should say a silent thanks to **Walter Hagen** each time they stretch a check between their fingers. It was Walter who made professional golf what it is." Hagen once described his approach to life: "Don't hurry, don't worry, you're only here for a short visit so be sure to smell the flowers along the way."

Hagen also sought to improve the status of professional golfers. Prior to 1920, they were not considered gentlemen and were not allowed in the clubhouse at many open tournaments, notably, the U.S. Open. At the 1920 U.S. Open, held at Inverness Club in Toledo, Ohio, Hagen protested this treatment, and the club allowed the professionals to use the clubhouse during the tournament. The professional golfers gave Inverness a grandfather clock in thanks. It was inscribed with the following message: "God measures men by what they are/Not by what they in wealth possess/This message chimes afar/The voice of Inverness."

HAM-AND-EGG. Ham-and-egg refers to a **four-ball** match in which a team of two golfers scores very well without either partner playing exceptionally well. When a team ham-and-eggs well, one partner may be completely out of a hole, while the other partner comes through for a good score on that hole. If this continues over several holes, with each partner contributing approximately equal amounts, the team is said to be ham-and-egging it. In the converse situation, where one partner plays extremely well, while the other is often out of the hole, the player who plays well is said to be carrying the team.

HANDICAP. A handicap is a measure of a player's ability. It is calculated by subtracting the **course rating**s from a factored average of a certain number of the player's most recent scores. Over the years, the factored average has changed. Currently, after turning in 20 scores for handicap purposes, a player computes the average of the 10 best scores minus the course rating on which the rounds took place. This number is then multiplied by 0.96 to determine the final handicap. Handicaps are usually assigned from zero to 36, with a zero handicap player being roughly someone who can average **par** golf on good days. This player, termed a "**scratch golfer**," is considered a high quality player. However, there are actually lower handicaps, called "plus handicaps." A +2 handicap belongs to someone whose 10 best scores averaged approximately two under course rating, or, basically, par on most courses. As a way of comparison, golfers on the **PGA Tour** would likely have handicaps ranging from +4 to +8 (notably, **Tiger Woods**).

Handicaps are a way to equalize players of unequal ability and enable them to play competitive matches against each other. If a 10 handicap player plays against a 4 handicap player, the better player will give the 10-handicapper six shots, virtually always given as one shot on six holes in match play. Most courses rank their holes in degree of difficulty. The six shots would be given as one shot on each of the six highest ranked holes. **Stroke-play** handicap tournaments are also common at country clubs. All players play stroke play, and then their handicaps are subtracted from their final scores to derive net scores, with the lowest net score winning.

HANSON, BEVERLY. B. 5 December 1924, Fargo, North Dakota, United States. Beverly Hanson grew up in North Dakota. She attended the University of North Dakota, and later, Mills College in Oakland, California. In addition to her golf ability, she was a top bassoonist, playing with civic orchestras. As an **amateur**, she won the 1949 Texas Women's Open and the 1960 **U.S. Women's Amateur.** In 1960, she also played on the **Curtis Cup** team. Turning **professional** in 1951, she won the first **LPGA** event in which she competed and went on to win 17 times on the LPGA through the mid-1960s. She won three major championships—the inaugural **LPGA Championship** in 1955, the 1956 **Western Open**, and the 1958 **Titleholders**. In 1958, she was the leading money winner on the LPGA.

HARBOUR TOWN GOLF LINKS. Harbour Town Golf Links is a **golf course** on Hilton Head Island, South Carolina. It is the site of the Heritage Tournament on the **PGA Tour**. The Heritage, held annually since 1969, has had various corporate sponsors. The course, designed by **Pete Dye** and **Jack Nicklaus** and opened in 1967, is considered by many the first great course built by those two architects, who worked together for a few years. The course is relatively short but has very tight **fairways**, very small greens, and tight bunkering that make it very challenging to play. The final two holes run along Calibogue Sound on the Intracoastal Waterway.

HARLOW, ROBERT ELSING "BOB." B. 21 October 1889, Newburyport, Massachusetts, United States; D. 15 November 1954, Pinehurst, North Carolina, United States. Bob Harlow was a promoter of the game who was elected to the **World Golf Hall of Fame** for his efforts. He is considered by many the father of the **PGA Tour**. In the 1920s, when such a tour did not exist, pros only played various events around the country. But Harlow had a vision of a true tour and promoted it, often selling the idea of a local tournament to the Chambers of Commerce around the country. He first served as a business manager for **Walter Hagen** and was later the tournament manager of the PGA Tour from 1930 to 1935. In 1947, in what may be his most lasting contribution, Harlow founded *Golf World* magazine, the newsmagazine of golf.

HARMON, EUGENE CLAUDE "BUTCH," JR. B. 28 August 1943, New Rochelle, New York, United States. Butch Harmon is the son of Claude Harmon, the 1948 Masters Champion and a renowned club **professional**. Butch is one of the world's best-known golf instructors, known primarily for his work with **Tiger Woods** during his early professional years. Harmon played golf at the University of Houston, and then had a brief **PGA Tour** career (1969–1971) after a stint in the U.S. Army. He also taught **Greg Norman** and, more recently, **Phil Mickelson**. Harmon has established several teaching centers in his native Houston. He has two brothers, Craig and Bill Harmon, who are golf professionals.

HARRINGTON, PÁDRAIG "PADDY." B. 31 August 1971, Ballyroan, Dublin, Ireland. Pádraig Harrington, considered the greatest ever Irish **professional** golfer, has won three major championships—the **Open Championship (British Open)** in 2007 and 2008 and the **PGA Championship** in 2008. Harrington played on the **Walker Cup** team for Great Britain and Ireland in 1995, and then turned professional, joining the European Tour in 1996. He won the 1996 Spanish Open, but did not win again until 2000. Since then, he has had at least one win every year on the European Tour, and he won the Order of Merit in 2006. Harrington now splits his time between the U.S. **PGA Tour** and the **European PGA Tour**, playing frequently in the **United States** since 2005. Through 2009, he has won 11 times on the European Tour, five times on the U.S. PGA Tour, and is a six-time Irish PGA champion. He has played for Europe at five **Ryder Cup** matches—1999, 2002, 2004, 2006, and 2008. Harrington is a distant cousin of NFL quarterback Joey Harrington and the 1995 World Series of Poker Champion Dan Harrington.

HARRISON, ERNEST JOSEPH "DUTCH." B. 29 March 1910, Conway, Arkansas, United States; D. 19 June 1982, St. Louis, Missouri, United States. Dutch Harrison was a top American **professional** who had a very long career on the **PGA Tour**. He turned professional in 1930 and eventually won 18 tournaments on the PGA Tour. He was named to the **Ryder Cup** team in 1947, 1949, and 1951. Harrison placed in the top 10 at major championships nine times but never managed to win one. He finished third at the 1939 **PGA Championship** and third at the 1960 **U.S. Open**, the latter, when he was 50 years old. He also placed fourth at the 1950 U.S. Open and 1954 **Masters**. Harrison won the **Vardon Trophy** in 1954 for the lowest scoring average on tour.

HASKELL BALL. In 1898, Coburn Haskell of Cleveland developed a **golf ball** with a solid core that was wrapped with tightly wound rubber thread. It had a thin outer shell made, for many years, from balata. This was termed the Haskell ball and was a big improvement over the **guttie**, then the most popular ball in golf. By 1905, the Haskell ball had virtually replaced the guttie among top players. The basic design of the Haskell ball is similar to modern golf balls of the 21st century but with some modifications.

HAVEMEYER TROPHY. The Havemeyer Trophy is given to the winner of the **U.S. Amateur** Championship. It was donated by Theodore Havemeyer, the first president of the **USGA**, who made his fortune with the American Sugar Refining Company, which he founded with his brother, Henry.

HAYNIE, SANDRA JANE. B. 4 June 1943, Fort Worth, Texas, United States. Sandra Haynie was one of the top **LPGA professionals** in the 1960s and 1970s. She had a long career, playing on the LPGA from 1962 to 1989. Haynie won 42 tournaments, among them four major championships—1965 and 1974 **LPGA Championship**, 1974 **U.S. Open**, and the 1982 **Du Maurier Classic**. She was second on the LPGA money list five times and was in the top 10 every year from 1963 to 1975. Haynie struggled throughout her career with health issues, battling arthritis in her back and knees, which caused her to take several breaks from the tour to recover. In 1977, the arthritis and ulcers made her cut back to only a few tournaments a year, although she returned in the 1980s to play a fuller schedule. She has since become a fund-raiser for the National Arthritis Foundation. After her playing career, she became a well-known instructor with Sandra Haynie Golf Experiences at Castle Hills Golf Club in Carrollton, Texas.

HAZARDS. Hazards are areas of a **golf course** that are specifically designated as such and consist of three types—**bunkers**, **water hazards**, and **lateral water hazards**. The entry for each type in this dictionary contains details of the rules pertaining to each. The main rule is that a player's club cannot be grounded in a hazard. A player may play the ball from a hazard at any time, although in water hazards, this is not always possible. Another rule pertaining to hazards relates to hitting a **wrong ball**. Unlike **through the green**, a player is not entitled to identify the ball. The player may uncover enough sand or dirt on top of the ball to see the top of the ball, but that is all. However, if the player plays a wrong ball in the hazard, there is no resulting penalty.

HEZLET (-ROSS), MARY ELIZABETH LINZEE "MAY." B. 1882, Gibraltar; D. 27 December 1978, Sandwich, Kent, England. May Hezlet was one of three Irish sisters who starred in **amateur** golf. In 1899, May Hezlet won the Irish Ladies' Closed Championship, her first of five victories in that event, including three consecutive wins in 1904 to 1906, with her final victory coming in 1908. Twice she defeated her sister Florence in the final. The third sister was Violet. May Hezlet won the **British Ladies' Amateur** three times, in 1902, 1904, and 1907. A brother, Charles Hezlet, was runner-up in the **Amateur Championship** (**British Amateur**) in 1914, played on the British **Walker Cup** team, and won the Irish Amateur several times. May Hezlet published one of the first golf books for **women**, *Ladies Golf*, in 1904, with a second edition published in 1907. In 1912, she contributed to *The New Book of Golf* by **Horace Hutchinson**.

HICKS (-HARB), HELEN L. B. 11 February 1911, Cedarhurst, New York, United States; D. 16 December 1974. Helen Hicks was a pioneering American female **professional** golfer. She was a top **amateur**, twice reaching the final of the **U.S. Women's Amateur**, losing in 1931 to **Glenna Collett Vare** and in 1933 to **Virginia Van Wie**. She was the Canadian Amateur Champion in 1929, won three New York Women's Amateurs, and two Metropolitan Women's Amateurs. In 1934, Hicks turned professional to endorse clubs by Wilson Sporting Goods, one of the first female athletes to sign an endorsement contract. She won two tournaments considered major championships, the 1937 **Women's Western Open** and the 1940 **Titleholders**. Hicks was one of the 13 founders of the **LPGA** in 1950.

HICKS (-NEWELL), ELIZABETH "BETTY." B. 16 November 1920, Long Beach, California, United States. Betty Hicks won the **U.S. Women's Amateur** in 1941 and turned **professional** later that year. In 1944, she, **Hope Seignious**, and **Ellen Griffin** formed the **Women's Professional Golf Association**, the forerunner of the **LPGA.** Via a coin flip among the three, Hicks became the WPGA's first president. As a player, Hicks never managed to win a professional event but did finish second in the **U.S. Women's Open** in 1948 and 1954, and third in 1957. Hicks has been inducted into numerous Halls of Fame, including the LPGA Teaching and Club Professional Hall of Fame, the Long Beach Golf Hall of Fame, San Jose Sports Hall of Fame, the Women's Sports Foundation International Hall of Fame, and the California Golf Writers Hall of Fame. She was named the 1999 Ellen Griffin Rolex award winner for her contributions to **women**'s golf.

HIGUCHI, HISAKO "CHAKO." B. 13 October 1945, Kawagoe City, Saitama Prefecture, Japan. Chako Higuchi was the first great female Japanese **professional** player, winning over 70 professional tournaments. Most of these were in **Japan**, but in 1977, Higuchi won the **LPGA Championship**, making her the only Japanese player, male or female, to win a major championship. She also won the Australian Women's Open in 1974 and the Colgate European Women's Open in 1976. Higuchi has served as commissioner of the Japanese LPGA since 1994.

HILTON, HAROLD HORSFALL. B. 12 January 1869, West Kirby, Merseyside, England; D. 5 March 1942, Westcote, Gloucestershire, England. Harold Hilton was one of the first great **amateur** golfers. In 1892, he won the **Open Championship (British Open)**, only the second amateur to win that title, and he repeated that victory in 1897. Hilton won four Amateur Championships (British Amateur)—1900, 1901, 1911, and 1913—and was **U.S. Amateur** champion in 1911, winning both titles that year. He later became a golf writer. Hilton was inducted into the **World Golf Hall of Fame** in 1978.

HIRONO GOLF CLUB. Hirono Golf Club is among the world's top courses, often considered the best course in **Japan**. The course, designed by well-known British architect **Charles Alison,** opened in 1932. Hirono Golf Club has been ranked one of the top courses in the world by *Golf Magazine*'s panel of experts. The course is located 15 miles northwest of Kobe, Japan, and measures 6,925 yards from the back tees. It has hosted most of the major Japanese championships.

HOGAN, WILLIAM BEN "THE HAWK," "BANTAM BEN," "THE WEE ICE MON." B. 13 August 1912, Stephenville, Texas, United States; D. 25 July 1997, Fort Worth, Texas, United States. Ben Hogan is one of the greatest players of all-time, rivaling **Jack Nicklaus**, **Bob Jones**, and **Tiger Woods** in any discussion of the greatest ever. He was born to a poor family and grew up caddieing alongside **Byron Nelson**. He started on the tour in the late 1930s but went broke and returned to the Fort Worth area. There, he worked odd jobs, including dealing cards, while practicing during the day. Hogan was the first proponent of long hours on the practice tee, and his practice habits are still legendary. It is often said that nobody worked harder at the game than he did. After getting back on tour, he finally won a **PGA Tour** event in 1940 and then won three consecutively, all in North Carolina.

His career was interrupted by World War II, but in 1946, he won his first major championship, the **PGA Championship**, and 13 tournaments in all that year. In 1948, Hogan dominated the PGA Tour, winning the **U.S. Open** and PGA Championship, and 10 tournaments overall. After winning two tournaments in January 1949 and with his preeminence on tour established, he and his wife, Valerie, elected to drive back to Fort Worth for a holiday. Outside Van Horn, Texas, on a foggy stretch of road on the morning of 2 February 1949, a Greyhound bus crashed head-on into the Hogans' car, nearly killing Ben Hogan, who had thrown himself across his wife's lap to protect her. His pelvis was crushed; he broke his clavicle, several ribs, and an ankle, and while recovering, he developed blood clots that traveled to his lungs (pulmonary embolism). His life was saved by a then risky operation in which the vena cava was tied off to prevent further blood clots. It was not certain if he would walk again, and high-level competitive golf was considered unlikely.

But in 1950, Hogan returned, tying **Sam Snead** for first at the **Los Angeles Open**, only to lose in a play-off. Later that year, Hogan won his second U.S. Open. In 1951, he again won two major titles, his first **Masters** and the U.S. Open. Defending his title at the U.S. Open, he shot a final round 67 on the very difficult **Oakland Hills** course, after which Hogan famously said, "I am glad I brought this course, this monster, to its knees." After winning only one tournament in 1952, the **Colonial National Invitational**, he returned in 1953 with one of the greatest years in golf history, winning all three majors he entered—the Masters, U.S. Open, and the **Open Championship (British Open)**. It was his only entry in the British Championship and cemented his fame and reputation as, at the time, the greatest golfer ever.

Hogan is usually considered the greatest tournament ball striker ever, the results of his hours of assiduous practice. He wrote two books, *Power Golf*, and his legendary *Five Lessons: The Modern Fundamentals of Golf*, often considered the greatest golf instructional book ever written. Hogan finished his career with 64 wins on the

PGA Tour and nine major championships. He played in the Open Championship only once, and after his 1949 accident, he never again entered the PGA Championship, then held at **match play**, until it was converted to **stroke play** in the 1960s. By then, he was well past his prime. Hogan also started the Ben Hogan Company, a golf club and ball manufacturing company that was one of the top golf manufacturers in the 1960s, 1970s, and 1980s. He was known by some as a dour, hard man who did not suffer fools gladly, but he was a loyal friend to those who knew him well. A movie of his life, *Follow the Sun* (starring Glenn Ford as Hogan), details his early life, the bus accident, and his recovery. Hogan was a charter member of the **World Golf Hall of Fame** in 1974. *See also* HOGAN'S ALLEY.

HOGAN'S ALLEY. **Ben Hogan** was such an iconic figure in golf that there are several different places in the world called "Hogan's Alley." Hogan was from Fort Worth, Texas, and played frequently at Colonial Country Club in Fort Worth, site of the **Colonial National Invitational**. He won that tournament five times, and the course is often referred to as Hogan's Alley. In 1946–1948, Hogan won two **Los Angeles Open**s and the 1948 **U.S. Open** at **Riviera Country Club**, also called "Hogan's Alley." Finally, at **Carnoustie Golf Links** in **Scotland**, site of Hogan's only appearance, and victory, in the **Open Championship** (**British Open**) in 1953, Hogan played the very difficult par-five sixth in an unusual manner that most pros avoided. The shortest route to the hole was down the left side of the narrow **fairway**, but that required a drive to be placed expertly between out-of-bounds on the left and a deep, large fairway bunker. Hogan chose this route in every round of the Open and never missed the narrow fairway, which has since become known as "Hogan's Alley."

HOLE. A golf hole on the **putting green** must have a diameter of no more than 4¼ inches (108 mm) and must be at least 4 inches (101.6 mm) deep. Most holes have a plastic liner and the liner must be sunk at least 1 inch (25.4 mm) below the putting green surface.

HOLED. As defined in the **Rules of Golf**, a player's ball is holed when it is at rest within the circumference of the hole, and all of it is below the level of the lip of the hole. The only time this really becomes of importance is when a player hits a shot from off the green that becomes trapped against the side of the hole and the **flagstick**. In such a case, the ball is not usually fully below the level of the lip of the hole and is therefore not holed. However, by rule, the player may gently move the flagstick to see if the ball will drop to the bottom of the hole or at least below the lip of the hole. It is then holed.

HOLE-IN-ONE. A hole-in-one occurs when a player scores a one on a hole, holing the ball with the tee shot. It almost always occurs on a par-three hole, although, more rarely, it can occur on a par-four, when it is also a **double eagle**. A hole-in-one is considered the ultimate feat for most club **amateurs**, but most touring pros have made multiple "aces" in their career. At country clubs, tradition holds that any player who makes a hole-in-one must buy drinks for the entire membership that day. Many clubs will sponsor hole-in-one insurance to protect a player from having to pay out exorbitant amounts of drink money.

HOLLINS, MARION. B. 3 December 1892, East Islip, Long Island, New York, United States; D. 28 August 1944, Pacific Grove, California, United States. Marion Hollins was a wealthy socialite who became an outstanding athlete in numerous sports, golf among them, including tennis, equestrian, shooting, and auto racing. In 1912, Hollins was first noticed in the golf world when she was runner-up at the Metropolitan Women's Amateur. She entered her first **U.S. Women's Amateur** in 1913 and won the title in 1921, defeating **Alexa Stirling** in the final. During her career, she won three Metropolitan Women's Amateurs, eight Pebble Beach Championships, and was captain of the 1932 U.S. **Curtis Cup** team.

In the 1920s, she began developing **golf courses**, and eventually developed three of the best-known courses in the **United States**. The first was on Long Island, the Women's National Golf and Tennis Club, one of the first U.S. clubs exclusively for **women**. She hired **Ernest Jones** to be the head **professional** there, but eventually stole him away for her next venture. Moving to California, Hollins started Pasatiempo Golf Club in Santa Cruz. There she enlisted **Alister MacKenzie** to help design Pasatiempo and later worked with him on

Cypress Point Club on the Monterey Peninsula, her third course and one of the greatest in the country. It was his work on Pasatiempo and Cypress Point, spurred by Hollins' influence, that led to MacKenzie being selected by **Bob Jones** and **Clifford Roberts** to design the Augusta National. MacKenzie asked Hollins to come to Augusta for a site inspection, which greatly angered Roberts, who was a misanthrope and had other biases. MacKenzie told him, "She has been associated with me in three golf courses and not only are her own ideas valuable, but she is thoroughly conversant in regard to the character of work I like. I want her views and her personal impressions in regard to the way the work is being carried out. I do not know of any man who has sounder ideas."

Her dream was Pasatiempo Resort, and she spent most of her millions supporting the dream and lost some of it in the Great Depression. Because she had to sell it off, she lost rights to the resort. She moved to Monterey Peninsula, where it is said she died of a broken heart. *See also* GOLF COURSE ARCHITECTURE.

HONOR. By definition in the **Rules of Golf**, the player who is to play first from the teeing ground is said to have the honor. The honor is accorded on the first tee by draw of a tournament committee in formal matches or tournaments. On subsequent holes, the honor is given to the player or side who made the lower or lowest score on the previous hole. If a previous hole was tied, the honor reverts to the player or side who had the honor on the previous hole.

THE HONOURABLE COMPANY OF EDINBURGH GOLFERS. The Honourable Company of Edinburgh Golfers is one of the oldest golf clubs in the world, with club records dating back to at least 1744, although it is suspected that the club is much older. In 1744, the club produced the first known **Rules of Golf**, in preparation for its club tournament, the Silver Club. The Honourable Company of Edinburgh Golfers was originally based in Leith and played a five-hole course there until 1836, when it moved to **Musselburgh**, playing the nine-hole public course there. In 1891, the Honourable Company built a private course in **Muirfield** and has played there since that time. The club has hosted the **Open Championship** numerous times, first at Musselburgh in the 19th century, then at Muirfield in the 20th century.

HOOK. A hook is a shot that travels sharply from right-to-left for a right-handed player or left-to-right for a left-handed player. The milder form of a hook is a draw. A hook may be a player's preferred shape of shot, although better players try to play only mild curves, either draws or fades. A hook may also be an errant shot, ending up well off the **fairway**. A hook is caused by releasing the club too early, over-releasing the club, or an outside-in clubhead path with a closed face. More severe forms of the shot are called "**duck hook**," "snap hook," or "pull hook."

HOOTERS TOUR. The Hooters Tour is a men's golf tour in the **United States**, which was started in 1988 as a developmental tour for players trying to make their way to the **PGA Tour**. It is the third-highest-ranked tour in the United States, after the PGA Tour and the **Nationwide Tour** (formerly **Hogan, Nike**, **Buy.com Tour**). Hooters Tour players are essentially playing for their own entry fees, although some sponsorship enables the tour to pay out slightly more than entry fee money. Former Hooters Tour players who have since starred on the PGA Tour and won major championships include Stewart Cink, **John Daly**, **Jim Furyk**, **Lee Janzen**, Zach Johnson, Tom Lehman, Shaun Micheel, and David Toms. Chad Campbell, who became a top PGA Tour player, holds the Hooters Tour record for most tournament wins with13.

HOPE, LESLIE TOWNES "BOB." B. 29 May 1903, Eltham, London, England; D. 27 July 2003, Toluca Lake, California, United States. Bob Hope, who lived to 100 years of age, remains one of America's iconic comedians. He made numerous movies, told jokes all over the nation and the world, and often traveled far and wide on USO Tours to host shows for the U.S. military, often putting himself at risk to support the nation's soldiers. And he loved the game of golf, which he often played in concert with his friend, **Bing Crosby**, with whom he made over 20 movies. In 1962, Hope started the Bob Hope Desert Classic, often called the "Palm Springs Desert Classic" because it is held in that California desert community but usually just called "The Hope." The tournament is a five-day **pro-am** in which teams of three **amateurs**, many of them celebrity guests, play with **PGA Tour** stars. Each team plays with a different **professional** on each of the first four days, and the pros finish up their tournament on the fifth day. At his best, Hope played to a four **handicap** and competed in the 1951 **British Amateur** Championship. For his promotion of the game, he was inducted into the **World Golf Hall of Fame** in 1983.

HOSEL. The hosel is the connection of the clubhead to the golf shaft.

HOYLAKE. *See* ROYAL LIVERPOOL GOLF CLUB.

HOYT, BEATRIX. B. 5 July 1880, Southampton, Long Island, New York, United States; D. 14 August 1963, Thomasville, Georgia, United States. Beatrix Hoyt was one of the first great female **amateurs** in the **United States**. She grew up in New York suburbs to a wealthy family that afforded her the leisure time for golf. She was the granddaughter of Salmon P. Chase, secretary of the treasury under President Abraham Lincoln, and later, chief justice of the Supreme Court. Hoyt grew up playing **Shinnecock Hills** and in 1896 won the **U.S. Women's Amateur**, remaining the youngest ever to win it until 1971, when **Laura Baugh** surpassed her record. Hoyt won it again in 1897 and 1898, one of only five players to win it three times consecutively. In 1900, she lost in the semifinals to **Margaret Curtis** and then retired from competitive golf to pursue a career in sculpture and landscape painting.

HUTCHINSON, HORATIO GORDON "HORACE." B. 16 May 1859, North Devon, Devon, England; D. 1932. Horace Hutchinson twice won the **British Amateur** (1886 and 1887), but became better known as one of the first great golf writers. He wrote 14 books on golf, beginning in 1886 with *Hints on the Game of Golf*, a book of golf instruction. He is probably best known for *The Badminton Library: Golf* and *British Golf Links* (1897), a large-format book with multiple photographs of the best courses of the British Isles and France. Hutchinson was a prolific writer who authored over 50 books on varied subjects including cricket, shooting, and fishing.

HUTCHISON, JACK FOWLER "JOCK,"JR. B. 6 June 1884, St. Andrews, Fife, Scotland; D. 27 September 1977, Evanston, Illinois, United States. Jock Hutchison was one of the greatest American **professionals** in the era before a **PGA Tour** existed. He won the 1920 **PGA Championship** and won the **Open Championship (British Open)** in 1921. Hutchison also won the 1920 and 1923 **Western Open** and the 1921 **North and South Open**, when those were major American titles. In 1937, Hutchison became the first winner of the Senior PGA Championship and won that title again in 1947.

HYBRID CLUB. Hybrid clubs are a new addition to the standard set of golf clubs. These clubs are a cross between a **fairway wood/**metal and a **long iron**. With the loft of a long iron and the thicker sole of a smaller fairway wood/metal, hybrids enable a player to move the ball over 200 yards, often from tight lies or the rough. On **professional** tours, it is now very common for professionals to carry at least one hybrid, often dropping out a long iron to stay under the 14-club limit.

– I –

INKSTER, JULI SIMPSON. B. 24 June 1960, Santa Cruz, California, United States. Juli Inkster is one of the greatest U.S. female **professionals** at the turn of the 21st century. She first achieved fame when she won three consecutive **U.S. Women's Amateur** Championships (1980–1982), becoming only the fifth player to win that title in three straight years, after **Beatrix Hoyt**, **Alexa Stirling**, **Glenna Collett Vare**, and **Virginia Van Wie**. After graduating from San Jose State in 1982, Inkster turned **professional** in 1983. She has won 31 tournaments on the **LPGA**, including seven major titles—**U.S. Women's Open** (1999, 2002), **LPGA Championship** (1999, 2000), **Kraft Nabisco (Dinah Shore)** (1984, 1989), and the **Du Maurier Classic** (1984). Inkster has played on nine **Solheim Cup** teams, the most ever by an American player, and was inducted into the **World Golf Hall of Fame** in 2000. She has done all of this while remaining a devoted mother, raising her two girls, Hayley and Cori.

INSIDE THE LEATHER. "Inside the leather" is a term used by club players in casual matches in which all putts that are "inside the leather" are conceded. In this type of concession, a player's putter is used to measure the distance of the ball from the hole. In the original form of inside the leather, the measurement was from the grip end of the club to the end of the grip, or about 12 inches. But this later evolved to be from the clubhead to the grip, or about 24 inches. Therefore, all putts within two feet of the cup are conceded. Long putters have made this more difficult to police accurately between players in a match. The term is never used in tournament golf.

INTERNATIONAL FEDERATION OF PGA TOURS. The International Federation of PGA Tours was formed in 1996 to help globalize the game of golf. The original founding members were the U.S. **PGA Tour**, the **European PGA Tour**, the Japan Golf Tour, the **Australian PGA Tour**, and the Sunshine Tour (**South Africa**). The Asian Tour joined in 1999, and the Canadian Tour became an associate member in 2000. In 2007, the Tour de las Américas (South/Central America) became an associate member. In 2009, the Canadian Tour and Tour de las Américas were made full members, and the group had a major expansion, adding the China Golf Association, the Professional Golf Tour of India, and the Korea Professional Golfers' Association. It also added six major ladies tours: the **LPGA** Tour, the **Ladies European Tour**, the Australian Ladies Professional Golf Tour, the Japan LPGA, the Korean LPGA, and the Ladies Asian Golf Tour. In 1999, the International Federation of PGA Tours founded the World Golf Championships. It also runs the **World Golf Ranking**.

INTERNATIONAL GOLF FEDERATION (IGF). The International Golf Federation is, in a sense, the international ruling body of golf. The group, originally known as the World Amateur Golf Council, was formed in 1958 to organize the **World Amateur Team Championship** for men and **women**. In the late 1990s, the name was changed to the World Golf Council, and at about that time, it began to make entreaties to the International Olympic Committee (IOC) to return golf to the Olympic program. A first attempt, in 2001, to name golf to the 2008 Olympic program failed. After that, attempting to be more in line with other international sports federations, the group's name was changed to the International Golf Federation in 2003. In

October 2009, the IGF was successful when golf was restored to the Olympic program, beginning with the 2016 **Olympic Games**. The IGF has never truly been the international governing body of the sport. The ruling body in the **United States** and Mexico has always been the **USGA**, while the **R&A** has been the ruling body in Great Britain and the remainder of the world. The two organizations, however, were co-supporters of the IGF, which was effectively a shadow organization. With golf on the Olympic program, it is likely that this will now change, and the IGF will probably become the true ruling body of the sport internationally.

INWARD NINE. Inward nine refers to the back nine. In **Scotland**, most of the courses went away from the clubhouse for the front nine, referred to as the "**outward nine**," and then returned to the clubhouse on the back nine, referred to as the "inward nine." This is the source of the terms "going out in . . ." for the score on the front nine, and "coming in in . . ." for the score on the back nine.

IRELAND. The first known **golf course** in Ireland is considered to be Royal Curragh, dating to 1856. It was formerly established as Curragh Golf Club in County Kildare in 1883, but the game was played in the country back to at least the early 19th century. In 1886, British politician A. J. Balfour was appointed the Irish chief secretary. An avid golfer, Balfour is credited with sparking interest in the sport in the Emerald Isle.

In 1891, the Golfing Union of Ireland was formed, which makes it the world's oldest golf governing body. The Golfing Union oversees courses, tournaments, junior golf programs, and the game throughout the country. The Irish Ladies Golf Union was formed in 1893, making it the oldest ladies golf federation in the world. The **Open Championship (British Open)** was played for the only time in Ireland in 1951 at the **Royal Portrush Golf Club** in Northern Ireland. Ireland is renowned for several challenging and beautiful golf courses, including Royal Portrush, **Royal County Down**, **Ballybunion**, and **Lahinch**. Ireland has about 350 golf courses and trails only **Scotland**, **Australia**, and New Zealand in golf courses per capita, with Northern Ireland ranking fifth in the world.

IRWIN, HALE SPENCER, JR. B. 3 June 1945, Joplin, Missouri, United States. Hale Irwin is a U.S. **professional** who has starred on both the **PGA Tour** and the Senior PGA Tour. An excellent athlete, Irwin played football at the University of Colorado, where he was a two-time All–Big Eight defensive back, and in 1967, he won the **NCAA Golf Championship**. Turning pro in 1968, Irwin won 20 tournaments on the PGA Tour, including three major championships, all in the **U.S. Open**, winning in 1974, 1979, and 1990. On the PGA Tour, he played on five **Ryder Cup** teams. As a senior, for several years, Irwin was the top player on the **Champions Tour**, winning 45 tournaments, and through 2009, he is the all-time leading money winner on that tour. Irwin was inducted into the **World Golf Hall of Fame** in 1992.

– J –

JACKLIN, ANTHONY "TONY," CBE. B. 7 July 1944, Scunthorpe, England. Tony Jacklin was the first great British player of the post–World War II era. In golf-mad Great Britain, Jacklin achieved legend status when, in 1969, he became the first British player in 18 years to win the **Open Championship (British Open)**. In 1970, he added a victory in the **U.S. Open** at Hazeltine National, the first and, through 2009, only European to win that title after World War II. Jacklin won eight events on the European Tour, though it was only formed in 1972—after his best years. He also won four events on the U.S. **PGA Tour**. Jacklin played on seven **Ryder Cup** teams, all from 1967 to 1979, and captained the European side in 1983, 1985, 1987, and 1989. He was inducted into the **World Golf Hall of Fame** in 2002.

JACOBS, JOHN, OBE. B. 14 March 1925, Lindrick, Yorkshire, England. John Jacobs was a British touring **professional** from the 1950s who had some success without ever dominating European golf. He won the 1957 Dutch Open and South African PGA and played in the 1955 **Ryder Cup**. Better known as a golf teacher, he is the finest European teaching professional of his era. He was the first director-general of the European Tour, serving from 1971 to 1975, and he captained the European Ryder Cup team in 1979 and 1981.

JACOBSEN, PETER ERLING. B. 4 March 1954, Portland, Oregon, United States. Peter Jacobsen grew up in Oregon, attended the University of Oregon, and turned **professional** in late 1976, qualifying for the **PGA Tour** on his only attempt at **Q School**. He has had a solid PGA career, winning seven titles but no major championships. He did win the 2004 **U.S. Senior Open** and the 2006 Senior Players Championship, which are major titles on the **Champions Tour**. Jacobsen is best known for his outgoing manner and is one of golf's most colorful personalities. Jacobsen has used his popularity to become a top golf entrepreneur. He formed his own golf management company, Peter Jacobsen Sports, which sponsors and runs several professional and **pro-am** tournaments, notably, the Fred Meyer Challenge, a three-day charity event in his native Oregon. He has done work in golf announcing on network television and **Golf Channel**. In his early days on tour, Jacobsen was known for his golf swing imitations of other professional players, which developed into a popular skit he often gave to the galleries on the practice range. With tour pros **Payne Stewart** and Mark Lye, Jacobsen formed a musical group, Jake Trout and the Flounders.

JAMESON, ELIZABETH MAY "BETTY." B. 9 May 1919, Norman, Oklahoma, United States; D. 7 February 2009, Boynton Beach, Florida, United States. Betty Jameson was one of the 13 founding members of the **LPGA.** Jameson played the tour from 1948 through 1963, winning 10 events, including three major tournaments, the 1942 and 1954 **Women's Western Open**, and the 1947 **U.S. Women's Open**. She was also **U.S. Women's Amateur** Champion in 1939 and 1940. In 1952, she donated the trophy for lowest scoring average on the **LPGA**, which she requested be named in honor of her golf hero, **Glenna Collett Vare**. Jameson became a member of the LPGA Hall of Fame in 1967.

JANZEN, LEE MCLEOD. B. 28 August 1964, Austin, Minnesota, United States. Lee Janzen took up golf at the age of 12, when his family moved from Baltimore to Florida. He attended Florida Southern College, leading the team to the 1985 and 1986 NCAA Division II championships and winning the 1986 individual title. He turned **professional** later that year and joined the **PGA Tour** in 1990, winning his first tour event in 1992, the Northern Telecom Open. He has won 10 events through 2009, including the 1993 and 1998 **U.S. Open**, his two major victories, and the "fifth major," the 1995 **Players Championship**. Janzen played on the **Ryder Cup** team in 1993 and 1997.

JAPAN. The history of golf in Japan can be traced to Ryoichiro Arai, a Japanese businessman in the silk trade, who traveled to the **United States** and first played golf in 1900 at the Northfield Links, which later became the Atlantic City Golf Club. During his travels back and forth to Japan, he brought word of the game to his native country, especially after he was given his own set of **golf clubs** in 1902 by Andrew Carnegie, after they met at Pinehurst. Although the game began to be played with some regularity in the 1910s, Japanese golf exploded after the 1957 **Canada Cup** victory of **Torakichi "Pete" Nakamura** and Koichi Ono at Kasumigaseki. Over the next few years, the game became very popular, and **country club** memberships became prohibitively expensive for all but the very rich. According to *Business Week*, at the peak of Japan's market wealth in the late 1980s, the combined value of memberships represented roughly 10 percent of the nation's gross domestic product. Japan now has about 3,000 **golf courses**, more than any other nation other than the United States. Japan has a men's and **women**'s **professional** golf tour. The oldest tournament, the Japanese Open, was first held in 1927, and the Japanese Women's Open was first held in 1968.

JAPANESE PGA TOUR. The Japanese PGA Tour was founded in 1973 and is the third major international **professional** tour, after the U.S. **PGA Tour** and the **European PGA Tour**. The organizing body is the Japan Golf Tour Organization (JGTO), which also oversees the Japan Challenge Tour, a developmental tour. The top player on this tour has been **Masashi "Jumbo" Ozaki**, who won 94 tournaments and earned over two billion yen, leading the money list 12 times between 1973 and 1998.

JENKINS, DANIEL THOMAS "DAN." B. 2 December 1928, Fort Worth, Texas, United States. Dan Jenkins is one of the best-known golf writers of the second half of the 20th century. He started as a newspaper writer in his native Fort Worth and later, moved to the *Dallas Times Herald*. He wrote for many years for *Sports Illustrated*, but in the past 20 years, he has written for *Golf Digest*. In the 1970s, Jenkins began writing novels and became famous for a football novel, *Semi-Tough*, that was made into a movie starring Burt Reynolds and Kris Kristofferson. Jenkins followed this with his best-known golf book, *Dead Solid Perfect*, which was also made into a movie, albeit a less memorable one. Jenkins wrote about **Ben Hogan** for many years and championed Hogan's place as the greatest player ever.

JIGGER. "Jigger" was the name of a high-lofted club in the era when **golf clubs** had names and not numbers. It resembled a modern **wedge** or chipping iron.

JONES, ERNEST. B. 25 October 1887, Manchester, England; D. 31 July 1965, Glen Head, Long Island, New York, United States. **Ernest Jones** was one of the first well-known teaching **professionals**. He became an assistant golf professional at Chislehurst Golf Club at the age of 18. In March 1916, serving in World War I, Jones lost his right leg below the knee. He was able to return to playing golf, shooting 72 a few months later on one leg. He was later fitted with a prosthesis. Jones' teaching philosophy was built on the concept of "swing the clubhead." He popularized this term and used it to teach, among others, **Virginia Van Wie**, **Glenna Collett Vare**, and **Lawson Little**. Jones was posthumously inducted into the World Golf Teachers Hall of Fame.

JONES, REES. B. 16 September 1941, Montclair, New Jersey, United States. Rees Jones is the son of noted **golf course architect Robert Trent Jones Sr.**, and he eventually followed in his father's career. Rees Jones studied at Yale and the Harvard Graduate School of Design. After graduation, he joined his father's design company and helped him design or remodel over 100 courses. In 1974, Rees Jones started his own course architecture company. He has designed or redesigned over 100 golf courses in his career. In addition to designing numerous well-known courses, among them **Pinehurst** No. 7, he has helped redesign many classic courses, among them **The Country Club** (Brookline, Massachusetts), Atlanta Athletic Club, and East Lake Country Club (Atlanta, Georgia). Rees Jones was president of the **American Society of Golf Course Architects.** In 2004, he received the Old Tom Morris Award from the **Golf Course Superintendents Association of America**, an award given to his father in 1987. He has championed environmentally sensitive courses. His older brother, **Robert Trent Jones Jr.**, is also a top golf course architect.

JONES, ROBERT TRENT "BOBBY," JR. B. 24 July 1939, Montclair, New Jersey, United States. Robert Trent Jones Jr. is the son of noted **golf course architect Robert Trent Jones Sr**. and the brother of architect **Rees Jones**. Bobby Jones attended Yale University, did graduate work at Stanford University, and then joined his father's design firm. In the late 1960s, he broke away to form his own company and has since designed or remodeled over 250 courses. Jones was president of the **American Society of Golf Course Architects** and chairman of the California State Parks and Recreation Commission.

JONES, ROBERT TRENT, SR. B. 20 June 1906, Ince, England; D. 14 June 2000, Fort Lauderdale, Florida, United States. Robert Trent Jones was a top **golf course architect** in the **United States**. He came to this country as a young boy and later attended Cornell University, where he designed the back nine of the university's golf course. After his graduation, he formed a partnership with Canadian **Stanley Thompson**, and they designed several Canadian courses. In the late 1930s, Trent Jones, as he was known, broke off and established his own **golf course** design firm. He is among the most prolific U.S. golf course designers ever. He is credited with over 500 designs, many of which are overseas, inspiring the aphorism, "The sun never sets on a Robert Trent Jones golf course." His original designs include Point O'Woods (Benton Harbor, Michigan), Bellerive (Creve Coeur, Missouri), Hazeltine National (Chaska, Minnesota), the Golden Horseshoe Gold Course (Williamsburg, Virginia), **Spyglass Hill** (Pebble Beach, California), Firestone North (Akron, Ohio), and Royal Ka'anapali (Maui, Hawaii). He is credited with redesigning numerous championship courses, including **Augusta National**, **Oakland Hills**, **Baltusrol**, **Olympic Club**, Oak Hill, and **Southern Hills**. Trent Jones was inducted into the **World Golf Hall of Fame** in 1987, and that year, he also received the Old Tom Morris Award from the **Golf Course Superintendents Association of America**. Two of his sons, **Rees Jones** and **Robert Trent Jones Jr.**, have also become well-known golf course architects.

JONES, ROBERT TYRE "BOB" OR "BOBBY," JR. B. 17 March 1902, Atlanta, Georgia, United States; D. 18 December 1971, Atlanta, Georgia, United States. Bobby Jones, who preferred the name "Bob," is the greatest **amateur** golfer of all time and was considered, until the advent of **Ben Hogan**, and later **Jack Nicklaus** and **Tiger Woods**, the greatest player ever. He won 13 major championships, all national titles, when the **U.S. and British Amateurs** were major titles. Jones was a golf prodigy who went to the third round of the 1916 U.S. Amateur when he was only 14 and won the Georgia Amateur that same year. On the national stage, much was expected of Jones, but he struggled for several years. It was later written that he had seven lean years, followed by seven great years. In 1923, he broke through to win the **U.S. Open**. From 1923 to 1930, he won four U.S. Opens (1923, 1926, 1929, 1930), five U.S. Amateurs (1924, 1925, 1927, 1928, 1930), three **British Opens** (1926, 1927, 1930), and one British Amateur (1930). His greatest year, perhaps the greatest year by any golfer, was 1930, when he won the U.S. Open, British Open, U.S. Amateur, and British Amateur. Termed by golf writer George Trevor "the impregnable quadrilateral," it is now called the "**Grand Slam**."

After his annus mirabilis, Jones retired from competitive play. A graduate of Georgia Tech and Emory Law who also studied law at Harvard, he never turned **professional**, practicing law instead. But in the early 1930s, he became a professional when he filmed a series of golf instructional movies. In 1932, he and **Clifford Roberts** began building a club in Augusta, Georgia, the **Augusta National Golf Club**, which was to be a winter club for many of their wealthy northern friends. The club became the home of the **Masters**, later one of the renowned golf championships. Jones played in it himself several times (through 1948) but never contended. In 1945, along with **Robert Trent Jones,** Bob Jones helped design and build the Peachtree Country Club in Atlanta. Jones stopped playing after 1948 when he was diagnosed with syringomyelia, a degenerative spinal cord condition, which would eventually cause his death. In his later years, he was wheelchair bound. Renowned golf writer **Herbert Warren Wind** wrote of him, "He faced the best life has to offer, and the worst, with equal grace."

Jones received numerous honors. He became a charter member of the **World Golf Hall of Fame** in 1974. In 1958, he was only the second American, after Benjamin Franklin, made a freeman of the City of **St. Andrews, Scotland**. An exchange scholarship, the Robert T. Jones Scholarship, was established between Georgia Tech, Emory, and the University of St. Andrews. *See also* BOB JONES AWARD.

– K –

KAWANA HOTEL GOLF COURSE. The Fuji Course at the Kawana Hotel Golf Course is considered by many the best course in **Japan** and the entire Orient. It was designed by **Charles Alison** and opened in 1936. He wrote of it, "This paradise is at least two hours from Yokohama, and much of the journey is along a narrow and earth quaked road, cut in the rocky coast. It lies among the hills beyond the hot springs of Ito on a pine-covered plateau bordered by red cliffs which descend down to the blue sea. From a wooded bay, a mile distant, a fishing village sends out boats with brown sails to complete the last detail of a perfect scene." Many golf tournaments have been held on the Fuji course, among them the 1960 **World Amateur Team Championship** for the **Eisenhower Trophy**. It was recently the site of the well-known Fuji Sankei Classic.

KEELER, OSCAR BANE "O. B.," "POP." B. 4 June 1882, Chicago, Illinois, United States; D. 15 October 1950, Atlanta, Georgia, United States. O. B. Keeler was an Atlanta sportswriter who wrote for most of his career for the *Atlanta Journal*. He was the personal writer for **Bob Jones** during Jones' great years in the 1920s. They met when Keeler covered Jones' victory at the 1916 Georgia State Amateur at age 14. Keeler helped Jones write his autobiography, *Down the Fairway*, in 1927, and later assisted him with a radio series. Keeler covered over 80 major golf championships and witnessed all 13 of Jones' major titles.

KIAWAH ISLAND GOLF RESORT. Kiawah Island Golf Resort is a resort with five **golf courses** on Kiawah Island, South Carolina, near Charleston. The most famous course on the island, by far, is the Ocean Course. Designed by **Pete Dye** and opened in 1974, it has numerous holes bordering the Atlantic Ocean. The Ocean Course was the site of the 1991 **Ryder Cup**, one of the most hotly contested ever held and often called the "War on the Shore." It also hosted the 2007 Senior PGA Championship. The Ocean Course is extremely difficult, made more so by frequent high winds whipping off the sea. From the tournament tees, the Ocean Course measures 7,356 yards with a **par** of 72. It has a **course rating** of 77.2 and a **slope** of 144, and it has unmarked tee boxes that can stretch the course to 7,873 yards. It was featured in the 2000 film *The Legend of Bagger Vance* and has been named a Certified Audubon Cooperative Sanctuary by Audubon International. The other courses at Kiawah Island are Turtle Point (Jack Nicklaus, designer), Osprey Point (**Tom Fazio,** designer), Oak Point (Clyde Johnston, designer), and Cougar Point (originally Marsh Point, redesigned by **Gary Player** in 1996).

KIKUYU GRASS. Kikuyu is a type of **grass**, technically known as *Pennisetum clandestinum*, which grows on **golf courses**, mostly in California, **Australia**, and Africa. It is a stoloniferous grass with a very thick, tough blade, which makes playing out of kikuyu rough very difficult. Because of its stolons, kikuyu is aggressive and often overgrows other planted grasses.

KING, BETSY. B. 13 August 1955, Reading, Pennsylvania, United States. Betsy King was a U.S. **professional** on the **LPGA.** She attended Furman University, graduating in 1976, and joined the LPGA in 1977. She won 34 LPGA tournaments, 20 from 1984 to 1989 when she was the top player in the world. King was named Player of the Year three times, won two scoring titles, and won three money titles. She won six major titles—two **U.S. Women's Open**s (1989, 1990), one **LPGA Championship** (1992), and three **Kraft Nabisco** (**Dinah Shore**) (1987, 1990, 1997). King played on the **Solheim Cup** team five times and was captain of the team in 2007. She was inducted into the **World Golf Hall of Fame** in 1995. King, known for her Christian faith, served several missions overseas preaching the gospel, notably in Korea.

KINGSTON HEATH GOLF CLUB. Kingston Heath Golf Club, located in Heatherton, a southeast suburb of Melbourne, is one of **Australia**'s top **golf courses**. It has hosted most of the major Australian championships, including the **Australian Open** seven times and the Australian Match Play Championship seven times. The course, designed by 1905 Australian Open champion Dan Soutar and built by **Royal Melbourne greenkeeper** M. A. Morcom, opened in 1925. It was an unusual **par** 82, with 12 par-fives and only two par-threes. It was redesigned several times, with the bunkers redone by **Alister MacKenzie**, and now measures 6,352 meters (6,947 yards) for men at par 72.

KIRK BELL, MARGARET ANNE "PEGGY." B. 28 October 1921, Findlay, Ohio, United States. Peggy Kirk Bell was a top **amateur** in the 1940s, winning the Ohio Amateur three times and the 1949 **Titleholders** and **North and South** titles. She attended Boston University and graduated from Rollins College. After playing on the 1950 **Curtis Cup** team, Peggy Kirk turned **professional** and was one of the founding members of the **LPGA.** She played for several years but is much better known as a golf teacher and as the owner of Pine Needles Resort in Southern Pines, North Carolina, which she founded with her husband, Warren "Bullet" Bell, a former NBA player. Peggy Kirk Bell has received virtually every award in golf, including the **USGA**'s **Bob Jones Award**, the **William D. Richardson Award** from the **Golf Writers Association of America**, the LPGA's Ellen Griffin Rolex Award, and the **National Golf Foundation**'s Joe Graffis Award. She has received honorary doctorates from the University of Findlay, Methodist College (North Carolina), and Sandhills Community College (North Carolina), and she is a member of seven Halls of Fame.

KITE, THOMAS OLIVER "TOM," JR. B. 9 December 1949, McKinney, Texas, United States. A native of Austin, Texas, Tom Kite starred at the University of Texas, where he helped the team win two NCAA team titles and shared the 1972 NCAA individual title with his teammate **Ben Crenshaw**. Kite turned **professional** in late 1972, winning the 1973 Rookie of the Year award, and continues to play through 2009 on the **Champions Tour**. In his career, he won 19

PGA events, including the 1992 **U.S. Open** at Pebble Beach, his only major title. Kite won the **Vardon Trophy** in 1980 and 1981. He was Golf Writers Player of the Year in 1981 and the PGA Player of the Year in 1989. Kite played on seven **Ryder Cup** teams (1979, 1981, 1983, 1985, 1987, 1989, and 1993) and was the captain in 1997. In 1979, Kite received the **Bob Jones Award** from the **USGA** for distinguished sportsmanship in golf. He was inducted into the **World Golf Hall of Fame** in 2004.

KLASS, BEVERLY. B. 8 November 1956, Tarzana, California, United States. After she won the National Pee Wee Championship by 65 shots, Beverly Klass became famous in 1966 when she turned **professional** as a fourth grader, at age nine, and attempted to play on the **LPGA**, spurred on by her father. The LPGA sought an injunction and enacted a minimum-age limit for the tour. Klass regained her **amateur status**, won over 25 tournaments in the Los Angeles area in the next six years, and briefly played on the men's golf team at Pierce College. In 1976, she joined the LPGA again and played for 13 years on tour. Her best year was 1984, when she was 41st on the money list with two second-place finishes. She later recounted tales of how her father forced her to play and beat her when she would not practice. Klass became a teaching professional at Turtle Bay Golf Club in West Palm Beach, Florida, after she left the LPGA in 1988.

KNOCKDOWN SHOT. *See* PUNCH SHOT.

KNUDSON, GEORGE ALFRED CHRISTIAN, CM. B. 28 June 1937, Winnipeg, Manitoba, Canada; D. 24 January 1989, Toronto, Ontario, Canada. George Knudson was one of the greatest Canadian **professionals**. He won the Manitoba Open in 1958–1960, the Ontario Open in 1960 and 1961, and then began playing the U.S. **PGA Tour**. He won eight tournaments on the PGA Tour and in 1968 was **World Cup** Champion with Al Balding. He never won a major championship but placed second at the 1969 **Masters**. Knudson was known for his technically proficient golf swing and his ball striking. He is a member of **Canada**'s Sports Hall of Fame, the Canadian Golf Hall of Fame, the Manitoba Sports Hall of Fame, and was made a member of the Order of Canada.

KRAFT NABISCO (DINAH SHORE). The Kraft Nabisco is one of the four major tournaments on the **LPGA.** Sponsored by singer **Dinah Shore,** the event began in 1972. It was called the Colgate Dinah Shore from 1972 to 1981 and did not achieve official major status until 1983. From 1982 to 1999, the event continued on as the Nabisco Dinah Shore. Shore's name was then dropped officially, and in 2000–2001, the event was the Nabisco Championship. Since 2002, it is the Kraft Nabisco Championship, but players still often call it the "Dinah Shore." It has always been held at Mission Hills Country Club in Rancho Mirage, California. In 1988, **Amy Alcott** won the event for a second time and jumped into the lake surrounding the 18th green to celebrate her triumph. This has since become an annual tradition, with the champion always taking the leap, most memorably in 1991 when Alcott won again and jumped in with Dinah Shore. Three players have won the event three times—Alcott, **Betsy King**, and **Annika Sörenstam**. Appendix 3 includes a list of champions.

– L –

LACOSTE (-PRADO-PIÑERO), CATHERINE. B. 27 June 1945, Paris, France. Catherine Lacoste was the daughter of French tennis legend René Lacoste, one of the Four Musketeers of French tennis of the 1920s. However, her mother, **Simone de la Chaume,** winner of the 1927 **British Ladies' Amateur** Championship, was a golfer. Catherine Lacoste, best known for winning the 1967 **U.S. Women's Open** as an **amateur**, is, through 2009, the only amateur to win that championship. She won the 1969 **U.S. Women's Amateur** and mimicked her mother that year by also winning the British Ladies' Amateur. Lacoste played on the French team that won the inaugural **World Amateur Golf Team Championships** in 1964, and played for France at the 1966, 1968, 1970, 1974, 1976, and 1978 World Championships. She never turned **professional**. She is on the board of Lacoste, the French sportswear company founded by her father.

LADIES EUROPEAN TOUR. Founded in 1978 and based in Great Britain, the Ladies European Tour, which has evolved over the years, is a **professional** tour for **women**. In 1978, the Women's Professional Golf Association (WPGA) was formed as part of the PGA of Great Britain and Ireland. The name changed in 1988 to the Women Professional Golfers' European Tour Limited, headquartered at Tytherington Club in Cheshire, **England**. In 1998, the name became the European Ladies' Professional Golf Association. The group took its current name in July 2000 and relocated to the Buckinghamshire Golf Club, just outside London. The tour has struggled to retain membership and compete against the **LPGA.** In 2005, the tour dismissed its chief executive, the fifth in eight years. The 2008 Ladies European Tour had 26 events, and in 2009, it had 23.

LADIES' GOLF UNION. The Ladies' Golf Union (LGU) was founded in 1893 and is the governing body of golf for **women** in Great Britain and Ireland. It conducts several tournaments: the **Ladies' British Open Amateur (British Ladies' Amateur)**, Ladies' British Open Amateur Stroke Play Championship, **Women's British Open**, Senior Ladies' British Open Amateur, and Girls' British Open Amateur. The LGU also cosponsors several team competitions: Girls' Home International Matches, Seniors' Home International Matches (both of which are between teams from **England**, **Scotland**, **Ireland**, and Wales), the **Solheim Cup**, and the Vagliano Trophy, which contests a team from Great Britain and Ireland against a team from Continental Europe.

LAG PUTT. A lag putt is a long putt, the distance of which is not precisely defined. Basically, any putt that is so long that a player does not reasonably expect to make it, can be considered a lag putt. In that situation, the player is simply trying to move the ball close enough to the hole to ensure holing the ball in two putts.

LAHINCH GOLF CLUB. Lahinch Golf Club, often called the "**St. Andrews** of Ireland," is a club in County Clare on the west coast of **Ireland**. The club was founded in 1892 and is situated between the towns of Ennistymon and Miltown Malbay. The original course, or Old Course, was redesigned in 1894 by **Old Tom Morris** and then again in 1927 by **Alister MacKenzie**. The Old Course has been the site of the South of Ireland Championship since 1895 and has hosted all the major Irish championships. The club has a second course for members.

LANCOME TROPHY. The Lancome Trophy (known in French as "Le Trophée Lancôme") was a **professional** invitational held in France from 1970 to 2003. The original tournament was suggested by French golf fan Gaëtan Mourgue d'Algue to Pierre Menet, then chairman of the Lancôme Company. The tournament was held at the Saint-Nom-La-Bretèche Club. It was originally organized by **Mark McCormack**'s IMG Company, which lent it an air of importance, because McCormack was able to bring many of the world's best players to the tournament. The Lancome Trophy was an invitational in its early years and was one of the more important international championships. The event was made a part of the **European PGA Tour** in 1982. When the French Golfing Federation (Fédération Française de Golf) tried to upgrade the **French Open** tournament in the late 1990s, the Lancome Trophy was given less emphasis, and it was discontinued after the 2003 event. Appendix 4 includes a list of champions.

LANGER, BERNHARD. B. 27 August 1957, Anhausen, Bavaria, Germany. Bernhard Langer is Germany's greatest golfer ever. He turned **professional** in 1976 and has played primarily on the **European PGA Tour**, where he has won 40 tournaments. Langer has also won two major titles, the **Masters** in 1985 and 1993. He won one other tournament on the **PGA Tour**, the Sea Pines Heritage Classic in 1985. Langer played on 10 European **Ryder Cup** teams (1981–1997, 2002), captained the 2004 team, and was inducted into the **World Golf Hall of Fame** in 2001. Langer has won the German Open 12 times. He has persevered to become a great player despite many problems over the years with the **yips**, and he became one of the first top players to putt with a split-hand technique using a long putter.

LATERAL WATER HAZARDS. A lateral water hazard is a type of **water hazard** on a **golf course**. It is marked with red stakes or lines, as opposed to yellow stakes or lines for a water hazard. Lateral water hazards usually run roughly parallel to the play of the hole. When a ball is hit into a lateral water hazard, the player has three options: 1) play the ball as it lies from within the hazard; 2) take a stroke and distance penalty, replaying the shot from the spot where the ball was hit; or 3) drop a ball on either side of the lateral hazard within two club lengths of the point where the ball last crossed the margin of the lateral hazard.

LAUNCH ANGLE. "Launch angle" is the term that refers to the angle at which the ball leaves the clubface as it begins its flight. The term became popular in the 1990s with the use of computerized video of golf swings and ball flight and is used almost exclusively in reference to **drivers**. It enables the study of a golf player's swing and resultant launch angle in an effort to optimize both and maximize driving distance.

LAZARO, JOSEPH "JOE." B. 1918, Waltham, Massachusetts, United States. Joe Lazaro was one of the greatest blind players in golf history. He lost his sight in 1944 while serving in World War II, when a German land mine exploded nearby. He played in his first blind National Championship in 1950 and continued to play in the Senior Division into the 21st century. Lazaro was a nine-time National Blind Champion and twice won the International Championships. He has received numerous awards including the 1970 **Ben Hogan Award**, given to a player who overcomes a disability to continue playing golf and the 1984 PGA Man of the Year Award. In 2007, he became a charter member of the **United States Blind Golf Association** (USBGA) Hall of Fame. In 1995, the USBGA established the Joe Lazaro Award, given each year to the most improved player at the National Championship.

LEAD TAPE. Lead tape is adhesive tape, made heavy by lead components. Through its use, better players make fine adjustments to the weight of their clubs. They may add a slight amount of weight to the head, to the heel, or to the toe of the club in an attempt to balance the club to their liking. It was popular on the **PGA Tour** through the 1980s, but with the advent of newer clubs, which are better designed and balanced, it is now less common.

LEADBETTER, DAVID B. N. B. 1952, Worthing, England. David Leadbetter is one of the best-known golf teachers of the 1990s and 21st century. He has taught many of the players on the **PGA Tour**, **LPGA**, **European PGA Tour**, and **Champions Tour**. Leadbetter's students have won over 100 worldwide **professional** victories and a dozen major championships. He established the David Leadbetter Golf Academies, which train junior players, now with over 30 locations in 13 countries. He is the author of seven best-selling golf instructional books.

LEITCH, CHARLOTTE CECILIA PITCAIRN "CECIL." B. 13 April 1891, Silloth, Cumberland, England; D. 16 September 1977, London, Greater London, England. Cecil Leitch was a British **amateur** player. She won four **British Ladies' Amateur** Championships (1914, 1920, 1921 [giving her three consecutive because of World War I], and 1926), a record shared with **Joyce Wethered**. Leitch also won the Canadian Women's Amateur title and five French Ladies' Amateur championships.

LEMA, ANTHONY DAVID "TONY" "CHAMPAGNE TONY." B. 25 February 1934, Oakland, California, United States; D. 24 July 1966, Lansing, Illinois, United States. Tony Lema was a very popular American **professional** of the 1960s who left the golf world all too soon. Lema grew up in Oakland, California. His father died when he was three, and his mother raised four children on welfare. He joined the Marine Corps when he was 17 and became an assistant golf pro after his discharge in 1955. He quickly improved his game and joined the **PGA Tour** in 1957. Lema struggled for a few years but in 1962 won his first tournament. Leading after three rounds at the Orange County Invitational, he told the press that if he won, he would serve champagne to the media the next day. He won, served the champagne, and became known as "Champagne Tony." In his four good years on the PGA Tour, Lema won 12 tournaments and one major championship, the 1964 **Open Championship (British Open)**. He finished second at the 1963 **Masters**. He was very popular with the fans because of his good looks, his golf talent, and his bon vivant personality. Lema died tragically in 1966. En route to an exhibition near Chicago, the private plane in which he was flying crashed, killing both pilots, Tony Lema, and his wife.

LIFT, CLEAN, AND PLACE. Lift, clean, and place is a specific type of **winter rule** or **preferred lie**. It is a local rule only and is not recognized by the **Rules of Golf** because it violates the principle of playing the ball "as it lies." However, pro tours do use it when a course is in poor condition. In club golf, when "preferred lies" are permitted, a player will simply roll the ball around with the clubhead until they get the lie they want. In lift, clean, and place, the player must mark the original spot of the ball, clean the ball, and then place it back in the desired lie, usually within one club length of the original spot, although that may vary according to the local rule. Once placed, the ball may not be moved again. Lift, clean, and place is usually played only in **fairways**, although it may be played **through the green** when the course is in very poor condition.

LINKS. A links course is a style of **golf course**, most associated with courses in **Scotland**. It is also an often misused term—many golf courses are called links courses when, in fact, very few outside of Scotland are actually links courses. A links course proper is a course built on land created when the sea receded. The land is said to "link" the mainland and the sea, and only a course built on such linksland is properly called a "links course." By this strict definition, it is said that no true links course exists in the **United States**, although many courses claim to be links courses. Links courses in Scotland are usually very flat, virtually treeless, and are protected by fierce winds blowing off the ocean.

LITTLE, SALLY. B. 12 October 1951, Cape Town, Cape Province, South Africa. Sally Little was a **South African** female **professional** who was based in the **United States** for most of her career. She became a U.S. citizen in August 1982. She turned pro in 1971, earning Rookie of the Year honors that year on the **LPGA.** During her career, which lasted through 2005, she won 15 LPGA events, including two major championships, the 1980 **LPGA Championship** and the 1988 **Du Maurier Classic**. She also won the 1982 **Kraft Nabisco (Dinah**

Shore) Championship before it was a major. Little's greatest year was 1982, when she won four tournaments and was third on the money list for the year. She also won three tournaments in 1979 and 1981 and two in 1980.

LITTLE, WILLIAM LAWSON, JR. B. 23 June 1910, Newport, Rhode Island, United States; D. 1 February 1968, Monterey, California, United States. Lawson Little is known for winning the "Little Slam" when he won the **U.S. and British Amateur** titles in both 1934 and 1935. Although it appeared that the Stanford grad would remain an amateur, he turned **professional** in 1936. His professional career saw him win eight tournaments on the **PGA Tour**, including one major, the 1940 **U.S. Open**, but it did not quite fulfill the promise of 1934–1935. With the cancelation of major events during World War II, he lost interest in golf and focused his efforts on stock investing. In the days before the limit of 14 clubs in a golf bag, Little was known for carrying multiple extra clubs, having as many as 26 in his bag at any one time, and this was the impetus for the **USGA** and **R&A** to implement the 14-club rule. Little won the 1935 Sullivan Award, given to the nation's top amateur athlete, and played on the 1934 **Walker Cup** team. He is a member of the Stanford Athletic Hall of Fame and was inducted into the **World Golf Hall of Fame** in 1980.

LITTLER, GENE ALEC "GENE THE MACHINE." B. 21 July 1930, San Diego, California, United States. Gene Littler had one of the smoothest swings in golf history, which inspired the nickname, "Gene the Machine." In 1953, Littler won the **U.S. Amateur** and played on the **Walker Cup** team. In 1954, he won a **PGA Tour** event, the San Diego Open, as an amateur, a feat that didn't occur again until 1985, when Scott Verplank won the **Western Open**. Littler turned **professional** at the end of 1954 and won four tournaments on the PGA Tour in 1955. He won 29 tournaments on the PGA Tour, among them, one major title, the 1961 **U.S. Open** at **Oakland Hills**. He finished second at the 1954 U.S. Open and lost play-offs at the 1970 **Masters** and 1977 **PGA Championship**. Littler played on **Ryder Cup** teams in 1961, 1963, 1965, 1967, 1969, 1971, and 1975. He received the 1973 **Bob Jones Award**, for distinguished sportsmanship in golf. Littler was inducted into the **World Golf Hall of Fame** in 1990.

LOB WEDGE. A lob wedge is a highly lofted wedge, sometimes called an "L-wedge," used for short pitches and shots from the **fairway**. The lob wedge was the brainchild of **Dave Pelz**, a former NASA scientist, who, in the 1970s and 1980s, made a very scientific study of putting and the short game. He determined that most **professionals** would benefit from carrying more than the then standard two wedges, a pitching and **sand wedge**. **Tom Kite**, who worked with Pelz, started carrying the lob wedge as a third wedge and popularized the concept on the **PGA Tour**. The result was the more-lofted lob wedge, which has varying lofts usually in the 56 degrees–60 degrees range. More lofted lob wedges, up to 64 degrees, sometimes called X-wedges, are used by professionals. *See also* FLOP SHOT.

LOCAL RULES. Local rules are rules established by any tournament committee to deal with special or abnormal conditions related to a specific course or competition. The **Rules of Golf** have an extensive appendix dealing with Rules of Golf, giving specific recommendations for certain local rules. The most well-known local rule deals with **preferred lies**, sometimes called "**winter rules**." Winter rules violate the basic tenet of the game to "play the ball as it lies" by allowing improvement of the player's lie. Usually this rule applies only to the "**fairway**"(a term not actually defined in the rule book), but it may be allowed anywhere "**through the green**," which refers to the entire course, except the teeing grounds, **putting greens**, and **hazards**. Most local rules allowing improvement of a player's lie are not terribly specific at the club level: they simply tell the players that they may improve their lies. At the **professional** level, on the pro tours, the rule is quite specific, and is called "**lift, clean, and place**." This usually allows the player to lift the ball, either through the green, in a closely mown area, or in the fairway, depending on the specifics of the rule, clean the ball, and replace it by hand. It must be placed no closer to the hole and usually within one club length of the original placement of the ball. On the **PGA Tour**, the players and **caddie**s often term this "picking it up and running with it."

Other local rules deal with environmentally sensitive areas: playing from **ground under repair**, obstructions and temporary obstructions, how to deal with power lines and cables, and stones in bunkers. Temporary obstruction rules are important for major championships because television towers often cause problems with sightlines for players playing a shot.

LOCKE, ARTHUR D'ARCY "BOBBY." B. 20 November 1917, Germiston, South Africa; D. 9 March 1987, Johannesburg, South Africa. Bobby Locke was the first great **South African** player, preceding **Gary Player**. Locke looked nothing like an athlete, with a paunch and several chins, but he was the greatest putter of his era. Even that, however, defied all logic since he hit all his putts with an inside-out stroke that looked like he hooked his putts, which mimicked the natural shape of his full shots. Locke won 38 tournaments in his native South Africa, and was a four-time champion at the **Open Championship (British Open)** (1949, 1950, 1952, 1957). He also played in the **United States** beginning in 1946, winning 11 **PGA Tour** events, including six in 1947 alone. His victory at the 1948 Chicago Victory Open was by a margin of 16 shots, still a record for the PGA Tour. Locke was controversially banned from the PGA Tour in 1949–1950, officially because of problems with playing commitments, but some felt it was a response by American pros to his success. He was allowed to play again in 1951, and he did play a few events in 1949–1950, but he never returned to full-time play in the United States. Locke was inducted into the **World Golf Hall of Fame** in 1977.

LONG IRONS. Long irons refer to the lowest numbered iron clubs, such as the 1-iron, 2-iron, 3-iron, and occasionally, the 4-iron. These are now becoming scarce items in the bags of many players. At one time, the mark of a great player was the ability to play long irons. Since the advent of metal woods and **hybrid clubs**, as well as the modern trend to carry multiple wedges, many players are carrying only one or two long irons, and some players carry none. In addition, the longer driving distances have made it less necessary to use long irons on par-fours. The 1-iron, formerly often used as a driving iron on shorter par-fours, is rarely seen nowadays, and there are many

professional players who carry no iron longer than a 4-iron. *See also* GOLF CLUBS.

LONGEST DRIVERS. Over the history of golf, there have been many players renowned for their ability to drive a golf ball a long way, and after all, "chicks dig the long ball." The first player renowned for his driving length was **Ted Blackwell**, a British **amateur**. On the **PGA Tour**, the first notable long driver was **Jimmy Thomson**. Thomson won multiple long-driving contests when they were often held prior to PGA Tour events. Among the top players, **Sam Snead** was known for his long drives. In the 1960s, the next longest driver among the pros was **George Bayer**, a very large man at over 6 feet 5 inches and 250 lbs. The longest tour player of the 1970s was Jim Dent, and in the early 1990s, **John Daly** became known for his ability to hit a ball a long way. In the early 1970s, a National Long Drive Championship emerged, open to all players, and many players were able to hit a ball longer than the pros, who, of necessity, had to sacrifice some distance for accuracy. One of the winners of this event was **Art Sellinger**, who won it twice. Sellinger took the concept and enlarged it, organizing a tour of several events, called Long Drivers of America. The main event on the tour is still the RE/MAX National Long Drive Championship. The most famous winner of this event is Canadian **Jason Zuback**, who has won the title five times.

LONGHURST, HENRY CARPENTER. B. 18 March 1909, Bedford, Bedfordshire, England; D. 21 July 1978, Cuckfield, West Sussex, England. Henry Longhurst was an **amateur** player in **England.** He won the 1936 German Amateur and finished second at the French and Swiss Amateur Championships. In addition, he captained the Cambridge University golf team. But it is as a golf writer and announcer that he is best known. He wrote a golf column for the *Sunday Times* (London) from 1947 to 1972, and contributed to *Golf Illustrated*. Longhurst was the first golf commentator for the BBC and later announced golf tournaments on U.S. television. He was a parliament member for Acton during World War II.

LOOP. Loop refers to a round made by a caddie, and caddies are often referred to as "loopers." The most famous reference to this is by Carl

Spackler, the Bill Murray character in **Caddyshack**, who begins his description of his encounter with the Dalai Lama by noting, "So I jump ship in Hong Kong and make my way over to Tibet, and I get on as a looper at a course over in the Himalayas. A looper, you know, a caddie, a looper, a jock."

LOOSE IMPEDIMENTS. The **Rules of Golf** define "loose impediments" as "natural objects including: stones, leaves, twigs, branches and the like; dung, and; worms and insects and casts or heaps made by them; provided they are not: fixed or growing; solidly embedded, or; adhering to the ball. Sand and loose soil are loose impediments on the **putting green**, but not elsewhere. Snow and natural ice, other than frost, are either **casual water** or loose impediments, at the option of the player. Dew and frost are not loose impediments." A player may move a loose impediment before playing a shot, except in a **hazard**. However, care must be taken in doing so, for if the ball moves while moving a loose impediment, it is considered that the player caused the ball to move and a penalty stroke is added to the player's score.

LOPEZ (-MELTON-KNIGHT), NANCY. B. 6 January 1957, Torrance, California, United States. Nancy Lopez was a U.S. **professional** who merits inclusion in any discussion of the greatest ever **women** players. Lopez first became known when she won the New Mexico Women's Amateur at the age of only 12. She was **U.S. Girls' Junior** champion in 1972 and 1974 and then played collegiately at the University of Tulsa, placing second at the 1975 **U.S. Women's Open** as an amateur. Sadly, her loss at that tournament was repeated during her career—the only hole on her résumé is the failure to win the U.S. Women's Open. Lopez turned professional in 1977, and in her first full year on tour—1978—she won nine tournaments, including five in a row, a record for the **LPGA.** She followed this with eight wins in 1979, and finished her LPGA career with 48 wins. She won the **LPGA Championship** three times, in 1975, 1985, and 1989, and these are her only major titles. She finished second four times at the U.S. Women's Open. Lopez's record could have been even greater, but she played only parts of some years due to pregnancy and giving birth to several children. She was inducted into the **World Golf**

Hall of Fame in 1987. Lopez is married to Ray Knight, former major league baseball player.

LOS ANGELES OPEN. The Los Angeles Open is the longest running **PGA Tour** event that is not a major championship. The tournament first took place in 1926, at the Los Angeles Country Club. Over the next few years, the tournament rotated among various courses in the Los Angeles area, but it is most associated with **Riviera Country Club**, which hosted the tournament in 1945–1953 and continuously since 1973. **Babe Zaharias** played in the 1938 event (and later, the 1945 event), held at Griffith Park Golf Course, making her the first woman to play in a PGA Tour event. The tournament has had several corporate sponsors, Nissan (1987–2007) and Northern Trust (current) being the best known, and from 1971 to 1983, it was hosted by entertainer Glen Campbell and was known as the Glen Campbell Los Angeles Open. In 2009, the tournament announced that it would grant a yearly exemption, named the **Charlie Sifford** Exemption, in honor of the pioneering black player, in the name of diversity in golf. The tournament was won four times by **Macdonald Smith** and **Lloyd Mangrum** and three times by **Ben Hogan** and **Arnold Palmer**.

LOST BALL. By definition in the **Rules of Golf**, a ball is deemed lost if 1) it is not found or identified by the player within five minutes after the player's side or their **caddies** have begun to search for it; 2) the player has made a stroke at a substituted ball; or 3) the player has made a stroke at a **provisional ball** from the place where the original ball is likely to be or from a point nearer the hole than that place. Time spent playing a **wrong ball** is not counted in the five-minute period allowed for search. When a ball is declared lost, the player entails a stroke-and-distance penalty—one stroke is added to the player's score, and the player must play another ball from as near as possible to the spot from which the previous shot was played.

LOUIS, JOE "THE BROWN BOMBER" (NÉ JOSEPH LOUIS BARROW). B. 13 May 1914, near La Fayette, Chambers County, Alabama, United States; D. 12 April 1981, Las Vegas, Nevada, United States. Joe Louis was one of the greatest athletes ever. He reigned as heavyweight boxing champion longer than any other man in history, from 1937 to 1949, a total of 12 years with the crown. With Jesse Owens, in the 1930s, he was one of the first blacks to cross the color barrier and gain appeal among all races. He finished his career with a record of 65 wins and 3 losses, 51 wins by knockout. Louis won the heavyweight title in 1937 against James J. Braddock and held it until his retirement in March 1949. He came out of retirement for financial reasons in 1950, losing two fights to Ezzard Charles and Rocky Marciano at the end of his career. He fought two epic bouts against German Max Schmeling, losing by knockout in 1936, and winning the rematch for the heavyweight title in June 1938 by a knockout at 2:04 of the first round.

Louis' hobby was golf and he used his fame and his passion for the game to help blacks gain entry to the segregated game. In 1952, he was invited to play in the San Diego Open, one of the first African Americans to play a **PGA Tour** event. Louis later gave financial support to assist the careers of several black **professional** golfers, including **Bill Spiller**, **Ted Rhodes**, and **Charlie Sifford**. His son, Joe Louis Barrow Jr., became director of **The First Tee**. Joe Louis was given posthumous membership in the **PGA of America**. He was buried at Arlington National Cemetery, an exception being made in his case by President Ronald Reagan.

LOVE, DAVIS MILTON, III. B. 13 April 1964, Charlotte, North Carolina, United States. Davis Love is the son of renowned teaching pro Davis Love Jr., who played numerous tour events with some success while a club **professional**. Davis Love III attended the University of North Carolina and turned professional in 1985. He has been a steady winner for most of his career, winning 20 events from 1987 to 2008. He won the 1997 **PGA Championship**, his only major title. Love also teamed with **Fred Couples** to win the **World Cup of Golf** four times consecutively from 1992 to 1995. Early in his career, Love was known as one of the longest **drivers** in golf. In the 1990s, Love began a subsidiary career as a **golf course** designer.

LPGA (LADIES' PROFESSIONAL GOLF ASSOCIATION). The LPGA was founded in 1950 by 13 **women** players. It was preceded by another women's **professional** tour, the **Women's Professional Golfer's Association (WPGA)**, founded in 1944, which lasted only five years. The LPGA is primarily based in the **United States**, although recently, the tour has hosted events internationally—in **Canada**, Mexico, Korea, Singapore, and Great Britain. It is the best-known professional tour for women in the world. The tour was originally dominated by American players, but since the mid-1980s, a large influx of international players has changed the face of the LPGA. Since about 1990, the best players have been non-Americans, notably, **Annika Sörenstam**, **Karrie Webb**, and more recently, **Lorena Ochoa**. In addition, in the 2000s, a number of Korean players moved to the fore, the best known being **Pak Se-Ri**.

With the tour primarily based in the United States, this influx of international players has led to some problems with the popularity of the LPGA. In addition, since 2007–2008, due to the difficult economic times, the tour has lost several tournaments and has struggled somewhat. This led, in 2008, to the players ousting Carolyn Bivens, who was LPGA commissioner at the time, and at the end of 2009, a new commissioner was selected, Michael Whan. At one of his early press conferences, he announced that the 2010 LPGA will consist of only 24 tournaments, down from 31 in 2007, and only 14 of those will be in the United States. The LPGA also has a section for women club professionals, but it is mostly associated with the LPGA events.

LPGA CHAMPIONSHIP. The LPGA Championship started in 1955 and has always been a major championship for **women professionals** in the **United States**. Unlike the **U.S. Open**, **U.S. Women's Open**, and men's **PGA Championship**, the LPGA has usually been held for several consecutive years at one course, under a sponsorship agreement. The LPGA has also usually had a title sponsor, which over the years has been Mazda, McDonald's, and Wegmans, with major sponsorship also given by AIG and Coca-Cola. The tournament has taken place 12 times at the Jack Nicklaus Golf Center in Kings Island, Ohio. **Mickey Wright** won the event four times, the most ever, with five players winning three titles—**Kathy Whitworth**, **Nancy Lopez**, **Patty Sheehan**, **Pak Se-Ri**, and **Annika Sörenstam**. Appendix 3 includes a list of champions.

LYLE, ALEXANDER WALTER BARR "SANDY," MBE. B. 9 February 1958, Shrewsbury, England. Though born in **England**,

Sandy Lyle is considered a Scottish **professional**, based on his father's heritage. Lyle played on the 1977 **Walker Cup** team and turned professional later that year. He won two major championships, the 1985 **Open Championship (British Open)** and the 1988 **Masters**. Lyle won 18 times on the **European PGA Tour** and six times on the U.S. **PGA Tour**, including the 1987 Players Championship. He led the European Order of Merit in 1979, 1980, and 1985. Lyle's form fell off after his Masters title, at a very young age, and he has not been a contender in major professional events since the early 1990s.

LYON, GEORGE SEYMOUR. B. 27 July 1858, Richmond Hill, Ontario, Canada; D. 11 May 1938, Toronto, Ontario, Canada. George Lyon came to golf very late, preferring more athletic pursuits. His first love was cricket and in 1894 he made 234 not out, at the time a world record. He took up golf at the age of 37 and despite an unorthodox swing, quickly became the top **amateur** in **Canada**. He won the Canadian Amateur Championship in 1898 and won that title seven times in all. He lost in the final of the 1906 **U.S. Amateur** and in 1908 went to the semifinals of the **British Amateur**. Lyon defeated **Chandler Egan** in the final of the 1904 **Olympic** golf championship. Lyon's business career was in insurance and he served in the Canadian military with Queen's Own Rifles and served at the Metis uprising in 1885.

– M –

MACDONALD, CHARLES BLAIR. B. 14 November 1855, Niagara Falls, Ontario, Canada; D. 21 April 1939, Southampton, New York, United States. Charles Blair Macdonald was the first **U.S. Amateur** champion, but he is best known as one of the earliest **golf course architects** in the **United States**. Macdonald studied at St. Andrews University and was tutored there by **Old Tom Morris**. After college, he returned to Chicago and became a stockbroker. In the late 1880s, he joined with several associates to form the Chicago Golf Club, one of the five founding clubs of the **USGA.** Macdonald designed the **golf course**, which at first was nine holes but expanded to 18 in 1893.

Shortly thereafter, Macdonald was a driving force in the formation of the USGA and subsequently won the 1895 U.S. Amateur, the first ever held. In 1900, he moved to New York to work with a Wall Street brokerage firm, and in 1908, he and a group founded the **National Golf Links of America**. After searching for a site for the club, they settled on **links**-type land near Southampton, New York, on Long Island. Macdonald designed and built the course, considered one of the classics of golf architecture. Macdonald was inducted into the **World Golf Hall of Fame** in 2007.

MacKENZIE, ALISTER. B. 30 August 1870, Wakefield, Yorkshire, England; D. 6 January 1934, Santa Cruz, California, United States. Alister MacKenzie was one of the greatest of the early **golf course architects** in the **United States**. Born in **Scotland**, where he trained as a surgeon, MacKenzie left medicine after World War I and worked in Great Britain designing courses with Harry S. Colt and **Charles Alison**. In the 1920s, MacKenzie moved to the United States. He designed numerous courses, and the quality of his very best work rivals that of any other architect. MacKenzie is best known as the architect of the **Augusta National Golf Club.** His other top designs include **Cypress Point Club**, **Lahinch Golf Club** (Old Course), Pasatiempo Golf Club, **Royal Melbourne Golf Club**, and the Scarlet Course at Ohio State.

MAIDEN, STEWART. B. 13 February 1884, Barry, Angus, Scotland; D. 4 November 1948, Atlanta, Georgia, United States. Stewart Maiden's claim to golf fame lies in the fact that he was the only teacher of **Bob Jones**, the greatest-ever **amateur** player and among the very best players ever. Born in **Scotland**, Maiden came to the **United States** in 1908 to take a position as head **professional** at East Lake **Golf Club** in Atlanta, where he first met Bob Jones. Maiden also taught top woman amateur **Alexa Stirling**.

MAJOR CHAMPIONSHIPS. *See* GRAND SLAM.

MALLON, MARGARET MARY ELIZABETH "MEG." B. 14 April 1963, Natick, Massachusetts, United States. Meg Mallon has been a top female **professional** on the **LPGA** Tour since her graduation from Ohio State University. Mallon started on tour in 1987 and has won 18 tournaments on the LPGA, including four major championships. She won the **LPGA Championship** and **U.S. Women's Open** in 1991, added the **Du Maurier Classic** in 2000, and won the U.S. Women's Open for a second time in 2004. Mallon has played for the United States eight times in the **Solheim Cup**.

MANGRUM, LLOYD EUGENE. B. 1 August 1914, Trenton, Texas, United States; D. 17 November 1973, Apple Valley, California, United States. Lloyd Mangrum was one of the greatest players of his generation, but he receives little mention today for his feats. Mangrum won 36 **PGA Tour** events, including the 1946 **U.S. Open**, but he had the bad timing to play in the era of **Ben Hogan**, **Byron Nelson**, and **Sam Snead**, which prevented him from winning more tournaments. This is shown by his major record, which includes four second-place finishes and five third-place finishes. He played for the United States in the 1947, 1949, 1951, and 1953 **Ryder Cups**. Mangrum's career was interrupted by World War II, in which he won two Purple Hearts, including one for being wounded in the Battle of the Bulge. He was the leading winner on the PGA Tour in 1951 and won the **Vardon Trophy** for lowest scoring average in 1951 and 1953. Mangrum had a relaxed demeanor on the course but was a hard man off the course. He is also known for his pencil-thin mustache and smooth swing.

MANN (-HARDY), CAROL A. B. 3 February 1941, Buffalo, New York, United States. Carol Mann attended the University of North Carolina at Greensboro (UNC-G) and joined the **LPGA** in 1961. She became one of the best players of her era but never quite reached the top, having to play against **Mickey Wright** and **Kathy Whitworth**, who dominated women's golf in the 1960s and 1970s. Mann still managed to win 38 tournaments on the LPGA, including two major titles, the 1964 **Western Open** and 1965 **U.S. Women's Open**. Mann is probably the tallest player ever among women golfers, at 6 feet 3 inches (191 cm). Mann has become a well-known golf instructor, teaching out of The Woodlands in the Houston, Texas, area. During her tour career, she was LPGA president from 1973 to 1976, and from 1985 to 1989, she served as president of the Women's Sports Foundation.

MARTIN, CASEY. B. 2 June 1972, Eugene, Oregon, United States. Casey Martin was a U.S. **professional** golfer who later became golf coach at his hometown University of Oregon. He was born with a congenital defect, Klippel-Trenaunay-Weber syndrome, which is a vascular disorder that inhibits blood return from the veins. In Martin's case, it affected his right leg and made it very difficult for him to walk a **golf course**. Despite this, he became quite a good player, earning a scholarship to Stanford University, where he played on the team with **Tiger Woods**. After college, as his condition worsened, Martin attempted successfully to qualify for the **PGA Tour**. And while doing so, he sued the PGA Tour for the right to use a golf cart in competition under the Americans with Disabilities Act. Martin was eventually successful and won the right to use a golf cart on the PGA Tour. But he never was highly successful on tour and eventually left competition to become a college golf coach. *See also* CASEY MARTIN RULING.

MARTIN, ROBERT "BOB." B. 1853, South Toll, Cupar, Fife, Scotland; D. 1917, Strathkiness, Fife, Scotland. Bob Martin was an early Scottish **professional** who played at **St. Andrews** and won the **Open Championship (British Open)** twice, in 1876 and 1885. His victory in 1876 was won in a play-off walkover over Davie Strath, who did not appear. On the 17th hole in the final round, Strath had struck a player on the green, and there were calls for his disqualification, but the committee decided to hold the play-off while a protest was lodged. Strath, however, refused to play. Martin also finished second in the Open in 1875 and 1887. He began caddieing at age 11, and then went into clubmaking. He also worked as a shepherd as a youth and won his first tournament while still in that occupation, defeating **Old Tom Morris** in the process.

MASHIE. In the 19th century, irons were not called by numbers as they are now but rather, by names. A mashie was a mid-iron, approximating what is known as a 5-iron today. *See also* GOLF CLUBS.

MASSY, ARNAUD. B. 6 July 1877, Biarritz, Pyrénées-Atlantiques, France; D. 16 April 1950, Étretat, Seine-Maritime, Normandy, France. Even now, over 100 years after his best playing days, Arnaud Massy is still the greatest-ever French **professional**. He learned the game as a **caddie** in Biarritz and later traveled to **Scotland** to hone his golf game there. In 1906, he won the inaugural **French Open**, his first of four titles in that event. In 1907, he won the **Open Championship (British Open)**, the only major championship ever won by a French golfer, making him the first Continental player to win the Open, something not repeated until 1979 by **Seve Ballesteros**. Massy fought in World War I and was wounded in Verdun, but returned to golf after the war, winning a gold medal at the 1919 Inter-Allied Games, a sort of military Olympics. He worked as a club professional for most of his career and played in the few tournaments available to him at the time. After the war, he won the 1925 French Open and the 1927 and 1928 Spanish Open.

THE MASTERS. The Masters is a tournament held annually in early April at the **Augusta National Golf Club** in Augusta, Georgia. It is one of the four major championships of golf and is the only one held annually at the same course. The tournament started in 1934 as the brainchild of **Bob Jones**. Jones and his associate, **Clifford Roberts**, built the course as a winter retreat for many of their wealthy northern friends. They decided to invite many of Jones' **professional** friends from his golf career to play in an invitational tournament, which was at first called the Augusta National Invitation Tournament. The event has become possibly the best-known tournament in the world. The Masters was won six times by **Jack Nicklaus**, four times by **Arnold Palmer** and **Tiger Woods**, and three times by **Jimmy Demaret** and **Sam Snead**.

A number of traditions help perpetuate the Masters' reputation. The tournament is now always opened by a retired, venerated player or players, who hit a ceremonial tee shot on the first day of the tournament. This is now Arnold Palmer, soon to be joined by Jack Nicklaus, but in past years it was **Byron Nelson**, **Gene Sarazen**, Sam Snead, and in earlier years (1963–1973), Fred McLeod and **Jock Hutchison**, who would actually play a ceremonial nine holes. On the Tuesday before the Masters starts, a Champions Dinner is held at the club, in which all past champions return for a friendly evening together, with the menu chosen by the defending champion, who also picks up the tab. This was started in 1952 by **Ben Hogan**. On Wednesday afternoon, before the tournament, the contestants play a par-three event on the par-three course that is adjacent to the main course on the grounds of the club. Another tradition is that no winner of the par-three event has ever gone on to win the Masters. Finally, on the last day, at the victory ceremony, the winner of the Masters is awarded a green jacket, which is exactly the same as the club jacket worn by the members. The green jacket was first given to the winner in 1949, Sam Snead. All Masters champions are made honorary members of Augusta National.

The **golf course**, Augusta National, is one of the best-known courses in the world. It was designed by Jones, in concert with **Alister MacKenzie**, on rolling land that was formerly a tree nursery. The course is actually quite hilly with very difficult, very fast, and highly sloped greens that are the hallmark of the course. There is very little rough, and the course is fairly open, with driving not at a premium. The course design mandates that players place their approach shots in the best position to attack the hole and avoid placing them above the hole, where recovery is sometimes next to impossible.

The tournament is highly acclaimed by the players, who look forward to receiving the coveted invitation to the event. But it has had its share of controversy. In the 1960s and early 1970s, the controversy concerned black players, who were not invited to the tournament. The event is held in the deep South in Georgia, and there were rumors that the membership would not allow a black player to compete. The most egregious absentee was **Charlie Sifford**, a top player on the **PGA Tour** who won a few PGA Tour events but was never invited to the Masters. **Pete Brown**, another African American PGA Tour champion, also never played in the tournament. Finally in 1975, **Lee Elder** broke the color barrier at the Masters, after he won the 1974 Monsanto Open. In that year, any PGA Tour victory qualified a player for the Masters. The club itself had no black members until 1990, when Ron Townsend, president of Gannett Television, accepted an invitation to join.

Another major controversy over the club's membership occurred in 2002 when **women**'s groups, notably the National Council of

Women's Organizations, led by their chairperson, Martha Burk, demanded that women be admitted to the club, as long as the club continued to host the Masters. Burk demanded a boycott of the tournament sponsors' products that were advertised on television. Augusta National responded by broadcasting the 2003 and 2004 tournaments with no commercials and no sponsors. Through 2009, Augusta National still has no female members. Appendix 2 includes a list of champions.

MATCH PLAY. Match play is a type of golf competition in which play is by holes rather than strokes. Players win a match if they have won more holes than their competition. Match play is contested in a head-to-head, or team-to-team, single elimination tournament, similar to a tennis tournament, with the winner of a match advancing to the next round. In match play, scores are given as 1 up, 2 up, etc. (or 1 down, 2 down, etc.), displaying how many more holes a player or team has won than the competition. A match ends when a player or team is more holes ahead than there are holes remaining to play. Final scores are displayed in the following ways: 3 & 2, 4 & 3, 5 & 4, or 1 up, 2 up—3 & 2 means the player is three holes up (ahead) with only two holes to play. If a match is tied after 18 holes (or 36 holes), the players play extra holes, with the first player to win a hole winning the match. Match play was the original form of competition of golf, played in the British Isles in the early 19th century. It was replaced at the **professional** level by **stroke play**, but match play is still very popular in club golf and in **amateur** tournaments. *See also* DORMIE; GIMME.

MAXWELL, PERRY DUKE. B. 13 June 1879, Princeton, Kentucky, United States; D. 17 November 1952, Tulsa, Oklahoma, United States. Perry Maxwell was a **golf course architect** who worked for many years with **Alister MacKenzie**, but he eventually formed his own firm and designed numerous courses by himself. He did at least 70 original designs and redesigned about 50 more courses, in 21 states. With MacKenzie, he designed the Ohio State University Scarlet Course, the University of Michigan Golf Course, and Crystal Downs Country Club in Michigan. With his son, Press, he designed **Prairie Dunes Country Club** in Hutchinson, Kansas. Maxwell is best known for his designs of **Southern Hills** in Tulsa, and Colonial Country Club in Fort Worth. Both courses have hosted the **U.S. Open** and numerous other major championships. He is responsible for numerous renovations and redesigns, among them **Pine Valley**, **Augusta National**, and **Merion**.

MAXWELL-BERNING, SUZANNE, "SUSIE." B. 22 July 1941, Pasadena, California, United States. Susie Maxwell grew up in California. She attended college at Oklahoma City University, where she played on the men's golf team. She turned **professional** after college and joined the **LPGA** in 1964, winning the Rookie of the Year Award. Her first LPGA victory was the 1965 **Women's Western Open**, at the time, a major championship. She won 11 times on the LPGA, and of those, four were major championships. Besides the 1965 Western, she won the **U.S. Women's Open** three times, in 1968, 1972, and 1973. After her tour career wound down in the 1980s she became a teaching professional. Her brother, Roger Maxwell, was a well-known PGA club professional, originally at Camelback Country Club in Scottsdale, Arizona.

McCORD, GARY DENNIS. B. 23 May 1948, San Gabriel, California, United States. Gary McCord is a former **professional** golfer who has become better known as a golf announcer on television. McCord turned professional in 1971 and played on the **PGA Tour** from 1974 through the later 1980s. He never won a tournament on tour but placed second at the 1975 and 1977 Greater Milwaukee Open. Known for his handlebar mustache, he joined CBS Sports in 1986 as a golf analyst and has become famous for his witticisms and funny commentary. He has played a little bit on the **Champions Tour**, winning two tournaments. In 1977, McCord partnered with Bill Mallon to set a PGA Tour record for the fastest round ever played (since broken by **Greg Norman** and **Mark O'Meara**)—1 hour, 26 minutes—in the final round of the Heritage Classic at **Harbour Town**.

McCORMACK, MARK HUME. B. 6 November 1930, Chicago, Illinois, United States; D. 16 May 2003, New York, New York, United States. Mark McCormack was the first man to establish himself as a major sports agent. McCormack was a fair player as well. He played on the golf team at the College of William & Mary before going to Yale Law School. While at William & Mary he met a Wake Forest player, **Arnold Palmer**, and when Palmer hit it big, he asked McCormack to represent him. This quickly spiraled into a major business, and McCormack formed the International Management Group (IMG), the largest sports promotional business in the world. In addition to representing athletes in all sports and branching out to the entertainment industry, IMG organizes many sports events. McCormack's and IMG's current and former clients, in addition to Palmer, include **Jack Nicklaus**, **Gary Player**, **Greg Norman**, **Tiger Woods**, Chris Evert, Björn Borg, Michael Schumacher, and Pete Sampras—a true who's who of the greatest in their respective sports in various eras. McCormack was inducted into the **World Golf Hall of Fame** in 2006 and the International Tennis Hall of Fame in 2008, the only person in both halls. His second wife was Betsy Nagelsen, a two-time doubles champion at tennis' Australian Open.

McDERMOTT, JOHN JOSEPH, JR. B. 12 August 1891, Philadelphia, Pennsylvania, United States; D. 2 August 1971, Norristown, Pennsylvania, United States. John McDermott was the first golfer born in the **United States** to win the **U.S. Open**. He learned the game **caddieing** in his hometown Philadelphia and won the **U.S. Open** in 1911 at Chicago Golf Club. In 1912, McDermott successfully defended his title at the Buffalo Country Club. In 1913, he won the **Western Open**, the second most important American tournament in that era. But later that year, he lost his entire savings in the stock market and began a downward spiral into depression. He also made a seemingly innocuous comment after winning a tournament in Delaware by eight shots, stating, "We hope our foreign visitors had a good time, but we don't think they did, and are sure they won't win the National Open." Considered very rude for the time, the **USGA** considered barring him from the 1913 U.S. Open, but he played and finished eighth. In 1914, he traveled to Great Britain to play in the **Open Championship** (he had finished equal fifth in 1913) but missed a ferry, was late for his qualifying round, and never got to play. He booked passage to return on the *Kaiser Wilhelm II*, but it collided with a grain ship in the English Channel, and McDermott spent several hours adrift in a lifeboat before being rescued. He played the 1914 U.S. Open but did not factor, and later that summer, with his depression worsening, he collapsed in his pro shop at Atlantic City Country Club. McDermott never played another round of golf, spending the rest of his life in a psychiatric hospital in Norristown, Pennsylvania.

McKAY, JIM (NÉ JAMES KENNETH "JIM" McMANUS). B. 24 September 1921, Philadelphia, Pennsylvania, United States; D. 7 June 2008, Monkton, Maryland, United States. An American sportscaster, Jim McKay achieved his greatest fame as the "Voice of the Olympics," in the **United States**, but he was also known for hosting ABC Sports golf telecasts for over two decades. He was host or cohost on U.S. television broadcasting the Olympics an unprecedented seven times: six times for ABC Sports—1976 and 1984 for the **Olympic Games**, and the Olympic Winter Games consecutively from 1976 through 1988—and for CBS in 1960. At the 1972 Olympics in Munich, McKay broadcast the news reports of the horrific Israeli hostage massacre, and he was on the air in the United States for over 15 consecutive hours. He was the one who eventually told the world, in his own poignant words, "They're all gone." He received an Emmy for that broadcast, one of 10 individual Emmys won by McKay, nine for sportscaster of the year and one for lifetime achievement. McKay was the lead announcer for ABC on golf telecasts, notably the **U.S. Open** for most of the 1970s and early 1980s.

McLEAN, JAMES CRAIG "JIM." B. 1951. Jim McLean was a top **amateur** player in the Pacific Northwest, playing golf at the University of Houston and competing several times in the **U.S. Open** and once at the **Masters**. He later became a club **professional** and teacher. After his competitive professional career faltered, he started as an assistant and became head pro at Quaker Ridge Country Club in Scarsdale, New York. McLean quickly developed a reputation as a top teacher and is now one of best golf instructors in the world. He has worked with numerous golf professionals and started the Jim McLean Golf School, which is open to amateurs and pros. There are currently six such schools in the **United States**, the first one starting at **Doral Golf Resort**, where McLean has been based since the late 1980s. In 1994, McLean was named PGA Teaching Professional of the Year.

MEDALIST. In **match play** tournaments, there is often a **stroke play** qualifying round, or rounds, which qualifies players to advance to the match play portion of the tournament. The winner of the qualifying round is called the medalist, and that player is seeded first in the match play draw.

MEDINAH COUNTRY CLUB. Medinah Country Club is a private club in Medinah, Illinois, near Chicago, that is known for its No. 3 course, which has hosted three **U.S. Opens** (1949, 1975, 1990) and two **PGA Championships** (1999, 2006). The club has three courses, swimming facilities, and an ornate Byzantine-style clubhouse renowned for its architectural features. Lake Kadijah winds through the grounds of the course and features on several holes of the No. 3 course. The courses were originally designed by **Tom Bendelow**, although No. 3 has been redesigned several times in preparation for major events. The club was founded in 1924 by the Medinah Shriners, who eventually allowed non-Shriners to become members. Medinah is scheduled to host the 2012 **Ryder Cup**.

MEMBER-GUEST. A member-guest is a popular form of **country club** tournament and is often the most important event at a club. For the event, each club member who participates invites one or more guests to partner with in a club tournament, in various formats. The major member-guest event at most tournaments is held over three or four days in midsummer, often in a **match play** tournament. But in addition, many clubs will hold one-day member-guests, usually held in a **stroke play** format. It serves as a way to introduce the club to people and frequently is a source of revenue for the club as well. Large member-guests often have **Calcutta** pools associated with them in which members and their guests may buy shares in their teams.

THE MEMORIAL TOURNAMENT. The Memorial Tournament is a **PGA Tour** invitational hosted by **Jack Nicklaus** at his self-designed course, Muirfield Village Golf Club, in Dublin, Ohio. The event was first started in 1976 and was won that year by Roger Maltbie. Since it is by invitation only, the tournament has a restricted field. Each year, the tournament honors one of the greats of golf by inducting that player into what they call the Champions Club. **Tiger Woods** has won the event four times through 2009, the most ever.

MERION GOLF CLUB. Merion Golf Club is a private club in Ardmore, Pennsylvania, near Philadelphia that has hosted multiple championship tournaments. The club has 36 holes, with a West Course and an East Course, with most of the major championships played on the East Course. The club was founded in 1896 when members of the Merion Cricket Club (founded 1865) opened a **golf course**. In 1910, **Hugh Wilson** designed and built a new course on the current site. Wilson spent several months in 1910 in **Scotland** and **England** to get ideas for the course, and North Berwick Golf Course particularly influenced him. The East Course was opened in 1912 and the West Course in 1914. Through 2009, **Merion** has hosted 17 **USGA** Championships, more than any other club. The course has hosted four **U.S. Opens**, in 1934, 1950, 1971, and 1981, and is scheduled to host the 2013 U.S. Open. The course has also been the site for the **U.S. Amateur**, **U.S. Women's Amateur**, **U.S. Girl's Junior**, the **Walker Cup**, the **Curtis Cup**, and the **World Amateur Team Championship** (Eisenhower Trophy).

Merion is somewhat short for a major championship course in the 21st century but is very tight, with narrow **fairways** and very small, heavily bunkered greens with steep slopes. Merion is unique among American golf courses because it does not have flags atop its "flagsticks" but rather wicker baskets. The wicker baskets originated with a woman who lived near the course, who wove wicker baskets. She donated the baskets to the club, and Merion has a tradition that anyone who wins a USGA event there receives a wicker basket top.

Merion is probably best known for two championships, the 1930 U.S. Amateur and the 1950 U.S. Open. In 1930, **Bob Jones** won the U.S. Amateur at Merion to complete his **Grand Slam** of golf. In 1950, **Ben Hogan** won the U.S. Open in a play-off, signaling his recovery from the bus accident of February 1949 that nearly ended his life. Merion Golf Club became a National Historic Landmark in 1992.

METROPOLITAN AMATEUR. The Metropolitan Amateur, usually called simply the "Met," is an **amateur** championship hosted by the Metropolitan Golf Association since 1899. The event is held at various clubs around metropolitan New York. The event has been won five or more times by several different players—seven by Frank Strafaci (1938–1954), six by Robert Gardner, including five consecutively from 1960 to 1964, and five by Dick Siderowf (1968–1989), George Zahringer (1982–1987), and **Jerry Travers** (1906–1913).

METROPOLITAN OPEN. The Metropolitan Open is an open championship held at various clubs around metropolitan New York since 1905, making it the third oldest open championship in the **United States**, after the **U.S. Open** and the **Western Open**. With the Western Open essentially defunct after the 2006 edition, the Metropolitan Open now trails only the **U.S. Open** among annually held championships in the United States. Hosted by the Metropolitan Golf Association, the event was part of the **PGA Tour** from the tour's inception in the late 1920s through the 1940s and was actually a major championship during that time. The event was won four times by **Alex Smith** from 1905 to 1913, and three times consecutively by **Walter Hagen**, in 1916, 1919, and 1920. The 2009 event was won by former Duke golfer Andrew Giuliani, son of former New York City mayor Rudy Giuliani.

MICKELSON, PHILIP ALFRED "PHIL," "LEFTY," "PHILLY MICK." B. 16 June 1970, San Diego, California, United States. Phil Mickelson, an active American touring **professional**, is one of the three or four greatest players in the world for over a decade now. Mickelson attended Arizona State, where he won three **NCAA Championships** and three Haskins Awards (1990–1992) as the top collegiate golfer. He also won the 1990 **U.S. Amateur**, the only left-hander to win that title, and he won the 1991 Northern Telecom Tucson Open as an amateur, only the fourth amateur to win a **PGA Tour** event. Turning pro shortly after college, Mickelson has won 36 PGA Tour events through 2009. He has won three major championships, the 2004 and 2006 **Masters**, and the 2005 **PGA Championship**.

Mickelson, who long held the title of "Best Player Never to Win a Major Championship," struggled for a decade to win a major until breaking through at the 2004 Masters. After winning his three majors, he had another chance in 2006 in the **U.S. Open** at **Winged Foot**.

Leading well into the fourth round, he came to the 72nd hole with a one-shot lead but drove into the left rough. He then tried a risky recovery, which led to a double **bogey** and handed the championship to Geoff Ogilvy. At the victory ceremony, Mickelson noted, "What an idiot I am." The attempted recovery is typical of Mickelson, who is known for his daring play. This has made him a gallery favorite and occasionally has paid off in big ways, but it has also led to some disasters. Mickelson is very popular with golf fans and is also known for his generosity in charitable giving.

MIDDLECOFF, EMMETT CARY. B. 6 January 1921, Halls, Tennessee, United States; D. 1 September 1998, Memphis, Tennessee, United States. Cary Middlecoff was one of the greatest players of the 1950s, after giving up an early career as a dentist. He won 40 tournaments on the **PGA Tour**, including the 1955 **Masters** and the 1949 and 1956 **U.S. Open**. Middlecoff won the **Vardon Trophy** for the lowest scoring average on tour in 1956 and played on three **Ryder Cup** teams, in 1952, 1955, and 1959. In addition to his prowess as a player, Middlecoff was known as a very slow player and for a lengthy pause at the top of his backswing. He was inducted into the **World Golf Hall of Fame** in 1986.

MID-IRONS. Mid-irons are the middle irons in a full set. They usually include the 4-iron, 5-iron, and 6-iron. As players have started using fewer and fewer long irons, this term is not used much anymore, and some **professional** and **amateur** players often carry nothing longer than a 4-iron in their bags. *See also* GOLF CLUBS.

MILLER, JOHN LAURENCE "JOHNNY." B. 29 April 1947, San Francisco, California, United States. Johnny Miller was an **amateur** star who won the **U.S. Junior Amateur** in 1964. He attended Brigham Young University, where he played college golf. In 1966, he played in the **U.S. Open** at **Olympic Club**, near his home in San Francisco, finishing eighth as an amateur. He joined the **PGA Tour** in 1969 and won 25 PGA Tour events, his last two at the Pebble Beach Pro-Am in 1987 and 1994, several years after his last previous win in 1983. In 1974 and 1975, Miller was probably the best player in the world, dominating the tour in those years, especially early in the years, in the desert tournaments in Arizona and California. His victories were especially emphatic. He won the 1974 Kaiser International by eight shots, the 1975 Phoenix Open by 15 shots, the second largest margin ever on the **PGA Tour**, and the next week, the 1975 Tucson Open by nine shots. He did this with some of the most precise iron play ever seen.

Miller won two major titles. In 1973, seemingly out of contention after the third round, he won the U.S. Open at fabled **Oakmont** when he shot 63 in the final round, a U.S. Open record at the time, and often considered the greatest round ever played. In 1976, he won the **Open Championship (British Open)**. Tall, blond, and handsome, Miller made a great deal of money in endorsements and backed off the PGA Tour in the late 1970s, playing less and less often, not really motivated to win further tournaments. Miller has since become a golf analyst for NBC Television, where he is quite outspoken, making him popular with the fans but often not well liked by the players.

MILLS, MARY. B. 19 January 1940, Laurel, Mississippi, United States. Mary Mills grew up in rural Mississippi and attended Millsaps College, where she majored in philosophy and played on the men's golf team. She won eight straight titles (1954–1961) in the Mississippi Women's Amateur. In 1962, she turned **professional** and won the **LPGA** Rookie of the Year Award that year. She played the LPGA through the early 1980s, winning nine tournaments, including three majors, the 1963 **U.S. Women's Open** and the 1964 and 1973 **LPGA Championships**. In the early 1990s, Mills returned to college at Florida International University, earning a master's degree in landscape architecture. She now designs **golf courses** and is a top teaching professional.

MINIATURE GOLF. Miniature golf is a smaller version of golf that is played on special putting courses. In 1867, the **Royal and Ancient Golf Club of St. Andrews** designed a putting course in the town of **St. Andrews.** Called the "Himalayas," it still operates today and is open to public play. Miniature golf is often found in resort towns, where courses are often played by tourists, many times in or near beach or lake towns. Many of these miniature **golf courses** are quite tricked up and do not resemble anything near a true putting competition. However, certain variants of miniature golf courses have been more realistic, notably those of Putt-Putt, which has conducted tournaments and national championships under the aegis of the Professional Putters Association (PPA). There is a World Minigolf Sport Federation, which governs the game in various guises in the **United States** and Europe and conducts a biennial world championship.

MONTGOMERIE, COLIN STUART "MONTY," OBE. B. 23 June 1963, Glasgow, Scotland. Colin Montgomerie was one of the greatest European players of the late 1980s and 1990s, but he struggled to win a major championship or any tournament when he ventured to the U.S. **PGA Tour**. As an **amateur**, Montgomerie played in the 1985 and 1987 **Walker Cup** and then turned **professional** in 1988. On the European Tour, he has won 31 tournaments through 2009 and was the leader of the Order of Merit from 1993 to 1999, a record number of years. Monty has been ranked as high as number two in the world and has played for Great Britain in the **Ryder Cup** continuously from 1991 to 2006. His failure to win a major title has led to him being given the unofficial title of "Best Player Never to Have Won a Major Championship." Montgomerie has finished second five times at majors—the 1994, 1997, and 2006 **U.S. Open**, the 1995 **PGA Championship**, and the 2005 **Open Championship (British Open)**. At times, Montgomerie has had a dour appearance on the course, and therefore, many U.S. fans have not accepted him. This has led to some difficult times as American galleries have gotten on him a bit, often quite unfairly.

MORRIS, THOMAS MITCHELL "TOM" OR "OLD TOM," SR. B. 16 June 1821, St. Andrews, Fife, Scotland; D. 24 May 1908, St. Andrews, Fife, Scotland. Old Tom Morris is the first tournament champion in golf and the pioneer of Scottish **professional** golf. He apprenticed under **Allan Robertson**, the top player in the world in the era before the **Open Championship (British Open)**, but Old Tom soon surpassed his teacher in playing ability. Old Tom Morris won the Open Championship in 1861, 1862, 1864, and 1867, still the oldest ever victor at the age of 46 in 1867. Old Tom's son, **Young Tom Morris**, became an even greater player, winning four consecutive Open Championships before dying at only 24 years of age. Old

Tom Morris was known for more than his playing ability. He was a renowned clubmaker, ballmaker (in the age of the **featherie**), club professional, and course designer, and is often called the "father of modern greenkeeping." Old Tom died a few weeks after sustaining injuries while falling down the stairs of the **St. Andrews** clubhouse.

MORRIS, THOMAS MITCHELL "TOM" OR "YOUNG TOM," JR. B. 20 April 1851, St. Andrews, Fife, Scotland; D. 25 December 1875, St. Andrews, Fife, Scotland. Young Tom Morris was the son of **Old Tom Morris**, one of the first great champions of golf. But Young Tom became the better player, and his father admitted that as well. A true phenom, Young Tom won the **Open Championship (British Open)** in 1868 when he was only 17 years of age. He then won again in 1869 and 1870, retiring the championship belt. With no belt to play for, the tournament was cancelled in 1871, but Morris returned to win his fourth consecutive title in 1872. He was then equal third in 1873 and second in 1874. In early September 1875, Young Tom partnered his father in a challenge match against Willie and Mungo Park, when he received a telegram that his young wife, pregnant with their first child, was very sick. Though he rushed home, they both died before he arrived. Young Tom Morris died three months later, with the official cause of death listed as "heartbreak."

MUIRFIELD. Muirfield, the home of the **Honourable Company of Edinburgh Golfers**, is one the great **links** courses of the British Isles, located in Gullane, East Lothian, **Scotland**, alongside the Firth of Forth. The course has been the host of the **Open Championship (British Open)** 15 times. It has also hosted the **British Senior Open**, the **Amateur Championship (British Amateur)**, the **Ryder Cup**, the **Walker Cup**, and the **Curtis Cup**. The Honourable Company of Edinburgh Golfers is one of the oldest golf clubs in the world, with club records dating to 1744. It was first located at Leith, Scotland, then at **Musselburgh**, both **public courses**, before the private Muirfield was built in 1891. **Jack Nicklaus** has often stated that Muirfield was his favorite course in the Open rota (he won his first Open Championship there in 1966), and he named his own club in Dublin, Ohio, after it, Muirfield Village Golf Club.

MULLIGAN. A mulligan is a golf shot that is basically a "do-over." Many club players will allow a player on the first tee to hit a second tee ball, choosing the better of the two shots, and this is termed a "mulligan." "Mulligan" is occasionally used to refer to any "do-over" shot in an informal game, but used properly, the term refers only to the second shot on the first tee. A mulligan is not allowed in any formal match or tournament. The origin of the term is uncertain but there are several theories. One relates to a Canadian player named David Mulligan, who often played what he called a "correction shot" off the first tee and his friends named the shot for him. He became the manager of the Waldorf-Astoria Hotel in New York and brought the concept to the **United States** and his club, **Winged Foot**. Another theory is that the shot was named after a New Jersey locker room attendant, Buddy Mulligan, who often replayed his opening tee shot. The term has also been attributed to Thomas Mulligan, an Anglo-Irish aristocrat, who felt that a player should have an opportunity on the first tee to get off to a good start. By this definition, a player may take several attempts on the first tee, until they are happy with the shot, often called "hit 'til you're happy."

MUNICIPAL COURSES. In the **United States**, courses are usually designated as public or private. **Public courses** may be played by anybody who pays the green fee. One subset of public courses are municipal courses, which are courses owned by towns or counties. Municipal courses are often very, very busy courses, because they tend to have lower green fees and are frequented by players who may not be able to play at exclusive courses. But there are some municipal courses that are quite good, notably **Bethpage Black** at Bethpage State Park on Long Island (technically owned by New York State, and not a municipality), which has twice hosted the **U.S. Open**, in 2002 and 2009; and Torrey Pines in San Diego, which hosted the 2008 U.S. Open. Another notable course, near Boston, is Ponkapoag Golf Course, a **Donald Ross** course, which has hosted numerous local tournaments, but has fallen into disrepair in recent years.

MUSSELBURGH LINKS. Musselburgh is one of the oldest **golf courses** still in existence. There is evidence that golf was played there regularly in the late 17th century, and there are rumors that Mary Queen of Scots played golf there in the 16th century. The course is located in Musselburgh, East Lothian, **Scotland**. The course originally had seven holes, but an eighth was added in 1838, and it was made a full nine-hole course, as it remains today at **par** 34, in 1870. Musselburgh was one of the three courses used for the original rotation for the **Open Championship (British Open)**, along with **Prestwick** and the **Old Course** at **St. Andrews**. Musselburgh hosted six Open Championships, in 1873, 1877, 1880, 1883, 1886, and 1889. One of Musselburgh's legacies to the game is in the size of the golf hole. The instrument used to cut holes on **putting greens** was 4¼ inches in diameter at Musselburgh, but other courses in the 19th century used different diameters. In 1893, the **R&A** adopted the Musselburgh hole diameter as the standard for the game, which has remained to this day. Musselburgh is now a public golf course, owned by the East Lothian Town Council.

– N –

NAGLE, KELVIN DAVID GEORGE "KEL." B. 21 December 1920, North Sydney, New South Wales, Australia. Kel Nagle was one of the first great **Australian professionals**. He won 61 tournaments on the **Australian PGA Tour**, 30 more than **Greg Norman**, who is second on that all-time list. Nagle won the 1960 **Open Championship (British Open)**, narrowly defeating **Arnold Palmer**, who had already won the **Masters** and **U.S. Open** in 1960. With **Peter Thomson**, Nagle won the World Cup in 1954 and 1959. He later won the 1971, 1973, and 1975 PGA Senior Championship in the **United States**. Nagle was inducted into the **World Golf Hall of Fame** in 2007.

NAKAMURA, TORAKICHI "PETE," "TORA-SAN." B. 17 September 1915, Yokohama, Kanagawa Prefecture, Japan; D. 11 February 2008, Zama, Kanagawa Prefecture, Japan. Pete Nakamura was the first great Japanese **professional** in a country where the sport became very popular in the 1950s and 1960s. In 1957, Nakamura and Koichi Ono led **Japan** to the team victory at the **Canada Cup**, with Nakamura also winning the individual title, which often gets credit for starting the golf boom in Japan. A three-time winner of the Japanese Open, in 1958, Nakamura became the first Japanese golfer to play in the **Masters**. He also won the Japanese PGA four times and the Japanese PGA Senior twice. Nakamura later became a golf administrator and became president of the Japanese LPGA in 1974.

NANTZ, JAMES WILLIAM, "JIM," III. B. 17 May 1959, Charlotte, North Carolina, United States. Although born in Charlotte, Jim Nantz grew up in New Jersey. He was a good junior player and attended the University of Houston on a golf scholarship, rooming with future **PGA Tour** players **Fred Couples** and Blaine McAlister. But he never pursued **professional** golf, instead majoring in broadcasting in college, and has become one of the top golf announcers on U.S. television. Nantz joined CBS Television in 1985 and has become their lead tower announcer on all their televised golf broadcasts. He is also known for announcing the NFL and college basketball (especially the Final Four), and he was the lead announcer at both the 1992 and 1994 Olympic Winter Games. Nantz received an honorary doctorate from Houston in 2001. He received the Basketball Hall of Fame's Curt Gowdy award for sportscasting. In 2009, he won a Sports Emmy for Outstanding Play-by-Play Sports Personality.

NASSAU. A "Nassau" is a betting game played by club golfers, which is probably the most popular betting game in golf. A Nassau is almost always held at **match play**, usually either in singles or **four-ball** matches. Three points are awarded, one point to the winner of the front nine, one point to the winner of the back nine, and one point to the winner of the full round. A set amount of money is bet on each point, so a player may win the match 3-0 and win three times that set amount. However, Nassaus get more complicated because of press bets. In a press bet, a player may press and start a new match at that point. Usually, a press is allowed any time a player goes 2 down. But occasionally, presses are allowed when a player goes 1 down. Thus there could be, theoretically, up to nine bets on a side. Presses are usually at the option of the player who is down, but in some forms of the Nassau, players will play "automatics," in which the press bet automatically occurs whenever a player goes 2 down, or even more rarely, when the player goes 1 down. The origin of the Nassau is usually credited to John B. Coles Tappan, the club captain at Nassau Country Club in New York, who is said to have invented the game in 1900. *See also* CALCUTTA.

NATIONAL AMPUTEE GOLF ASSOCIATION (NAGA). The National Amputee Golf Association was formed in 1954 through the inspiration of Dale Bourisseau, a World War II veteran who had a leg amputated due to injuries sustained in the war. He contacted similar veterans and encouraged them to stay active by playing golf. Bourisseau and 11 others started NAGA, which now has over 2,000 members in the **United States** and 17 other nations. NAGA holds annual national championships and sponsors regional and local championships throughout the United States. NAGA also started the First Swing Program, which teaches adaptive golf to people with physical disabilities, with over 30 clinics held across the United States every year. Another NAGA effort is the Golf for the Physically Challenged program, which enables many to realize that they can play the game and have fun outdoors. In 1989, to assist a growing number of physical, occupational, and recreational therapists who realized that golf could be used as a means for rehabilitation, NAGA brought its First Swing program to hospitals and rehabilitation centers throughout the United States. Many amputees and physically challenged individuals have rediscovered their sense of personal pride through participation in these NAGA golf programs.

NATIONAL GOLF FOUNDATION (NGF). The National Golf Foundation is a consulting group based in Jupiter, Florida, that assists companies in the golf business. It was founded in 1936 by golf writer **Herb Graffis** and his brother, Joe Graffis. The NGF describes itself as "the industry leader in providing relevant information and insights on the business of golf, offering golf-business research, information and consulting services to companies and organizations worldwide." There are over 6,000 member companies affiliated with the National Golf Foundation.

NATIONAL GOLF LINKS OF AMERICA. The National Golf Links of America is a **links**-style course in Southampton, on Long Island. It was designed by **Charles Blair Macdonald** and was opened in 1908. The course is adjacent to **Shinnecock Hills Golf Club**. The "National," as it is called, is a shorter, slightly quirky course but is one of the finest examples of early **golf course architecture** in the **United States**. The National hosted the first **Walker Cup** in 1922 and has been selected to host the 2013 Walker Cup.

NATIONWIDE TOUR. The Nationwide Tour, which was started in 1990, is the current name of the developmental tour for the U.S. **PGA Tour**. It was formerly known as the Ben Hogan Tour (1990–1992), the Nike Tour (1993–1999), and the Buy.com Tour (2000–2002), and became the Nationwide Tour in 2003. The Nationwide Tour rivals the **European PGA Tour** for being the second strongest pro tour in the world. It is one of nine tours that award points toward the **World Golf Ranking**. At the end of each season, the top 25 players on the Nationwide Tour money list earn PGA Tour cards. A player may also advance to the PGA Tour by winning three Nationwide Tour events in a single calendar year, termed a "battlefield promotion." Numerous top PGA players started their careers on the Nationwide Tour or one of its ancestors, among them Tom Lehmann, Chad Campbell, Stewart Cink, Zach Johnson, and Jeff Maggert. Players qualify for the Nationwide Tour via the PGA Tour **Q School** (or Qualifying School). The top finishers at that event, usually about 25, earn PGA Tour Cards. The next 50 players earn cards to play on the Nationwide Tour. Players may also qualify each week for Nationwide events via a Monday qualifying tournament. Former PGA Tour winners may play on the Nationwide Tour when they are 48 or 49 years of age, as a way to prepare for the **Champions Tour**.

NCAA GOLF CHAMPIONSHIP. The NCAA Golf Championship, technically, the "NCAA Division I Men's Golf Championships," is one of the top **amateur** golf tournaments in the world. It takes place on different courses annually and awards a team championship and an individual championship. With many international amateurs playing college golf in the **United States**, the NCAA brings together one of the strongest fields in amateur golf each year. The individual title was won three times each by **Ben Crenshaw** and **Phil Mickelson**. Yale University has won the most team titles, with 21, but most of those were early in the 20th century, their last title coming in 1943. The University of Houston holds the modern record, with 16 titles since 1956, including 12 of 15 from 1956 to 1970. The NCAA has also conducted championships for Division II schools since 1963 and Division III schools since 1975. Appendix 6 includes a list of champions.

NCAA WOMEN'S GOLF CHAMPIONSHIP. The NCAA Women's Golf Championship for Division I schools has been contested since 1982. Prior to that time, Intercollegiate Championships for **women** were conducted by the Association for Intercollegiate Athletics for Women (AIAW) from 1966 to 1982. In 1982, both the AIAW and NCAA conducted national collegiate championships, both won by Kathy Baker and the University of Tulsa. From 1941 to 1965, women competed in national collegiate championships conducted by the Division for Girls and Women's Sports (DGWS). These were the first national collegiate championships in any sport for women. They were contested under the aegis of several different organizations, initially, the American Alliance for Health, Physical Education, and Recreation (AAHPER), and later, the Commission on Intercollegiate Athletics for Women (CIAW). The NCAA has also conducted championships for Division II and Division III schools, since 1996. From 1996 to 1999, this was a combined Division II/III event, but there have been separate tournaments since 2000. In Division I, no woman has ever won two AIAW or two NCAA golf championships, although Kathy Baker, as noted above, won both titles in 1982. Charlotte Williams won two titles in Division II in 2003 and 2004 for Rollins College, and two Division III titles for Methodist College in 2005 and 2006, winning four consecutive national collegiate championships. Appendix 7 includes a list of champions.

NEAREST POINT OF RELIEF. The nearest point of relief as defined in the **Rules of Golf** is an important concept for tournament play because it strictly delineates how a player may take relief in certain situations. On television, one will often see players carefully marking their nearest point of relief, usually assisted by a rules official. Nearest point of relief is used to take relief from **ground under repair**, from an immovable obstruction, or from the wrong **putting green**.

To find the nearest point of relief, the player takes a stance with the club to be used for the next shot, demonstrating that complete relief from the situation is being. Thus, in taking relief from ground under repair, it must be demonstrated that the player is no longer standing in ground under repair. The point at which the ball would lie if the player were to play a ball from that stance is then marked, usually with a tee. This is the nearest point of relief. The player then must drop the ball within one club length of this point. The one club length may be measured with any club, and the longest club in the bag is always chosen, often the **driver**. At **PGA Tour** orientation, players are reminded to remove their head covers when making such a measurement. Another tee will mark the second point, and the ball should be dropped between the two tees, being certain to drop no nearer the hole. Once a correct drop has been made, the player or official will announce that the "**ball is in play**" and play resumes from that point. If after dropping the ball, it rolls nearer the hole, back into the area from which relief is sought, or into a hazard, the ball must be re-dropped. If it does so again, the player is entitled to place the ball at the point where it struck the ground on the second drop, which is usually marked by the rules official or the player's **caddie**.

NELSON, JOHN BYRON "LORD BYRON," JR. B. 4 February 1912, Waxahachie, Texas, United States; D. 26 September 2006, Roanoke, Texas, United States. Byron Nelson is virtually always included in any list of the top ten golfers of all time. A native Texan, Nelson grew up around Fort Worth, **caddieing** at Glen Garden County Club, as did **Ben Hogan**. Later, with Hogan and **Sam Snead**, Nelson formed the Great Triumvirate of the 1940s. Nelson turned **professional** in 1932 and won his first **PGA Tour** event, the New Jersey Open, in 1935. He won 52 events on the PGA Tour, including five major championships, the 1939 **U.S. Open**, the 1937 and 1942 **Masters**, and the 1940 and 1945 **PGA Championship**. Nelson played in the **Open Championship** (**British Open**) only once, in 1937, placing fifth. In 1945, Nelson enjoyed one of the greatest years in golf, possibly the greatest ever. He won 18 PGA tournaments that year, an unrivaled record, and won 11 of them consecutively. The second best mark is six in a row by Hogan and **Tiger Woods** (twice). The 11 consecutive victories is considered the one absolutely unbreakable golf record. After 1945, Nelson withdrew from the golf scene. He did not stop competing fully, winning some tournaments through the 1955 **French Open**, but he never again played the PGA Tour full-time, preferring to spend time on a ranch he had bought in Texas. Had he continued playing, it is likely his record would have been even greater.

Nelson was one of the finest gentlemen in the game of golf. Until his death, he hosted the Byron Nelson Classic held at various courses in Dallas. In 1974, Nelson received the **Bob Jones Award** from the **USGA** for distinguished sportsmanship in golf, and he was inducted into the **World Golf Hall of Fame** in the same year. In 1997, the PGA Tour gave him their Lifetime Achievement Award. Shortly after his death, he was posthumously honored with the Congressional Gold Medal.

NELSON, LARRY GENE. B. 10 September 1947, Fort Payne, Alabama, United States. Larry Nelson came late to the game of golf, starting to play at 21 years of age, after returning from service in Vietnam. He taught himself to play by studying **Ben Hogan**'s book *Five Lessons: The Modern Fundamentals of Golf*. Nelson turned **professional** in 1971 and qualified for the **PGA Tour** in 1974. He won his first PGA Tour event in 1979, the Jackie Gleason-Inverrary Classic, and eventually won 10 events on tour. Nelson won three majors, the **PGA Championship** in 1981 and 1987, and the 1983 **U.S. Open**. He also won 19 times on the **Champions Tour**. Nelson was on the **Ryder Cup** team in 1979, 1981, and 1987.

NEUMANN, LISELOTTE "LOTTA." B. 20 May 1966, Finspång, Sweden. Though her records were surpassed by **Annika Sörenstam**, Lotta Neumann was the first great Swedish golfer, male or female, and she is responsible for the golf boom that occurred in the Scandanavian country. After playing for Sweden in the 1982 and 1984 **World Amateur Team Championships**, Neumann turned **professional** in 1985. She joined the **LPGA** in 1988 and that same year won her first tournament, starting rather auspiciously by winning the **U.S. Women's Open** at Baltimore Country Club. It was her only major championship, but she was a runner-up in majors five times and placed third four times. Neumann won 13 times on the LPGA. She won the 1994 **Women's British Open**. Neumann played for Europe in the **Solheim Cup** in 1990, 1992, 1994, 1996, 1998, and 2000. She and Sörenstam won the 2006 Women's World Cup for Sweden.

NIBLICK. In the 19th century, irons were not called by numbers as they are now but rather by names. A niblick was a short iron that approximated today's 9-iron, or wedge. *See also* GOLF CLUBS.

NICKLAUS, JACK WILLIAM "THE GOLDEN BEAR." B. 21 January 1940, Dublin, Ohio, United States. Jack Nicklaus, in the opinion of many, is the greatest golfer of all time. Nicklaus grew up near Columbus, Ohio, and attended Ohio State University, winning the Ohio Open when he was only 16 (in 1956). He won the **NCAA Championship** in 1961 and the **U.S. Amateur** in 1959 and 1961. Nicklaus' greatest performance as an amateur likely came at the 1960 **World Amateur Team Championship**. Played at venerable **Merion Golf Club**, Nicklaus won the individual title by 13 shots with a score of 269, 11-under-par. It was thought for a time that Nicklaus would remain an **amateur**, to emulate his idol, **Bob Jones**, but in 1962, he did turn **professional**. Although he struggled a bit in his first few months on tour, Nicklaus won the 1962 **U.S. Open** for his first professional victory, defeating **Arnold Palmer** in a play-off. At the time, Palmer was the greatest, and most popular, player in the world, but Nicklaus soon surpassed him in victories and major titles.

On the **PGA Tour,** Nicklaus won 73 tournaments, second all-time after **Sam Snead**, and now being challenged by **Tiger Woods**. More important, Nicklaus won 18 major professional titles, sometimes listed as 20 majors because the U.S. Amateur used to be considered a major championship, surpassing the record of his idol, Jones. Woods is challenging this record, with 14 through 2009, but Nicklaus also finished second in majors 19 times, giving him 37 placements in the top two at major championships, a record Woods is not approaching. Nicklaus won his last major improbably at the 1986 **Masters**, when he was 46 years of age and past his prime. He had not won a major since 1980, when he won the U.S. Open and the PGA. Nicklaus played on six **Ryder Cup** teams and led the PGA Tour money list eight times. He also won 10 tournaments on the **Champions Tour**, even though he played that tour only sporadically.

In his senior years, Nicklaus has emphasized his career as a **golf course architect**. He first began designing courses in the late 1960s with Desmond Muirhead and later with **Pete Dye**. He soon formed his own course design company. His course credits include **Harbour Town Golf Links**, his own Muirfield Village in Dublin, Ohio, and **Glen Abbey** near Toronto, longtime home of the **Canadian Open**, which was his first solo design. Nicklaus has hosted the **Memorial Tournament** at Muirfield Village since 1976. Nicklaus became a charter member of the **World Golf Hall of Fame** in 1974.

NIKE TOUR. *See* NATIONWIDE TOUR.

NORMAN, GREGORY JOHN, "GREG," "THE GREAT WHITE SHARK," "THE SHARK," AM. B. 10 February 1955, Mount Isa, Queensland, Australia. Greg Norman is the best-known **Australian** golfer ever, and one of the most popular players of the 1980s and 1990s. Tall with a wispy waist and almost white-blond hair, he was known as "The Great White Shark," later shortened to "The Shark," which also signified his aggressive playing style. Norman turned **professional** when he was 20 and began playing the European Tour the next year. He won his first of five **Australian Opens** in 1980 and joined the U.S. **PGA Tour** in 1981. Norman has played all over the world, winning 20 tournaments on the U.S. PGA Tour, 14 on the **European PGA Tour**, and 31 on the **Australian PGA Tour**. He won two major championships, the 1986 and 1993 **Open Championship (British Open)**. But that fails to tell the story of Norman in major championships.

Greg Norman was expected to win multiple major titles, and he challenged many times, but had difficulty winning. In 1986, he actually completed what some have called the "Saturday Slam," when he led all four major championships after the third round. But he won only the Open Championship that year, losing to **Jack Nicklaus**' comeback at the **Masters** at the age of 46, and watching Bob Tway hole a bunker shot on the 72nd hole of the **PGA Championship** at Inverness. Norman also finished second at the 1984 and 1995 **U.S. Open**, losing the 1984 title in a play-off to **Fuzzy Zoeller**, the 1989 Open Championship, and the 1993 PGA. But it was the Masters that may forever haunt him. In 1987, he lost a play-off to Larry Mize who holed a long chip shot on the second play-off hole, the 11th, from an almost impossible position to the right of the green. In 1996, Norman led the Masters by six shots over **Nick Faldo**. He seemed to finally be in position to win the tournament he most wanted, but in the final round he shot 78, while Faldo played a flawless 67 to win by five shots, with Norman again finishing second.

But Norman has done well for himself. His good looks, easy smile, and classy acceptance of some very difficult losses made him extremely popular among fans. His length and straightness off the tee also attracted fans. Norman was described by Jack Nicklaus as the straightest long **driver** in the history of the game. Endorsement dollars flooded his way, and through some investments in golf companies that were later bought out, Norman became the richest golfer ever, until the advent of **Tiger Woods**. Great White Shark Enterprises has its hand in many ventures, including **golf course** design and a wine label. Norman was a former part owner and chairman of MacGregor Golf. Norman has been married twice, the second time in 2008 to tennis star Chris Evert, but in late 2009, they announced that they were separating after one year of marriage.

NORMAN, MURRAY IRWIN "MOE." B. 10 July 1929, Kitchener, Ontario, Canada; D. 4 September 2004, Kitchener, Ontario, Canada. Moe Norman was a Canadian **professional** golfer who is somewhat of an urban legend in the world of golf. He is often considered the greatest ball striker in the history of the game, a title bestowed on him by none other than **Sam Snead**. To hone his ball-striking skills, Norman practiced possibly more than any player ever, often hitting 1,200 balls a day. He played competitively in **Canada** and was elected a member of the Canadian Golf Hall of Fame. But Norman was quirky, and some people considered him an "idiot savant of golf." He was shy, and spoke rapidly, often repeating all his phrases twice.

NORTH AND SOUTH AMATEUR. The North and South Amateur is a men's **match play amateur** tournament that has been one of the top amateur events in the **United States** since its inception in 1901. It is always held on the No. 2 course at **Pinehurst** Resort. The event is somewhat invitational, but non-invited players may enter qualifying rounds to get into the match-play format. The greatest number of wins in the event is seven by George Dunlap between 1931 and 1942. Appendix 6 includes a list of champions.

NORTH AND SOUTH OPEN. The North and South Open was a **professional** event from 1902 to 1951 and was a part of the **PGA Tour** from its inception in the late 1920s. Always held at the No. 2 Course at **Pinehurst** Resort, prior to World War II, it was a major professional championship. Many of the leading pros of the era won the tournament, notably **Ben Hogan** in 1940, his first PGA Tournament victory. The most wins in the event was six by Alex Ross, between 1902 and 1915, which include the first event in 1902. Ross' better-known brother, **Donald Ross**, who designed the early Pinehurst courses, including No. 2, won it three times, in 1903, 1905, and 1906. Appendix 4 includes a list of champions.

NORTH AND SOUTH WOMEN'S AMATEUR. The North and South Women's Amateur is a **match play** tournament for female amateurs, which has been held annually since 1903. It is always held on the No. 2 course at **Pinehurst** Resort. The event is somewhat invitational, but non-invited players may enter qualifying rounds to get into the match-play format. The greatest number of wins in the event is six by three players—**Glenna Collett Vare** from 1922 to 1930, Estelle Lawson Page from 1937 to 1945, and Barbara McIntire from 1957 to 1971. Appendix 7 includes a list of champions.

NORTH, ANDREW STEWART "ANDY." B. 9 March 1950, Thorp, Wisconsin, United States. Andy North grew up in Wisconsin. He played golf at the University of Florida, where he was a three-time All-American, and won the 1971 **Western Amateur**. North turned **professional** in 1972 and would win three tournaments on the **PGA Tour**. But two of those were biggies. In 1978 and 1985, North won the **U.S. Open**. His other victory came at the 1977 American Express Westchester Classic. A tall man, but not an overly long hitter, North was known for his putting stroke, which certainly helped him on U.S. Open greens. In 1993, North began a second career as a golf analyst for ESPN and has continued in that capacity through 2009.

– O –

O'CONNOR, CHRISTY "HIMSELF," SR. B. 21 December 1924, Knocknacarra, County Galway, Ireland. Christy O'Connor was the first great Irish **professional**. He began his golf career as a **caddie** at the Galway Club. He turned professional in 1946 and played in every **Ryder Cup** from 1955 to 1973, setting a record of 10 appearances, later broken by **Nick Faldo**. In the years before a formal European Tour, O'Connor won a significant British professional tournament every year from 1955 to 1970, winning 43 professional events in all. He never managed to win the **Open Championship (British Open)**, his best finish being second in 1965. In 1961 and 1962, he led the British Order of Merit. As a senior, he won the U.S. PGA Senior Championship six times and the World Senior Championship twice, in 1976 and 1977. O'Connor was inducted into the **World Golf Hall of Fame** in 2009. His son, **Christy O'Connor Jr.**, also became a top Irish professional player.

O'CONNOR, CHRISTY "JUNIOR," JR. B. 19 August 1948, Galway, County Galway, Ireland. Christy O'Connor Jr. is the son of **Christy O'Connor**, and both were top Irish **professionals**. Junior turned professional in 1967 and played almost exclusively on the European Tour, until his senior years. He twice played on the **Ryder Cup** team and won four European Tour events. As a senior, he competed in both the U.S. and Europe, winning two events on each tour.

OAKLAND HILLS COUNTRY CLUB. Oakland Hills Country Club is a private club in Bloomfield, Michigan, not far from Detroit. It has two courses, the North and South. The South Course has hosted numerous **professional** championships. The club was opened in 1916, and what would become the South Course, designed by renowned **golf course architect Donald Ross,** was opened on 13 June 1918. The club's first professional was **Walter Hagen**. Oakland Hills is best known for hosting the **U.S. Open** six times, in 1924, 1937, 1951, 1961, 1985, and 1996. In 1951, the South Course was redesigned for the U.S. Open by **Robert Trent Jones**, who made it extremely difficult. **Ben Hogan** won the championship with a score of 287, 7-over-par, which includes a final round 67, one of only two rounds under **par** all week. After shooting that final round, Hogan memorably stated, "I am glad I brought this course, this monster, to its knees." Oakland Hills has also hosted the **Western Open**, the **PGA Championship**, the **U.S. Amateur**, the **U.S. Senior Open**, and the **Ryder Cup**.

OAKMONT COUNTRY CLUB. Oakmont Country Club is a club near Pittsburgh, in Oakmont, Pennsylvania. It is one of the classic **golf courses** of the penal school of golf architecture. It is one of the best-known courses in the **United States** and has hosted the **U.S. Open** eight times—in 1927, 1935, 1953, 1962, 1973, 1983, 1994, and 2007. It is also scheduled to host the 2016 U.S. Open. Oakmont is extremely difficult and is routinely listed among the top 10 courses in the country, with a **course rating** of 77.5 as of 2009. The course was designed by Henry Fownes, a Pittsburgh native who designed only one golf course, and opened in 1903. Oakmont is especially known for its greens, often considered the fastest greens in golf. Its bunkers were originally furrowed with a heavy, toothed rake to make them even more difficult, and the original course had over 300 bunkers. Oakmont has also hosted the **U.S. Women's Open**, **U.S. Amateur**, and **PGA Championship**. At the 1973 U.S. Open, **Johnny Miller** recorded one of golf's most famous rounds when he came from behind in the fourth round to win the tournament by shooting 63, at the time a U.S. Open record.

OBSTRUCTIONS. The **Rules of Golf** define an obstruction as "anything artificial, including the artificial surfaces and sides of roads and paths and manufactured ice, except: a) objects defining **out-of-bounds**, such as walls, fences, stakes, and railings; b) any part of an immovable artificial object that is out-of-bounds; and c) any construction declared by the Committee to be an integral part of the course." The definition further states, "An obstruction is a movable obstruction if it may be moved without unreasonable effort, without unduly delaying play and without causing damage. Otherwise it is an immovable obstruction. The Committee may make a Local Rule declaring a movable obstruction to be an immovable obstruction." On the **PGA Tour** or at other televised golf events, the committee always has a local rule for temporary immovable obstructions, basically referring to television towers. When these obstruct a player's swing or stance or when they obstruct a player's line of play between the ball and the hole, the player is entitled to drop the ball at the nearest point of relief.

OCHOA REYES (-CONESA), LORENA. B. 15 November 1981, Guadalajara, Mexico. Lorena Ochoa is a female Mexican **professional** who ascended to the number one spot in the **World Golf Ranking** in 2007. Ochoa was a superb junior player, winning over 60 tournaments in Mexico. She attended college at the University of Arizona, where she was NCAA Player of the Year in 2001 and 2002, winning the **NCAA** title both her freshman and sophomore years. After her sophomore year, Ochoa turned professional and played on the Futures Tour, where she was the Player of the Year. She joined the **LPGA** in 2003 and won her first two tournaments in 2004. In April 2007, she surpassed **Annika Sörenstam** to become the top ranked player in the world. From 2004 to 2009, she won 29 LPGA events, including two majors, the 2007 **Women's British Open** and the 2008 **Kraft Nabisco (Dinah Shore).** This makes her eligible for the **World Golf Hall of Fame**, although she will not be strictly eligible until 2012, after completing 10 years on tour. Ochoa was the 2006 Associated Press Female Athlete of the Year. Ochoa has formed Ochoa Sports Management, which serves as her agent and runs the LPGA Corona Championship, a tour event in Mexico, and the Ochoa Invitational, a charity event.

OFFSET. Offset is a measurement used in club design. If one follows the center line of a golf shaft down to the ground, the clubface may precisely touch that line, in which case the club has no offset. However, most clubs have some offset, such that the clubface is recessed, by a curve in the **hosel**, so that the clubface is slightly posterior to the extended line of the shaft. Clubs are usually designed with a set amount of offset, and short irons will often have more offset. Among better players, such as touring pros, when they request a new set of clubs, the amount of offset on each iron is usually among the design characteristics they will specify.

OKAMOTO, AYAKO. B. 2 April 1951, Akitsu, Hiroshima, Japan. Ayako Okamoto followed **Chako Higuchi** as the star of Japanese **women**'s golf. Okamoto won 44 tournaments in Japan and won 17 times on the **LPGA** from 1982 to 1992. Her best year was 1987 when she won four tournaments on the LPGA and was voted the Player of the Year. She was unfortunate in never winning a major championship, placing second six times, including a play-off loss in 1987 for the **U.S. Women's Open** to **Laura Davies**. Okamoto returned to the Japanese LPGA in 1993 and played on that tour until 2005. She was inducted into the **World Golf Hall of Fame** in 2005.

OLAZÁBAL MANTEROLA, JOSÉ MARÍA, "OLLIE." B. 5 February 1966, Hondarribia, Basque Country, Spain. José María Olazábal is a Spanish **professional** golfer who followed **Seve Ballesteros** as the best player from that country. Olazábal grew up in the Basque Country and won the 1984 **British Amateur** when he was only 18. He turned professional in 1986, finishing second that year in the European Tour Order of Merit. Olazábal mostly focused on the **European PGA Tour** through the 1990s, playing in America only for the major championships. He has won 23 times on the European PGA Tour and six times on the U.S. **PGA Tour**, with two major championship victories, at the 1994 and 1999 **Masters**. In 2001, Olazábal switched over to playing the U.S. PGA Tour full-time for a few years, but he has won only once since that time, in 2002 at the Buick Invitational. Olazábal was on the European **Ryder Cup** teams in 1987, 1989, 1991, 1993, 1997, 1999, and 2006, often partnering with Ballesteros, and will captain the team in 2012. He overcame severe medical issues in the mid-1990s, eventually being diagnosed with rheumatoid arthritis, which severely affected his feet and made it difficult for him to walk the course.

OLD COURSE. *See* ST. ANDREWS.

OLYMPIC CLUB. The Olympic Club is a San Francisco–based athletic club best known for one of its **golf courses**, the Lake Course, which has hosted four **U.S. Opens**, in 1955, 1966, 1987, and 1998, and is scheduled to host the 2012 U.S. Open. Olympic Club was founded as an inner-city athletic club in 1860, making it the oldest athletic club in the **United States**. In 1917, the club took over the Lakeside Club, and eventually would have 45 holes, including a small nine-hole course, the Cliffs Course, and the Ocean Course, also a championship course. It still has a downtown city clubhouse. The Lakeside course was eventually replaced by a new course designed by Willie Watson, and is usually called the Lake Course. In 1927, after damage from landslides, Sam Whiting rebuilt both courses and the Lake Course was redesigned by **Robert Trent Jones** in preparation for the 1955 U.S. Open. The Ocean Course sustained heavy storm damage in the early 1990s and was rebuilt by **Tom Weiskopf**. Olympic Club has also hosted the **U.S. Amateur** (1958, 1981) and **U.S. Junior Amateur** (2004).

The most famous U.S. Open at Olympic likely occurred in 1955 when **Ben Hogan** was trying to win his fifth title. Leading on the final day, he was tied by unheralded **Jack Fleck**, who defeated Hogan the next day in a major upset. Another important U.S. Open at Olympic occurred in 1966 when **Arnold Palmer** blew a seven-shot lead on the back nine of the final round and lost the championship the next day to **Billy Casper** in a play-off. Palmer never won another major championship. In its early years, Olympic Club was known for many **amateur** sports and contributed numerous athletes to U.S. Olympic teams. Another member of Olympic Club was James J. Corbett, a world **professional** heavyweight boxing champion.

OLYMPIC GAMES. Golf has been on the program of the Olympic Games twice, in 1900 and 1904. In 1900, an individual **stroke play** event for men and **women** took place at the Compiègne Club, north of Paris. In 1904, two men's events were contested, an individual **match play** tournament and a team stroke play event, at the Glen Echo Golf Club in St. Louis. Golf was scheduled to be on the program of the 1908 and 1920 Olympic Games, in London and Antwerp, Belgium, respectively, but neither tournament was held. In 1908, the **R&A** had concerns about the **amateur status** of some of the players, and the entry was quite poor, so the tournament was cancelled. The 1920 Olympic golf event had almost no entrants, and it was also cancelled.

Golf has not been on the Olympic Program since then. In the early 1990s, Billy Payne, the president of the Atlanta Committee for the

Olympic Games (ACOG), the organizing committee for the 1996 Atlanta Olympics, announced plans to hold an Olympic golf event at Augusta National. Unfortunately, Payne had not cleared those plans with the International Olympic Committee (IOC), which was quite upset with the announcement. The tournament was never held, but Payne was later elected a member of Augusta National, which some say was the rationale for his announcement, and in 2006, he was made chairman of the Augusta National.

The World Amateur Golf Council, later called the **International Golf Federation**, began attempts around 2000 to return golf to the Olympic Games. In 2005, a bid by golf's ruling bodies for the sport to be included on the 2012 Olympic program was rejected. At the time, the bid did not have the support of the **PGA Tour**. But the PGA Tour soon decided that supporting Olympic golf would be beneficial for the game. In October 2009, the IOC voted to return golf to the Olympics, beginning with the 2016 Olympics in Rio de Janeiro, Brazil.

O'MEARA, MARK FRANCIS. B. 13 January 1957, Goldsboro, North Carolina, United States. Although born in North Carolina, Mark O'Meara grew up in California, where he played golf at Long Beach State, winning the 1979 **U.S. Amateur** title. In his **PGA Tour** career, he won 16 times, including two majors in 1998, the **Masters** and **Open Championship (British Open)**. In that year, he also won the **World Match Play Championship**, moving to second in the **World Golf Ranking**, trailing only **Tiger Woods**, who had become a close friend, and for whom O'Meara served as a mentor in his early **professional** years. O'Meara competed often internationally, winning the 1986 Australian Masters and the 1997 **Lancome Trophy**. He won four times on the **European PGA Tour** and twice on the **Japanese PGA Tour**.

ONE (1)-IRON. The one-iron is the longest iron club. It is very rarely used nowadays. The advent of more modern iron heads, with perimeter weighting and larger faces, has changed the loft of many irons. Most 3-irons now are close to the former 1-iron in loft, thus making a 1-iron now so flat that gaining loft with it is difficult. The ability to play a 1-iron and the other long irons was once considered the hallmark of top players. In addition to play off the **fairway**, the 1-iron was often used as a driving iron off the tee, enabling the player to get sufficient distance with increasing accuracy, for tighter driving holes. *See also* GOLF CLUBS.

THE OPEN CHAMPIONSHIP (BRITISH OPEN). The Open Championship is the original golf championship, first held in 1860. It is one of the four **professional** major championships of golf. In the mid-19th century the greatest player in the game was, by acclamation, **Allan Robertson**. Robertson played in the era before major tournaments and made his fame in challenge matches. After his death in 1859, it was decided to contest an annual golf championship to determine "the champion golfer." In fact, at the victory ceremony at the end of the tournament, the champion is always introduced to the crowd as the "Champion Golfer of the Year." The first event was played at **Prestwick Golf Club** on 17 October 1860, over 36 holes, which was three rounds of Prestwick's 12-hole **links**, and was won by **Willie Park Sr.** Park and all winners from 1860 to 1870 were given a championship belt—a red Moroccan belt with silver clasps donated by the members of Prestwick. However, in 1870, **Young Tom Morris** won his third consecutive title, retiring the belt, and the event was not held in 1871. When it resumed in 1872, won again by Young Tom, the belt was replaced by a small trophy, known as the **Claret Jug**, which remains the trophy to this day.

Prestwick hosted the first 11 championships, 1860–1870. When the championship resumed in 1872, it was elected to rotate the tournament among three courses, a rota. This rota consisted of **Prestwick**, **St. Andrews**, and the **Honourable Company of Edinburgh Golfers**, now commonly known as **Muirfield**, but in that era, the Honourable Company was based at **Musselburgh**. The championship was held over 36 holes from 1860 to 1891 and increased to 72 holes in 1892. Play-offs were initially over 36 holes but later play-offs were over 18 holes. In 1988, the Open became the first major championship to institute a 4-hole play-off, won that year by Mark Calcavecchia.

The early Open was always held in **Scotland**, the first English course to host the event being **Royal St. George's Golf Club** in 1894. In that year, the championship rota was expanded to other clubs. Prestwick, which was becoming somewhat antiquated, last hosted the championship in 1925. Currently, the Open rota consists of nine courses, five in Scotland—St. Andrews, **Turnberry**, **Carnoustie**, Muirfield, and **Royal Troon**; and four in **England**—**Royal Birkdale**, **Royal Lytham and St. Annes**, **Royal St. George's**, and **Royal Liverpool**, commonly known as Hoylake. The event was held once in **Ireland**, in 1951 at **Royal Portrush**.

The Open Championship was the greatest championship in the game through the 1910s but in the 1920s, the U.S. Open began to challenge it. With the growing superiority of American players, the Open was pushed back to secondary status in the 1930s and after World War II. Travel to Great Britain made it difficult for American players to compete in the British Open, but this changed when **Arnold Palmer** made the trip in 1960, finishing second. He won in 1961 and 1962, when he was the greatest player in the game and easily the most popular. His trips to Britain restored luster to the tournament, which now has at least equal status with the U.S. Open as the biggest championship in golf. The championship was won six times by **Harry Vardon**, which is the record. Four players won the event five times—**James Braid**, **J. H. Taylor**, **Peter Thomson**, and **Tom Watson**. Appendix 2 includes a list of champions.

OPEN DE FRANCE. *See* FRENCH OPEN.

ORCUTT (-CREWS), MAUREEN. B. 1 April 1907, New York, New York, United States; D. 9 January 2007, Durham, North Carolina, United States. Maureen Orcutt was a top **amateur** player from the New York area who won 10 Metropolitan Women's Amateur titles, her first in 1926 and her last in 1968. Although she never won the **U.S. Women's Amateur**, losing in the final in 1927 and 1936, Orcutt won the Women's Eastern Amateur seven times (between 1925 and 1949), the Canadian Amateur in 1930 and 1931, and the **North and South Women's Amateur** three times. She played on four **Curtis Cup** teams. As a senior, she won the **USGA Senior Women's Amateur** in 1962 and 1966. In 1937, Orcutt became one of the first female sportswriters, working for the *New York Times*. Orcutt was inducted into the New York State Hall of Fame in 1991. She spent her senior years in Durham, North Carolina, where she served for many years as a volunteer at Durham Regional Hospital.

ORIGINS OF THE GAME. Golf is like most sports in that its origins are not precisely known. The standard version is that golf began in northern **Scotland** in the 15th century, but similar games are likely much older than that. There is evidence of a game similar to golf being played in China during the Song Dynasty (960–1279), a game called *chuíw án*, played with several clubs and a ball. Even older than that is the Roman game *paganica*, played with a bent stick to strike a wool or feathered ball. The game was brought by the Romans to Britain and some consider it a forerunner of the game of golf. But the game is likely more closely related to hockey (field) or the Celtic games of shinty and hurling or possibly, even polo or lacrosse. The French played a game called *chole*, as far back as 1353, that some consider an antecedent of golf, but it is more similar to hockey (field). Another possible antecedent was a game called *cambuca* in Britain or *chambot* in France. It was later called *pall mall*, or *malle*, and uses a mallet to strike a wooden ball. Finally, a Persian game, *chaugán*, may have had some similarities to golf.

But the first game that is most likely a forerunner of modern golf originated in the low countries of Europe, often called *kolven* or *kolf*. Records exist of such a game in the 13th century. In February 1297, on Boxing Day, there are records of this game, in which contestants used a stick to strike a leather ball into a target several hundred meters distant, being played in Loenen aan de Vecht. The Dutch word, *kolf*, means club, and the name "golf" is thought to be derived from it.

But if the game started elsewhere, the origin of the modern game is usually traced to Scotland. In the 15th century, the Scottish Parliament passed several acts banning the practice of the game, along with football (soccer), because the two sports were interfering with archery practice, which was necessary for national defense. The first was passed in 1457 by James II, King of Scotland, and it was reaffirmed in 1471 and 1491. In 1502, the ban on golf was lifted. The first written evidence of golf at **St. Andrews** dates to 1552, but the evidence documents that the game had been played there for many years by that time. By 1567, Mary Queen of Scots was known to have played golf, and the game had definitely taken hold in Scotland by that time.

OSCAR BROWN. *See* OUT-OF-BOUNDS.

OUIMET, FRANCIS DESALES. B. 8 May 1893, Brookline, Massachusetts, United States; D. 3 September 1967, Newton, Massachusetts, United States. Francis Ouimet grew up near Boston and learned the game of golf as a **caddie** at **The Country Club.** He soon became a top **amateur**, won the Massachusetts Amateur in 1913, and was then asked to submit an entry to the **U.S. Open** for that year, to be held at The Country Club in Brookline. Almost inexplicably, Ouimet won the championship in a play-off over British stars **Harry Vardon** and **Ted Ray**. Considered the greatest upset in golf history, it was also responsible for making the game much more popular in the **United States**. Ouimet won the **U.S. Amateur** in 1914 and repeated that title in 1931. He played on the first eight **Walker Cup** teams and served as captain of the team four times. In 1955, he was the first winner of the **Bob Jones Award**, given by the **USGA** for distinguished sportsmanship in golf. He is a member of numerous golf halls of fame and in 1958 was the first American elected as captain of the **Royal and Ancient Golf Club of St. Andrews**. His other significant tournament victories include the 1917 **Western Amateur**, 1914 French Amateur, 1920 **North and South Amateur**, 1932 Massachusetts Open, and the Massachusetts Amateur, which he won six times.

OUT-OF-BOUNDS. The Rules of Golf define out-of-bounds as "any area beyond the boundaries of the course, or any area so designated by a tournament committee." A ball hit out-of-bounds must be replayed as near as possible from the spot of the previous shot and a one-stroke penalty must be taken. This is termed "stroke-and-distance." Out-of-bounds is usually marked by a series of white stakes. The boundary line extends from the inside of any two adjacent stakes and vertically upward and downward along that line. Out-of-bounds may also be marked by a line on the ground, in which case the line itself is out-of-bounds. A ball is considered out-of-bounds when all of it lies out-of-bounds, but a player may stand out-of-bounds to play a ball that is in bounds. Tour players will often refer to a ball that is out-of-bounds as "Oscar Browned," or "O.B."

OUTSIDE AGENCY. The **Rules of Golf** define "outside agency" as "any agency not part of the match or, in **stroke play**, not part of the competitor's side, and includes a referee, a marker, an observer, and a forecaddie." Wind and water are not considered outside agencies. A spectator is an outside agency, and if a ball strikes a spectator, or any outside agency, the player simply plays the ball from where it comes to rest.

OUTWARD NINE. "Outward nine" refers to the front nine. In **Scotland**, most of the courses went out away from the clubhouse for the front nine, referred to as the "outward nine," and then returned to the clubhouse on the back nine, referred to as the "**inward nine**." This is the source of the terms "going out in . . ." for the score on the front nine, and "coming in in . . ." for the score on the back nine.

OZAKI, MASASHI "JUMBO." B. 24 January 1947, Kaifu District, Tokushima, Japan. Jumbo Ozaki is considered the greatest ever Japanese **professional** player. He started out as a professional baseball player, pitching from 1965 to 1967 in Japanese leagues, but turned professional in golf in 1970 and won the Japanese PGA in 1971. Jumbo eventually won 94 tournaments on the Japanese Tour and led the money list 12 times (1973, 1974, 1977, 1988, 1990, 1992, 1994–1998); both are records. Known for his size, hence the name "Jumbo," and his driving length, Ozaki was ranked in the World Top 10 for over 200 weeks between 1988 and 1998. He played in the **Masters** 18 times, with a best finish of eighth in 1973. He also finished sixth at the 1989 **U.S. Open**. Ozaki played sporadically on the U.S. **PGA Tour** from 1972 to 1989, never winning a tournament but with a best finish of fourth at the 1993 Memorial Tournament. Both of his brothers, Tateo "Jet" Ozaki and Naomichi "Joe" Ozaki, are professional golfers.

– P –

PAK SE-RI. B. 28 September 1977, Daejeon, Republic of Korea (South). Pak Se-Ri is a Korean female **professional** who has been a pioneer for that nation, credited with inspiring a huge influx of great Korean female players.. Properly called "Pak Se-Ri" by Korean naming traditions, she is incorrectly known in the golf world by the Western style "Se-Ri Pak." Pak turned pro in 1996 and came to the

United States to play the **LPGA** full-time in 1998. That year she won two major championships, the **U.S. Women's Open** and **LPGA Championship**. She has won 24 events on the LPGA despite taking off parts of 2005–2006. She suffered some "burnout" and said she needed time to restore some balance in her life. She has won five majors, the two cited above in 1998, the 2001 **Women's British Open**, and the LPGA again in 2002 and 2006. Pak was inducted into the **World Golf Hall of Fame** in 2007, the youngest ever living inductee. Pak won the Jamie Farr Classic in Toledo, Ohio, in 1988, 1999, 2001, 2003, and 2007, only the third LPGA player to have won a single tournament five times.

PALMER, ARNOLD DANIEL "ARNIE," "THE KING." B. 10 September 1929, Latrobe, Pennsylvania, United States. He is not the greatest golfer ever, having been surpassed in his own generation by **Jack Nicklaus**. But Arnold Palmer may be the most popular golfer, and possibly, the most important, to play the game. He learned the game from his father, Deacon Palmer, at Latrobe Country Club, in a small Pennsylvania town, and he later attended Wake Forest University. His first major title was the 1954 **U.S. Amateur** and he turned **professional** the next year, winning the **Canadian Open** in 1955 for his first **PGA Tour** victory. It was the first of his 62 PGA Tour wins from 1955 to 1973, which also include seven major titles—the **Masters** in 1958, 1960, 1962, and 1964; the **Open Championship** (**British Open**) in 1961 and 1962, and the **U.S. Open** in 1960.

Palmer's career was marked by his failure to complete a career **Grand Slam**, never winning the **PGA Championship**, although he finished second in the event three times. Palmer also placed second at the U.S. Open four times, a record at the time. In 1960, he won the Masters and U.S. Open and coined the terminology for the modern Grand Slam when he decided to travel to Great Britain and play the Open Championship at **St. Andrews**. Palmer claimed that any player winning those three events and the PGA in a single year would duplicate the **amateur** Grand Slam of **Bob Jones**. This has never occurred in one calendar year, though Palmer challenged it in 1960, placing second at St. Andrews. He won the title the next two years, and his appearance there resurrected the Open Championship, which had not been as popular or important after World War II.

Palmer almost defined the word "charisma" as applied to pro athletes. Handsome, with wide shoulders, huge forearms, and a narrow waist, he radiated sex appeal to galleries who adopted him as their own. His enormous galleries were called "Arnie's Army." His background from a Pennsylvania coal-mining town, and his attitude that gave the impression he would want to go have a beer with you as your friend, made him the everyman's player. Seemingly, every man wanted to be him, and every woman wanted to bed him. Palmer also came along at the advent of television and made the sport popular on the tube as well. He was known for his come-from-behind victories, often achieved by his gambling, swashbuckling play, which were termed "Arnie's Charges." **Frank Beard**, a pro in the 1960s and 1970s, made the case that Palmer so popularized golf that all professionals owed him at least 25 cents from every dollar they made. Because of his importance to the game, he has been termed "The King." Palmer's charisma and popularity made him extremely wealthy, and even after his best years were behind him, he was often among the top athletes in terms of endorsement dollars earned. But his appeal and the fact that Jack Nicklaus came along and surpassed his records almost masked the fact that Palmer was definitely one of the greatest players in the history of the game. He won 29 PGA Tour events from 1960 to 1963, was the best player in the game from 1958 to 1964, and played on six **Ryder Cup** teams—1961, 1963, 1965, 1967, 1971, and 1973—captaining the team in 1963 and 1975.

Palmer was inducted into the **World Golf Hall of Fame** in 1974 and in 1998 was given the PGA Lifetime Achievement Award. His other honors are too numerous to list. His charitable work includes the Arnold Palmer Pavilion at the University of Pittsburgh Medical Center and the Arnold Palmer Hospital for Children in Orlando, Florida. Palmer is also an excellent private pilot and has flown his own jet since the early 1960s.

PAR. "Par" was originally defined as the score an expert player should make on a particular hole and, by extension, on a full round on a particular **golf course**. It was first used in tournament golf at the 1911 **U.S. Open**, when the **USGA** defined it as "perfect play without any flukes and under ordinary weather conditions, always allowing for two strokes on each **putting green**." High-level **professionals** now play tournaments in well under par, but for club or **amateur** players, the attempt to match par on a course is still a major goal. *See also* BOGEY.

PAR-THREE COURSES. A par-three course is one that contains only par-three holes, thus having a par of 54 for 18 holes or 27 for nine-hole courses. They are often built when there is no room for a full-sized **golf course**. They are sometimes termed "executive courses," but this is incorrect; executive courses are simply shorter versions of full-size courses, usually with multiple par-threes and a few short par-fours.

PARK, WILLIAM "WILLIE" OR "AULD WILLIE," SR. B. 30 June 1833, Musselburgh, Scotland; D. 25 July 1903, Musselburgh, Scotland. Willie Park was one of the early great players in **Scotland** in the 19th century. Like many early pros, he learned the game as a **caddie**. He is best known as the first winner of the **Open Championship (British Open)** in 1860. He eventually won the championship four times, adding victories in 1863, 1866, and 1875, and finished second four times. In 1854, Park began playing challenge matches against **Allan Robertson** and **Old Tom Morris**, winning many of them. He was known for his long drives, causing Robertson to say, "Willie frichtens us wi' his long driving." His brother, Mungo Park, won the title in 1874, and his son, **Willie Park Jr.**, won in 1887 and 1889.

PARK, WILLIE, JR. B. 4 February 1864, Musselburgh, East Lothian, Scotland; D. 24 May 1925, Musselburgh, Scotland. Willie Park Jr. was the son of **Willie Park Sr.**, the first Open Champion in 1860 and a four-time winner of the title. His uncle, Mungo Park, also won the **Open Championship (British Open)** in 1874. As a youth, Willie Jr. worked in both club and ball making. He won his first tournament at age 17. He eventually won the Open Championship twice, in 1887 and 1889. He excelled at the short game but was a wild **driver**. His titles opened business opportunities, and he had offices for his club and ball making business in London and New York. He was one of the first to mass produce the new **gutta percha** balls. Willie Park Jr. was the first great **golf course architect**, designing over 170 courses in Britain, **Canada**, and the **United States**, among them

Sunningdale Old, which is his masterpiece. His daughter Dorothy was runner-up in the 1937 **British Ladies' Amateur** Championship.

PEBBLE BEACH GOLF LINKS. Pebble Beach is one of the most famous **golf courses** in the world. Considered by many the most beautiful golf course in the world, it sits on the Monterey Peninsula, winding its way among the forests, with several holes bordering the Pacific Ocean. Pebble Beach hosted the **U.S. Open** in 1972, 1982, 1992, and 2000 (and will host again in 2010), and it was the first publicly accessible golf course to host the event. While technically a **public course**, tee times are hard to get because of the popularity of the course, and it is quite expensive, with greens fees approaching $500 for a round. Pebble Beach was designed by Jack Neville and Douglas Grant and opened in February 1919. In 1947, it became the host course for the **Bing Crosby Pro-Am**, which is still held there, although now it is known as the AT&T Pebble Beach National Pro-Am. The course was the site of the 1961 **U.S. Amateur** (won by **Jack Nicklaus**, who also won the 1972 U.S. Open there) and the 1977 **PGA Championship**.

PELZ, DAVID T. "DAVE." B. October 1939. Dave Pelz is a golf teacher and innovator, best known for teaching putting and the short game. Pelz has an unlikely background, having studied physics at Indiana University, where he played on the golf team. Pelz then joined NASA as a physicist, while continuing to play **amateur** golf at Columbia Country Club in the Washington, D.C. area. In the early 1970s, he designed the Teacher Putter, a putter with two prongs on its clubface that forced a player to hit the ball in the absolute center of the clubface or the ball would shoot off sideways and go only a few feet. It became a very popular training aid among **professionals**, and in 1976, Pelz left NASA to form Preceptor Golf, which made and marketed the Teacher Putter. Over the next few years, Pelz's scientific background enabled him to design many innovations to clubs and training devices. Preceptor went bankrupt in 1986, but Pelz moved on to form Dave Pelz Golf, Inc., which continued to build training devices. He has also started putting and short game schools, the Dave Pelz Scoring Game Schools, and teaches many touring professionals, most notably **Phil Mickelson**.

PENICK, HARVEY MORRISON. B. 23 October 1904, Austin, Texas, United States; D. 2 April 1995, Austin, Texas, United States. Harvey Penick was a club **professional** at Austin Country Club from 1923 to 1973, where he became a top golf instructor. His most notable pupils include **Ben Crenshaw** and **Tom Kite**, but he also taught **Mickey Wright** and **Betsy Rawls**. Penick is best known for his book, *Harvey Penick's Little Red Book*, which was published in 1992 and became the best-selling golf book ever published. A small book, it contains short aphorisms and suggestions that make it very easy to read and understand. Penick was inducted into the **World Golf Hall of Fame** in 2002.

PEPPER (-MOCHRIE), DOTTIE. B. 17 August 1965, Saratoga Springs, New York, United States. Dottie Pepper was a U.S. **professional** golfer known for her competitive, and sometimes fiery, demeanor on the course. Growing up in upstate New York, Pepper won the 1981 New York Women's Amateur and then played collegiately at Furman University, where she was named All-American three times. Pepper joined the **LPGA** in 1988 and won 17 tournaments on tour, including the 1992 and 1999 **Kraft Nabisco (Dinah Shore)** championships, her two major victories. Pepper led the U.S. LPGA money list in 1992 and played on six **Solheim Cup** teams. She retired after the 2004 season, having been hampered by injuries in her last three years on tour, and has since become a golf broadcaster and a golf writer, with a weekly column in *Sport Illustrated*'s golf section.

PGA CHAMPIONSHIP. The PGA Championship was originally the national championship of American golf **professionals**, technically, the championship of the **PGA of America**. But it has expanded into a **PGA Tour** event that is one of golf's four major championships. It is always the last of the majors to take place each year, ending the major championship season. The championship started in 1916 and was won by **Jim Barnes** at Siwanoy Country Club in Eastchester, New York. Originally, the PGA was held at **match play** and continued in that manner through 1957, changing to the more standard 72-hole **stroke play** event in 1958. The event rotates to different courses each year and has been played on some of the top U.S. courses. The event has always been open to **club professional** members of the PGA of America, but in the last few decades, fewer and fewer club pros have been invited, as the championship has tried to better its fields by inviting more international players high up in the **World Golf Ranking**. Currently, the field includes 20 spots for club professionals, who have to qualify for the event at the PGA Club Pro Championship. Both **Jack Nicklaus** and **Walter Hagen** have won the event five times. The PGA champion receives the **Wanamaker Trophy**, named for Rodman Wanamaker, a department store magnate. Appendix 2 includes a list of champions.

PGA OF AMERICA. The Professional Golfers Association of America, usually shortened to the PGA of America, is the organization that governs golf **professionals** in the **United States**, most notably club professionals. The group was founded in 1916 and is now headquartered in Palm Beach Gardens, Florida. The PGA of America defines as its mission: "to promote enjoyment and involvement in golf among the general public, as well as to contribute to the game's growth by producing services to golf professionals and the industry. The PGA seeks to accomplish this mission by enhancing the skills of the PGA Professionals and expanding playing opportunities for the general public, employers and manufactures. Through these efforts, The PGA elevates the standards of the PGA Professional's vocation, enhances the economic well-being of the individual PGA member, stimulates interest in the game of golf and promotes the overall vitality of the game."

Essentially, the purpose of the PGA of America is to promote the game of golf via the club professionals and to help further their status and job enhancements. Club professionals become PGA members by taking various levels of educational courses, passing a written test, serving as an apprentice for several years, and passing a playing ability test. The PGA conducts several events including the **PGA Championship**, Senior PGA Championship, PGA Grand Slam of Golf, and the **Ryder Cup**. Originally, the PGA of America was in charge of running the **PGA Tour**. But in 1968, the touring professionals formed their own division within the PGA, termed the Tournament Players Division. This was renamed the PGA Tour in 1975. While U.S. PGA Tour members become members of the PGA of America, the PGA Tour is basically autonomous. *See also* SMITH, HORTON.

PGA TOUR. The PGA Tour is the leading **professional** golf tour in the world. It conducts tournaments, mostly in the **United States**. The PGA Tour was originally run by the **PGA of America**, but the touring pros broke away in 1968, forming their own subdivision within the PGA, named the Tournament Players Division. This was renamed the PGA Tour in 1975. While U.S. PGA Tour members become members of the PGA of America, the PGA Tour is basically autonomous. Because of some marketing disputes with the PGA, the name was briefly changed to the TPA (Tournament Players Association) Tour from August 1981 to March 1982. The PGA Tour actually operates three tours; the PGA Tour, the **Nationwide Tour** (a developmental tour), and the **Champions (Senior) Tour**. The organization is headquartered in Ponte Vedra Beach, Florida. The tour is led by a commissioner, of which there have been three since its formation in 1968—**Joe Dey** (1968–1974), **Deane Beman** (1974–1994), and since 1994, **Tim Finchem**.

PICARD, HENRY GILFORD. B. 28 November 1906, Plymouth, Massachusetts, United States; D. 30 April 1997, Charleston, South Carolina, United States. Henry Picard played on the **PGA Tour** mostly in the 1930s, winning 26 PGA Tour events, which include major championships at the 1938 Masters and the 1939 PGA. He was twice on the **Ryder Cup** team, in 1935 and 1937. Early in his career, Picard was the club **professional** at Charleston Country Club, but during the Depression the club was broke and let him go, which forced him to turn to tournament golf for money. After World War II, he became a noted club professional and teacher, working at many clubs around the country. His pupils included both **Ben Hogan** and **Sam Snead**. His teaching was based on principles he learned from renowned golf instructor Alex Morrison. Picard eventually settled back in Charleston, where he lived out his days. He was inducted into the **World Golf Hall of Fame** posthumously in 2006.

PINE VALLEY GOLF CLUB. Pine Valley Golf Club is a club in southern New Jersey that is always ranked among the greatest courses in the United States and the world. It is considered by many the hardest **golf course** in the world. It is a "men-only" club. The golf course is a classic example of penal architecture, and wayward shots are severely punished. The course runs through the pine forests of southern Jersey, is tightly wooded, and has numerous, very difficult bunkers. Founded in 1913, it was designed by George Crump and was his first and only golf course design. There are several design features on the course, notably a huge **fairway** cross-bunker on the 7th hole, termed "Hell's Half Acre." On the short par-three 10th hole, a very small, very deep bunker, just in front of the green is so deep and small that it is difficult to get into and even more difficult to extricate one's ball from it. It has been named the "Devil's Asshole."

PINEHURST. Pinehurst is a series of resort **golf courses** in the small village of Pinehurst, set in the sandhills of south-central North Carolina. The resort is famous for its golf courses, of which there are now eight. The most famous of these is Pinehurst No. 2, which is among the classic golf courses of the world. The village and the resort were founded in the late 1890s by Boston soda fountain magnate James Walker Tufts, with the first course opened in 1898, although it was really developed by his grandson, **Richard Tufts**. Pinehurst No. 2 was designed by the renowned architect **Donald Ross** and is acclaimed as his greatest work. The No. 2 course opened in 1907, although Ross settled in the area and continued to make changes to it throughout his life.

Pinehurst was home to the **North and South Open**, which was a major **professional** championship through World War II, from 1901 to 1951. It also hosts the **North and South Amateur**, since 1901, and the **North and South Women's Amateur**, since 1903. Pinehurst was the site of the 1999 and 2005 **U.S. Open** and hosted the 1951 **Ryder Cup**. In 2014, it is scheduled to host the U.S. Open and **U.S. Women's Open** in back-to-back weeks, the first time that will be attempted.

PITCH SHOT. A pitch shot is made by a player, around the green, using a lofted club, often a **wedge** of some sort. The ball is pitched higher into the air than a **chip shot**, which is usually struck fairly low to the ground. The ball usually stops fairly quickly. When it continues to run a bit, it is termed a "**pitch-and-run**." The more extreme variant of a pitch shot is the **flop shot**.

PITCH-AND-RUN. A pitch-and-run is a variant of a **pitch shot**, or the chip-and-run/**chip shot**. In a pitch-and-run, a player uses a lofted club around the green, often a **wedge** of some sort, and pitches the ball higher into the air than a chip shot, which is usually struck fairly low to the ground. In a pitch-and-run, the ball will still run a bit after hitting the green, although not as much as a chip shot or a chip-and-run.

PLAYER, GARY "THE BLACK KNIGHT." B. 1 November 1935, Johannesburg, South Africa. Gary Player is a **South African professional** who is among the greatest players of all time. He also internationalized the game of golf, traveling to play on all continents, and often boasted that he had flown more miles than any man alive. During his career, he won 24 **PGA Tour** events, including nine major championships. These include the 1959 **Open Championship (British Open)**, which he won again in 1968 and 1974; the **Masters** in 1961, 1974, and 1978; the **PGA Championship** in 1962 and 1971; and the **U.S. Open** in 1965. When Player won the 1965 U.S. Open, it made him only the fourth golfer (after **Gene Sarazen**, **Ben Hogan**, and **Jack Nicklaus**) to complete the career professional **Grand Slam**. In the 1960s, Player formed, with Nicklaus and **Arnold Palmer**, what was often termed the "Big Three" of professional golf, and in fact, they appeared for several years in a televised series of golf matches that used that name. Player won 19 events on the **Champions (Senior) Tour** in the **United States**. His greatest year was 1974 when he won the Masters and the Open Championship. Player also won the **South African Open** 13 times, the South African Masters 10 times, the South African PGA five times, and the **Australian Open** seven times. He was individual World Cup champion in 1965 and 1977 and won the **World Match Play Championship** at Wentworth, **England**, five times between 1965 and 1973.

Player was relatively small, at only 5 feet 8 inches (173 cm), and realized early in his career that he needed to learn to drive the ball farther to succeed at the top levels. He did this by embracing physical fitness—lifting weights, running, and doing fingertip push-ups, which he popularized—and he has continued as a fitness proselytizer into his seventies. His superb physical conditioning allowed him to win professional championships in six decades—from the 1950s to the 2000s. He was the only golfer in the 20th century to win the

Open Championship in three decades (1959, 1968, 1974). In addition to his physical conditioning, Player was known for his work ethic, practicing as much as, or more than, any other professional of his era, rivaling Ben Hogan in time spent on the practice tee. Player is often considered the greatest sand bunker player in the history of golf, which he claims is due to his long hours of practice.

Player was inducted into the **World Golf Hall of Fame** in 1974. He was voted "Sportsman of the Century" by South Africa in 2000. In 1966, Gary Player received the **Bob Jones Award** from the **USGA** in recognition of distinguished sportsmanship in golf. Player has also established a successful **golf course** design business. Early in his career, Player was often harassed by apartheid opponents, because of South Africa's support of that racist policy. But Player was an outspoken critic of apartheid and often financially supported black golfers and athletes in South Africa, notably by arranging for tours of South Africa by golfer **Lee Elder** and tennis player Arthur Ashe.

THE PLAYERS CHAMPIONSHIP. The Players Championship is the annual championship of players on the U.S. **PGA Tour**. It is not a major, but many players consider it the fifth major, and there is some support to list it as such officially. This is because The Players Championship annually has the strongest field of any golf tournament. It invites the top 50 players in the world based on the **World Golf Ranking** and the top players on the U.S. PGA Tour, also based on the World Golf Ranking. The event began in 1974 and was held at several different clubs from 1974 to 1976. In 1977, it moved to Sawgrass Country Club in Ponte Vedra Beach, Florida, and in 1982, it moved across town to the TPC at Sawgrass, where it has been since. The course was designed by **Pete Dye** and has been redesigned and rebuilt twice. It is best known for the 17th hole, a very short par-three made difficult by an island green. The Players Championship is known for offering the largest purse of any annually held golf tournament. The event was won three times by **Jack Nicklaus** (1974, 1976, 1978) and twice each by **Fred Couples**, **Steve Elkington**, **Davis Love III**, and **Hal Sutton**. Appendix 2 includes a list of champions.

POA ANNUA. *Poa Annua* is the genus and species of a creeping, fibrous, rootstock meadow grass. It is technically a weed on **golf**

courses and is often difficult to eradicate. Because it creeps and overgrows other **grass**, it will often infest **putting greens**. *Poa annua* can actually make a fairly nice putting surface just after it has been cut, since it is tough and can be cut quite short. The problem is that it grows quickly and often erratically, and later in the day, *Poa annua* greens are often very uneven, causing great difficulty with putting. *Poa annua* **fairways**, on the other hand, can be very nice to play off, because the tough, thick roots of the grass allow them to be cut short, and the ball sits up very well on them. However, because of *Poa annua*'s green-infesting problems, many courses try to eradicate it.

PORTER CUP. The Porter Cup is one of the top U.S. **amateur** golf tournaments. It has been held annually at the Niagara Falls Country Club in Lewiston, New York, since 1959. In its first year, it was called the International Invitation at Niagara Falls Country Club, with most of the players coming from Western New York and Southern Ontario. It was renamed the "Porter Cup" in 1960, with a trophy donated by Alex L. Porter, a local businessman. The tournament became synonymous with the name "Dick Harvey," a club member who assiduously recruited the nation's top amateur players to come to Niagara Falls each August to compete in the Porter Cup. He made certain that they were treated royally by the club members. Harvey died in 1978, and his position was taken by Dr. William McMahon, "Doc," who continued to recruit the world's best amateurs. The Porter Cup now has a Senior Division, with the players competing for the Harvey Cup. There is a small monument on the course, near the confluence of the 3rd, 4th, 6th, and 7th holes, known as "Doc's Corner," in honor of McMahon. Similar to the **Masters**, the Porter Cup gives its champion a green jacket at the trophy presentation, which has been won by, among others, **Ben Crenshaw**, **Phil Mickelson**, **Jay Sigel**, Bobby Clampett, John Harris, and John Cook. Appendix 6 includes a list of champions.

POST, SANDRA, CM. B. 4 June 1948, Oakville, Ontario, Canada. Sandra Post is the greatest ever Canadian female **professional** golfer. She turned pro in 1968, winning the **LPGA Championship** in her rookie year, her only major title, and was the 1968 LPGA Rookie of the Year. She then struggled for 10 years but won seven **LPGA**

events between 1978 and 1981 and played the tour through 1984. She was inducted into the Canadian Sports Hall of Fame and the **Royal Canadian Golf Association** Hall of Fame in 1988. At the end of the 20th century, Post was voted the number eight female athlete of the century in **Canada**. She was honored as a member of the Order of Canada in 2003.

POT BUNKER. A pot bunker is a type of **bunker**, usually a **fairway** bunker, which is very small and very deep. Basically, when one drives into a pot bunker, there is no chance to play out toward the green, unless the shot is only a short **wedge**. Players usually have to play a blast shot out sideways back to the fairway. Thus, pot bunkers are to be avoided at all costs. They are more popular on courses in **Scotland**, where many of the original bunkers could be termed "pot bunkers" because of their steep faces.

POWELL, RENÉE. B. 4 May 1946, Canton, Ohio, United States. Renée Powell was an American **LPGA** member who was a pioneer African American top female **professional** player. Powell was the second black to play on the LPGA, following **Althea Gibson**, and played from 1967 to 1980. She began playing in her native Ohio, where her father, William Powell, became the first African American to design, build, and operate a **golf course** in the **United States**. She attended Ohio University and Ohio State University, captaining the **women**'s golf team at both schools. Powell became the head professional at Clearview Golf Club in East Canton, Ohio, her father's old course. She is a member of the Ohio Golf Hall of Fame, and has received numerous honors for her pioneering career and the grace with which she handled some difficult times. In 2003, Powell was given the First Lady of Golf Award; in 2007, she received the Rolex For the Love of the Game Award; and in 2008, St. Andrews University awarded her an honorary doctor of laws (LL.D.) degree.

PRACTICE PUTTING GREEN. Most courses have a practice putting green on which players will warm up briefly before a round, striking a few putts, especially to get a feel for the speed of the greens. Better players will often use practice greens after rounds to work on their putting strokes, and many tournament players will spend hours on them daily.

PRACTICE RANGE. Most courses have practice ranges, sometimes termed "driving ranges," although that term is often reserved for stand-alone ranges where players may practice their driving exclusively. At most better courses, practice ranges have a closely mowed area where a player may practice shots of any type off **grass** that approximates the **fairways** of the **golf course** and where they may hit **drivers**. Many more modern courses have huge expanses of land set aside for the practice range. Here players can hit all types of shots in all conditions, moving around and varying their shots according to the wind or the shape of shot they wish to practice. The prototype of this sort of range was built in the 1970s by **Jack Nicklaus** at his signature course, Muirfield Village, in Dublin, Ohio. *See also* DRIVING RANGE.

PRAIRIE DUNES COUNTRY CLUB. Prairie Dunes is a course in Hutchinson, Kansas, somewhat off the beaten path, that is one of the great **golf course** designs in the **United States**. It was originally designed by **Perry Maxwell**, who built nine holes in 1937. His son, Press, designed the second nine holes, which opened in 1957. The course is unusual in that it looks like a wide-open **links** course, though it is far from the ocean. Many people who play it say it reminds them more of a British seaside links than an American course. The course has hosted several **USGA** Championships, including the 2002 **U.S. Women's Open**, the 2006 **U.S. Senior Open**, the 1988 **U.S. Mid-Amateur**, the 1995 **USGA Senior Amateur**, three **U.S. Women's Amateur** Championships, and the 1986 **Curtis Cup** match. Prairie Dunes has also been the site of the **Trans-Mississippi Amateur** five times.

PREFERRED LIES. Preferred lies is a local rule that allows a player to improve the lie of the ball before playing a shot. Preferred lies violate the basic tenet of the game to "play the ball as it lies," and instead allows the ball's lie to be improved. Usually this rule is applied in the "**fairway**," a term not actually defined in the rule book, but it may be allowed anywhere "**through the green**," which refers to the entire course, except the **teeing ground**, **putting green**, and **hazards**. Most **local rules** allowing a player to improve the lie are not terribly specific at the club level, simply stating that lies may be improved. At the **professional** level, on the pro tours, the rule is quite specific, and is called "**lift, clean, and place**." This usually permits the player to lift the ball, either through the green, in a closely mown area, or in the fairway, depending on how the rule is written, clean the ball, and replace it by hand. It must be placed no closer to the hole and usually within one club length of the original location of the ball. On the **PGA Tour**, the players and caddies often term this "picking it up and running with it." Preferred lies are ostensibly used to protect the **golf course** in adverse conditions, such as poor fairway conditions, although critics of the rule argue that this works in reverse, because the ball is moved to the area of the best condition, which further injures the golf course.

PRESIDENTS CUP. The Presidents Cup is a biennial team match between a team of U.S. **professionals** and a team of international professionals from outside of Europe. The event was first held in 1994 to give non-European internationals a chance to compete in a team match against the **United States**. It is held in alternate years from the **Ryder Cup**. The event takes place over four days, with **foursomes** and **four-ball** matches held on the first three days. On the final day, all 12 players on each team play a series of singles matches. The location alternates between a U.S. course and an international course. Appendix 5 includes a list of champions.

PRESTWICK GOLF CLUB. Prestwick is one of the most renowned early Scottish **links**, located 30 miles southwest of Glasgow. The club was founded in 1851, with **Old Tom Morris** as the first club **professional**, known then as "Keeper of the Green, Ball and Club Maker." Prestwick was the first host of the **Open Championship** (**British Open**) and hosted the first 12 events from 1860 to 1870 and 1872 (it was not held in 1871). Originally, the winner of the tournament received a red Moroccan belt with silver clasps, which the Prestwick members purchased at a cost of £25. Prestwick remained in the Open rota until 1925, when it hosted its 24th and final Open Championship, won by **Jim Barnes**. Prestwick has also hosted the **Amateur**

Championship (British Amateur) 11 times, most recently in 2001. Prestwick originally had only 12 holes, and the early British Opens were held at 36 holes (through 1891), which consisted of three trips around Prestwick's links. The course's best-known obstacle is the River Pow, or the Pow Burn, which flows through the course and comes into play on several holes.

PRICE, NICHOLAS RAYMOND LEIGE "NICK." B. 28 January 1957, Durban, South Africa. Though born in **South Africa**, Nick Price grew up in Zimbabwe (then Rhodesia). He turned **professional** in 1977 and played in South Africa until moving to the European Tour and eventually the U.S. **PGA Tour** in 1983. In the early 1990s, Price was world ranked number one for 43 weeks in 1993–1994. During his career, he won 18 PGA Tour events, including three major championships, the 1992 and 1994 **PGA Championships** and the **Open Championship (British Open)** in 1994. He also won five events on the European Tour, although he did not play there much after 1983. Price was inducted into the **World Golf Hall of Fame** in 2003.

PRO SHOP. The pro shop, often called the "golf shop," is the area at a **golf course** where players often visit prior to starting their rounds. At **public courses**, this is mandatory as it is usually where the players pay their green fee, allowing them to play. At private courses, players may visit the pro shop to buy golf balls and pick up tees or other equipment prior to playing or to register for use of a golf cart. Both public and private course pro shops usually sell merchandise, including golf balls, clubs, shoes, and clothing. Pro shops are usually run by a head golf **professional**, assisted by one or more assistant golf pros. The money earned from sales of merchandise in a pro shop is usually split, by contract, between the head golf professional and the club.

PRO-AMS. Pro-ams are events in which a **professional** plays with one or more **amateur** partners. They are ubiquitous on the U.S. **PGA Tour** and are virtually always held before every tournament on Wednesday. Usually, in these pro-ams, a PGA Tour player partners with four amateurs in a fivesome. The amateurs, or their corporate sponsors, pay significant amounts of money to play in this format, and this money is used to help support the event or its charities. Two events on the PGA Tour feature longer pro-ams: the **Bob Hope** Desert Classic, in which pros play with three different amateurs on the first four days of a five-round tournament, and the former **Bing Crosby** Pro-Am, now the AT&T Pebble Beach National Pro-Am, in which the pros play with a single amateur partner for the first three days of a four-round tournament. At Pebble Beach, the pro-am teams may also play on the fourth day, with the leading teams making a cut to do so. There are many other pro-ams held in golf. In the **United States**, many PGA Sections sponsor pro-ams, allowing the section's club professionals to play with their members. Some clubs will also sponsor local pro-ams to which they invite top professionals, often from the PGA Tour, **Champions Tour**, or **Nationwide Tour**. Some of these are well-known charity events, such as the Fred Meyer Challenge in Portland, Oregon (hosted by **Peter Jacobsen**), and the CVS Classic in Rhode Island, hosted by PGA Tour pros Brad Faxon and Billy Andrade.

PROFESSIONAL. A professional, as opposed to an **amateur**, is a golfer who plays the game for money or makes money working as a club or teaching professional. There are two main categories of **professionals** in golf: "**Golf professional**" is usually the term reserved for a pro who works at a **golf course**, running the **pro shop**, teaching and giving lessons, conducting tournaments, and helping members or **public course** players enjoy their day at the course. "Professional golfer," on the other hand, is the term usually used for a pro who makes a living playing in tournaments. There may be some overlap, but at the highest level of professional golf, it is extremely rare for tournament players to work at clubs anymore, although they may represent the club as the touring professional. However, golf professionals do play in tournaments, often locally, and they may sometimes play in more prestigious tournaments.

PROFESSIONAL GOLFER. *See* GOLF PROFESSIONAL.

PROFESSIONAL GOLFERS ASSOCIATION OF AMERICA. *See* PGA OF AMERICA.

PROVISIONAL BALL. A provisional ball is a ball played under rule 27-2 when a player's ball *may* be lost outside a **water hazard** or *may* be **out-of-bounds**, but the player isn't sure. The player must announce that a provisional ball will be played. A provisional ball becomes the **ball in play** if it is determined that the original ball is lost outside a water hazard or out-of-bounds. A provisional ball cannot be played for a ball that the player thinks may be in a water hazard or in an **unplayable lie** (a mistake often made by non-tournament players). If either of these situations is found to exist, the provisional ball must be abandoned, and the player must proceed under the rules governing whichever of these situations exists.

PUBLIC COURSES. Public **golf courses** are, quite simply, golf courses that are open to the public. Players pay a green fee every time they play a round rather than paying annual dues, such as at a private club. Public golf courses are quite popular in the **United States** and Great Britain and actually host more play than private courses in these countries. Some public courses are quite good, notably **Bethpage Black**, **Pebble Beach,** and **Pinehurst**. There is a subset of public courses, usually termed "**resort courses**," of which Pebble and Pinehurst are classic examples. These courses are technically open to the public, but they are part of upscale resorts, and they can be very expensive to play. Another subset of public courses is **municipal courses**, which is a public course owned and operated by a governmental authority, usually a town or city.

PULL HOOK. *See* DUCK HOOK.

PUNCH SHOT. A punch shot, often called a "knockdown shot," is a type of shot played to keep the ball lower than its normal flight. It is usually used in windy conditions to keep the ball under the wind. Punch shots will travel lower than normal for the club used but have fairly good spin and good stopping action on the green, because they have to be hit very crisply. Punch shots are hit in a number of ways—one may play the ball back in the stance a bit, hit down more firmly through impact, shorten the follow-thru a bit, and/or keep the hands lower into the follow-thru just beyond impact.

PUTTER. The putter is the **golf club** used to roll a ball on the **putting green** in an attempt to place the ball in the hole. Historically, the putter is the shortest club in the bag, although that has changed in recent years. It has the least loft of any club—usually from 3 degrees to 7 degrees. Putters have the most variability of any club in terms of clubhead design, with one restriction being that the length of the clubhead from heel to toe must be more than the length from face to back end. Putters are the only clubs that may have a grip that is noncircular in cross-section, although it must be symmetrical. In the late 1960s, **Sam Snead** began a new putting style that was called "croquet style," in which he putted with the club between his legs and swung the putter like a croquet mallet. This was soon outlawed and a rule was adopted that disallows a player to stand astride the putting line, or an extension of that line, while making a putt. In the early 1980s, players, especially senior players, began to play with very long putters, often termed "belly putters" because the club rested against a player's belly. When using a belly putter, the golfer usually uses a split-hand grip with the top hand stabilizing the club against the belly, while the bottom hand swings the club. Putters are the only clubs that are not restricted to a maximum length of 48 inches (121.9 cm). Long putters may also have a split grip, one for the top hand and one for the lower swinging hand.

Tournament golfers are particularly finicky about their putters, and many players have found one putter and stuck with it throughout their careers. Notable among these are **Bob Jones**, whose blade putter was called Calamity Jane; **Ben Crenshaw**, who began using a Wilson 8802 putter in high school and continued using it throughout his career (mostly); and **Gary Player**, who used many putters, but is best known for a blade putter with a black face that he used for most of the 1970s. On the other hand, some golfers change putters frequently, always seeking that magic perfect roller. **Arnold Palmer** was famous in his later career for trying multiple putters and was known to have over 1,000 different models in his workshop in Latrobe, Pennsylvania.

Putters are divided into blade- and mallet-headed models. Mallet-type putters have predominated recently. Blades have a thin, very narrow clubhead, while a mallet has a thicker, heavier clubhead. Mallets are now often designed with perimeter weighting, which have higher moments of inertia and turn off-line less with off-center hits. The first forerunner of this style was the Ping putter, which in the 1960s had weight distribution at the extreme inner and outer ends of the clubhead.

PUTTING GREENS. Putting greens are the smooth, closely mowed surfaces surrounding the hole and **flagstick**, on which the golfer uses a putter to roll the ball into the hole. For the purposes of the **Rules of Golf**, a ball is considered to be on a putting green when all of it lies on the putting green. The short-cut **grass** on a putting green accommodates the putting, or rolling, of the ball along the ground by the player, in an effort to place the ball in the hole. The green contains the hole, which has a mandatory diameter of 4¼ inches (108 mm). Greens are made of various grasses, but **bent grass** predominates in nontropical climates, with **Bermuda grass** used in warmer regions. Putting greens are cut closer than any other surface of the **golf course**, with some greens now cut to the length of only 3/32nds of an inch.

Better grasses and turfgrass management have allowed greens to be mowed very close, increasing the "speed" of the greens, which measures how far a ball will roll when struck by a standard force. Green speed is now measured by a device called a **Stimpmeter**, which is a V-shaped inclined plane, with a slot at the top for a ball. The Stimpmeter is placed on the green on a flat surface, and it is gradually raised slowly until the ball leaves the slot, rolls down the inclined plane, and then rolls for a certain distance on the green. Distances of greater than 10 feet on the Stimpmeter have been a standard for fast greens, but with the newer greens and tighter mowing, Stimp speeds of 12–13, and even up to 15 feet, now occasionally occur.

Putting greens have various designs, which are at the discretion of the **golf course architect**. Many great courses have become so because of the design of their greens, the paradigm of this class being the **Augusta National Golf Club**. Greens may be flat, sloped, or have raised surfaces, or levels. They may be somewhat circular, L-shaped, long and thin, or any combination of these basic shapes. As greens have become faster with better technology, extremely sloped greens are no longer as feasible as they were in the early 20th century. Very fast, sloped greens can be almost impossible to putt well on, and they limit the number of possible hole locations, since holes should be located on relatively flat areas. *See also* FALSE FRONT; PRACTICE PUTTING GREEN.

PUTT-PUTT. *See* MINIATURE GOLF.

– Q –

Q SCHOOL, OR QUALIFYING SCHOOL. "Q School" is the term for the qualifying school that allows **professionals** to become members of the **PGA Tour**, **LPGA**, or **European PGA Tour**. The first Q School took place in 1965 for the PGA Tour and was at first an annual school. The top players in the school, which is just an extra-long tournament, receive "Tour Cards," a highly desired commodity among professionals. For a few years in the late 1960s and early 1970s, qualifying schools for the PGA Tour were held twice annually. For the PGA Tour, so many players now enter that a series of rounds, or stages, are necessary, with the leaders at each stage advancing to the final qualifying tournament. The final Q School is considered by most professionals the most pressure-packed tournament they ever play, because it determines how they make a living for the coming year. On the PGA Tour, the top 20–25 players in the final Q School now receive Tour Cards, with the next 50 players receiving cards to play on the **Nationwide Tour** (the developmental tour of the PGA Tour). The final stage is now a six-round tournament, though in some early years of the Q School, it was eight rounds.

The European PGA Tour also has a Qualifying School, which is now contested over three stages, with the final stage consisting of six rounds over two courses, usually held in Spain. The LPGA also has a Qualifying School, with two stages, with the best 40 players now awarded LPGA Cards.

QUAST (-DECKER-WELTS-SANDER), ANNE. B. 31 August 1937, Everett, Washington, United States. Anne Quast was a top female American **amateur** with a very long career, which enabled her to make the **Curtis Cup** team in four decades. Quast attended Stanford University and won the **U.S. Women's Amateur** title three times, in 1958, 1961, and 1963 and lost in the final in 1965, 1968, and 1973. She won the **British Ladies' Amateur** in 1980. After turning 50, she (by then Anne Sander) won the **USGA Senior Women's Amateur** in 1987, 1989, 1990, and 1993. She was on the **Curtis Cup** team eight times—in 1958, 1960, 1962, 1966, 1968, 1974, 1984, and 1990—a record later bettered by **Carol Semple-Thompson**. Quast is a member of the Stanford University Hall of Fame, the Washington Sports Hall of Fame, and the Pacific Northwest Golf Association Hall of Fame.

– R –

R&A. *See* ROYAL AND ANCIENT GOLF CLUB OF ST. ANDREWS.

RABBIT. Rabbit is a term applied to **professional** golfers who are near the bottom of the touring professional food chain. The term came about in the 1950s when there was very little money to be had at the bottom of the money list in any tournament, and it was referred to as "picking up scraps of lettuce." The players who rarely finished near the top in tournaments were left to scramble for these lettuce scraps and were termed rabbits. In the 1960s and 1970s, when the **PGA Tour** was not "all-exempt," Monday qualifying was held every week, and this was often the only way non-exempt players could get into tournaments. The players who were non-exempt and forced to play in Monday qualifiers were often derisively called "rabbits."

RANKIN, JUDY TORLUEMKE. B. 18 February 1945, St. Louis, Missouri, United States. Judy Rankin was a U.S. **professional** who was one of the first teenage phenoms of **women**'s golf. As Judy Torluemke, she won the 1959 Missouri Amateur when only 14, and was low amateur at the 1960 **U.S. Women's Open**. Torluemke turned pro at 17 and joined the **LPGA** in 1962. Her first LPGA win came in 1968, and she won 26 LPGA events from 1968 through 1979. She led the LPGA money list in 1976 and 1977 when she won six and five tournaments, respectively. She married Yippy Rankin in 1967, taking that name. Back problems caused her retirement in 1983, but she has forged a career as an analyst on televised golf events. Rankin was inducted into the **World Golf Hall of Fame** in 2000.

RAWLS, ELIZABETH EARLE "BETSY." B. 4 May 1928, Spartanburg, South Carolina, United States. Betsy Rawls was one of the greatest female players in the first decade of the **LPGA**, the 1950s. Born in South Carolina, she attended the University of Texas, where she majored in physics. Rawls joined the LPGA in 1951 and won 39 tournaments during the 1950s. She went of to win 55 LPGA events in her career, including eight major championships. Her majors include four wins at the **U.S. Women's Open** (1951, 1953, 1957, 1960), a record Rawls shares with **Mickey Wright**. Rawls also won the **LPGA Championship** twice (1959, 1969) and the **Women's Western Open** twice (1952, 1959). She continued to play competitively into the 1970s. In the late 1970s, she became tournament director for the LPGA. In 1996, she received the **Bob Jones Award** from the **USGA** for distinguished sportsmanship in golf. She became a charter member of the LPGA Hall of Fame in 1967.

RAY, EDWARD RIVERS G. "TED." B. 28 March 1877; D. 26 August 1943. Ted Ray was a British **professional** from the Isle of Jersey. A stocky man with a fine mustache that surrounded an ever-present pipe, he was known for his long driving. He won the **Open Championship (British Open)** in 1912 and the **U.S. Open** in 1920, on a tour of the **United States**. Ray also toured the United States in 1913 with **Harry Vardon**, and they tied for first at the U.S. Open, losing a fabled play-off to **Francis Ouimet**. Ray was a club professional at Oxhey Golf Club, near Watford, Herts, from 1912 to 1941, retiring due to ill health.

RAYNOR, SETH JAGGER. B. 7 May 1874, Southampton, Long Island, New York, United States; D. 23 January 1926, Palm Beach, Florida, United States. Seth Raynor was an American **golf course architect** who got his start as an assistant to **Charles Blair Macdonald** in the building of the **National Golf Links**. After they finished that course, Raynor assisted Macdonald on several other courses, and in 1914, he opened his own course design firm. His work was known to be dependable, as he virtually always finished the courses on time and within budget constraints. He used the natural design of the land as much as possible and tried to do as little earth moving as possible. Among his best-known courses are the following: Camargo Club, Cincinnati, Ohio; Country Club of Charleston, Charleston, South Carolina; Yale Golf Course, New Haven, Connecticut; Dunes Course at Monterey Peninsula Country Club, Pebble Beach, California; Sleepy Hollow Country Club, Scarborough, New York; Fox Chapel Golf Club, Pittsburgh, Pennsylvania; Greenwich Country Club, Greenwich, Connecticut; Mid Ocean Club in Bermuda; Old White Course at the Greenbrier Resort, White Sulphur Springs, West Virginia; and Waialae Country Club, Honolulu, Hawaii.

REDAN/REDAN HOLE. "Redan" is a type of golf hole that was popularized by **Charles Blair Macdonald** when he designed the fourth hole at the **National Golf Links**, which he based on the design of the 15th hole at the West Links in North Berwick, **Scotland**. A Redan hole has a longer, somewhat narrow green, which is set at a diagonal to the intended approach shot. It is usually sloped toward the rear of the green, with a large bunker, or bunkers, guarding that portion of the green. It can make for a very difficult approach shot, because of the diagonal nature of the green and its sloping away from the approach shot. The player must hit a shot that is not only the correct distance but also close to the correct line, or the ball will miss the green; thus, Redan holes leave little margin for error.

REES, DAVID JAMES "DAI," CBE. B. 31 March 1913, Fontygary, Glamorgan, Wales; D. 10 September 1983, London, Greater London, England. Dai Rees was a top British **professional** of the 1930s, 1940s, and 1950s who won numerous tournaments in Great Britain and on the Continent, but never succeeded in taking the **Open Championship (British Open)**. He was runner-up in the Open three times—1953, 1954, and 1961. Rees won the News of the World Match Play four times, in 1936, 1938, 1949, and 1950, losing in the final in 1967 and 1969 when he was well into his 50s. He was Swiss Open champion in 1956, 1959, and 1963, and he won the British Masters in 1950 and 1962. He is best remembered in British golf for captaining the 1957 Ryder Cup team, which defeated the **United**

States in a rare win in that era. He was a five-time **Ryder Cup** captain, in 1955, 1957, 1959, 1961, and 1967.

RESORT COURSE. A resort course is, technically, a **public golf course** although it is an upscale version. Resort courses are built near or within nice resorts, typically with many amenities at the resort and the golf club, but allow play by the guests staying at the resort. Many courses in Florida or near seaside resorts can be considered resort courses. Among the best-known resort courses are **Pinehurst** No. 2 in Pinehurst, North Carolina, and **Pebble Beach Golf Links** in California.

RHODES, THEODORE "TED," "RAGS." B. 9 November 1913, Nashville, Tennessee, United States; D. 4 July 1969, Nashville, Tennessee, United States. Ted Rhodes was one of the greatest ever African American players, but he was never given much chance to show his skills on a national stage. In most of his lifetime, blacks were banned from the **PGA Tour** by the Caucasian-only clause. After learning his game as a **caddie** in Nashville at Belle Meade Country Club, Rhodes did play in the 1948 **U.S. Open**, opening with 70 at **Riviera** before struggling a bit and finishing 51st. He also played the U.S. Open in 1949 but failed to make the cut. Rhodes played mostly on the **United Golfers Association** (UGA) tour, a tour for blacks in the **United States**. He was the biggest winner on that tour, winning over 150 events. Rhodes also taught golf to **Joe Louis** and Billy Eckstine and traveled some with Louis, serving as his valet and golf instructor. In 2009, Rhodes was granted posthumous membership by the **PGA of America**.

RIVIERA COUNTRY CLUB. Riviera Country Club is a course in Pacific Palisades, California. It has been a frequent host of the **Los Angeles Open** and was the site of the 1948 **U.S. Open** and the **PGA Championship** in 1983 and 1995. The course was designed by **George Thomas** with some assistance from **Alister MacKenzie** and opened in 1926. After World War II, the course was known as "**Hogan's Alley**," named for **Ben Hogan**, who won the Los Angeles Open three times in the 1940s and the 1948 U.S. Open there. The club also hosted the equestrian events at the 1932 **Olympic Games**, in Los Angeles.

ROBERTS, CLIFFORD. B. 6 March 1894, Morning Sun, Iowa, United States; D. 29 September 1977, Augusta, Georgia, United States. Clifford Roberts was a wealthy investment banker who, with **Bob Jones**, founded the **Augusta National Golf Club**, home of the **Masters**. Roberts served as chairman of the Masters Tournament from 1934 to 1976. Roberts made his fortune as a partner with Reynolds & Company. He was a controversial figure, who was not well liked by many golfers. He was considered responsible for the failure of the Masters to invite a black player until **Lee Elder** broke the color barrier there in 1975. Roberts committed suicide, shooting himself at night on the grounds of the Augusta National. His body was found the next morning on the par-three course. He was inducted into the **World Golf Hall of Fame** in 1978.

ROBERTSON, ALLAN. B. 1 September 1815, St. Andrews, Fife, Scotland; D. 11 September 1859, St. Andrews, Fife, Scotland. Allan Robertson is recorded as the first golf **professional**, and he is the first golfer considered the greatest player in the world. He was a professional who came along before the **Open Championship (British Open)**, which started in 1860. In fact, it is said that Robertson was so good that the Open was started after his death to determine his successor as the champion golfer. Robertson was also the first golfer to break 80 on the Old Course at **St. Andrews**. He made his reputation mostly playing in challenge matches, but he made most of his money as a **featherie-**ball maker and clubmaker and was the finest ball and club maker of his time. When the **guttie** came along in the 1840s, he was very upset because it reduced his featherie-making income.

RODRIGUEZ, JUAN ANTONIO "CHI-CHI." B. 23 October 1935, Rio Piedras, Puerto Rico. Chi-Chi Rodriguez was a Puerto Rican **professional** who made his name on the **PGA Tour**. A humorous man, who was very outgoing with the galleries, Rodriguez was a very long hitter for a man of his small stature. He won eight tournaments on the PGA Tour and 22 on the Champions (Senior) Tour. Among other pros, Rodriguez was considered one of the best bunker players in the world. Rodriguez started in golf as a **caddie** but joked that he was so small that he started out as a ball marker. He had a celebratory act after making a birdie or long putt: He would handle his putter as though it were a sword, doing a toreador dance. Then, sometimes, he would place his straw hat over the hole, ostensibly to keep the ball from getting out. Rodriguez was extremely generous to other players and the less fortunate. He received the **Bob Jones Award** in 1989 from the **USGA** for distinguished sportsmanship in golf, and in 1992, he was inducted into the **World Golf Hall of Fame**.

ROSS, DONALD JAMES. B. 23 November 1872, Dornoch, Scotland; D. 26 April 1948, Raleigh, North Carolina, United States. Donald Ross was the first great **golf course architect** in the **United States** and is among the greatest ever. Born in **Scotland**, he apprenticed under **Old Tom Morris** at **St. Andrews** before immigrating to the United States in 1899, where he served as an assistant pro at Oakley Country Club, in Watertown, Massachusetts. Ross was quite a good player, winning three **North and South Opens** (1903, 1905, 1906) and two Massachusetts Opens (1905, 1911).

In 1900, Ross became the golf **professional** at **Pinehurst**, where he began his course design career, eventually building four of the five Pinehurst courses (there are now eight). His most famous design is Pinehurst No. 2, one of the premier **golf courses** in the United States. He also designed Oak Hill and **Oakland Hills**, courses that have hosted the **U.S. Open**. He designed courses all over the country, but his courses are almost ubiquitous in New England and North Carolina. Ross was a founding member and the first president of the **American Society of Golf Course Architects**, which was formed at Pinehurst in 1947. He was inducted into the **World Golf Hall of Fame** in 1977. Ross' brother, Alex, won the 1907 U.S. Open.

ROUGH. "Rough" is an odd word in the world of golf. Every golfer knows what it is, but the word is not in the **Rules of Golf**. For years, **Augusta National Golf Club**, home of the **Masters**, was famous for not having rough, but then, strangely, longer **grass** appeared in the 1990s, but they called it the "first cut," and the club still adamantly denies the existence of rough on the course. Rough is **fairway**-type grass that is allowed to grow longer, bordering the sides of the fairway. At major championships (other than the Masters), notably the **U.S. Open**, the rough is sometimes allowed to grow extremely long (up to 4½ inches), making recovery from off the fairway very difficult, thus placing a premium on straight driving.

Some tournament courses have gradations of rough, often termed the "first cut" and "second cut," with the first cut being shorter and less difficult to recover from. In addition to the difficulty of making solid ball contact in longer grass, rough causes problems for **professionals** because the long grass prevents a player from putting much spin on the ball. Such a shot, often termed a "**flyer**," will hit a green and roll uncontrollably, making it difficult to get the ball close to the hole from the rough. Most country clubs do not have significant amounts of rough because it makes play difficult and slow, with players losing balls and hitting poor shots. In the Rules of Golf, there is no distinction between the fairway and the rough, which are considered parts of **through the green**.

THE ROYAL AND ANCIENT GOLF CLUB OF ST. ANDREWS. The Royal and Ancient, often abbreviated "R&A," is really two distinct entities. The Royal and Ancient Golf Club of St. Andrews is the club based in St. Andrews, **Scotland**. It has seven **golf courses**, but the most famous of these is the Old Course, which has been the site of many **Open Championships (British Open)**. All the courses are **public courses**. The seven courses are the Old Course, New Course, Jubilee Course, Eden Course, and three newer courses, the Balgove Course, a nine-hole course opened in 1972, the Strathtyrum Course (1993), and the Castle Course (2008). The Royal and Ancient Golf Club of St. Andrews is one of the original Scottish clubs and is often considered the home of golf. It was founded in 1754 as the Society of St. Andrews Golfers, taking its current name in 1834.

The Royal and Ancient Golf Club was the governing body for golf in the British Isles, but in 2004, this role was separated from the golf club, and a new group of companies, called the "R&A, Ltd." was formed. The R&A serves as the governing body of golf in all countries except the **United States** and Mexico, which are governed by the **USGA.** The current R&A consists of eight committees: Rule and Equipment Committee, Course Management Committee, Championship Committee, **Amateur Status** Committee, Golf Development Committee, External Fund Committee, General Committee, and Research Committee. The R&A conducts 11 championships and international matches. The tournaments are the **Open Championship (British Open)**, the **Amateur Championship (British Amateur)**, **British Boys Amateur**, British Mid-Amateur, British Seniors Open Amateur, **British Senior Open**, and the Junior Open Championships for boys and girls less than 16. The matches it conducts are the Boys Home Internationals—between teams of boys from **England**, Scotland, Wales, and All-**Ireland**; the **Walker Cup**—amateur matches between the United States and the British Isles, co-organized with the USGA; the St. Andrews Trophy—a men's amateur team competition between Great Britain–Ireland and Continental Europe; and the Jacques Léglise Trophy—a boys amateur team competition between Great Britain–Ireland and Continental Europe. The R&A does not conduct the **Women's British Open** or **British Ladies' Amateur**, which are organized by the **Ladies' Golf Union**. Appendix 11 includes a list of captains of the Royal and Ancient.

ROYAL BIRKDALE GOLF CLUB. Royal Birkdale Golf Club is in Southport, **England**, and is one of the courses in the rotation (rota) of the **Open Championship (British Open)**. Royal Birkdale first hosted in 1954 and has since hosted the event nine times, most recently in 2008. The club was founded in 1889 and gained royal status in 1951. It was designed by **J. H. Taylor** and Frederick Hawtrey. Royal Birkdale first hosted a major event in 1946 when the **Amateur Championship (British Amateur)** took place there. That event has only returned to the course twice. The course has also hosted the **Women's British Open**, the **Ryder Cup**, the **Walker Cup**, and the **Curtis Cup**.

ROYAL CANADIAN GOLF ASSOCIATION (RCGA). The Royal Canadian Golf Association is the governing body of golf in **Canada**. It was founded in June 1895 as the Royal Ottawa Golf Club, becoming the RCGA in 1896. The original RCGA was formed among 10 clubs: **Royal Montréal Golf Club**; Royal Québec Golf Club; Royal Ottawa Golf Club; Kingston Golf Club; Toronto Golf Club; Rosedale Golf Club; Hamilton Golf and Country Club; London Golf Club; Winnipeg Golf Club; and Victoria Golf Club. In 1895, the group organized the first Canadian Amateur Championship, held the Canadian Ladies' Amateur Championship for the first time in 1901, and added the **Canadian Open** in 1904. In 1924, the Canadian Ladies' Golf Union took over the Canadian Ladies' Amateur, running it until 2005, when the group merged with the RCGA. The RCGA now runs several other national championships, notably the Canadian Women's Open (formerly the **Du Maurier Classic**), Canadian Junior Championship, Canadian Junior Girls' Championship, Canadian Senior Championship, Canadian Senior Women's Championship, Canadian Mid-Amateur Championship, Canadian Senior Match Play Championship, Future Links Series, and the CN Canadian Women's Tour. The RCGA also conducts the Willingdon Cup Matches for the Interprovincial Championship and provides Canadian teams for international play.

ROYAL COUNTY DOWN GOLF CLUB. Royal County Down is an iconic Irish **links** course. The club has two courses, the Championship Course and the Annesley Links. The Championship Course at Royal County Down is virtually always included in any list of the great courses of the world. It was originally designed by **Old Tom Morris** and opened in 1889. The course later saw minor redesigns by George Combe, **Harry Vardon**, and **Harry Colt**. Royal County Down has hosted three **British Senior Opens** (2000–2002), the **Amateur Championship (British Amateur)** in 1970 and 1999, eight **British Ladies' Amateur** Championships, the 1968 **Curtis Cup**, and the 2007 **Walker Cup**.

ROYAL DORNOCH GOLF CLUB. Royal Dornoch is a club in Dornoch, Sutherland, **Scotland**. The club has two courses, the Championship Course, a **links** course on the Dornoth Firth, and the Struie Course. Dornoch is in the very far north of Scotland, and it has never hosted a major championship because of its inaccessibility. However, it attracts touring **professionals**, who will travel there to play it, having heard of its wonders from other players. The Championship Course design is attributed to **Old Tom Morris**. It opened in 1877, and the club gained royal status in 1906.

ROYAL LIVERPOOL GOLF CLUB. Royal Liverpool Golf Club is in Merseyside, Northwest **England**, and is one of the courses on the rotation (rota) of the **Open Championship** (**British Open**). It was founded in 1869 and became royal in 1871, based on the patronage given by the Duke of Connaught, one of Queen Victoria's sons. The club is located in the small town of Hoylake on the Wirral Peninsula, and it is often referred to simply as Hoylake. Hoylake has hosted the Open Championship (British Open) 11 times, the **Amateur Championship (British Amateur)** 18 times, the **British Ladies' Amateur** (1896, 1989, 1996), the **Walker Cup** (1983), and the **Curtis Cup** (1992).

ROYAL LYTHAM AND ST. ANNES GOLF CLUB. Royal Lytham and St. Annes is located in Lytham St. Annes, Lancashire, **England**. It is one of the courses on the rotation (rota) of the **Open Championship (British Open)**. It first hosted the event in 1926, when it was won by **Bob Jones**, moved into the rota in 1952, and has conducted the championship 10 times through 2001. The course has also hosted the **Women's British Open** four times. Royal Lytham and St. Annes was the first site of the **British Ladies' Amateur** Championship in 1893. The course is somewhat unusual among major championship courses, because the opening hole is a par-three.

ROYAL MELBOURNE GOLF CLUB. Royal Melbourne Golf Club is the most famous course in **Australia**. It has been a frequent host to the **Australian Open** and hosted the 1959 **World Cup** (then the **Canada Cup**), the 1970 World Cup, the 1998 **President's Cup**, and will host the President's Cup again in 2011. The course was founded in 1891 as the Melbourne Golf Club, achieving royal status in 1895. There are two courses at the club—the West Course and East Course. The club moved to its current site in the early 1920s, and the West Course was the original course on site, designed by **Alister MacKenzie**. The East Course opened in 1932, designed by Australian golfer Alex Russell. The current tournament layout is a composite course of the best holes from the two courses. Royal Melbourne is known for its extremely fast greens.

ROYAL MONTRÉAL GOLF CLUB. Royal Montréal Golf Club is the oldest continuously operated club in North America, having been founded in 1873. However, the club has had several locations, starting with a nine-hole course at Fletcher's Field in Mount Royal Park. In 1959, 45 holes were built at the current location in Île-Bizard,

Québec, all designed by Dick Wilson. The championship layout was the Blue Course, which is on most lists of the top 100 courses in the world. Royal Montréal was one of the founding clubs of the **Royal Canadian Golf Association**. The course has hosted the **Canadian Open** and Canadian Amateur numerous times and in 2007 hosted the President's Cup matches.

ROYAL PORTRUSH GOLF CLUB. Royal Portrush is located in County Antrim in Northern Ireland. It is one of the greatest Irish **links** courses and is the only Irish course to ever host the **Open Championship (British Open)**, which it did in 1951, with **Max Faulkner** winning. In 1947, Fred Daly, a member of the club, became the first Irishman to win the Open. There are two full courses at the club, but the Dunluce Links is the championship layout, and it has been ranked as high as number three among non-U.S. courses in various lists of the world's best **golf courses**. It also hosted the **British Senior Open** in 1995–1999 and 2004. The club opened in 1888 as the County Club and became the Royal County Club in 1892 under the patronage of the Duke of York. It became Royal Portrush in 1895. The second course is called the Valley Course. A shorter course, it is often played by beginners, seniors, and **women**. There is also a short nine-hole pitch-and-putt course. The Dunluce Links is situated on the North Antrim Causeway Coast, wedged between giant sand hills, with views of the Donegal hills to the west, the Isle of Islay and Southern Hebrides to the north, and the Giant's Causeway and the Skerries to the east. The course is overlooked by the ruins of 13th-century Dunluce Castle, from which the course takes its name.

ROYAL ST. GEORGE'S GOLF CLUB. Royal St. George's is a British **golf course** that is in the rota of clubs that host the **Open Championship (British Open)**. The course is located in Sandwich, Kent, **England**, and was founded in 1887 in an area of wild dunelands. The Open was first held there in 1894, and the course has hosted the championship 13 times, with the 2011 Open scheduled. Royal St. George's was taken off the Open rota after 1949 but returned in 1981 and has hosted the championship four times since. The club has also hosted the **Amateur Championship (British Amateur)** 13 times. The course was described in Ian Fleming's novel *Goldfinger*, although he called it Royal St. Marks, and the movie's golf scenes were shot at Stoke Poges Golf Club.

ROYAL TROON GOLF CLUB. Royal Troon is a **links** course located in Troon, South Ayrshire, **Scotland**. It is used in the rotation (rota) of the **Open Championship (British Open)**. The Open was first held there in 1923, but it didn't move onto the rota until 1950, and it has hosted the Open eight times. Royal Troon has two courses, the Old Course and the Portland Course, with championships played on the Old Course. The club was founded in 1878.

RUB OF THE GREEN. A rub of the green occurs when a ball in motion is accidentally deflected or stopped by any **outside agency**. Play then proceeds under Rule 19-1 of the **Rules of Golf**. Specifically, **through the green** or in a **hazard**, the player will play the ball wherever it came to rest. If that cannot be determined (usually when a bird or other animal picks up the ball and takes off with it), the player should drop a ball as near to the original place where the ball came to rest as can be determined. On the putting green, if a moving ball is stopped or deflected by an outside agency, the stroke is cancelled and should be replayed.

RULES OF GOLF. The Rules of Golf govern how the game of golf is played. The earliest known Rules of Golf, drafted by the **Honourable Company of Edinburgh Golfers** in March 1744, consisted of only 13 rules:

1. You must Tee your Ball within a Club's length of the Hole.
2. Your Tee must be upon the Ground.
3. You are not to change the Ball which you Strike off the Tee.
4. You are not to remove Stones, Bones or any Break Club, for the sake of playing your Ball, Except upon the fair Green within a Club's length of your Ball.
5. If your Ball comes among watter, or any wattery filth, you are at liberty to take out your Ball & bringing it behind the hazard and Teeing it, you may play it with any Club and allow your Adversary a Stroke for so getting out your Ball.
6. If your Balls be found any where touching one another, You are to lift the first Ball, till you play the last.

7. At Holling, you are to play your Ball honestly for the Hole, and not to play upon your Adversary's Ball, not lying in your way to the Hole.
8. If you should lose your Ball, by its being taken up, or any other way, you are to go back to the Spot, where you struck last, & drop another Ball, And allow your adversary a Stroke for the misfortune.
9. No man at Holling his Ball, is to be allowed, to mark his way to the Hole with his Club, or anything else.
10. If a Ball be stopp'd by any Person, Horse, Dog or anything else, The Ball so stop'd must be play'd where it lyes.
11. If you draw your Club in Order to Strike, & proceed so far in the Stroke as to be bringing down your Club; If then, your Club shall break, in any way, it is to be Accounted a Stroke.
12. He whose Ball lyes farthest from the Hole is obliged to play first.
13. Neither Trench, Ditch or Dyke, made for the preservation of the Links, nor the Scholar's Holes, or the Soldier's Lines, Shall be accounted a Hazard; But the Ball is to be taken out and play'd with any Iron Club.

For many years, there were two sets of rules, codifed by the **USGA** and the **R&A**. Beginning in 1952, the two groups standardized the rules, publishing a new set every two years, usually with some minor changes. However, it was not until 1990 that the two sets of rules truly became one, as both groups settled upon a standard set for the game. The biggest difference for many years was that the R&A allowed play with a 1.62 inch diameter ball, while the USGA ball was standardized at 1.68 inches.

There are three basic premises governing the Rules of Golf: 1) play the ball as it lies, 2) play the course as you find it, and 3) if unable to do either "1" or "2," do what is fair. There are currently 34 rules, with many sub-rules, and sub-sub-rules. In addition, the USGA and R&A publish a book called *Decisions on the Rules of Golf*, which are specialized rulings that have been standardized over the years, based on questions that have come up in competitive play. There have been several popular books written on the Rules of Golf: delineating its history—*Rules of the Green: A History of the Rules of Golf*, by Kenneth Chapman; and attempting to simplify the rules for the club player—*The Rules of Golf in Plain English* by Jeffrey Kuhn and Bryan Garner; and *Golf Rules: Plain and Simple* by Mark

Russell and John Andrisani. *See also* ALTERNATE BALL; BALL IN PLAY; BALL MARKER; BEST-BALL; BETTER-BALL; BUNKERS; CASUAL WATER; COEFFICIENT OF RESTITUTION; CONCEDED PUTT; FLAGSTICK; FORECADDIE; FOUR-BALL; FOURSOMES; GIMME; HAZARDS; HOLED; LATERAL WATER HAZARDS; LOCAL RULES; LOOSE IMPEDIMENTS; LOST BALL; MATCH PLAY; MULLIGAN; OBSTRUCTIONS; OUT-OF-BOUNDS; OUTSIDE AGENCY; PREFERRRED LIES; PROVISIONAL BALL; SPIKE MARKS; STABLEFORD SYSTEM; STROKE PLAY; STYMIE; UNPLAYABLE LIE; WATER HAZARDS; WINTER RULES; WRONG BALL.

RUNYAN, PAUL SCOTT "LITTLE POISON." B. 12 July 1908, Hot Springs, Arkansas, United States; D. 17 March 2002, Palm Springs, California, United States. Paul Runyan was one of the shortest hitters to ever reach the top levels of golf. He won 29 events on the **PGA Tour** from 1930 to 1941. He was at his best in 1933, with nine wins, and 1934, with seven wins, including the 1934 **PGA Championship**. In 1938, he defeated **Sam Snead** in the finals to win the PGA again, prevailing 8 & 7 despite being outdriven by Snead by 50 yards or more on most holes. Runyan was known for his short game and his ability as a putter, and later became a renowned teacher, specializing in the short game. Runyan played on two **Ryder Cup** teams (1933, 1935). He was inducted into the **World Golf Hall of Fame** in 1990. He is also a member of the World Golf Teachers Hall of Fame and the Arkansas Hall of Fame, and he was a recipient of the **Harvey Penick** Lifetime Teaching Award

RYDER CUP. The Ryder Cup is a biennial men's **professional** team competition, currently played between the **United States** and a European team. The event began in 1927 with a trophy donated by **Samuel Ryder**, a seed merchant from Hertfordshire, and was originally contested between the United States and Great Britain. There were two unofficial competitions between U.S. and British professionals that preceded the actual **Ryder Cup**. In 1921, the British defeated the Americans 9-3, and in 1926, they won easily, 13½-1½. Samuel Ryder was a spectator at the second match in 1926 and suggested the biennial trophy, which he donated. The competition remained between the United States and Great Britain until 1973, when the British side was enlarged to include Great Britain and Ireland. But the event was lopsided, with the United States winning all the matches except three, those of 1929, 1933, and 1957, through 1977. Thus, in 1979, the event was changed to include a European team instead of a British side. The European team first won in 1985 and has since bested the United States, winning seven of twelve matches, with the 1989 match halved. Since the addition of European players, the event has become hotly contested and one of the most anticipated events of the golf year. It was always held on odd-numbered years through 1999, but in 2001, the events of 9/11 necessitated cancellation of the Ryder Cup. It was held in 2002 and is now held in even-numbered years.

The format of the competition has changed over the years. From 1927 to 1959, it consisted of two days, with the first day devoted to four **foursomes** matches and the second day to eight singles matches, all held at 36 holes, for a total of 12 points. In 1961, all matches were changed to 18 holes, doubling the number of matches, to eight, and points, to 24. The event was expanded to the current three days in 1963 and from 1963 to 1975, it consisted of eight foursome matches on the first day, eight **four-ball** matches on the second day, and 16 singles matches on the final day, for 32 points. In 1977, the event consisted of five foursomes matches, five four-ball matches, and 10 singles matches on the final day, for 20 points. Since the 1979 match, the event has been standardized at four foursomes and four four-ball matches on each of the first two days, and 12 singles matches on the final day, for 28 points.

There have been a number of famous Ryder Cup competitions. In 1969, the event was very close and came down to the final match between **Jack Nicklaus** and **Tony Jacklin**. On the final green, after Nicklaus had holed out, Jacklin was left with a three-foot putt to tie the match, and if he missed, the United States would win. Nicklaus did not give him the chance, conceding the putt and telling him, "I don't think you would have missed that putt, but in these circumstances, I would never give you the opportunity."

After Europe had won the Cup in 1985 and 1987, and retained it with a tie in 1989, the 1991 match at **Kiawah Island Golf Resort** in South Carolina was eagerly anticipated by the Americans, hoping to regain the cup. It was termed the "War on the Shore" and was closely contested, the U.S. team eventually winning 14½-13½. The course was extremely difficult, and high winds on the final day made scores in the high 70s and low 80s common, adding to the drama. During four-ball play, **Paul Azinger** and **Seve Ballesteros** had a heated argument when Ballesteros accused Azinger of cheating, and it looked for a moment like they might need to be separated.

In 1999, the event was held at **The Country Club** in Brookline, Massachusetts, following European wins in 1995 and 1997. After the first two days of play, Europe led 10-6 and appeared headed for another easy victory. But U.S. captain **Ben Crenshaw** gave an inspiring speech and showed a motivational movie the night before the final day, and the United States played very well in singles to eke out a victory, 14½-13½. The critical match came down to Justin Leonard on the 17th green, playing against **José María Olazábal**. The Ryder Cup was square, and their match was also square. Olazábal played his second shot to about 20 feet, with Leonard barely reaching the green, 50 feet away on the wrong level. But Leonard holed his sea roller, which made the gallery riotous, and the U.S. team and their wives ran onto the green to embrace Leonard. Olazábal was upset, as was the entire European team, thinking that it violated the etiquette of the game and that the players and their wives had run over the Spaniard's line. Olazábal missed his putt, lost the match on 18, and the United States prevailed. The Americans apologized in their press conference but noted that Olazábal's frequent partner, Seve Ballesteros, was well-known for his gamesmanship during the Ryder Cup. Appendix 5 includes a list of champions, scores, and captains.

RYDER, SAMUEL. B. 24 March 1858, Walton-le-Dale, Lancashire, England; D. 2 January 1936, London, England. Samuel Ryder was a British seed merchant and golf enthusiast who donated the trophy for the biennial men's **professional** team competition between the **United States** and now Europe, known as the **Ryder Cup**. There were two unofficial matches between the U.S. and British professionals, in 1921 and 1926. In 1926, Ryder was in the gallery and suggested making this a biennial event, offering to donate a £250 gold trophy for the competition. Ryder had started working for his father in the florist and seed business, but discord between the two led him to join a rival merchant in London. Ryder then began selling seed packets via post, and he eventually became quite wealthy. He entered politics in 1903, served on the town council in St. Albans, was mayor of St. Albans in 1905, and then served as a town councillor until 1916.

RYEGRASS. Ryegrass is any of nine species of a tufted, perennial **grass** of genus *Lolium*. Ryegrass grows best in cooler climates. It is a soft, not very tough grass. It is often used on **golf courses**, especially in the winter, when many courses will overseed their greens and **fairways** with ryegrass, which survives the cooler weather well and protects the underlying grass. Many courses in the south and west will overseed in the winter with ryegrass because it is a deep, bright green color. Warmer climate grasses, such as **fescue** or **Bermuda**, become dormant in the winter and turn a soft brown, which is not attractive to club members or resort guests. By overseeding with ryegrass, the club keeps up the appearance of the course, the greens and fairways staying a bright green.

– S –

ST. ANDREWS. St. Andrews is a town in Fife, **Scotland**, located on the east coast of Scotland, bordering the North Sea. It is often called the "home of golf," because the **Royal and Ancient Golf Club of St. Andrews** is based there. The town has seven public **golf courses**, of which the Old Course is the most famous, having hosted the **Open Championship (British Open)** many times. The other courses are the New Course, Jubilee Course, Eden Course, and three newer courses, the Balgove Course, a nine-hole course opened in 1972, the Strathtyrum Course (1993), and the Castle Course (2008). The town is also home to St. Andrews University, the third-oldest university in the English-speaking world.

ST. GEORGE'S GOLF and COUNTRY CLUB. St. George's Golf and Country Club is a top Canadian course, located in the Toronto suburb of Islington. Originally called Royal York Golf Club, the club was built in 1909, coordinated with the design of the Royal York Hotel in Toronto. The **golf course**, however, wasn't built until 1929.

It was designed by Canadian **golf course architect Stanley Thompson**. In 1946, the club changed its name to St. George's Golf and Country Club. It has hosted the **Canadian Open** four times and the Canadian Women's Open (**Du Maurier Classic**) five times.

SAND WEDGE. A sand wedge is a golf club specifically designed for getting one's ball out of a sand trap, or **bunker**. It is occasionally called a "sand iron." Prior to the advent of **lob wedges**, the sand wedge was usually the most lofted and heaviest club in the bag. In addition to its loft, the sand wedge works because its bottom sole is thicker and wider than a pitching wedge or lob wedge, creating bounce so that the club doesn't dig into the sand but instead slides through it. The sand wedge is the only club that can be attributed to one person for its popularization, and that was **Gene Sarazen**, the great **professional** of the 1920s and 1930s. Sarazen was unhappy with his bunker play and tinkered with his wedge, adding thickness to the sole to create bounce. He then used the club to win the 1932 **British Open**, which made it very popular. A sand wedge may also be used for pitching and for short **fairway** shots.

SANDBAGGER. "Sandbagger" is a derisive term for someone who cheats by trying to play at a higher **handicap** than he or she actually carries. For example, if a player who is new to a group, and is not known by the other players, carries an 8 handicap but tells the other players that his or her handicap is higher, say, 12 or 14, then that player is a sandbagger. A sandbagger has to be careful not to choose too high a number, since this is definitely frowned upon in club matches. When a player who is honest about his or her handicap has a particularly good round and plays better than the handicap suggests, that player will often be jokingly accused by playing partners of "sandbagging it."

SANDER, ANNE. *See* ANNE QUAST.

SANDERS, DOUG. B. 24 July 1933, Cedartown, Georgia, United States. Doug Sanders was a top American **professional** who won 20 **PGA Tour** events during his career. He turned pro in 1956 after winning the 1956 **Canadian Open** as an **amateur**. He never managed a major title, but was a runner-up at the 1959 **PGA Championship**, the 1961 **U.S. Open**, and the **Open Championship (British Open)** in 1966 and 1970. He also placed third in the PGA in 1960 and 1961. Sanders' loss at the 1970 British Open was particularly painful because he missed a three-foot putt on the 72nd hole at **St. Andrews** that would have won him the title. He fell back to a tie with **Jack Nicklaus** and lost the play-off the next day. Sanders had the shortest backswing in the professional game, which made him a slightly shorter hitter but a very accurate **driver** of the ball off the tee. For all his golfing feats, however, he was best known as the most flamboyant dresser on the PGA Tour.

SANDS, CHARLES EDWARD. B. 22 December 1865, New York, New York, United States; D. 9 August 1945, Brookville, New York, United States. Charles Sands is one of only two American men to compete in three different **Olympic** sports. (The other is Frank Kugler,who competed in athletics, weightlifting, and wrestling. Sheila Taormina also accomplished this, competing in swimming, triathlon, and modern pentathlon.) In October 1900, Sands shot rounds of 81-84 to win the first Olympic golf championship. He probably did not care, since golf was not his favorite, or best, sport, even though he finished second in the first **U.S. Amateur** ever held—in 1895. Charles Sands was primarily a court tennis player. He was the only American to win the Racquette d'Or, which he received at the Tuileries Gardens in Paris in 1899 and 1900. In 1905, he won his only American championship in court tennis. In 1908, court tennis was an Olympic sport, under the original French name of *jeu de paume*. Sands played but lost in the first round. It was not his first appearance in Olympic tennis. In 1900, while in Paris for the Racquette d'Or competition, he played in the Olympic lawn tennis event but lost in the early rounds.

SANDY. A "sandy" refers to getting a ball up-and-down from a sand **bunker**. In many club matches, players bet on specific feats on the course, such as making **birdies** or **eagles** naturally (without strokes). Many times, these side bets include a payoff for making a sandy. Among **professional** players, a sandy is something they expect to do, and most pros will get up-and-down from sand bunkers very frequently if they have a good lie, and as a result, the term is not used by pros to any extent.

SARAZEN, GENE "THE SQUIRE" (NÉ EUGENIO SARACENI). B. 27 February 1902, Harrison, New York, United States; D. 13 May 1999, Naples, Florida, United States. Like many **professionals** of the 1920s, Eugenio Saraceni started in golf as a **caddie** in his youth. After playing in a few tournaments, he changed his name to Gene Sarazen and became the first golfer to win the current career professional **Grand Slam**, winning the **U.S. Open** (1922, 1932), **PGA Championship** (1922, 1923, 1933), **Open Championship (British Open)** (1932), and **Masters** (1935). During his career, he won 39 PGA Tournaments. With **Walter Hagen** and **Bob Jones**, he made up the great golfing triumvirate of the 1920s, often considered the Golden Age of Sport. Sarazen played on six **Ryder Cup** teams and became a charter member of the **World Golf Hall of Fame** in 1974. He was the smallest-ever great champion at only 5 feet 5 inches (165 cm), but was still a fairly long hitter. He always competed wearing knickers, or plus-fours.

Sarazen was known for popularizing the **sand wedge**, which he developed in the early 1930s when he became frustrated with his own bunker play. He was also known for his victory at the second Masters Tournament in 1935. Playing with Walter Hagen in the final group, Sarazen was three shots behind with four holes to play when he holed a 4-wood shot on the par-five 15th for a **double eagle**. That made up all three shots at once and enabled him to tie **Craig Wood**, whom he defeated the next day in a play-off. In 1973, Sarazen played in his final Open Championship, at Troon, and made a **hole-in-one** on the Postage Stamp, the par-three 8th hole. Sarazen played Wilson clubs and was on the Wilson staff for 75 years, from 1923 until his death.

Sarazen was a great ambassador for the game of golf. From 1981 to 1999, he, **Sam Snead**, and **Byron Nelson** were the ceremonial starters on the first tee of the Masters. In the 1960s, he was a popular host of the American televised golf series, **Shell's Wonderful World of Golf**. He received the 1992 **Bob Jones Award** from the **USGA** for distinguished sportsmanship in golf. In 1996, he received the first **PGA Tour** Lifetime Achievement Award. In 1978, he was awarded an honorary degree from Siena College, and in 1998, he and his wife endowed the Gene and Mary Sarazen Scholarship at that school.

SCORECARD. The scorecard is used in tournament golf to record the scores of the players. A player does not keep his own scorecard; it is filled out by one of the player's playing partners. The scorecard must be signed by both the player and the player keeping score. However, the player is responsible for his own ultimate score and must correct any errors on it prior to signing it. According to the **Rules of Golf**, a player who signs for a higher score on any hole than actually made must accept the higher score rather than the actual score. At the 1968 Masters, this occurred when **Roberto De Vicenzo** finished the final round with what appeared to be a 65, tying Bob Goalby for the title. But De Vicenzo signed for a four on the 17th hole, when he actually made a three. He had to accept that score, changing his final round to 66 dropping him one shot behind Goalby, and making him ineligible for a play-off. Goalby won the tournament as a result.

If a player signs for a score on any hole that is lower than the actual score made, that player is disqualified. This also occurred at a major championship, the 1957 **U.S. Women's Open** at **Winged Foot**. Hawaii's Jackie Pung appeared to have won the tournament, shooting a final round 72 for 298, but it was discovered that her scorecard listed a five on the fourth hole when she actually made a six. Her playing partner, **Betty Jameson**, had filled out the card. Pung did not catch the error and was disqualified, giving the title to **Betsy Rawls**. A player is only responsible for the hole-by-hole scores. If they are correct, but when added, the total score is incorrect, the total is corrected with no penalty to the player.

SCOTCH FOURSOMES. "Scotch foursome" is **foursomes** play in which a man and woman play together, making up a team and hitting alternate shots, as in typical foursome play. It is sometimes referred to as "mixed foursomes" or colloquially, "mixies."

SCOTLAND. Scotland is considered the home of golf. Although golf's origins are **obscure**, golf was played in Scotland as early as the 15th century, although similar games to golf may have originated earlier in the Low Countries of Europe. Scotland claims to be the home of golf because it popularized the game in the 19th century. Many Scottish **golf professionals** immigrated to the **United States** to work at newly formed clubs, bringing the game from the "old country" to the colonies. Scotland is also the home of the first major golf championship, the **Open Championship (British Open).** While it is the Open Championship of Great Britain and is now held almost as often in **England** as it is in Scotland, the championship started in 1860 and was always held in Scotland until the 1894 edition. The greatest players of the 19th century were Scottish **professionals**, including **Allan Robertson**, **Old Tom Morris**, and **Young Tom Morris**. But in the 1920s, the U.S. players surpassed those from Great Britain, and Scotland has never again been the dominant nation in international golf competitions. Scotland remains the nation with the most **golf courses** per capita.

SCOTT, LADY MARGARET RACHEL. B. 5 April 1874, Westminster, London, England; D. 27 January 1938, London, Greater London, England. Lady Margaret Scott was the first great player in the **women**'s game. She won the first three **British Ladies' Amateur** championships, in 1893–1895, and then retired from golf. Scott was the daughter of John Scott, the third Earl of Eldon. Three of her brothers were also top players: Michael Scott won the 1933 **Amateur Championship (British Amateur)**, Osmund Scott was runner-up at the 1905 British Amateur, and Denys Scott played in the tournament several times. Lady Scott married the Honorable Frederick Gustavus Hamilton-Russell in 1897.

SCRAMBLE. In a scramble tournament, two or four persons play together as a team. On each shot, the team selects the best shot hit by any of the players, then they all play the next shot from that spot. This process continues with each shot until the ball is holed. This leads to very low scores. It is a popular format for **pro-am** tournaments and is often played at **country clubs**. The event may be played either with or without **handicaps**. The event has several variations and several different names. In an Ambrose tournament, a group handicap is applied. In a Texas Scramble, four tee balls are played, and each player then plays a second shot, with the scramble beginning after the second shot. This format is rarely used nowadays; it was occasionally called a "Super-Ball" or "Fort Lauderdale" tournament.

SCRATCH GOLFER. A scratch golfer is one who has attained a **handicap** of 0. It is the hallmark of an expert **amateur** golfer, although handicaps may be lower than scratch. Handicaps lower than scratch are referred to as "plus handicaps," and a player may be a +1, +2, or even lower. Most top college amateurs at the better Division I programs and many top amateurs playing in state or national tournaments are scratch golfers, so it is not unusual. Male touring **professionals** would likely have very low plus handicaps if such a term were ever used in reference to a pro, possibly as low as +6 to +8.

SEIGNIOUS, HOPE. B. 4 January 1919, Orangeburg, South Carolina, United States; D. July 1968, Ware, South Carolina, United States. Hope Seignious is almost unknown to the golf world today but deserves acknowledgment as one of the pioneers of **women**'s **professional** golf. Born to a wealthy cotton broker in South Carolina, she and her family moved to Michigan when she was a child, where she began playing golf at the Clinton Valley Country Club. After losing in the final of the 1936 Western Girls' Junior, Seignious won the Detroit Women's Golf Association Championship for five straight years, from 1936 to 1940. She played in the 1938 **U.S. Women's Amateur**, losing in the third round, made it to the quarterfinals in the Western Women's Amateur in 1937 and 1938, was runner-up in the 1937 Michigan Women's Amateur, and placed seventh at the 1939 Women's All-American Open. In 1944, Seignious, along with **Ellen Griffin** and **Betty Hicks**, formed the **Women's Professional Golf Association (WPGA)**, the first such organization for women golfers. That same year, Seignious was hired as an assistant golf professional at Starmount Forest in Greensboro, North Carolina.

She served as secretary-treasurer and tournament director for the WPGA, and in 1946 she was able to hold the first **U.S. Women's Open**, with prize money donated by the Spokane Athletic Round Table. In 1947, Seignious tapped her father's fortune to support the second U.S. Women's Open. By then, she was head professional at the North Shore Country Club in Milwaukee, Wisconsin, one of the first women ever to be a head professional in the **United States**. She again managed and organized the U.S. Women's Open, in 1948, and was able to get the WPGA schedule up to seven events, but the WPGA lacked financial support and died out in late 1949. Women's professional golf was resurrected in 1950 with the formation of the **LPGA.** Seignious was an only child and never married. After starting a **miniature golf course** in Greensboro with Kathryn Hemphill, a top local professional, she began a trucking company in the Greensboro area and disappeared from public life. Her pioneering story is now only a shadow and a vague memory for women golfers.

SELLINGER, ART. B. 6 May 1965, Brooklyn, New York, United States. Art Sellinger was one of the longest **drivers** in golf history but is better known as a promoter of long-driving competitions. Sellinger won the National Long Drive Championship twice and now owns the Long Drivers of America tour, which promotes and conducts the RE/MAX World Long Drive Championship.

SEMINOLE GOLF CLUB. Seminole Golf Club is a **golf course** in Juno Beach, Florida, that is one of the greatest courses in the **United States**. It has never hosted a major championship and is a very exclusive, very private club. The course was designed in the 1920s by **Donald Ross** when E. F. Hutton and Martin Sweeney asked him to lay out the finest course in Florida. From the 1930s to 1961, the club hosted the Latham Invitational Pro-Am, which paired a member with a touring pro and was associated with one of the largest **Calcutta** pools in the country. The course was the winter training ground of **Ben Hogan**, who would spend several weeks there preparing for the **Masters**.

SEMPLE-THOMPSON, CAROL. B. 27 October 1948, Sewickley, Pennsylvania, United States. Carol Semple is a career **amateur** player who has compiled one of the greatest records of any female golfer. Semple attended Hollins College in Virginia, graduating in 1970. She won her first major title in 1973 at the **U.S. Women's Amateur**, and in 1974, she added the **British Ladies' Amateur**. She won two **U.S. Women's Mid-Amateur** titles and the **USGA Senior Women's Amateur** from 1999 to 2002. Playing by the name "Carol Semple-Thompson" later in her career, she was on four winning World Amateur Team Champions. She received the 2003 **Bob Jones Award** from the **USGA** for distinguished sportsmanship in golf, and in 2008, she was inducted into the **World Golf Hall of Fame**.

SENIOR TOUR. *See* CHAMPIONS TOUR.

SEWGOLUM, SEWSUNKER "PAPWA." B. 1930, Natal, South Africa; D. 6 July 1978, Durban, Natal, South Africa. Sewsunker "Papwa" Sewgolum was an ethnic Indian golfer who grew up in **South Africa** and highlighted the struggle of nonwhites to compete in sports in the era of apartheid. Sewgolum won the 1963 and 1965 Natal Open, in 1965 defeating **Gary Player**, who befriended Sewgolum and supported his career. But when he won tournaments he was forced to receive his trophies outside because he was not allowed in clubhouses in that era in South Africa. Sewgolum won the Dutch Open in 1959, 1960, and 1964. In 2003, he was posthumously awarded a Silver Medal in the Order of Ikhamanga by the president of South Africa for excellent achievements in sports. Sewgolum was likely the best player ever who hit all his shots cross-handed, or left-hand low.

SHAFT STIFFNESS. Golf club shafts come in various stiffnesses. These are usually termed "extra-stiff (X)," "stiff (S)," "regular (R)," and "flexible (F)." However, with the advent of graphite and hybrid shafts, the measurement of shaft stiffness has become more precise, with some shafts having stiffness measured in numbers. Early **graphite shafts** came in stiffnesses from 1 to 15, with 15 being the stiffest. Stiffness can be varied by players by moving the shaft deeper into the **hosel**, bringing the first "flex-step" on a shaft closer to the clubhead, termed "tipping." Thus, a **professional** might describe a club as "stiff, tipped an inch," which indicates a club of intermediate stiffness, between stiff and extra-stiff. A much more precise measurement of shaft and club stiffness exists, termed "frequency matching." In this method, a club is struck with a standardized force and the vibration frequency is measured. Similar clubs should have similar frequency, although this measurement is affected by other factors besides shaft stiffness, such as clubhead weight and club length.

SHANK. A shank is a very poor golf shot in which the ball is struck on the very inside of the clubface, such that part of the ball hits the **hosel**. A shank travels a very short distance and almost diagonally to the right (for a right-handed player). Shanks are greatly feared because they often occur in bunches and getting rid of the shanks can be difficult.

SHEEHAN, PATTY. B. 27 October 1956, Middlebury, Vermont, United States. Patty Sheehan played college golf at the University of Nevada and San Jose State. As an **amateur**, she was runner-up at the 1979 **U.S. Women's Amateur** and won the 1980 AIAW title. She also played on the 1980 **Curtis Cup** team. Sheehan turned **professional** later in 1980 and was **LPGA** Rookie of the Year in 1981 and LPGA Player of the Year in 1983. During her career, she won 35 LPGA events, including six major championships—the LPGA in 1983, 1984, and 1993, the **U.S. Women's Open** in 1992 and 1994, and the **Kraft Nabisco (Dinah Shore)** in 1996. Sheehan's father was a collegiate ski coach at Middlebury College, and Patty was an accomplished skier before settling on golf as a career.

SHELL'S WONDERFUL WORLD OF GOLF. *Shell's Wonderful World of Golf* was a televised golf show that started in 1962 and ran through 1970. It was the most popular golf show of the era. Each week, it showed an 18-hole match in a different part of the world, although some shows were played on U.S. courses. It focused on the different courses and the tourist sites in other countries. The match was usually between a U.S. **professional** and a local professional or occasionally a top **amateur**. Both men and **women** pros were featured, but there were usually only one or two shows a year for women. The show was hosted by **Jimmy Demaret** and **Gene Sarazen**. The show was revived in 1994 and ran through 2003 but was not a weekly show in that period, often being shown only one to three times per year. Notable matches include a 1962 match at **Pine Valley** in New Jersey between **Gene Littler** and **Byron Nelson** and a 1965 match between **Ben Hogan** and **Sam Snead** at Houston Golf Club.

SHINNECOCK HILLS GOLF CLUB. Shinnecock Hills Golf Club, located near Southampton, Long Island, is highly regarded. The course, a Willie Davis–designed 12-hole course, was first opened in 1891 for the members. Workers on the course included many local Native Americans of the Shinnecock Nation, which gave the club its name. In addition to its course, Shinnecock Hills is famous for its dramatic shingle-style clubhouse, which was designed by Stanford White. In 1893, Shinnecock Hills added a nine-hole ladies course, and the next year, **Willie Dunn** came over from **Scotland** and added six holes to the main course, bringing it to a full 18 holes. The ladies course was abandoned in 1901, allowing for a redesign and lengthening of the original course, which was done by **Charles Blair Macdonald** and **Seth Raynor**. The course was again redesigned, this time by William Flynn, in 1937, giving it its current layout. One of the five founding clubs of the **USGA**, Shinnecock Hills hosted the **U.S. Open** and **U.S. Amateur** in 1896. It was not used for a major championship again until 1986, when the U.S. Open took place there, won by **Raymond Floyd**. The U.S. Open was also held there in 1995 and 2004.

SHIPPEN, JOHN MATTHEW, JR. B. 2 December 1879, Anacostia, Washington, D.C., United States; D. 20 May 1968, Newark, New Jersey, United States. John Shippen was an early African American pioneer of golf. He is often described as being Native American on his mother's side, but his daughter later stated that he was 100 percent black. Shippen lived on the Shinnecock Indian Reservation on Long Island, near the **Shinnecock Hills Golf Club**. He worked as a minister on the reservation and as a **caddie** at the course. Shippen entered the 1896 **U.S. Open** at Shinnecock Hills, but when the other **professional** players found out about his entry and the entry of Oscar Bunn, a full-blooded Shinnecock, they threatened to boycott the championship. The **USGA** president, Theodore Havemeyer, stated that the championship would be held in any case, even if the only players were Shippen and Bunn. Shippen played and finished tied for fifth. He played in four other U.S. Opens (1899, 1900, 1902, 1908), with a best finish of fifth in 1896 and 1902. Shippen later worked as a club professional and clubmaker, first at the Marine and Field Club in Brooklyn, but mostly at Shady Rest Golf Course in New Jersey. In 2009, he became an honorary member of the **PGA of America**.

SHORE, FRANCES ROSE "DINAH." B. 29 February 1916, Winchester, Tennessee, United States; D. 24 February 1994, Beverly Hills, California, United States. Dinah Shore was a well-known American singer and entertainer who broke into show business on radio in the late 1930s, singing duets with Frank Sinatra. She was a star of early American television, hosting her own show, which had various titles, from 1951 to 1961. She won 10 Emmy Awards and earned nine gold records. Shore took up golf after a polio attack in her youth prevented her from playing many sports. She became the first female member of the Hillcrest Country Club in Los Angeles, and later played often at Mission Hills Country Club in Rancho Mirage, near Palm Springs. Shore's golf contribution is mostly related to her hosting of the Dinah Shore tournament, which has had several different names during its lifetime. The **LPGA** event began at Mission Hills in 1972 and has been an LPGA major championship since 1983. She was inducted into the LPGA Hall of Fame and **World Golf Hall of Fame** in 1994. *See also* KRAFT NABISCO (DINAH SHORE).

SHORT IRONS. The short irons are the higher-lofted irons in a set of clubs. Historically, the term includes the 7-iron, 8-iron, and 9-iron, and the **wedges**. Short irons are used when the golfer gets closer to the hole. They are often described as "scoring clubs" because, due to the shorter distance of the shot, they often allow the player to place the ball very close to the hole. *See also* GOLF CLUBS.

SHOTGUN START. "Shotgun start" refers to a way of starting a tournament, usually a club tournament. In a shotgun start, instead of all players starting on the 1st hole, or 1st and 10th holes, the groups are distributed around the course, and players may start on any hole. In a classic shotgun start, 18 groups play, with one group starting on each hole, but, more often, there will be two groups starting on the par-fours and par-fives. Play begins at a designated time or when a horn signal is given. The term arose because, formerly, a shotgun blast was used to let players know when to start. Players still play a full stipulated round, 18 holes, ending on the hole prior to the one on which they started.

SHUTE, HERMON DENSMORE "DENNY." B. 25 October 1904, Cleveland, Ohio, United States; D. 13 May 1974, Akron, Ohio, United States. Denny Shute was a student at Case Western Reserve in Cleveland. After graduation, he became a **professional** golfer. As an **amateur**, he won the 1923 and 1925 West Virginia Amateur and the 1927 Ohio Amateur. In the 1930s, he won 15 **PGA Tour** events, including three major championships—the 1933 Open Championship (**British Open**) and the 1936 and 1937 **PGA Championship**. His back-to-back PGA titles were not equaled until **Tiger Woods** did so in 1999 and 2000. Shute played on the **Ryder Cup** team in 1931, 1933, and 1937. He was a very quiet man who was a short hitter, but he made up for it with deadly accurate iron play. Shute was inducted into the **World Golf Hall of Fame** in 2008.

SIFFORD, CHARLIE. B. 2 June 1922, Charlotte, North Carolina, United States. Charlie Sifford was one of the pioneers of African American golf. He was a great player, but he never reached his potential because of the many obstacles to blacks in his era. He learned the game as a **caddie** and later became an instructor to both Billy Eckstine and **Joe Louis**. Blacks could not play on the **PGA Tour** until 1961 because of the clause restricting membership to "players of Caucasian race." For that reason, Sifford played on the **United Golfers Association** (UGA) tour and won many tournaments on that tour, including five straight Negro National Opens from 1952 to 1956, and seven in all. Sifford won the 1957 Long Beach Open, which was cosponsored by the PGA but not an official PGA event. He eventually won two official PGA Tour events, the 1967 Greater Hartford Open and the 1969 **Los Angeles Open**. In 1975, Sifford won the PGA Seniors' Championship. For all his achievements, Sifford was never invited to play in the **Masters**, an affront that cannot be reasonably defended. That color line was finally broken in 1975 by **Lee Elder**. Sifford's biography told the tale of his struggles against discrimination, exemplified by the title *Just Let Me Play*.

In 2004, Charles Sifford was inducted into the **World Golf Hall of Fame**, the first African American member. He was inducted by **Gary Player**, who fought against apartheid in his native **South Africa**. Sifford was awarded an honorary doctor of laws degree from St. Andrews University in 2006. In 2009, the Northern Trust Open created the Charlie Sifford Exemption, to be given to a player who represents the advancement of diversity in golf.

SIGEL, ROBERT JAY. B. 13 November 1943, Bryn Mawr, Pennsylvania, United States. Jay Sigel played college golf at Wake Forest. He graduated in 1967, but a hand injury during his senior year caused him to forgo a **professional** career. Instead, he settled back near his native Philadelphia, opened an insurance business, and became a top career **amateur** player—or so it seemed. Sigel was one of the nation's top amateurs in the 1970s and 1980s. He won the 1979 **British Amateur**, back-to-back 1982 and 1983 **U.S. Amateurs**, back-to-back 1983 and 1984 **U.S. Mid-Amateurs**, and three titles each at regular stops on the amateur circuit, the **Porter Cup**, the **Sunnehanna Amateur**, and the Northeast Amateur. In Philadelphia, he won the Philadelphia Open six times between 1975 and 1987. And then he ended it, turning professional in 1992 and joining the Champions (Senior) Tour in 1993. From 1994 to 2003, Sigel won eight events on the **Champions Tour**, including the 1996 Senior Tour Championship, and he was Rookie of the Year in 1994.

Sigel continued to run his insurance business while on breaks from the tour, but he eventually sold the business to Century Business Services. Sigel sits on the Corporate Advisory Board for the American Cancer Society and is president of the Greater Philadelphia Scholastic Golf Association and the Philadelphia Chapter of the First Tee. At his home course, Aronimink Golf Club, he hosts the Annual Jay Sigel Invitational Golf Tournament, the proceeds of which benefit prostate cancer research at the University of Pennsylvania.

SINGH, VIJAY. B. 22 February 1963, Lautoka, Fiji. Vijay Singh is a Fijian **professional** who is one of the top professionals in the world. He is known for his long hours on the practice tee. He grew up on the Pacific island and turned professional in 1982, winning his first tournament in 1984 at the Malaysian PGA Championship. In 1985, Singh was suspended from the Asian Tour when he was alleged to have altered his scorecard in a tournament. He worked as a club pro in Malaysia for several years before winning the 1988 Nigerian Open and qualifying for the 1989 European Tour. From 1989 to 1992, Singh won four tournaments on the European Tour and moved to the U.S. **PGA Tour** in 1993. He is one of those rare players who continue to improve as they get older. He has continued to improve even into his forties and through 2009 has won 34 PGA Tour events and 13 on the **European PGA Tour**, with 22 of the PGA Tour wins coming after he turned 40. These include three major championships, the 1998 and 2004 **PGA Championship**, and the 2000 **Masters**. Singh led the U.S. PGA Tour money list, in 2003, 2004, and 2008, and won the 2008 FedEx Cup. He was inducted into the **World Golf Hall of Fame** in 2006. He has twice held the number one **World Golf Ranking**, the only other player to do so in the era of **Tiger Woods**.

Singh has been somewhat of a controversial player on the PGA Tour. He is very outspoken, notably in 2003 when he criticized the choice to allow Annika Sörenstem to play at the Colonial Invitational, saying she "didn't belong" on the men's tour. The media have been quick to criticize him. However, many players have defended Singh, telling of his honesty, his work ethic, and how willing he has been to help other players. In 2005, Singh was appointed a goodwill ambassador by the Fijian government.

SKINS GAME. "Skins" is a type of golf match in which players or teams win holes, or "skin." The skin must be won outright, with no ties. If two players tie for best score on a hole, the skin is carried over to the next hole. Thus, the holes near the end of a nine or full round can often be contested for multiple skins. The winner of the skins game is the player or team who wins the most skins. In club competition, a set amount of money is usually given for each skin. The winning player receives payment from all the other players or teams. Thus, in a singles skins game, if the winning player has 9 skins (A), and the other three have 4 (B), 3 (C), and 2 (D) skins, and each skin is worth $10, the winner, player A, receives $50 from player B, the difference between 9 and 4 multiplied by 10, $60 from player C, and $70 from player D. Player B receives $10 from player C and $20 from player D, and player C receives $10 from player D, although effectively all that money accrues to Player A.

In 1983, the Skins Game became a made-for-television event, played in the late fall. It began the practice of having small, invitational golf events of varying, somewhat different from standard, tournament formats near the end of, or after, the **PGA Tour** schedule. This has become known as the "Silly Season" but often provides huge payments to the invited players, notably **Fred Couples**, who has become known as the "King of the Silly Season" because of his five wins in the event. The Skins Game has been held continuously through 2009 but is much less popular than it was in the 1980s. Appendix 4 includes a list of champions.

SLICE. A slice is a shot that travels sharply from left to right for a right-handed player or right to left for a left-handed player. A slice is often hit unintentionally by lesser skilled players who have not learned how to properly release the club near impact or strike the ball on an outside-in clubhead path. Almost no tournament players play a slice as their preferred shot shape, although the milder variant of it, the **fade**, is often played by **professionals** because it is easily controlled. A slice is often derisively called a "banana ball." Many beginners, or poorer players, will take golf lessons simply to learn how to stop hitting a slice.

SLOPE. The slope rating of a **golf course** is a measure of its difficulty. Each slope rating is based upon the scores a scratch golfer and **bogey** golfer are expected to shoot from a certain set of tees. When these scores are charted on a graph, the line showing the difference in their scores forms a slope. The slope of a more difficult course is steeper than the slope of an easier course and produces a higher slope rating. A slope of 113 signifies a course of average difficulty, 155 is the highest possible slope, and 55 is the lowest. Whatever the exact slope rating, the net result, when using handicaps, is that players receive more strokes on a more difficult course and fewer strokes on an easier course. In addition, weaker players receive more strokes than stronger players as course difficulty increases, because the gap between their scores increases. The slope system was designed and implemented by the **USGA** in the early 1980s.

SMITH, ALEX. B. 1872, Carnoustie, Angus, Scotland; D. 21 April 1930, Baltimore, Maryland, United States. Alex Smith was born in Scotland and came to the **United States** in the late 1890s with his brothers, Willie and **Mac Smith**. Willie was the better golfer initially, winning the 1899 **U.S. Open**, but Alex Smith later won that title twice, in 1906 and 1910. They were his only recognized major titles, but Smith also won the **Western Open** twice (1903, 1906) and the **Metropolitan Open** four times (1905, 1909, 1910, 1913), when they were the next most important (after the majors) tournaments in the game. Smith was a club **professional** primarily, starting at the Washington Park Golf Club in Chicago and spending many years at Wykagyl Country Club near New York. He was also a pro in the winter at Belleaire Country Club in Clearwater, Florida. Smith died in a Baltimore sanitarium from tuberculosis.

SMITH, HORTON. B. 22 May 1908, Springfield, Missouri, United States; D. 15 October 1963, Detroit, Michigan, United States. Horton Smith was a U.S. **professional** who is best known for winning the first Masters Tournament in 1934. During his career, he won 32 **PGA Tour** events, with a best year of eight wins in 1929. He won two major titles, the 1934 and 1936 **Masters**. Smith played on five **Ryder Cup** teams, 1929, 1931, 1933, 1935, and 1937. Smith spent many years as head professional at Detroit Golf Club after his playing career ended and served as president of the **PGA of America** from 1952 to 1954. The PGA of America annually gives the Horton Smith Award to a club professional who makes "outstanding and continuing contributions to PGA education." He received the 1962 **Bob Jones Award** from the **USGA** in recognition of distinguished sportsmanship in golf. Smith was inducted into the **World Golf Hall of Fame** in 1990.

SMITH, MacDONALD "MAC." B. 18 March 1892, Carnoustie, Scotland; D. 31 August 1949, Glendale, California, **United States**. Mac Smith is among the greatest players never to have won a major championship. Born in Scotland, Smith and his brothers immigrated to the United States, where both Willie Smith (1899) and **Alex Smith** (1906, 1910) won the **U.S. Open**. Mac Smith's best finish in the event was his loss in a play-off in 1910 to brother Alex and **John McDermott**. During his career, which mostly preceded the **PGA Tour**, he won 24 of the top **professional** events in the country. Despite never winning an official major, he won the **Western Open** three times (1912, 1925, 1933), the **Metropolitan Open** twice (1926, 1931), and the **North and South Open** in 1925, when all three were among the major professional events in the United States.

SMITH, RICK. B. 1958, Michigan, United States. Rick Smith is a top teaching **professional** who is known for working with many of the **PGA Tour** players. His students have included **Phil Mickelson**, **Lee Janzen**, **Greg Norman**, **Vijay Singh**, **David Duval**, and Raymond Floyd. Smith is an entrepreneur. He formed Rick Smith

Enterprises, Inc., which helped him set up golf academies at Treetops Resort in Gaylord, Michigan, which is co-owned by Smith, and Tiburon Golf Club in Naples, Florida. Smith is frequently on television giving golf instruction, beginning in 1994 with "The Rick Smith Signature Series" on ESPN. He signed an exclusive contract in 1999 with the **Golf Channel**. In 2003, he began hosting the first "Big Break" series on the Golf Channel. Smith has also worked as a course designer, best known for his Signature Course at his own Treetops Resort. He has written numerous books and magazine articles, and his awards include National Teacher of the Year, National Golf Professional of the Year, and National Merchandiser of the Year.

SNAKE. Although one may find snakes on **golf courses**, the golf term actually refers to sinking a very long putt. The term arose because such a putt may curve several times during its course to the hole, resembling a long, slinky snake.

SNAP HOOK. *See* DUCK HOOK.

SNEAD, SAMUEL JACKSON, "SAM," "SLAMMIN' SAMMY." B. 27 May 1912, Ashwood, Virginia, United States; D. 23 May 2002, Hot Springs, Virginia, United States. Sam Snead is among the greatest players of all time, and many consider him to have had the finest golf swing ever. He grew up in the hills of western Virginia and learned to play by hitting apples with a club made from a tree branch with a knob on the end. A talented natural athlete who was a very long **driver**, Snead had the longest career of any great player, winning tournaments from the 1930s to the 1960s and placing third at the 1974 **PGA Championship** when he was 62 years of age. He holds several records on tour for being the oldest to accomplish certain feats: He is the oldest player to win a **PGA Tour** event (52 years 312 days at the 1965 Greater Greensboro Open). He is the oldest player to make a cut at a major (67 years old at the 1979 PGA). He is the oldest player to make a PGA Tour cut (67 years 82 days at the 1979 Westchester Classic). And he is the first and, through 2009, only player to shoot his age on the PGA Tour, which he did by shooting 67 at the 1979 Quad Cities Open.

Snead joined the PGA Tour in 1937, winning five events in his first year. He won 82 PGA Tour events (a record), which include seven major titles. He won three Masters (1948, 1952, 1954), three PGA Championships (1942, 1949, 1951), and one **Open Championship (British Open)** (1946). Unfortunately, Snead never won the **U.S. Open**, a championship in which he finished second four times—1937, 1947, 1949, and 1953. Snead won the Greater Greensboro Open eight times, still a record for most wins in a single event on tour. Snead won the PGA Seniors title six times, in 1964, 1965, 1967, 1970, 1972, and 1973. Snead was the leading money winner on the PGA Tour in 1938, 1949, and 1950, and he won the **Vardon Trophy** for low scoring average those three years and in 1955. He played on seven **Ryder Cup** teams (1937, 1947, 1949, 1951, 1953, 1955, 1959) and captained the team in 1951, 1959, and 1969. Snead was inducted into the **World Golf Hall of Fame** in 1974 as a charter member. In 1998, he received the PGA Tour Lifetime Achievement Award.

SOLHEIM CUP. The Solheim Cup is a biennial team match for female **professionals**, with a team from the **United States** playing a team from Europe. The event, named for **Karsten Solheim**, who founded the Ping Golf Club company, was first held in 1990 and was held in even-numbered years through 2000. Because the events of 9/11 in 2001 caused the cancellation of the 2001 Ryder Cup until 2002 and even years thereafter, the Solheim Cup resumed in 2003 and now takes place in odd-numbered years. The current format of the event is precisely the same as the **Ryder Cup**. With 12 players on each team, it takes place over three days. Players compete in four **foursomes** matches and four **four-ball** matches on each of the first two days and then 12 singles matches on the final day. Through 2009, the match has been held 11 times, with the United States winning eight matches. The Solheim Cup alternates between a U.S. site and a European site. There is also a Junior Solheim Cup, contested between teams of U.S. and European junior girls. Appendix 5 includes a list of champions, scores, and captains.

SOLHEIM, KARSTEN. B. 15 September 1911, Bergen, Norway; D. 16 February 2000, Phoenix, Arizona, United States. Karsten Solheim moved with his family to Seattle, Washington, when he was only two years old. He later enrolled at the University of Washington, but financial problems forced him to drop out in his sophomore year. He went into the workplace, and, studying on his own, he became an engineer for General Electric (GE). His engineering background led him to start designing better putter heads. His first was one called the "Anser," which had weight far out on the periphery, causing it to rotate less off-line on off-center hits. The original design also made a "ping" sound when struck, leading Solheim to call his clubs "Ping." In 1967, the putters became so popular that he left his job at GE and formed Karsten Manufacturing, which built Ping putters. By 1970, the company added a full line of irons and eventually woods, and it became one of the most popular club lines in the world. The company also pioneered the use of investment casting techniques for irons, as opposed to the traditional method of forged iron heads that were shaped by clubmakers. Solheim became a very wealthy man because of his club company and became a philanthropist, especially supporting **women**'s golf. He sponsored several **LPGA** events, and in 1990, he was the driving force behind the creation of the **Solheim Cup**, a women's **professional** team competition between U.S. and European teams. Karsten Solheim was inducted into the **World Golf Hall of Fame** in 2001. *See also* GOLF CLUBS.

SÖRENSTAM (-ESCH-MCGEE), ANNIKA. B. 9 October 1970, Bro, Sweden. Annika Sörenstam merits consideration in any discussion of the greatest ever female golfers. Sörenstam grew up in Sweden. She played college golf in 1991–1992 at the University of Arizona, winning the 1991 NCAA title as a freshman. She turned **professional** after her sophomore year but failed to advance through the **LPGA Q School** and played one year on the **Ladies' European Tour** in 1993. She qualified for the LPGA the next year, winning the Rookie of the Year title in 1994. She moved to the top of **women**'s golf in 1995 when she won the **U.S. Women's Open**, led the money list, won the **Vare Trophy** for the lowest scoring average, and became LPGA Player of the Year. Sörenstam won Player of the Year eight times and six Vare Trophies. She retired after the 2008 season, having won 72 LPGA events and 90 female professional events worldwide. These include 10 major championships—the 1995, 1996, and 2006 U.S. Women's Open, the 2003–2005 **LPGA Championship**, the **Kraft Nabisco (Dinah Shore)** in 2001, 2002, and 2005, and the **Women's British Open** in 2003. Sörenstam totally dominated the tour during this era, winning five or more tournaments in six years—11 in 2002, 10 in 2005, 8 in 2004, 6 in 1997 and 2003, and 5 in 2000.

Sörenstam was one of the first women golfers to emphasize physical fitness, and she credits her fitness with adding yards to her drive and taking her to the top of the women's game. In 2003, she was invited to play on the **PGA Tour** at the **Colonial National Invitational**, the first woman to play on the men's tour since **Babe Zaharias** in 1945. She opened with a solid 71 but missed the cut. Sörenstam was inducted into the **World Golf Hall of Fame** in 2003. In her retirement, she started a clothing line for women golfers and is involved in multiple **golf course** design projects.

SOUTH AFRICA. Golf was first played in South Africa in 1885 at Waterloo Green, Wynberg, near Cape Town. The first club was the Cape **Golf Club**, now the Royal Cape Golf Club. The South African Amateur was first contested in 1892, and the South African Open started in 1903. The governing body of South African golf, the South African Golf Union, was formed in 1910, followed by the South African Ladies Golf Union in 1914. South Africa has produced several notable **professional** players, including **Bobby Locke**, **Ernie Els**, **Retief Goosen**, and, among **women**, **Sally Little**. But the greatest South African golfer ever is **Gary Player**, who is among the greatest players of all time and the first truly international champion of golf. South Africa has had a men's professional tour since the 1960s, now called the "Sunshine Tour." It is a member of the International Federation of PGA Tours.

Even at the club level, golf is very competitive in South Africa, and most clubs hold tournaments every Wednesday and Saturday throughout the year. On those days, in order to be able to play at the club, one must play in the tournament.

SOUTH AFRICAN OPEN. The South African Open is the South African national championship. It is open to players from any nation and has been contested since 1903. The event is held at various courses.

Gary Player has won the most South African Open titles, with 13. Because of apartheid, the tournament was restricted to whites only until 1972, although **Sewsunker "Papwa" Sewgolum**, who was of Indian origin, played in the championship several times, placing second in 1963. The championship has been part of the **European PGA Tour** since 1997. Appendix 4 includes a list of champions.

SOUTHERN HILLS COUNTRY CLUB. Southern Hills Country Club is a private club in Tulsa, Oklahoma, best known for hosting the **U.S. Open** three times and the **PGA Championship** four times. The club was founded in 1936, with a **golf course**, which is usually ranked among the top courses in the country, designed by **Perry Maxwell**. It hosted the U.S. Open in 1958, 1977, and 2001 and the PGA Championship in 1970, 1982, 1994, and 2007. Southern Hills was also the site of the Tour Championship in 1995 and 1996. The course is noted for the multitude of national championships that have been held there. It also hosted the **U.S. Amateur** (1965 and 2009), the **U.S. Women's Amateur** (1946), the **U.S. Junior Amateur** (1953), the **USGA Senior Amateur** (1961), and the inaugural **U.S. Women's Mid-Amateur** in 1987.

SPACE COAST GOLF TOUR. The Space Coast Golf Tour was one of the very first mini-tours and the only truly successful one, lasting more than a few years. The tour was first founded in 1973 by former **PGA Tour** player J. C. Goosie, with events conducted almost exclusively in Florida. In the days before the **Nationwide** (Hogan/Nike/Buy.com) and **Hooters Tour**, players who did not qualify for the PGA Tour had few playing options. The Space Coast Tour and a few other similar mini-tours provided them an opportunity to continue playing in competitive events. There is little money to be won on mini-tours because players usually play for their own money, their entry fees being used to fund the tournament. The Space Coast Golf Tour lasted from 1973 into the 21st century, suspending operations in 2008 only to restart the tour in late 2009.

SPIKE MARKS. Spike marks are marks made on **putting greens** by the spikes on a golf shoe. These are now less common with the advent of plastic spikes that are not as long or sharp. After putting out, players should always repair any damage they make to putting greens with their spikes, if they realize they have done so. Unlike ball marks, by rule, spike marks cannot be repaired before putting, regardless of whether the spike marks were made by the current putter or a previous player.

SPILLER, BILL. B. 25 October 1913, Tishomingo, Oklahoma, United States; D. 1988. Bill Spiller was one of the great early black players but was denied a chance to play at the highest levels because of discrimination by the **PGA of America**, which then ran the **PGA Tour**. Spiller attempted to play in the 1948 Richmond Open but was denied because of the PGA of America's Caucasian-only clause. He sued the PGA of America, along with fellow African American great **Ted Rhodes**, but they withdrew their suit when the PGA of America promised to eliminate the Caucasian-only clause. But the PGA reneged on its promise. In 1952, Spiller was invited to play in the San Diego Open, but PGA of America President **Horton Smith** told the tournament's sponsors that this was against its rules. Spiller again threatened to sue, and Smith stated that he would change the rules, but nothing was done. It was not until November 1961 that the PGA of America removed the offensive clause. By then, Spiller was 48 years old and well past his playing prime. But he had led the way for future generations of black players, including **Charlie Sifford**, **Lee Elder**, and eventually, **Tiger Woods**. In 2009, the PGA of America granted posthumous honorary membership to Spiller.

SPOON. "Spoon" is the old name for a 3-wood, dating to the era when golf clubs were known by names and not numbers. The term is now rarely used. *See also* GOLF CLUBS.

SPYGLASS HILL GOLF COURSE. Spyglass Hill Golf Course is on the Monterey Peninsula in California. It was designed by **Robert Trent Jones** Sr. and opened in March 1966. The course is one of the three courses on which the **Bing Crosby** Pro-Am, now the AT&T National Pro-Am, has taken place. The course is extremely difficult and is probably the most difficult of the three courses that host the **pro-am**. The course opens with five holes that run near Seventeen-Mile Drive, with clear views of the Pacific Ocean. The holes meander through sand dunes and ice plants. The course then turns inland, with the final 13 holes routed through the redwood forests of Monterey Peninsula, giving the appearance of two distinctly different courses.

STABLEFORD SYSTEM. The Stableford System is a scoring system used for tournaments that was developed around 1900 by Dr. Frank Barney Gorton Stableford (1870–1959). In Stableford scoring, the highest score, not the lowest score, wins. Points are awarded on each hole based on the player's score in relation to **par**. There are many variations of the system. However, in the classic system defined in the **Rules of Golf**, points are awarded on each hole as follows:

Two or more over fixed score	0
One over fixed score	1
Fixed score	2
One under fixed score	3
Two under fixed score	4
Three under fixed score	5
Four under fixed score	6

The fixed score is almost always par. Stableford scoring is a popular format, used for some club tournaments, but it is rarely used in major competition. On the **PGA Tour**, the International, a tournament held near Denver, was conducted under modified Stableford scoring from 1986 to 2006. On the European Tour, the ANZ Championship was played under modified Stableford scoring in 2002–2004. Two different **Champions Tour** events have used Stableford scoring. The modified Stableford System used at the International and the ANZ Championship is as follows:

Double eagle	+8 points
Eagle	+5 points
Birdie	+2 points
Par	0 points
Bogey	–1 point
Double bogey or worse	–3 points

See also MATCH PLAY; STROKE PLAY.

STACY, HOLLIS. B. 16 March 1954, Savannah, Georgia, United States. Hollis Stacy was an American female **professional** player. Stacy became known to the golf world when she won the **U.S. Girls' Junior** Championship three consecutive years (1969–1971), a feat still not matched. Her 1969 win at the age of 15 also made her the youngest at that time to win the title. As an **amateur**, Stacy attended Rollins College, won the 1970 **North and South Women's Amateur**, and played on the 1972 **Curtis Cup** team. She turned professional in 1974. During her **LPGA** career, she won 18 professional tournaments, including four major championships, notably, the **U.S. Women's Open** three times—in 1977, 1978, and 1984. She also won the 1984 **Du Maurier Classic**. In 2009, Hollis Stacy's little sister, Martha Stacy-Leach, won the **U.S. Women's Mid-Amateur** Championship.

STEPHENSON, JAN LYNNE. B. 22 December 1951, Sydney, New South Wales, Australia. Jan Stephenson was one of the best-known **women professionals**, as much for her beauty as for her golf game, of the 1970s and 1980s. She joined the **LPGA** in 1974, earning Rookie of the Year honors. She won 16 LPGA events, including three major championships, the 1981 **Du Maurier Classic**, the 1982 **LPGA Championship**, and the 1983 **U.S. Women's Open**. Stephenson was a very attractive blonde who openly embraced her looks as a marketing approach. She once posed in a bathtub, covered only by golfballs, and later in a pin-up calendar. She was in favor of the LPGA using sex appeal to sell its product, a view not fully endorsed by the other female professionals. More recently, she has done significant charitable work, including serving as chairperson of the National Multiple Sclerosis Society. In 2003, Stephenson caused some controversy when she stated, "Asians are killing the [LPGA] Tour," referring to the large influx of Koreans winning on the tour. She called for quotas on international players, perhaps forgetting that she was one herself, but later apologized for her remarks.

STEWART, WILLIAM PAYNE. B. 30 January 1957, Springfield, Missouri, United States; D. 25 October 1999, en route from Orlando to Dallas, airplane crashing near Aberdeen, South Dakota, United States. Payne Stewart was a top American **professional** of the 1980s and 1990s. He was known for his flowing, syrupy golf swing and his wardrobe, which often included plus fours. After graduating from Southern Methodist University (SMU), Stewart attempted to qualify for the **PGA Tour** but failed twice and played in Asia for two years. He earned his PGA Tour Card in 1982 and won his first event at the 1982 Quad Cities Open. Stewart eventually won eight PGA Tour events, including three major championships, the 1989 **PGA Championship** and the 1991 and 1999 **U.S. Open**. Stewart played on five **Ryder Cup** teams, in 1987, 1989, 1991, 1993, and 1999. Stewart died tragically. He was flying on a private plane from Orlando to Dallas to discuss building a **golf course** for SMU. The plane lost pressurization shortly after takeoff, and all aboard apparently died of hypoxia before the plane crashed into an abandoned field in Mina, near Aberdeen, South Dakota. In his honor, the PGA Tour instituted the Payne Stewart Award, given each year to a player who shows respect for the traditions of the game, commitment to uphold the game's heritage of charitable support, and professional and meticulous presentation of himself and the sport through his dress and conduct.

STEWART-STREIT, MARLENE, CM, OONT. B. 9 March 1934, Cereal, Alberta, Canada. Marlene Stewart-Streit is **Canada**'s greatest-ever female **amateur** player, and was the first Canadian golfer inducted into the **World Golf Hall of Fame**, in 2004. It is difficult to list her numerous tournament victories. Stewart-Streit won the Canadian Ladies' Amateur 11 times, the Ontario Ladies' Amateur 11 times, and eventually won 43 Canadian or provincial titles. She also won the 1953 **British Ladies' Amateur**, the 1956 **U.S. Women's Amateur**, the 1963 Australian Women's Amateur, and the **North and South Women's Amateur** in 1956 and 1974. As a senior, Stewart-Streit won the **USGA Senior Women's Amateur** three times, the last in 2003 when she was 69 years old, making her the oldest person to ever win a **USGA** event. In 1965–1966, she played in televised matches on **Shell's Wonderful World of Golf**, defeating Marilynn Smith in 1965 and losing to **Mickey Wright** in 1966. To keep her **amateur status**, she donated what she won to a fund supporting Canadian Junior Women's Golf, which still supports those players. Stewart-Streit was made an Officer of the Order of Canada (CM) in 1967 and a member of the Order of Ontario (OOnt.) in 2006. She is in Canada's Sports Hall of Fame, the Canadian Golf Hall of Fame, and the Ontario Golf Hall of Fame.

STIMPMETER. The Stimpmeter is a device that measures the speed of **putting greens**. It was developed in the 1930s by Edward S. Stimpson Sr., who was the 1935 Massachusetts Amateur Champion. Watching the **U.S. Open** at **Oakmont** in 1935, Stimpson thought the greens were overly fast and decided to develop a method to quantify green speed. The Stimpmeter is a three-foot-long bar, with a V-shaped groove. At 30 inches from one end, a small notch in the groove allows a golf ball to rest in the groove. To measure green speed, one places the Stimpmeter flat on a green, usually selecting a reasonably flat portion of the green. The Stimpmeter is then gradually raised, lifting the end that contains the notch and the golf ball, until gravity pulls the ball from the notch, usually at about 20 degrees, and down the groove. The ball rolls down the Stimpmeter and rolls for a certain distance on the green. The distance is measured in feet and the number of feet is the "Stimp reading" for the green. For better precision, several readings in opposite directions are used and then averaged. The **USGA** pioneered the use of the Stimpmeter, first using it to measure green speed at the U.S. Open in 1978. The USGA has developed the following classification scheme for describing green speed for regular membership play:

Slow greens:	<7½
Medium greens:	7½–8½
Fast greens:	>8½

For club tournament play, the USGA has the following classification:

Slow greens:	<8½
Medium greens:	8½–9½
Fast greens:	>9½

In reality, U.S. Open green speeds now tend to be at least 10½. Very fast greens on the **PGA Tour** and major championships may now measure 12–13 feet and have even approached 15 feet on the fastest greens.

STIRLING (-FRASER), ALEXA. B. 5 September 1897, Atlanta, Georgia, United States; D. 15 April 1977, Ottawa, Ontario, Canada. Alexa Stirling was one of the first great American female players. Stirling won the 1916 **U.S. Women's Amateur** and then, after the war, won it again in 1919 and 1920, for three consecutive victories. She grew up playing at East Lake Country Club alongside junior boy phenom **Bob Jones**, later considered the greatest player in the world. Stirling won the 1920 and 1934 Canadian Women's Amateur. She eventually settled in Ottawa, Ontario, after her marriage to Canadian doctor W. G. Fraser. She was a runner-up at the U.S. Women's Amateur in 1921, 1923, and 1925 and the Canadian Women's Amateur in 1921 and 1925. She is a member of the Georgia Sports Hall of Fame, Georgia Golf Hall of Fame, and the Canadian Golf Hall of Fame.

STOCKTON, DAVID KNAPP "DAVE." B. 2 November 1941, San Bernardino, California, United States. Dave Stockton attended the University of Southern California (USC) and turned **professional** in 1964, joining the **PGA Tour** in 1965. He played the tour through the mid-1980s, winning 10 tournaments between 1967 and 1976. These include two major championships, the 1970 and 1976 **PGA Championship**. Stockton played for the **United States** at the 1971 and 1977 **Ryder Cup** matches and captained the team in 1991 at **Kiawah Island** in the "War on the Shore." Stockton began playing the **Champions (Senior) Tour** in 1991 and won 14 titles, including three of the senior majors—the 1992 and 1994 Senior Players Championship and the 1996 **U.S. Senior Open**. Stockton's son, Dave Stockton Jr., has also played on the PGA Tour but with less success. Dave Stockton was known for his short game and putting stroke, and he has become a putting instructor to many current PGA Tour players, notably **Phil Mickelson**.

STRANAHAN, FRANK RICHARD "THE TOLEDO STRONGMAN." B. 5 August 1922, Toledo, Ohio, United States. Frank Stranahan was the top **amateur** in the country in the late 1940s and early 1950s, although he never managed to win the **U.S. Amateur**. Stranahan was from a wealthy family His father was the heir to the Champion Sparkplug Company fortune, which enabled him to play year-round as an amateur. He won the 1948 and 1950 **Amateur**

Championship (British Amateur), the 1947 and 1948 Canadian Amateur, and the **North and South Amateur** in 1946, 1949, and 1952. Stranahan was one of the first golfers to lift weights, which led to his being called the "Toledo Strongman." In 1954, Stranahan finally turned **professional** and played for most of the 1950s on the **PGA Tour**, winning two tournaments, the 1958 **Los Angeles Open** and the 1955 Eastern Open. Stranahan dropped out of competitive golf in the 1960s but continued to lift weights, and later ran marathons. He eventually became devoted to a hyper-healthy diet along with his exercising, maintaining that his goal was to live over 100 years.

STRANGE, CURTIS NORTHRUP. B. 30 January 1955, Norfolk, Virginia, United States. Curtis Strange is the son of Tom Strange, a top Virginia **professional** who died at a young age from cancer. Curtis attended Wake Forest University, where he won the **NCAA** individual title as a freshman and led Wake Forest to the team crown. He turned professional at the end of 1976 but failed to earn his **PGA Tour** Card. He did, however, join the tour in 1978. In his career on the PGA Tour he won 17 events, including back-to-back titles at the 1988 and 1989 **U.S. Open**, the first player to defend that championship since **Ben Hogan** in 1950 and 1951. Strange was the PGA Tour leading money winner in 1985, 1987, and 1988, the latter year becoming the first player to win over $1 million (U.S.) in a single season. The best player in the world for the last half of the 1980s, Strange never won another tournament after the 1989 U.S. Open. He played on five **Ryder Cup** teams in 1983, 1985, 1987, 1989, and 1995. Strange was inducted into the **World Golf Hall of Fame** in 2007. He has played sporadically on the **Champions Tour** and has spent some time as a television broadcaster for golf events.

STRAUSBAUGH, WILLIAM "BILL." *See* BILL STRAUSBAUGH AWARD.

STROKE. The **Rules of Golf** define a stroke as "the forward movement of the club made with the intention of striking at and moving the ball, but if a player checks his downswing voluntarily before the clubhead reaches the ball he has not made a stroke." In golf, "stroke" may also refer to strokes given in a **handicap** match, or net tournament, in accordance with a player's handicap.

STROKE PLAY. Stroke play is one of the two major formats of competition in golf, the other being **match play**. Stroke is also known as "medal play," although the **Rules of Golf** only use the term "stroke play." Stroke play entails the counting of strokes in a round of golf. The player with the lowest total of strokes at the end of the designated number of rounds wins the competition. Most **professional** tournaments are stroke play events, usually over 72 holes, although the **LPGA** and **Champions (Senior) Tour** play a number of events over 54 holes. At the end of the regulation competition, if there is a tie for first place, a play-off is held to determine the champion. This is often a sudden-death hole-by-hole play-off, but the **Open Championship (British Open)** uses a four-hole play-off format, and the **PGA Championship** uses a three-hole play-off format. The **U.S. Open** continues to use a full 18-hole play-off in the event of a tie. *See also* ALTERNATE BALL.

STYMIE. The stymie is the blocking or obstructing of the hole with one's golf ball, that is, one player's ball being between the hole and another player's ball. At one time, it was permitted in the Rules of Golf. In singles **match play** when one player's ball obstructed the other's putting line, the player closer to the hole did not have to lift the ball, unless the two balls were within six inches of one another. In the era of the stymie, most scorecards were designed to be six inches in length and were used to measure the gap between the balls. The stymie led to some difficult tactical situations. Players had to learn to play over or around a stymie, often chipping with a wedge when the balls were near the hole. If a player's ball struck the ball at rest and knocked it into the cup, the ball was considered to have been holed on its previous shot. If the resting ball was struck and moved on the green, that player could either play from there or return to the original spot of the ball. There were several variations of the stymie. Originally, a player could not avoid a stymie by conceding the player's next putt. But in 1920, this rule was changed, and the putt could be conceded, the ball having to be lifted. In 1941, the **USGA** changed the rule so that any ball within six inches of the hole had to be lifted if the opposing player requested it. In 1952, both the USGA and the **R&A** banished the stymie.

SUGGS, MAE LOUISE. B. 7 September 1923, Atlanta, Georgia, United States. Louise Suggs was one of the founders of the **LPGA** and one of the pioneers of **women**'s **professional** golf. Suggs started out with a very successful **amateur** career in the era before there was a women's professional golf tour. She was Georgia State Women's Amateur champion in 1940 and 1942, Southern Women's Amateur champion in 1941 and 1947, won the **Women's Western Amateur** and Open in 1946 and 1947, and won three **North and South Women's Amateurs**, in 1942, 1946, and 1948. In 1947, Suggs won the **U.S. Women's Amateur** and added the **British Ladies' Amateur** in 1948. She won three professional tournaments as an amateur, the 1946 and 1947 **Women's Western Open** and the 1946 **Titleholders**. Suggs turned professional in 1948 and won 55 tournaments on the LPGA, winning at least one tournament every year from 1946 to 1962. She won 11 major championships: **U.S. Women's Open**—1949, 1952, **LPGA Championship**—1957, **Titleholders Championship**—1946, 1954, 1956, 1959, and the **Western Open**—1946, 1947, 1949, 1953.

Suggs was inducted into the LPGA Hall of Fame as an inaugural member in 1967 and into the **World Golf Hall of Fame** in 1979. She served as LPGA president from 1955 to 1957. In 2007, Suggs received the **Bob Jones Award** from the **USGA** in recognition of distinguished sportsmanship in golf. The LPGA Rookie of the Year Award is named in her honor.

SUNNEHANNA AMATEUR. The Sunnehanna Amateur is one of the top **amateur** tournaments in the **United States**. It is held at the Sunnehanna Country Club in Johnstown, Pennsylvania, usually early in June. The event is strictly invitational and is considered the equivalent of the Masters among U.S. amateurs. To qualify, a player must win a tournament at the level of a state amateur championship or higher, such as a regional or national title. A few other special invitations are also given, usually to older amateurs who have played in the tournament several times. Its champions include many great future touring **professionals**, among them Billy Andrade, Scott Verplank, Bobby Clampett, Lucas Glover, John Cook, and **Ben Crenshaw**. The Sunnehanna used to have a fun event prior to the start of the tournament called the "Rat Race." It consisted of teams of four players playing four of the club's holes (3rd through 6th), each player having one club only. In addition, all rules of etiquette were waved, which led to players yelling as another player was swinging, or players throwing water at a swinging player, or other such shenanigans. Appendix 6 includes a list of champions.

SUNNINGDALE GOLF CLUB. Sunningdale Golf Club is in Berkshire, just west of London. It was founded in 1900, the original course designed by **Willie Park Jr.**, and opened for play in 1901. It is rare among well-known British courses in that it is not a **links**, being instead a parkland course. The course never hosted an **Open Championship (British Open)**, but it has hosted the **Women's British Open**, the **British Senior Open**, the European Open, the 1987 **Walker Cup**, the 1975 European Women's Open, the British Masters, and the News of the World Match Play Championship. The course is unusual in that it begins with two opening par-fives. The club has 36 holes, the original course being called the "Old Course." The New Course, designed by **Harry Colt**, opened in 1923.

SUTTON, HAL EVAN. B. 28 April 1958, Shreveport, Louisiana, United States. Hal Sutton was the top **amateur** of the late 1970s and early 1980s and won the 1980 College Player of the Year Award. He also won the **U.S. Amateur**, **Western Amateur**, **North and South Amateur**, and the Northeast Amateur in that same year. After turning pro in 1981, he quickly became a star on the **PGA Tour**, winning the 1982 Walt Disney World Golf Classic. His best year was 1983, when he won his only major, the **PGA Championship**. That same year, he won **The Players Championship**, was PGA Player of the Year, and he led the money list. After four more wins, two in 1985 and two in 1986, he fell from grace and almost lost his playing card in the early 1990s. Sutton did not win again until the 1995 BC Open, but then he resurrected his game, winning seven PGA Tour events from 1995 to 2001 and ending his PGA Tour career with 15 wins. He won the 1998 Tour Championship, and his other big win was the 2000 Players Championship, where he stiffed a 4-iron on the 72nd hole to hold off **Tiger Woods**, famously calling out on television as the final approach shot was in the air, "Be the right one . . . today." Sutton is known for his charitable work and giving and especially for helping New Orleans recover after Hurricane Katrina. He played on four **Ryder Cup** teams and captained the 2004 team.

SWEET SPOT. The sweet spot refers to a point on a clubface. When a player strikes the ball on the sweet spot, there is no torque of the clubface, and the contact is said to be solid, or pure. The goal of every shot is for the player to hit the sweet spot. Technically, a sweet spot is an infinitesimal point on the clubface, with any deviation of contact from that spot resulting in some minor torque that may throw the ball off-line a bit. However, modern golf clubs are often built with heel-and-toe weighting, or cavity-backs, which increases a clubface's moment of inertia. When a shot is struck away from the sweet spot, the amount of torque that results depends on how far the impact is from the sweet spot and the club's moment of inertia. The larger the moment of inertia, the less torque there is on the clubface, which results in less sidespin and causes the club to effectively have a larger sweet spot, although this use of the term is not technically correct.

SWINGWEIGHT. Swingweight is a measure of a **golf club**'s weight and playing characteristics. Swingweight is affected by a club's overall weight and the distribution of that weight. Thus, a club with a very light shaft and a heavier clubhead will have a heavier swingweight. Swingweight is expressed as an alpha numeric, such as D-2, C-8, or E-3, with the higher letters and numbers representing heavier clubs. Most club players will use clubs with swingweights in the D-0 to D-4 range. Women players will often use clubs in the C-6 to D-0 range. **Professionals** will usually use heavier clubs, often getting up into the high Ds, or even low Es.

– T –

TAIT, FREDERICK GUTHRIE "FREDDIE." B. 11 January 1870, Edinburgh, Scotland; D. 7 February 1900, Koodoosberg, South Africa. Freddie Tait was a Scottish **amateur** player known for his excellent play, his long driving ability, and his bravery as a soldier. Tait was schooled at the Royal Military Academy Sandhurst and joined the 2nd Battalion, Leinster Regiment, eventually joining the 2nd Battalion, the Black Watch. However, he continued to compete, winning the **Amateur Championship (British Amateur)** in 1896 and 1898, and placing third at the **Open Championship (British Open)** in 1896 and 1897. In January 1893, at the **Old Course** in **St. Andrews**, Tait was credited with a drive of 341 yards, at the time, the longest ever with a **gutta percha** ball.

Tait rejoined his battalion for active service in October 1899 and was sent to **South Africa** during the Boer War, where he served with the Kimberley Relief Force. He was wounded at the Battle of Magersfontein and again a few weeks later at Koodoosberg, where his last words were, "They have got me this time." In his name, a bed was endowed at the Scottish South African Hospital, and a ward was built and named after him at the Cottage Hospital, St. Andrews. The Freddie Tait Cup is given annually to the low amateur in the **South African Open**.

TAKEAWAY. The takeaway is the initial movement of the club away from the golf ball in a golf swing. Instructor **Jim Flick** has insisted for years that this is a bad term and prefers "swingaway" because the club should be swung away from the ball. Nevertheless, "takeaway" is pretty firmly entrenched in golf instructor lingo.

TAYLOR, JOHN HENRY "J. H." B. 19 March 1871, Northam, Devon, England; D. 10 February 1962, Northam, Devon, England. J. H. Taylor was part of the Great Triumvirate of Golf, with **James Braid** and **Harry Vardon,** in the late 19th century and first decade of the 20th century. Taylor learned the game as a **caddie** at Royal North Devon Golf Club and turned **professional** when he was 19. He served as the pro at Royal Mid-Surrey Golf Club from 1899 to 1946. His fame as a player rested on his five wins in the **Open Championship (British Open)**, a mark bettered only by Vardon and equaled by Braid, **Peter Thomson**, and **Tom Watson**. Taylor won in 1894, 1895, 1900, 1909, and 1913. Taylor founded and was the first chairman of the British PGA. Later in life, he became a **golf course architect**, his most notable design being **Royal Birkdale**. Taylor captained the 1933 British **Ryder Cup** team.

TEEING GROUNDS (TEEBOX). By definition in the **Rules of Golf**, the teeing ground, often called "**teebox**," is the area from which a player begins the play on each hole. Tees are closely mown areas that are usually kept shorter than all areas of the course except the **putting green**. The teeing ground is defined by two markers, and extends backward, away from the hole, two clublengths in depth from the markers. Most **golf courses** have several different tees on each hole, usually either three or four. The different tees are for golfers of differing abilities, with the longest tees usually called the "championships tees" and the shortest tees usually called the "ladies' tees" or the "senior tees." The tees are usually of different colors, with the championship tees often blue, the middle tees white, and the shortest tees red. If a course has four sets of tees, the championship tees may be gold or black, with the next longest tees blue.

TELEVISION. Television has been very influential in popularizing the game of golf. The first nationally televised golf tournament was the 1953 Tam O'Shanter World Championship of Golf. The television audience was stunned by the finish, in which Lew Worsham came to the last hole trailing Chandler Harper by one shot. But Worsham holed a full-wedge shot approach for an **eagle** two, winning by one shot. The 1954 **U.S. Open,** played at **Baltusrol Golf Club**, was televised nationally for the first time, although parts of the 1947 U.S. Open were televised locally in St. Louis. Television and **Arnold Palmer** soon became the perfect match, as the charismatic "King of Golf" thrilled millions with his many famous charges and his come-from-behind victories. For many years, the tournaments were able to show only the final few holes, often only the 15th through the 18th holes. In the 1970s, the holes shown were expanded greatly, with the 1977 U.S. Open showing all 18 holes for the first time.

But the next big change in televised golf came in 1995 when the Golf Channel was launched as a 24-7 channel devoted to televising and talking about golf. It was started by an Alabama entrepreneur, Joseph Gibbs (not the football coach/NASCAR owner), but appropriately enough, one of the major investors was Arnold Palmer. Although the Golf Channel struggled in its early years, it has become very popular and profitable and has led to a proliferation of specific cable sports channels, devoted to tennis, football, baseball, and

Olympic sports. In 2007, the Golf Channel signed a 15-year contract to be the exclusive cable channel of the **PGA Tour**. Today, all PGA Tour events are televised in some form due to this contract, and the Golf Channel also shows many **LPGA** and **European PGA Tour** events.

TEXAS WEDGE. "Texas wedge" refers to the use of a putter from well off the **putting green**. It got this name because many Texas courses, prior to watering systems coming into vogue, had very hard-packed turf with closely mown **grass** around the greens, and putting from off the green was quite easy, actually easier than chipping.

THIN. "Thin" refers to a slight mis-hit in which the **golf club** does not fully impact the golf ball but instead hits high up on the ball's surface. In a thin shot, no divot is taken, and the club is swung on a path slightly elevated to the intended plane.

THION DE LA CHAUME, SIMONE. *See* DE LA CHAUME, SIMONE.

THOMAS, GEORGE CLIFFORD, JR. B. 3 October 1873, Philadelphia, Pennsylvania, United States; D. 23 February 1932, Beverly Hills, California, United States. George Thomas was an American **golf course architect** known for many of the courses he designed in the 1910s and 1920s. He was prominent in California, with his best-known courses being **Riviera Country Club**, Bel-Air Country Club, and the North Course at the Los Angeles Country Club. In the era in which he worked, large earth-moving equipment was not available for golf course construction, so he tended to follow the contours of the land, allowing his courses to blend into the natural surroundings. Thomas preferred wide **fairways** and a more strategic approach to golf course design, believing that although **hazards** had importance, they should not be penal.

THOMPSON, ALVIN CLARENCE "TITANIC" (NÉ ALVIN CLARENCE THOMAS). B. 1892, Rogers, Arkansas, United States; D. 1974. Titanic Thompson is the best-known gambler and hustler in golf history. He was actually an expert golfer, but his skill lay in being able to figure the odds on any bet and stacking the bet in his own favor. In addition, he was used to playing for large sums of money, which often brought pressure to his opponents and caused them to crack under the pressure. Titanic Thompson was also an excellent card player and crack shot, and many of his bets involved card games and shooting skills. *See also* GAMBLING.

THOMPSON, STANLEY. B. 18 September 1894, Toronto, Ontario, Canada; D. 4 January 1953, Toronto, Ontario, Canada. Stanley Thompson is the best-known Canadian **golf course architect**. He designed courses from 1912 to 1952, most of them in **Canada**. The Stanley Thompson Society documents 178 courses designed by Thompson, with 144 of them in Canada. He started building courses with George Cumming, longtime head **professional** at the Toronto Golf Club. Thompson's best-known courses include the **Banff Springs Hotel Golf Course**, the Jasper Park Golf Course in Alberta, and the **St. George's Golf and Country Club** in Toronto. In 1946, Thompson and **Donald Ross** cofounded the **American Society of Golf Course Architects** (ASGCA). Thompson was inducted into the Canadian Golf Hall of Fame in 1980.

THOMSON, JAMES LAURIE "JIMMY." B. 29 October 1908, North Berwick, Scotland; D. June 1985. Jimmy Thomson was born in **Scotland**, came to the **United States** in 1922, and established himself as a U.S. **professional**. He was the longest **driver** in golf during his career. Thomson did not have many **PGA Tour** wins, recording only two, the 1936 Richmond Open and 1938 **Los Angeles Open**, but he did place second at the 1935 and 1936 **U.S. Open** and lost in the final of the 1936 **PGA Championship** to **Denny Shute**. He first played in the U.S. Open in 1925 when he was only 17 years old, placing 16th. Thomson's length off the tee was legendary. He won numerous driving contests, including a best-recorded drive of 380 yards, several times. During the 1929 **Open Championship (British Open)**, he drove the 375-yard 11th hole at **Muirfield**, and at the 1935 U.S. Open at **Oakmont**, he was the first player ever to reach the 595-yard 12th hole in two shots. Thomson was also a club professional, as were many players in that era, working at the Broadmoor

County Club in Colorado Springs, and Lakewood Country Club in Los Angeles.

THOMSON, PETER WILLIAM. B. 23 August 1929, Melbourne, Victoria, Australia. Peter Thomson was the first great Australian player known internationally. He made his fame by winning the **Open Championship (British Open)** five times, in 1954–1956, 1958, and 1965. While Thomson's victories in the 1950s came against fields that did not have the top American players, his 1965 victory established his ability to beat the best in the world. Thomson played briefly on the U.S. **PGA Tour** in 1953–1956, winning one tournament, the 1956 Texas Invitational. He won over 30 **professional** tournaments in **Australia**, including eight victories at the New Zealand Open and three at the **Australian Open**. He also won 26 times in European professional events before the era of the **European PGA Tour**. Besides his Open championships, these wins include the News of the World Match Play event in 1954, 1961, 1966, and 1967. Thomson captained the International team at the 1998 President's Cup. He was inducted into the **World Golf Hall of Fame** in 1988.

THROUGH THE GREEN. "Through the green" is a defined term in the **Rules of Golf**. It includes the entire area of the **golf course** except the **teeing ground**, the **putting green**, and **hazards**. Many of the rules refer to areas "through the green," and the rules do not include any references to "**fairway**" and "**rough**," which basically constitute what is considered "through the green."

TIGER TEES. This is the term used for the very back tees, usually on a course with four sets of tees. It is so named because the tees are often located well back into the woods, away from other tees, and are difficult to find, and it was jokingly said that one needed to be careful of the tigers back there. The term has nothing to with **Tiger Woods** and predates him by several decades.

TILGHMAN, KELLY. B. 6 August 1969, North Myrtle Beach, South Carolina, United States. Kelly Tilghman is a golf announcer on the **Golf Channel**. Tilghman played college golf at Duke University, and she briefly attempted a **professional** career, but never qualified for the **LPGA**. She played in Europe, Asia, and **Australia** from 1992 to 1996. Tilghman joined the Golf Channel in 1996. She moved up the ranks to become lead broadcaster for **PGA Tour** events after the PGA Tour signed a contract with the Golf Channel in 2007 allowing it to host early round coverage of all its events. Tilghman is unfortunately best known for a remark she made on the air in January 2008 in reference to **Tiger Woods**. Discussing Woods' dominance of the PGA Tour, Tilghman said the only thing the other players could do was to "lynch him in a back alley." With Woods' ethnic background, the reference to lynching was particularly offensive and brought outcries from various do-gooders, notably the Reverend Al Sharpton, for the Golf Channel to fire Tilghman. She was suspended for two weeks but remained on the air. Woods and his agent realized Tilghman meant no offense and voiced their support for her, which defused the incident.

TILLINGHAST, ALBERT WARREN "A. W." B. 7 May 1876, Philadelphia, Pennsylvania, United States; D. 19 May 1942, Toledo, Ohio, United States. A. W. Tillinghast was one of the greatest **golf course architects** in golf history, known for both the quality and number of courses he designed. He is credited with over 260 course designs. His most famous courses have been around New York, notably **Winged Foot Golf Club**, **Baltusrol Golf Club**, Quaker Ridge Golf Club, and **Bethpage Black**. He also designed Newport Country Club, Inverness Club, and the Five Farms Course at Baltimore Country Club, all sites of major open or **amateur** championships. Other courses for which he completed the original design include San Francisco Golf Club and the Philadelphia Cricket Club. Tillinghast was an entrepreneur of golf. He organized and conducted several tournaments, most notably the Shawnee Open in the Poconos on a course he designed, Shawnee-on-the-Delaware. He wrote for numerous golf magazines and wrote books as well.

TIPS. "Tips" refers to playing a **golf course** from the very back edge of the longest tees available, thus playing the course at its absolute fullest length. It is often a form of lingo on **professional** tours, where the pros often rate anything in terms of **handicap** and the level of tees involved. Thus, a pretty sunset might be a "4 from the blues," while poor service in a restaurant might be an "18 from the reds." The ultimate compliment is to be a "scratch from the tips."

TITLEHOLDERS CHAMPIONSHIP. The Titleholders Championship was one of the original major championships for **women**. It was first contested in 1937, held at the Augusta Country Club, adjacent to **Augusta National Golf Club**, and the tournament fancied itself a "female **Masters**." Until 1948, the event was a mixture of **amateurs** and **professionals** but no prize money was offered. It became a fixture on the **LPGA** but was discontinued in 1966. In 1972, the Titleholders was held for one final time. In the 1990s, an **LPGA** event, also called the Titleholders, was held at other clubs from 1996 to 1999, but it was not a major championship. **Patty Berg** won the Titleholders seven times, a record. **Louise Suggs** won four times, and **Babe Zaharias** won three times. Appendix 3 includes a list of champions.

TITLEIST. "Titleist" is a brand name of the Acushnet Company, headquartered near Buzzards Bay, Massachusetts. "Titleist" refers to the company's headline brand of **golf balls**, which is the best-known golf ball in the world. Acushnet began manufacturing the Titleist in the 1940s, and it has been the best-selling ball in golf and on the pro tours since the 1960s. Acushnet makes various brands of the Titleist for players of varying abilities, with the current top brands played by pros being the Pro V1 and the Pro V1x. Acushnet also makes **golf clubs** but is known primarily for the Titleist golf ball.

TOSKI, ROBERT JOHN "BOB" (NÉ ROBERT JOHN ALGUSTOSKI). B. 18 September 1926, Haydenville, Massachusetts, United States. Bob Toski was one of the top **professional** players of the 1950s but has become much better known as a golf teacher. Toski played on the **PGA Tour** from 1949 to 1956. He led the money list in 1954 when he won George May's World Championship at Tam O'Shanter Club in Chicago, which offered a then-record $50,000 to the winner. Toski won four times on the PGA Tour in 1954 and five times in all. In the late 1960s, Toski became famous as an instructor, teaching several professionals and helping to start the *Golf Digest*

Golf Schools. Toski has written several books on golf instruction and is a member of the World Golf Teachers Hall of Fame.

TOURNAMENT PLAYERS CHAMPIONSHIP. *See* THE PLAYERS CHAMPIONSHIP.

TPC SAWGRASS. TPC Sawgrass, which stood originally for Tournament Players' Club Sawgrass, is a **golf course** in Ponte Vedra Beach, Florida, near Jacksonville. It is the annual site of the **The Players' Championship**, considered the de facto fifth major championship by many touring pros. There are two courses at the club, the Stadium Course and the Valley Course. The tournament is held on the Stadium Course. The U.S. **PGA Tour** has its headquarters at the club. The Stadium Course was designed by **Pete Dye** and opened in 1980. It first hosted The Players' in 1982, then called the Tournament Players' Championship. The course was widely criticized by the pros when it first opened. The well-known pro and architect **Ben Crenshaw**, usually the most gracious of pros, said that it was "Star Wars golf," designed by Darth Vader. However, Dye made some changes to the course over the years, making it much more playable and acceptable to the pros. The signature hole is the 17th, a short par-three to an island green. Although the shot requires only a wedge or up to an 8-iron at most, for the pros, missing the green puts the ball in the water and necessitates another shot from the tee or the drop area. It has been estimated that more than 100,000 balls per year are put in the water surrounding that green.

TRANS-MISSISSIPPI AMATEUR CHAMPIONSHIP (TRANS-MISS). The Trans-Mississippi Amateur, or simply the "Trans-Miss," is one of the top **amateur** championships in the **United States**. Held since 1901, it rotates to various courses but always to one west of, or near, the Mississippi River. For years, the field was open, but in 1987, it converted to a Mid-Amateur event, limited to players 25 years of age or greater. The tournament has historically been contested at **match play**. But in 2010, the event will change to a Champions Division, with no age restriction, and a Senior Division, for players 55 and older, both of which will be held at 54 holes **stroke play**. Past champions of the Trans-Miss include **Jack Nicklaus**, Charles Coe, **Deane Beman**, **Ben Crenshaw**, and Gary Koch.

The Trans-Miss began in 1901 as a challenge match between Omaha Country Club and St. Joseph Country Club of Missouri. Later in 1901, the players formed the Trans-Mississippi Golf Association, which has always sponsored the tournament, with these original clubs: Cedar Rapids Country Club; Denver Country Club; Des Moines Golf and Country Club; Dubuque Golf Club; Evanston Golf Club; Kansas City Country Club; Holdredge Country Club; Leavenworth Country Club; Leavitt Country Club; Norton Country Club; Omaha Country Club; St. Joseph Country Club; Town and Gown Golf Club of Colorado Springs; and Wichita Country Club. Appendix 6 includes a list of champions.

TRAVERS, JEROME DUNSTAN "JERRY." B. 19 May 1887, New York, New York, United States; D. 29 March 1951, East Hartford, Connecticut, United States. Jerry Travers was one of the early greats of **amateur** golf in the **United States**, winning four **U.S. Amateur** titles, in 1907, 1908, 1912, and 1913. Living around New York, Travers won the **Metropolitan Amateur** five times, in 1906, 1907, 1911, 1912, and 1913 and the New Jersey Amateur four times, in 1907, 1908, 1911, and 1913. Travers also won the **U.S. Open** in 1915, the second amateur to win that title. Although he was not known as a strong **stroke player**, he was considered the finest **match player** in the world in his prime. Travers was born to a wealthy family, which gave him the opportunity to play when he wished. But in the 1929 stock market crash, he and his family lost much of their fortune, and he then turned **professional**, giving lessons and exhibitions to make money for his family. Travers was inducted into the **World Golf Hall of Fame** in 1976.

TRAVIS, WALTER JOHN "THE OLD MAN." B. 10 January 1862, Maldon, Victoria, Australia; D. 31 July 1927, Denver, Colorado, United States. Walter Travis was one of the great American **amateurs** of the first decade of the 20th century. Born in **Australia**, he came to the **United States** in 1886 and settled in New York City, where he sold hardware and construction products for an Australian-based firm. Travis did not take up golf until 1896, when he was 34 years old, but he quickly learned the game, entering the **U.S. Amateur** for the first time in 1898 and making the semifinals. Travis eventually won the U.S. Amateur three times, in 1900, 1901, and 1903. In 1904, Travis traveled to Great Britain to compete in the **Amateur Championship (British Amateur)** and won that title. His victory was controversial. Travis used a center-shafted putter in his U.S. Amateur victories, and his putting was the best part of his game. He used the center-shafted putter in Britain, but the controversy caused it to be banned by the **R&A** in 1909. Travis' other titles include five victories in the **Metropolitan Amateur**, three in the **North and South Amateur**, and the 1913 and 1914 Cuban Amateur. At age 53, Travis won the 1915 Metropolitan Amateur and then retired from competitive play the next year due to issues related to his amateur status.

TREVINO, LEE BUCK "THE MERRY MEX." B. 1 December 1939, Dallas, Texas, United States. Lee Trevino was a Mexican-American **professional** who was among the greatest players in the world from the late 1960s through the early 1980s. Trevino grew up in a poor family and learned the game in Dallas as a **caddie**. He taught himself with long hours of practice, which he continued even after he entered the Marine Corps at 17. After he was discharged, he made money by playing in big-money matches, a notable one in Dallas against **PGA Tour** star Raymond Floyd. Trevino went on the PGA Tour in 1967, finished a remarkable fifth that year at the **U.S. Open**, and was named Rookie of the Year. He bettered that in 1968 when he won the U.S. Open at Oak Hill Country Club. Trevino won 29 tournaments on the PGA Tour, including six major titles—the U.S. Open in 1968 and 1971, the **PGA Championship** in 1974 and 1984, and the **Open Championship (British Open)** in 1971 and 1972. Trevino played on six **Ryder Cup** teams and won the **Vardon Trophy** for low scoring average on the PGA Tour five times. He also won 29 tournaments on the Champions (Senior) Tour.

Trevino continued to be one of the hardest workers on tour, known for long hours on the practice tee. His swing was unusual: he aimed left with a strong grip, swung quickly, and blocked everything to produce a slight fade. But he was one of the greatest ball strikers in golf history. The only thing that kept him from dominating the tour was the fact that he was only an average-length **driver**, and he could not fully overcome the advantage that long drivers had, notably **Jack Nicklaus**. Trevino was known for his humor, seemingly speaking to everyone on the course and cracking jokes. He was a very funny man and used the humor to help ease pressure, but when it came time to play the shot, he was quite serious.

Trevino's greatest year was 1971 when he won the U.S., Canadian, and British Opens, received the Hickok Belt as the top professional athlete of the year, and was named *Sports Illustrated*'s "Sportsman of the Year." He was inducted into the **World Golf Hall of Fame** in 1981.

TROPHÉE LANCÔME. *See* LANCOME TROPHY.

TUFTS, RICHARD SISE. B. 16 March 1896, Medford, Massachusetts, United States; D. 17 December 1980, Pinehurst, North Carolina, United States. Richard Tufts was the grandson of James Walker Tufts, who founded the **Pinehurst** Resort in North Carolina. Richard Tufts eventually ran the resort for his father and became a top golf administrator. He became president of the **USGA** in 1956–1957 and was captain of the 1963 **Walker Cup** team. Tufts was the head of Pinehurst until the resort was bought by Diamondhead Corporation in 1973. He was inducted into the **World Golf Hall of Fame** in 1992.

TURFGRASS RESEARCH AND MANAGEMENT. Turfgrass research and management is done at many universities in the **United States** and throughout the world. In the golf world, such research has been funded since the early 1980s by the **USGA**, which provides grants to many of these universities. The research looks at development of better or tougher grasses, control of insects and other pests, ways to use pesticides more judiciously, methods to lessen water use on **golf courses**, and ways to protect and preserve the environment. The USGA funds research projects in five categories: integrated turfgrass management; physiology, genetics and breeding; golf course construction; environmental impact; and outreach programs. The USGA also funds the Green Section, which provides agronomists to solve smaller regional problems on golf courses. In addition to funds being provided to university programs, the USGA assists the **Golf**

Course Superintendents Association of America, Turfgrass Producers International, and the National Turfgrass Evaluation Program. *See also* AGRONOMY.

TURNBERRY. Turnberry is a golf resort in South Ayrshire, in southwest **Scotland**, bordering the Firth of Clyde. The resort has three **golf courses**, the Ailsa Course being the best known. It has hosted the **Open Championship (British Open)** four times, in 1977, 1986, 1994, and 2009. The other two courses are the Kintyre Course and the nine-hole Arran course. The Ailsa Course is named for Ailsa Craig, an uninhabited rock island located in the Firth of Clyde, which is visible from several holes. Turnberry was used as an airbase during both World War I and II, and a memorial to lost airmen can be found on the hill above the 12th green on the Ailsa course. Turnberry also hosted the **Women's British Open** in 2002.

Turnberry hosted two great Open Championships, both involving **Tom Watson**. In 1977, he and **Jack Nicklaus** dueled in the final 36 holes, with Watson winning by one shot, as he shot 65-65 on the weekend, to Nicklaus' 65-66. The battle has been called the "Duel in the Sun." The two were so dominant that the third-place finisher in the event, **Hubert Green**, was 10 shots back of Nicklaus. In their honor, the 18th hole on the Ailsa Course has been renamed "Duel in the Sun."

In 2009, Watson, by then 59 years old, inexplicably led the Open at Turnberry through three rounds and, in fact, held a one-shot lead standing on the 72nd tee. But Watson's second shot to 18, played with a firm 8-iron, went through the green. With the hole cut in the back, he did not get up and down, falling into a tie with Stewart Cink, who defeated Watson in the four-hole play-off.

TURNESA, WILLIAM P. "WILLIE." B. 20 January 1914, Elmsford, New York, United States; D. 16 June 2001, Sleepy Hollow, New York, United States. Willie Turnesa was an American **amateur**, who came from a famous golfing family that produced seven well-known golfing brothers. Of the seven, all turned **professional** except Willie. The brothers were Phil Turnesa (1896–1987), Frank Turnesa (1898–1949), Joe Turnesa (1901–1991), Mike Turnesa (1907–2000), Doug Turnesa (1909–1972), and Jim Turnesa (1912–1971). Jim won the only professional major in the group, the 1952 **PGA Championship**, although Joe placed second at the 1926 **U.S. Open** and 1927 PGA. But it is Willie who remains the best known for his amateur exploits. Willie won the 1947 **British Amateur** and the **U.S. Amateur** in 1938 and 1948. He played on the **Walker Cup** team in 1947, 1949, and 1951, captaining the 1951 team, and served as president of the Metropolitan Golf Association and the New York State Golf Association.

– U –

UNITED GOLFERS ASSOCIATION (UGA). The United Golfers Association was a **professional** tour for African Americans in the days before they were allowed to play the **PGA Tour**. The PGA Tour had a Caucasian-only clause, which was quite controversial and was not rescinded until 1961. This necessitated a separate tour for black players. The UGA was founded in 1926 by Massachusetts golf enthusiast Robert Hawkins. It became the home for such top black players as **Ted Rhodes**, **Bill Spiller**, **Pete Brown**, and **Charlie Sifford**. Both Brown and Sifford credited the UGA with giving them the chance to develop their games and eventually succeed on the PGA Tour, but the rule change came too late for Rhodes and Spiller. The UGA Tour was at its apex from 1946 to 1961 when **Joe Louis** and bandleader Billy Eckstine supported black golfers and the tour. Louis frequently played in UGA events as an **amateur**. The top event was the National Negro Open, won seven times by Sifford and four times by Brown. When the PGA Tour, then run by the **PGA of America**, eliminated its Caucasian-only clause in 1961, blacks became eligible for the PGA Tour, which led to the demise of the United Golfers Association.

UNITED STATES. The game of golf first appeared in the United States in the 18th century. with the first mention in Charleston, South Carolina, at the South Carolina Golf Club. The first permanent club was the Oakhurst Club in White Sulphur Springs, West Virginia, which opened in 1884. But the club did not last long, and the oldest club in the United States is usually considered to be the St. Andrews'

Golf Club in Yonkers, New York, formed by a group of players in 1888 who called themselves the "Apple Tree Gang," led by Scottish émigré John Reid. The **USGA** was formed in December 1894 and the **U.S. Amateur** and **U.S. Open** were held for the first time in 1895. Many of the early clubs and best players were Scottish **professionals** who had settled in the United States. By the 1920s, the United States had the best players in the world, notably **Bob Jones** and **Walter Hagen**, and that dominance has not waned to this day. In later years, U.S. dominance was led by **Ben Hogan**, **Byron Nelson**, **Sam Snead**, **Arnold Palmer**, **Jack Nicklaus**, **Tom Watson**, and today, **Tiger Woods**. But since the early 1980s, many international players have challenged this dominance. And although U.S. **women professionals** have been preeminent since the formation of the **LPGA** in 1950, they have also been challenged in recent years by players from Sweden, Korea, and Mexico.

Golf is very popular in the United States as a participant sport, although less so in recent years. The **National Golf Foundation** estimated in 2005 that 4.6 million Americans played 25 or more rounds per year, and 26 million played some golf in the same year. But that was down from 6.9 million and 30 million, respectively, in 2000. As of 2008, there are approximately 17,000 **golf courses** in the United States, which places the country eighth in the world in terms of number of courses per capita.

UNITED STATES BLIND GOLFERS ASSOCIATION (USBGA). The United States Blind Golfers Association was formed in 1953 by Bob Allman, a blind lawyer and golfer. But the first National Blind Golfers Championship was held in 1946, won by Clint Russell, who lost his sight in 1924 when a tire exploded in his face. The Mission Statement of the United States Blind Golfers Association notes that "the United States Blind Golf Association is organized and operated for the purposes of benefiting blind and vision-impaired persons and promoting the public good through programs that advance, and increase public awareness of golf among the blind and vision-impaired throughout the United States." The organization now annually hosts the USBGA National Championship, usually at different sites throughout the country, although from 1990 to 1997, it was held at the Lake Buena Vista Club near Disney World in Florida. The championship is now cosponsored by The Lions Clubs International. In 1978, the **Ken Venturi** Guiding Eyes Classic started in Mount Kisco, New York, which is considered the "Masters" for blind golfers. A team match between the **United States** and Great Britain, the Stewart Cup, was held in 1991, 1993, and 1995. In 1998, the USBGA was one of nine founding groups of the International Blind Golf Association.

UNPLAYABLE LIE. An unplayable lie is a **Rule of Golf** that specifies the options available to a player who is not able to reasonably play a shot from where the ball lies. The applicable rule is Rule 28, which allows a player three options, to be taken with a one-shot penalty: 1) play the ball from where it was originally played, thus taking a stroke and distance penalty; 2) take a drop at the nearest point of relief, no closer to the hole, within two club lengths from the ball's position; or 3) keeping the point of the unplayable lie between the player and the hole, the player may go back an unlimited distance and drop the ball at that point. The **ball in play** may be cleaned prior to dropping, and Rule 28 states that the player is the sole judge of whether or not the ball is unplayable. The ball may be ruled unplayable anywhere on the course, including a **bunker**, except in **water hazards**.

UP-AND-DOWN. "Up-and-down" refers to making a recovery for **par** when one misses the green in regulation, thus taking only two shots from there to hole the ball. The ability to get up-and-down effectively is the hallmark of a player with a solid short game and a requirement in high-level tournament golf.

U.S. AMATEUR. The U.S. Amateur is the top **amateur** golf championship in the **United States** and possibly the world, rivaled only by the **Amateur Championship (British Amateur)**. The championship was first officially held in 1895. In 1894, there were two tournaments that billed themselves as National Amateur championships, one won by William Lawrence and the other by Laurence Stoddart. This prompted **Charles Blair Macdonald**, the runner-up in both events, to call for a national governing body for golf, and the **USGA** was formed late in 1894. In 1895, the USGA held the first U.S. Amateur and **U.S. Open**; the first U.S. Amateur was won by Macdonald.

The U.S. Amateur was always held at **match play** until 1965, when it was converted to a 72-hole **stroke play** event. However, this lasted only a few years, and in 1973, the championship returned to match play and remains a match play event to this day. The championship is now held late in the summer, near the end of August, and ends the summer amateur circuit for the top players. While the event was often won by career amateurs for many years, it is now usually a stepping-stone for top collegiate and amateur players who are planning to turn **professional**.

The U.S. Amateur rotates around various courses in the United States. Local qualifying is held around the country to determine the final field. The championship now consists of on-site 36-hole qualifying to choose 64 players for match play. Thus, the final site actually consists of two courses, with the main course being used for match play. The championship has been won by many of the top professionals, including **Jack Nicklaus**, **Tiger Woods**, **Arnold Palmer**, and **Phil Mickelson**. The most wins in the event is five by **Bob Jones**, with **Jerry Travers** winning four times, and **Walter Travis** and Woods three times. Appendix 6 includes a list of champions.

U.S. AMATEUR PUBLIC LINKS CHAMPIONSHIP (U.S. PUBLINX). The U.S. Amateur Public Links Championship, usually shortened to the U.S. Publinx, is a **USGA** championship open only to players who play on public **golf courses**, barring any player who is a member of a private club. The event was first held in 1922. The championship has sectional qualifying, with 36 holes of on-site qualifying at the main site, followed by 64 players competing in **match play**. Carl Kauffmann won the event three times, and seven players have won the event twice. Appendix 8 includes a list of champions.

U.S. GIRLS' JUNIOR. The U.S. Girls' Junior is a national championship conducted by the **USGA** for girls 17 years old or younger. It was first held in 1949, won by Marlene Bauer. The event takes place at various courses around the country. **Hollis Stacy** won the event three times consecutively (1969–1971), and **Nancy Lopez** won it twice in 1972 and 1974. Many great **LPGA** players have won the event, notably **Mickey Wright**, **JoAnne Carner**, **Amy Alcott**, Michelle McGann, and Kelli Kuehne. The championship is conducted at

match play, with players qualifying regionally. Appendix 8 includes a list of champions.

U.S. JUNIOR AMATEUR. The U.S. Junior Amateur is a national championship conducted by the **USGA** for boys 17 years old or younger. It was first held in 1948, won that year by Dean Lind. Regional qualifiers are held to advance players to **stroke play** qualifying at the final site, followed by **match play** rounds to determine a champion. Only one player has won the event more than once, **Tiger Woods**, who won in 1991–1993. Several other champions later starred on the **PGA Tour**, notably **Gay Brewer**, Mason Rudolph, Tommy Jacobs, **Johnny Miller**, Gary Koch, and Willie Wood. Appendix 8 includes a list of champions.

U.S. MID-AMATEUR. The U.S. Mid-Amateur Championship is a **USGA** championship, first played in 1981, which is open to players 25 years of age or older. The championship was founded in response to the trend of top **amateur** players, those competing in the **U.S. Amateur** and other major amateur tournaments, to come almost exclusively from the ranks of college players. The Mid-Amateur was designed to be contested among those who were already several years out of college and were more likely to be career amateurs. The championship is rotated to different clubs each year. The format is **match play** among 64 players, who have survived 36 holes of on-site qualifying. The winner receives an automatic invitation to play in the **Masters. Jay Sigel** won the championship three times, while four players have won it twice: Tim Jackson, John "Spider" Miller, Nathan Smith, and Jim Stuart. Appendix 8 includes a list of champions.

U.S. OPEN. The U.S. Open is the U.S. national golf championship, conducted annually by the **USGA.** In the early days of the tournament, it was known as the National Open. The championship is always held in mid-June, finishing on the third Sunday, usually Father's Day. The championship is a 72-hole **stroke play** event that is contested on various courses chosen several years in advance. Unlike the **Open Championship (British Open)**, the U.S. Open does not have a set rotation (rota) of courses for the championship. But there have been certain well-known courses that have hosted the event multiple times, among them **Oakmont**, which has hosted eight U.S. Opens (1927, 1935, 1953, 1962, 1973, 1983, 1994, and 2007), and **Baltusrol**, which has hosted seven (1903, 1915, 1936, 1954, 1967, 1980 and 1993).

The U.S. Open courses are specially prepared for the championship, and the event is known for its difficult conditions, including very fast greens, narrow **fairways**, and thick rough bordering the fairways. The prototype of this occurred in 1951 at **Oakland Hills Country Club** when **Robert Trent Jones** was brought in to modify the course for the championship. The rough was grown to over six inches in length, and nobody broke **par** in the first three rounds. Only **Ben Hogan** (67) and Clayton Heafner (69) shot rounds under par, both in the fourth round. After winning the Open, Hogan noted, "I'm glad I brought this course, this monster, to its knees." Many players think that the USGA has gone overboard, in certain years, in an attempt to defend a course's reputation and keep the winning score around par. Modern **professionals** routinely shoot well under par in most events. In 1974, the U.S. Open was held at **Winged Foot**, and the winning score, by **Hale Irwin**, was 287, 7-over-par. After the first two rounds, then–USGA president Sandy Tatum was asked if they were trying to embarrass the world's greatest players. He famously replied, "We're not trying to embarrass them, we're trying to identify them."

The first U.S. Open was played in 1895 at Newport Country Club. Eleven players entered the 36-hole event, held in one day, and the winner was Horace Rawlins, who received a first-prize purse of $150. The event remained at 36 holes in 1896 and 1897, but became the standard 72 holes in 1898. The U.S. Open is the only major championship that still decides its champion, in the event of a tie, by using a full 18-hole play-off. Actually, in early years of the event, the play-offs were 36 holes, with the last 36-hole play-off occurring in 1931. In that year, Billy Burke and George Von Elm tied, and in the 36-hole play-off they tied again, at 149. They then actually played another 36 holes, with Burke prevailing after 144 total holes, 148-149. In 1939, the next U.S. Open play-off occurred and was to be held at 18 holes between **Byron Nelson**, **Craig Wood**, and **Denny Shute**. However, Nelson and Wood tied with 68 in the play-off and played another 18 holes to determine the champion, Nelson winning, 70-73. The first simple 18-hole play-off occurred in 1940, when **Lawson Little** defeated **Gene Sarazen**, 70-73.

The U.S. Open now receives about 9,000 entries. Entrants must be either a professional or an **amateur** with a **handicap** index of no more than 1.4, but with no gender or age restrictions. The U.S. Open final field consists of 156 players, with approximately 50–60 players exempted by virtue of several qualifying standards. The remainder of the field is filled by two rounds of qualifying, local qualifying and sectional qualifying. The sectional qualifying is contested over 36 holes at several sites around the country. Local qualifying was also 36 holes, but is now contested at 18 holes. It takes place in most states, with a few states having more than one site.

The U.S. Open has been won four times by four players—**Willie Anderson** in 1901 and 1903–1905; **Bob Jones** in 1923, 1926, 1929, and 1930; Ben Hogan in 1948, 1950, 1951, and 1953; and **Jack Nicklaus** in 1962, 1967, 1972, and 1980. The championship was not held in 1917–1918 and 1942–1945 because of World War I and II. In 1942, the USGA conducted the Hale America National Open Championship, raising money for the war effort. The tournament was won by Ben Hogan, who insisted throughout his life that he had won five U.S. Opens, because he received the same medal there as he had for his other four championships. The USGA does not consider the Hale America National Open to have been a U.S. Open and credits Hogan with only four wins. Appendix 2 includes a list of champions.

U.S. SENIOR OPEN. The U.S. Senior Open is a major championship for seniors, conducted by the **USGA.** It is open to players 50 years old or greater, although the age limit was originally 55. The event was first held in 1980. It rotates around various courses throughout the country. The U.S. Senior Open has been won three times by Miller Barber and twice by Allen Doyle, **Hale Irwin**, **Jack Nicklaus**, and **Gary Player**. Appendix 8 includes a list of champions.

U.S. WOMEN'S AMATEUR. The U.S. Women's Amateur Championship is the top female **amateur** championship in the **United States**. Conducted by the **USGA**, the event was first held in 1895, one month after the **U.S. Open** and **U.S. Amateur**, at the Meadow Brook Club on Long Island. The championship is contested at **match**

play. It rotates among different courses throughout the United States. The Robert Cox Trophy, donated by Robert Cox, a member of British Parliament, is awarded to the winner. **Glenna Collett Vare** won the title six times, which is the record. The event was won five times by **JoAnne Gunderson Carner**. Seven players have won the title three times—**Beatrix Hoyt**, **Margaret Curtis**, **Dorothy Campbell**, **Alexa Stirling**, **Virginia Van Wie**, **Anne Quast**, and **Juli Inkster**. Appendix 7 includes a list of champions.

U.S. WOMEN'S AMATEUR PUBLIC LINKS (U.S. WOMEN'S PUBLINX). The U.S. Women's Amateur Public Links Championship, usually shortened to the U.S. Women's Publinx, or WAPL, is a **USGA** championship open only to female players who play on public **golf courses**, barring any player who is a member of a private club. The event first took place in 1977. The tournament has sectional qualifying, with 36 holes of on-site qualifying at the main site, followed by 64 players competing in **match play**. Four players have won the event twice: Kelly Fuiks, Lori Castillo, Pearl Sinn, and Jo Jo Robertson. **Michelle Wie** won the event in 2003 when she was only 13 years old, and she played in the event in 2000 when she was only 10. Appendix 8 includes a list of champions.

U.S. WOMEN'S MID-AMATEUR. The U.S. Women's Mid-Amateur is a **USGA** championship, first played in 1987, which is open to players 25 years of age or older. The championship started as a female response to the **U.S. Mid-Amateur**, which is open to men. It is designed for golfers several years out of college, who are more likely to be career **amateurs**. Appendix 8 includes a list of champions.

U.S. WOMEN'S OPEN. The U.S. Women's Open Championship is the female equivalent of the **U.S. Open**. Conducted by the **USGA**, it is the national championship for **women** in the **United States** and is one of the four major championships played by women. The event was first held in 1946 at Spokane Country Club, when it was won by **Patty Berg** in a **match play** format. Since 1947, the event has been conducted at 72-holes **stroke play**. The event took place from 1946 to 1948 under the auspices of the **Women's Professional Golf Association**, and from 1949 to 1952, it was conducted by the

LPGA. It came under the USGA umbrella in 1953. The event rotates among courses throughout the United States, and it has been held three times at the Atlantic City Country Club and the Pine Needles Lodge and Golf Club. The event is open to any professional or **amateur** golfer with a **handicap** index of 4.4 or lower. The event has a full field of 156 players, of which about half are exempted based on past performance. Since 2002, the remainder of the field qualifies via a two-stage process, with 18 holes of local qualifying followed by 36 holes of sectional qualifying. Through 2001, qualifying was a single-stage process of 36 holes only, and in 2010, the championship will once again revert to single-stage qualifying. Two players have won the U.S. Women's Open four times—**Betsy Rawls** and **Mickey Wright**. Four players have won three titles—**Susie Berning**, **Annika Sörenstam**, **Hollis Stacy**, and **Babe Zaharias**. Appendix 3 includes a list of champions.

USGA (UNITED STATES GOLF ASSOCIATION). The USGA, or in full, the United States Golf Association, is the governing body of golf in the **United States**, its territories and possessions, and Mexico. The organization was formed on 22 December 1894, when five of the top clubs in the United States—Chicago Golf Club, **The Country Club**, **Shinnecock Hills Golf Club**, Newport Country Club, and St. Andrews Golf Club—organized to conduct national championships for **amateurs** and an open championship. The original name was the Amateur Golf Association of the United States, but the name was changed in 1895. The USGA now has over 9,700 member golf or country clubs. It is headquartered at Far Hills, New Jersey, and is led by an executive committee, with day-to-day affairs under the direction of an executive director, currently **David Fay**.

The USGA conducts 13 national championships annually in the United States—the **U.S. Open**, **U.S. Women's Open**, **U.S. Amateur**, **U.S. Women's Amateur**, **U.S. Mid-Amateur**, **U.S. Women's Mid-Amateur**, **U.S. Senior Open**, **USGA Senior Amateur**, **USGA Women's Senior Amateur**, **U.S. Junior Amateur**, **U.S. Girls' Junior**, **U.S. Public Links Championship, and the U.S. Women's Public Links Championship**. In addition, the organization hosts two team events biennially: USGA Men's State Team Championship and USGA Women's State Team Championship. It also cohosts the **Walker Cup** and **Curtis Cup** biennially with the **R&A** and the **Ladies' Golf Union**, respectively, which are team amateur matches for men and **women**. Finally, the USGA helps administer, via the **International Golf Federation** (IGF), two **World Amateur Team Championships**, with men competing for the **Eisenhower Trophy** and women, for the **Espirito Santo Trophy**.

The USGA also promotes the game of golf in the United States and the world. It has formed the USGA Foundation, which provides grants to programs for the underprivileged and golfers with disabilities, and is a large contributor to the First Tee Program. It also tests **golf clubs** and golf balls for conformance to the **Rules of Golf** and helps underwrite turfgrass research for **golf courses**. With the R&A, the USGA is responsible for writing the Rules of Golf and making decisions on them. The USGA is also responsible for defining and maintaining the **handicap** system in the United States. It awards the **Bob Jones Award** annually, given since 1955 to an individual for distinguished sportsmanship in golf. Appendix 11 includes a list of USGA presidents.

USGA SENIOR AMATEUR. The USGA Senior Amateur is a **USGA** championship for male **amateurs** who are 55 years old or older. The first event was held in 1955. The championship is rotated to different clubs each year. The format is **match play** among 64 players who have survived 36 holes of on-site qualifying. There was an earlier senior national championship, conducted by the U.S. Senior Golf Association, which was not affiliated with the USGA and which had been held at Apawamis Golf Club in Rye, New York, since the early 1900s. The USGA Senior Amateur has been won three times by Lew Oehmig and 12 different players have won it twice. Senior Amateur contestants have been permitted to ride in carts since 1969. Appendix 8 includes a list of champions.

USGA SENIOR WOMEN'S AMATEUR. The USGA Senior Women's Amateur is a **USGA** championship for female **amateurs** who are 50 years old or older. The first event was held in 1962. The format began as a 54-hole **stroke play** competition over three days. In 1997, it was changed to a **match play** event. Carolyn Cudone has won the event five times, with three players winning it four times:

Dorothy Germain Porter, **Anne Quast-Decker-Welts-Sander**, and **Carol Semple-Thompson**. Appendix 8 includes a list of champions.

– V –

VALDERRAMA GOLF CLUB. *See* CLUB DE GOLF VALDERRAMA.

VAN DONCK, FLORY. B. 23 June 1912, Tervuren, Brabant, Belgium; D. 1992. Flory Van Donck was the greatest player in Continental Europe in the early years after World War II, and is considered the best Belgian player ever. He won multiple national Open championships in Europe, including the Dutch Open five times, the Belgian Open five times, the **French Open** three times, the Italian Open four times, the German Open twice, the Swiss Open twice, and one victory each at the Portuguese Open and Venezuelan Open. Van Donck won the Belgian PGA title 16 times. Van Donck never managed a major title, finishing second twice at the **Open Championship (British Open)** in 1956 and 1959, but in 1960, he won the individual title at the **Canada Cup** (World Cup).

VAN PELT, SCOTT. B. 1967, Brookeville, Maryland, United States. Scott Van Pelt is an American sportscaster who is now an anchor on SportsCenter on ESPN. He has a special interest in golf, based on his early career at the **Golf Channel**. Van Pelt attended the University of Maryland, majoring in radio/television and film. Shortly after his college graduation, he worked at WTTG-TV, a Fox affiliate station in Washington, D.C. He was hired by the Golf Channel as an anchor and reporter. There, he was a studio cohost of Golf Central, Leaderboard Report, and occasionally hosted Viewer's Forum. Van Pelt was at the Golf Channel from 1994 to 2000, and then moved to ESPN, where he is one of the sports network's top golf correspondents. He also anchors Sports Center, usually, the 11 p.m. edition, and is the host of his own show, "The Scott Van Pelt Show," on ESPN Radio.

VAN WIE, VIRGINIA. B. 9 February 1909, Chicago, Illinois, United States; D. 18 February 1997, Big Rapids, Michigan, United States.

Virginia Van Wie was one of the greatest **women amateurs** in the **United States**. A Chicago native, Van Wie won three **U.S. Women's Amateur** titles, all consecutively from 1932 to 1934. She lost in the final in 1928 and 1930, both times to **Glenna Collett Vare**. Van Wie played on the first **Curtis Cup** team in 1932 and was on the team again in 1934. She retired from competition in 1935 and taught golf in the Chicago area for more than 30 years. In 1950, Van Wie was inducted into the Women's Golf Hall of Fame.

VARDON, HARRY. B. 9 May 1870, Grouville, Isle of Jersey, Great Britain; D. 20 March 1937, Totteridge, Hertfordshire, England. Harry Vardon was the first player in the 20th century to be considered the greatest player ever. Vardon's fame was based on his winning the **Open Championship (British Open)** six times, still a record. He also won the 1900 **U.S. Open** and was runner-up in that event in 1913 and 1920. His 1900 U.S. Open victory occurred during a tour of the **United States** in which he played more than 80 matches throughout the country. He won at least 60 **professional** tournaments in an era before organized professional tours. He suffered in his later career from tuberculosis, which possibly prevented him from winning more. Vardon popularized a style of golf grip, the overlap, which he used and which is often called the Vardon grip. The **Vardon Trophy** is given annually by the **PGA Tour** for the lowest scoring average. Vardon became a charter member of the **World Golf Hall of Fame** in 1974.

VARDON TROPHY. The Vardon Trophy is an award given by the **PGA of America** to the **PGA Tour** player with the lowest scoring average for the year. It is named for British golfing great **Harry Vardon** and was first awarded in 1937. Since 1980, the PGA Tour has given a similar award, the **Byron Nelson Award**, to the player with the lowest adjusted scoring average, relative to par. The Vardon Trophy was won eight times by **Tiger Woods**, five times by **Billy Casper** and **Lee Trevino**, and four times by **Arnold Palmer** and **Sam Snead**. The Byron Nelson Award was won nine times by Tiger Woods and five times by **Greg Norman**. Appendix 10 includes a list of recipients.

VARE, GLENNA COLLETT. B. 20 June 1903, New Haven, Connecticut, United States; D. 3 February 1989, Gulfstream, Florida, United States. Glenna Collett Vare dominated **women**'s golf in the era before **professional** golf existed for women. She competed in her first **U.S. Women's Amateur** in 1919, at only 16, and in 1921, she was the medalist at that championship. She was Women's Amateur champion six times, still a record, winning in 1922, 1925, 1928–1930, and 1935. From 1928 to 1931, she won an astounding 16 consecutive major amateur championships. In her career, she won the **North and South Women's Amateur** six times and the Women's Eastern Amateur six times. Collett Vare played on the first **Curtis Cup** team in 1932 and was player/captain in 1934, 1936, 1938, and 1948. In her honor, the **LPGA** awards the **Vare Trophy** to the player with the lowest scoring average for the year. She was inducted into the **World Golf Hall of Fame** in 1975.

VARE TROPHY. The Vare Trophy is an award given by the **LPGA** to the player with the lowest scoring average for the year. It is named for U.S. **amateur** great **Glenna Collett Vare** and was first awarded in 1953. The trophy was donated by LPGA founder **Betty Jameson**, who asked that it be named in honor of her golfing heroine. The Vare Trophy was won six times by **Kathy Whitworth** and **Annika Sörenstam**, and five times by **Mickey Wright** and **JoAnne Carner**. Appendix 10 includes a list of recipients.

VENTURI, KENNETH "KEN." B. 15 May 1931, San Francisco, California, United States. Ken Venturi was a U.S. **professional**, perhaps best known to the current generation as a golf broadcaster. Venturi grew up in the Bay Area and became a top **amateur** player. In 1956, he led the **Masters** and appeared set to become the first amateur to win that title. But in heavy winds on the final day, he shot 80 and lost by one shot to Jackie Burke. To this day, no amateur has won the Masters. Mentored by **Byron Nelson**, Venturi turned professional in 1956 and quickly became one of the top players on the **PGA Tour**, winning 10 tournaments in 1957–1960. But then, he inexplicably lost his game and was close to quitting the tour. Gradually in 1964, his game improved and he placed third at the Thunderbird Classic the week before the **U.S. Open**.

At that 1964 U.S. Open, Venturi came through for his greatest win. In the third round on Saturday, in scorching heat at the Congressional Country Club, Venturi shot 66 despite shooting two late **bogeys** when he was in the midst of near collapse from heat exhaustion. In that era, the players shot 36 holes on the final day. He was treated between rounds by Dr. John Everett, who advised him not to play the final round. But he refused and went out to play, paired with young pro Raymond Floyd. Venturi was on the brink of collapse throughout the round, but he somehow managed to shoot 70 and won the event by four shots. Walking very slowly, at a pace that would now warrant a penalty, on the 71st hole, Venturi apologized to **USGA** official **Joe Dey,** who told him, "Hold your head up, and keep walking, Kenny. You're about to be a champion." When he made his final shot, a 20-foot putt for a **par** on the 72nd hole, he raised his arms to his head and proclaimed, "My God, I've won the Open." Venturi, tears streaming down his face, was too weak at that point to get to the hole, so Floyd retrieved the ball and handed it to him. In the scoring tent, Venturi could not read his scorecard correctly, nor remember all his hole scores. Dey looked at it, over Venturi's shoulder, and advised him, "Sign it, Kenny. It's correct." His victory is considered the most dramatic in U.S. Open history.

Venturi won twice more in 1964 and once in 1966 despite ongoing problems with carpal tunnel syndrome in his hands. He retired with 14 PGA Tour victories. In 1967, he became a broadcaster on PGA Tour events with CBS Sports, spending 35 years in the booth before retiring in 2002. Venturi played on the 1965 **Ryder Cup** Team. He became *Sports Illustrated*'s "Sportsman of the Year" in 1964.

VON NIDA, NORMAN GUY. B. 14 February 1914, Strathfield, New South Wales, Australia; D. 20 May 2007, Gold Coast, Queensland, Australia. Norman Von Nida was the first great Australian golfer. He played mostly "Down Under." He won the Queensland Amateur in 1932 and turned pro the next year. In **Australia,** he won multiple **professional** titles, including the following: **Australian Open**—3; Australian PGA—3; Queensland Open—6; New South Wales Open—5; New South Wales PGA—4. Von Nida played briefly in Great Britain after World War II, placing second on the Order of Merit in 1946 and in 1947 winning seven events in Britain and topping the Order of Merit. He played in Britain again in 1948 and then returned permanently to Australia. He played the **Open Championship (British Open)** five times—1946–1950 and 1952—with best finishes of third in 1948 and fourth in 1946. In addition to his playing ability, Von Nida was known for his temper on the course. The Australian PGA developmental tour is named after him, the Von Nida Tour.

VOTAW, TY MICHAEL. B. 12 February 1962, Salem, Ohio, United States. Ty Votaw is a golf administrator who earned a law degree from the University of North Carolina in 1987, after graduating from Ohio University in 1984. After graduation from law school, he worked for the law firm of Taft, Stettinius & Hollister in Ohio. He joined the **LPGA** in 1991 as its general counsel and he served as LPGA commissioner from 1999 to 2005. In 2005, he left the LPGA and joined the **PGA Tour**, becoming an executive vice president and in charge of International Affairs for the PGA Tour. In 2009, Votaw was the point person for the successful efforts to have golf restored to the Olympic program. He is married to Sophie Gustafson, a Swedish player who plays on the LPGA.

– W –

WADKINS, JEROME LANSTON "LANNY." B. 5 December 1949, Richmond, Virginia, United States. Lanny Wadkins was a phenom as a junior player and **amateur** out of Richmond, Virginia. He attended Wake Forest University, won the 1970 **U.S. Amateur,** and turned **professional** in 1971 after his junior year. He was the 1972 PGA Rookie of the Year and was one of the top professionals in the world through the 1970s and into the 1980s. Wadkins won 21 tournaments on the **PGA Tour**, including the 1977 **PGA Championship**, his only major, although he finished second four times in other majors. He also won the 1979 **Players Championship**, the "fifth major," was voted PGA Player of the Year in 1985, and was inducted into the **World Golf Hall of Fame** in 2009. Known for his confident, borderline cocky, attitude, Wadkins was a top match player and very tough in money matches against other pros. None other than **Lee Trevino**

said of him, "He was the gutsiest sumbitch I've ever met." Wadkins used his **match play** ability to play well on eight **Ryder Cup** teams between 1977 and 1993. Not a long hitter, Wadkins was very accurate with his **driver** and irons, which enabled him to overcome his lack of length. His swagger and pinpoint accuracy enabled him to fire at every pin, which he did. From 2002 to 2007, he worked as a golf analyst for CBS Sports. Wadkins' younger brother, Bobby Wadkins, also played for many years on the PGA Tour and **Champions Tour**.

WAGGLE. Waggle is the loose movement of the club and hands, often back-and-forth but occasionally up-and-down, as the player addresses the ball prior to beginning the swing, or takeaway. **Ben Hogan** wrote much of one chapter about the waggle in his famous book *Five Lessons: The Modern Fundamentals of Golf*. He considered it an absolute necessity to get the swing in motion and to mimic some of the motions one was trying to create in the golf swing. Hogan noted, "The bridge between the address and the actual start of the backswing is the waggle. . . . It is an extremely important part of shotmaking. Far from being just a lot of minute details, it is a sort of miniature practice swing, an abbreviated 'dry run' for the shot coming up."

WALKER, GEORGE HERBERT "BERT." B. 11 June 1875, St. Louis, Missouri, United States; D. 24 June 1953, New York, New York, United States. Bert Walker was an American banker and businessman known for being the donor of the **Walker Cup**, given to the winning team in the biennial U.S.-Great Britain **amateur** team matches. Walker made his fortune first with G. H. Walker & Co. and later with W. A. Harriman & Co., both banking and investment firms. He served as president of the **USGA** from 1919 to 1920, and his son-in-law, Prescott Bush, served as USGA president from 1934 to 1935. Walker was also the grandfather of U.S. president George H. W. Bush and the great-grandfather of President George W. Bush, both noted golf enthusiasts.

WALKER CUP. The Walker Cup is a biennial team match played between teams of male **amateurs** representing the **United States** and Great Britain–Ireland. The event began officially in 1922, although there was an unofficial match held in 1921. From 1922 to 1924, it was held annually but has since been contested biennially. Held in even-numbered years prior to World War II, the event switched to odd-numbered years in 1947. The competition alternates locations between a U.S. course and a course in Great Britain or **Ireland**. The trophy itself was donated and is named for **George Herbert Walker**, who was president of the **USGA** in 1919–1920 and was the grandfather of U.S. president George H. W. Bush and great-grandfather of U.S. president George W. Bush. Each team has 10 players who compete against each other in **foursomes**, **four-ball**, and singles competitions over three days. The United States leads the series 33-7, but leads in the last 11 matches only 6-5. Appendix 5 includes a list of champions, scores, and captains.

WANAMAKER TROPHY. The Wanamaker Trophy is the trophy given to the winner of the U.S. **PGA Championship**. It was donated by Rodman Wanamaker, owner of the Wanamaker Department Store in Philadelphia, and was given for the first PGA Championship in 1916.

WARD, EDWARD HARVIE, JR. B. 8 December 1925, Tarboro, North Carolina, United States; D. 4 September 2004, Pinehurst, North Carolina, United States. Harvie Ward grew up in North Carolina and attended his state school, the University of North Carolina, and while there, won the 1949 **NCAA Championship** and the 1948 **North and South Amateur**. He then began a heralded **amateur** career in the 1950s, winning the 1952 **British Amateur**, the 1954 Canadian Amateur, and back-to-back **U.S. Amateur**s in 1955 and 1956. Ward is one of only two men, the other being Dick Chapman, to have won those three major amateur titles. In 1957, the **USGA** revoked Ward's **amateur status**, ruling that he had taken excess expense money, but he was reinstated in 1958. He played on the **Walker Cup** team in 1953, 1955, and 1959.

Ward was one of the great gentleman amateurs of the game. In 1974, he turned **professional**, almost 50 years old and with no Senior Tour yet available to him. He spent many years as a club professional at Foxfire Country Club in the **Pinehurst** area and often held court as a raconteur at several different Pinehurst clubs. He won the 1977 North Carolina Open and played occasionally on the **Senior PGA Tour** in the 1980s. Ward was inducted into the North Carolina Sports Hall of Fame in 1965, the Carolinas Golf Reporters Association-Carolinas Golf Hall of Fame in 1981, and the Carolinas PGA Hall of Fame in 1996. He was a friend to all who met him.

WASTE BUNKER. A waste bunker is a large **bunker** on a **golf course**, usually along the **fairway**, which may contain sand, but more often simply contains wasteland, grasses, dirt, or wild areas. Play from a waste bunker can be quite difficult because of the variety of **hazards** one may encounter. The most famous waste bunker is a large bunker on the seventh hole at **Pine Valley** called "Hell's Half Acre," which is often considered the largest bunker in the world.

WATER HAZARDS. A water hazard is a **hazard** on a **golf course** that, usually, contains water. There are two types of **water hazards**—water hazards and **lateral water hazards**. The **Rules of Golf** define a water hazard as follows:

> A water hazard is any sea, lake, pond, river, ditch, surface drainage ditch or other open water course (whether or not containing water) and anything of a similar nature on the course. All ground or water within the margin of a water hazard is part of the water hazard. The margin of the water hazard extends vertically upwards and downwards. Stakes and lines defining the margins of water hazards are in the hazards. Such stakes are obstructions. A ball is in a water hazard when it lies in or any part of it touches the water hazard. Stakes or lines used to define a water hazard must be yellow. When both stakes and lines are used to define water hazards, the stakes identify the hazard and the lines define the hazard margin. The committee may make a local rule prohibiting play from an environmentally-sensitive area defined as a water hazard.

Lateral water hazards are defined as follows by the Rules of Golf:

> A lateral water hazard is a water hazard or that part of a water hazard so situated that it is not possible or is deemed by the committee to be impracticable to drop a ball behind the water hazard in accordance with rule 26-1b. That part of a water hazard to be played as a lateral water hazard should be distinctively marked. A ball is in a lateral water hazard when it lies in or any part of it touches the lateral water hazard.

> Stakes or lines used to define a lateral water hazard must be red. When both stakes and lines are used to define lateral water hazards, the stakes identify the hazard and the lines define the hazard margin. The committee may make a local rule prohibiting play from an environmentally-sensitive area defined as a lateral water hazard. The committee may define a lateral water hazard as a water hazard.

Rule 26 of the Rules of Golf refers to the procedure when a ball is hit into a water hazard. First of all, it may be played, if that is possible. If not possible, the player has several options. One is to take a stroke-and-distance penalty: one stroke is added to the player's score, and another ball is played from the spot of the previous shot. Second, the player may drop behind the water hazard, keeping the spot at which the ball crossed the margin of the hazard between the point of the drop and on a line to the hole. There is no limit to how far behind the margin of the hazard the player may drop the ball. Third, and applicable to only a lateral water hazard, the player may drop the ball within two club lengths of the margin of the hazard where the ball last crossed the margin and no nearer the hole. One oddity of this final drop rule, not well known to most players, is that the player may drop the ball on either side of the lateral hazard, in this case, using a point on the opposite margin of the hazard.

Water hazards usually increase the difficulty of a golf course and are the hallmark of a very difficult golf course. There are several famous water hazards in golf, usually on well-known courses. At Pebble Beach, the Pacific Ocean borders several holes, including the 6th, 7th, 8th, 9th, 10th, 17th, and 18th, but most notably the 18th, which parallels the ocean, which borders the left side of the **fairway** for its entire length. At Augusta National, Rae's Creek is a small creek that borders the 12th and 13th holes. Its small section directly in front of the par-three 12th hole is its most well-known hazard. On the well-televised back nine during the **Masters**, television watchers also know of the ponds that border the 11th, 12th, 13th, 15th, and 16th holes, which have often played havoc with players' shots. On the **Old Course at St. Andrews**, the Swilcan Burn is a small creek bordering the front of the green on the 1st hole. It also runs in front of the 18th tee, although it does not come into play on that hole. A few well-known courses have no water hazards, notably **Winged Foot** and **Pinehurst**. Pinehurst actually has one hazard on the 16th hole, but it is not in play for tournament golfers.

WATSON, THOMAS STURGES "TOM." B. 4 September 1949, Kansas City, Missouri, United States. Tom Watson is a U.S. **professional** who, in the late 1970s and early 1980s, was the greatest player in the world. After playing college golf at Stanford, Watson joined the **PGA Tour** in 1971. He struggled a bit for the first few years in attempts to win tournaments but finally broke through in June 1974 at the **Western Open**. During his PGA Tour career, Watson won 39 tournaments, including eight major championships. Watson won the **Open Championship (British Open)** five times—in 1975, 1977, 1980, 1982, and 1983; the **Masters** in 1977 and 1981; and the **U.S. Open** in 1982. He never succeeded in winning the career **Grand Slam.** He came close several times but never managed to win the **PGA Championship**. Watson has played well on the **Champions (Senior) Tour**, winning 12 times through 2009. In 2009, Watson almost made golf history at **Turnberry**, which had been the site of one of his greatest triumphs when he memorably defeated **Jack Nicklaus** in what was effectively a two-man duel at the 1977 Open Championship. Watson was almost 60 years old at the 2009 Open Championship but held the lead after three rounds and in the final round continued to lead as he stood on the 72nd tee. But his 8-iron second shot was too strong and went through the green. When he failed to get up and down from there he fell back into a tie with Stewart Cink, who defeated Watson in the four-hole play-off.

Watson was named PGA Player of the Year six times (1977–1980, 1982, 1984), a record at the time, since broken by **Tiger Woods**, who has been accorded that honor 10 times (through 2009). Watson also received the **Vardon Trophy** for lowest scoring average on the PGA Tour in 1977–1979. He played on four **Ryder Cup** teams (1977, 1981, 1983, and 1989) and was captain of the team in 1993. Watson received the 1987 **Bob Jones Award** from the **USGA** for distinguished sportsmanship in golf. He was inducted into the **World Golf Hall of Fame** in 1988.

WEBB, KARRIE ANNE. B. 21 December 1974, Ayr, Queensland, Australia. Karrie Webb is the best female player yet produced by

Australia and one of the greatest ever from any country. In the late 1990s, she briefly interrupted the reign of **Annika Sörenstam** as the world's number-one-ranked player. Webb began her **professional** career in 1994 on the Ladies' European Tour and joined the **LPGA** in 1996. She won her second tournament on the LPGA and through 2009 has won 36 LPGA tournaments. Her greatest years were 1999 and 2000, when she won six and seven tournaments, respectively, with two major championships in 2000. Her titles, to date, include seven major championships—the **Du Maurier Classic** in 1999, the **Kraft Nabisco (Dinah Shore)** in 2000 and 2006, the LPGA in 2001, the **U.S. Women's Open** in 2000 and 2001, and the **Women's British Open** in 2002. After 2002, Webb struggled a bit for three years, winning one tournament in 2003, one in 2004, and going winless in 2005. But she returned to her old form in 2006, winning five events on tour. In 2005, she was inducted into the **World Golf Hall of Fame**.

WEDGES. Wedges are the most highly lofted clubs in a set of irons. There are several different types, notably pitching wedges, **sand wedges**, and **lob wedges**. When clubs were designated by names and not numbers, early wedges were called **niblicks**, which were effectively the same as a modern pitching wedge. In some older sets of clubs, after the advent of numbers, wedges were occasionally called 10-irons.

A pitching wedge is used for fairly short shots from the **fairway** and may be used to pitch the ball around the greens. Sand wedges are slightly more lofted than pitching wedges and have a thickened, raised bottom sole that allows a player to hit from sand bunkers without the leading edge of the club digging into the sand and ruining the shot. The sand wedge is attributed to **Gene Sarazen**, who popularized it in the early 1930s. Sand wedges are the preferred club for sand bunker shots but may also be played from the fairway or for pitching around the greens. In the 1990s, players began adding a third wedge (and occasionally a fourth) to their set of irons, usually dropping out a long iron. This wedge is the most lofted of all and is termed a "lob wedge," because it is usually used to lob the ball up very dramatically in pitching shots around the green. Lob wedges will often have a loft of up to 60 degrees, with a few players, notably **Phil Mickelson**, using a very lofted wedge of up to 64 degrees, sometimes called an "X-wedge," for "extreme lob wedge." Lob wedges can also be played from the fairway for very short shots, often around 60–80 yards. Pitching wedges, through the 1970s, had lofts of about 48 degrees–54 degrees, but in the 1980s, with the new technology in iron design that allowed for greater loft on all shots, all iron clubs began to be de-lofted, and modern pitching wedges usually have lofts of about 46 degrees–50 degrees. Sand wedges now usually have lofts of about 54 degrees–58 degrees. When players carry four wedges, as many **professionals** now do, the fourth wedge may be called a gap wedge, which will have lofts of about 50 degrees–54 degrees.

WEIR, MICHAEL RICHARD, "MIKE," CM, OONT. B. 12 May 1970, Sarnia, Ontario. Mike Weir has been the top Canadian **professional** of the 1990s and early 21st century. A left-handed player, Weir became the first Canadian to win a major professional title when he triumphed at the 2003 **Masters.** It also made him only the second lefty to win a major title, following **Bob Charles** at the 1963 **Open Championship (British Open)**. Weir played college golf at Brigham Young University and turned professional in 1992. He played initially on the Canadian Tour, leading the Canadian Order of Merit in 1997, and joined the **PGA Tour** in 1998. Weir has won six times on the PGA Tour through 2009, his first win coming in 1999. He was ranked in the World Top 10 for over 100 weeks from 2001 to 2005. Weir started his own line of wines, produced by Creekside Estate Winery, and is opening his own winery. He has formed the Mike Weir Foundation, whose charitable work supports the Children's Miracle Network. Weir was appointed to the Order of Ontario in 2003 and became a Member of the Order of **Canada** in 2007.

WEISKOPF, THOMAS DANIEL "TOM." B. 9 November 1942, Massillon, Ohio, United States. Tom Weiskopf is one of the most talented golfers in history, noted for his beautiful golf swing, his ability to drive the ball a long way, but also for some difficulty turning that talent into tournament victories. Weiskopf followed **Jack Nicklaus** at Ohio State University, and many considered him more talented than Nicklaus. He turned **professional** in 1964, but did not win his first PGA Tournament until 1968. He would eventually win 16 times on the **PGA Tour**, winning from 1968 to his final win at the 1982 **Western Open**. His greatest year was 1973, when he won five times, including the **Canadian Open** and the **Open Championship (British Open)**, his only major title. Weiskopf's greatest disappointments came at **Augusta National** in the **Masters**, a tournament he dearly wanted to win. He finished second there four times, a record, in 1969, 1972, 1974, and 1975. The 1975 tournament was one of the greatest ever, with Weiskopf, Nicklaus, and **Johnny Miller** all very close on the back nine on Sunday, but Nicklaus prevailed, as he often did. At the victory ceremony in Butler Cabin, Weiskopf was obviously distraught and stated firmly, "Someday I will win this tournament." But it was never to be. Weiskopf has played sporadically on the **Champions (Senior) Tour**, winning four tournaments, including the 1995 **U.S. Senior Open**. He has not played much as a senior because he is heavily involved in a **golf course** design business, for which he has become quite well known, especially for his Scottish design, Loch Lomond.

WELTS, ANNE. *See* ANNE QUAST.

WENTWORTH CLUB. Wentworth Club is a famous club and **golf course** in Virginia Water, Surrey, a southwestern suburb of London. It was founded in 1926. The club has 63 holes, with three full 18-hole courses and a nine-hole par-three course. The best known of the courses is the West Course, designed by **Harry Colt** in 1926. The West Course has hosted the **World Match Play Championship** from 1964 to 2008 and the British **PGA Championship** since 1984. It also hosted the 1953 **Ryder Cup** and the 1956 **Canada Cup**. The headquarters of the PGA European Tour are located at the club, and each year, it hosts the tour's BMW PGA Championship. Wentworth Club is surrounded by the Wentworth Estate, an exclusive private enclave, which is home to many top golfers and celebrities, among them **Ernie Els**, who became Wentworth's "worldwide touring **professional**" in 2005. Wentworth also boasts a Tennis and Health Club. In 2004, Richard Caring, a fashion industry tycoon, purchased the club for £130 million.

WESTERN AMATEUR. The Western Amateur is a top **amateur** tournament in the **United States**, usually considered the most prestigious after the **U.S. Amateur**. It is organized by the Western Golf Association (WGA). The event was first held in 1899, and has been held continuously since, except during the world wars. Until 1970, the tournament was rotated among various courses, but in 1971, the tournament made a "permanent" home at Point O'Woods Golf and Country Club in Benton Harbor, Michigan. However, after the 2008 tournament, it was announced that the Point would no longer host the tournament, and the WGA would again rotate the sites. The Western has an unusual format, consisting of a 72-hole **stroke play** qualifying event, which advances 16 players to **match play**. Making the match play portion of the tournament, termed the "Sweet 16," is an honor among top amateurs. The winner of the tournament receives the George R. Thorne Championship Trophy. Past champions read like a *Who's Who* of top golfers, including **Ben Crenshaw**, Justin Leonard, **Phil Mickelson**, **Jack Nicklaus**, **Francis Ouimet**, **Tiger Woods**, **Curtis Strange**, **Hal Sutton**, **Lanny Wadkins**, and **Tom Weiskopf**. Appendix 6 includes a list of champions.

WESTERN OPEN. The Western Open, founded by the Western Golf Association in 1899, was, for many years, the second most prestigious championship in the **United States**. It took place continuously from 1899 to 2006. In 2007, it became known as the BMW Championship. It is no longer an open championship, since **amateurs** are no longer invited, but it is still run by the Western Golf Association. The championship was rotated among various courses in the Midwest until 1974. Then, it began to be held at Butler National Golf Club, in Oak Brook, Illinois, near Chicago, an all-men's club and one of the hardest courses on the **PGA Tour**. The Western Open took place at Butler National from 1974 to 1990. But in 1990, the PGA Tour ruled that all their tournaments had to take place on courses that had no discrimination in their membership policies, which eliminated all-men's clubs such as Butler National. From 1991 until its demise in 2006, the Western Open took place at the Dubsdread Course at Cog Hill Golf and Country Club, in Lemont, Illinois, also near Chicago. The BMW Championship continued to take place at Cog Hill, a public **golf course**, in 2007–2009, but will now be rotated among three courses—Cog Hill, Crooked Stick Golf Club (Carmel, Indiana), and Bellerive Country Club (St. Louis). Appendix 4 includes a list of champions.

WETHERED, JOYCE (LADY HEATHCOAT-AMORY). B. 17 November 1901, Surrey, England; D. 18 November 1997, London, Greater London, England. Joyce Wethered is usually considered the greatest British **woman** player ever and is often listed in the top 10 of all-time women golfer lists, although she had a relatively short career. Wethered won the English Ladies' Championship five consecutive years, from 1920 to 1924, and was **British Ladies' Amateur** Champion four times, in 1922, 1924, 1925, and 1929. She effectively retired after her 1929 title but returned in 1932 to play in the first **Curtis Cup**. Wethered grew up playing at Worplesdon Golf Club in Surrey, often accompanied by her brother, Roger, who also became a top **British Amateur**. She married Sir John Heathcoat-Amory in 1924, becoming Lady Heathcoat-Amory. Lady Heathcoat-Amory was inducted into the **World Golf Hall of Fame** in 1925. **Bob Jones** often said she had the finest golf swing he had ever seen, man or woman. *See also* WETHERED, ROGER.

WETHERED, ROGER. B. 3 January 1899, Surrey, England; D. 12 March 1983, Wimbledon, Greater London, England. Roger Wethered was a top British **amateur** of the 1920s and the brother of **Joyce Wethered**. After serving briefly in World War I, Roger Wethered attended Christ Church College, Oxford, where he played on the golf team. In 1921, he tied for first at the **Open Championship (British Open)** with **Jock Hutchison**, losing the title to Hutchison in a 36-hole play-off. Wethered won the **Amateur Championship (British Amateur)** only once, in 1923, but was a runner-up in 1928 and 1930. He was soundly trounced in the 1930 final by **Bob Jones**, who was in the midst of winning the **Grand Slam**. Wethered was elected captain of the **Royal and Ancient Golf Club of St. Andrews** in 1939, taking office in 1946.

WHITWORTH, KATHY. B. 27 September 1939, Monahans, Texas, United States. Kathy Whitworth won more **professional** golf tournaments than any other woman player ever. Growing up in New

Mexico, Whitworth won the 1957 and 1958 New Mexico Women's State Amateur Championship and turned professional late in 1958. After winning her first **LPGA** event in 1962, she went on to win 88 LPGA tournaments, her last in 1985. Whitworth won seven or more tournaments in seven calendar years—1963, 1965–1969, and 1973, with her best year being 1968, when she won 10 times. During that period, she was LPGA Player of the Year seven times and won the **Vare Trophy** for lowest scoring average on the tour seven times. Whitworth won six major championships during her career, the 1965 and 1966 **Titleholders**, the 1967 **Western Open**, and the **LPGA Championship** in 1967, 1971, and 1975. The only trophy missing from her mantel is the **U.S. Women's Open**, in which her best finish was second place in 1971. Whitworth was inducted into the **World Golf Hall of Fame** in 1975.

WIE, MICHELLE SUNG "THE BIG WIESY" (NÉE WIE SEONG-MI). B. 11 October 1989, Honolulu, Hawaii. Michelle Wie is a U.S. **professional** prodigy who learned to play in Hawaii. She began to play at age four and immediately showed enormous talent. When she was 10, she qualified for the **U.S. Women's Publinx** Championship. In 2001, she won the Hawaii Women's Stroke Play Championship and the Jennie K. Wilson Women's Invitational, the most prestigious **women**'s **amateur** event in Hawaii. Wie grew into a tall (6 feet 1 inch [185 cm]), lovely young lady, who possessed a powerful golf swing and drove the ball prodigious distances for someone her age, male or female. **Johnny Miller** and **David Leadbetter** proclaimed it the best swing in golf, when she was young. She was expected to dominate the women's game, and in 2002, she won the Hawaii Women's Open by 13 shots over former **LPGA** player Cindy Rarick. In 2003, she won the U.S. Women's Publinx at only 13 years of age.

In 2005, Wie began to play in professional events, both on the LPGA and the men's **PGA Tour**. She almost made the cut at the men's Hawaiian Open in 2006, missing by only four shots, a stunning performance for a 16-year-old girl. She finished the 2006 **U.S. Women's Open** in third place, coming to the final holes with a chance to win. But in 2007, she elected not to immediately pursue the LPGA full-time, instead choosing to attend Stanford University, where her father had once been a professor. In addition, she sustained a wrist injury that year that greatly hampered her playing. It cost her most of the 2007 and part of the 2008 seasons. In late 2008, Wie entered the LPGA Q School and qualified to play the LPGA in 2009, where she placed 16th on the money list for the year with two second-place and two third-place finishes. Finally, in November 2009, Wie broke through to win on the LPGA, claiming the **Lorena Ochoa** Invitational in Guadalajara, Mexico.

Michelle Wie has been a great enigma. Possessed of tremendous talent and ability, her biggest failure has been her inability to win. She did not win a golf tournament of any type between 2003 and late 2009. Some people in the golf world feel her parents pushed her too much into playing against professionals, male and female. The **LPGA** would love to see her begin to win consistently because her marketing potential, with her beauty, her driving length, and winsome golf swing, is unlimited. But the world still waits on the next great female player and wonders if that player will be Michelle Wie.

WILLIAM D. RICHARDSON AWARD. The William D. Richardson Award is given by the **Golf Writers Association of America (GWAA)** to an individual who has made consistent outstanding contributions to the game of golf. The award was first given out in 1948. Winners since that time include **Dwight Eisenhower**, **Bob Hope**, **Jack Nicklaus**, and **Nancy Lopez**. Appendix 11 includes a list of recipients.

WILSON, HUGH IRVINE. B. 13 November 1879, Philadelphia, Pennsylvania, United States; D. 3 February 1925, Bryn Mawr, Pennsylvania, United States. **Hugh Wilson** was a U.S. **golf course architect**, most well known for his design of **Merion Golf Club** West Course in Philadelphia in 1911. He also helped finish the layout of **Pine Valley**, often considered the hardest golf course in the world. Wilson studied at Princeton University, where he played on the golf team and was the club champion at Aronimink in Philadelphia. Chosen to design **Merion** in 1910, Wilson spent several months in **Scotland** and **England** to develop ideas for the course, being especially influenced by the North Berwick Golf Club. Wilson eventually built both courses at Merion, adding the East Course in 1914, and designed several other courses in the Pennsylvania area, notably Phoenixville Country Club and Reading Country Club.

WIND, HERBERT WARREN. B. 11 August 1916, Brockton, Massachusetts, United States; D. 30 May 2005, Bedford, Massachusetts, United States. Herbert Warren Wind was an American writer who wrote frequently on golf. Wind was a Yale graduate who also earned a master's degree in English literature at Cambridge University. He was a writer for the *New Yorker*, and covered golf and other sports for that magazine from 1947 to 1953. He then moved to *Sports Illustrated* from 1954 to 1960, before returning to the *New Yorker*, where he spent the rest of his career, which ended in 1990. Wind coined the term **Amen Corner**, describing the 11th, 12th, and 13th holes at **Augusta National**, where the **Masters** tournament was often decided. His best-known golf book, which he authored solely, was *The Story of American Golf*, published in 1948, with a second edition in 1975. In 1957, with **Ben Hogan**, Wind coauthored *Five Lessons: The Modern Fundamentals of Golf*, which became the best selling golf instructional book ever. Wind was elected to the **World Golf Hall of Fame** in 2008. The **USGA** named its annual book award (the Herbert Warren Wind Book Award) in his honor.

WINGED FOOT GOLF CLUB. Winged Foot is a golf club in Mamaroneck, New York, with two courses. Both courses were designed by **A. W. Tillinghast** and are of championship caliber. The West Course, in particular, has hosted numerous major championships, notably the **U.S. Open** in 1929, 1959, 1974, 1984, and 2006, the **U.S. Amateur** in 2004, and the 1997 **PGA Championship**. The East Course, which is slightly shorter, hosted the **U.S. Women's Open** in 1957 and 1972, and the **U.S. Senior Open** in 1980.

WINTER RULES. *See* PREFERRED LIES.

WOMEN. Women have played golf for almost the entire recorded history of the game, going back to Mary Queen of Scots, in the 16th century. Women have also competed in tournaments since the 19th century, with the first major event being the **British Ladies' Amateur**, which began in 1893. The **United States** soon followed, with the **U.S. Women's Amateur**, started in 1895. Unlike the men's game, which featured **professionals** from the early 19th century, women's **professional** golf took longer to develop. The first attempts to start a **women**'s professional game began in the mid-1940s in the United States, with the formation of the **Women's Professional Golf Association (WPGA)** in 1945. It failed after a few years, but it was succeeded by the **LPGA (Ladies' Professional Golf Association)** in 1950, created by 13 founding members. The LPGA is the longest continuously run women's professional sporting organization, although it has had some problems with finding sponsors during the global recession in 2008–2009. But its success has led to women's professional tours in Great Britain and Europe, **Japan**, and a smaller one in **Australia**. There are also international team matches for women, similar to men, with U.S. and European professionals contesting the **Solheim Cup**, and teams of **amateurs** from the United States and Great Britain–Ireland playing for the **Curtis Cup**.

At the club level, women play golf frequently. **Golf courses** are usually designed with special sets of tees for women, often called "ladies' tees." These allow women to play a slightly shorter golf course to make up for their shorter relative driving distance compared to men. A few all-women clubs have existed, beginning with the Morris County Golf Club in Morristown, New Jersey, which later became a men's club. The Women's National Golf and Tennis Club on Long Island, New York, was another. It later became Glen Head Country Club, a club now open to both men and women. There are several associations of women golfers, but not a single golf or country club currently exists as a women-only club in the United States.

WOMEN'S BRITISH OPEN. The Women's British Open is a major championship for female **professionals** conducted by the **Ladies' Golf Union** of Great Britain. The tournament was first held in 1976, but has been a major since only 2001. The tournament rotates to various sites, although there is not a set rota, as there is for the **Open Championship (British Open)**. The Women's British Open took place at Woburn Golf and Country Club from 1987 to 1996. It has been contested 12 times at that course, and four times each at **Sunningdale**, **Royal Lytham and St. Anne's**, and **Royal Birkdale**. The tournament has been won three times each by **Karrie Webb** and

Sherri Steinhauer, although each won it only one time when it was a major. The only other multiple winner is Debbie Massey, who won in 1980 and 1981. Appendix 3 includes a list of champions.

WOMEN'S PROFESSIONAL GOLF ASSOCIATION (WPGA). The Women's Professional Golf Association (WPGA) was the first professional tour for **women** in the **United States** and was the forerunner of the **LPGA.** The WPGA started in 1944 through the pioneering efforts of **Betty Hicks**, **Ellen Griffin**, and **Hope Seignious**. Hicks served as the first president, Griffin as vice-president, and Seignious as secretary-treasurer and tournament director. In 1946, the WPGA sponsored the first **U.S. Women's Open**, with most of the purse donated by the Spokane Athletic Round Table. The second U.S. Women's Open was held in 1947, with most of the money coming from Seignious' father's cotton fortune. The WPGA never had much of a tour; only seven to nine pros competed in 1947, and only seven tournaments were held in total—the U.S. Women's Open, the **Titleholders**, **Women's Western Open**, George S. May's All-American Open, Women's Texas Open, the Tampa Open, and the Hardscrabble Open. In 1945, Seignious attempted to get the WPGA subsumed into the **PGA of America**, which turned her down. In 1946, the Golf Manufacturers' Association turned down her request for financial assistance. With no capital, the WPGA died out after the 1948 season, officially suspending operations in December 1949, but it was soon replaced by the LPGA, led by the star power of **Babe Zaharias**.

WOMEN'S WESTERN OPEN. The Women's Western Open, conducted by the Western Golf Association, was one of the first **women**'s **professional** tournaments. The tournament was held from 1930 to 1967 and was always one of the women's major championships during its lifetime. The event was won seven times by **Patty Berg** and four times each by **Babe Zaharias** and **Louise Suggs**. Appendix 3 includes a list of champions.

WOMEN'S WORLD AMATEUR TEAM CHAMPIONSHIP. The Women's World Amateur Team Championship is an international event for teams of three **amateurs**. It was organized by the **Inter-**

national Golf Federation, with the first event being held at the Saint-Germain Golf Club in France in 1964. Through 2008, the event was won 13 times by the **United States**, twice each by **Australia**, France, Spain, and Sweden, and once each by Korea (South) and **South Africa**. The event is held biennially and is rotated among various courses of the world. The event began in 1964 when the U.S. **Curtis Cup** team was asked to play an informal match against France after the Curtis Cup matches in Wales. The **USGA** accepted the invitation but suggested that other nations be invited, which was done, with the event organized by Vicomtesse de Saint Sauveur of France and Mrs. Henri Prunaret of the United States. The Vicomtesse asked some Portuguese friends, Ricardo and Silvia Espirito Santo, to donate a gold-plated bowl that they possessed and that had originally been owned by Tsar Nicholas II of Russia. It was purchased in auction after the Russian Revolution in 1917. This is now known as the **Espirito Santo Trophy** and is given to the winning team at the Women's World Amateur Team Championship. Appendix 5 includes a list of champions and captains.

WOOD SHAFTS. Golf club shafts were originally made of wood, usually hickory. It was not until the 1920s that steel shafts became available, and these were legalized by the **USGA** in only 1924. Wood shafts were lighter than steel, had more flex, and some thought a better feel. But because of the vagaries of wood varieties, wood shafts were not nearly as consistent throughout a set as steel shafts. Because of the softer feel of wood shafts, they continued to be used in putters into the 1970s but then died out fully.

WOOD, CRAIG RALPH. B. 18 November 1901, Lake Placid, New York, United States; D. 7 May 1968, Palm Beach, Florida, United States. Craig Wood was a U.S. **professional** golfer who was a top player on the **PGA Tour** in the 1930s and 1940s. Wood won his first PGA Tour event in 1928 and his last in 1944, winning 21 in all during his career. This includes two major championships, the **Masters** and **U.S. Open**. He won both titles in 1941, the first time anyone had won both of those events in the same year. Wood also lost all four of the current major professional championships in play-offs, a feat later repeated by **Greg Norman**. Wood was a longtime club professional at **Winged Foot Golf Club**. Craig Wood played on the **Ryder Cup** team in 1931, 1933, and 1935 and was elected to the **World Golf Hall of Fame** in 2008.

WOODS, ELDRICK TONT "TIGER." B. 30 December 1975, Cypress, California, United States. Tiger Woods has been the greatest player in golf since 1997 and, with **Jack Nicklaus**, **Ben Hogan**, and **Bob Jones,** warrants inclusion in any discussion of who is the greatest golfer of all time. Woods was a golf prodigy, actually appearing on "The Mike Douglas Show," as a three year old, hitting golf balls. Woods won numerous junior tournaments and in 1991 won the **U.S. Junior Amateur** when only 15, at the time the youngest ever to win that title. Woods went on to repeat in 1992 and 1993 and is still the only player to win the U.S. Junior three times. In 1994–1996, Woods repeated that feat at the **U.S. Amateur**, winning it three times consecutively and winning a USGA event in six consecutive years. This also gave him six straight years as a national champion. Woods attended Stanford University, winning the 1996 NCAA title in his sophomore year, before turning pro at the end of 1996 after his third U.S. Amateur title. In his first abbreviated year on the **PGA Tour**, via sponsor invitations, Woods won two tournaments, which allowed him to bypass Q School.

Woods first major as a **professional** was the 1997 **Masters**, but he started poorly with a 40 on the front nine. However, he recovered with 30 on the back nine for 70 and won that tournament with a record-tying 270, and a record 12-shot margin. It presaged his coming dominance of the **PGA Tour**. Over the next 13 years, through 2009, Woods has won 14 major championships and 71 PGA Tour events. The major record is second to Nicklaus' 18, and the tour wins are third to **Sam Snead** and Nicklaus. Woods has stated that his goal is to better Nicklaus' record of 18 major championships, and, since he is only 34 in 2010, both records appear in jeopardy. Woods' greatest year to date has been 2000, in which he won nine tournaments, including six consecutive and three majors. Woods won the 2000 **U.S. Open** by 15 shots at Pebble Beach, then the **Open Championship (British Open)** by six shots at **St. Andrews**, and then the PGA by one shot. In April 2001, Woods won his second Masters title, making him the holder of all four major championships, which had never been done before.

Many purists demurred that a **Grand Slam** had to be won in a calendar year, but Tiger's feat is often called the Tiger Slam.

Woods has now been PGA Player of the Year 10 times (through 2009), won the **Vardon Trophy** for lowest scoring average on the PGA Tour eight times, and led the PGA Tour money list eight times, all through 2008. He is one of the most popular athletes of all time, his popularity in golf rivaling that of **Arnold Palmer** in the early 1960s. Due to many endorsements, he is probably the richest athlete ever, and in 2009, it was estimated that he was the first athlete to become a billionaire from his tournament earnings and endorsements, although Woods denied that. Woods has broken many sociological barriers because of his mixed ethnicity. He was born to Earl Woods, a part-black, part–Native American, former Green Beret, who met his mother, Kutilda Punsawad, a Thai native of mixed Thai, Chinese, and Dutch origin, while he was stationed in Vietnam. Tiger was named for a close friend of Earl Woods, who died in Vietnam. Tiger has often described his ethnic makeup as "Cablinasian," referring to his Caucasian, black, Native American, and Asian ancestry.

As a player, Woods started out as one of the longest hitters on the PGA Tour. He is still quite long, but has been surpassed by others in the game. His only flaw seems to be some wild driving, but his recovery ability (short game and putting) is unsurpassed and allows him to contend in tournaments when he seems to be hitting it all over the course. When Woods drives the ball well, he is virtually unbeatable. Woods has also emphasized physical fitness, and his practice and workout routines are legendary among other players.

In 2004, Woods married Elin Nordegren, a former Swedish model. He met her when she was working as a nanny for Swedish golfer Jesper Parnevik. In late 2009, great controversy enveloped their relationship when Woods was involved in an accident at 2:30 a.m. outside their home, hitting a fire hydrant and a tree. There were rumors of a domestic dispute, and it then appeared that Woods had been involved in several extramarital affairs, threatening the marriage. Woods has made several statements on his Web site, including an apology for his infidelity, but has not spoken about the situation publicly. Several of his major sponsors have dropped their sponsorship because of the controversy, and in December 2009, he announced he was taking an indefinite leave of absence from the game.

WOOSNAM, IAN HAROLD, "WOOSIE," OBE. B. 2 March 1958, Oswestry, Shropshire, England. Ian Woosnam is a Welsh **professional** golfer who was one of the "Big Five" European players of the 1980s, with **Seve Ballesteros**, **Nick Faldo**, **Bernhard Langer**, and **Sandy Lyle**. Woosie turned professional in 1976 and started on the **European PGA Tour** in 1979. He concentrated on that tour, although he played in the **United States** some, and was leader of the Order of Merit in 1987 and 1990. In all, Woosnam won 29 tournaments on the European PGA Tour and twice on the U.S. **PGA Tour**. Both his U.S. victories came in 1991 within a few weeks of one another. In 1991, he won the New Orleans tournament in late March and two weeks later won the **Masters**, his only major championship. He also won the **World Match Play Championship** at Wentworth, **England**, three times—in 1987, 1990, and 2001. Woosie played for the European **Ryder Cup** team at eight consecutive matches from 1983 to 1997. Woosnam is one of the shortest ever players among top professionals, at only 5 feet 4½ inches (164 cm), but was a very long hitter despite his height.

WORLD AMATEUR TEAM CHAMPIONSHIP. The World Amateur Team Championship is an international event for teams of four **amateurs** that has been held since 1958. Organized by the **International Golf Federation**, the first event was held at **St. Andrews**. The winning team receives the **Eisenhower Trophy**, named for U.S. president **Dwight D. Eisenhower**. Through 2008, the event has been won 13 times by the **United States**, four times by Great Britain–Ireland, three times by **Australia**, with six other nations winning one title each. The event is held biennially and is rotated among various courses of the world. When the World Amateur Golf Council, the original name of the International Golf Federation, was formed in 1958, Eisenhower held an initial meeting at the Rose Garden near the White House, stating, "I suggest, aside from the four hotshot golfers you bring, that you take along some high-handicap fellows and let them play at their full **handicaps** . . . this way golf doesn't become so important." This led to the Delegates and Duffers Cup, which is contested among the officials and nonplaying captains at the tournament. Appendix 5 includes a list of champions and captains.

WORLD CUP OF GOLF. The World Cup is an annual **professional stroke play** tournament contested by two-man teams, one from each nation. The event was first held in 1953 and was originally known as the **Canada Cup.** It was changed to the World Cup in 1967 and the World Cup of Golf in 1993. The event has been rotated among courses throughout the world, but in 2007, it moved to Mission Hills Golf Club in China, which has agreed to host the event through 2018. The original format in 1953 was 36 holes stroke play, but from 1954 to 1999, the event was contested over 72 holes, with a team and individual champion named. In 2000, the event changed to four rounds, alternating between **foursomes** and **four-ball** play, and there is no longer an individual champion named. The **United States** has won by far the most team titles, with 23. Appendix 5 includes a list of champions and captains.

WORLD GOLF CHAMPIONSHIPS (WGC). The World Golf Championships are a series of events for male **professionals** that were started in 1999 by agreement of the major professional tours around the world, who organized to form the International Federation of PGA Tours. There have usually been four (occasionally three) events in each year. They are invitational, with players qualifying by their performance on the various PGA Tours. The idea of an international golf tour was actually first broached in the early 1990s by **Greg Norman**, but the idea was shunned by the U.S. **PGA Tour**. However, only a few years later, the PGA Tour embraced the idea, but Norman was never involved in the actual setup of the events, an affront that greatly angered him. The events are supposed to rotate around the world, hosted by the various tours. However, in reality, most of them have been held in the **United States**. **Tiger Woods** has absolutely dominated the series (not unusual), winning 16 of the 39 events that have been contested through 2009. Appendix 9 includes a list of champions.

WORLD GOLF FOUNDATION (WGF). The World Golf Foundation is a nonprofit organization made up of most of the leaders of the golf industry. It was founded in 1994 to oversee the **World Golf Hall of Fame** and promote the game of golf. The WGF gives its mission statement as "a not-for-profit organization created to unite the golf industry and those who love the game in support of initiatives that promote, enhance the growth of and provide access to the game of golf, while preserving golf's traditional values and also passing them on to others." In 1999, the WGF also created the **Golf 20/20** program, which organizes golf industry leaders in an attempt to continue growth of the game. *See also* THE FIRST TEE.

WORLD GOLF HALL OF FAME. Golf has had several halls of fame. In 1940, the **PGA of America** formed the PGA Hall of Fame, and the **LPGA** formed the Hall of Fame of Women's Golf in 1951. That hall had four charter members, **Patty Berg**, **Betty Jameson**, **Louise Suggs**, and **Babe Zaharias**, but was mostly inactive until 1967, when it was moved to Augusta, Georgia, and was renamed the LPGA Hall of Fame. In 1974, the World Golf Hall of Fame was started. It was originally based at **Pinehurst**, North Carolina, and had 13 charter members. In the early 1980s, the PGA of America merged their hall of fame with the World Golf Hall of Fame, and the LPGA Hall of Fame followed suit in 1998. In 1994, the **World Golf Foundation** was formed to promote the game, and it made plans to relocate the World Golf Hall of Fame to St. Augustine, Florida, near the headquarters of the PGA Tour. This took place officially in 1998. The new building contains exhibits on the game's history, heritage, and greatest players. Players may be inducted into the World Golf Hall of Fame in one of five categories—PGA Tour/Champions (Senior) Tour, LPGA, International, Lifetime Achievement, and Veterans. There are membership requirements for each of the five categories. Appendix 1 includes a list of members of the World Golf Hall of Fame.

WORLD GOLF RANKING. World golf rankings began in 1968 when **Mark McCormack** began to publish an unofficial year-end list in his yearly book, *World of Professional Golf Annual*. McCormack did this from 1968 to 1985. In 1986, an official world golf ranking was instituted for men, with the impetus coming from the Championship Committee of the **Royal and Ancient Golf Club of St. Andrews.** The R&A was looking for a better way to rank players for automatic invitations to the **Open Championship (British Open)**. The first player ranked number one in 1986 was **Bernhard Langer**. The rankings now award points based on finishes and strengths of field in the major professional tours (*See* INTERNATIONAL FEDERATION OF PGA TOURS). The rankings are now used to determine automatic invitations to all of the major golf championships and the **World Golf Championships** events. Through 2009, 12 players have been ranked number one, **Tiger Woods** enjoying the longest time at the top, with over 580 weeks, followed by **Greg Norman**, who was number one for 331 weeks.

WORLD MATCH PLAY CHAMPIONSHIP. The World Match Play Championship was founded in 1964 by **Mark McCormack**, who often used it as a vehicle for the many golfers in his International Management Group (IMG) stable. It became the best-known **professional match play** tournament in the world, with a select, very strong field of 12–16 players competing in 36-hole matches at the **Wentworth Club**, near London. The event was held there from 1964 to 2008, but in 2009, it shifted to Finca Cortesín Golf Club in Casares, near Málaga, Spain. The tournament was originally sponsored by Piccadilly, but later had Suntory, Toyota, Cisco, Volvo, and HSBC as name sponsors. The event has always offered one of the largest purses in golf. It is played in the fall, near the end of the regular tour seasons. The tournament has been won seven times by **Ernie Els** and five times each by **Gary Player** and **Seve Ballesteros**. Appendix 4 includes a list of champions.

WRIGHT, JOHN BENTLEY "BEN." B. 1932. Ben Wright is a former CBS broadcaster who worked on televised golf events in the **United States**. He was educated at London University and later became a golf correspondent for the *Daily Dispatch* in Manchester, **England**, and then the *Daily Mirror* in London. He began work as a golf broadcaster for the BBC in 1961 and as a freelance writer. In 1972, Wright began work for CBS Sports in the United States and worked for the CBS network for almost 24 years. In late 1995, Wright was embroiled in controversy when a reporter interviewed him for the *Wilmington News Journal* (Delaware), and he made remarks about the **LPGA.** The reporter quoted him as saying that the LPGA was hampered by lesbians in the sport, and that **women**

were handicapped in golf because of their breasts getting in the way of their swings. Wright initially denied making either remark but later said that if he had said them, they were off the record. Amidst a media uproar, he was released by CBS Sports. Wright then had some difficulties with alcohol abuse and depression, but later moved to the Asheville, North Carolina, area, spent some time at the Betty Ford Clinic, and recovered. He continues to write golf articles and does some local broadcasting for a Charlotte, North Carolina, station.

WRIGHT, MARY KATHRYN "MICKEY." B. 14 February 1935, San Diego, California, United States. Mickey Wright was an American female **professional** who is always mentioned in any discussion of the greatest female golfer of all time. She grew up in San Diego, attended Stanford for two years, and first achieved national notice when she won the 1952 **U.S. Girls' Junior** title. In 1954, she played in her only **U.S. Women's Amateur**, losing in the final. She also finished fourth that year at the **U.S. Women's Open** and then turned professional in 1955, winning her first event on the **LPGA** in 1956. From 1956 to 1969, Wright won 68 tournaments on the LPGA before semiretiring, although she returned to win the 1973 **Dinah Shore**. During those years, she absolutely dominated the LPGA, never more so than from 1961 to 1964, when she won 44 tournaments, winning 10 or more each year. She won 10 in 1961–1962, 11 in 1964, and a record 13 in 1963 that stands to this day. Wright was so popular on the LPGA that she felt pressure to play all the time, and she played over 30 tournaments per year in 1961–1963, before cutting back slightly to 27 in 1964. The effort to stay at the top and the pressure to play most of the tournaments led to her early retirement, and although she played regularly through 1969, she cut back her schedule after 1964. **Kathy Whitworth**, who holds the record of 88 LPGA victories, has been quoted as saying, "I maintain that she could have won 100 tournaments if she hadn't quit early."

Wright won every major tournament available to her, 13 in all. These include a record four wins at the U.S. Women's Open (1958–1959, 1961, 1964) (equaled by **Betsy Rawls**), a record four victories at the **LPGA Championship** (1958, 1960, 1961, 1963), three victories at the **Women's Western Open** (1962, 1963, 1966), and the **Titleholders** in 1961 and 1962. She was the LPGA's leading money winner in 1961–1964 and won the **Vare Trophy** for lowest scoring average from 1960 to 1964. Wright also won four or more tournaments in a single year in six other years—1958 (5), 1959 (4), 1960 (6), 1966 (7), 1967 (4), and 1968 (4). In 1961–1962, Wright held all four major titles at the same time, a feat later accomplished among men by **Tiger Woods** and called the Tiger Slam. Both **Ben Hogan** and **Byron Nelson** said that Wright had the finest golf swing of any golfer, male or female.

Wright was elected to the LPGA Hall of Fame in 1964 and became a charter member of the **World Golf Hall of Fame** in 1974. She was the Associated Press Female Athlete of the Year in 1963 and 1964. In 1999, Wright was named the greatest female golfer of the 20th century by the Associated Press, and in 2000, *Golf Digest* magazine named her the ninth greatest golfer and the greatest female golfer ever. She was the recipient of the 2010 **Bob Jones Award**, given by the **USGA** for distinguished sportsmanship in golf.

WRIGHT, WILLIAM A. "BILL." B. 1936, Kansas City, Missouri, United States. Bill Wright was born in Kansas City. His family moved to the Pacific Northwest when he was 12, eventually settling in Seattle. A good athlete, he led his high school basketball team to the city championship as a power forward, and he became the city junior golf champion. An African American, Wright expected that golf scholarship offers would be forthcoming. But he was recruited by only Western Washington State College in Bellingham, Washington, where he was not permitted to practice at the same course as the rest of the team. But Wright still progressed enough to win the 1960 NAIA Individual Golf Championship. It was his second national title. In 1959, Wright played in the **U.S. Amateur Public Links Championship** in Denver, at Wellshire Golf Club. He defeated Don Essig, the 1957 champion, in the semifinals, and then won the title by defeating Frank Campbell, a reinstated **professional**, 3 & 2 in the final. This made Wright the first black man to win a **USGA** championship.

When the **PGA of America** rescinded its Caucasian-only clause in its by-laws in November 1961, Wright had a chance to compete as a pro. He did play some, but had difficulty finding sponsorship to allow him to play. He was on and off the tour, always having to qualify, and often sleeping in a YMCA for lack of money. He eventually played in one **U.S. Open** (1966) and five **U.S. Senior Opens**. Wright ended up as a teaching pro in the Los Angeles area, a victim of the era in which he grew up.

WRONG BALL. A wrong ball is any ball other than the player's **ball in play**, a **provisional ball**, or an **alternate ball** played in **stroke play**, when a player is not sure of a ruling. A wrong ball includes another player's ball, any abandoned ball, or the player's original ball when it is no longer the ball in play.

– Y –

YIPS. The yips is a movement disorder that affects putting. It often manifests by twitching and jerking motions during a putting stroke and leads to very poor putting. The cause of the yips is not known, although it has actually been studied by neurologists at the Mayo Clinic, but many great players have been afflicted with the problem at various times.

– Z –

ZAHARIAS, MILDRED ELLA "BABE" DIDRIKSON. B. 26 June 1911, Port Arthur, Texas, United States; D. 27 September 1956, Galveston, Texas, United States. One of seven children of Norwegian immigrants, Babe Didrikson Zaharias is often considered the greatest female athlete of all time and is often in a discussion of the greatest female golfer ever. Babe played almost every sport but became famous to the American sporting public with her feats in track and field in 1932. Her track career was brief but brilliant and her performance at the 1932 AAU meet remains among the greatest in sporting history. In the space of 2½ hours, she competed in eight events, winning four of them outright and finishing equal first in another. As the only representative of her club, Employers Casualty AA of Dallas, she won the national team championship. The powerful Illinois Women's

AC, who fielded more than 20 athletes, finished in second place. The score was Didrikson—30 points, Illinois Women's—22 points.

At the 1932 Olympics, Babe opened her Olympic campaign by winning the javelin on her first throw with a new Olympic record. She then equaled the world record (11.8) in the heats of the 80 meter hurdles and the following day brought the record down to 11.7, as she took her second gold medal. Finally she placed second in the high jump after a controversial jump-off with Jean Shiley. The judges ruled that Didrikson had dived over the bar, although she had been using the same style throughout the competition. Prior to the games, Babe was already voted an all-American in basketball for three years and, as a 17 year old, she twice broke the world javelin record in 1930. Babe forfeited her **amateur status** after the Olympics by allowing her name to be used in an automobile advertisement, so she turned her attention to golf and was easily the greatest woman golfer of her era.

In 1934, Babe won the first tournament she entered and, until cancer ended her career in 1955, she won multiple major titles, including the 1946 **U.S. Women's Amateur** and the 1947 **British Ladies' Amateur** (the first American to ever win both of those championships). She also played in three men's **PGA Tour** events in 1945, making all three cuts at the Los Angeles, Phoenix, and Tucson Opens. From 1948 to 1951, she was the leading money winner on the **LPGA**, during the first four years of its existence (**WPGA** in 1948–1949), and she won 41 LPGA sanctioned events in her career. These include 10 major **professional** titles, the **U.S. Women's Open** in 1948, 1950, and 1954, the **Women's Western Open** in 1940, 1944, 1945, and 1950, and the **Titleholders** in 1947, 1950, and 1952. Better known professionally by her married name of Babe Zaharias, she was diagnosed with colon cancer in 1953 but recovered after major surgery to win the 1954 U.S. Women's Open and two tournaments in 1955, before dying from cancer at the age of 44.

Babe was the most popular golfer of her day, male or female, and it has been said her popularity in golf is rivaled by only **Arnold Palmer**'s. Her awards are almost too numerous to mention. In 1950, she was voted the Greatest Female Athlete of the First Half of the Century. She was named Female Athlete of the Year by the Associated Press six times. In 1999, the Associated Press selected her as

Woman Athlete of the 20th Century, while *Sports Illustrated* placed her second behind the heptathlete Jackie Joyner-Kersee. She is a member of the LPGA Hall of Fame and the **World Golf Hall of Fame**. In 1957, she was posthumously given the **Bob Jones Award** by the **USGA** in recognition of distinguished sportsmanship in golf.

ZOELLER, FRANK URBAN "FUZZY," JR. B. 11 November 1951, New Albany, Indiana, United States. Fuzzy Zoeller was a top American **professional** of the 1970s and 1980s. Zoeller started on the **PGA Tour** in 1973 after playing college golf at the University of Houston. He won 10 events on the PGA Tour, including two major championships, the 1979 **Masters** and the 1984 **U.S. Open**. His Masters win was accomplished in his first appearance in the tournament, making him one of only three people to have won in his first attempt at Augusta National. Zoeller was given the 1985 **Bob Jones Award** by the **USGA**, after his victory in the 1984 U.S. Open at **Winged Foot**. Zoeller won that championship in a play-off with **Greg Norman**. On the 72nd hole, Zoeller was in the **fairway** when Norman made a long putt on the green, which Zoeller thought was for a birdie to win the event. Zoeller graciously waved a white flag, his towel, over his head, conceding to what he thought was Norman's winning putt.

Zoeller was one of the most popular players, among both the other players and the galleries. He was quick with a smile and would talk to almost anybody. In 1997, Zoeller was embroiled in controversy at the **Masters**. As **Tiger Woods** was winning the tournament easily, Zoeller was asked for his comments after the third round. He made some comments about how Tiger had the tournament wrapped up, and all he had to do was to decide what to serve at the Champions Dinner the next year. But his comments had some demeaning racial connotations; he was derided in the press and lost some endorsement sponsors as a result. Most of the players, knowing Zoeller, knew he was joking around and supported him, and Woods eventually accepted his apology.

ZOYSIA. Zoysia refers to one of eight species of a creeping-type **grass**, all in the genus *Zoysia*. They are native to Asia and Australasia but are planted on many courses in the **United States** in tropical climates. Zoysia is a stoloniferous grass, somewhat similar to **Ber-**

muda, and is very tough. When Zoysia grows into rough, it can be like steel wool, making it very difficult to extract one's ball.

ZUBACK, JASON. B. 24 April 1970, Lethbridge, Alberta, Canada. Jason Zuback is one of the longest **drivers** in golf history. He has won the RE/MAX World Long Drive Championship five times, a record. He won four consecutively in 1996–1999 and won it again in 2006. He has won many other long-drive events. His longest competitive drive was 506 yards, at the 2003 Pinnacle Distance Challenge in Denver. That was done at altitude, but his 1997 winning drive in the World Long Drive Championship was 412 yards, the longest ever in that competition.

Approaching the 13th green at Augusta National, fabled home of the Masters.

The frightening 16th hole at Cypress Point Club, a 230-yard carry over the Pacific Ocean.

The Old Course at St. Andrews, looking onto the 17th green, the Road Hole, and down the 18th fairway, with the renowned clubhouse in the background.

The 18th green at the legendary Pebble Beach Golf Links, overlooking Monterey Bay and the Pacific Ocean.

The Royal Melbourne Golf Club, a renowned course in Australia.

The terrifying island green of the 17th hole at the TPC Sawgrass.

John Ball, eight-time winner of the Amateur Championship (British Amateur).

The Spaniard Seve Ballesteros.

Patty Berg, whose 15 major-championship victories is a female record.

Pat Bradley, winner of six major championships and 31 LPGA events.

Walter Hagen, the first famous showman of golf, winner of 11 major championships.

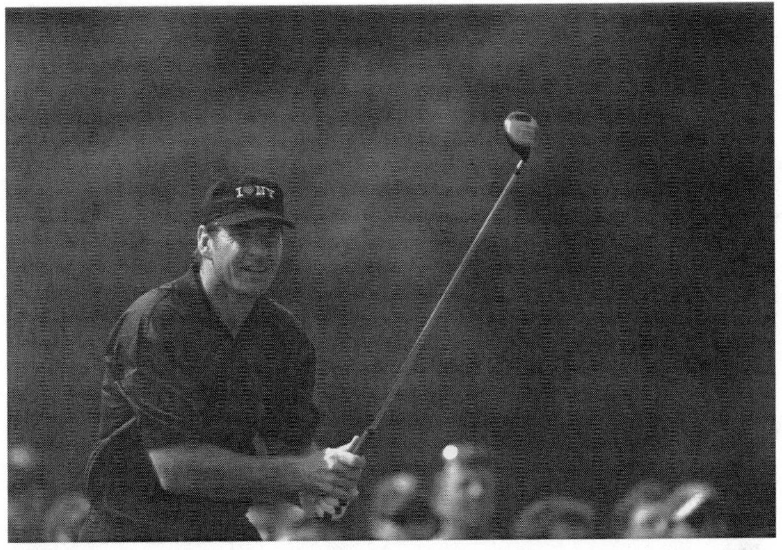

Sir Nick Faldo, winner of six major championships—three Masters and three Open Championships (British Open).

Ben Hogan receiving the U.S. Open trophy, with his wife, Valerie.

Juli Inkster, three-time U.S. Women's Amateur champion and winner of multiple LPGA titles.

Bobby Jones, the greatest ever amateur player.

Betsy King with the U.S. Women's Open trophy.

Meg Mallon, two-time U.S. Women's Open champion and winner of four major championships.

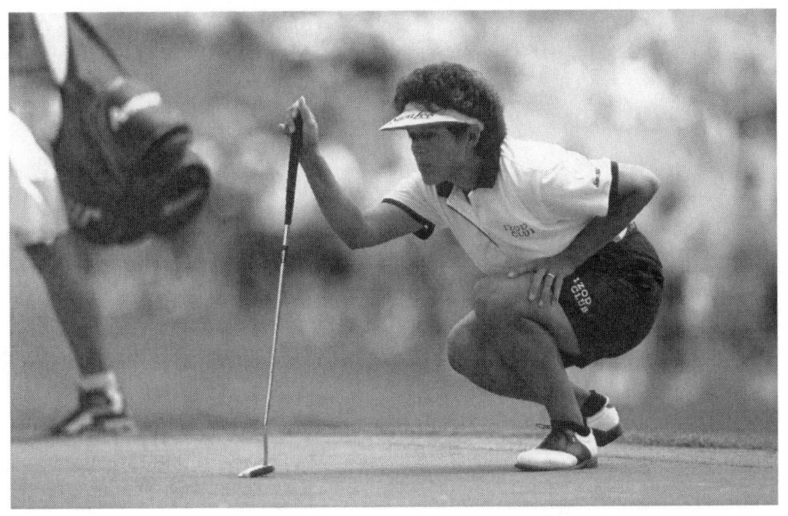

Nancy Lopez, the leading female player of the late 1970s and 1980s.

Phil Mickelson, one of the most popular players ever, winner of 37 PGA Tour events through 2009.

Johnny Miller, a dominant player in the mid-1970s.

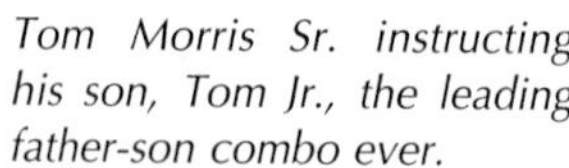

Tom Morris Sr. instructing his son, Tom Jr., the leading father-son combo ever.

Byron Nelson, winner of 11 consecutive PGA Tour events in 1945, one of the finest gentlemen in the game.

Jack Nicklaus while winning the 1972 U.S. Open at Pebble Beach.

Greg Norman, a great Australian player.

Lorena Ochoa, the number-one ranked woman player from 2007 to 2009.

Gary Player, the first international golf superstar.

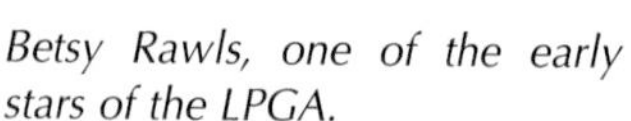

Betsy Rawls, one of the early stars of the LPGA.

Gene Sarazen, the first man to complete the career professional Grand Slam.

Pak Se-Ri, the Korean superstar whose multiple victories have made the game popular on the Korean peninsula.

Patty Sheehan, winner of six major championships and 35 LPGA events.

A young Sam Snead, winner of over 80 PGA Tour events, the most ever.

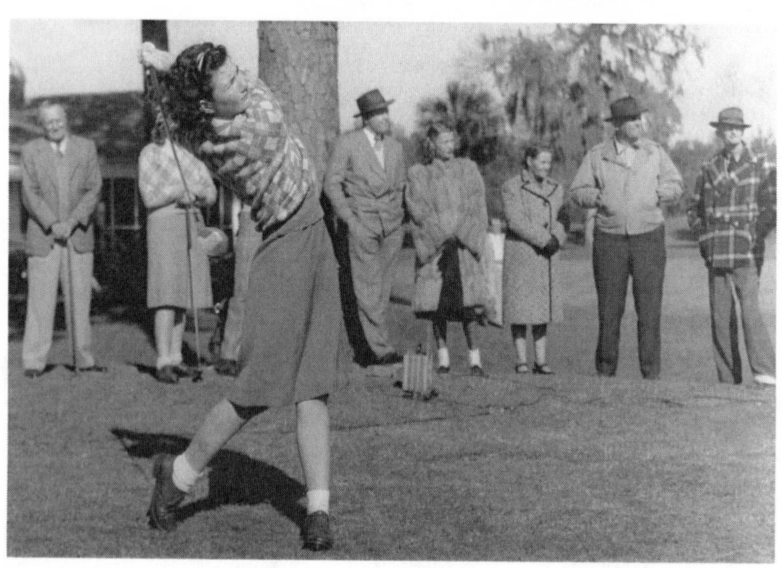

Louise Suggs, one of the founders of the LPGA and an early star of women's golf.

Lee Trevino receiving the 1968 U.S. Open trophy, with runner-up Jack Nicklaus in the background.

Harry Vardon, six-time winner of the Open Championship (British Open).

Tom Watson, winner of eight major championships, including five at the Open Championship (British Open).

Karrie Webb, Australia's best-known female player.

Joyce Wethered, Lady Heathcoat-Amory, one of the finest female British amateur players.

Two legends in women's amateur golf: Joyce Wethered on the left, and Glenna Collett-Vare on the right.

Kathy Whitworth, who won more LPGA events than any other player.

Michelle Wie, the woman who might be queen of women's golf—someday.

Tiger Woods, who has been the leading golfer for more than a decade.

Babe Zaharias, probably the greatest modern-day female athlete.

Mickey Wright, voted the greatest female player of the 20th century.

Appendixes

Following is a series of appendixes. The first lists the members of the World Golf Hall of Fame through 2009 (including one who will be inducted in 2012, Lorena Ochoa). The following appendixes list the champions of most of the important golf championships since 1860—professional, amateur, male, female. Space limitations preclude any information other than the year, champions, venues, and locations, except in the case of team events. We have also included a series of appendixes that list the recipients of most of the major golf awards. There are many, many other important tournaments worldwide and many other awards, but we have tried to choose those we feel are the most significant. In order, they are as follows:

1. World Golf Hall of Fame
2. Men's Major Professional Champions
3. Women's Major Professional Champions
4. Other Professional Champions
5. International Team Events
6. Men's Major Amateur Champions
7. Women's Major Amateur Champions
8. Other USGA Champions
9. Other International Champions
10. Professional Tour Awards
11. Other Awards

APPENDIX 1. WORLD GOLF HALL OF FAME

Men

1974	Walter Hagen	United States
1974	Ben Hogan	United States
1974	Robert T. Jones Jr.	United States
1974	Byron Nelson	United States
1974	Jack Nicklaus	United States
1974	Francis Ouimet	United States
1974	Arnold Palmer	United States
1974	Gary Player	South Africa
1974	Gene Sarazen	United States
1974	Sam Snead	United States
1974	Harry Vardon	Isle of Jersey
1975	Willie Anderson	Scotland
1975	Fred Corcoran	United States
1975	Joseph Dey	United States
1975	Chick Evans	United States
1975	Young Tom Morris	Scotland
1975	John Henry Taylor	England
1976	Tommy Armour	Scotland / United States
1976	James Braid	Scotland
1976	Old Tom Morris	Scotland
1976	Jerome Travers	United States
1977	Bobby Locke	South Africa
1977	John Ball	England
1977	Herb Graffis	United States
1977	Donald Ross	Scotland
1978	Billy Casper	United States
1978	Harold Hilton	England
1978	Bing Crosby	United States
1978	Clifford Roberts	United States
1979	Walter Travis	United States
1980	Henry Cotton	England
1980	Lawson Little	United States
1981	Ralph Guldahl	United States

1981	Lee Trevino	United States
1982	Julius Boros	United States
1983	Jimmy Demaret	United States
1983	Bob Hope	United States
1986	Cary Middlecoff	United States
1987	Robert Trent Jones Sr.	United States
1988	Bob Harlow	United States
1988	Peter Thomson	Australia
1988	Tom Watson	United States
1989	Jim Barnes	England / United States
1989	Roberto De Vicenzo	Argentina
1989	Ray Floyd	United States
1990	Bill Campbell	United States
1990	Gene Littler	United States
1990	Paul Runyan	United States
1990	Horton Smith	United States
1992	Harry Cooper	United States
1992	Hale Irwin	United States
1992	Chi Chi Rodriguez	Puerto Rico
1992	Richard Tufts	United States
1996	Johnny Miller	United States
1997	Seve Ballesteros	Spain
1997	Nick Faldo	England
1998	Lloyd Mangrum	United States
2000	Jack Burke Jr.	United States
2000	Deane Beman	United States
2000	Michael Bonallack	England
2000	Neil Coles	England
2000	John Jacobs	England
2001	Greg Norman	Australia
2001	Payne Stewart	United States
2001	Bernhard Langer	Germany
2001	Allan Robertson	Scotland
2001	Karsten Solheim	United States
2002	Ben Crenshaw	United States
2002	Tony Jacklin	England

2002	Tommy Bolt	United States
2002	Harvey Penick	United States
2003	Nick Price	Zimbabwe
2003	Leo Diegel	United States
2004	Charlie Sifford	United States
2004	Isao Aoki	Japan
2004	Tom Kite	United States
2005	Bernard Darwin	England
2005	Alister MacKenzie	England
2005	Willie Park Sr.	Scotland
2006	Vijay Singh	Fiji
2006	Larry Nelson	United States
2006	Henry Picard	United States
2006	Mark McCormack	United States
2007	Joe Carr	Ireland
2007	Hubert Green	United States
2007	Charles Blair Macdonald	Canada / United States
2007	Kel Nagle	Australia
2007	Curtis Strange	United States
2008	Bob Charles	New Zealand
2008	Pete Dye	United States
2008	Denny Shute	United States
2008	Herbert Warren Wind	United States
2008	Craig Wood	United States
2009	Christy O'Connor Sr.	Ireland
2009	José María Olazábal	Spain
2009	Lanny Wadkins	United States
2009	Dwight D. Eisenhower	United States

Women

1951	Betty Jameson	United States
1951	Patty Berg	United States
1951	Louise Suggs	United States
1951	Babe Zaharias	United States
1960	Betsy Rawls	United States
1964	Mickey Wright	United States

1975	Glenna Collett Vare	United States
1975	Joyce Wethered	England
1975	Kathy Whitworth	United States
1977	Sandra Haynie	United States
1977	Carol Mann	United States
1978	Dorothy Campbell-Hurd-Howe	Scotland / United States
1982	JoAnne Carner	United States
1987	Nancy Lopez	United States
1991	Pat Bradley	United States
1993	Patty Sheehan	United States
1994	Dinah Shore	United States
1995	Betsy King	United States
1999	Amy Alcott	United States
2000	Beth Daniel	United States
2000	Juli Inkster	United States
2000	Judy Rankin	United States
2001	Donna Caponi	United States
2001	Judy Bell	United States
2002	Marlene Bauer Hagge	United States
2003	Hisako "Chako" Higuchi	Japan
2003	Annika Sörenstam	Sweden
2004	Marlene Stewart Streit	Canada
2005	Ayako Okamoto	Japan
2005	Karrie Webb	Australia
2006	Marilynn Smith	United States
2007	Pak Se-Ri	Korea (South)
2008	Carol Semple Thompson	United States
2012	Lorena Ochoa	Mexico

APPENDIX 2. MEN'S MAJOR PROFESSIONAL CHAMPIONS

The Open Championship (British Open)

1860	Willie Park Sr.	Scotland	Prestwick Golf Club	Prestwick, South Ayrshire, Scotland
1861	Old Tom Morris	Scotland	Prestwick Golf Club	Prestwick, South Ayrshire, Scotland
1862	Old Tom Morris	Scotland	Prestwick Golf Club	Prestwick, South Ayrshire, Scotland
1863	Willie Park Sr.	Scotland	Prestwick Golf Club	Prestwick, South Ayrshire, Scotland
1864	Old Tom Morris	Scotland	Prestwick Golf Club	Prestwick, South Ayrshire, Scotland
1865	Andrew Strath	Scotland	Prestwick Golf Club	Prestwick, South Ayrshire, Scotland
1866	Willie Park Sr.	Scotland	Prestwick Golf Club	Prestwick, South Ayrshire, Scotland
1867	Old Tom Morris	Scotland	Prestwick Golf Club	Prestwick, South Ayrshire, Scotland
1868	Young Tom Morris	Scotland	Prestwick Golf Club	Prestwick, South Ayrshire, Scotland
1869	Young Tom Morris	Scotland	Prestwick Golf Club	Prestwick, South Ayrshire, Scotland

1870	Young Tom Morris	Scotland	Prestwick Golf Club	Prestwick, South Ayrshire, Scotland
1871	No Championship			
1872	Young Tom Morris	Scotland	Prestwick Golf Club	Prestwick, South Ayrshire, Scotland
1873	Tom Kidd	Scotland	St. Andrews Links, Old Course	St. Andrews, Fife, Scotland
1874	Mungo Park	Scotland	Musselburgh Links	Musselburgh, East Lothian, Scotland
1875	Willie Park Sr.	Scotland	Prestwick Golf Club	Prestwick, South Ayrshire, Scotland
1876	Bob Martin	Scotland	St. Andrews Links, Old Course	St. Andrews, Fife, Scotland
1877	Jamie Anderson	Scotland	Musselburgh Links	Musselburgh, East Lothian, Scotland
1878	Jamie Anderson	Scotland	Prestwick Golf Club	Prestwick, South Ayrshire, Scotland
1879	Jamie Anderson	Scotland	St. Andrews Links, Old Course	St. Andrews, Fife, Scotland
1880	Bob Ferguson	Scotland	Musselburgh Links	Musselburgh, East Lothian, Scotland
1881	Bob Ferguson	Scotland	Prestwick Golf Club	Prestwick, South Ayrshire, Scotland

1882	Bob Ferguson	Scotland	St. Andrews Links, Old Course	St. Andrews, Fife, Scotland
1883	Willie Fernie	Scotland	Musselburgh Links	Musselburgh, East Lothian, Scotland
1884	Jack Simpson	Scotland	Prestwick Golf Club	Prestwick, South Ayrshire, Scotland
1885	Bob Martin	Scotland	St. Andrews Links, Old Course	St. Andrews, Fife, Scotland
1886	David Brown	Scotland	Musselburgh Links	Musselburgh, East Lothian, Scotland
1887	Willie Park Jr.	Scotland	Prestwick Golf Club	Prestwick, South Ayrshire, Scotland
1888	Jack Burns	Scotland	St. Andrews Links, Old Course	St. Andrews, Fife, Scotland
1889	Willie Park Jr.	Scotland	Musselburgh Links	Musselburgh, East Lothian, Scotland
1890	John Ball (amateur)	England	Prestwick Golf Club	Prestwick, South Ayrshire, Scotland
1891	Hugh Kirkaldy	Scotland	St. Andrews Links, Old Course	St. Andrews, Fife, Scotland
1892	Harold Hilton (amateur)	England	Muirfield Links	Gullane, East Lothian, Scotland
1893	William Auchterlonie	Scotland	Prestwick Golf Club	Prestwick, South Ayrshire, Scotland

1894	John Henry Taylor	England	Royal St. George's Golf Club	Sandwich, Kent, England
1895	John Henry Taylor	England	St. Andrews Links, Old Course	St. Andrews, Fife, Scotland
1896	Harry Vardon	Isle of Jersey	Muirfield Links	Gullane, East Lothian, Scotland
1897	Harold Hilton (amateur)	England	Royal Liverpool Golf Club	Hoylake, England
1898	Harry Vardon	Isle of Jersey	Prestwick Golf Club	Prestwick, South Ayrshire, Scotland
1899	Harry Vardon	Isle of Jersey	Royal St. George's Golf Club	Sandwich, Kent, England
1900	John Henry Taylor	England	St. Andrews Links, Old Course	St. Andrews, Fife, Scotland
1901	James Braid	Scotland	Muirfield Links	Gullane, East Lothian, Scotland
1902	Sandy Herd	Scotland	Royal Liverpool Golf Club	Hoylake, England
1903	Harry Vardon	Isle of Jersey	Prestwick Golf Club	Prestwick, South Ayrshire, Scotland
1904	Jack White	Scotland	Royal St. George's Golf Club	Sandwich, Kent, England
1905	James Braid	Scotland	St. Andrews Links, Old Course	St. Andrews, Fife, Scotland
1906	James Braid	Scotland	Muirfield Links	Gullane, East Lothian, Scotland

1907	Arnaud Massy	France	Royal Liverpool Golf Club	Hoylake, England
1908	James Braid	Scotland	Prestwick Golf Club	Prestwick, South Ayrshire, Scotland
1909	John Henry Taylor	England	Royal Cinque Ports Golf Club	Deal, Kent, England
1910	James Braid	Scotland	St. Andrews Links, Old Course	St. Andrews, Fife, Scotland
1911	Harry Vardon	Isle of Jersey	Royal St. George's Golf Club	Sandwich, Kent, England
1912	Ted Ray	Isle of Jersey	Muirfield Links	Gullane, East Lothian, Scotland
1913	John Henry Taylor	England	Royal Liverpool Golf Club	Hoylake, England
1914	Harry Vardon	Isle of Jersey	Prestwick Golf Club	Prestwick, South Ayrshire, Scotland
1920	George Duncan	Scotland	Royal Cinque Ports Golf Club	Deal, Kent, England
1921	Jock Hutchison	United States	St. Andrews Links, Old Course	St. Andrews, Fife, Scotland
1922	Walter Hagen	United States	Royal St. George's Golf Club	Sandwich, Kent, England
1923	Arthur Havers	England	Royal Troon Golf Club	Troon, South Ayrshire, Scotland
1924	Walter Hagen	United States	Royal Liverpool Golf Club	Hoylake, England

1925	Jim Barnes	United States	Prestwick Golf Club	Prestwick, South Ayrshire, Scotland
1926	Bob Jones (amateur)	United States	Royal Lytham & St. Annes Golf Club	Lytham and St. Annes, Lancashire, England
1927	Bob Jones (amateur)	United States	St. Andrews Links, Old Course	St. Andrews, Fife, Scotland
1928	Walter Hagen	United States	Royal St. George's Golf Club	Sandwich, Kent, England
1929	Walter Hagen	United States	Muirfield Links	Gullane, East Lothian, Scotland
1930	Bob Jones (amateur)	United States	Royal Liverpool Golf Club	Hoylake, England
1931	Tommy Armour	Scotland / United States	Carnoustie Golf Links	Carnoustie, Angus, Scotland
1932	Gene Sarazen	United States	Prince's Golf Club	Sandwich, Kent, England
1933	Denny Shute	United States	St. Andrews Links, Old Course	St. Andrews, Fife, Scotland
1934	Henry Cotton	England	Royal St. George's Golf Club	Sandwich, Kent, England
1935	Alf Perry	England	Muirfield Links	Gullane, East Lothian, Scotland
1936	Alf Padgham	England	Royal Liverpool Golf Club	Hoylake, England
1937	Henry Cotton	England	Carnoustie Golf Links	Carnoustie, Angus, Scotland

1938	Reg Whitcombe	England	Royal St. George's Golf Club	Sandwich, Kent, England
1939	Richard Burton	England	St. Andrews Links, Old Course	St. Andrews, Fife, Scotland
1946	Sam Snead	United States	St. Andrews Links, Old Course	St. Andrews, Fife, Scotland
1947	Fred Daly	Northern Ireland	Royal Liverpool Golf Club	Hoylake, England
1948	Henry Cotton	England	Muirfield Links	Gullane, East Lothian, Scotland
1949	Bobby Locke	South Africa	Royal St. George's Golf Club	Sandwich, Kent, England
1950	Bobby Locke	South Africa	Royal Troon Golf Club	Troon, South Ayrshire, Scotland
1951	Max Faulkner	England	Royal Portrush Golf Club	Portrush, County Antrim, Northern Ireland
1952	Bobby Locke	South Africa	Royal Lytham & St. Annes Golf Club	Lytham and St. Annes, Lancashire, England
1953	Ben Hogan	United States	Carnoustie Golf Links	Carnoustie, Angus, Scotland
1954	Peter Thomson	Australia	Royal Birkdale Golf Club	Southport, Merseyside, England
1955	Peter Thomson	Australia	St. Andrews Links, Old Course	St. Andrews, Fife, Scotland

1956	Peter Thomson	Australia	Royal Liverpool Golf Club	Hoylake, England
1957	Bobby Locke	South Africa	St. Andrews Links, Old Course	St. Andrews, Fife, Scotland
1958	Peter Thomson	Australia	Royal Lytham & St. Annes Golf Club	Lytham and St. Annes, Lancashire, England
1959	Gary Player	South Africa	Muirfield Links	Gullane, East Lothian, Scotland
1960	Kel Nagle	Australia	St. Andrews Links, Old Course	St. Andrews, Fife, Scotland
1961	Arnold Palmer	United States	Royal Birkdale Golf Club	Southport, Merseyside, England
1962	Arnold Palmer	United States	Royal Troon Golf Club	Troon, South Ayrshire, Scotland
1963	Bob Charles	New Zealand	Royal Lytham & St. Annes Golf Club	Lytham and St. Annes, Lancashire, England
1964	Tony Lema	United States	St. Andrews Links, Old Course	St. Andrews, Fife, Scotland
1965	Peter Thomson	Australia	Royal Birkdale Golf Club	Southport, Merseyside, England
1966	Jack Nicklaus	United States	Muirfield Links	Gullane, East Lothian, Scotland
1967	Roberto De Vicenzo	Argentina	Royal Liverpool Golf Club	Hoylake, England
1968	Gary Player	South Africa	Carnoustie Golf Links	Carnoustie, Angus, Scotland

1969	Tony Jacklin	England	Royal Lytham & St. Annes Golf Club	Lytham and St. Annes, Lancashire, England
1970	Jack Nicklaus	United States	St. Andrews Links, Old Course	St. Andrews, Fife, Scotland
1971	Lee Trevino	United States	Royal Birkdale Golf Club	Southport, Merseyside, England
1972	Lee Trevino	United States	Muirfield Links	Gullane, East Lothian, Scotland
1973	Tom Weiskopf	United States	Royal Troon Golf Club	Troon, South Ayrshire, Scotland
1974	Gary Player	South Africa	Royal Lytham & St. Annes Golf Club	Lytham and St. Annes, Lancashire, England
1975	Tom Watson	United States	Carnoustie Golf Links	Carnoustie, Angus, Scotland
1976	Johnny Miller	United States	Royal Birkdale Golf Club	Southport, Merseyside, England
1977	Tom Watson	United States	Turnberry, Ailsa Course	Turnberry, South Ayrshire, Scotland
1978	Jack Nicklaus	United States	St. Andrews Links, Old Course	St. Andrews, Fife, Scotland
1979	Seve Ballesteros	Spain	Royal Lytham & St. Annes Golf Club	Lytham and St. Annes, Lancashire, England
1980	Tom Watson	United States	Muirfield Links	Gullane, East Lothian, Scotland

1981	Bill Rogers	United States	Royal St. George's Golf Club	Sandwich, Kent, England
1982	Tom Watson	United States	Royal Troon Golf Club	Troon, South Ayrshire, Scotland
1983	Tom Watson	United States	Royal Birkdale Golf Club	Southport, Merseyside, England
1984	Seve Ballesteros	Spain	St. Andrews Links, Old Course	St. Andrews, Fife, Scotland
1985	Sandy Lyle	Scotland	Royal St. George's Golf Club	Sandwich, Kent, England
1986	Greg Norman	Australia	Turnberry, Ailsa Course	Turnberry, South Ayrshire, Scotland
1987	Nick Faldo	England	Muirfield Links	Gullane, East Lothian, Scotland
1988	Seve Ballesteros	Spain	Royal Lytham & St. Annes Golf Club	Lytham and St. Annes, Lancashire, England
1989	Mark Calcavecchia	United States	Royal Troon Golf Club	Troon, South Ayrshire, Scotland
1990	Nick Faldo	England	St. Andrews Links, Old Course	St. Andrews, Fife, Scotland
1991	Ian Baker-Finch	Australia	Royal Birkdale Golf Club	Southport, Merseyside, England

1992	Nick Faldo	England	Muirfield Links	Gullane, East Lothian, Scotland
1993	Greg Norman	Australia	Royal St. George's Golf Club	Sandwich, Kent, England
1994	Nick Price	Zimbabwe	Turnberry, Ailsa Course	Turnberry, South Ayrshire, Scotland
1995	John Daly	United States	St. Andrews Links, Old Course	St. Andrews, Fife, Scotland
1996	Tom Lehman	United States	Royal Lytham & St. Annes Golf Club	Lytham and St. Annes, Lancashire, England
1997	Justin Leonard	United States	Royal Troon Golf Club	Troon, South Ayrshire, Scotland
1998	Mark O'Meara	United States	Royal Birkdale Golf Club	Southport, Merseyside, England
1999	Paul Lawrie	Scotland	Carnoustie Golf Links	Carnoustie, Angus, Scotland
2000	Tiger Woods	United States	St. Andrews Links, Old Course	St. Andrews, Fife, Scotland
2001	David Duval	United States	Royal Lytham & St. Annes Golf Club	Lytham and St. Annes, Lancashire, England
2002	Ernie Els	South Africa	Muirfield Links	Gullane, East Lothian, Scotland
2003	Ben Curtis	United States	Royal St. George's Golf Club	Sandwich, Kent, England

2004	Todd Hamilton	United States	Royal Troon Golf Club	Troon, South Ayrshire, Scotland
2005	Tiger Woods	United States	St. Andrews Links, Old Course	St. Andrews, Fife, Scotland
2006	Tiger Woods	United States	Royal Liverpool Golf Club	Hoylake, England
2007	Pádraig Harrington	Ireland	Carnoustie Golf Links	Carnoustie, Angus, Scotland
2008	Pádraig Harrington	Ireland	Royal Birkdale Golf Club	Southport, Merseyside, England
2009	Stewart Cink	United States	Turnberry, Ailsa Course	Turnberry, South Ayrshire, Scotland

U.S. Open

1895	Horace Rawlins	England	Newport Country Club	Newport, Rhode Island
1896	James Foulis	Scotland	Shinnecock Hills Golf Club	Southampton, New York
1897	Joe Lloyd	England	Chicago Golf Club	Wheaton, Illinois
1898	Fred Herd	Scotland	Myopia Hunt Club	South Hamilton, Massachusetts
1899	Willie Smith	Scotland	Baltimore Country Club, Roland Park Course	Timonium, Maryland
1900	Harry Vardon	Isle of Jersey	Chicago Golf Club	Wheaton, Illinois
1901	Willie Anderson	Scotland	Myopia Hunt Club	South Hamilton, Massachusetts
1902	Laurie Auchterlonie	Scotland	Garden City Golf Club	Garden City, New York

1903	Willie Anderson	Scotland	Baltusrol Golf Club	Springfield, New Jersey
1904	Willie Anderson	Scotland	Glen View Club	Golf, Illinois
1905	Willie Anderson	Scotland	Myopia Hunt Club	South Hamilton, Massachusetts
1906	Alex Smith	Scotland	Onwentsia Club	Lake Forest, Illinois
1907	Alex Ross	Scotland	Philadelphia Cricket Club, St. Martin's Course	Philadelphia, Pennsylvania
1908	Fred McLeod	Scotland	Myopia Hunt Club	South Hamilton, Massachusetts
1909	George Sargent	England	Englewood Golf Club	Englewood, New Jersey
1910	Alex Smith	Scotland	Philadelphia Cricket Club, St. Martin's Course	Philadelphia, Pennsylvania
1911	John McDermott	United States	Chicago Golf Club	Wheaton, Illinois
1912	John McDermott	United States	Country Club of Buffalo	Williamsville, New York
1913	Francis Ouimet (amateur)	United States	The Country Club	Brookline, Massachusetts
1914	Walter Hagen	United States	Midlothian Country Club	Midlothian, Illinois
1915	Jerome Travers (amateur)	United States	Baltusrol Golf Club	Springfield, New Jersey
1916	Chick Evans (amateur)	United States	Minikahda Club	Minneapolis, Minnesota
1919	Walter Hagen	United States	Brae Burn Country Club	West Newton, Massachusetts
1920	Ted Ray	Isle of Jersey	Inverness Club	Toledo, Ohio

1921	Jim Barnes	England / United States	Columbia Country Club	Chevy Chase, Maryland
1922	Gene Sarazen	United States	Skokie Country Club	Glencoe, Illinois
1923	Bob Jones (amateur)	United States	Inwood Country Club	Inwood, New York
1924	Cyril Walker	England	Oakland Hills Country Club, South Course	Bloomfield Hills, Michigan
1925	Willie Macfarlane	Scotland	Worcester Country Club	Worcester, Massachusetts
1926	Bob Jones (amateur)	United States	Scioto Country Club	Columbus, Ohio
1927	Tommy Armour	Scotland / United States	Oakmont Country Club	Oakmont, Pennsylvania
1928	Johnny Farrell	United States	Olympia Fields Country Club, North Course	Olympia Fields, Illinois
1929	Bob Jones (amateur)	United States	Winged Foot Golf Club, West Course	Mamaroneck, New York
1930	Bob Jones (amateur)	United States	Interlachen Country Club	Edina, Minnesota
1931	Billy Burke	United States	Inverness Club	Toledo, Ohio
1932	Gene Sarazen	United States	Fresh Meadow Country Club	Great Neck, New York
1933	Johnny Goodman (amateur)	United States	North Shore Golf Club	Glenview, Illinois
1934	Olin Dutra	United States	Merion Golf Club, East Course	Ardmore, Pennsylvania

1935	Sam Parks Jr.	United States	Oakmont Country Club	Oakmont, Pennsylvania
1936	Tony Manero	United States	Baltusrol Golf Club, Upper Course	Springfield, New Jersey
1937	Ralph Guldahl	United States	Oakland Hills Country Club, South Course	Bloomfield Hills, Michigan
1938	Ralph Guldahl	United States	Cherry Hills Country Club	Cherry Hills Village, Colorado
1939	Byron Nelson	United States	Philadelphia Country Club, Spring Mill Course	Gladwyne, Pennsylvania
1940	Lawson Little	United States	Canterbury Golf Club	Beachwood, Ohio
1941	Craig Wood	United States	Colonial Country Club	Fort Worth, Texas
1946	Lloyd Mangrum	United States	Canterbury Golf Club	Beachwood, Ohio
1947	Lew Worsham	United States	St. Louis Country Club	St. Louis, Missouri
1948	Ben Hogan	United States	Riviera Country Club	Pacific Palisades, California
1949	Cary Middlecoff	United States	Medinah Country Club, Course No. 3	Medinah, Illinois
1950	Ben Hogan	United States	Merion Golf Club, East Course	Ardmore, Pennsylvania
1951	Ben Hogan	United States	Oakland Hills Country Club, South Course	Bloomfield Hills, Michigan
1952	Julius Boros	United States	Northwood Club	Dallas, Texas
1953	Ben Hogan	United States	Oakmont Country Club	Oakmont, Pennsylvania
1954	Ed Furgol	United States	Baltusrol Golf Club, Lower Course	Springfield, New Jersey

1955	Jack Fleck	United States	Olympic Club, Lake Course	San Francisco, California
1956	Cary Middlecoff	United States	Oak Hill Country Club, East Course	Rochester, New York
1957	Dick Mayer	United States	Inverness Club	Toledo, Ohio
1958	Tommy Bolt	United States	Southern Hills Country Club	Tulsa, Oklahoma
1959	Billy Casper	United States	Winged Foot Golf Club, West Course	Mamaroneck, New York
1960	Arnold Palmer	United States	Cherry Hills Country Club	Cherry Hills Village, Colorado
1961	Gene Littler	United States	Oakland Hills Country Club, South Course	Bloomfield Hills, Michigan
1962	Jack Nicklaus	United States	Oakmont Country Club	Oakmont, Pennsylvania
1963	Julius Boros	United States	The Country Club	Brookline, Massachusetts
1964	Ken Venturi	United States	Congressional Country Club	Bethesda, Maryland
1965	Gary Player	South Africa	Bellerive Country Club	St. Louis, Missouri
1966	Billy Casper	United States	Olympic Club, Lake Course	San Francisco, California
1967	Jack Nicklaus	United States	Baltusrol Golf Club, Lower Course	Springfield, New Jersey
1968	Lee Trevino	United States	Oak Hill Country Club, East Course	Rochester, New York
1969	Orville Moody	United States	Champions Golf Club, Cypress Creek Course	Houston, Texas

1970	Tony Jacklin	England	Hazeltine National Golf Club	Chaska, Minnesota
1971	Lee Trevino	United States	Merion Golf Club, East Course	Ardmore, Pennsylvania
1972	Jack Nicklaus	United States	Pebble Beach Golf Links	Pebble Beach, California
1973	Johnny Miller	United States	Oakmont Country Club	Oakmont, Pennsylvania
1974	Hale Irwin	United States	Winged Foot Golf Club, West Course	Mamaroneck, New York
1975	Lou Graham	United States	Medinah Country Club, Course No. 3	Medinah, Illinois
1976	Jerry Pate	United States	Atlanta Athletic Club, Highlands Course	Duluth, Georgia
1977	Hubert Green	United States	Southern Hills Country Club	Tulsa, Oklahoma
1978	Andy North	United States	Cherry Hills Country Club	Cherry Hills Village, Colorado
1979	Hale Irwin	United States	Inverness Club	Toledo, Ohio
1980	Jack Nicklaus	United States	Baltusrol Golf Club, Lower Course	Springfield, New Jersey
1981	David Graham	Australia	Merion Golf Club, East Course	Ardmore, Pennsylvania
1982	Tom Watson	United States	Pebble Beach Golf Links	Pebble Beach, California
1983	Larry Nelson	United States	Oakmont Country Club	Oakmont, Pennsylvania

1984	Fuzzy Zoeller	United States	Winged Foot Golf Club, West Course	Mamaroneck, New York
1985	Andy North	United States	Oakland Hills Country Club, South Course	Bloomfield Hills, Michigan
1986	Ray Floyd	United States	Shinnecock Hills Golf Club	Southampton, New York
1987	Scott Simpson	United States	Olympic Club, Lake Course	San Francisco, California
1988	Curtis Strange	United States	The Country Club	Brookline, Massachusetts
1989	Curtis Strange	United States	Oak Hill Country Club, East Course	Rochester, New York
1990	Hale Irwin	United States	Medinah Country Club, Course No. 3	Medinah, Illinois
1991	Payne Stewart	United States	Hazeltine National Golf Club	Chaska, Minnesota
1992	Tom Kite	United States	Pebble Beach Golf Links	Pebble Beach, California
1993	Lee Janzen	United States	Baltusrol Golf Club, Lower Course	Springfield, New Jersey
1994	Ernie Els	South Africa	Oakmont Country Club	Oakmont, Pennsylvania
1995	Corey Pavin	United States	Shinnecock Hills Golf Club	Southampton, New York
1996	Steve Jones	United States	Oakland Hills Country Club, South Course	Bloomfield Hills, Michigan
1997	Ernie Els	South Africa	Congressional Country Club	Bethesda, Maryland
1998	Lee Janzen	United States	Olympic Club, Lake Course	San Francisco, California

1999	Payne Stewart	United States	Pinehurst Resort, No. 2 Course	Pinehurst, North Carolina
2000	Tiger Woods	United States	Pebble Beach Golf Links	Pebble Beach, California
2001	Retief Goosen	South Africa	Southern Hills Country Club	Tulsa, Oklahoma
2002	Tiger Woods	United States	Bethpage State Park, Black Course	Farmingdale, New York
2003	Jim Furyk	United States	Olympia Fields Country Club, North Course	Olympia Fields, Illinois
2004	Retief Goosen	South Africa	Shinnecock Hills Golf Club	Southampton, New York
2005	Michael Campbell	New Zealand	Pinehurst Resort, No. 2 Course	Pinehurst, North Carolina
2006	Geoff Ogilvy	Australia	Winged Foot Golf Club, West Course	Mamaroneck, New York
2007	Ángel Cabrera	Argentina	Oakmont Country Club	Oakmont, Pennsylvania
2008	Tiger Woods	United States	Torrey Pines Golf Course, South Course	La Jolla, California
2009	Lucas Glover	United States	Bethpage State Park, Black Course	Farmingdale, New York

PGA Championship

1916	Jim Barnes	England / United States	Siwanoy Country Club	Eastchester, New York

1919	Jim Barnes	England / United States	Engineers Country Club	Roslyn Harbor, New York
1920	Jock Hutchison	United States	Flossmoor Country Club	Flossmoor, Illinois
1921	Walter Hagen	United States	Inwood Country Club	Inwood, New York
1922	Gene Sarazen	United States	Oakmont Country Club	Oakmont, Pennsylvania
1923	Gene Sarazen	United States	Pelham Country Club	Pelham Manor, New York
1924	Walter Hagen	United States	French Lick Springs Resort, Hill Course	French Lick, Indiana
1925	Walter Hagen	United States	Olympia Fields Country Club, North Course	Olympia Fields, Illinois
1926	Walter Hagen	United States	Salisbury Golf Club, Red Course	East Meadow, New York
1927	Walter Hagen	United States	Cedar Crest Country Club	Dallas, Texas
1928	Leo Diegel	United States	Baltimore Country Club, Five Farms, East Course	Timonium, Maryland
1929	Leo Diegel	United States	Hillcrest Country Club	Los Angeles, California
1930	Tommy Armour	Scotland / United States	Fresh Meadow Country Club	Great Neck, New York
1931	Tom Creavy	United States	Wannamoisett Country Club	Rumford, Rhode Island
1932	Olin Dutra	United States	Keller Golf Course	Saint Paul, Minnesota

1933	Gene Sarazen	United States	Blue Mound Golf & Country Club	Wauwatosa, Wisconsin
1934	Paul Runyan	United States	Park Country Club	Williamsville, New York
1935	Johnny Revolta	United States	Twin Hills Golf & Country Club	Oklahoma City, Oklahoma
1936	Denny Shute	United States	Pinehurst Resort, No. 2 Course	Pinehurst, North Carolina
1937	Denny Shute	United States	Pittsburgh Field Club	O'Hara Township, Pennsylvania
1938	Paul Runyan	United States	Shawnee Inn & Golf Resort	Smithfield Township, Pennsylvania
1939	Henry Picard	United States	Pomonok Country Club	Flushing, New York
1940	Byron Nelson	United States	Hershey Country Club, West Course	Hershey, Pennsylvania
1941	Vic Ghezzi	United States	Cherry Hills Country Club	Cherry Hills Village, Colorado
1942	Sam Snead	United States	Seaview Country Club	Atlantic City, New Jersey
1944	Bob Hamilton	United States	Manito Golf and Country Club	Spokane, Washington
1945	Byron Nelson	United States	Moraine Country Club	Dayton, Ohio
1946	Ben Hogan	United States	Portland Golf Club	Portland, Oregon
1947	Jim Ferrier	Australia	Plum Hollow Country Club	Detroit, Michigan
1948	Ben Hogan	United States	Norwood Hills Country Club	St. Louis, Missouri

1949	Sam Snead	United States	Hermitage Country Club	Richmond, Virginia
1950	Chandler Harper	United States	Scioto Country Club	Columbus, Ohio
1951	Sam Snead	United States	Oakmont Country Club	Oakmont, Pennsylvania
1952	Jim Turnesa	United States	Big Spring Country Club	Louisville, Kentucky
1953	Walter Burkemo	United States	Birmingham Country Club	Birmingham, Michigan
1954	Chick Harbert	United States	Keller Golf Course	Saint Paul, Minnesota
1955	Doug Ford	United States	Meadowbrook Country Club	Detroit, Michigan
1956	Jack Burke Jr.	United States	Blue Hill Country Club	Canton, Massachusetts
1957	Lionel Hebert	United States	Miami Valley Golf Club	Dayton, Ohio
1958	Dow Finsterwald	United States	Llanerch Country Club	Havertown, Pennsylvania
1959	Bob Rosburg	United States	Minneapolis Golf Club	Minneapolis, Minnesota
1960	Jay Hebert	United States	Firestone Country Club, South Course	Akron, Ohio
1961	Jerry Barber	United States	Olympia Fields Country Club, North Course	Olympia Fields, Illinois
1962	Gary Player	South Africa	Aronimink Golf Club	Newtown Square, Pennsylvania
1963	Jack Nicklaus	United States	Dallas Athletic Club, Blue Course	Dallas, Texas
1964	Bobby Nichols	United States	Columbus Country Club	Columbus, Ohio
1965	Dave Marr	United States	Laurel Valley Golf Club	Ligonier, Pennsylvania
1966	Al Geiberger	United States	Firestone Country Club, South Course	Akron, Ohio

1967	Don January	United States	Columbine Country Club	Columbine Valley, Colorado
1968	Julius Boros	United States	Pecan Valley Golf Club	San Antonio, Texas
1969	Ray Floyd	United States	NCR Country Club, South Course	Kettering, Ohio
1970	Dave Stockton	United States	Southern Hills Country Club	Tulsa, Oklahoma
1971	Jack Nicklaus	United States	PGA National Golf Club	Palm Beach Gardens, Florida
1972	Gary Player	South Africa	Oakland Hills Country Club, South Course	Bloomfield Hills, Michigan
1973	Jack Nicklaus	United States	Canterbury Golf Club	Beachwood, Ohio
1974	Lee Trevino	United States	Tanglewood Park, Championship Course	Clemmons, North Carolina
1975	Jack Nicklaus	United States	Firestone Country Club, South Course	Akron, Ohio
1976	Dave Stockton	United States	Congressional Country Club	Bethesda, Maryland
1977	Lanny Wadkins	United States	Pebble Beach Golf Links	Pebble Beach, California
1978	John Mahaffey	United States	Oakmont Country Club	Oakmont, Pennsylvania
1979	David Graham	Australia	Oakland Hills Country Club, South Course	Bloomfield Hills, Michigan

1980	Jack Nicklaus	United States	Oak Hill Country Club, East Course	Rochester, New York
1981	Larry Nelson	United States	Atlanta Athletic Club, Highlands Course	Duluth, Georgia
1982	Ray Floyd	United States	Southern Hills Country Club	Tulsa, Oklahoma
1983	Hal Sutton	United States	Riviera Country Club	Pacific Palisades, California
1984	Lee Trevino	United States	Shoal Creek Country Club	Shoal Creek, Alabama
1985	Hubert Green	United States	Cherry Hills Country Club	Cherry Hills Village, Colorado
1986	Bob Tway	United States	Inverness Club	Toledo, Ohio
1987	Larry Nelson	United States	PGA National Golf Club	Palm Beach Gardens, Florida
1988	Jeff Sluman	United States	Oak Tree Golf Club	Edmond, Oklahoma
1989	Payne Stewart	United States	Kemper Lakes Golf Club	Long Grove, Illinois
1990	Wayne Grady	Australia	Shoal Creek Country Club	Shoal Creek, Alabama
1991	John Daly	United States	Crooked Stick Golf Club	Carmel, Indiana
1992	Nick Price	Zimbabwe	Bellerive Country Club	St. Louis, Missouri
1993	Paul Azinger	United States	Inverness Club	Toledo, Ohio
1994	Nick Price	Zimbabwe	Southern Hills Country Club	Tulsa, Oklahoma
1995	Steve Elkington	Australia	Riviera Country Club	Pacific Palisades, California
1996	Mark Brooks	United States	Valhalla Golf Club	Louisville, Kentucky

1997	Davis Love III	United States	Winged Foot Golf Club, West Course	Mamaroneck, New York
1998	Vijay Singh	Fiji	Sahalee Country Club	Sammamish, Washington
1999	Tiger Woods	United States	Medinah Country Club, Course No. 3	Medinah, Illinois
2000	Tiger Woods	United States	Valhalla Golf Club	Louisville, Kentucky
2001	David Toms	United States	Atlanta Athletic Club, Highlands Course	Duluth, Georgia
2002	Rich Beem	United States	Hazeltine National Golf Club	Chaska, Minnesota
2003	Shaun Micheel	United States	Oak Hill Country Club, East Course	Rochester, New York
2004	Vijay Singh	Fiji	Whistling Straits, Straits Course	Kohler, Wisconsin
2005	Phil Mickelson	United States	Baltusrol Golf Club, Lower Course	Springfield, New Jersey
2006	Tiger Woods	United States	Medinah Country Club, Course No. 3	Medinah, Illinois
2007	Tiger Woods	United States	Southern Hills Country Club	Tulsa, Oklahoma
2008	Pádraig Harrington	Ireland	Oakland Hills Country Club, South Course	Bloomfield Hills, Michigan
2009	Yang Yong-Eun	Korea (South)	Hazeltine National Golf Club	Chaska, Minnesota

The Masters

1934	Horton Smith	United States	Augusta National Golf Club	Augusta, Georgia
1935	Gene Sarazen	United States	Augusta National Golf Club	Augusta, Georgia
1936	Horton Smith	United States	Augusta National Golf Club	Augusta, Georgia
1937	Byron Nelson	United States	Augusta National Golf Club	Augusta, Georgia
1938	Henry Picard	United States	Augusta National Golf Club	Augusta, Georgia
1939	Ralph Guldahl	United States	Augusta National Golf Club	Augusta, Georgia
1940	Jimmy Demaret	United States	Augusta National Golf Club	Augusta, Georgia
1941	Craig Wood	United States	Augusta National Golf Club	Augusta, Georgia
1942	Byron Nelson	United States	Augusta National Golf Club	Augusta, Georgia
1946	Herman Keiser	United States	Augusta National Golf Club	Augusta, Georgia
1947	Jimmy Demaret	United States	Augusta National Golf Club	Augusta, Georgia
1948	Claude Harmon	United States	Augusta National Golf Club	Augusta, Georgia
1949	Sam Snead	United States	Augusta National Golf Club	Augusta, Georgia
1950	Jimmy Demaret	United States	Augusta National Golf Club	Augusta, Georgia
1951	Ben Hogan	United States	Augusta National Golf Club	Augusta, Georgia
1952	Sam Snead	United States	Augusta National Golf Club	Augusta, Georgia
1953	Ben Hogan	United States	Augusta National Golf Club	Augusta, Georgia
1954	Sam Snead	United States	Augusta National Golf Club	Augusta, Georgia
1955	Cary Middlecoff	United States	Augusta National Golf Club	Augusta, Georgia
1956	Jack Burke Jr.	United States	Augusta National Golf Club	Augusta, Georgia
1957	Doug Ford	United States	Augusta National Golf Club	Augusta, Georgia
1958	Arnold Palmer	United States	Augusta National Golf Club	Augusta, Georgia

1959	Art Wall Jr.	United States	Augusta National Golf Club	Augusta, Georgia
1960	Arnold Palmer	United States	Augusta National Golf Club	Augusta, Georgia
1961	Gary Player	South Africa	Augusta National Golf Club	Augusta, Georgia
1962	Arnold Palmer	United States	Augusta National Golf Club	Augusta, Georgia
1963	Jack Nicklaus	United States	Augusta National Golf Club	Augusta, Georgia
1964	Arnold Palmer	United States	Augusta National Golf Club	Augusta, Georgia
1965	Jack Nicklaus	United States	Augusta National Golf Club	Augusta, Georgia
1966	Jack Nicklaus	United States	Augusta National Golf Club	Augusta, Georgia
1967	Gay Brewer	United States	Augusta National Golf Club	Augusta, Georgia
1968	Bob Goalby	United States	Augusta National Golf Club	Augusta, Georgia
1969	George Archer	United States	Augusta National Golf Club	Augusta, Georgia
1970	Billy Casper	United States	Augusta National Golf Club	Augusta, Georgia
1971	Charles Coody	United States	Augusta National Golf Club	Augusta, Georgia
1972	Jack Nicklaus	United States	Augusta National Golf Club	Augusta, Georgia
1973	Tommy Aaron	United States	Augusta National Golf Club	Augusta, Georgia
1974	Gary Player	South Africa	Augusta National Golf Club	Augusta, Georgia
1975	Jack Nicklaus	United States	Augusta National Golf Club	Augusta, Georgia
1976	Ray Floyd	United States	Augusta National Golf Club	Augusta, Georgia
1977	Tom Watson	United States	Augusta National Golf Club	Augusta, Georgia
1978	Gary Player	South Africa	Augusta National Golf Club	Augusta, Georgia
1979	Fuzzy Zoeller	United States	Augusta National Golf Club	Augusta, Georgia
1980	Seve Ballesteros	Spain	Augusta National Golf Club	Augusta, Georgia
1981	Tom Watson	United States	Augusta National Golf Club	Augusta, Georgia
1982	Craig Stadler	United States	Augusta National Golf Club	Augusta, Georgia

1983	Seve Ballesteros	Spain	Augusta National Golf Club	Augusta, Georgia
1984	Ben Crenshaw	United States	Augusta National Golf Club	Augusta, Georgia
1985	Bernhard Langer	West Germany	Augusta National Golf Club	Augusta, Georgia
1986	Jack Nicklaus	United States	Augusta National Golf Club	Augusta, Georgia
1987	Larry Mize	United States	Augusta National Golf Club	Augusta, Georgia
1988	Sandy Lyle	Scotland	Augusta National Golf Club	Augusta, Georgia
1989	Nick Faldo	England	Augusta National Golf Club	Augusta, Georgia
1990	Nick Faldo	England	Augusta National Golf Club	Augusta, Georgia
1991	Ian Woosnam	Wales	Augusta National Golf Club	Augusta, Georgia
1992	Fred Couples	United States	Augusta National Golf Club	Augusta, Georgia
1993	Bernhard Langer	Germany	Augusta National Golf Club	Augusta, Georgia
1994	José María Olazábal	Spain	Augusta National Golf Club	Augusta, Georgia
1995	Ben Crenshaw	United States	Augusta National Golf Club	Augusta, Georgia
1996	Nick Faldo	England	Augusta National Golf Club	Augusta, Georgia
1997	Tiger Woods	United States	Augusta National Golf Club	Augusta, Georgia
1998	Mark O'Meara	United States	Augusta National Golf Club	Augusta, Georgia
1999	José María Olazábal	Spain	Augusta National Golf Club	Augusta, Georgia
2000	Vijay Singh	Fiji	Augusta National Golf Club	Augusta, Georgia
2001	Tiger Woods	United States	Augusta National Golf Club	Augusta, Georgia
2002	Tiger Woods	United States	Augusta National Golf Club	Augusta, Georgia
2003	Mike Weir	Canada	Augusta National Golf Club	Augusta, Georgia
2004	Phil Mickelson	United States	Augusta National Golf Club	Augusta, Georgia
2005	Tiger Woods	United States	Augusta National Golf Club	Augusta, Georgia
2006	Phil Mickelson	United States	Augusta National Golf Club	Augusta, Georgia

2007	Zach Johnson	United States	Augusta National Golf Club	Augusta, Georgia
2008	Trevor Immelman	South Africa	Augusta National Golf Club	Augusta, Georgia
2009	Ángel Cabrera	Argentina	Augusta National Golf Club	Augusta, Georgia

Tournament Players Championship (1974–1987); The Players Championship (1988–2009)

1974	Jack Nicklaus	United States	Atlanta Country Club	Marietta, Georgia
1975	Al Geiberger	United States	Colonial Country Club	Fort Worth, Texas
1976	Jack Nicklaus	United States	Inverrary Country Club	Ft. Lauderdale, Florida
1977	Mark Hayes	United States	Sawgrass Country Club	Ponte Vedra Beach, Florida
1978	Jack Nicklaus	United States	Sawgrass Country Club	Ponte Vedra Beach, Florida
1979	Lanny Wadkins	United States	Sawgrass Country Club	Ponte Vedra Beach, Florida
1980	Lee Trevino	United States	Sawgrass Country Club	Ponte Vedra Beach, Florida
1981	Ray Floyd	United States	Sawgrass Country Club	Ponte Vedra Beach, Florida
1982	Jerry Pate	United States	The TPC at Sawgrass	Ponte Vedra Beach, Florida
1983	Hal Sutton	United States	The TPC at Sawgrass	Ponte Vedra Beach, Florida
1984	Fred Couples	United States	The TPC at Sawgrass	Ponte Vedra Beach, Florida
1985	Calvin Peete	United States	The TPC at Sawgrass	Ponte Vedra Beach, Florida
1986	John Mahaffey	United States	The TPC at Sawgrass	Ponte Vedra Beach, Florida
1987	Sandy Lyle	Scotland	The TPC at Sawgrass	Ponte Vedra Beach, Florida
1988	Mark McCumber	United States	The TPC at Sawgrass	Ponte Vedra Beach, Florida
1989	Tom Kite	United States	The TPC at Sawgrass	Ponte Vedra Beach, Florida
1990	Jodie Mudd	United States	The TPC at Sawgrass	Ponte Vedra Beach, Florida

1991	Steve Elkington	Australia	The TPC at Sawgrass	Ponte Vedra Beach, Florida
1992	Davis Love III	United States	The TPC at Sawgrass	Ponte Vedra Beach, Florida
1993	Nick Price	Zimbabwe	The TPC at Sawgrass	Ponte Vedra Beach, Florida
1994	Greg Norman	Australia	The TPC at Sawgrass	Ponte Vedra Beach, Florida
1995	Lee Janzen	United States	The TPC at Sawgrass	Ponte Vedra Beach, Florida
1996	Fred Couples	United States	The TPC at Sawgrass	Ponte Vedra Beach, Florida
1997	Steve Elkington	Australia	The TPC at Sawgrass	Ponte Vedra Beach, Florida
1998	Justin Leonard	United States	The TPC at Sawgrass	Ponte Vedra Beach, Florida
1999	David Duval	United States	The TPC at Sawgrass	Ponte Vedra Beach, Florida
2000	Hal Sutton	United States	The TPC at Sawgrass	Ponte Vedra Beach, Florida
2001	Tiger Woods	United States	The TPC at Sawgrass	Ponte Vedra Beach, Florida
2002	Craig Perks	New Zealand	The TPC at Sawgrass	Ponte Vedra Beach, Florida
2003	Davis Love, III	United States	The TPC at Sawgrass	Ponte Vedra Beach, Florida
2004	Adam Scott	Australia	The TPC at Sawgrass	Ponte Vedra Beach, Florida
2005	Fred Funk	United States	The TPC at Sawgrass	Ponte Vedra Beach, Florida
2006	Stephen Ames	Trinidad and Tobago / Canada	The TPC at Sawgrass	Ponte Vedra Beach, Florida
2007	Phil Mickelson	United States	The TPC at Sawgrass	Ponte Vedra Beach, Florida
2008	Sergio García	Spain	The TPC at Sawgrass	Ponte Vedra Beach, Florida
2009	Henrik Stenson	Sweden	The TPC at Sawgrass	Ponte Vedra Beach, Florida

APPENDIX 3. WOMEN'S MAJOR PROFESSIONAL CHAMPIONS

U.S. Women's Open

1946	Patty Berg	United States	Spokane Country Club	Spokane, Washington
1947	Betty Jameson	United States	Starmount Forest Country Club	Greensboro, North Carolina
1948	Babe Zaharias	United States	Atlantic City Country Club	Northfield, New Jersey
1949	Louise Suggs	United States	Prince Georges Golf and Country Club	Landover, Maryland
1950	Babe Zaharias	United States	Rolling Hills Country Club	Wichita, Kansas
1951	Betsy Rawls	United States	Druid Hills Golf Club	Atlanta, Georgia
1952	Louise Suggs	United States	Bala Golf Club	Philadelphia, Pennsylvania
1953	Betsy Rawls	United States	Country Club of Rochester	Rochester, New York
1954	Babe Zaharias	United States	Salem Country Club	Peabody, Massachusetts
1955	Fay Crocker	Uruguay	Wichita Country Club	Wichita, Kansas
1956	Kathy Cornelius	United States	Northland Country Club	Duluth, Minnesota
1957	Betsy Rawls	United States	Winged Foot Golf Club, East Course	Mamaroneck, New York
1958	Mickey Wright	United States	Forest Lake Country Club	Bloomfield Hills, Michigan
1959	Mickey Wright	United States	Churchill Valley Country Club	Pittsburgh, Pennsylvania

1960	Betsy Rawls	United States	Worcester Country Club	Worcester, Massachusetts
1961	Mickey Wright	United States	Baltusrol Golf Club, Lower Course	Springfield, New Jersey
1962	Murle Lindstrom	United States	Dunes Golf and Beach Club	Myrtle Beach, South Carolina
1963	Mary Mills	United States	Kenwood Country Club, Kenview Course	Cincinnati, Ohio
1964	Mickey Wright	United States	San Diego Country Club	Chula Vista, California
1965	Carol Mann	United States	Atlantic City Country Club	Northfield, New Jersey
1966	Sandra Spuzich	United States	Hazeltine National Golf Club	Chaska, Minnesota
1967	Catherine Lacoste (amateur)	France	Homestead, Cascades Course	Hot Springs, Virginia
1968	Susie Maxwell-Berning	United States	Moselem Springs Golf Club	Fleetwood, Pennsylvania
1969	Donna Caponi	United States	Scenic Hills Country Club	Pensacola, Florida
1970	Donna Caponi	United States	Muskogee Country Club	Muskogee, Oklahoma
1971	JoAnne Carner	United States	Kahkwa Club	Erie, Pennsylvania
1972	Susie Maxwell-Berning	United States	Winged Foot Golf Club, East Course	Mamaroneck, New York
1973	Susie Maxwell-Berning	United States	Country Club of Rochester	Rochester, New York

1974	Sandra Haynie	United States	La Grange Country Club	La Grange, Illinois
1975	Sandra Palmer	United States	Atlantic City Country Club	Northfield, New Jersey
1976	JoAnne Carner	United States	Rolling Green Golf Club	Springfield, Pennsylvania
1977	Hollis Stacy	United States	Hazeltine National Golf Club	Chaska, Minnesota
1978	Hollis Stacy	United States	Country Club of Indianapolis	Indianapolis, Indiana
1979	Jerilyn Britz	United States	Brooklawn Country Club	Fairfield, Connecticut
1980	Amy Alcott	United States	Richland Country Club	Nashville, Tennessee
1981	Pat Bradley	United States	La Grange Country Club	La Grange, Illinois
1982	Janet Anderson	United States	Del Paso Country Club	Sacramento, California
1983	Jan Stephenson	Australia	Cedar Ridge Country Club	Tulsa, Oklahoma
1984	Hollis Stacy	United States	Salem Country Club	Peabody, Massachusetts
1985	Kathy Guadagnino	United States	Baltusrol Golf Club, Upper Course	Springfield, New Jersey
1986	Jane Geddes	United States	NCR Country Club	Kettering, Ohio
1987	Laura Davies	England	Plainfield Country Club	Edison, New Jersey
1988	Liselotte Neumann	Sweden	Baltimore Country Club, Five Farms, East Course	Baltimore, Maryland

1989	Betsy King	United States	Indianwood Golf and Country Club, Old Course	Lake Orion, Michigan
1990	Betsy King	United States	Atlanta Athletic Club, Riverside Course	Duluth, Georgia
1991	Meg Mallon	United States	Colonial Country Club	Fort Worth, Texas
1992	Patty Sheehan	United States	Oakmont Country Club	Oakmont, Pennsylvania
1993	Lauri Merten	United States	Crooked Stick Golf Club	Carmel, Indiana
1994	Patty Sheehan	United States	Indianwood Golf and Country Club, Old Course	Lake Orion, Michigan
1995	Annika Sörenstam	Sweden	Broadmoor Golf Club, East Course	Colorado Springs, Colorado
1996	Annika Sörenstam	Sweden	Pine Needles Lodge and Golf Club	Southern Pines, North Carolina
1997	Alison Nicholas	England	Pumpkin Ridge Golf Club, Witch Hollow Course	North Plains, Oregon
1998	Pak Se-Ri	Korea (South)	Blackwolf Run Golf Course	Kohler, Wisconsin
1999	Juli Inkster	United States	Old Waverly Golf Club	West Point, Mississippi
2000	Karrie Webb	Australia	Merit Club	Gurnee, Illinois
2001	Karrie Webb	Australia	Pine Needles Lodge and Golf Club	Southern Pines, North Carolina

2002	Juli Inkster	United States	Prairie Dunes Golf Club	Hutchinson, Kansas
2003	Hilary Lunke	United States	Pumpkin Ridge Golf Club, Witch Hollow Course	North Plains, Oregon
2004	Meg Mallon	United States	Orchards Golf Club	South Hadley, Massachusetts
2005	Birdie Kim	Korea (South)	Cherry Hills Country Club	Cherry Hills Village, Colorado
2006	Annika Sörenstam	Sweden	Newport Country Club	Newport, Rhode Island
2007	Cristie Kerr	United States	Pine Needles Lodge and Golf Club	Southern Pines, North Carolina
2008	Park In-Bee	Korea (South)	Interlachen Country Club	Edina, Minnesota
2009	Ji Eun-Hee	Korea (South)	Saucon Valley Country Club, Old Course	Bethlehem, Pennsylvania

LPGA Championship

1955	Beverly Hanson	United States	Orchard Ridge Country Club	Fort Wayne, Indiana
1956	Marlene Bauer Hagge	United States	Forest Lake Country Club	Detroit, Michigan
1957	Louise Suggs	United States	Churchill Valley Country Club	Pittsburgh, Pennsylvania

1958	Mickey Wright	United States	Sheraton Hotel Country Club	French Lick, Indiana
1959	Betsy Rawls	United States	Sheraton Hotel Country Club	French Lick, Indiana
1960	Mickey Wright	United States	Sheraton Hotel Country Club	French Lick, Indiana
1961	Mickey Wright	United States	Stardust Country Club	Las Vegas, Nevada
1962	Judy Kimball	United States	Stardust Country Club	Las Vegas, Nevada
1963	Mickey Wright	United States	Stardust Country Club	Las Vegas, Nevada
1964	Mary Mills	United States	Stardust Country Club	Las Vegas, Nevada
1965	Sandra Haynie	United States	Stardust Country Club	Las Vegas, Nevada
1966	Gloria Ehret	United States	Stardust Country Club	Las Vegas, Nevada
1967	Kathy Whitworth	United States	Pleasant Valley Country Club	Sutton, Massachusetts
1968	Sandra Post	Canada	Pleasant Valley Country Club	Sutton, Massachusetts
1969	Betsy Rawls	United States	Concord Golf Course	Kiamesha Lake, New York
1970	Shirley Englehorn	United States	Pleasant Valley Country Club	Sutton, Massachusetts
1971	Kathy Whitworth	United States	Pleasant Valley Country Club	Sutton, Massachusetts
1972	Kathy Ahern	United States	Pleasant Valley Country Club	Sutton, Massachusetts

1973	Mary Mills	United States	Pleasant Valley Country Club	Sutton, Massachusetts
1974	Sandra Haynie	United States	Pleasant Valley Country Club	Sutton, Massachusetts
1975	Kathy Whitworth	United States	Pine Ridge Golf Course	Lutherville, Maryland
1976	Betty Burfeindt	United States	Pine Ridge Golf Course	Lutherville, Maryland
1977	Chako Higuchi	Japan	Bay Tree Golf Plantation	Myrtle Beach, South Carolina
1978	Nancy Lopez	United States	Jack Nicklaus Sports Center at Kings Island	Mason, Ohio
1979	Donna Caponi	United States	Jack Nicklaus Sports Center at Kings Island	Mason, Ohio
1980	Sally Little	South Africa	Jack Nicklaus Sports Center at Kings Island	Mason, Ohio
1981	Donna Caponi	United States	Jack Nicklaus Sports Center at Kings Island	Mason, Ohio
1982	Jan Stephenson	Australia	Jack Nicklaus Sports Center at Kings Island	Mason, Ohio
1983	Patty Sheehan	United States	Jack Nicklaus Sports Center at Kings Island	Mason, Ohio
1984	Patty Sheehan	United States	Jack Nicklaus Sports Center at Kings Island	Mason, Ohio

1985	Nancy Lopez	United States	Jack Nicklaus Sports Center at Kings Island	Mason, Ohio
1986	Pat Bradley	United States	Jack Nicklaus Sports Center at Kings Island	Mason, Ohio
1987	Jane Geddes	United States	Jack Nicklaus Sports Center at Kings Island	Mason, Ohio
1988	Sherri Turner	United States	Jack Nicklaus Sports Center at Kings Island	Mason, Ohio
1989	Nancy Lopez	United States	Jack Nicklaus Sports Center at Kings Island	Mason, Ohio
1990	Beth Daniel	United States	Bethesda Country Club	Bethesda, Maryland
1991	Meg Mallon	United States	Bethesda Country Club	Bethesda, Maryland
1992	Betsy King	United States	Bethesda Country Club	Bethesda, Maryland
1993	Patty Sheehan	United States	Bethesda Country Club	Bethesda, Maryland
1994	Laura Davies	England	The DuPont Country Club	Wilmington, Delaware
1995	Kelly Robbins	United States	The DuPont Country Club	Wilmington, Delaware
1996	Laura Davies	England	The DuPont Country Club	Wilmington, Delaware
1997	Christa Johnson	United States	The DuPont Country Club	Wilmington, Delaware
1998	Pak Se-Ri	Korea (South)	The DuPont Country Club	Wilmington, Delaware
1999	Juli Inkster	United States	The DuPont Country Club	Wilmington, Delaware
2000	Juli Inkster	United States	The DuPont Country Club	Wilmington, Delaware
2001	Karrie Webb	Australia	The DuPont Country Club	Wilmington, Delaware
2002	Pak Se-Ri	Korea (South)	The DuPont Country Club	Wilmington, Delaware
2003	Annika Sörenstam	Sweden	The DuPont Country Club	Wilmington, Delaware

2004	Annika Sörenstam	Sweden	The DuPont Country Club	Wilmington, Delaware
2005	Annika Sörenstam	Sweden	Bulle Rock Golf Course	Havre de Grace, Maryland
2006	Pak Se-Ri	Korea (South)	Bulle Rock Golf Course	Havre de Grace, Maryland
2007	Suzann Pettersen	Norway	Bulle Rock Golf Course	Havre de Grace, Maryland
2008	Yani Tseng	Taiwan	Bulle Rock Golf Course	Havre de Grace, Maryland
2009	Anna Nordqvist	Sweden	Bulle Rock Golf Course	Havre de Grace, Maryland

Kraft Nabisco/Dinah Shore

1972	Jane Blalock	United States	Mission Hills Country Club	Rancho Mirage, California
1973	Mickey Wright	United States	Mission Hills Country Club	Rancho Mirage, California
1974	Jo Ann Prentice	United States	Mission Hills Country Club	Rancho Mirage, California
1975	Sandra Palmer	United States	Mission Hills Country Club	Rancho Mirage, California
1976	Judy Rankin	United States	Mission Hills Country Club	Rancho Mirage, California
1977	Kathy Whitworth	United States	Mission Hills Country Club	Rancho Mirage, California
1978	Sandra Post	Canada	Mission Hills Country Club	Rancho Mirage, California

1979	Sandra Post	Canada	Mission Hills Country Club	Rancho Mirage, California
1980	Donna Caponi	United States	Mission Hills Country Club	Rancho Mirage, California
1981	Nancy Lopez	United States	Mission Hills Country Club	Rancho Mirage, California
1982	Sally Little	South Africa	Mission Hills Country Club	Rancho Mirage, California
1983	Amy Alcott	United States	Mission Hills Country Club	Rancho Mirage, California
1984	Juli Inkster	United States	Mission Hills Country Club	Rancho Mirage, California
1985	Alice Miller	United States	Mission Hills Country Club	Rancho Mirage, California
1986	Pat Bradley	United States	Mission Hills Country Club	Rancho Mirage, California
1987	Betsy King	United States	Mission Hills Country Club	Rancho Mirage, California
1988	Amy Alcott	United States	Mission Hills Country Club	Rancho Mirage, California
1989	Juli Inkster	United States	Mission Hills Country Club	Rancho Mirage, California
1990	Betsy King	United States	Mission Hills Country Club	Rancho Mirage, California

1991	Amy Alcott	United States	Mission Hills Country Club	Rancho Mirage, California
1992	Dottie Mochrie (-Pepper)	United States	Mission Hills Country Club	Rancho Mirage, California
1993	Helen Alfredsson	Sweden	Mission Hills Country Club	Rancho Mirage, California
1994	Donna Andrews	United States	Mission Hills Country Club	Rancho Mirage, California
1995	Nanci Bowen	United States	Mission Hills Country Club	Rancho Mirage, California
1996	Patty Sheehan	United States	Mission Hills Country Club	Rancho Mirage, California
1997	Betsy King	United States	Mission Hills Country Club	Rancho Mirage, California
1998	Pat Hurst	United States	Mission Hills Country Club	Rancho Mirage, California
1999	Dottie (Mochrie-) Pepper	United States	Mission Hills Country Club	Rancho Mirage, California
2000	Karrie Webb	Australia	Mission Hills Country Club	Rancho Mirage, California
2001	Annika Sörenstam	Sweden	Mission Hills Country Club	Rancho Mirage, California

2002	Annika Sörenstam	Sweden	Mission Hills Country Club	Rancho Mirage, California
2003	Patricia Meunier-Lebouc	France	Mission Hills Country Club	Rancho Mirage, California
2004	Grace Park	Korea (South)	Mission Hills Country Club	Rancho Mirage, California
2005	Annika Sörenstam	Sweden	Mission Hills Country Club	Rancho Mirage, California
2006	Karrie Webb	Australia	Mission Hills Country Club	Rancho Mirage, California
2007	Morgan Pressel	United States	Mission Hills Country Club	Rancho Mirage, California
2008	Lorena Ochoa	Mexico	Mission Hills Country Club	Rancho Mirage, California
2009	Brittany Lincicome	United States	Mission Hills Country Club	Rancho Mirage, California

British Women's Open

1976	Jenny Lee Smith	England	Fulford, York Golf Club	York, England
1977	Vivien Saunders	England	Lindrick Golf Club	Worksop, Nottinghamshire, England
1978	Janet Melville	England	Foxhills Golf & Country Club	

1979	Alison Sheard	South Africa	Southport and Ainsdale Golf Club	Southport, Lancashire, England
1980	Debbie Massey	United States	Wentworth Club	Virginia Water, Surrey, England
1981	Debbie Massey	United States	Northumberland Golf Club	High Gosforth Park, Newcastle-upon-Tyne, England
1982	Marta Figueras-Dotti	Spain	Royal Birkdale Golf Club	Southport, Merseyside, England
1984	Ayako Okamoto	Japan	Woburn Golf and Country Club	Woburn, Buckinghamshire, England
1985	Betsy King	United States	Moortown Golf Club	Leeds, Yorkshire, England
1986	Laura Davies	England	Royal Birkdale Golf Club	Southport, Merseyside, England
1987	Alison Nicholas	England	Woburn Golf and Country Club	Woburn, Buckinghamshire, England
1988	Corinne Dibnah	Australia	Woburn Golf and Country Club	Woburn, Buckinghamshire, England
1989	Jane Geddes	United States	Woburn Golf and Country Club	Woburn, Buckinghamshire, England
1990	Helen Alfredsson	Sweden	Woburn Golf and Country Club	Woburn, Buckinghamshire, England

1991	Penny Grice-Whittaker	England	Woburn Golf and Country Club	Woburn, Buckinghamshire, England
1992	Patty Sheehan	United States	Woburn Golf and Country Club	Woburn, Buckinghamshire, England
1993	Karen Lunn	Australia	Woburn Golf and Country Club	Woburn, Buckinghamshire, England
1994	Liselotte Neumann	Sweden	Woburn Golf and Country Club	Woburn, Buckinghamshire, England
1995	Karrie Webb	Australia	Woburn Golf and Country Club	Woburn, Buckinghamshire, England
1996	Emilee Klein	United States	Woburn Golf and Country Club	Woburn, Buckinghamshire, England
1997	Karrie Webb	Australia	Sunningdale Golf Club	London, Greater London, England
1998	Sherri Steinhauer	United States	Royal Lytham & St. Annes Golf Club	Lytham and St. Annes, Lancashire, England
1999	Sherri Steinhauer	United States	Woburn Golf and Country Club	Woburn, Buckinghamshire, England
2000	Sophie Gustafson	Sweden	Royal Birkdale Golf Club	Southport, Merseyside, England
2001	Pak Se-Ri	Korea (South)	Sunningdale Golf Club	London, Greater London, England

2002	Karrie Webb	Australia	Turnberry, Ailsa Course	Turnberry, South Ayrshire, Scotland
2003	Annika Sörenstam	Sweden	Royal Lytham & St. Annes Golf Club	Lytham and St. Annes, Lancashire, England
2004	Karen Stupples	England	Sunningdale Golf Club	London, Greater London, England
2005	Jang Jeong	Korea (South)	Royal Birkdale Golf Club	Southport, Merseyside, England
2006	Sherri Steinhauer	United States	Royal Lytham & St. Annes Golf Club	Lytham and St. Annes, Lancashire, England
2007	Lorena Ochoa	Mexico	St. Andrews Links, Old Course	St. Andrews, Fife, Scotland
2008	Jiyai Shin	Korea (South)	Sunningdale Golf Club	London, Greater London, England
2009	Catriona Matthew	Scotland	Royal Lytham & St. Annes Golf Club	Lytham and St. Annes, Lancashire, England

Titleholders Championship

1937	Patty Berg (amateur)	United States	Augusta Country Club	Augusta, Georgia
1938	Patty Berg (amateur)	United States	Augusta Country Club	Augusta, Georgia
1939	Patty Berg (amateur)	United States	Augusta Country Club	Augusta, Georgia
1940	Betty Hicks (amateur)	United States	Augusta Country Club	Augusta, Georgia
1941	Dorothy Kirby (amateur)	United States	Augusta Country Club	Augusta, Georgia

1942	Dorothy Kirby (amateur)	United States	Augusta Country Club	Augusta, Georgia
1946	Louise Suggs (amateur)	United States	Augusta Country Club	Augusta, Georgia
1947	Babe Zaharias (amateur)	United States	Augusta Country Club	Augusta, Georgia
1948	Patty Berg	United States	Augusta Country Club	Augusta, Georgia
1949	Peggy Kirk (amateur)	United States	Augusta Country Club	Augusta, Georgia
1950	Babe Zaharias	United States	Augusta Country Club	Augusta, Georgia
1951	Pat O'Sullivan (amateur)	United States	Augusta Country Club	Augusta, Georgia
1952	Babe Zaharias	United States	Augusta Country Club	Augusta, Georgia
1953	Patty Berg	United States	Augusta Country Club	Augusta, Georgia
1954	Louise Suggs	United States	Augusta Country Club	Augusta, Georgia
1955	Patty Berg	United States	Augusta Country Club	Augusta, Georgia
1956	Louise Suggs	United States	Augusta Country Club	Augusta, Georgia
1957	Patty Berg	United States	Augusta Country Club	Augusta, Georgia
1958	Beverly Hanson	United States	Augusta Country Club	Augusta, Georgia
1959	Louise Suggs	United States	Augusta Country Club	Augusta, Georgia
1960	Fay Crocker	Uruguay	Augusta Country Club	Augusta, Georgia
1961	Mickey Wright	United States	Augusta Country Club	Augusta, Georgia
1962	Mickey Wright	United States	Augusta Country Club	Augusta, Georgia
1963	Marilynn Smith	United States	Augusta Country Club	Augusta, Georgia
1964	Marilynn Smith	United States	Augusta Country Club	Augusta, Georgia
1965	Kathy Whitworth	United States	Augusta Country Club	Augusta, Georgia
1966	Kathy Whitworth	United States	Augusta Country Club	Augusta, Georgia
1972	Sandra Palmer	United States	Augusta Country Club	Augusta, Georgia

Women's Western Open

1930	Mrs. Lee Mida	United States	Arcadia Country Club	Arcadia, Wisconsin
1931	June Beebe	United States	Midlothian Country Club	Midlothian, Illinois
1932	Jane Weiller	United States	Ozaukee Country Club	Mequon, Wisconsin
1933	June Beebe	United States	Olympia Fields Country Club	Olympia Fields, Illinois
1934	Marian McDougall	United States	Portland Golf Club	Portland, Oregon
1935	Opal Hill	United States	Sunset Ridge Country Club	Northfield, Illinois
1936	Opal Hill	United States	Topeka Country Club	Topeka, Kansas
1937	Betty Hicks (amateur)	United States	Beverly Country Club	Chicago, Illinois
1938	Bea Barrett (amateur)	United States	Broadmoor Golf Club, East Course	Colorado Springs, Colorado
1939	Helen Dettweiler	United States	Westwood Country Club	St. Louis, Missouri
1940	Babe Zaharias	United States	Blue Mound Golf & Country Club	Milwaukee, Wisconsin
1941	Patty Berg	United States	Town & Country Club	St. Paul, Minnesota
1942	Betty Jameson	United States	Elmhurst Country Club	Elmhurst, Pennsylvania
1943	Patty Berg	United States	Glen Oak Country Club	Glen Ellyn, Illinois
1944	Babe Zaharias (amateur)	United States	Park Ridge Country Club	Park Ridge, Illinois
1945	Babe Zaharias (amateur)	United States	Highland Golf & Country Club	Indianapolis, Indiana
1946	Louise Suggs (amateur)	United States	Wakonda Club	Des Moines, Iowa

1947	Louise Suggs (amateur)	United States	Capital City Country Club	Tallahassee, Florida
1948	Patty Berg	United States	Skycrest Country Club	Prairie View, Illinois
1949	Louise Suggs	United States	Oklahoma City Golf & Country Club	Oklahoma City, Oklahoma
1950	Babe Zaharias	United States	Cherry Hills Country Club	Cherry Hills Village, Colorado
1951	Patty Berg	United States	Whitemarsh Valley Country Club	Whitemarsh Township, Pennsylvania
1952	Betsy Rawls	United States	Skokie Country Club	Glencoe, Illinois
1953	Louise Suggs	United States	Capital City Country Club	Tallahassee, Florida
1954	Betty Jameson	United States	Glen Fora Country Club	Waukegan, Illinois
1955	Patty Berg	United States	Maple Bluff Country Club	Madison, Wisconsin
1956	Beverly Hanson	United States	Wakonda Club	Des Moines, Iowa
1957	Patty Berg	United States	Montgomery Country Club	Montgomery, Alabama
1958	Patty Berg	United States	Kahkwa Club	Erie, Pennsylvania
1959	Betsy Rawls	United States	Rainier Golf & Country Club	Seattle, Washington
1960	Joyce Ziske	United States	Beverly Country Club	Chicago, Illinois

1961	Mary Lena Faulk	United States	Belle Meade Country Club	Nashville, Tennessee
1962	Mickey Wright	United States	Montgomery Country Club	Montgomery, Alabama
1963	Mickey Wright	United States	Maple Bluff Country Club	Madison, Wisconsin
1964	Carol Mann	United States	Scenic Hills Country Club	Pensacola, Florida
1965	Susie Maxwell	United States	Beverly Country Club	Chicago, Illinois
1966	Mickey Wright	United States	Rainbow Springs Country Club	Mukwonago, Wisconsin
1967	Kathy Whitworth	United States	Pekin Country Club	Pekin, Illinois

Du Maurier Classic/Canadian Open

1973	Jocelyne Bourassa	Canada	Montreal Municipal Golf Club	Montréal, Québec
1974	Carole Jo Callison	United States	Candiac Golf Club	Candiac, Québec
1975	JoAnne Carner	United States	St. George's Golf & Country Club	Islington, Ontario
1976	Donna Caponi	United States	Cedar Brae Golf & Country Club	Scarborough, Ontario
1977	Judy Rankin	United States	Club de Golf Lachute	Lachute, Québec

1978	JoAnne Carner	United States	St. George's Golf & Country Club	Islington, Ontario
1979	Amy Alcott	United States	Richelieu Valley Golf Club	Sainte-Julie, Québec
1980	Pat Bradley	United States	St. George's Golf & Country Club	Islington, Ontario
1981	Jan Stephenson	Australia	Summerlea Golf & Country Club	Montréal, Québec
1982	Sandra Haynie	United States	St. George's Golf & Country Club	Islington, Ontario
1983	Hollis Stacy	United States	Beaconsfield Golf Club	Pointe-Claire, Québec
1984	Juli Inkster	United States	St. George's Golf & Country Club	Islington, Ontario
1985	Pat Bradley	United States	Beaconsfield Golf Club	Pointe-Claire, Québec
1986	Pat Bradley	United States	Board of Trade Country Club	Woodbridge, Ontario
1987	Jody Rosenthal	United States	Club de Golf Islesmere	Sainte-Dorothée, Québec
1988	Sally Little	United States	Vancouver Golf Club	Vancouver, British Columbia

1989	Tammie Green	United States	Beaconsfield Golf Club	Pointe-Claire, Québec
1990	Cathy Johnston-Forbes	United States	Westmount Golf & Country Club	Montréal, Québec
1991	Nancy Scranton	United States	Vancouver Golf Club	Vancouver, British Columbia
1992	Sherri Steinhauer	United States	St. Charles Country Club	Winnipeg, Manitoba
1993	Brandie Burton	United States	London Hunt & Country Club	London, Ontario
1994	Martha Nause	United States	Ottawa Hunt and Golf Club	Ottawa, Ontario
1995	Jenny Lidback	United States	Beaconsfield Golf Club	Pointe-Claire, Québec
1996	Laura Davies	England	Edmonton Country Club	Edmonton, Alberta
1997	Colleen Walker	United States	Glen Abbey Golf Course	Oakville, Ontario
1998	Brandie Burton	United States	Essex Golf & Country Club	Windsor, Ontario
1999	Karrie Webb	Australia	Priddis Greens Golf & Country Club	Calgary, Alberta
2000	Meg Mallon	United States	Royal Ottawa Golf Club	Gatineau, Québec
2001	Annika Sörenstam	Sweden	Angus Glen Golf Club, North Course	Markham, Ontario

2002	Meg Mallon	United States	Summerlea Golf & Country Club	Montréal, Québec
2003	Beth Daniel	United States	Point Grey Golf & Country Club	Vancouver, British Columbia
2004	Meg Mallon	United States	Legends on the Niagara	Niagara, Ontario
2005	Meena Lee	Korea (South)	Glen Arbour Golf Course	Halifax, Nova Scotia
2006	Cristie Kerr	United States	London Hunt & Country Club	London, Ontario
2007	Lorena Ochoa	Mexico	Royal Mayfair Golf & Country Club	Edmonton, Alberta
2008	Katherine Hull	Australia	Ottawa Hunt and Golf Club	Ottawa, Ontario
2009	Suzann Pettersen	Norway	Priddis Greens Golf & Country Club	Calgary, Alberta

APPENDIX 4. OTHER PROFESSIONAL CHAMPIONS

Australian Open

1904	Michael Scott (amateur)	Australia	The Australian Golf Club	Sydney, New South Wales
1905	Dan Soutar	Australia	Royal Melbourne Golf Club	Melbourne, Victoria
1906	Carnegie Clark (amateur)	Australia	Royal Sydney Golf Club	Sydney, New South Wales
1907	Michael Scott (amateur)	Australia	Royal Melbourne Golf Club	Melbourne, Victoria
1908	Clyde Pearce (amateur)	Australia	The Australian Golf Club	Sydney, New South Wales
1909	Claude Felstead (amateur)	Australia	Royal Melbourne Golf Club	Melbourne, Victoria
1910	Carnegie Clark (amateur)	Australia	Royal Adelaide Golf Club	Adelaide, South Australia
1911	Carnegie Clark (amateur)	Australia	Royal Sydney Golf Club	Sydney, New South Wales
1912	Ivo Whitton (amateur)	Australia	Royal Melbourne Golf Club	Melbourne, Victoria
1913	Ivo Whitton (amateur)	Australia	Royal Melbourne Golf Club	Melbourne, Victoria
1920	Joe Kirkwood Sr.	Australia	The Australian Golf Club	Sydney, New South Wales
1921	Arthur Le Fevre	Australia	Royal Melbourne Golf Club	Melbourne, Victoria
1922	Charlie Campbell	Australia	Royal Sydney Golf Club	Sydney, New South Wales

1923	Tom Howard	Australia	Royal Adelaide Golf Club	Adelaide, South Australia
1924	A. Russell (amateur)	Australia	Royal Melbourne Golf Club	Melbourne, Victoria
1925	Fred Popplewell	Australia	The Australian Golf Club	Sydney, New South Wales
1926	Ivo Whitton (amateur)	Australia	Royal Adelaide Golf Club	Adelaide, South Australia
1927	Rufus Stewart	Australia	Royal Melbourne Golf Club	Melbourne, Victoria
1928	Fred Popplewell	Australia	Royal Sydney Golf Club	Sydney, New South Wales
1929	Ivo Whitton (amateur)	Australia	Royal Adelaide Golf Club	Adelaide, South Australia
1930	Frank Eyre	Australia	Metropolitan Golf Club	Melbourne, Victoria
1931	Ivo Whitton (amateur)	Australia	The Australian Golf Club	Sydney, New South Wales
1932	Mick Ryan (amateur)	Australia	Royal Adelaide Golf Club	Adelaide, South Australia
1933	Lou Kelly	Australia	Royal Melbourne Golf Club	Melbourne, Victoria
1934	Billy Bolger	Australia	Royal Sydney Golf Club	Sydney, New South Wales
1935	Fergus McMahon	Australia	Royal Adelaide Golf Club	Adelaide, South Australia
1936	Gene Sarazen	United States	Metropolitan Golf Club	Melbourne, Victoria
1937	George Naismith	Australia	The Australian Golf Club	Sydney, New South Wales

1938	Jim Ferrier (amateur)	Australia	Royal Adelaide Golf Club	Adelaide, South Australia
1939	Jim Ferrier (amateur)	Australia	Royal Melbourne Golf Club	Melbourne, Victoria
1946	Ossie Pickworth	Australia	Royal Sydney Golf Club	Sydney, New South Wales
1947	Ossie Pickworth	Australia	Royal Queensland Golf Club	Brisbane, Queensland
1948	Ossie Pickworth	Australia	Kingston Heath Golf Club	Melbourne, Victoria
1949	Eric Cremin	Australia	The Australian Golf Club	Sydney, New South Wales
1950	Norman Von Nida	Australia	Kooyonga Golf Club	Adelaide, South Australia
1951	Peter Thomson	Australia	Metropolitan Golf Club	Melbourne, Victoria
1952	Norman Von Nida	Australia	Lake Karrinyup Country Club	Perth, Western Australia
1953	Norman Von Nida	Australia	Royal Melbourne Golf Club	Melbourne, Victoria
1954	Ossie Pickworth	Australia	Kooyonga Golf Club	Adelaide, South Australia
1955	Bobby Locke	South Africa	Gailes Golf Club	Brisbane, Queensland
1956	Bruce Crampton	Australia	Royal Sydney Golf Club	Sydney, New South Wales
1957	Frank Phillips	Australia	Kingston Heath Golf Club	Melbourne, Victoria
1958	Gary Player	South Africa	Kooyonga Golf Club	Adelaide, South Australia
1959	Kel Nagle	Australia	The Australian Golf Club	Sydney, New South Wales

1960	Bruce Devlin (amateur)	Australia	Lake Karrinyup Country Club	Perth, Western Australia
1961	Frank Phillips	Australia	Victoria Golf Club	Melbourne, Victoria
1962	Gary Player	South Africa	Royal Adelaide Golf Club	Adelaide, South Australia
1963	Gary Player	South Africa	Royal Melbourne Golf Club	Melbourne, Victoria
1964	Jack Nicklaus	United States	The Lakes Golf Club	Sydney, New South Wales
1965	Gary Player	South Africa	Kooyonga Golf Club	Adelaide, South Australia
1966	Arnold Palmer	United States	Royal Queensland Golf Club	Brisbane, Queensland
1967	Peter Thomson	Australia	Commonwealth Golf Club	Melbourne, Victoria
1968	Jack Nicklaus	United States	Lake Karrinyup Country Club	Perth, Western Australia
1969	Gary Player	South Africa	Royal Sydney Golf Club	Sydney, New South Wales
1970	Gary Player	South Africa	Kingston Heath Golf Club	Melbourne, Victoria
1971	Jack Nicklaus	United States	Royal Hobart Golf Club	Hobart, Tasmania
1972	Peter Thomson	Australia	Kooyonga Golf Club	Adelaide, South Australia
1973	J. C. Snead	United States	Royal Queensland Golf Club	Brisbane, Queensland
1974	Gary Player	South Africa	Victoria Golf Club	Melbourne, Victoria

1975	Jack Nicklaus	United States	The Australian Golf Club	Sydney, New South Wales
1976	Jack Nicklaus	United States	The Australian Golf Club	Sydney, New South Wales
1977	David Graham	Australia	The Australian Golf Club	Sydney, New South Wales
1978	Jack Nicklaus	United States	The Australian Golf Club	Sydney, New South Wales
1979	Jack Newton	Australia	Metropolitan Golf Club	Melbourne, Victoria
1980	Greg Norman	Australia	The Lakes Golf Club	Sydney, New South Wales
1981	Bill Rogers	United States	Victoria Golf Club	Melbourne, Victoria
1982	Bob Shearer	Australia	The Australian Golf Club	Sydney, New South Wales
1983	Peter Fowler	Australia	Kingston Heath Golf Club	Melbourne, Victoria
1984	Tom Watson	United States	Royal Melbourne Golf Club	Melbourne, Victoria
1985	Greg Norman	Australia	Royal Melbourne Golf Club	Melbourne, Victoria
1986	Rodger Davis	Australia	Metropolitan Golf Club	Melbourne, Victoria
1987	Greg Norman	Australia	Royal Melbourne Golf Club	Melbourne, Victoria
1988	Mark Calcavecchia	United States	Royal Sydney Golf Club	Sydney, New South Wales
1989	Peter Senior	Australia	Kingston Heath Golf Club	Melbourne, Victoria
1990	John Morse	United States	The Australian Golf Club	Sydney, New South Wales
1991	Wayne Riley	Australia	Royal Melbourne Golf Club	Melbourne, Victoria
1992	Steve Elkington	Australia	The Lakes Golf Club	Sydney, New South Wales

1993	Brad Faxon	United States	Metropolitan Golf Club	Melbourne, Victoria
1994	Robert Allenby	Australia	Royal Sydney Golf Club	Sydney, New South Wales
1995	Greg Norman	Australia	Kingston Heath Golf Club	Melbourne, Victoria
1996	Greg Norman	Australia	The Australian Golf Club	Sydney, New South Wales
1997	Lee Westwood	England	Metropolitan Golf Club	Melbourne, Victoria
1998	Greg Chalmers	Australia	Royal Adelaide Golf Club	Adelaide, South Australia
1999	Aaron Baddeley (amateur)	Australia	Royal Sydney Golf Club	Sydney, New South Wales
2000	Aaron Baddeley	Australia	Kingston Heath Golf Club	Melbourne, Victoria
2001	Stuart Appleby	Australia	The Grand Golf Club	Gilston, Queensland
2002	Stephen Allan	Australia	Victoria Golf Club	Melbourne, Victoria
2003	Peter Lonard	Australia	Moonah Links	Mornington Peninsula, Victoria
2004	Peter Lonard	Australia	The Australian Golf Club	Sydney, New South Wales
2005	Robert Allenby	Australia	Moonah Links	Mornington Peninsula, Victoria
2006	John Senden	Australia	Royal Sydney Golf Club	Sydney, New South Wales
2007	Craig Parry	Australia	The Australian Golf Club	Sydney, New South Wales
2008	Tim Clark	South Africa	Royal Sydney Golf Club	Sydney, New South Wales

Canadian Open

1904	John Oke	England	Royal Montreal Golf Club	Montreal, Québec
1905	George Cumming	Scotland	Toronto Golf Club	Toronto, Ontario
1906	Charles Murray	Canada	Royal Ottawa Golf Club	Gatineau, Québec
1907	Percy Barrett	England	Lambton Golf Club	Toronto, Ontario
1908	Albert Murray	Canada	Royal Montreal Golf Club	Montreal, Québec
1909	Karl Keffer	Canada	Toronto Golf Club	Toronto, Ontario
1910	Daniel Kenny	United States	Lambton Golf Club	Toronto, Ontario
1911	Charles Murray	Canada	Royal Ottawa Golf Club	Gatineau, Québec
1912	George Sargent	England	Rosedale Golf Club	Toronto, Ontario
1913	Albert Murray	Canada	Royal Montreal Golf Club	Montreal, Québec
1914	Karl Keffer	Canada	Toronto Golf Club	Mississauga, Ontario
1919	James Douglas Edgar	England	Hamilton Golf and Country Club	Ancaster, Ontario
1920	James Douglas Edgar	England	Rivermead Golf Club	Aylmer, Québec
1921	William Trovinger	United States	Toronto Golf Club	Mississauga, Ontario
1922	Al Watrous	United States	Mt. Bruno Golf Club	Mt. Bruno, Québec
1923	Clarence Hackney	Scotland	Lakeview Golf Club	Mississauga, Ontario
1924	Leo Diegel	United States	Mt. Bruno Golf Club	Mt. Bruno, Quebec
1925	Leo Diegel	United States	Lambton Golf Club	Toronto, Ontario
1926	MacDonald Smith	Scotland	Royal Montreal Golf Club	Montreal, Québec

1927	Tommy Armour	Scotland / United States	Toronto Golf Club	Mississauga, Ontario
1928	Leo Diegel	United States	Rosedale Golf Club	Toronto, Ontario
1929	Leo Diegel	United States	Kanawaki Golf Club	Kahnawake, Québec
1930	Tommy Armour	Scotland / United States	Hamilton Golf and Country Club	Ancaster, Ontario
1931	Walter Hagen	United States	Mississauga Golf & Country Club	Mississauga, Ontario
1932	Harry Cooper	England	Ottawa Hunt	Ottawa, Ontario
1933	Joe Kirkwood Sr.	Australia	Royal York Golf Club	Toronto, Ontario
1934	Tommy Armour	Scotland / United States	Lakeview Golf Club	Toronto, Ontario
1935	Gene Kunes	United States	Summerlea Golf & Country Club	Montréal, Québec
1936	Lawson Little	United States	St. Andrews Golf Club	Toronto, Ontario
1937	Harry Cooper	England	St. Andrews Golf Club	Toronto, Ontario
1938	Sam Snead	United States	Mississauga Golf & Country Club	Mississauga, Ontario
1939	Harold "Jug" McSpaden	United States	Riverside Country Club	Saint John, New Brunswick

1940	Sam Snead	United States	Scarboro Golf & Country Club	Scarborough, Ontario
1941	Sam Snead	United States	Lambton Golf Club	Toronto, Ontario
1942	Craig Wood	United States	Mississauga Golf & Country Club	Mississauga, Ontario
1945	Byron Nelson	United States	Thornhill Golf Club	Thornhill, Ontario
1946	George Fazio	United States	Beaconsfield Golf Club	Pointe-Claire, Québec
1947	Bobby Locke	South Africa	Scarboro Golf & Country Club	Scarborough, Ontario
1948	Charles Congdon	United States	Shaughnessy Heights Golf Club	Vancouver, British Columbia
1949	Dutch Harrison	United States	St. George's Golf and Country Club	Toronto, Ontario
1950	Jim Ferrier	Australia	Royal Montreal Golf Club	Montreal, Québec
1951	Jim Ferrier	Australia	Mississauga Golf & Country Club	Mississauga, Ontario
1952	Johnny Palmer	United States	St. Charles Country Club	Winnipeg, Manitoba
1953	Dave Douglas	United States	Scarboro Golf & Country Club	Scarborough, Ontario
1954	Pat Fletcher	Canada	Point Grey Golf Club	Vancouver, British Columbia
1955	Arnold Palmer	United States	Weston Golf and Country Club	Toronto, Ontario

1956	Doug Sanders (amateur)	United States	Beaconsfield Golf Club	Pointe-Claire, Québec
1957	George Bayer	United States	Westmount Golf & Country Club	Kitchener, Ontario
1958	Wes Ellis	United States	Mayfair Golf & Country Club	Edmonton, Alberta
1959	Doug Ford	United States	Islesmere Golf & Country Club	Montreal, Québec
1960	Art Wall Jr.	United States	St. George's Golf and Country Club	Toronto, Ontario
1961	Jacky Cupit	United States	Niakwa Country Club	Winnipeg, Manitoba
1962	Ted Kroll	United States	Le Club Laval-sur-le-Lac	Laval-sur-le-Lac, Québec
1963	Doug Ford	United States	Scarboro Golf & Country Club	Scarborough, Ontario
1964	Kel Nagle	Australia	Pinegrove Country Club	St. Luc, Québec
1965	Gene Littler	United States	Mississaugua Golf & Country Club	Mississauga, Ontario
1966	Don Massengale	United States	Shaughnessy Golf & Country Club	Vancouver, British Columbia
1967	Billy Casper	United States	Montreal Municipal Golf Course	Montreal, Québec
1968	Bob Charles	New Zealand	St. George's Golf and Country Club	Toronto, Ontario

1969	Tommy Aaron	United States	Pine Grove Golf & Country Club	St. Luc, Quebec
1970	Kermit Zarley	United States	London Hunt & Country Club	London, Ontario
1971	Lee Trevino	United States	Richelieu Valley Golf & Country Club	Ste. Julie de Vercheres, Quebec
1972	Gay Brewer	United States	Cherry Hill Club	Ridgeway, Ontario
1973	Tom Weiskopf	United States	Richelieu Valley Golf & Country Club	Ste. Julie de Vercheres, Quebec
1974	Bobby Nichols	United States	Mississaugua Golf & Country Club	Mississauga, Ontario
1975	Tom Weiskopf	United States	Royal Montreal Golf Club	Ile Bizard, Quebec
1976	Jerry Pate	United States	Essex Golf & Country Club	Windsor, Ontario
1977	Lee Trevino	United States	Glen Abbey Golf Course	Oakville, Ontario
1978	Bruce Lietzke	United States	Glen Abbey Golf Course	Oakville, Ontario
1979	Lee Trevino	United States	Glen Abbey Golf Course	Oakville, Ontario
1980	Bob Gilder	United States	Royal Montreal Golf Club	Ile Bizard, Quebec
1981	Peter Oosterhuis	England	Glen Abbey Golf Course	Oakville, Ontario
1982	Bruce Lietzke	United States	Glen Abbey Golf Course	Oakville, Ontario
1983	John Cook	United States	Glen Abbey Golf Course	Oakville, Ontario
1984	Greg Norman	Australia	Glen Abbey Golf Course	Oakville, Ontario
1985	Curtis Strange	United States	Glen Abbey Golf Course	Oakville, Ontario

1986	Bob Murphy	United States	Glen Abbey Golf Course	Oakville, Ontario
1987	Curtis Strange	United States	Glen Abbey Golf Course	Oakville, Ontario
1988	Ken Green	United States	Glen Abbey Golf Course	Oakville, Ontario
1989	Steve Jones	United States	Glen Abbey Golf Course	Oakville, Ontario
1990	Wayne Levi	United States	Glen Abbey Golf Course	Oakville, Ontario
1991	Nick Price	Zimbabwe	Glen Abbey Golf Course	Oakville, Ontario
1992	Greg Norman	Australia	Glen Abbey Golf Course	Oakville, Ontario
1993	David Frost	South Africa	Glen Abbey Golf Course	Oakville, Ontario
1994	Nick Price	Zimbabwe	Glen Abbey Golf Course	Oakville, Ontario
1995	Mark O'Meara	United States	Glen Abbey Golf Course	Oakville, Ontario
1996	Dudley Hart	United States	Glen Abbey Golf Course	Oakville, Ontario
1997	Steve Jones	United States	Royal Montreal Golf Club	Ile Bizard, Québec
1998	Billy Andrade	United States	Glen Abbey Golf Course	Oakville, Ontario
1999	Hal Sutton	United States	Glen Abbey Golf Course	Oakville, Ontario
2000	Tiger Woods	United States	Glen Abbey Golf Course	Oakville, Ontario
2001	Scott Verplank	United States	Royal Montreal Golf Club	Ile Bizard, Québec
2002	John Rollins	United States	Angus Glen Golf Club, South Course	Markham, Ontario
2003	Bob Tway	United States	Hamilton Golf and Country Club	Ancaster, Ontario
2004	Vijay Singh	Fiji	Glen Abbey Golf Course	Oakville, Ontario
2005	Mark Calcavecchia	United States	Shaughnessy Golf & Country Club	Vancouver, British Columbia

2006	Jim Furyk	United States	Hamilton Golf and Country Club	Ancaster, Ontario
2007	Jim Furyk	United States	Angus Glen Golf Club, North Course	Markham, Ontario
2008	Chez Reavie	United States	Glen Abbey Golf Course	Oakville, Ontario
2009	Nathan Green	Australia	Glen Abbey Golf Course	Oakville, Ontario

South African Open

1903	Laurie Waters	South Africa	Port Elizabeth Golf Club	Port Elizabeth, South Africa
1904	Laurie Waters	South Africa	Johannesburg Golf Club	Johannesburg, South Africa
1905	A. G. Gray	South Africa	Bloemfontein Golf Club	Bloemfontein, South Africa
1906	A. G. Gray	South Africa	East London Golf Club	London, England
1907	Laurie Waters	South Africa	Kimberley Golf Club	Kimberley, British Columbia
1908	George Fotheringham	South Africa	Port Elizabeth Golf Club	Port Elizabeth, South Africa
1909	John Fotheringham	South Africa	Potchefstroom Golf Club	Potchefstroom Northern Province, South Africa
1910	George Fotheringham	South Africa	Royal Cape Golf Club	Cape Town, South Africa

1911	George Fotheringham	South Africa	Durban Country Club	Durban, KwaZulu-Natal, South Africa
1912	George Fotheringham	South Africa	Potchefstroom Golf Club	Potchefstroom, Northern Province, South Africa
1913	James Prentice (amateur)	South Africa	Kimberley Golf Club	Kimberley, British Columbia
1914	George Fotheringham	South Africa	Royal Cape Golf Club	Cape Town, South Africa
1919	W. H. Horne	South Africa	Durban Country Club	Durban, KwaZulu-Natal, South Africa
1920	Laurie Waters	South Africa	Johannesburg Golf Club	Johannesburg, South Africa
1921	Jock Brews	South Africa	Port Elizabeth Golf Club	Port Elizabeth, South Africa
1922	Fred Jangle	South Africa	Royal Port Alfred Golf Club	Port Alfred, Eastern Cape, South Africa
1923	Jock Brews	South Africa	Royal Cape Golf Club	Cape Town, South Africa
1924	Bertie Elkin	South Africa	Durban Country Club	Durban, KwaZulu-Natal, South Africa
1925	Sid Brews	South Africa	Johannesburg Golf Club	Johannesburg, South Africa
1926	Jock Brews	South Africa	Port Elizabeth Golf Club	Port Elizabeth, South Africa

1927	Sid Brews	South Africa	Maccauvlei Golf Club	Vereeniging, Gauteng, South Africa
1928	Jock Brews	South Africa	Durban Country Club	Durban, KwaZulu-Natal, South Africa
1929	Archie Tosh	South Africa	Royal Cape Golf Club	Cape Town, South Africa
1930	Sid Brews	South Africa	East London Golf Club	London, England
1931	Sid Brews	South Africa	Port Elizabeth Golf Club	Port Elizabeth, South Africa
1932	Charles McIlvenny	South Africa	Mowbray Golf Club	Cape Town, South Africa
1933	Sid Brews	South Africa	Maccauvlei Golf Club	Vereeniging, Gauteng, South Africa
1934	Sid Brews	South Africa	Humewood Golf Club	Port Elizabeth, South Africa
1935	Bobby Locke (amateur)	South Africa	Parkview Golf Club	Eagan, Minnesota
1936	Clarence Olander	South Africa	Royal Cape Golf Club	Cape Town, South Africa
1937	Bobby Locke (amateur)	South Africa	East London Golf Club	London, England
1938	Bobby Locke	South Africa	Maccauvlei Golf Club	Vereeniging, Gauteng, South Africa
1939	Bobby Locke	South Africa	Durban Country Club	Durban, KwaZulu-Natal, South Africa
1940	Bobby Locke	South Africa	Humewood Golf Club	Port Elizabeth, South Africa
1946	Bobby Locke	South Africa	Royal Johannesburg Golf Club	Johannesburg, South Africa

1947	Ronnie Glennie (amateur)	South Africa	Mowbray Golf Club	Cape Town, South Africa
1948	Mickey Janks (amateur)	South Africa	East London Golf Club	London, England
1949	Sid Brews	South Africa	Maccauvlei Golf Club	Vereeniging, Gauteng, South Africa
1950	Bobby Locke	South Africa	Durban Country Club	Durban, KwaZulu-Natal, South Africa
1951	Bobby Locke	South Africa	Houghton le Spring Golf Club	Houghton, Tyne and Wear, England
1952	Sid Brews	South Africa	Humewood Golf Club	Port Elizabeth, South Africa
1953	Jimmy Boyd (amateur)	South Africa	Royal Cape Golf Club	Cape Town, South Africa
1954	Reg Taylor (amateur)	South Africa	East London Golf Club	London, England
1955	Bobby Locke	South Africa	Zwartkop Country Club	Zwartkop, Gauteng, South Africa
1956	Gary Player	South Africa	Durban Country Club	Durban, KwaZulu-Natal, South Africa
1957	Harold Henning	South Africa	Humewood Golf Club	Port Elizabeth, South Africa
1958	Arthur Stewart (amateur)	South Africa	Bloemfontein Golf Club	Bloemfontein, South Africa
1959	Denis Hutchinson (amateur)	South Africa	Royal Johannesburg Golf Club	Johannesburg, South Africa
1960	Gary Player	South Africa	Mowbray Golf Club	Cape Town, South Africa

1961	Retief Waltman	South Africa	East London Golf Club	London, England
1962	Harold Henning	South Africa	Houghton le Spring Golf Club	Houghton, Tyne and Wear, England
1963 (spring)	Retief Waltman	South Africa	Durban Country Club	Durban, KwaZulu-Natal, South Africa
1963 (fall)	Allan Henning	South Africa	Bloemfontein Golf Club	Bloemfontein, South Africa
1965	Gary Player	South Africa	Royal Cape Golf Club	Cape Town, South Africa
1966	Gary Player	South Africa	Houghton le Spring Golf Club	Houghton, Tyne and Wear, England
1967	Gary Player	South Africa	East London Golf Club	London, England
1968	Gary Player	South Africa	Houghton le Spring Golf Club	Houghton, Tyne and Wear, England
1969	Gary Player	South Africa	Durban Country Club	Durban, KwaZulu-Natal, South Africa
1970	Tommy Horton	England	Royal Durban	Durban, South Africa
1971	Simon Hobday	South Africa	Mowbray Golf Club	Cape Town, South Africa
1972	Gary Player	South Africa	Royal Johannesburg Golf Club	Johannesburg, South Africa
1973	Bob Charles	New Zealand	Durban Country Club	Durban, KwaZulu-Natal, South Africa
1974	Bobby Cole	South Africa	Royal Johannesburg Golf Club	Johannesburg, South Africa

1975	Gary Player	South Africa	Mowbray Golf Club	Cape Town, South Africa
1976	Gary Player	South Africa	Durban Country Club	Durban, KwaZulu-Natal, South Africa
1976	Dale Hayes	South Africa	Houghton le Spring Golf Club	Houghton, Tyne and Wear, England
1977	Gary Player	South Africa	Royal Johannesburg Golf Club	Johannesburg, South Africa
1978	Hugh Baiocchi	South Africa	Mowbray Golf Club	Cape Town, South Africa
1979	Gary Player	South Africa	Houghton le Spring Golf Club	Houghton, Tyne and Wear, England
1980	Bobby Cole	South Africa	Durban Country Club	Durban, KwaZulu-Natal, South Africa
1981	Gary Player	South Africa	Royal Johannesburg Golf Club	Johannesburg, South Africa
1982	No tournament due to two events in 1976			
1983	Charlie Bolling	United States	Royal Cape Golf Club	Cape Town, South Africa
1984	Tony Johnstone	Zimbabwe	Houghton le Spring Golf Club	Houghton, Tyne and Wear, England
1985	Gavan Levenson	South Africa	Royal Durban Golf Club	Durban, South Africa
1986	David Frost	South Africa	Royal Johannesburg Golf Club	Johannesburg, South Africa

1987	Mark McNulty	Zimbabwe	Mowbray Golf Club	Cape Town, South Africa
1988	Wayne Westner	South Africa	Durban Country Club	Durban, KwaZulu-Natal, South Africa
1989	Fred Wadsworth	United States	Glendower	Dowerglen, Gauteng, South Africa
1990	Trevor Dodds	Namibia	Royal Cape Golf Club	Cape Town, South Africa
1991	Wayne Westner	South Africa	Durban Country Club	Durban, KwaZulu-Natal, South Africa
1992	Ernie Els	South Africa	Houghton le Spring Golf Club	Houghton, Tyne and Wear, England
1993 (spring)	Clinton Whitelaw	South Africa	Glendower	Dowerglen, Gauteng, South Africa
1993 (winter)	Tony Johnstone	Zimbabwe	Durban Country Club	Durban, KwaZulu-Natal, South Africa
1994	No tournament due to two events in 1993			
1995	Retief Goosen	South Africa	Randpark Golf Club	Johannesburg, South Africa
1996	Ernie Els	South Africa	Royal Cape Golf Club	Cape Town, South Africa
1997	Vijay Singh	Fiji	Glendower	Dowerglen, Gauteng, South Africa
1998	Ernie Els	South Africa	Durban Country Club	Durban, KwaZulu-Natal, South Africa

1999	David Frost	South Africa	Stellenbosch Golf Club	Cape Town, South Africa
2000	Mathias Grönberg	Sweden	Randpark Golf Club	Johannesburg, South Africa
2001	Mark McNulty	Zimbabwe	East London Golf Club	East London, East Cape, South Africa
2002	Tim Clark	South Africa	Durban Country Club	Durban, KwaZulu-Natal, South Africa
2003	Trevor Immelman	South Africa	Erinvale Golf Club	Somerset West, Western Cape, South Africa
2004	Trevor Immelman	South Africa	Erinvale Golf Club	Somerset West, Western Cape, South Africa
2005 (spring)	Tim Clark	South Africa	Durban Country Club	Durban, KwaZulu-Natal, South Africa
2005 (winter)	Retief Goosen	South Africa	The Links, Fancourt	Blanco, George, South Africa
2006	Ernie Els	South Africa	Humewood Golf Club	Port Elizabeth, South Africa
2007	James Kingston	South Africa	Pearl Valley Golf Estates	Franschooek, Cape Winelands, South Africa
2008	Richard Sterne	South Africa	Pearl Valley Golf Estates	Franschooek, Cape Winelands, South Africa

Western Open

1899	Willie Smith	United States	Glen View Club	Golf, Illinois
1901	Laurie Auchterlonie	Scotland	Midlothian Country Club	Midlothian, Illinois
1902	Willie Anderson	United States	Euclid Club	Cleveland Heights, Ohio
1903	Alex Smith	United States	Milwaukee Country Club	River Hills, Wisconsin
1904	Willie Anderson	United States	Kent Country Club	Grand Rapids, Michigan
1905	Arthur Smith	United States	Cincinnati Golf Club	Cincinnati, Ohio
1906	Alex Smith	United States	Homewood Country Club	Flossmoor, Illinois
1907	Robert Simpson	United States	Hinsdale Golf Club	Clarendon Hills, Illinois
1908	Willie Anderson	United States	Normandie Golf Club	St. Louis, Missouri
1909	Willie Anderson	United States	Skokie Country Club	Glencoe, Illinois
1910	Chick Evans (amateur)	United States	Beverly Country Club	Chicago, Illinois
1911	Robert Simpson	United States	Kent Country Club	Grand Rapids, Michigan
1912	MacDonald Smith	United States	Idlewild Country Club	Flossmoor, Illinois
1913	John McDermott	United States	Memphis Country Club	Memphis, Tennessee
1914	Jim Barnes	United States	Interlachen Country Club	Edina, Minnesota
1915	Tom McNamara	United States	Glen Oak Country Club	Glen Ellyn, Illinois
1916	Walter Hagen	United States	Blue Mound Golf & Country Club	Milwaukee, Wisconsin
1917	Jim Barnes	United States	Westmoreland Country Club	Wilmette, Illinois
1919	Jim Barnes	United States	Mayfield Country Club	Lyndhurst, Ohio
1920	Jock Hutchison	United States	Olympia Fields Country Club, South Course	Olympia Fields, Illinois
1921	Walter Hagen	United States	Oakwood Club	Cleveland Heights, Ohio

1922	Mike Brady	United States	Oakland Hills Country Club	Bloomfield Hills, Michigan
1923	Jock Hutchison	United States	Colonial Country Club	Cordova, Tennessee
1924	Bill Mehlhorn	United States	Calumet Country Club	Homewood, Illinois
1925	MacDonald Smith	United States	Youngstown Country Club	Youngstown, Ohio
1926	Walter Hagen	United States	Highland Golf & Country Club	Indianapolis, Indiana
1927	Walter Hagen	United States	Olympia Fields Country Club, North Course	Olympia Fields, Illinois
1928	Abe Espinosa	United States	North Shore Country Club	Glenview, Illinois
1929	Tommy Armour	United States	Ozaukee Country Club	Mequon, Wisconsin
1930	Gene Sarazen	United States	Indianwood Golf & Country Club	Lake Orion, Michigan
1931	Ed Dudley	United States	Miami Valley Golf Club	Dayton, Ohio
1932	Walter Hagen	United States	Canterbury Golf Club	Beachwood, Ohio
1933	MacDonald Smith	United States	Olympia Fields Country Club, North Course	Olympia Fields, Illinois
1934	Harry Cooper	United States	Country Club of Peoria	Peoria Heights, Illinois
1935	Johnny Revolta	United States	South Bend Country Club	South Bend, Indiana
1936	Ralph Guldahl	United States	Davenport Country Club	Pleasant Valley, Iowa
1937	Ralph Guldahl	United States	Canterbury Golf Club	Beachwood, Ohio
1938	Ralph Guldahl	United States	Westwood Country Club	St. Louis, Missouri
1939	Byron Nelson	United States	Medinah Country Club	Medinah, Illinois
1940	Jimmy Demaret	United States	River Oaks Country Club	Houston, Texas

1941	Ed Oliver	United States	Phoenix Golf Club	Phoenix, Arizona
1942	Herman Barron	United States	Phoenix Golf Club	Phoenix, Arizona
1946	Ben Hogan	United States	Sunset Country Club	St. Louis, Missouri
1947	Johnny Palmer	United States	Salt Lake City Country Club	Salt Lake City, Utah
1948	Ben Hogan	United States	Brookfield Country Club	Clarence, New York
1949	Sam Snead	United States	Keller Golf Course	Saint Paul, Minnesota
1950	Sam Snead	United States	Brentwood Country Club	Los Angeles, California
1951	Marty Furgol	United States	Davenport Country Club	Pleasant Valley, Iowa
1952	Lloyd Mangrum	United States	Westwood Country Club	St. Louis, Missouri
1953	Dutch Harrison	United States	Bellerive Country Club	St. Louis, Missouri
1954	Lloyd Mangrum	United States	Kenwood Country Club	Cincinnati, Ohio
1955	Cary Middlecoff	United States	Portland Golf Club	Portland, Oregon
1956	Mike Fetchick	United States	Presidio Golf Club	San Francisco, California
1957	Doug Ford	United States	Plum Hollow Country Club	Southfield, Michigan
1958	Doug Sanders	United States	Red Run Golf Club	Royal Oak, Michigan
1959	Mike Souchak	United States	Pittsburgh Field Club	O'Hara Township, Pennsylvania
1960	Stan Leonard	Canada	Western Golf & Country Club	Redford, Michigan
1961	Arnold Palmer	United States	Blythefield Country Club	Belmont, Michigan
1962	Jacky Cupit	United States	Medinah Country Club	Medinah, Illinois
1963	Arnold Palmer	United States	Beverly Country Club	Chicago, Illinois
1964	Chi Chi Rodriguez	Puerto Rico	Tam O'Shanter Country Club	Niles, Illinois
1965	Billy Casper	United States	Tam O'Shanter Country Club	Niles, Illinois

1966	Billy Casper	United States	Medinah Country Club	Medinah, Illinois
1967	Jack Nicklaus	United States	Beverly Country Club	Chicago, Illinois
1968	Jack Nicklaus	United States	Olympia Fields Country Club, North Course	Olympia Fields, Illinois
1969	Billy Casper	United States	Midlothian Country Club	Midlothian, Illinois
1970	Hugh Royer Jr.	United States	Beverly Country Club	Chicago, Illinois
1971	Bruce Crampton	Australia	Olympia Fields Country Club, North Course	Olympia Fields, Illinois
1972	Jim Jamieson	United States	Sunset Ridge Country Club	Northfield, Illinois
1973	Billy Casper	United States	Midlothian Country Club	Midlothian, Illinois
1974	Tom Watson	United States	Butler National Golf Club	Oak Brook, Illinois
1975	Hale Irwin	United States	Butler National Golf Club	Oak Brook, Illinois
1976	Al Geiberger	United States	Butler National Golf Club	Oak Brook, Illinois
1977	Tom Watson	United States	Butler National Golf Club	Oak Brook, Illinois
1978	Andy Bean	United States	Butler National Golf Club	Oak Brook, Illinois
1979	Larry Nelson	United States	Butler National Golf Club	Oak Brook, Illinois
1980	Scott Simpson	United States	Butler National Golf Club	Oak Brook, Illinois
1981	Ed Fiori	United States	Butler National Golf Club	Oak Brook, Illinois
1982	Tom Weiskopf	United States	Butler National Golf Club	Oak Brook, Illinois
1983	Mark McCumber	United States	Butler National Golf Club	Oak Brook, Illinois
1984	Tom Watson	United States	Butler National Golf Club	Oak Brook, Illinois
1985	Scott Verplank (amateur)	United States	Butler National Golf Club	Oak Brook, Illinois
1986	Tom Kite	United States	Butler National Golf Club	Oak Brook, Illinois

1987	D. A. Weibring	United States	Butler National Golf Club	Oak Brook, Illinois
1988	Jim Benepe	United States	Butler National Golf Club	Oak Brook, Illinois
1989	Mark McCumber	United States	Butler National Golf Club	Oak Brook, Illinois
1990	Wayne Levi	United States	Butler National Golf Club	Oak Brook, Illinois
1991	Russ Cochran	United States	Cog Hill Golf & Country Club, #4	Lemont, Illinois
1992	Ben Crenshaw	United States	Cog Hill Golf & Country Club, #4	Lemont, Illinois
1993	Nick Price	Zimbabwe	Cog Hill Golf & Country Club, #4	Lemont, Illinois
1994	Nick Price	Zimbabwe	Cog Hill Golf & Country Club, #4	Lemont, Illinois
1995	Billy Mayfair	United States	Cog Hill Golf & Country Club, #4	Lemont, Illinois
1996	Steve Stricker	United States	Cog Hill Golf & Country Club, #4	Lemont, Illinois
1997	Tiger Woods	United States	Cog Hill Golf & Country Club, #4	Lemont, Illinois
1998	Joe Durant	United States	Cog Hill Golf & Country Club, #4	Lemont, Illinois
1999	Tiger Woods	United States	Cog Hill Golf & Country Club, #4	Lemont, Illinois
2000	Robert Allenby	Australia	Cog Hill Golf & Country Club, #4	Lemont, Illinois

2001	Scott Hoch	United States	Cog Hill Golf & Country Club, #4	Lemont, Illinois
2002	Jerry Kelly	United States	Cog Hill Golf & Country Club, #4	Lemont, Illinois
2003	Tiger Woods	United States	Cog Hill Golf & Country Club, #4	Lemont, Illinois
2004	Stephen Ames	Trinidad / Canada	Cog Hill Golf & Country Club, #4	Lemont, Illinois
2005	Jim Furyk	United States	Cog Hill Golf & Country Club, #4	Lemont, Illinois
2006	Trevor Immelman	South Africa	Cog Hill Golf & Country Club, #4	Lemont, Illinois

French Open

1906	Arnaud Massy	France	La Boulie Golf Club	Ile-de-France
1907	Arnaud Massy	France	La Boulie Golf Club	Ile-de-France
1908	John Henry Taylor	England	La Boulie Golf Club	Ile-de-France
1909	John Henry Taylor	England	La Boulie Golf Club	Ile-de-France
1910	James Braid	Scotland	La Boulie Golf Club	Ile-de-France
1911	Arnaud Massy	France	La Boulie Golf Club	Ile-de-France
1912	Jean Gassiat	France	La Boulie Golf Club	Ile-de-France
1913	George Duncan	Scotland	Chantilly National Golf & Country Club	Centreville, Virginia

1914	James Douglas Edgar	England	Golf du Touquet	Côte d'Opale, Pas-de-Calais
1920	Walter Hagen	United States	La Boulie Golf Club	Ile-de-France
1921	Aubrey Boomer	England	Golf du Touquet	Côte d'Opale, Pas-de-Calais
1922	Aubrey Boomer	England	La Boulie Golf Club	Ile-de-France
1923	James Ockenden	England	Dieppe-Pourville Golf Club	Dieppe, Normandy
1924	Cyril Tolley (amateur)	England	La Boulie Golf Club	Ile-de-France
1925	Arnaud Massy	France	Chantilly Golf Club	Ile-de-France
1926	Aubrey Boomer	England	Golf de Saint-Cloud	Garches
1927	George Duncan	Scotland	Golf de Saint-Germain	Saint-German-en-Laye
1928	Cyril Tolley (amateur)	England	La Boulie Golf Club	Ile-de-France
1929	Aubrey Boomer	England	Golf Country Club de Fourqueux	Fourqueux
1930	Ernest Whitcombe	England	Dieppe-Pourville Golf Club	Dieppe, Normandy
1931	Aubrey Boomer	England	Deauville Golf Club	Deauville, Normandy
1932	Arthur Lacey	England	Golf de Saint-Cloud	Garches
1933	Bert Gadd	England	Chantilly Golf Club	Ile-de-France
1934	Sid Brews	South Africa	Dieppe-Pourville Golf Club	Dieppe, Normandy

1935	Sid Brews	South Africa	Golf du Touquet	Côte d'Opale, Pas-de-Calais
1936	Marcel Dallemagne	France	Golf de Saint-Germain	Saint-German-en-Laye
1937	Marcel Dallemagne	France	Golf de Saint-Cloud	Garches
1938	Marcel Dallemagne	France	Golf Country Club de Fourqueux	Fourqueux
1939	Martin Pose	Argentina	Golf du Touquet	Côte d'Opale, Pas-de-Calais
1946	Henry Cotton	England	Golf de Saint-Cloud	Garches
1947	Henry Cotton	England	Chantilly Golf Club	Ile-de-France
1948	Firmin Cavalo	France	Golf de Saint-Cloud	Garches, France
1949	Ugo Grappasonni	Italy	Golf de Saint-Germain	Saint-German-en-Laye
1950	Roberto De Vicenzo	Argentina	Chantilly Golf Club	Ile-de-France
1951	Hassan Hassanein	Egypt	Golf de Saint-Cloud	Garches
1952	Bobby Locke	South Africa	Golf de Saint-Germain	Saint-German-en-Laye
1953	Bobby Locke	South Africa	La Boulie Golf Club	Ile-de-France
1954	Flory Van Donck	Belgium	Golf de Saint-Cloud	Garches
1955	Byron Nelson	United States	La Boulie Golf Club	Ile-de-France
1956	Ángel Miguel	Spain	Deauville Golf Club	Deauville, Normandy
1957	Flory Van Donck	Belgium	Golf de Saint-Cloud	Garches

1958	Flory Van Donck	Belgium	Golf de Saint-Germain	Saint-German-en-Laye
1959	Dave Thomas	Wales	La Boulie Golf Club	Ile-de-France
1960	Roberto De Vicenzo	Argentina	Golf de Saint-Cloud	Garches
1961	Kel Nagle	Australia	La Boulie Golf Club	Ile-de-France
1962	Alan Murray	Australia	Golf de Saint-Germain	Saint-German-en-Laye
1963	Bruce Devlin	Australia	Golf de Saint-Cloud	Garches
1964	Roberto De Vicenzo	Argentina	Chantilly Golf Club	Ile-de-France
1965	Ramón Sota	Spain	Saint-Nom-la-Bretèche Golf Club	Saint-Nom-la-Bretèche
1966	Denis Hutchinson	South Africa	La Boulie Golf Club	Ile-de-France
1967	Bernard Hunt	England	Golf de Saint-Germain	Saint-German-en-Laye
1968	Peter Butler	England	Golf de Saint-Cloud	Garches
1969	Jean Garaïalde	France	Saint-Nom-la-Bretèche Golf Club	Saint-Nom-la-Bretèche
1970	David Graham	Australia	Golf de Chantaco	Biarritz
1971	Lu Liang-Huan	Chinese Taipei	Biarritz La Nivelle	Biarritz
1972	Barry Jaeckel	United States	Biarritz La Nivelle	Biarritz
1973	Peter Oosterhuis	England	La Boulie Golf Club	Ile-de-France
1974	Peter Oosterhuis	England	Chantilly Golf Club	Ile-de-France

1975	Brian Barnes	Scotland	La Boulie Golf Club	Ile-de-France
1976	Vincent Tshabalala	South Africa	Golf du Touquet	Côte d'Opale, Pas-de-Calais
1977	Seve Ballesteros	Spain	Golf du Touquet	Côte d'Opale, Pas-de-Calais
1978	Dale Hayes	South Africa	Golf International Barrière La Baule	La Baule-Escoublac, Loire-Atlantique
1979	Bernard Gallacher	Scotland	Golf Club Lyon	Villette d'Anthon, Lyon
1980	Greg Norman	Australia	Golf de Saint-Cloud	Garches
1981	Sandy Lyle	Scotland	Golf de Saint-Germain	Saint-German-en-Laye
1982	Seve Ballesteros	Spain	Saint-Nom-la-Bretèche Golf Club	Saint-Nom-la-Bretèche
1983	Nick Faldo	England	La Boulie Golf Club	Ile-de-France
1984	Bernhard Langer	Germany	Golf de Saint-Cloud	Garches
1985	Seve Ballesteros	Spain	Golf de Saint-Germain	Saint-German-en-Laye
1986	Seve Ballesteros	Spain	La Boulie Golf Club	Ile-de-France
1987	José Rivero	Spain	Golf de Saint-Cloud	Garches
1988	Nick Faldo	England	Chantilly Golf Club	Ile-de-France
1989	Nick Faldo	England	Chantilly Golf Club	Ile-de-France
1990	Philip Walton	Ireland	Chantilly Golf Club	Ile-de-France

1991	Eduardo Romero	Argentina	Le Golf National	Guyancourt
1992	Miguel Ángel Martín	Spain	Le Golf National	Guyancourt
1993	Costantino Rocca	Italy	Le Golf National	Guyancourt
1994	Mark Roe	England	Le Golf National	Guyancourt
1995	Paul Broadhurst	England	Le Golf National	Guyancourt
1996	Robert Allenby	Australia	Le Golf National	Guyancourt
1997	Retief Goosen	South Africa	Le Golf National	Guyancourt
1998	Sam Torrance	Scotland	Le Golf National	Guyancourt
1999	Retief Goosen	South Africa	Golf du Médoc Hôtel et Spa	Le Pian Médoc, Louens
2000	Colin Montgomerie	Scotland	Le Golf National	Guyancourt
2001	José María Olazábal	Spain	Golf Club Lyon	Villette d'Anthon, Lyon
2002	Malcolm MacKenzie	England	Le Golf National	Guyancourt
2003	Philip Golding	England	Le Golf National	Guyancourt
2004	Jean-François Remésy	France	Le Golf National	Guyancourt
2005	Jean-François Remésy	France	Le Golf National	Guyancourt
2006	John Bickerton	England	Le Golf National	Guyancourt
2007	Graeme Storm	England	Le Golf National	Guyancourt
2008	Pablo Larrazábal	Spain	Le Golf National	Guyancourt
2009	Martin Kaymer	Germany	Le Golf National	Guyancourt

North and South Open

1902	Alex Ross	United States	Pinehurst Resort, No. 2 Course	Pinehurst, North Carolina
1903	Donald Ross	United States	Pinehurst Resort, No. 2 Course	Pinehurst, North Carolina
1904	Alex Ross	United States	Pinehurst Resort, No. 2 Course	Pinehurst, North Carolina
1905	Donald Ross	United States	Pinehurst Resort, No. 2 Course	Pinehurst, North Carolina
1906	Donald Ross	United States	Pinehurst Resort, No. 2 Course	Pinehurst, North Carolina
1907	Alex Ross	United States	Pinehurst Resort, No. 2 Course	Pinehurst, North Carolina
1908	Alex Ross	United States	Pinehurst Resort, No. 2 Course	Pinehurst, North Carolina
1909	Fred McLeod	United States	Pinehurst Resort, No. 2 Course	Pinehurst, North Carolina
1910	Alex Ross	United States	Pinehurst Resort, No. 2 Course	Pinehurst, North Carolina
1911	Gil Nicholls	United States	Pinehurst Resort, No. 2 Course	Pinehurst, North Carolina
1912	Tom McNamara	United States	Pinehurst Resort, No. 2 Course	Pinehurst, North Carolina
1913	Tom McNamara	United States	Pinehurst Resort, No. 2 Course	Pinehurst, North Carolina
1914	Gil Nicholls	United States	Pinehurst Resort, No. 2 Course	Pinehurst, North Carolina
1915	Alex Ross	United States	Pinehurst Resort, No. 2 Course	Pinehurst, North Carolina
1916	Jim Barnes	United States	Pinehurst Resort, No. 2 Course	Pinehurst, North Carolina
1917	Mike Brady	United States	Pinehurst Resort, No. 2 Course	Pinehurst, North Carolina
1918	Walter Hagen	United States	Pinehurst Resort, No. 2 Course	Pinehurst, North Carolina
1919	Jim Barnes	United States	Pinehurst Resort, No. 2 Course	Pinehurst, North Carolina
1920	Fred McLeod	United States	Pinehurst Resort, No. 2 Course	Pinehurst, North Carolina
1921	Jock Hutchison	United States	Pinehurst Resort, No. 2 Course	Pinehurst, North Carolina
1922	Pat O'Hara	United States	Pinehurst Resort, No. 2 Course	Pinehurst, North Carolina
1923	Walter Hagen	United States	Pinehurst Resort, No. 2 Course	Pinehurst, North Carolina

1924	Walter Hagen	United States	Pinehurst Resort, No. 2 Course	Pinehurst, North Carolina
1925	MacDonald Smith	United States	Pinehurst Resort, No. 2 Course	Pinehurst, North Carolina
1926	Bobby Cruickshank	United States	Pinehurst Resort, No. 2 Course	Pinehurst, North Carolina
1927	Bobby Cruickshank	United States	Pinehurst Resort, No. 2 Course	Pinehurst, North Carolina
1928	Billy Burke	United States	Pinehurst Resort, No. 2 Course	Pinehurst, North Carolina
1929	Horton Smith	United States	Pinehurst Resort, No. 2 Course	Pinehurst, North Carolina
1930	Paul Runyan	United States	Pinehurst Resort, No. 2 Course	Pinehurst, North Carolina
1931	Wiffy Cox	United States	Pinehurst Resort, No. 2 Course	Pinehurst, North Carolina
1932	Johnny Golden	United States	Pinehurst Resort, No. 2 Course	Pinehurst, North Carolina
1933	Joe Kirkwood Sr.	United States	Pinehurst Resort, No. 2 Course	Pinehurst, North Carolina
1934	Henry Picard	United States	Pinehurst Resort, No. 2 Course	Pinehurst, North Carolina
1935	Paul Runyan	United States	Pinehurst Resort, No. 2 Course	Pinehurst, North Carolina
1936	Henry Picard	United States	Pinehurst Resort, No. 2 Course	Pinehurst, North Carolina
1937	Horton Smith	United States	Pinehurst Resort, No. 2 Course	Pinehurst, North Carolina
1938	Vic Ghezzi	United States	Pinehurst Resort, No. 2 Course	Pinehurst, North Carolina
1939	Byron Nelson	United States	Pinehurst Resort, No. 2 Course	Pinehurst, North Carolina
1940	Ben Hogan	United States	Pinehurst Resort, No. 2 Course	Pinehurst, North Carolina
1941	Sam Snead	United States	Pinehurst Resort, No. 2 Course	Pinehurst, North Carolina
1942	Ben Hogan	United States	Pinehurst Resort, No. 2 Course	Pinehurst, North Carolina
1943	Bobby Cruickshank	United States	Pinehurst Resort, No. 2 Course	Pinehurst, North Carolina
1944	Bob Hamilton	United States	Pinehurst Resort, No. 2 Course	Pinehurst, North Carolina
1945	Cary Middlecoff (amateur)	United States	Pinehurst Resort, No. 2 Course	Pinehurst, North Carolina
1946	Ben Hogan	United States	Pinehurst Resort, No. 2 Course	Pinehurst, North Carolina

1947	Jim Turnesa	United States	Pinehurst Resort, No. 2 Course	Pinehurst, North Carolina
1948	Toney Penna	United States	Pinehurst Resort, No. 2 Course	Pinehurst, North Carolina
1949	Sam Snead	United States	Pinehurst Resort, No. 2 Course	Pinehurst, North Carolina
1950	Sam Snead	United States	Pinehurst Resort, No. 2 Course	Pinehurst, North Carolina
1951	Tommy Bolt	United States	Pinehurst Resort, No. 2 Course	Pinehurst, North Carolina

Lancome Trophy (Trophée Lancôme) (France)

1970	Tony Jacklin	England	Saint-Nom-la-Bretèche Golf Club	Saint-Nom-la-Bretèche
1971	Arnold Palmer	United States	Saint-Nom-la-Bretèche Golf Club	Saint-Nom-la-Bretèche
1972	Tommy Aaron	United States	Saint-Nom-la-Bretèche Golf Club	Saint-Nom-la-Bretèche
1973	Johnny Miller	United States	Saint-Nom-la-Bretèche Golf Club	Saint-Nom-la-Bretèche
1974	Billy Casper	United States	Saint-Nom-la-Bretèche Golf Club	Saint-Nom-la-Bretèche
1975	Gary Player	South Africa	Saint-Nom-la-Bretèche Golf Club	Saint-Nom-la-Bretèche
1976	Seve Ballesteros	Spain	Saint-Nom-la-Bretèche Golf Club	Saint-Nom-la-Bretèche
1977	Graham Marsh	Australia	Saint-Nom-la-Bretèche Golf Club	Saint-Nom-la-Bretèche

1978	Lee Trevino	United States	Saint-Nom-la-Bretèche Golf Club	Saint-Nom-la-Bretèche
1979	Johnny Miller	United States	Saint-Nom-la-Bretèche Golf Club	Saint-Nom-la-Bretèche
1980	Lee Trevino	United States	Saint-Nom-la-Bretèche Golf Club	Saint-Nom-la-Bretèche
1981	David Graham	Australia	Saint-Nom-la-Bretèche Golf Club	Saint-Nom-la-Bretèche
1982	David Graham	Australia	Saint-Nom-la-Bretèche Golf Club	Saint-Nom-la-Bretèche
1983	Seve Ballesteros	Spain	Saint-Nom-la-Bretèche Golf Club	Saint-Nom-la-Bretèche
1984	Sandy Lyle	Scotland	Saint-Nom-la-Bretèche Golf Club	Saint-Nom-la-Bretèche
1985	Nick Price	Zimbabwe	Saint-Nom-la-Bretèche Golf Club	Saint-Nom-la-Bretèche
1986	Seve Ballesteros	Spain	Saint-Nom-la-Bretèche Golf Club	Saint-Nom-la-Bretèche
	Bernhard Langer	West Germany	Saint-Nom-la-Bretèche Golf Club	Saint-Nom-la-Bretèche
1987	Ian Woosnam	Wales	Saint-Nom-la-Bretèche Golf Club	Saint-Nom-la-Bretèche
1988	Seve Ballesteros	Spain	Saint-Nom-la-Bretèche Golf Club	Saint-Nom-la-Bretèche

1989	Eduardo Romero	Argentina	Saint-Nom-la-Bretèche Golf Club	Saint-Nom-la-Bretèche
1990	José María Olazábal	Spain	Saint-Nom-la-Bretèche Golf Club	Saint-Nom-la-Bretèche
1991	Frank Nobilo	New Zealand	Saint-Nom-la-Bretèche Golf Club	Saint-Nom-la-Bretèche
1992	Mark Roe	England	Saint-Nom-la-Bretèche Golf Club	Saint-Nom-la-Bretèche
1993	Ian Woosnam	Wales	Saint-Nom-la-Bretèche Golf Club	Saint-Nom-la-Bretèche
1994	Vijay Singh	Fiji	Saint-Nom-la-Bretèche Golf Club	Saint-Nom-la-Bretèche
1995	Colin Montgomerie	Scotland	Saint-Nom-la-Bretèche Golf Club	Saint-Nom-la-Bretèche
1996	Jesper Parnevik	Sweden	Saint-Nom-la-Bretèche Golf Club	Saint-Nom-la-Bretèche
1997	Mark O'Meara	United States	Saint-Nom-la-Bretèche Golf Club	Saint-Nom-la-Bretèche
1998	Miguel Ángel Jiménez	Spain	Saint-Nom-la-Bretèche Golf Club	Saint-Nom-la-Bretèche
1999	Pierre Fulke	Sweden	Saint-Nom-la-Bretèche Golf Club	Saint-Nom-la-Bretèche
2000	Retief Goosen	South Africa	Saint-Nom-la-Bretèche Golf Club	Saint-Nom-la-Bretèche

2001	Sergio García	Spain	Saint-Nom-la-Bretèche Golf Club	Saint-Nom-la-Bretèche
2002	Alex Čejka	Germany	Saint-Nom-la-Bretèche Golf Club	Saint-Nom-la-Bretèche
2003	Retief Goosen	South Africa	Saint-Nom-la-Bretèche Golf Club	Saint-Nom-la-Bretèche

World Match Play Championship

1964	Arnold Palmer	United States	Wentworth Club	Virginia Water, Surrey, England
1965	Gary Player	South Africa	Wentworth Club	Virginia Water, Surrey, England
1966	Gary Player	South Africa	Wentworth Club	Virginia Water, Surrey, England
1967	Arnold Palmer	United States	Wentworth Club	Virginia Water, Surrey, England
1968	Gary Player	South Africa	Wentworth Club	Virginia Water, Surrey, England
1969	Bob Charles	New Zealand	Wentworth Club	Virginia Water, Surrey, England
1970	Jack Nicklaus	United States	Wentworth Club	Virginia Water, Surrey, England
1971	Gary Player	South Africa	Wentworth Club	Virginia Water, Surrey, England
1972	Tom Weiskopf	United States	Wentworth Club	Virginia Water, Surrey, England
1973	Gary Player	South Africa	Wentworth Club	Virginia Water, Surrey, England
1974	Hale Irwin	United States	Wentworth Club	Virginia Water, Surrey, England
1975	Hale Irwin	United States	Wentworth Club	Virginia Water, Surrey, England
1976	David Graham	Australia	Wentworth Club	Virginia Water, Surrey, England
1977	Graham Marsh	Australia	Wentworth Club	Virginia Water, Surrey, England
1978	Isao Aoki	Japan	Wentworth Club	Virginia Water, Surrey, England

1979	Bill Rogers	United States	Wentworth Club	Virginia Water, Surrey, England
1980	Greg Norman	Australia	Wentworth Club	Virginia Water, Surrey, England
1981	Seve Ballesteros	Spain	Wentworth Club	Virginia Water, Surrey, England
1982	Seve Ballesteros	Spain	Wentworth Club	Virginia Water, Surrey, England
1983	Greg Norman	Australia	Wentworth Club	Virginia Water, Surrey, England
1984	Seve Ballesteros	Spain	Wentworth Club	Virginia Water, Surrey, England
1985	Seve Ballesteros	Spain	Wentworth Club	Virginia Water, Surrey, England
1986	Greg Norman	Australia	Wentworth Club	Virginia Water, Surrey, England
1987	Ian Woosnam	Wales	Wentworth Club	Virginia Water, Surrey, England
1988	Sandy Lyle	Scotland	Wentworth Club	Virginia Water, Surrey, England
1989	Nick Faldo	England	Wentworth Club	Virginia Water, Surrey, England
1990	Ian Woosnam	Wales	Wentworth Club	Virginia Water, Surrey, England
1991	Seve Ballesteros	Spain	Wentworth Club	Virginia Water, Surrey, England
1992	Nick Faldo	England	Wentworth Club	Virginia Water, Surrey, England
1993	Corey Pavin	United States	Wentworth Club	Virginia Water, Surrey, England
1994	Ernie Els	South Africa	Wentworth Club	Virginia Water, Surrey, England
1995	Ernie Els	South Africa	Wentworth Club	Virginia Water, Surrey, England
1996	Ernie Els	South Africa	Wentworth Club	Virginia Water, Surrey, England
1997	Vijay Singh	Fiji	Wentworth Club	Virginia Water, Surrey, England
1998	Mark O'Meara	United States	Wentworth Club	Virginia Water, Surrey, England
1999	Colin Montgomerie	Scotland	Wentworth Club	Virginia Water, Surrey, England
2000	Lee Westwood	England	Wentworth Club	Virginia Water, Surrey, England
2001	Ian Woosnam	Wales	Wentworth Club	Virginia Water, Surrey, England

2002	Ernie Els	South Africa	Wentworth Club	Virginia Water, Surrey, England
2003	Ernie Els	South Africa	Wentworth Club	Virginia Water, Surrey, England
2004	Ernie Els	South Africa	Wentworth Club	Virginia Water, Surrey, England
2005	Michael Campbell	New Zealand	Wentworth Club	Virginia Water, Surrey, England
2006	Paul Casey	England	Wentworth Club	Virginia Water, Surrey, England
2007	Ernie Els	South Africa	Wentworth Club	Virginia Water, Surrey, England
2008	No tournament			
2009	Ross Fisher	England	Finca Cortesín Golf Club	Casares, Spain

Belgian Open

1910	Arnaud Massy	France	Ravenstein, Royal Golf Club of Belgium	Tervuren
1911	Charles Mayo		Ravenstein, Royal Golf Club of Belgium	Tervuren
1912	George Duncan	Scotland	Ravenstein, Royal Golf Club of Belgium	Tervuren
1913	Tom Ball	England	Golf Club Lombardsijde	Lombardsijde
1914	Tom Ball	England	Royal Antwerp Golf Club	Antwerp
1920	Rowland Jones	England	Royal Zoute Golf Club	Knokke-Heist
1921	Eugène Lafitte	France	Ravenstein, Royal Golf Club of Belgium	Tervuren
1922	Aubrey Boomer	England	Ravenstein, Royal Golf Club of Belgium	Tervuren

1923	Percy Boomer	England	Ravenstein, Royal Golf Club of Belgium	Tervuren
1924	Walter Hagen	United States	Royal Zoute Golf Club	Knokke-Heist
1925	Eugène Lafitte	France	Royal Antwerp Golf Club	Antwerp
1926	Aubrey Boomer	England	Royal Zoute Golf Club	Knokke-Heist
1927	Marcel Dallemagne	France	Royal Zoute Golf Club	Knokke-Heist
1928	Albert Tingey Jr.	England	Ravenstein, Royal Golf Club of Belgium	Tervuren
1929	Sid Brews	South Africa	Royal Antwerp Golf Club	Antwerp
1930	Henry Cotton	England	Ravenstein, Royal Golf Club of Belgium	Tervuren
1931	Arthur Lacey	England	Royal Golf Club des Fagnes	Spa
1932	Arthur Lacey	England	Ravenstein, Royal Golf Club of Belgium	Tervuren
1933	Auguste Boyer	France	Royal Golf Club des Fagnes	Spa
1934	Henry Cotton	England	Royal Waterloo Golf Club	Lasne
1935	W. J. Branch		Ravenstein, Royal Golf Club of Belgium	Tervuren
1936	Auguste Boyer	France	Royal Golf Club des Fagnes	Spa
1937	Marcel Dallemagne	France	Royal Zoute Golf Club	Knokke-Heist
1938	Henry Cotton	England	Royal Waterloo Golf Club	Lasne
1939	Flory Van Donck	Belgium	Ravenstein, Royal Golf Club of Belgium	Tervuren

1946	Flory Van Donck	Belgium	Royal Waterloo Golf Club	Lasne
1947	Flory Van Donck	Belgium	Royal Golf Club des Fagnes	Spa
1948	W. S. Forrester		Ravenstein, Royal Golf Club of Belgium	Tervuren
1949	Jimmy Adams	Scotland	Royal Golf Club des Fagnes	Spa
1950	Roberto DeVicenzo	Argentina	Royal Zoute Golf Club	Knokke-Heist
1951	Albert Pelissier	France	Royal Latem Golf Club	St-Martens-Latem
1952	Antonio Cerdá	Argentina	Royal Golf Club des Fagnes	Spa
1953	Flory Van Donck	Belgium	Royal Waterloo Golf Club	Lasne
1954	Dai Rees	Wales	Royal Antwerp Golf Club	Antwerp
1955	Dave Thomas	Wales	Royal Golf Club des Fagnes	Spa
1956	Flory Van Donck	Belgium	Royal Latem Golf Club	St-Martens-Latem
1957	Bernard Hunt	England	Royal Latem Golf Club	St-Martens-Latem
1958	Ken Bousfield	England	Ravenstein, Royal Golf Club of Belgium	Tervuren
1978	Noel Ratcliffe	Australia	Ravenstein, Royal Golf Club of Belgium	Tervuren
1979	Gavan Levenson	South Africa	Royal Waterloo Golf Club	Lasne
1987	Eamonn Darcy	Ireland	Royal Waterloo Golf Club	Lasne
1988	José María Olazábal	Spain	Golf du Bercuit	Grez-Doiceau
1989	Gordon Brand Jr.	England	Royal Waterloo Golf Club	Lasne
1990	Ove Sellberg	Sweden	Royal Waterloo Golf Club	Lasne

1991	Per-Ulrik Johansson	Sweden	Royal Waterloo Golf Club	Lasne
1992	Miguel Ángel Jiménez	Spain	Royal Zoute Golf Club	Knokke-Heist
1993	Darren Clarke	Northern Ireland	Royal Zoute Golf Club	Knokke-Heist
1994	Nick Faldo	England	Royal Zoute Golf Club	Knokke-Heist
1998	Lee Westwood	England	Royal Zoute Golf Club	Knokke-Heist
1999	Robert Karlsson	Sweden	Royal Zoute Golf Club	Knokke-Heist
2000	Lee Westwood	England	Royal Zoute Golf Club	Knokke-Heist

British Masters

1946	Bobby Locke	South Africa	Stoneham Golf Club	Hampshire, England
1946	Jimmy Adams	Scotland	Stoneham Golf Club	Hampshire, England
1947	Arthur Lees	England	Little Aston Golf Club	Streetly, Sutton Coldfield, England
1948	Norman Von Nida	Australia	Sunningdale Golf Club	London, Greater London, England
1949	Charlie Ward	England	St. Andrews Links, Old Course	St. Andrews, Fife, Scotland
1950	Dai Rees	Wales	Royal Liverpool Golf Club	Hoylake, England

1951	Max Faulkner	England	Wentworth Club	Virginia Water, Surrey, England
1952	Harry Weetman	England	Mere Golf & Country Club	Knutsford, Cheshire, England
1953	Harry Bradshaw	Ireland	Sunningdale Golf Club	London, Greater London, England
1954	Bobby Locke	South Africa	Prince's Golf Club	Sandwich, Kent, England
1955	Harry Bradshaw	Ireland	Little Aston Golf Club	Streetly, Sutton Coldfield, England
1956	Christy O'Connor Sr.	Ireland	Prestwick Golf Club	Prestwick, South Ayrshire, Scotland
1957	Eric Brown	Scotland	Notts Golf Club	Ashfield, Nottinghamshire, England
1958	Harry Weetman	England	Little Aston Golf Club	Streetly, Sutton Coldfield, England
1959	Christy O'Connor Sr.	Ireland	Portmarnock Golf Club	Portmarnock, Fingal, Ireland
1960	James Hitchcock	England	Sunningdale Golf Club	London, Greater London, England
1961	Peter Thomson	Australia	Royal Porthcawl Golf Club	Porthcawl, South Wales, Wales
1962	Dai Rees	Wales	Wentworth Club	Virginia Water, Surrey, England
1963	Bernard Hunt	England	Little Aston Golf Club	Streetly, Sutton Coldfield, England

1964	Cobie Legrange	South Africa	Royal Birkdale Golf Club	Southport, Merseyside, England
1965	Bernard Hunt	England	Portmarnock Golf Club	Portmarnock, Fingal, Ireland
1966	Neil Coles	England	Lindrick Golf Club	Worksop, Nottinghamshire, England
1967	Tony Jacklin	England	Royal St. George's Golf Club	Sandwich, Kent, England
1968	Peter Thomson	Australia	Sunningdale Golf Club	London, Greater London, England
1969	Cobie Legrange	South Africa	Little Aston Golf Club	Streetly, Sutton Coldfield, England
1970	Brian Huggett	Wales	Royal Lytham & St. Annes Golf Club	Lytham and St. Annes, Lancashire, England
1971	Maurice Bembridge	England	St. Pierre Golf & Country Club	Chepstow, Wales
1972	Bob Charles	New Zealand	Northumberland Golf Club	High Gosforth Park, Newcastle-upon-Tyne, England
1973	Tony Jacklin	England	St. Pierre Golf & Country Club	Chepstow, Wales
1974	Bernard Gallacher	Scotland	St. Pierre Golf & Country Club	Chepstow, Wales

1975	Bernard Gallacher	Scotland	Ganton Golf Club	Ganton, North Yorkshire, England
1976	Baldovino Dassù	Italy	St. Pierre Golf & Country Club	Chepstow, Wales
1977	Guy Hunt	England	Lindrick Golf Club	Worksop, Nottinghamshire, England
1978	Tommy Horton	England	St. Pierre Golf & Country Club	Chepstow, Wales
1979	Graham Marsh	Australia	Woburn Golf and Country Club	Woburn, Buckinghamshire, England
1980	Bernhard Langer	West Germany	St. Pierre Golf & Country Club	Chepstow, Wales
1981	Greg Norman	Australia	Woburn Golf and Country Club	Woburn, Buckinghamshire, England
1982	Greg Norman	Australia	St. Pierre Golf & Country Club	Chepstow, Wales
1983	Ian Woosnam	Wales	St. Pierre Golf & Country Club	Chepstow, Wales
1985	Lee Trevino	United States	Woburn Golf and Country Club	Woburn, Buckinghamshire, England
1986	Seve Ballesteros	Spain	Woburn Golf and Country Club	Woburn, Buckinghamshire, England

1987	Mark McNulty	Zimbabwe	Woburn Golf and Country Club	Woburn, Buckinghamshire, England
1988	Sandy Lyle	Scotland	Woburn Golf and Country Club	Woburn, Buckinghamshire, England
1989	Nick Faldo	England	Woburn Golf and Country Club	Woburn, Buckinghamshire, England
1990	Mark James	England	Woburn Golf and Country Club	Woburn, Buckinghamshire, England
1991	Seve Ballesteros	Spain	Woburn Golf and Country Club	Woburn, Buckinghamshire, England
1992	Christy O'Connor Jr.	Ireland	Woburn Golf and Country Club	Woburn, Buckinghamshire, England
1993	Peter Baker	England	Woburn Golf and Country Club	Woburn, Buckinghamshire, England
1994	Ian Woosnam	Wales	Woburn Golf and Country Club	Woburn, Buckinghamshire, England
1995	Sam Torrance	Scotland	Collingtree Park Golf Club	Northampton, England
1996	Robert Allenby	Australia	Collingtree Park Golf Club	Northampton, England
1997	Greg Turner	New Zealand	Forest of Arden Hotel & Country Club	Warwickshire, England

1998	Colin Montgomerie	Scotland	Forest of Arden Hotel & Country Club	Warwickshire, England
1999	Bob May	United States	Woburn Golf and Country Club	Woburn, Buckinghamshire, England
2000	Gary Orr	Scotland	Woburn Golf and Country Club	Woburn, Buckinghamshire, England
2001	Thomas Levet	France	Woburn Golf and Country Club	Woburn, Buckinghamshire, England
2002	Justin Rose	England	Woburn Golf and Country Club	Woburn, Buckinghamshire, England
2003	Greg Owen	England	Forest of Arden Hotel & Country Club	Warwickshire, England
2004	Barry Lane	England	Forest of Arden Hotel & Country Club	Warwickshire, England
2005	Thomas Bjørn	Denmark	Forest of Arden Hotel & Country Club	Warwickshire, England
2006	Johan Edfors	Sweden	The Belfry	Sutton Coldfield, England
2007	Lee Westwood	England	The Belfry	Sutton Coldfield, England
2008	Gonzalo Fernández-Castaño	Spain	The Belfry	Sutton Coldfield, England

Dutch Open

Year	Winner	Country	Club	Location
1912	George Pannell	England	Koninklijke Haagsche Golf & Country Club	Den Haag, Zuid Holland
1915	Gerry del Court van Krimpen	Netherlands	Koninklijke Haagsche Golf & Country Club	Den Haag, Zuid Holland
1916	Charles Bryce	England	Noordwijkse Golfclub	Noordwijk, Zuid Holland
1917	Jacob Oosterveer	Netherlands	Koninklijke Haagsche Golf & Country Club	Den Haag, Zuid Holland
1918	Florent Gevers (amateur)	Netherlands	Doornsche Golfclub	Doorn, Utrecht
1919	Dirk Oosterveer	Netherlands	Koninklijke Haagsche Golf & Country Club	Den Haag, Zuid Holland
1920	Henry Burrows	England	Kennemer Golf & Country Club	Zandvoort, Noord Holland
1921	Henry Burrows	England	Domburgsche Golf Club	Domburg, Zeeland
1922	George Pannell	England	Noordwijkse Golfclub	Noordwijk, Zuid Holland
1923	Henry Burrows	England	Hilversumsche Golf Club	Hilversum, Noord Holland
1924	Aubrey Boomer	France	Koninklijke Haagsche Golf & Country Club	Den Haag, Zuid Holland
1925	Aubrey Boomer	France	Koninklijke Haagsche Golf & Country Club	Den Haag, Zuid Holland

1926	Aubrey Boomer	France	Koninklijke Haagsche Golf & Country Club	Den Haag, Zuid Holland
1927	Percy Boomer	France	Koninklijke Haagsche Golf & Country Club	Den Haag, Zuid Holland
1928	Ernest Whitcombe	England	Koninklijke Haagsche Golf & Country Club	Den Haag, Zuid Holland
1929	J. H. Taylor	England	Hilversumsche Golf Club	Hilversum, Noord Holland
1930	Jacob Oosterveer	Netherlands	Koninklijke Haagsche Golf & Country Club	Den Haag, Zuid Holland
1931	Frank Dyer	Netherlands	Kennemer Golf & Country Club	Zandvoort, Noord Holland
1932	Auguste Boyer	France	Koninklijke Haagsche Golf & Country Club	Den Haag, Zuid Holland
1933	Marcel Dallemagne	France	Kennemer Golf & Country Club	Zandvoort, Noord Holland
1934	Sid Brews	South Africa	Utrechtse Golf Club de Pan	Bosch en Duin, Utrecht
1935	Sid Brews	South Africa	Kennemer Golf & Country Club	Zandvoort, Noord Holland
1936	Flory Van Donck	Belgium	Hilversumsche Golf Club	Hilversum, Noord Holland
1937	Flory Van Donck	Belgium	Utrechtse Golf Club de Pan	Bosch en Duin, Utrecht

1938	Alf Padgham	England	Koninklijke Haagsche Golf & Country Club	Den Haag, Zuid Holland
1939	Bobby Locke	South Africa	Kennemer Golf & Country Club	Zandvoort, Noord Holland
1946	Flory Van Donck	Belgium	Hilversumsche Golf Club	Hilversum, Noord Holland
1947	Joop Ruhl	Netherlands	Eindhovensche Golfclub	Valkenswaard, Noord-Brabant
1948	Cecil Denny	England	Hilversumsche Golf Club	Hilversum, Noord Holland
1949	Jimmy Adams	Scotland	Koninklijke Haagsche Golf & Country Club	Den Haag, Zuid Holland
1950	Roberto De Vicenzo	Argentina	Noord-Brabantsche Golfclub Toxandria	Breda, Noord-Brabant
1951	Flory Van Donck	Belgium	Kennemer Golf & Country Club	Zandvoort, Noord Holland
1952	Cecil Denny	England	Hilversumsche Golf Club	Hilversum, Noord Holland
1953	Flory Van Donck	Belgium	Eindhovensche Golfclub	Valkenswaard, Noord-Brabant
1954	Ugo Grappasonni	Italy	Koninklijke Haagsche Golf & Country Club	Den Haag, Zuid Holland

1955	Alfonso Angelini	Italy	Kennemer Golf & Country Club	Zandvoort, Noord Holland
1956	Antonio Cerdá	Argentina	Eindhovensche Golfclub	Valkenswaard, Noord-Brabant
1957	John Jacobs	England	Hilversumsche Golf Club	Hilversum, Noord Holland
1958	Dave Thomas	Wales	Kennemer Golf & Country Club	Zandvoort, Noord Holland
1959	Sewsunker "Papwa" Sewgolum	South Africa	Koninklijke Haagsche Golf & Country Club	Den Haag, Zuid Holland
1960	Sewsunker "Papwa" Sewgolum	South Africa	Eindhovensche Golfclub	Valkenswaard, Noord-Brabant
1961	Brian Wilkes	South Africa	Kennemer Golf & Country Club	Zandvoort, Noord Holland
1962	Brian Huggett	Wales	Eindhovensche Golfclub	Valkenswaard, Noord-Brabant
1963	Retief Waltman	South Africa	Koninklijke Haagsche Golf & Country Club	Den Haag, Zuid Holland
1964	Sewsunker "Papwa" Sewgolum	South Africa	Eindhovensche Golfclub	Valkenswaard, Noord-Brabant

1965	Ángel Miguel	Spain	Noord-Brabantsche Golfclub Toxandria	Breda, Noord-Brabant
1966	Ramón Sota	Spain	Kennemer Golf & Country Club	Zandvoort, Noord Holland
1967	Peter Townsend	England	Koninklijke Haagsche Golf & Country Club	Den Haag, Zuid Holland
1968	John Cockin	England	Hilversumsche Golf Club	Hilversum, Noord Holland
1969	Guy Wolstenholme	England	Utrechtse Golf Club de Pan	Bosch en Duin, Utrecht
1970	Vicente Fernández	Argentina	Eindhovensche Golfclub	Valkenswaard, Noord-Brabant
1971	Ramón Sota	Spain	Kennemer Golf & Country Club	Zandvoort, Noord Holland
1972	Jack Newton	Australia	Koninklijke Haagsche Golf & Country Club	Den Haag, Zuid Holland
1973	Doug McClelland	England	Koninklijke Haagsche Golf & Country Club	Den Haag, Zuid Holland
1974	Brian Barnes	Scotland	Hilversumsche Golf Club	Hilversum, Noord Holland
1975	Hugh Baiocchi	South Africa	Hilversumsche Golf Club	Hilversum, Noord Holland

1976	Seve Ballesteros	Spain	Kennemer Golf & Country Club	Zandvoort, Noord Holland
1977	Bob Byman	United States	Kennemer Golf & Country Club	Zandvoort, Noord Holland
1978	Bob Byman	United States	Noordwijkse Golfclub	Noordwijk, Zuid Holland
1979	Graham Marsh	Australia	Noordwijkse Golfclub	Noordwijk, Zuid Holland
1980	Seve Ballesteros	Spain	Hilversumsche Golf Club	Hilversum, Noord Holland
1981	Harold Henning	South Africa	Haagsche Golf & Country Club	Wassenaar, Zuid Holland
1982	Paul Way	England	Utrechtse Golf Club de Pan	Bosch en Duin, Utrecht
1983	Ken Brown	Scotland	Kennemer Golf & Country Club	Zandvoort, Noord Holland
1984	Bernhard Langer	West Germany	Rosendaelsche Golfclub	Arnhem, Gelderland
1985	Graham Marsh	Australia	Noordwijkse Golfclub	Noordwijk, Zuid Holland
1986	Seve Ballesteros	Spain	Noordwijkse Golfclub	Noordwijk, Zuid Holland
1987	Gordon Brand Jr.	Scotland	Hilversumsche Golf Club	Hilversum, Noord Holland

1988	Mark Mouland	Wales	Hilversumsche Golf Club	Hilversum, Noord Holland
1989	José María Olazábal	Spain	Kennemer Golf & Country Club	Zandvoort, Noord Holland
1990	Stephen McAllister	Scotland	Kennemer Golf & Country Club	Zandvoort, Noord Holland
1991	Payne Stewart	United States	Noordwijkse Golfclub	Noordwijk, Zuid Holland
1992	Bernhard Langer	Germany	Noordwijkse Golfclub	Noordwijk, Zuid Holland
1993	Colin Montgomerie	Scotland	Noordwijkse Golfclub	Noordwijk, Zuid Holland
1994	Miguel Ángel Jiménez	Spain	Hilversumsche Golf Club	Hilversum, Noord Holland
1995	Scott Hoch	United States	Hilversumsche Golf Club	Hilversum, Noord Holland
1996	Mark McNulty	Zimbabwe	Hilversumsche Golf Club	Hilversum, Noord Holland
1997	Sven Strüver	Germany	Hilversumsche Golf Club	Hilversum, Noord Holland
1998	Stephen Leaney	Australia	Hilversumsche Golf Club	Hilversum, Noord Holland
1999	Lee Westwood	England	Hilversumsche Golf Club	Hilversum, Noord Holland

2000	Stephen Leaney	Australia	Noordwijkse Golfclub	Noordwijk, Zuid Holland
2001	Bernhard Langer	Germany	Noordwijkse Golfclub	Noordwijk, Zuid Holland
2002	Tobias Dier	Germany	Hilversumsche Golf Club	Hilversum, Noord Holland
2003	Maarten Lafeber	Netherlands	Hilversumsche Golf Club	Hilversum, Noord Holland
2004	David Lynn	England	Hilversumsche Golf Club	Hilversum, Noord Holland
2005	Gonzalo Fernández-Castaño	Spain	Hilversumsche Golf Club	Hilversum, Noord Holland
2006	Simon Dyson	England	Kennemer Golf & Country Club	Zandvoort, Noord Holland
2007	Ross Fisher	England	Kennemer Golf & Country Club	Zandvoort, Noord Holland
2008	Darren Clarke	Northern Ireland	Kennemer Golf & Country Club	Zandvoort, Noord Holland
2009	Simon Dyson	England	Kennemer Golf & Country Club	Zandvoort, Noord Holland

European PGA Championship

1972	Tony Jacklin	England	Wentworth Club	Virginia Water, Surrey, England

1973	Peter Oosterhuis	England	Wentworth Club	Virginia Water, Surrey, England
1974	Maurice Bembridge	England	Wentworth Club	Virginia Water, Surrey, England
1975	Arnold Palmer	United States	Royal St. George's Golf Club	Sandwich, Kent, England
1976	Neil Coles	England	Royal St. George's Golf Club	Sandwich, Kent, England
1977	Manuel Piñero	Spain	Royal St. George's Golf Club	Sandwich, Kent, England
1978	Nick Faldo	England	Royal Birkdale Golf Club	Southport, Merseyside, England
1979	Vicent Fernández	Argentina	St. Andrews Links, Old Course	St. Andrews, Fife, Scotland
1980	Nick Faldo	England	Royal St. George's Golf Club	Sandwich, Kent, England
1981	Nick Faldo	England	Ganton Golf Club	Ganton, North Yorkshire, England
1982	Tony Jacklin	England	Hillside Golf Club	Southport, England
1983	Seve Ballesteros	Spain	Royal St. George's Golf Club	Sandwich, Kent, England
1984	Howard Clark	England	Wentworth Club	Virginia Water, Surrey, England
1985	Paul Way	England	Wentworth Club	Virginia Water, Surrey, England
1986	Rodger Davis	England	Wentworth Club	Virginia Water, Surrey, England
1987	Bernhard Langer	West Germany	Wentworth Club	Virginia Water, Surrey, England

1988	Ian Woosnam	Wales	Wentworth Club	Virginia Water, Surrey, England
1989	Nick Faldo	England	Wentworth Club	Virginia Water, Surrey, England
1990	Mike Harwood	England	Wentworth Club	Virginia Water, Surrey, England
1991	Seve Ballesteros	Spain	Wentworth Club	Virginia Water, Surrey, England
1992	Tony Johnstone	England	Wentworth Club	Virginia Water, Surrey, England
1993	Bernhard Langer	West Germany	Wentworth Club	Virginia Water, Surrey, England
1994	José Maria Olazábal	Spain	Wentworth Club	Virginia Water, Surrey, England
1995	Bernhard Langer	West Germany	Wentworth Club	Virginia Water, Surrey, England
1996	Costantino Rocco	Italy	Wentworth Club	Virginia Water, Surrey, England
1997	Ian Woosnam	Wales	Wentworth Club	Virginia Water, Surrey, England
1998	Colin Montgomerie	Scotland	Wentworth Club	Virginia Water, Surrey, England

1999	Colin Montgomerie	Scotland	Wentworth Club	Virginia Water, Surrey, England
2000	Colin Montgomerie	Scotland	Wentworth Club	Virginia Water, Surrey, England
2001	Andrew Oldcorn	Scotland	Wentworth Club	Virginia Water, Surrey, England
2002	Anders Hansen	Sweden	Wentworth Club	Virginia Water, Surrey, England
2003	Ignacio Garrido	Spain	Wentworth Club	Virginia Water, Surrey, England
2004	Scott Drummond	Scotland	Wentworth Club	Virginia Water, Surrey, England
2005	Ángel Cabrera	Spain	Wentworth Club	Virginia Water, Surrey, England
2006	David Howell	England	Wentworth Club	Virginia Water, Surrey, England
2007	Anders Hansen	Sweden	Wentworth Club	Virginia Water, Surrey, England
2008	Miguel Ángel Jiménez	Spain	Wentworth Club	Virginia Water, Surrey, England
2009	Paul Casey	England	Wentworth Club	Virginia Water, Surrey, England

German Open

1911	Harry Vardon	Isle of Jersey		
1912	J. H. Taylor	England	Baden-Baden Golf Club	Baden-Baden
1926	Percy Alliss	England	Sporting Club Berlin	Berlin
1927	Percy Alliss	England	Sporting Club Berlin	Berlin
1928	Percy Alliss	England	Sporting Club Berlin	Berlin,
1929	Percy Alliss	England	Sporting Club Berlin	Berlin
1930	Auguste Boyer	France	Baden-Baden Golf Club	Baden-Baden
1931	René Golias	France	Sporting Club Berlin	Berlin
1932	Auguste Boyer	France	Mittelrheinischer Golf-Club Bad Ems	Bad Ems
1933	Percy Alliss	England	Mittelrheinischer Golf-Club Bad Ems	Bad Ems
1934	Alf Padgham	England	Mittelrheinischer Golf-Club Bad Ems	Bad Ems
1935	Auguste Boyer	France	Mittelrheinischer Golf-Club Bad Ems	Bad Ems
1936	Auguste Boyer	France	Berlin Golf & Country Club	Wannsee
1937	Henry Cotton	England	Mittelrheinischer Golf-Club Bad Ems	Bad Ems
1938	Henry Cotton	England	Frankfurt Golf Club	Frankfurt
1939	Henry Cotton	England	Mittelrheinischer Golf-Club Bad Ems	Bad Ems
1951	Antonio Cerdá	Argentina	Hamburg Golf Club	Falkenstein, Hamburg
1952	Antonio Cerdá	Argentina	Hamburg Golf Club	Falkenstein, Hamburg
1953	Flory Van Donck	Belgium	Frankfurt Golf Club	Frankfurt
1954	Bobby Locke	South Africa	Krefeld Golf Club	Krefeld

1955	Ken Bousfield	England	Hamburg Golf Club	Falkenstein, Hamburg
1956	Flory Van Donck	Belgium	Frankfurt Golf Club	Frankfurt
1957	Harry Weetman	England	Köln-Refrath Golf Club	Köln
1958	Fidel de Luca	Argentina	Krefeld Golf Club	Krefeld
1959	Ken Bousfield	England	Hamburg Golf Club	Falkenstein, Hamburg
1960	Peter Thomson	Australia	Köln-Refrath Golf Club	Köln
1961	Bernard Hunt	England	Krefeld Golf Club	Krefeld
1962	Bobby Verwey	South Africa	Hamburg Golf Club	Falkenstein, Hamburg
1963	Brian Huggett	Wales	Köln-Refrath Golf Club	Köln
1964	Roberto DeVicenzo	Argentina	Krefeld Golf Club	Krefeld
1965	Harold Henning	South Africa	Hamburg Golf Club	Falkenstein, Hamburg
1966	Bob Stanton	Australia	Frankfurt Golf Club	Frankfurt
1967	Donald Swaelens	Belgium	Krefeld Golf Club	Krefeld
1968	Barry Franklin	South Africa	Köln-Refrath Golf Club	Köln
1969	Jean Garaïalde	France	Frankfurt Golf Club	Frankfurt
1970	Jean Garaïalde	France	Krefeld Golf Club	Krefeld
1971	Neil Coles	England	Club zur Vahr	Earstedt
1972	Graham Marsh	Australia	Frankfurt Golf Club	Frankfurt
1973	Francisco Abreu	Spain	Hubbelrath Golf Club	Düsseldorf

1974	Simon Owen	New Zealand	Krefeld Golf Club	Krefeld
1975	Maurice Bembridge	England	Bremen Golf Club	Bremen
1976	Simon Hobday	South Africa	Frankfurt Golf Club	Frankfurt
1977	Tienie Britz	South Africa	Dusseldorf Golf Club	Düsseldorf
1978	Seve Ballesteros	Spain	Köln-Refrath Golf Club	Köln
1979	Tony Jacklin	England	Frankfurt Golf Club	Frankfurt
1980	Mark McNulty	Zimbabwe / Ireland	Berlin Golf & Country Club	Wannsee
1981	Bernhard Langer	West Germany	Hamburg Golf Club	Falkenstein, Hamburg
1982	Bernhard Langer	West Germany	Stuttgarter Golf-Club Solitude	Mönsheim
1983	Corey Pavin	United States	Köln-Refrath Golf Club	Köln
1984	Wayne Grady	Australia	Frankfurt Golf Club	Frankfurt
1985	Bernhard Langer	West Germany	Club zur Vahr	Earstedt
1986	Bernhard Langer	West Germany	Hubbelrath Golf Club	Düsseldorf
1987	Mark McNulty	Zimbabwe / Ireland	Frankfurt Golf Club	Frankfurt
1988	Seve Ballesteros	Spain	Frankfurt Golf Club	Frankfurt
1989	Craig Parry	Australia	Frankfurt Golf Club	Frankfurt

1990	Mark McNulty	Zimbabwe / Ireland	Hubbelrath Golf Club	Düsseldorf
1991	Mark McNulty	Zimbabwe / Ireland	Hubbelrath Golf Club	Düsseldorf
1992	Vijay Singh	Fiji	Hubbelrath Golf Club	Düsseldorf
1993	Bernhard Langer	Germany	Hubbelrath Golf Club	Düsseldorf
1994	Colin Montgomerie	Scotland	Hubbelrath Golf Club	Düsseldorf
1995	Colin Montgomerie	Scotland	Nippenburg Golf Club	Stuttgart
1996	Ian Woosnam	Wales	Nippenburg Golf Club	Stuttgart
1997	Ignacio Garrido	Spain	Schloß Nippenburg ETC	Stuttgart
1998	Stephen Allan	Australia	Sporting Club Berlin	Berlin
1999	Jarmo Sandelin	Sweden	Sporting Club Berlin	Berlin

Irish Open

1927	George Duncan	Scotland	Portmarnock Golf Club	Portmarnock, Fingal, Ireland
1928	Ernest Whitcombe	England	Royal County Down Golf Club	Newcastle, County Down, Northern Ireland
1929	Abe Mitchell	England	Portmarnock Golf Club	Portmarnock, Fingal, Ireland
1930	Charles Whitcombe	England	Royal Portrush Golf Club	Portrush, County Antrim, Northern Ireland
1931	Bob Kenyon	England	The Royal Dublin Golf Club	Dollymount, County Dublin, Ireland

1932	Alf Padgham	England	Cork Golf Club	County Cork, Ireland
1933	Bob Kenyon	England	Malone Golf Club	Belfast, County Antrim, Northern Ireland
1934	Syd Easterbrook	England	Portmarnock Golf Club	Portmarnock, Fingal, Ireland
1935	Ernest Whitcombe	England	Royal County Down Golf Club	Newcastle, County Down, Northern Ireland
1936	Reg Whitcombe	England	The Royal Dublin Golf Club	Dollymount, County Dublin, Ireland
1937	Bert Gadd	England	Royal Portrush Golf Club	Portrush, County Antrim, Northern Ireland
1938	Bobby Locke	South Africa	Portmarnock Golf Club	Portmarnock, Fingal, Ireland
1939	Arthur Lees	England	Royal County Down Golf Club	Newcastle, County Down, Northern Ireland
1946	Fred Daly	Northern Ireland	Portmarnock Golf Club	Portmarnock, Fingal, Ireland
1947	Harry Bradshaw	Ireland	Royal Portrush Golf Club	Portrush, County Antrim, Northern Ireland
1948	Dai Rees	Wales	Portmarnock Golf Club	Portmarnock, Fingal, Ireland
1949	Harry Bradshaw	Ireland	Belvoir Park Golf Club	Belfast, Northern Ireland
1950	Ossie Pickworth	Australia	The Royal Dublin Golf Club	Dollymount, County Dublin, Ireland
1953	Eric Brown	Scotland	Belvoir Park Golf Club	Belfast, Northern Ireland
1963	Bernard Hunt	England	Woodbrook Golf Club	County Wicklow, Ireland

1975	Christy O'Connor Jr.	Ireland	Woodbrook Golf Club	County Wicklow, Ireland
1976	Ben Crenshaw	United States	Portmarnock Golf Club	Portmarnock, Fingal, Ireland
1977	Hubert Green	United States	Portmarnock Golf Club	Portmarnock, Fingal, Ireland
1978	Ken Brown	Scotland	Portmarnock Golf Club	Portmarnock, Fingal, Ireland
1979	Mark James	England	Portmarnock Golf Club	Portmarnock, Fingal, Ireland
1980	Mark James	England	Portmarnock Golf Club	Portmarnock, Fingal, Ireland
1981	Sam Torrance	Scotland	Portmarnock Golf Club	Portmarnock, Fingal, Ireland
1982	John O'Leary	Ireland	Portmarnock Golf Club	Portmarnock, Fingal, Ireland
1983	Seve Ballesteros	Spain	The Royal Dublin Golf Club	Dollymount, County Dublin, Ireland
1984	Bernhard Langer	West Germany	The Royal Dublin Golf Club	Dollymount, County Dublin, Ireland
1985	Seve Ballesteros	Spain	The Royal Dublin Golf Club	Dollymount, County Dublin, Ireland
1986	Seve Ballesteros	Spain	Portmarnock Golf Club	Portmarnock, Fingal, Ireland
1987	Bernhard Langer	West Germany	Portmarnock Golf Club	Portmarnock, Fingal, Ireland
1988	Ian Woosnam	Wales	Portmarnock Golf Club	Portmarnock, Fingal, Ireland
1989	Ian Woosnam	Wales	Portmarnock Golf Club	Portmarnock, Fingal, Ireland
1990	José María Olazábal	Spain	Portmarnock Golf Club	Portmarnock, Fingal, Ireland
1991	Nick Faldo	England	Killarney Golf Club	Killarney, Ireland
1992	Nick Faldo	England	Killarney Golf Club	Killarney, Ireland
1993	Nick Faldo	England	Mount Juliet Conrad	Ireland

1994	Bernhard Langer	Germany	Mount Juliet Conrad	Ireland
1995	Sam Torrance	Scotland	Mount Juliet Conrad	Ireland
1996	Colin Montgomerie	Scotland	Druids Glen Golf Resort	Newtownmountkennedy, Ireland
1997	Colin Montgomerie	Scotland	Druids Glen Golf Resort	Newtownmountkennedy, Ireland
1998	David Carter	England	Druids Glen Golf Resort	Newtownmountkennedy, Ireland
1999	Sergio García	Spain	Druids Glen Golf Resort	Newtownmountkennedy, Ireland
2000	Patrik Sjöland	Sweden	Ballybunion Golf Club	County Kerry, Ireland
2001	Colin Montgomerie	Scotland	Fota Island Resort	Fota Island, County Cork, Ireland
2002	Søren Hansen	Denmark	Fota Island Resort	Fota Island, County Cork, Ireland
2003	Michael Campbell	New Zealand	Portmarnock Golf Club	Portmarnock, Fingal, Ireland
2004	Brett Rumford	Australia	County Louth Golf Club	County Louth, Ireland
2005	Stephen Dodd	Wales	Carton House Golf Club	Kildare, Ireland
2006	Thomas Bjørn	Denmark	Carton House Golf Club	Kildare, Ireland
2007	Pádraig Harrington	Ireland	Adare Golf Club	Country Limerick, Ireland
2008	Richard Finch	England	Adare Golf Club	Country Limerick, Ireland
2009	Shane Lowry (amateur)	Ireland	County Louth Golf Club	County Louth, Ireland

Italian Open

1925	Francesco Pasquali	Italy	Alpino Di Stresa Golf Club	Vezzo, Piemonte
1926	Auguste Boyer	France	Alpino Di Stresa Golf Club	Vezzo, Piemonte

1927	Percy Alliss	England	Alpino Di Stresa Golf Club	Vezzo, Piemonte
1928	Auguste Boyer	France	Villa d'Este	Cernobbio, Como, Lombardy
1929	René Golias	France	Villa d'Este	Cernobbio, Como, Lombardy
1930	Auguste Boyer	France	Villa d'Este	Cernobbio, Como, Lombardy
1931	Auguste Boyer	France	Villa d'Este	Cernobbio, Como, Lombardy
1932	Aubrey Boomer	England	Villa d'Este	Cernobbio, Como, Lombardy
1934	N. Nutley	England	Golf Club San Remo	San Remo, Liguria
1935	Percy Alliss	England	Golf Club San Remo	San Remo, Liguria
1936	Henry Cotton	England	Sestrieres Golf Club	Sestrieres, Piemonte
1937	Marcel Dallemagne	France	Golf Club San Remo	San Remo, Liguria
1938	Flory Van Donck	Belgium	Villa d'Este	Cernobbio, Como, Lombardy
1947	Flory Van Donck	Belgium	Golf Club San Remo	San Remo, Liguria
1948	Aldo Casera	Italy	Golf Club San Remo	San Remo, Liguria
1949	Hassan Hassanein	Egypt	Villa d'Este	Cernobbio, Como, Lombardy
1950	Ugo Grappasonni	Italy	Golf Club Olgiata	Roma, Lazio

1951	Jimmy Adams	Scotland	Golf Club Milano	Monza, Milano
1952	Eric Brown	Scotland	Golf Club Milano	Monza, Milano
1953	Flory Van Donck	Belgium	Villa d'Este	Cernobbio, Como, Lombardy
1954	Ugo Grappasonni	Italy	Villa d'Este	Cernobbio, Como, Lombardy
1955	Flory Van Donck	Belgium	Golf Club Lido de Venice	Venezia, Venezia
1956	Antonio Cerdá	Argentina	Golf Club Milano	Monza, Milano
1957	Harold Henning	South Africa	Villa d'Este	Cernobbio, Como, Lombardy
1958	Peter Alliss	England	Golf Club Varese	Luvinate, Lombardia
1959	Peter Thomson	Australia	Villa d'Este	Cernobbio, Como, Lombardy
1960	Brian Wilkes	South Africa	Golf Club Lido de Venice	Venezia, Venezia
1971	Ramón Sota	Spain	Golf Club Garlenda	Garlenda, Liguria
1972	Norman Wood	Scotland	Golf Club Monticello	Cassina Rizzardi, Como, Lombardy
1973	Tony Jacklin	England	Golf Club Olgiata	Roma, Lazio
1974	Peter Oosterhuis	England	Golf Club Lido de Venice	Venezia, Venezia
1975	Billy Casper	United States	Golf Club Monticello	Cassina Rizzardi, Como, Lombardy

1976	Baldovino Dassù	Italy	Is Molas Golf Club	Pula, Sardegna
1977	Ángel Gallardo	Spain	Golf Club Monticello	Cassina Rizzardi, Como, Lombardy
1978	Dale Hayes	South Africa	Golf Club Pevero	Costa Smeralda, Sardinia
1979	Brian Barnes	Scotland	Golf Club Monticello	Cassina Rizzardi, Como, Lombardy
1980	Massimo Mannelli	Italy	Circolo del Golf di Roma Acquasanta	Roma, Lazio
1981	José Maria Cañizares	Spain	Golf Club Milano	Monza, Milano
1982	Mark James	England	Is Molas Golf Club	Pula, Sardegna
1983	Bernhard Langer	West Germany	Ugolino Golf Club	Ugolino, Firenze
1984	Sandy Lyle	Scotland	Golf Club Milano	Monza, Milano
1985	Manuel Piñero	Spain	Molinetto Golf & Country Club	Formigine, Modena
1986	David Feherty	Northern Ireland	Albarella Golf Club	Venezia, Venezia
1987	Sam Torrance	Scotland	Golf Club Monticello	Cassina Rizzardi, Como, Lombardy
1988	Greg Norman	Australia	Golf Club Monticello	Cassina Rizzardi, Como, Lombardy
1989	Ronan Rafferty	Northern Ireland	Golf Club Monticello	Cassina Rizzardi, Como, Lombardy

1990	Richard Boxall	England	Golf Club Milano	Monza, Milano
1991	Craig Parry	Australia	Golf Club Castelconturbia	Agrate Conturbia, Novarra
1992	Sandy Lyle	Scotland	Golf Club Monticello	Cassina Rizzardi, Como, Lombardy
1993	Greg Turner	New Zealand	Golf Club Modena	Near Bologna
1994	Eduardo Romero	Argentina	Golf Club Marco Simone	Guidona, Roma, Lazio
1995	Sam Torrance	Scotland	Golf Club La Rovedine	Milano, Milano
1996	Jim Payne	England	Golf Club Bergamo	Almenno San Bartolomeo, Bergamo
1997	Bernhard Langer	Germany	Gardagolf Country Club	Brescia, Lombardy
1998	Patrik Sjöland	Sweden	Golf Club Castelconturbia	Agrate Conturbia, Novarra
1999	Dean Robertson	Scotland	Circolo Golf Torino La Mandria	Fiano, Torino
2000	Ian Poulter	England	Is Molas Golf Club	Pula, Sardegna
2001	Grégory Havret	France	Is Molas Golf Club	Pula, Sardegna
2002	Ian Poulter	England	Golf Club Olgiata	Roma, Lazio
2003	Mathias Grönberg	Sweden	Gardagolf Country Club	Brescia, Lombardy
2004	Graeme McDowell	Northern Ireland	Castello di Tolcinasco Golf & Country Club	Pieve Emanuel, Milano
2005	Steve Webster	England	Castello di Tolcinasco Golf & Country Club	Pieve Emanuel, Milano

2006	Francesco Molinari	Italy	Castello di Tolcinasco Golf & Country Club	Pieve Emanuel, Milano
2007	Gonzalo Fernández-Castaño	Spain	Castello di Tolcinasco Golf & Country Club	Pieve Emanuel, Milano
2008	Hennie Otto	South Africa	Castello di Tolcinasco Golf & Country Club	Pieve Emanuel, Milano
2009	Daniel Vancsik	Argentina	Royal Park I Roveri	Fiano, Torino

Japanese Open

1927	Rokuro Akahoshi	Japan	Hodogaya Country Club	Kanagawa
1928	Rokuzo Asami	Japan	Tokyo Golf Club, Komazawa Course	Tokyo
1929	Tomekichi Miyamoto	Japan	Ibaraki Country Club	Ibaraki
1930	Tomekichi Miyamoto	Japan	Ibaraki Country Club	Ibaraki
1931	Rokuzo Asami	Japan	Hodogaya Country Club	Kanagawa
1932	Tomekichi Miyamoto	Japan	Ibaraki Country Club	Ibaraki
1933	Kodekichi Nakamura	Japan	Kasumigaseki Country Club	Kanto, Honshu
1935	Tomekichi Miyamoto	Japan	Tokyo Golf Club, Asaka Course	Tokyo
1936	Tomekichi Miyamoto	Japan	Naruo Golf Club, Inagawa Course	near Osaka
1937	Chin Sei-Sui	Korea / Japan	Sagamihara Golf Club, East Course	Kanagawa

1938	Lin Man-Puku	Korea / Japan	Fujisawa Country Club	Fujisawa
1939	Toichira Toda	Japan	Hirono Golf Club	Kobe
1940	Tomekichi Miyamoto	Japan	Tokyo Golf Club, Asaka Course	Tokyo
1941	Tokuharu Nobuhara	Japan	Hodogaya Country Club	Kanagawa
1950	Yoshiro Hayashi	Japan	Abiko Golf Club	Chiba
1951	Son Shi-Kin	Chinese Taipei	Naruo Golf Club, Inagawa Course	near Osaka
1952	Torakichi “Pete” Nakamura	Japan	Kawana Golf Club, Fuji Course	Shizuoka
1953	Son Shi-Kin	Chinese Taipei	Higashi-Takarazuka Golf Club	Takarazuka, Hyogo
1954	Yoshiro Hayashi	Japan	Tokyo Golf Club	Tokyo
1955	Koichi Ono	Japan	Hirono Golf Club	Kobe
1956	Torakichi “Pete” Nakamura	Japan	Kasumigaseki Country Club	Kanto, Honshu
1957	Haruyoshi Kobari	Japan	Aichi Country Club, Higashiyama Course	Aichi
1958	Torakichi “Pete” Nakamura	Japan	Takanodai Country Club	Chiba
1959	Chen Ching-Po	Chinese Taipei	Sagamihara Golf Club, East Course	Kanagawa
1960	Haruyoshi Kobari	Japan	Hirono Golf Club	Kobe
1961	Kenji Hosoishi	Japan	Takanodai Country Club	Chiba
1962	Teruo Sugihara	Japan	Chiba Country Club, Umesato Course	Chiba
1963	Toichiro Toda	Japan	Yokkaichi Country Club	Yokkaichi

1964	Hideyo Sugimoto	Japan	Tokyo Golf Club	Tokyo
1965	Tadashi Kitta	Japan	Miyoshi Country Club	Miyoshi
1966	Seichi Sato	Japan	Sodegaura Country Club	Sodegaura
1967	Tadashi Kitta	Japan	Hirono Golf Club	Kobe
1968	Takaaki Kono	Japan	Sobu Country Club	Tokyo
1969	Hideyo Sugimoto	Japan	Ono Golf Club	Ono
1970	Mitsuhiro Kitta	Japan	Musashi Country Club, Toyooka Course	Saitama
1971	Yoshiro Hayashi	Japan	Aichi Country Club, Higashiyama Course	Aichi
1972	Hon Chang Sang	Singapore	Otone Country Club, East Course	Iwai City
1973	Ben Arda	Philippines	Ibaraki Country Club, West Course	Osaka
1974	Masashi "Jumbo" Ozaki	Japan	Central Golf Club, East Course	Asao
1975	Takashi Murakami	Japan	Kasugai Country Club, East Course	Aichi
1976	Kosaku Shimada	Japan	Central Golf Club, East Course	Asao
1977	Seve Ballesteros	Spain	Narashino Country Club	Chiba
1978	Seve Ballesteros	Spain	Yokohama Country Club, West Course	Yokohama
1979	Kuo Chie-Hsiung	Chinese Taipei	Hino Golf Club, King Course	Shiga

1980	Shoji Kikuchi	Japan	Sagamihara Golf Club, East Course	Kanagawa
1981	Yukata Hagawa	Japan	Nihon Line Golf Club, East Course	Gifu
1982	Akira Yabe	Japan	Musashi Country Club, Toyooka Course	Saitama
1983	Isao Aoki	Japan	Rokko Kokusai Golf Club	Hyogo
1984	Kouichi Uehara	Japan	Ranzan Country Club	Saitama
1985	Tsuneyuki Nakajima	Japan	Higashi Nagoya Country Club	Aichi
1986	Tsuneyuki Nakajima	Japan	Totsuka Country Club	Kanagawa
1987	Isao Aoki	Japan	Arima Royal Golf Club	Hyogo
1988	Masashi "Jumbo" Ozaki	Japan	Tokyo Golf Club	Tokyo
1989	Masashi "Jumbo" Ozaki	Japan	Nagoya Golf Club, Wago Course	Nagoya
1990	Tsuneyuki Nakajima	Japan	Otaru Country Club	Sapporo
1991	Tsuneyuki Nakajima	Japan	Shimonoseki Golf Club	Yamaguchi
1992	Masashi "Jumbo" Ozaki	Japan	Ryugasaki Country Club	Ryugasaki
1993	Seiki Okuda	Japan	Biwako Country Club, Ritto/Mikami Course	Ritto
1994	Masashi "Jumbo" Ozaki	Japan	Yokkaichi Country Club	Yokkaichi

1995	Toshimitsu Izawa	Japan	Kasumigaseki Country Club, East Course	Saitama
1996	Peter Teravainen	United States	Ibaraki Country Club, West Course	Osaka
1997	Craig Parry	Australia	Koga Golf Club	Fukuoka
1998	Hidemichi Tanaka	Japan	Oarai Golf Club	Ibaraki
1999	Naomichi Ozaki	Japan	Otaru Country Club, New Course	Sapporo
2000	Naomichi Ozaki	Japan	Takanodai Country Club	Chiba
2001	Taichi Teshima	Japan	Tokyo Golf Club	Tokyo
2002	David Smail	New Zealand	Shimonoseki Golf Club	Yamaguchi
2003	Keiichiro Fukabori	Japan	Nikko Country Club	Nikko
2004	Toru Taniguchi	Japan	Katayamazu Golf Club, Hakusan Course	Ishikawa
2005	Shingo Katayama	Japan	Hirono Golf Club	Kobe
2006	Paul Sheehan	Australia	Kasumigaseki Country Club, West Course	Saitama
2007	Toru Taniguchi	Japan	Sagamihara Golf Club, East Course	Kanagawa
2008	Shingo Katayama	Japan	Koga Golf Club	Fukuoka
2009	Ryuichi Oda	Japan	Musashi Country Club, Toyooka Course	Saitama

News of the World Match Play

Year	Winner	Country	Venue	Location
1903	James Braid	Scotland	Sunningdale Golf Club	London, Greater London, England
1904	J. H. Taylor	England	Royal Mid-Surrey Golf Club	Richmond, Surrey, England
1905	James Braid	Scotland	Walton Heath Golf Club	Walton-on-the-Hill, Surrey, England
1906	Sandy Herd	Scotland	Notts Golf Club	Ashfield, Nottinghamshire, England
1907	James Braid	Scotland	Sunningdale Golf Club	London, Greater London, England
1908	J. H. Taylor	England	Royal Mid-Surrey Golf Club	Richmond, Surrey, England
1909	Tom Ball	England	Walton Heath Golf Club	Walton-on-the-Hill, Surrey, England
1910	James Sherlock	England	Sunningdale Golf Club	London, Greater London, England
1911	James Braid	Scotland	Walton Heath Golf Club	Walton-on-the-Hill, Surrey, England
1912	Harry Vardon	Isle of Jersey	Sunningdale Golf Club	London, Greater London, England
1913	George Duncan	Scotland	Walton Heath Golf Club	Walton-on-the-Hill, Surrey, England

1919	Abe Mitchell	England	Walton Heath Golf Club	Walton-on-the-Hill, Surrey, England
1920	Abe Mitchell	England	Royal Mid-Surrey Golf Club	Richmond, Surrey, England
1921	Bert Seymour		Oxhey Park Golf Club	South Oxhey, Watford, England
1922	George Gadd		Sunningdale Golf Club	London, Greater London, England
1923	Reg Wilson		Walton Heath Golf Club	Walton-on-the-Hill, Surrey, England
1924	Ernest Whitcombe	England	Royal St. George's Golf Club	Sandwich, Kent, England
1925	Archie Compston	England	Moor Park Golf Club	Moor Park, Rickmansworth, England
1926	Sandy Herd	Scotland	Royal Mid-Surrey Golf Club	Richmond, Surrey, England
1927	Archie Compston	England	Walton Heath Golf Club	Walton-on-the-Hill, Surrey, England
1928	Charles Whitcombe	England	Stoke Poges Golf Club	Stoke Poges, Buckinghamshire, England
1929	Abe Mitchell	England	Wentworth Club	Virginia Water, Surrey, England
1930	Charles Whitcombe	England	Oxhey Park Golf Club	South Oxhey, Watford, England

1931	Alf Padgham	England	Royal Mid-Surrey Golf Club	Richmond, Surrey, England
1932	Henry Cotton	England	Moor Park Golf Club	Moor Park, Rickmansworth, England
1933	Percy Alliss	England	Purley Downs Golf Club	Sanderstead, Surrey, England
1934	J. J. Busson	England	Walton Heath Golf Club	Walton-on-the-Hill, Surrey, England
1935	Alf Padgham	England	Royal Mid-Surrey Golf Club	Richmond, Surrey, England
1936	Dai Rees	Wales	Oxhey Park Golf Club	South Oxhey, Watford, England
1937	Percy Alliss	England	Stoke Poges Golf Club	Stoke Poges, Buckinghamshire, England
1938	Dai Rees	Wales	Walton Heath Golf Club	Walton-on-the-Hill, Surrey, England
1940	Henry Cotton	England	Royal Mid-Surrey Golf Club	Richmond, Surrey, England
1945	Reg Horne	England	Walton Heath Golf Club	Walton-on-the-Hill, Surrey, England
1946	Henry Cotton	England	Royal Liverpool Golf Club	Hoylake, England
1947	Fred Daly	Northern Ireland	Royal Lytham and St. Annes Golf Club	Lytham and St. Annes, Lancashire, England
1948	Fred Daly	Northern Ireland	Royal Birkdale Golf Club	Southport, Merseyside, England

1949	Dai Rees	Wales	Walton Heath Golf Club	Walton-on-the-Hill, Surrey, England
1950	Dai Rees	Wales	Carnoustie Golf Links	Carnoustie, Angus, Scotland
1951	Harry Weetman	England	Royal Liverpool Golf Club	Hoylake, England
1952	Fred Daly	Northern Ireland	Walton Heath Golf Club	Walton-on-the-Hill, Surrey, England
1953	Max Faulkner	England	Ganton Golf Club	Ganton, North Yorkshire, England
1954	Peter Thomson	Australia	St. Andrews Links, Old Course	St. Andrews, Fife, Scotland
1955	Ken Bousfield	England	Walton Heath Golf Club	Walton-on-the-Hill, Surrey, England
1956	John Panton	Scotland	Royal Liverpool Golf Club	Hoylake, England
1957	Christy O'Connor Sr.	Ireland	Turnberry, Ailsa Course	Turnberry, South Ayrshire, Scotland
1958	Harry Weetman	England	Walton Heath Golf Club	Walton-on-the-Hill, Surrey, England
1959	David Snell		Royal Birkdale Golf Club	Southport, Merseyside, England
1960	Eric Brown	Scotland	Turnberry, Ailsa Course	Turnberry, South Ayrshire, Scotland
1961	Peter Thomson	Australia	Walton Heath Golf Club	Walton-on-the-Hill, Surrey, England

1962	Eric Brown	Scotland	Walton Heath Golf Club	Walton-on-the-Hill, Surrey, England
1963	Dave Thomas	Wales	Turnberry, Ailsa Course	Turnberry, South Ayrshire, Scotland
1964	Neil Coles	England	Walton Heath Golf Club	Walton-on-the-Hill, Surrey, England
1965	Neil Coles	England	Walton Heath Golf Club	Walton-on-the-Hill, Surrey, England
1966	Peter Thomson	Australia	Walton Heath Golf Club	Walton-on-the-Hill, Surrey, England
1967	Peter Thomson	Australia	Walton Heath Golf Club	Walton-on-the-Hill, Surrey, England
1968	Brian Huggett	Wales	Walton Heath Golf Club	Walton-on-the-Hill, Surrey, England
1969	Maurice Bembridge	England	Walton Heath Golf Club	Walton-on-the-Hill, Surrey, England
1970	Tommy Horton	England	Moor Park Golf Club	Moor Park, Rickmansworth, England
1972	John Garner		Moor Park Golf Club	Moor Park, Rickmansworth, England
1973	Neil Coles	England	Hillside Golf Club	Southport, England
1974	Jack Newton	Australia	Downfield Golf Club	Dundee, Scotland
1975	Eddie Polland	Northern Ireland	Lindrick Golf Club	Worksop, Nottinghamshire, England

1976	Brian Barnes	Scotland	Kings Norton Golf Club	Birmingham, Worcestershire, England
1977	Hugh Baiocchi	South Africa	Stoke Poges Golf Club	Stoke Poges, Buckinghamshire, England
1978	Mark James	England	Dalmahoy Country Club	Edinburgh, Scotland
1979	Des Smyth	Ireland	Fulford, York Golf Club	York, England

Open de España

1912	Arnaud Massy	France	Polo Golf Madrid	Madrid
1916	Ángel de la Torre	Spain	Real Club Puerta de Hierro	Madrid
1917	Ángel de la Torre	Spain	Real Club Puerta de Hierro	Madrid
1919	Ángel de la Torre	Spain	Real Club Puerta de Hierro	Madrid
1921	Eugène Lafitte	France	Real Club Puerta de Hierro	Madrid
1923	Ángel de la Torre	Spain	Real Club Puerta de Hierro	Madrid
1925	Ángel de la Torre	Spain	Real Club Puerta de Hierro	Madrid
1926	Joaquin Bernardino	Spain	Real Club Puerta de Hierro	Madrid

1927	Arnaud Massy	France	Real Club Puerta de Hierro	Madrid
1928	Arnaud Massy	France	Real Club Puerta de Hierro	Madrid
1929	Eugène Lafitte	France	Real Club Puerta de Hierro	Madrid
1930	Joaquin Bernardino	Spain	Real Club Puerta de Hierro	Madrid
1932	Gabriel Gonzalez	Spain	Real Club Puerta de Hierro	Madrid
1933	Gabriel Gonzalez	Spain	Real Club Puerta de Hierro	Madrid
1934	Joaquin Bernardino	Spain	Real Club Puerta de Hierro	Madrid
1935	Ángel de la Torre	Spain	Real Club Puerta de Hierro	Madrid
1941	Mariano Provencio	Spain	Real Club Puerta de Hierro	Madrid
1942	Gabriel Gonzalez	Spain	Club de Golf de San Cugat	Barcelona
1943	Mariano Provencio	Spain	Real Club Puerta de Hierro	Madrid
1944	Nicasio Sagardia	Spain	Pedreña Golf Club	Santander

1945	Carlos Celles	Spain	Real Club Puerta de Hierro	Madrid
1946	Marcelino Morcillo	Spain	Pedreña Golf Club	Santander
1947	Mario Gonzalez (amateur)	Brazil	Real Club Puerta de Hierro	Madrid
1948	Marcelino Morcillo	Spain	Neguri Golf Club	Algorta, Pais Vasco
1949	Marcelino Morcillo	Spain	Real Club Puerta de Hierro	Madrid
1950	Antonio Cerdá	Argentina	Real Club de Golf Cerdaña	Girona
1951	Mariano Provencio	Spain	Real Club Puerta de Hierro	Madrid
1952	Max Faulkner	England	Real Club Puerta de Hierro	Madrid
1953	Max Faulkner	England	Real Club Puerta de Hierro	Madrid
1954	Sebastian Miguel	France	Real Club Puerta de Hierro	Madrid
1955	Henry de Lamaze (amateur)	France	Real Club Puerta de Hierro	Madrid
1956	Peter Alliss	England	El Prat Golf Club	Barcelona
1957	Max Faulkner	England	Real Sociedad Hipica Española Club de Campo	Madrid

1958	Peter Alliss	England	Real Club Puerta de Hierro	Madrid
1959	Peter Thomson	Australia	El Prat Golf Club	Barcelona
1960	Sebastian Miguel	Spain	Real Sociedad Hipica Española Club de Campo	Madrid
1961	Ángel Miguel	Spain	Real Club Puerta de Hierro	Madrid
1963	Ramón Sota	Spain	El Prat Golf Club	Barcelona
1964	Ángel Miguel	Spain	Real Club de Golf Tenerife	Tenerife, Islas Canarias
1966	Roberto De Vicenzo	Argentina	Real Club de Golf Sotogrande	Sotogrande, Cádiz
1967	Sebastian Miguel	Spain	Club de Golf de San Cugat	Barcelona
1968	Bob Shaw	Australia	Neguri Golf Club	Algorta, Pais Vasco
1969	Jean Garaïalde	France	Real Club Puerta de Hierro	Madrid
1970	Ángel Gallardo	Spain	Las Brisas Nueva	Andalucia
1971	Dale Hayes	South Africa	El Prat Golf Club	Barcelona
1972	Antonio Garrido	Spain	Golf Platja de Pals	Girona
1973	Neil Coles	England	La Manga, South Course	Murcia
1974	Jerry Heard	United States	La Manga, South Course	Murcia

1975	Arnold Palmer	United States	La Manga, South Course	Murcia
1976	Eddie Polland	Northern Ireland	La Manga, South Course	Murcia
1977	Bernard Gallacher	Scotland	La Manga, South Course	Murcia
1978	Brian Barnes	Scotland	El Prat Golf Club	Barcelona
1979	Dale Hayes	South Africa	Torrequebrada Golf Club	Spain
1980	Eddie Polland	Northern Ireland	Escorpion Golf Club	Valencia
1981	Seve Ballesteros	Spain	El Prat Golf Club	Barcelona
1982	Sam Torrance	Scotland	Real Sociedad Hipica Española Club de Campo	Madrid
1983	Eamonn Darcy	Ireland	Las Brisas Nueva	Andalucia
1984	Bernhard Langer	West Germany	El Saler	Valencia
1985	Seve Ballesteros	Spain	Vallromanas Golf Club	Barcelona
1986	Howard Clark	England	La Moraleja I	Madrid
1987	Nick Faldo	England	Las Brisas Nueva	Andalucia
1988	Mark James	England	Pedreña Golf Club	Santander
1989	Bernhard Langer	West Germany	El Saler	Valencia
1990	Rodger Davis	Australia	Real Sociedad Hipica Española Club de Campo	Madrid
1991	Eduardo Romero	Argentina	Real Sociedad Hipica Española Club de Campo	Madrid

1992	Andrew Sherborne	England	Real Club Puerta de Hierro	Madrid
1993	Joakim Haeggman	Sweden	Real Club Puerta de Hierro	Madrid
1994	Colin Montgomerie	Scotland	Real Sociedad Hipica Española Club de Campo	Madrid
1995	Seve Ballesteros	Spain	Real Sociedad Hipica Española Club de Campo	Madrid
1996	Pádraig Harrington	Ireland	Real Sociedad Hipica Española Club de Campo	Madrid
1997	Mark James	England	La Moraleja II	Madrid
1998	Thomas Bjørn	Denmark	El Prat Golf Club	Barcelona
1999	Jarmo Sandelin	Sweden	Real Club Puerta de Hierro	Barcelona
2000	Brian Davis	England	PGA Golf de Catalunya Sa	Caldes De Malavella
2001	Robert Karlsson	Sweden	El Saler	Valencia

2002	Sergio García	Spain	El Cortijo Club de Campo	Islas Gran Canarias
2003	Kenneth Ferrie	England	Golf Costa Adeje	Tenerife, Islas Canarias
2004	Christian Cévaër	France	Fuerteventura Golf Club	Fuerteventura
2005	Peter Hanson	Sweden	San Roque Golf & Country Club	San Roque, Cádiz
2006	Niclas Fasth	Sweden	San Roque Golf & Country Club	San Roque, Cádiz
2007	Charl Schwartzel	South Africa	Centro Nacional de Golf	Madrid
2008	Peter Lawrie	Ireland	Real Club Puerta de Hierro	Sevilla
2009	Thomas Levet	France	PGA Golf de Catalunya Sa	Caldes De Malavella

Swiss Open (1923–1983), European Masters (1984–2009)

1923	Alec Ross	Scotland	Golf Engadin St. Moritz	Samedan, Graubünden
1924	Percy Boomer	England	Golf Engadin St. Moritz	Samedan, Graubünden
1925	Alec Ross	Scotland	Golf Engadin St. Moritz	Samedan, Graubünden
1926	Alec Ross	Scotland	Lucerne Golf Club	Lucerne, Lucerne
1929	Alex Wilson	England	Lucerne Golf Club	Lucerne, Lucerne

1930	Auguste Boyer	France	Golf Engadin St. Moritz	Samedan, Graubünden
1931	Marcel Dallemagne	France	Lucerne Golf Club	Lucerne, Lucerne
1934	Auguste Boyer	France	Golf Club de Lausanne	Lausanne, Vaud
1935	Auguste Boyer	France	Golf Club de Lausanne	Lausanne, Vaud
1936	Francis Francis (Amateur)	England	Golf Club de Lausanne	Lausanne, Vaud
1937	Marcel Dallemagne	France	Golf Engadin St. Moritz	Samedan, Graubünden
1938	Jean Saubabe	France	Zürich Zumikon Golf Club	Zumikon, Zürich
1939	Fifi Calavo	France	Golf Club Crans-sur-Sierre	Crans-Montana, Valais
1948	Ugo Grappasonni	Italy	Golf Club Crans-sur-Sierre	Crans-Montana, Valais
1949	Marcel Dallemagne	France	Golf Club Crans-sur-Sierre	Crans-Montana, Valais
1950	Aldo Casera	Italy	Golf Club Crans-sur-Sierre	Crans-Montana, Valais
1951	Eric Brown	Scotland	Golf Club Crans-sur-Sierre	Crans-Montana, Valais
1952	Ugo Grappasonni	Italy	Golf Club Crans-sur-Sierre	Crans-Montana, Valais
1953	Flory Van Donck	Belgium	Golf Club Crans-sur-Sierre	Crans-Montana, Valais
1954	Bobby Locke	South Africa	Golf Club Crans-sur-Sierre	Crans-Montana, Valais
1955	Flory Van Donck	Belgium	Golf Club Crans-sur-Sierre	Crans-Montana, Valais
1956	Dai Rees	Wales	Golf Club Crans-sur-Sierre	Crans-Montana, Valais

1957	Alfonso Angelini	Italy	Golf Club Crans-sur-Sierre	Crans-Montana, Valais
1958	Ken Bousfield	England	Golf Club Crans-sur-Sierre	Crans-Montana, Valais
1959	Dai Rees	Wales	Golf Club Crans-sur-Sierre	Crans-Montana, Valais
1960	Harold Henning	South Africa	Golf Club Crans-sur-Sierre	Crans-Montana, Valais
1961	Kel Nagle	Australia	Golf Club Crans-sur-Sierre	Crans-Montana, Valais
1962	Bob Charles	New Zealand	Golf Club Crans-sur-Sierre	Crans-Montana, Valais
1963	Dai Rees	Wales	Golf Club Crans-sur-Sierre	Crans-Montana, Valais
1964	Harold Henning	South Africa	Golf Club Crans-sur-Sierre	Crans-Montana, Valais
1965	Harold Henning	South Africa	Golf Club Crans-sur-Sierre	Crans-Montana, Valais
1966	Alfonso Angelini	Italy	Golf Club Crans-sur-Sierre	Crans-Montana, Valais
1967	Randall Vines	Australia	Golf Club Crans-sur-Sierre	Crans-Montana, Valais
1968	Roberto Bernardini	Italy	Golf Club Crans-sur-Sierre	Crans-Montana, Valais
1969	Roberto Bernardini	Italy	Golf Club Crans-sur-Sierre	Crans-Montana, Valais
1970	Graham Marsh	Australia	Golf Club Crans-sur-Sierre	Crans-Montana, Valais
1971	Peter Townsend	England	Golf Club Crans-sur-Sierre	Crans-Montana, Valais
1972	Graham Marsh	Australia	Golf Club Crans-sur-Sierre	Crans-Montana, Valais
1973	Hugh Baiocchi	South Africa	Golf Club Crans-sur-Sierre	Crans-Montana, Valais
1974	Bob Charles	New Zealand	Golf Club Crans-sur-Sierre	Crans-Montana, Valais
1975	Dale Hayes	South Africa	Golf Club Crans-sur-Sierre	Crans-Montana, Valais

1976	Manuel Piñero	Spain	Golf Club Crans-sur-Sierre	Crans-Montana, Valais
1977	Seve Ballesteros	Spain	Golf Club Crans-sur-Sierre	Crans-Montana, Valais
1978	Seve Ballesteros	Spain	Golf Club Crans-sur-Sierre	Crans-Montana, Valais
1979	Hugh Baiocchi	South Africa	Golf Club Crans-sur-Sierre	Crans-Montana, Valais
1980	Nick Price	Zimbabwe	Golf Club Crans-sur-Sierre	Crans-Montana, Valais
1981	Manuel Piñero	Spain	Golf Club Crans-sur-Sierre	Crans-Montana, Valais
1982	Ian Woosnam	Wales	Golf Club Crans-sur-Sierre	Crans-Montana, Valais
1983	Nick Faldo	England	Golf Club Crans-sur-Sierre	Crans-Montana, Valais
1984	Jerry Anderson	Canada	Golf Club Crans-sur-Sierre	Crans-Montana, Valais
1985	Craig Stadler	United States	Golf Club Crans-sur-Sierre	Crans-Montana, Valais
1986	José María Olazábal	Spain	Golf Club Crans-sur-Sierre	Crans-Montana, Valais
1987	Anders Forsbrand	Sweden	Golf Club Crans-sur-Sierre	Crans-Montana, Valais
1988	Chris Moody	England	Golf Club Crans-sur-Sierre	Crans-Montana, Valais
1989	Seve Ballesteros	Spain	Golf Club Crans-sur-Sierre	Crans-Montana, Valais
1990	Ronan Rafferty	Northern Ireland	Golf Club Crans-sur-Sierre	Crans-Montana, Valais
1991	Jeff Hawkes	South Africa	Golf Club Crans-sur-Sierre	Crans-Montana, Valais
1992	Jamie Spence	England	Golf Club Crans-sur-Sierre	Crans-Montana, Valais
1993	Barry Lane	England	Golf Club Crans-sur-Sierre	Crans-Montana, Valais

1994	Eduardo Romero	Argentina	Golf Club Crans-sur-Sierre	Crans-Montana, Valais
1995	Mathias Grönberg	Sweden	Golf Club Crans-sur-Sierre	Crans-Montana, Valais
1996	Colin Montgomerie	Scotland	Golf Club Crans-sur-Sierre	Crans-Montana, Valais
1997	Costantino Rocca	Italy	Golf Club Crans-sur-Sierre	Crans-Montana, Valais
1998	Sven Strüver	Germany	Golf Club Crans-sur-Sierre	Crans-Montana, Valais
1999	Lee Westwood	England	Golf Club Crans-sur-Sierre	Crans-Montana, Valais
2000	Eduardo Romero	Argentina	Golf Club Crans-sur-Sierre	Crans-Montana, Valais
2001	Ricardo González	Argentina	Golf Club Crans-sur-Sierre	Crans-Montana, Valais
2002	Robert Karlsson	Sweden	Golf Club Crans-sur-Sierre	Crans-Montana, Valais
2003	Ernie Els	South Africa	Golf Club Crans-sur-Sierre	Crans-Montana, Valais
2004	Luke Donald	England	Golf Club Crans-sur-Sierre	Crans-Montana, Valais
2005	Sergio García	Spain	Golf Club Crans-sur-Sierre	Crans-Montana, Valais
2006	Bradley Dredge	Wales	Golf Club Crans-sur-Sierre	Crans-Montana, Valais
2007	Brett Rumford	Australia	Golf Club Crans-sur-Sierre	Crans-Montana, Valais
2008	Jean-François Lucquin	France	Golf Club Crans-sur-Sierre	Crans-Montana, Valais
2009	Alexander Norén	Sweden	Golf Club Crans-sur-Sierre	Crans-Montana, Valais

Skins Games Winners

1983	Gary Player	South Africa
1984	Jack Nicklaus	United States
1985	Fuzzy Zoeller	United States
1986	Fuzzy Zoeller	United States
1987	Lee Trevino	United States
1988	Ray Floyd	United States
1989	Curtis Strange	United States
1990	Curtis Strange	United States
1991	Payne Stewart	United States
1992	Payne Stewart	United States
1993	Payne Stewart	United States
1994	Tom Watson	United States
1995	Fred Couples	United States
1996	Fred Couples	United States
1997	Tom Lehman	United States
1998	Mark O'Meara	United States
1999	Fred Couples	United States
2000	Colin Montgomerie	Scotland
2001	Greg Norman	Australia
2002	Mark O'Meara	United States
2003	Fred Couples	United States
2004	Fred Couples	United States
2005	Fred Funk	United States
2006	Stephen Ames	Trinidad & Tobago / Canada
2007	Stephen Ames	Trinidad & Tobago / Canada
2008	K. J. Choi	Korea (South)
2009	not held	

APPENDIX 5. INTERNATIONAL TEAM EVENTS: RYDER CUP

Year	Winning Team	Losing Team	Score	U.S. Captain	International Captain	Venue	Location
1927	United States	Great Britain	9½ - 2½	Walter Hagen	Ted Ray (JER)	Worcester Country Club	Worcester, Massachusetts
1929	Great Britain	United States	7 - 5	Walter Hagen	George Duncan (SCO)	Moortown Golf Club	Leeds, Yorkshire, England
1931	United States	Great Britain	9 - 3	Walter Hagen	Charles Whitcombe (ENG)	Scioto Country Club	Columbus, Ohio
1933	Great Britain	United States	6½ - 5½	Walter Hagen	John Henry Taylor (ENG)	Southport and Ainsdale Golf Club	Southport, Lancashire, England
1935	United States	Great Britain	9 - 3	Walter Hagen	Charles Whitcombe (ENG)	Ridgewood Country Club	Paramus, New Jersey
1937	United States	Great Britain	8 - 4	Walter Hagen	Charles Whitcombe (ENG)	Southport and Ainsdale Golf Club	Southport, Lancashire, England
1947	United States	Great Britain	11 - 1	Ben Hogan	Henry Cotton (ENG)	Portland Golf Club	Portland, Oregon

1949	United States	Great Britain	7 - 5	Ben Hogan	Charles Whitcombe (ENG)	Ganton Golf Club	Ganton, North Yorkshire, England
1951	United States	Great Britain	9½ - 2½	Sam Snead	Arthur Lacey (ENG)	Pinehurst Resort, No. 2 Course	Pinehurst, North Carolina
1953	United States	Great Britain	6½ - 5½	Lloyd Mangrum	Henry Cotton (ENG)	Wentworth Club	Virginia Water, Surrey, England
1955	United States	Great Britain	8 - 4	Chick Harbert	Dai Rees (WLS)	Thunderbird Country Club	Rancho Mirage, California
1957	Great Britain	United States	7½ - 4½	Jack Burke, Jr.	Dai Rees (WLS)	Lindrick Golf Club	Rotherham, Yorkshire, England
1959	United States	Great Britain	8½ - 3½	Sam Snead	Dai Rees (WLS)	Eldorado Golf Club	Indian Wells, California
1961	United States	Great Britain	14½ - 9½	Jerry Barber	Dai Rees (WLS)	Royal Lytham & St. Annes Golf Club	Lytham and St. Annes, Lancashire, England
1963	United States	Great Britain	23 - 9	Arnold Palmer	John Fallon (SCO)	Atlanta Athletic Club	Atlanta, Georgia

1965	United States	Great Britain	19½ - 12½	Byron Nelson	Harry Weetman (ENG)	Royal Birkdale Golf Club	Southport, Merseyside, England
1967	United States	Great Britain	23½ - 8½	Ben Hogan	Dai Rees (WLS)	Champions GC, Cypress Creek Course	Houston, Texas
1969	United States	Great Britain	16 - 16	Sam Snead	Eric Brown (SCO)	Royal Birkdale Golf Club	Southport, Merseyside, England
1971	United States	Great Britain	18½ - 13½	Jay Hebert	Eric Brown (SCO)	Old Warson Country Club	St. Louis, Missouri
1973	United States	Great Britain & Ireland	19 - 13	Jack Burke, Jr.	Bernard Hunt (ENG)	Muirfield Links	Gullane, East Lothian, Scotland
1975	United States	Great Britain & Ireland	21 - 11	Arnold Palmer	Bernard Hunt (ENG)	Laurel Valley Golf Club	Ligonier, Pennsylvania

1977	United States	Great Britain & Ireland	12½ - 7½	Dow Finsterwald	Brian Huggett (WLS)	Royal Lytham and St. Annes Golf Club	Lytham and St. Annes, Lancashire, England
1979	United States	Europe	17 - 11	Billy Casper	John Jacobs (ENG)	Greenbrier, Old White Course	White Sulphur Springs, West Virginia
1981	United States	Europe	18½ - 9½	Dave Marr	John Jacobs (ENG)	Walton Heath Golf Club	Walton-on-the-Hill, Surrey, England
1983	United States	Europe	14½ - 13½	Jack Nicklaus	Tony Jacklin (ENG)	PGA National Golf Club	Palm Beach Gardens, Florida
1985	Europe	United States	16½ - 11½	Lee Trevino	Tony Jacklin (ENG)	Belfry, Brabazon Course	Wishaw, Warwickshire, England
1987	Europe	United States	15 - 13	Jack Nicklaus	Tony Jacklin (ENG)	Muirfield Village Golf Club	Dublin, Ohio
1989	Europe	United States	14 - 14	Ray Floyd	Tony Jacklin (ENG)	Belfry, Brabazon Course	Wishaw, Warwickshire, England

1991	United States	Europe	14½ - 13½	Dave Stockton	Bernard Gallacher (SCO)	Kiawah Island Golf Resort, Ocean Course	Kiawah Island, South Carolina
1993	United States	Europe	15 - 13	Tom Watson	Bernard Gallacher (SCO)	Belfry, Brabazon Course	Wishaw, Warwickshire, England
1995	Europe	United States	14½ - 13½	Lanny Wadkins	Bernard Gallacher (SCO)	Oak Hill Country Club, East Course	Rochester, New York
1997	Europe	United States	14½ - 13½	Tom Kite	Seve Ballesteros (ESP)	Valderrama Golf Club	Sotogrande, Andalusia, Spain
1999	United States	Europe	14½ - 13½	Ben Crenshaw	Mark James (ENG)	The Country Club	Brookline, Massachusetts
2002	Europe	United States	15½ - 12½	Curtis Strange	Sam Torrance (SCO)	Belfry, Brabazon Course	Wishaw, Warwickshire, England
2004	Europe	United States	18½ - 9½	Hal Sutton	Bernhard Langer (GER)	Oakland Hills Country Club, South Course	Bloomfield Hills, Michigan

2006	Europe	United States	18½ - 9½	Tom Lehman	Ian Woosnam (WLS)	K Club, Palmer Course	Straffan, County Kildare, Ireland
2008	United States	Europe	16½ - 11½	Paul Azinger	Nick Faldo (ENG)	Valhalla Golf Club	Louisville, Kentucky

World Cup of Golf: Canada Cup (1953–1966), World Cup (1967–1992), World Cup of Golf (1993–2009)

Year	Indiv. Champion	Nation	Team Champions	Nation	Venue	Location
1953	Antonio Cerdá	Argentina	Antonio Cerdá/ Roberto De Vicenzo	Argentina	Beaconsfield Golf Club	Pointe-Claire, Québec, Canada
1954	Stan Leonard	Canada	Kel Nagle/ Peter Thomson	Australia	Le Club Laval-sur-le-Lac	Laval-sur-le-Lac, Quebec, Canada
1955	Ed Furgol	United States	Ed Furgol/ Chick Harbert	United States	Columbia Country Club	Chevy Chase, Maryland
1956	Ben Hogan	United States	Ben Hogan/ Sam Snead	United States	Wentworth Club	Virginia Water, Surrey, England

1957	Torakichi Nakamura	Japan	Torakichi Nakamura/ Koichi Ono	Japan	Kasumigaseki Country Club, East Course	Kanto, Honshu, Japan
1958	Ángel Miguel	Spain	Harry Bradshaw/ Christy O'Connor	Ireland	Club de Golf Ciudad de México	Ciudad de México, México
1959	Stan Leonard	Canada	Kel Nagle/ Peter Thomson	Australia	Royal Melbourne Golf Club	Melbourne, Australia
1960	Flory Van Donck	Belgium	Arnold Palmer/ Sam Snead	United States	Portmarnock Golf Club	Portmarnock, Fingal, Ireland
1961	Sam Snead	United States	Jimmy Demaret/ Sam Snead	United States	Hyatt Dorado Beach Resort	Dorado, Puerto Rico
1962	Roberto De Vicenzo	Argentina	Arnold Palmer/ Sam Snead	United States	Jockey Club	Buenos Aires, Argentina
1963	Jack Nicklaus	United States	Jack Nicklaus/ Arnold Palmer	United States	Saint-Nom-la-Bretèche Golf Club	Saint-Nom-la-Bretèche, France
1964	Jack Nicklaus	United States	Jack Nicklaus/ Arnold Palmer	United States	Royal Kaanapali Golf Resort	Lahaina, Maui, Hawaii

1965	Gary Player	South Africa	Harold Henning/ Gary Player	South Africa	Club de Campo Villa de Madrid	Madrid, Spain
1966	George Knudson	Canada	Jack Nicklaus/ Arnold Palmer	United States	Yomiuri Golf Club	Inagi-shi, Tokyo, Japan
1967	Arnold Palmer	United States	Jack Nicklaus/ Arnold Palmer	United States	Club de Golf Ciudad de México	Ciudad de México, México
1968	Al Balding	Canada	Al Balding/ George Knudson	Canada	Olgiata Golf Club	Roma, Italy
1969	Lee Trevino	United States	Orville Moody/ Lee Trevino	United States	Singapore Island Country Club, Island Golf Course	Singapore
1970	Roberto De Vicenzo	Argentina	Bruce Devlin/ David Graham	Australia	Jockey Club	Buenos Aires, Argentina
1971	Jack Nicklaus	United States	Jack Nicklaus/ Lee Trevino	United States	PGA National Golf Club	Palm Beach Gardens, Florida

1972	Hsieh Min-Nan	Chinese Taipei	Hsieh Min-Nan/ Lu Liang-Huan	Chinese Taipei	Royal Melbourne Golf Club	Melbourne, Australia
1973	Johnny Miller	United States	Johnny Miller/ Jack Nicklaus	United States	Las Brisas Golf Club	Marbella, Costa del Sol, Spain
1974	Bobby Cole	South Africa	Bobby Cole / Dale Hayes	South Africa	Lagunita Country Club	Caracas, Venezuela
1975	Johnny Miller	United States	Lou Graham/ Johnny Miller	United States	Navatanee Golf Club	Bangkok, Thailand
1976	Ernesto Perez Acosta	Mexico	Seve Ballesteros/ Manuel Piñero	Spain	Mission Hills Country Club,	Rancho Mirage, California
1977	Gary Player	South Africa	Seve Ballesteros/ Antonio Garrido	Spain	Wack Wack Golf & Country Club	Mandaluyong, Manila, Philippines
1978	John Mahaffey	United States	John Mahaffey/ Andy North	United States	Princeville at Hanalei, Makai Golf Course	Hanalei, Hawaii
1979	Hale Irwin	United States	Hale Irwin/John Mahaffey	United States	Glyfada Golf Club	Athens, Greece

1980	Sandy Lyle	Scotland	Dan Halldorson/ Jim Nelford	Canada	Club el Rincón de Cajica	Bogotá, Colombia
1982	Manuel Piñero	Spain	José María Cañizares/ Manuel Piñero	Spain	Pierre Marques Golf Course	Acapulco, Mexico
1983	Dave Barr	Canada	Rex Caldwell/ John Cook	United States	Pondok Indah Golf & Country Club	Jakarta, Indonesia
1984	José María Cañizares	Spain	José María Cañizares/ José Rivero	Spain	Olgiata Golf Club	Roma, Italy
1985	Howard Clark	England	Dave Barr/Dan Halldorson	Canada	La Quinta Resort & Club	La Quinta, California
1987	Ian Woosnam	Wales	David Llewellyn/Ian Woosnam	Wales	Kapalua Resort, Bay Course	Kapalua, Maui, HawaiiHawaii
1988	Ben Crenshaw	United States	Ben Crenshaw/ Mark McCumber	United States	Royal Melbourne Golf Club	Melbourne, Australia
1989	Peter Fowler	Australia	Peter Fowler/ Wayne Grady	Australia	Las Brisas Golf Club	Marbella, Costa del Sol, Spain

1990	Payne Stewart	United States	Torsten Giedeon/ Bernhard Langer	Germany	Grand Cypress Golf Club, North Course, Grand Cypress Resort	Orlando, Florida
1991	Ian Woosnam	Wales	Anders Forsbrand/ Per-Ulrik Johansson	Sweden	Golf Club de Querce	Roma, Italy
1992	Brett Ogle	Australia	Fred Couples/ Davis Love III	United States	Club de Golf la Moraleja	Madrid, Spain
1993	Bernhard Langer	Germany	Fred Couples/ Davis Love III	United States	Lake Nona Golf & Country Club	Orlando, Florida
1994	Fred Couples	United States	Fred Couples/ Davis Love III	United States	Hyatt Dorado Beach Resort	Dorado, Puerto Rico
1995	Davis Love III	United States	Fred Couples/ Davis Love III	United States	Mission Hills Golf Club	Shenzhen, China

1996	Ernie Els	South Africa	Ernie Els/Wayne Westner	South Africa	Erinvale Golf Club	Somerset West, Western Cape, South Africa
1997	Colin Montgomerie	Scotland	Pádraig Harrington/ Paul McGinley	Ireland	Kiawah Island Golf Resort, Ocean Course	Kiawah Island, South Carolina
1998	Scott Verplank	United States	David Carter/ Nick Faldo	England	Gulf Harbour Golf Course	Whangaparaoa, Auckland, New Zealand
1999	Tiger Woods	United States	Mark O'Meara/ Tiger Woods	United States	Mines Resort & Golf Club	Selangor, Malaysia
2000	not contested		David Duval/ Tiger Woods	United States	Buenos Aires Golf Club	Buenos Aires, Argentina
2001	not contested		Ernie Els/Retief Goosen	South Africa	The Taiheiyo Club, Gotemba Course	Shizuoka, Japan
2002	not contested		Toshimitsu Izawa/Shigeki Maruyama	Japan	Vista Vallarta Club de Golf, Nicklaus Course	Puerto Vallarta, Mexico

2003	not contested	Trevor Immelman/ Rory Sabbatini	South Africa	Kiawah Island Golf Resort, Ocean Course	Kiawah Island, South Carolina
2004	not contested	Paul Casey/ Luke Donald	England	Real Club de Golf de Seville	Seville, Spain
2005	not contested	Stephen Dodd/ Bradley Dredge	Wales	Victoria Clube de Golf Course	Algarve, Portugal
2006	not contested	Bernhard Langer/ Marcel Siem	Germany	Sandy Lane Resort, Country Club Course	Sandy Lane Resort, St. James, Barbados
2007	not contested	Colin Montgomerie/ Marc Warren	Scotland	Mission Hills Golf Club	Shenzhen, China
2008	not contested	Robert Karlsson/ Henrik Stenson	Sweden	Mission Hills Golf Club	Shenzhen, China
2009	not contested	Francesco Molinari/ Eduardo Molinari	Italy	Mission Hills Golf Club	Shenzhen, China

President's Cup

Year	Winning Team	Losing Team	Score	U.S. Captain	International Captain	Venue	Location
1994	United States	International	20- 12	Hale Irwin	David Graham (AUS)	Robert Trent Jones Golf Club	Gainesville, Virginia
1996	United States	International	16½ - 15½	Arnold Palmer	Peter Thomson (AUS)	Robert Trent Jones Golf Club	Gainesville, Virginia
1998	International	United States	20½ - 11½	Jack Nicklaus	Peter Thomson (AUS)	Royal Melbourne Golf Club	Melbourne, Australia
2000	United States	International	21½ - 10½	Ken Venturi	Peter Thomson (AUS)	Robert Trent Jones Golf Club	Gainesville, Virginia
2003	United States	International	17- 17	Jack Nicklaus	Gary Player (RSA)	Fancourt Hotel and Country Club Estate	George, Western Cape, South Africa
2005	United States	International	18½ - 15½	Jack Nicklaus	Gary Player (RSA)	Robert Trent Jones Golf Club	Gainesville, Virginia

2007	United States	International	19½ - 14½	Jack Nicklaus	Gary Player (RSA)	Royal Montréal Golf Club	Île Bizard, Québec, Canada
2009	United States	International	19½ - 14½	Fred Couples	Greg Norman (AUS)	Harding Park Golf Course	San Francisco, California

Solheim Cup

Year	Winning Team	Losing Team	Score	U.S. Captain	International Captain	Venue	Location
1990	United States	Europe	11½ - 4½	Kathy Whitworth	Mickey Walker (ENG)	Lake Nona Golf & Country Club	Orlando, Florida
1992	Europe	United States	11½ - 6½	Kathy Whitworth	Mickey Walker (ENG)	Dalmahoy Country Club	Edinburgh, Scotland
1994	United States	Europe	13 - 7	JoAnne Carner	Mickey Walker (ENG)	Greenbrier, Old White Course	White Sulphur Springs, West Virginia
1996	United States	Europe	17 - 11	Judy Rankin	Mickey Walker (ENG)	St. Pierre Golf & Country Club	Chepstow, Wales

1998	United States	Europe	16 - 12	Judy Rankin	Pia Nilsson (SWE)	Muirfield Village Golf Club	Dublin, Ohio
2000	Europe	United States	14½ - 11½	Pat Bradley	Dale Reid (SCO)	Loch Lomond Golf Club	Luss, Dunbartonshire, Scotland
2002	United States	Europe	15½ - 12½	Patty Sheehan	Dale Reid (SCO)	Interlachen Country Club	Edina, Minnesota
2003	Europe	United States	17½ - 10½	Patty Sheehan	Catrin Nilsmark (SWE)	Barsebäck Golf & Country Club	Löddeköpinge, Skåne, Sweden
2005	United States	Europe	15½ - 12½	Nancy Lopez	Catrin Nilsmark (SWE)	Crooked Stick Golf Club	Carmel, Indiana
2007	United States	Europe	16 - 12	Betsy King	Helen Alfredsson (SWE)	Halmstad GK	Halmstad, Sweden
2009	United States	Europe	16 - 12	Beth Daniel	Alison Nicholas (ENG)	Rich Harvest Farms	Sugar Grove, Illinois

Walker Cup

Year	Winning Team	Losing Team	Score	U.S. Captain	International Captain	Venue	Location
1922	United States	Great Britain & Ireland	8 - 4	William Fownes	Robert Harris (SCO)	National Golf Links of America	Southampton, New York
1923	United States	Great Britain & Ireland	6½ - 5½	Robert Gardner	Robert Harris (SCO)	St. Andrews Links, Old Course	St. Andrews, Fife, Scotland
1924	United States	Great Britain & Ireland	9 - 3	Robert Gardner	Cyril Tolley (ENG)	Garden City Golf Club	Garden City, New York
1926	United States	Great Britain & Ireland	6½ - 5½	Robert Gardner	Robert Harris (SCO)	St. Andrews Links, Old Course	St. Andrews, Fife, Scotland
1928	United States	Great Britain & Ireland	11 - 1	Bob Jones	William Tweddell (ENG)	Chicago Golf Club	Wheaton, Illinois

1930	United States	Great Britain & Ireland	10 - 2	Bob Jones	Roger Wethered (ENG)	Royal St. George's Golf Club	Sandwich, Kent, England
1932	United States	Great Britain & Ireland	9½ - 2½	Francis Ouimet	T. A. Torrance (SCO)	The Country Club	Brookline, Massachusetts
1934	United States	Great Britain & Ireland	9½ - 2½	Francis Ouimet	Michael Scott (ENG)	St. Andrews Links, Old Course	St. Andrews, Fife, Scotland
1936	United States	Great Britain & Ireland	10½ - 1½	Francis Ouimet	William Tweddell (ENG)	Pine Valley Golf Club	Pine Valley, New Jersey
1938	Great Britain & Ireland	United States	7½ - 4½	Francis Ouimet	John Beck (ENG)	St. Andrews Links, Old Course	St. Andrews, Fife, Scotland
1947	United States	Great Britain & Ireland	8 - 4	Francis Ouimet	John Beck (ENG)	St. Andrews Links, Old Course	St. Andrews, Fife, Scotland

1949	United States	Great Britain & Ireland	10 - 2	Francis Ouimet	Percy Lucas (ENG)	Winged Foot Golf Club, West Course	Mamaroneck, New York
1951	United States	Great Britain & Ireland	7½ - 4½	Willie Turnesa	Raymond Oppenheimer (ENG)	Royal Birkdale Golf Club	Southport, Merseyside, England
1953	United States	Great Britain & Ireland	9 - 3	Charles Yates	A. A. Duncan (WLS)	Kittansett Club	Marion, Massachusetts
1955	United States	Great Britain & Ireland	10 - 2	Bill Campbell	G. Alec Hill (ENG)	St. Andrews Links, Old Course	St. Andrews, Fife, Scotland
1957	United States	Great Britain & Ireland	8½ - 3½	Charlie Coe	Gerald Micklem (ENG)	Minikahda Club	Minneapolis, Minnesota
1959	United States	Great Britain & Ireland	9 - 3	Charlie Coe	Gerald Micklem (ENG)	Muirfield Links	Gullane, East Lothian, Scotland

1961	United States	Great Britain & Ireland	11 - 1	Jack Westland	Charles Lawrie (SCO)	Seattle Golf Club	Seattle, Washington
1963	United States	Great Britain & Ireland	12 - 8	Richard Tufts	Charles Lawrie (SCO)	Turnberry, Ailsa Course	Turnberry, South Ayrshire, Scotland
1965	United States	Great Britain & Ireland	11 - 11	John Fischer	Joe Carr (IRL)	Baltimore CC, Five Farms, East Course	Timonium, Maryland
1967	United States	Great Britain & Ireland	13 - 7	Jess Sweetser	Joe Carr (IRL)	Royal St. George's Golf Club	Sandwich, Kent, England
1969	United States	Great Britain & Ireland	10 - 8	Billy Joe Patton	Michael Bonallack (ENG)	Milwaukee Country Club	River Hills, Wisconsin
1971	Great Britain & Ireland	United States	13 - 11	John Winters	Michael Bonallack (ENG)	St. Andrews Links, Old Course	St. Andrews, Fife, Scotland

1973	United States	Great Britain & Ireland	14 - 10	Jess Sweetser	David Marsh (ENG)	The Country Club	Brookline, Massachusetts
1975	United States	Great Britain & Ireland	15½ - 8½	Ed Updegraff	David Marsh (ENG)	St. Andrews Links, Old Course	St. Andrews, Fife, Scotland
1977	United States	Great Britain & Ireland	16 - 8	Lewis Oehmig	Sandy Saddler (SCO)	Shinnecock Hills Golf Club	Southampton, New York
1979	United States	Great Britain & Ireland	15½ - 8½	Dick Siderowf	Rodney Foster (ENG)	Muirfield Links	Gullane, East Lothian, Scotland
1981	United States	Great Britain & Ireland	15 - 9	Jim Gabrielsen	Rodney Foster (ENG)	Cypress Point Club	Pebble Beach, California
1983	United States	Great Britain & Ireland	13½ - 10½	Jay Sigel	Charles Wilson Green (SCO)	Royal Liverpool Golf Club	Hoylake, England

1985	United States	Great Britain & Ireland	13 - 11	Jay Sigel	Charles Wilson Green (SCO)	Pine Valley Golf Club	Pine Valley, New Jersey
1987	United States	Great Britain & Ireland	16½ - 7½	Fred Ridley	Geoffrey Marks (ENG)	Sunningdale Golf Club	London, Greater London, England
1989	Great Britain & Ireland	United States	12½ - 11½	Fred Ridley	Geoffrey Marks (ENG)	Peachtree Golf Club	Atlanta, Georgia
1991	United States	Great Britain & Ireland	14 - 10	Jim Gabrielsen	George MacGregor (SCO)	Portmarnock Golf Club	Portmarnock, Fingal, Ireland
1993	United States	Great Britain & Ireland	19 - 5	Vinny Giles	George MacGregor (SCO)	Interlachen Country Club	Edina, Minnesota
1995	Great Britain & Ireland	United States	14 - 10	Downing Gray	Clive Brown (WLS)	Royal Porthcawl Golf Club	Porthcawl, South Wales, Wales

1997	United States	Great Britain & Ireland	18 - 6	Downing Gray	Clive Brown (WLS)	Quaker Ridge Golf Club	Scarsdale, New York
1999	Great Britain & Ireland	United States	15 - 9	Danny Yates	Peter McEvoy (ENG)	Nairn Golf Club	Nairn, Highlands, Scotland
2001	Great Britain & Ireland	United States	15 - 9	Danny Yates	Peter McEvoy (ENG)	Ocean Forest Golf Club	Sea Island, Georgia
2003	Great Britain & Ireland	United States	12½ - 11½	Bob Lewis Jr.	Garth McGimpsey (NIR)	Ganton Golf Club	Ganton, North Yorkshire, England
2005	United States	Great Britain & Ireland	12½ - 11½	Bob Lewis Jr.	Garth McGimpsey (NIR)	Chicago Golf Club	Wheaton, Illinois
2007	United States	Great Britain & Ireland	12½ - 11½	Buddy Marucci	Colin Dalgleish (SCO)	Royal County Down Golf Club	Newcastle, County Down, Northern Ireland

2009	United States	Great Britain & Ireland	16½ - 9½	Buddy Marucci	Colin Dalgleish (SCO)	Merion Golf Club, East Course	Ardmore, Pennsylvania

Curtis Cup

Year	Winning Team	Losing Team	Score	U.S. Captain	International Captain	Venue	Location
1932	United States	Great Britain & Ireland	5½ - 3½	Marion Hollins	Joyce Wethered (ENG)	Wentworth Club	Virginia Water, Surrey, England
1934	United States	Great Britain & Ireland	6½ - 2½	Glenna Collett Vare	Doris Chambers (ENG)	Chevy Chase Club	Chevy Chase, Maryland
1936	United States	Great Britain & Ireland	4½ - 4½	Glenna Collett Vare	Doris Chambers (ENG)	King's Course	Gleneagles, Scotland
1938	United States	Great Britain & Ireland	5½ - 3½	Frances Stebbins	R. H. Wallace-Williamson (SCO)	Essex County Club	Manchester-by-the-Sea, Massachusetts

1948	United States	Great Britain & Ireland	6½ - 2½	Glenna Collett Vare	Doris Chambers (ENG)	Royal Birkdale Golf Club	Southport, Merseyside, England
1950	United States	Great Britain & Ireland	7½ - 1½	Glenna Collett Vare	Diana Fishwick Critchley (ENG)	Country Club of Buffalo	Williamsville, New York
1952	Great Britain & Ireland	United States	5 - 4	Aniela Goldthwaite	Katherine Cairns (ENG)	Muirfield Links	Gullane, East Lothian, Scotland
1954	United States	Great Britain & Ireland	6 - 4	Edith Flippin	Baba Beck (IRL)	Merion Golf Club, East Course	Ardmore, Pennsylvania
1956	Great Britain & Ireland	United States	5 - 4	Edith Flippin	Zara Bolton (NIR)	Prince's Golf Club	Sandwich, Kent, England
1958	Great Britain & Ireland	United States	4½ - 4½	Virginia Dennehy	Daisy Ferguson (IRL)	Brae Burn Country Club	West Newton, Massachusetts

1960	United States	Great Britain & Ireland	6½ - 2½	Mildred Prunaret	Maureen Garrett (ENG)	Lindrick Golf Club	Worksop, Nottinghamshire, England
1962	United States	Great Britain & Ireland	8 - 1	Polly Riley	Frances Stephens (ENG)	Broadmoor Golf Club, East Course	Colorado Springs, Colorado
1964	United States	Great Britain & Ireland	10½ - 7½	Helen Hawes	Elsie Corlett (ENG)	Royal Porthcawl Golf Club	Porthcawl, South Wales, Wales
1966	United States	Great Britain & Ireland	13 - 5	Dorothy Germain Porter	Zara Bolton (NIR)	Homestead, Cascades Course	Hot Springs, Virginia
1968	United States	Great Britain & Ireland	10½ - 7½	Evelynn Monsted	Zara Bolton (NIR)	Royal County Down Golf Club	Newcastle, County Down, Northern Ireland
1970	United States	Great Britain & Ireland	11½ - 6½	Carolyn Cudone	Jeanne Bisgood (ENG)	Brae Burn Country Club	West Newton, Massachusetts

1972	United States	Great Britain & Ireland	10 - 8	Jean Ashley Crawford	Frances Stephens (ENG)	Western Gailes Golf Club	Ayrshire, Scotland
1974	United States	Great Britain & Ireland	13 - 5	Sis Choate	Belle Robertson (SCO)	San Francisco Golf Club	San Francisco, California
1976	United States	Great Britain & Ireland	11½ - 6½	Barbara McIntire	Belle Robertson (SCO)	Royal Lytham & St. Annes Golf Club	Lytham and St. Annes, Lancashire, England
1978	United States	Great Britain & Ireland	12 - 6	Helen Sigel Wilson	Carol Comboy (ENG)	Apawamis Club	Rye, New York
1980	United States	Great Britain & Ireland	13 - 5	Nancy Roth Syms	Carol Comboy (ENG)	St. Pierre Golf & Country Club	Chepstow, Wales
1982	United States	Great Britain & Ireland	14½ - 3½	Betty Probasco	Marie O'Donnell (IRL)	Denver Country Club	Denver, Colorado

1984	United States	Great Britain & Ireland	9½ - 8½	Phyllis “Tish” Preuss	Diane Bailey (ENG)	Muirfield Links	Gullane, East Lothian, Scotland
1986	Great Britain & Ireland	United States	13 - 5	Judy Bell	Diane Bailey (ENG)	Prairie Dunes Country Club	Hutchinson, Kansas
1988	Great Britain & Ireland	United States	11 - 7	Judy Bell	Diane Bailey (ENG)	Royal St. George’s Golf Club	Sandwich, Kent, England
1990	United States	Great Britain & Ireland	14 - 4	Leslie Shannon	Jill Thornhill (ENG)	Somerset Hills Country Club	Bernardsville, New Jersey
1992	Great Britain & Ireland	United States	10 - 8	Judy Oliver	Elizabeth Boatman (ENG)	Royal Liverpool Golf Club	Hoylake, England

1994	Great Britain & Ireland	United States	9 - 9	Lancy Smith	Elizabeth Boatman (ENG)	The Honors Course	Chattanooga, Tennessee
1996	Great Britain & Ireland	United States	11½ - 6½	Martha Lang	Ita Butler (IRL)	Killarney Golf Club, Killeen Course	Killarney, Ireland
1998	United States	Great Britain & Ireland	10 - 8	Barbara McIntire	Ita Butler (IRL)	Minikahda Club	Minneapolis, Minnesota
2000	United States	Great Britain & Ireland	10 - 8	Jane Bastanchury-Booth	Claire Dowling (ENG)	Ganton Golf Club	Ganton, North Yorkshire, England
2002	United States	Great Britain & Ireland	11 - 7	Mary Budke	Pam Benka (ENG)	Fox Chapel Golf Club	Pittsburgh, Pennsylvania

2004	United States	Great Britain & Ireland	10 - 8	Martha Kirouac	Ada O'Sullivan (IRL)	Formby Golf Club	Merseyside, England
2006	United States	Great Britain & Ireland	11½ - 6½	Carol Semple Thompson	Ada O'Sullivan (IRL)	Bandon Dunes Golf Resort, Pacific Duke Course	Bandon, Oregon
2008	United States	Great Britain & Ireland	13 - 7	Carol Semple Thompson	Mary McKenna (IRL)	St. Andrews Links, Old Course	St. Andrews, Fife, Scotland

World Amateur Team (Eisenhower Trophy)

Year	Winning Team	Runner-Up	Venue	Location
1958	Australia	United States	St. Andrews Links, Old Course	St. Andrews, Fife, Scotland
1960	United States	Australia	Merion Golf Club, East Course	Ardmore, Pennsylvania
1962	United States	Canada	Kawana Resort, Fuji Golf Course	It, Shizuoka, Japan

1964	Great Britain & Ireland	Canada	Olgiata Golf Club	Roma, Italy
1966	Australia	United States	Club de Golf Ciudad de México	Ciudad de México, México
1968	United States	Great Britain & Ireland	Royal Melbourne Golf Club	Melbourne, Australia
1970	United States	New Zealand	Real Club de la Puerta de Hierro	Madrid, Spain
1972	United States	Australia	Olivos Golf Club	Buenos Aires, Argentina
1974	United States	Japan	Casa de Campo	La Romana, Dominican Republic
1976	Great Britain & Ireland	Japan	Penina Golf Club	Portimão, Algarve, Portugal
1978	United States	Canada	Pacific Harbour Golf & Country Club	Suva, Viti Levu, Fiji
1980	United States	South Africa	Pinehurst Resort, No. 2 Course	Pinehurst, North Carolina
1982	United States	Japan	Golf Club de Lausanne	Lausanne, Switzerland
1984	Japan	United States	Royal Hong Kong Golf Club	Fanling, Hong Kong
1986	Canada	United States	Lagunita Country Club	Caracas, Venezuela
1988	Great Britain & Ireland	United States	Ullna Golf Club	Stockholm, Sweden
1990	Sweden	New Zealand	Christchurch Golf Club	Christchurch, New Zealand
1992	New Zealand	United States	Capilano Golf & Country Club / Marine Drive Golf Club	Vancouver, British Columbia, Canada

1994	United States	Great Britain & Ireland	The National Golf Club/La Boulie Golf Club	Versailles, France
1996	Australia	Sweden	Manila Southwoods Golf & Country Club	Manila, Philippines
1998	Great Britain & Ireland	Australia	Club de Golf Los Leones/Club de Golf La Dehesa	Santiago, Chile
2000	United States	Great Britain & Ireland	Sporting Club Berlin	Bad Saarow, Germany
2002	United States	France	Saujana Golf & Country Club	Kuala Lumpur, Malaysia
2004	United States	Spain	Westin Rio Mar Resort & Country Club	Río Grande, Puerto Rico
2006	Netherlands	Canada	De Zalze Golf Club/ Stellenbosch Golf Club	Cape Town, South Africa
2008	Scotland	United States	Royal Adelaide Golf Club/The Grange Golf Club	Adelaide, South Australia, Australia

World Women's Amateur Team (Espirito Santo Trophy)

Year	Winning Team	Runner-Up	Venue	Location
1964	France	United States	Golf de Saint-Germain	Saint-German-en-Laye, France
1966	United States	Canada	Club de Golf Ciudad de México	Ciudad de México, México

1968	United States	Australia	Victoria Golf Club	Cheltenham, Victoria, Australia
1970	United States	France	Club de Campo	Madrid, Spain
1972	United States	France	The Hindu Country Club	Buenos Aires, Argentina
1974	United States	Great Britain & Ireland	Casa de Campo	La Romana, Dominican Republic
1976	United States	France	Vilamoura Golf Club	Portimão, Algarve, Portugal
1978	Australia	Canada	Pacific Harbour Golf & Country Club	Suva, Viti Levu, Fiji
1980	United States	Australia	Pinehurst Resort, No. 2 Course	Pinehurst, North Carolina
1982	United States	New Zealand	Geneva Golf Club	Geneva, Switzerland
1984	United States	France	Royal Hong Kong Golf Club	Fanling, Hong Kong
1986	Spain	France	Lagunita Country Club	Caracas, Venezuela
1988	United States	Sweden	Drottningholm Golf Club	Stockholm, Sweden
1990	United States	New Zealand	Russley Golf Club	Christchurch, New Zealand
1992	Spain	Great Britain & Ireland	Marine Drive Golf Club	Vancouver, British Columbia, Canada
1994	United States	Korea (South)	The National Golf Club	Versailles, France
1996	Korea (South)	Italy	St. Elena Golf Club	Manila, Philippines
1998	United States	Italy	Prince of Wales Country Club	Santiago, Chile

2000	France	Korea (South)	Sporting Club Berlin	Bad Saarow, Germany
2002	Australia	Thailand	Saujana Golf & Country Club	Kuala Lumpur, Malaysia
2004	Sweden	Canada / United States	Rio Mar Country Club	Río Grande, Puerto Rico
2006	South Africa	Sweden	Stellenbosch Golf Club	Cape Town, South Africa
2008	Sweden	Spain	The Grange Golf Club	Adelaide, South Australia, Australia

APPENDIX 6. MEN'S MAJOR AMATEUR CHAMPIONS

British Amateur

1885	Allen MacFie	England	Royal Liverpool Golf Club	Hoylake, England
1886	Horace Hutchinson	England	St. Andrews Links, Old Course	St. Andrews, Fife, Scotland
1887	Horace Hutchinson	England	Royal Liverpool Golf Club	Hoylake, England
1888	John Ball	England	Prestwick Golf Club	Prestwick, South Ayrshire, Scotland
1889	Johnny Laidlay	Scotland	St. Andrews Links, Old Course	St. Andrews, Fife, Scotland
1890	John Ball	England	Royal Liverpool Golf Club	Hoylake, England
1891	Johnny Laidlay	Scotland	St. Andrews Links, Old Course	St. Andrews, Fife, Scotland
1892	John Ball	England	Royal St. George's Golf Club	Sandwich, Kent, England
1893	P. C. Anderson	Scotland	Prestwick Golf Club	Prestwick, South Ayrshire, Scotland
1894	John Ball	England	Royal Liverpool Golf Club	Hoylake, England
1895	Leslie Balfour-Melville	Scotland	St. Andrews Links, Old Course	St. Andrews, Fife, Scotland
1896	Freddie Tait	Scotland	Royal St. George's Golf Club	Sandwich, Kent, England
1897	Jack Allan	Scotland	Muirfield Links	Gullane, East Lothian, Scotland
1898	Freddie Tait	Scotland	Royal Liverpool Golf Club	Hoylake, England

1899	John Ball	England	Prestwick Golf Club	Prestwick, South Ayrshire, Scotland
1900	Harold Hilton	England	Royal St. George's Golf Club	Sandwich, Kent, England
1901	Harold Hilton	England	St. Andrews Links, Old Course	St. Andrews, Fife, Scotland
1902	Charles Hutchings	England	Royal Liverpool Golf Club	Hoylake, England
1903	Robert Maxwell	Scotland	Muirfield Links	Gullane, East Lothian, Scotland
1904	Walter Travis	United States	Royal St. George's Golf Club	Sandwich, Kent, England
1905	Arthur Barry	England	Prestwick Golf Club	Prestwick, South Ayrshire, Scotland
1906	James Robb	Scotland	Royal Liverpool Golf Club	Hoylake, England
1907	John Ball	England	St. Andrews Links, Old Course	St. Andrews, Fife, Scotland
1908	E. A. Lassen	England	Royal St. George's Golf Club	Sandwich, Kent, England
1909	Robert Maxwell	Scotland	Muirfield Links	Gullane, East Lothian, Scotland
1910	John Ball	England	Royal Liverpool Golf Club	Hoylake, England
1911	Harold Hilton	England	Prestwick Golf Club	Prestwick, South Ayrshire, Scotland
1912	John Ball	England	Royal North Devon Golf Club	Bideford, Devon, England
1913	Harold Hilton	England	St. Andrews Links, Old Course	St. Andrews, Fife, Scotland

1914	J. L. C. Jenkins	Scotland	Royal St. George's Golf Club	Sandwich, Kent, England
1920	Cyril Tolley	England	Muirfield Links	Gullane, East Lothian, Scotland
1921	Willie Hunter	Scotland	Royal Liverpool Golf Club	Hoylake, England
1922	Ernest Holderness	England	Prestwick Golf Club	Prestwick, South Ayrshire, Scotland
1923	Roger Wethered	England	Royal Cinque Ports Golf Club	Deal, Kent, England
1924	Ernest Holderness	England	St. Andrews Links, Old Course	St. Andrews, Fife, Scotland
1925	Robert Harris	Scotland	Royal North Devon Golf Club	Bideford, Devon, England
1926	Jess Sweetser	United States	Muirfield Links	Gullane, East Lothian, Scotland
1927	William Tweddell	England	Royal Liverpool Golf Club	Hoylake, England
1928	Phil Perkins	England	Prestwick Golf Club	Prestwick, South Ayrshire, Scotland
1929	Cyril Tolley	England	Royal St. George's Golf Club	Sandwich, Kent, England
1930	Bob Jones	United States	St. Andrews Links, Old Course	St. Andrews, Fife, Scotland
1931	Eric Martin-Smith	England	Royal North Devon Golf Club	Bideford, Devon, England
1932	John De Forest	England	Muirfield Links	Gullane, East Lothian, Scotland
1933	Michael Scott	England	Royal Liverpool Golf Club	Hoylake, England

1934	Lawson Little	United States	Prestwick Golf Club	Prestwick, South Ayrshire, Scotland
1935	Lawson Little	United States	Royal Lytham and St. Annes Golf Club	Lytham and St. Annes, Lancashire, England
1936	Hector Thomson	Scotland	St. Andrews Links, Old Course	St. Andrews, Fife, Scotland
1937	Robert Sweeny Jr.	United States	Royal St. George's Golf Club	Sandwich, Kent, England
1938	Charles Yates	United States	Royal Troon Golf Club	Troon, South Ayrshire, Scotland
1939	Alexander Kyle	Scotland	Royal Liverpool Golf Club	Hoylake, England
1946	James Bruen	Ireland	Royal Birkdale Golf Club	Southport, Merseyside, England
1947	Willie Turnesa	United States	Carnoustie Golf Links	Carnoustie, Angus, Scotland
1948	Frank Stranahan	United States	Royal St. George's Golf Club	Sandwich, Kent, England
1949	Samuel McCready	Ireland	Portmarnock Golf Club	Portmarnock, Fingal, Ireland
1950	Frank Stranahan	United States	St. Andrews Links, Old Course	St. Andrews, Fife, Scotland
1951	Dick Chapman	United States	Royal Porthcawl Golf Club	Porthcawl, South Wales, Wales
1952	Harvie Ward	United States	Prestwick Golf Club	Prestwick, South Ayrshire, Scotland

1953	Joe Carr	Ireland	Royal Liverpool Golf Club	Hoylake, England
1954	Douglas Bachli	Australia	Muirfield Links	Gullane, East Lothian, Scotland
1955	Joe Conrad	United States	Royal Lytham and St. Annes Golf Club	Lytham and St. Annes, Lancashire, England
1956	John Beharrell	England	Royal Troon Golf Club	Troon, South Ayrshire, Scotland
1957	Reid Jack	Scotland	Formby Golf Club	Merseyside, England
1958	Joe Carr	Ireland	St. Andrews Links, Old Course	St. Andrews, Fife, Scotland
1959	Deane Beman	United States	Royal St. George's Golf Club	Sandwich, Kent, England
1960	Joe Carr	Ireland	Royal Portrush Golf Club	Portrush, County Antrim, Northern Ireland
1961	Michael Bonallack	England	Turnberry, Ailsa Course	Turnberry, South Ayrshire, Scotland
1962	Richard Davies	United States	Royal Liverpool Golf Club	Hoylake, England
1963	Michael Lunt	England	St. Andrews Links, Old Course	St. Andrews, Fife, Scotland
1964	Gordon Clark	England	Ganton Golf Club	Ganton, North Yorkshire, England
1965	Michael Bonallack	England	Royal Porthcawl Golf Club	Porthcawl, South Wales, Wales
1966	Bobby Cole	South Africa	Carnoustie Golf Links	Carnoustie, Angus, Scotland

1967	Bob Dickson	United States	Formby Golf Club	Merseyside, England
1968	Michael Bonallack	England	Royal Troon Golf Club	Troon, South Ayrshire, Scotland
1969	Michael Bonallack	England	Royal Liverpool Golf Club	Hoylake, England
1970	Michael Bonallack	England	Royal County Down Golf Club	Newcastle, County Down, Northern Ireland
1971	Steve Melnyk	United States	Carnoustie Golf Links	Carnoustie, Angus, Scotland
1972	Trevor Homer	England	Royal St. George's Golf Club	Sandwich, Kent, England
1973	Dick Siderowf	United States	Royal Porthcawl Golf Club	Porthcawl, South Wales, Wales
1974	Trevor Homer	England	Muirfield Links	Gullane, East Lothian, Scotland
1975	Vinny Giles	United States	Royal Liverpool Golf Club	Hoylake, England
1976	Dick Siderowf	United States	St. Andrews Links, Old Course	St. Andrews, Fife, Scotland
1977	Peter McEvoy	England	Ganton Golf Club	Ganton, North Yorkshire, England
1978	Peter McEvoy	England	Royal Troon Golf Club	Troon, South Ayrshire, Scotland
1979	Jay Sigel	United States	Hillside Golf Club	Southport, England
1980	Duncan Evans	Wales	Royal Porthcawl Golf Club	Porthcawl, South Wales, Wales

1981	Phillipe Ploujoux	France	St. Andrews Links, Old Course	St. Andrews, Fife, Scotland
1982	Martin Thompson	England	Royal Cinque Ports Golf Club	Deal, Kent, England
1983	Philip Parkin	Wales	Turnberry, Ailsa Course	Turnberry, South Ayrshire, Scotland
1984	José María Olazábal	Spain	Formby Golf Club	Merseyside, England
1985	Garth McGimpsey	Northern Ireland	Royal Dornoch Golf Club	Dornoch, Scotland
1986	David Curry	England	Royal Lytham and St. Annes Golf Club	Lytham and St. Annes, Lancashire, England
1987	Paul Mayo	Wales	Prestwick Golf Club	Prestwick, South Ayrshire, Scotland
1988	Christian Hardin	Sweden	Royal Porthcawl Golf Club	Porthcawl, South Wales, Wales
1989	Stephen Dodd	Wales	Royal Birkdale Golf Club	Southport, Merseyside, England
1990	Rolf Muntz	Netherlands	Muirfield Links	Gullane, East Lothian, Scotland
1991	Gary Wolstenholme	England	Ganton Golf Club	Ganton, North Yorkshire, England
1992	Stephen Dundas	Scotland	Carnoustie Golf Links	Carnoustie, Angus, Scotland
1993	Iain Pyman	England	Royal Portrush Golf Club	Portrush, County Antrim, Northern Ireland
1994	Lee James	England	Nairn Golf Club	Nairn, Highlands, Scotland
1995	Gordon Sherry	Scotland	Royal Liverpool Golf Club	Hoylake, England

1996	Warren Bladon	England	Turnberry, Ailsa Course	Turnberry, South Ayrshire, Scotland
1997	Craig Watson	Scotland	Royal St. George's Golf Club	Sandwich, Kent, England
1998	Sergio García	Spain	Muirfield Links	Gullane, East Lothian, Scotland
1999	Graeme Storm	England	Royal County Down Golf Club	Newcastle, County Down, Northern Ireland
2000	Mikko Ilonen	Finland	Royal Liverpool Golf Club	Hoylake, England
2001	Michael Hoey	Northern Ireland	Prestwick Golf Club	Prestwick, South Ayrshire, Scotland
2002	Alejandro Larrazabal	Spain	Royal Porthcawl Golf Club	Porthcawl, South Wales, Wales
2003	Gary Wolstenholme	England	Royal Troon Golf Club	Troon, South Ayrshire, Scotland
2004	Stuart Wilson	Scotland	St. Andrews Links, Old Course	St. Andrews, Fife, Scotland
2005	Brian McElhinney	Ireland	Royal Birkdale Golf Club	Southport, Merseyside, England
2006	Julien Guerrier	France	Royal St. George's Golf Club	Sandwich, Kent, England
2007	Drew Weaver	United States	Royal Lytham and St. Annes Golf Club	Lytham and St. Annes, Lancashire, England
2008	Reinier Saxton	Netherlands	Westin Turnberry Resort	Turnberry, Scotland
2009	Matteo Manassero	Italy	Formby Golf Club	Merseyside, England

U.S. Amateur

1895	Charles Blair Macdonald	United States	Newport Country Club	Newport, Rhode Island

1896	H. J. Whigham	Scotland	Shinnecock Hills Golf Club	Southampton, New York
1897	H. J. Whigham	Scotland	Chicago Golf Club	Wheaton, Illinois
1898	Findlay Douglas	Scotland	Morris County Golf Club	Morristown, New Jersey
1899	H. M. Harriman	United States	Onwentsia Club	Lake Forest, Illinois
1900	Walter Travis	United States	Garden City Golf Club	Garden City, New York
1901	Walter Travis	United States	Atlantic City Country Club	Northfield, New Jersey
1902	Louis James	United States	Glen View Club	Golf, Illinois
1903	Walter Travis	United States	Nassau Country Club	Glen Cove, New York
1904	Chandler Egan	United States	Baltusrol Golf Club	Springfield, New Jersey
1905	Chandler Egan	United States	Chicago Golf Club	Wheaton, Illinois
1906	Eben Byers	United States	Englewood Golf Club	Englewood, New Jersey
1907	Jerome Travers	United States	Euclid Club	Cleveland Heights, Ohio
1908	Jerome Travers	United States	Garden City Golf Club	Garden City, New York

1909	Robert Gardner	United States	Chicago Golf Club	Wheaton, Illinois
1910	William Fownes Jr.	United States	The Country Club	Brookline, Massachusetts
1911	Harold Hilton	England	Apawamis Club	Rye, New York
1912	Jerome Travers	United States	Chicago Golf Club	Wheaton, Illinois
1913	Jerome Travers	United States	Garden City Golf Club	Garden City, New York
1914	Francis Ouimet	United States	Ekwanok Country Club	Manchester, Vermont
1915	Robert Gardner	United States	Country Club of Detroit	Detroit, Michigan
1916	Chick Evans	United States	Merion Golf Club, East Course	Ardmore, Pennsylvania
1919	S. Davidson Herron	United States	Oakmont Country Club	Oakmont, Pennsylvania
1920	Chick Evans	United States	Engineers' Country Club	Roslyn Harbor, New York
1921	Jesse Guilford	United States	St. Louis Country Club	St. Louis, Missouri
1922	Jess Sweetser	United States	The Country Club	Brookline, Massachusetts

1923	Max Marston	United States	Flossmoor Country Club	Flossmoor, Illinois
1924	Bob Jones	United States	Merion Golf Club, East Course	Ardmore, Pennsylvania
1925	Bob Jones	United States	Oakmont Country Club	Oakmont, Pennsylvania
1926	George Von Elm	United States	Baltusrol Golf Club, Lower Course	Springfield, New Jersey
1927	Bob Jones	United States	Minikahda Club	Minneapolis, Minnesota
1928	Bob Jones	United States	Brae Burn Country Club	West Newton, Massachusetts
1929	Harrison Johnston	United States	Pebble Beach Golf Links	Pebble Beach, California
1930	Bob Jones	United States	Merion Golf Club, East Course	Ardmore, Pennsylvania
1931	Francis Ouimet	United States	Beverly Country Club	Chicago, Illinois
1932	Ross Somerville	Canada	Baltimore CC, Five Farms, East Course	Timonium, Maryland
1933	George Dunlap	United States	Kenwood Country Club	Cincinnati, Ohio
1934	Lawson Little	United States	The Country Club	Brookline, Massachusetts

1935	Lawson Little	United States	The Country Club	Cleveland, Ohio
1936	John Fischer	United States	Garden City Golf Club	Garden City, New York
1937	Johnny Goodman	United States	Alderwood Country Club	Portland, Oregon
1938	Willie Turnesa	United States	Oakmont Country Club	Oakmont, Pennsylvania
1939	Bud Ward	United States	North Shore Country Club	Glenview, Illinois
1940	Dick Chapman	United States	Winged Foot Golf Club, West Course	Mamaroneck, New York
1941	Bud Ward	United States	Omaha Field Club	Omaha, Nebraska
1946	Ted Bishop	United States	Baltusrol Golf Club, Lower Course	Springfield, New Jersey
1947	Skee Riegel	United States	Pebble Beach Golf Links	Pebble Beach, California
1948	Willie Turnesa	United States	Memphis Country Club	Memphis, Tennessee
1949	Charlie Coe	United States	Oak Hill Country Club, East Course	Rochester, New York
1950	Sam Urzetta	United States	Minneapolis Golf Club	Minneapolis, Minnesota

1951	Billy Maxwell	United States	Saucon Valley Country Club, Old Course	Bethlehem, Pennsylvania
1952	Jack Westland	United States	Seattle Golf Club	Seattle, Washington
1953	Gene Littler	United States	Oklahoma City Golf & Country Club	Oklahoma City, Oklahoma
1954	Arnold Palmer	United States	Country Club of Detroit	Detroit, Michigan
1955	Harvie Ward	United States	Country Club of Virginia, James River Course	Richmond, Virginia
1956	Harvie Ward	United States	Knollwood Club	Lake Forest, Illinois
1957	Hillman Robbins	United States	The Country Club	Brookline, Massachusetts
1958	Charlie Coe	United States	Olympic Club, Lake Course	San Francisco, California
1959	Jack Nicklaus	United States	Broadmoor Golf Club, East Course	Colorado Springs, Colorado
1960	Deane Beman	United States	St. Louis Country Club	St. Louis, Missouri
1961	Jack Nicklaus	United States	Pebble Beach Golf Links	Pebble Beach, California
1962	Labron Harris Jr.	United States	Pinehurst Resort, No. 2 Course	Pinehurst, North Carolina

1963	Deane Beman	United States	Wakonda Club	Des Moines, Iowa
1964	Bill Campbell	United States	Canterbury Golf Club	Beachwood, Ohio
1965	Bob Murphy	United States	Southern Hills Country Club	Tulsa, Oklahoma
1966	Gary Cowan	Canada	Merion Golf Club, East Course	Ardmore, Pennsylvania
1967	Bob Dickson	United States	Broadmoor Golf Club, West Course	Colorado Springs, Colorado
1968	Bruce Fleisher	United States	Scioto Country Club	Columbus, Ohio
1969	Steve Melnyk	United States	Oakmont Country Club	Oakmont, Pennsylvania
1970	Lanny Wadkins	United States	Waverley Country Club	Portland, Oregon
1971	Gary Cowan	Canada	Wilmington Country Club, North Course	Wilmington, Delaware
1972	Vinny Giles	United States	Charlotte Country Club	Charlotte, North Carolina
1973	Craig Stadler	United States	Inverness Club	Toledo, Ohio
1974	Jerry Pate	United States	Ridgewood Country Club	Paramus, New Jersey

1975	Fred Ridley	United States	Country Club of Virginia, James River Course	Richmond, Virginia
1976	Bill Sander	United States	Bel-Air Country Club	Los Angeles, California
1977	John Fought	United States	Aronimink Golf Club	Newtown Square, Pennsylvania
1978	John Cook	United States	Plainfield Country Club	Edison, New Jersey
1979	Mark O'Meara	United States	Canterbury Golf Club	Beachwood, Ohio
1980	Hal Sutton	United States	Country Club of North Carolina	Southern Pines, North Carolina
1981	Nathaniel Crosby	United States	Olympic Club, Lake Course	San Francisco, California
1982	Jay Sigel	United States	The Country Club	Brookline, Massachusetts
1983	Jay Sigel	United States	North Shore Country Club	Glenview, Illinois
1984	Scott Verplank	United States	Oak Tree Golf Club	Edmond, Oklahoma
1985	Sam Randolph	United States	Montclair Golf Club	West Orange, New Jersey
1986	Buddy Alexander	United States	Shoal Creek Club	Shoal Creek, Alabama

1987	Billy Mayfair	United States	Jupiter Hills Club	Jupiter, Florida
1988	Eric Meeks	United States	Homestead, Cascades Course	Hot Springs, Virginia
1989	Chris Patton	United States	Merion Golf Club, East Course	Ardmore, Pennsylvania
1990	Phil Mickelson	United States	Cherry Hills Country Club	Cherry Hills Village, Colorado
1991	Mitch Voges	United States	The Honors Course	Chattanooga, Tennessee
1992	Justin Leonard	United States	Muirfield Village Golf Club	Dublin, Ohio
1993	John Harris	United States	Champions Golf Club, Cypress Creek Course	Houston, Texas
1994	Tiger Woods	United States	TPC at Sawgrass, Stadium Course	Sawgrass, Florida
1995	Tiger Woods	United States	Newport Country Club	Newport, Rhode Island
1996	Tiger Woods	United States	Pumpkin Ridge Golf Club, Witch Hollow Course	North Plains, Oregon
1997	Matt Kuchar	United States	Cog Hill Golf & Country Club, #4	Lemont, Illinois

1998	Hank Kuehne	United States	Oak Hill Country Club, East Course	Rochester, New York
1999	David Gossett	United States	Pebble Beach Golf Links	Pebble Beach, California
2000	Jeff Quinney	United States	Baltusrol Golf Club, Upper Course	Springfield, New Jersey
2001	Bubba Dickerson	United States	East Lake Golf Club	Atlanta, Georgia
2002	Ricky Barnes	United States	Oakland Hills Country Club	Bloomfield Hills, Michigan
2003	Nick Flanagan	Australia	Oakmont Country Club	Oakmont, Pennsylvania
2004	Ryan Moore	United States	Winged Foot Golf Club, West Course	Mamaroneck, New York
2005	Edoardo Molinari	Italy	Merion Golf Club, East Course	Ardmore, Pennsylvania
2006	Richie Ramsay	Scotland	Hazeltine National Golf Club	Chaska, Minnesota
2007	Colt Knost	United States	Olympic Club, Lake Course	San Francisco, California
2008	Danny Lee	New Zealand	Pinehurst Resort, No. 2 Course	Pinehurst, North Carolina
2009	An Byeong-hun	Korea (South)	Southern Hills Country Club	Tulsa, Oklahoma

Canadian Amateur

1895	Thomas Harley	Canada	Royal Ottawa Golf Club	Gatineau, Québec
1896	Stewart Gillespie	Canada	Le Club de Golf Royal Québec	Boischatel, Québec
1897	W. A. H. Kerr	Canada	Royal Montréal Golf Club	Île Bizard, Québec
1898	George Lyon	Canada	Toronto Golf Club	Toronto, Ontario
1899	Vere Brown	Canada	Royal Ottawa Golf Club	Gatineau, Québec
1900	George Lyon	Canada	Royal Montréal Golf Club	Île Bizard, Québec
1901	W. A. H. Kerr	Canada	Toronto Golf Club	Toronto, Ontario
1902	Fritz Martin	Canada	Royal Montréal Golf Club	Île Bizard, Québec
1903	George Lyon	Canada	Toronto Golf Club	Toronto, Ontario
1904	J. Percy Taylor	Canada	Royal Montréal Golf Club	Île Bizard, Québec
1905	George Lyon	Canada	Toronto Golf Club	Toronto, Ontario
1906	George Lyon	Canada	Royal Ottawa Golf Club	Gatineau, Québec
1907	George Lyon	Canada	Lambton Golf Club	Toronto, Ontario
1908	A. Wilson Jr.	Canada	Royal Montréal Golf Club	Île Bizard, Québec
1909	E. Legge	Canada	Toronto Golf Club	Toronto, Ontario
1910	Fritz Martin	Canada	Lambton Golf Club	Toronto, Ontario
1911	G. H. Hutton	Canada	Royal Ottawa Golf Club	Gatineau, Québec
1912	George Lyon	Canada	Royal Montréal Golf Club	Île Bizard, Québec
1913	G. H. Turpin	Canada	Toronto Golf Club	Toronto, Ontario
1914	George Lyon	Canada	Royal Ottawa Golf Club	Gatineau, Québec
1919	William McLuckie	Canada	Lambton Golf Club	Toronto, Ontario
1920	C. B. Grier	Canada	Beaconsfield Golf Club	Pointe-Claire, Québec

1921	Frank Thompson	Canada	Winnipeg Golf Club	Winnipeg, Manitoba
1922	C. C. Fraser	Canada	Hamilton Golf and Country Club	Ancaster, Ontario
1923	W. J. Thompson	Canada	Kanawaki Golf Club	Kahnawake, Québec
1924	Frank Thompson	Canada	Rosedale Golf Club	Toronto, Ontario
1925	Donald Carrick	Canada	Royal Ottawa Golf Club	Gatineau, Québec
1926	Ross Somerville	Canada	Toronto Golf Club	Toronto, Ontario
1927	Donald Carrick	Canada	Hamilton Golf and Country Club	Ancaster, Ontario
1928	Ross Somerville	Canada	Summerlea Golf & Country Club	Montréal, Québec
1929	Eddie Held	United States	Jasper Park Lodge Golf Club	Jasper, Alberta
1930	Ross Somerville	Canada	London Hunt & Country Club	London, Ontario
1931	Ross Somerville	Canada	Royal Montréal Golf Club	Île Bizard, Québec
1932	Gordon Taylor	Canada	Lambton Golf Club	Toronto, Ontario
1933	Albert Campbell	United States	Shaughnessy Heights Golf Club	Vancouver, British Columbia
1934	Albert Campbell	United States	Le Club Laval-sur-le-Lac	Laval-sur-le-Lac, Québec
1935	Ross Somerville	Canada	Hamilton Golf and Country Club	Ancaster, Ontario

1936	Fred Haas	United States	St. Charles Country Club	Winnipeg, Manitoba
1937	Ross Somerville	Canada	Ottawa Hunt and Golf Club	Ottawa, Ontario
1938	Ted Adams	United States	London Hunt & Country Club	London, Ontario
1939	Ken Black	Canada	Mt. Bruno Golf Club	Mt. Bruno, Québec
1946	Henry Martell	Canada	Mayfair Golf & Country Club	Edmonton, Alberta
1947	Frank Stranahan	United States	Le Club de Golf Royal Québec	Boischatel, Québec
1948	Frank Stranahan	United States	Hamilton Golf and Country Club	Ancaster, Ontario
1949	Dick Chapman	United States	Riverside Golf & Country Club	East Riverside, New Brunswick
1950	Bill Mawhinney	Canada	Saskatoon Golf & Country Club	Saskatoon, Saskatchewan
1951	Walter McElroy	Canada	Royal Ottawa Golf Club	Gatineau, Québec
1952	Larry Bouchery	United States	Capilano Golf & Country Club	Vancouver, British Columbia
1953	Don Cherry	United States	Kanawaki Golf Club	Kahnawake, Québec
1954	Harvie Ward	United States	London Hunt & Country Club	London, Ontario

1955	Moe Norman	Canada	Calgary Golf & Country Club	Calgary, Alberta
1956	Moe Norman	Canada	Fraser Edmundston Golf Club	Edmundston, New Brunswick
1957	Nick Weslock	Canada	St. Charles Country Club	Winnipeg, Manitoba
1958	Bruce Castator	Canada	Scarboro Golf & Country Club	Scarborough, Ontario
1959	John Johnston	Canada	Marine Drive Golf Club	Vancouver, British Columbia
1960	Keith Alexander	Canada	Ottawa Hunt and Golf Club	Ottawa, Ontario
1961	Gary Cowan	Canada	Edmonton Country Club	Edmonton, Alberta
1962	Reg Taylor	South Africa	Sunningdale Country Club	London, Ontario
1963	Nick Weslock	Canada	Riverside Golf & Country Club	East Riverside, New Brunswick
1964	Nick Weslock	Canada	Riverside Golf & Country Club	Saskatoon, Saskatchewan
1965	Bunky Henry	United States	Pine Ridge Golf Club	Winnipeg, Manitoba
1966	Nick Weslock	Canada	Summerlea Golf & Country Club	Montréal, Québec
1967	Stuart Jones	New Zealand	Royal Colwood Golf Club	Victoria, British Columbia
1968	Jim Doyle	Canada	Mayfair Golf & Country Club	Edmonton, Alberta
1969	Wayne MacDonald	Canada	Westmount Golf & Country Club	Montréal, Québec

1970	Allen Miller	United States	Ottawa Hunt and Golf Club	Ottawa, Ontario
1971	Dick Siderowf	United States	Oakfield Country Club	Grand Lake, Nova Scotia
1972	Doug Roxburgh	Canada	Earl Grey Golf Club	Calgary, Alberta
1973	George Burns II	United States	Summit Golf & Country Club	Richmond Hill, Ontario
1974	Doug Roxburgh	Canada	Niakwa Country Club	Winnipeg, Manitoba
1975	Jim Nelford	Canada	Riverside Golf & Country Club	East Riverside, New Brunswick
1976	Jim Nelford	Canada	Royal Colwood Golf Club	Victoria, British Columbia
1977	Rod Spittle	Canada	Hamilton Golf and Country Club	Ancaster, Ontario
1978	Rod Spittle	Canada	Le Club Laval-sur-le-Lac	Laval-sur-le-Lac, Québec
1979	Rafael Alarcon	Mexico	Brantford Golf & Country Club	Brantford, Ontario
1980	Greg Olson	Canada	Halifax Golf Club, New	Halifax, Nova Scotia
1981	Richard Zokol	Canada	Calgary Golf & Country Club	Calgary, Alberta
1982	Doug Roxburgh	Canada	Kanawaki Golf Club	Kahnawake, Québec
1983	Danny Mijovic	Canada	Capilano Golf & Country Club	Vancouver, British Columbia
1984	Bill Swartz	Canada	Sunningdale Country Club	London, Ontario
1985	Brent Franklin	Canada	Riverside Golf & Country Club	Saskatoon, Saskatchewan

1986	Brent Franklin	Canada	Derrick Golf and Winter Club	Edmonton, Alberta
1987	Brent Franklin	Canada	Mactaquac Provincial Park Golf Club	Fredericton, New Brunswick
1988	Doug Roxburgh	Canada	Gallaghers Canyon Golf & Country Club	Kelowna, British Columbia
1989	Peter Major	Canada	Oakfield Country Club	Grand Lake, Nova Scotia
1990	Warren Sye	Canada	Weston Golf and Country Club	Toronto, Ontario
1991	Jeff Kraemer	Canada	Royal Ottawa Golf Club	Gatineau, Québec
1992	Darren Ritchie	Canada	Riverside Golf & Country Club	East Riverside, New Brunswick
1993	Gary Simpson	Australia	Victoria Golf Club	Victoria, British Columbia
1994	Warren Sye	Canada	Hamilton Golf and Country Club	Ancaster, Ontario
1995	Garrett Willis	United States	Toronto Golf Club	Toronto, Ontario
1996	Rob McMillan	Canada	Glendale Country Club	Winnipeg, Manitoba
1997	Dale Goehring	Canada	The Links at Crowbush Cove	Charlottetown, Prince Edward Island
1998	Craig Matthew	Canada	Hillsdale Golf & Country Club	Mirabel, Québec
1999	Han Lee	United States	Rivershore Golf Club	Kamloops, British Columbia

2000	Han Lee	United States	Glendale Golf & Country Club	Edmonton, Alberta
2001	Gareth Paddison	New Zealand	Credit Valley Golf & Country Club	Mississauga, Ontario
2002	Dillard Pruitt	United States	Fraser Edmundston Golf Club	Edmundston, New Brunswick
2003	Richard Scott	Canada	Shaughnessy Golf & Country Club	Vancouver, British Columbia
2004	Darren Wallace	Canada	Beaconsfield Golf Club	Pointe-Claire, Québec
2005	Richard Scott	Canada	Bell Bay Golf Club	Baddeck, Nova Scotia
2006	Richard Scott	Canada	Mississauga Golf & Country Club	Mississauga, Ontario
2007	Nick Taylor	Canada	Riverside Golf & Country Club	Saskatoon, Saskatchewan
2008	Cam Burke	Canada	Paradise Canyon Golf Resort	Lethbridge, Alberta
2009	Cam Burke	Canada	Club de Golf le Blainvillier	Blainville, Québec

Western Amateur

1899	David Forgan	Glen View Club	Golf, Illinois
1900	William Waller	Onwentsia Club	Lake Forest, Illinois
1901	Phelps Hoyt	Midlothian Country Club	Midlothian, Illinois

1902	Chandler Egan	Chicago Golf Club	Wheaton, Illinois
1903	Walter Egan	Euclid Club	Cleveland Heights, Ohio
1904	Chandler Egan	Exmoor Country Club	Highland Park, Illinois
1905	Chandler Egan	Glen View Club	Golf, Illinois
1906	D. E. Sawyer	Glen Echo Country Club	St. Louis, Missouri
1907	Chandler Egan	Chicago Golf Club	Wheaton, Illinois
1908	Mason Phelps	Arsenal Golf Club	Rock Island, Illinois
1909	Chick Evans	Homewood Country Club	Flossmoor, Illinois
1910	Mason Phelps	Minikahda Club	Minneapolis, Minnesota
1911	Albert Seckel	Detroit Golf Club, North Course	Detroit, Michigan
1912	Chick Evans	Denver Country Club	Denver, Colorado
1913	Warren Wood	Homewood Country Club	Flossmoor, Illinois
1914	Chick Evans	Kent Country Club	Grand Rapids, Michigan
1915	Chick Evans	Mayfield Country Club	Cleveland, Ohio
1916	Heinrich Schmidt	Del Monte Golf & Country Club	Del Monte, California
1917	Francis Ouimet	Midlothian Country Club	Midlothian, Illinois
1919	Harry Legg	Sunset Hill Country Club	St. Louis, Missouri
1920	Chick Evans	Memphis Country Club	Memphis, Tennessee
1921	Chick Evans	Westmoreland Country Club	Wilmette, Illinois
1922	Chick Evans	Hillcrest Country Club	Kansas City, Missouri
1923	Chick Evans	Mayfield Country Club	Cleveland, Ohio
1924	Harrison Johnston	Hinsdale Country Club	Hinsdale, Illinois

1925	Keefe Carter	Lochmoor Club	Grosse Pointe Woods, Michigan
1926	Frank Dolp	White Bear Yacht Club	White Bear Lake, Minnesota
1927	Bon Stein	Seattle Golf Club	Seattle, Washington
1928	Frank Dolp	Bob O'Link Golf Club	Highland Park, Illinois
1929	Don Moe	Mission Hills Country Club	Mission Hills, Kansas
1930	John Lehman	Beverly Country Club	Chicago, Illinois
1931	Don Moe	Portland Golf Club	Portland, Oregon
1932	Gus Moreland	Rockford Country Club	Rockford, Illinois
1933	Jack Westland	Memphis Country Club	Memphis, Tennessee
1934	Zell Eaton	Twin Hills Golf & Country Club	Oklahoma City, Oklahoma
1935	Charles Yates	Broadmoor Golf Club, East Course	Colorado Springs, Colorado
1936	Paul Leslie	Happy Hollow Golf Club	Omaha, Nebraska
1937	Wilford Wehrle	Los Angeles Country Club, North Course	Los Angeles, California
1938	Bob Babbish	South Bend Country Club	South Bend, Indiana
1939	Harry Todd	Oklahoma City Golf & Country Club	Oklahoma City, Oklahoma
1940	Marvin Ward	Minneapolis Golf Club	Minneapolis, Minnesota
1941	Marvin Ward	Broadmoor Golf Club, East Course	Colorado Springs, Colorado
1942	Pat Abbott	Manito Golf & Country Club	Spokane, Washington
1946	Frank Stranahan	Northland Country Club	Duluth, Minnesota
1947	Marvin Ward	Wakonda Club	Des Moines, Iowa
1948	Skee Reigel	Wichita Country Club	Wichita, Kansas
1949	Frank Stranahan	Bellerive Country Club	St. Louis, Missouri
1950	Charlie Coe	Dallas Country Club	Dallas, Texas

1951	Frank Stranahan	South Bend Country Club	South Bend, Indiana
1952	Frank Stranahan	Exmoor Country Club	Highland Park, Illinois
1953	Dale Morey	Blythefield Country Club	Grand Rapids, Michigan
1954	Bruce Cudd	Broadmoor Golf Club	Seattle, Washington
1955	Eddie Merrins	Rockford Country Club	Rockford, Illinois
1956	Mason Rudolph	Belle Meade Country Club	Nashville, Tennessee
1957	Ed Updegraff	Old Warson Country Club	St. Louis, Missouri
1958	James (Billy) Key	Country Club of Florida	Delray Beach, Florida
1959	Ed Updegraff	Waverley Country Club	Portland, Oregon
1960	Tommy Aaron	Northland Country Club	Duluth, Minnesota
1961	Jack Nicklaus	New Orleans Country Club	New Orleans, Louisiana
1962	Art Hudnutt	Orchard Lake Country Club	Orchard Lake, Michigan
1963	Tom Weiskopf	Point O'Woods Golf & Country Club	Benton Harbor, Michigan
1964	Steve Oppermann	Tucson Country Club	Tucson, Arizona
1965	Bob E. Smith	Point O'Woods Golf & Country Club	Benton Harbor, Michigan
1966	Jim Wiechers	Pinehurst Resort, No. 2 Course	Pinehurst, North Carolina
1967	Bob E. Smith	Milburn Golf & Country Club	Overland Park, Kansas
1968	Rik Massengale	Grosse Ile Golf & Country Club	Grosse Ile, Michigan
1969	Steve Melnyk	Rockford Country Club	Rockford, Illinois
1970	Lanny Wadkins	Wichita Country Club	Wichita, Kansas
1971	Andy North	Point O'Woods Golf & Country Club	Benton Harbor, Michigan
1972	Gary Sanders	Point O'Woods Golf & Country Club	Benton Harbor, Michigan
1973	Ben Crenshaw	Point O'Woods Golf & Country Club	Benton Harbor, Michigan

1974	Curtis Strange	Point O'Woods Golf & Country Club	Benton Harbor, Michigan
1975	Andy Bean	Point O'Woods Golf & Country Club	Benton Harbor, Michigan
1976	John Stark	Point O'Woods Golf & Country Club	Benton Harbor, Michigan
1977	Jim Nelford	Point O'Woods Golf & Country Club	Benton Harbor, Michigan
1978	Bob Clampett	Point O'Woods Golf & Country Club	Benton Harbor, Michigan
1979	Hal Sutton	Point O'Woods Golf & Country Club	Benton Harbor, Michigan
1980	Hal Sutton	Point O'Woods Golf & Country Club	Benton Harbor, Michigan
1981	Frank Fuhrer	Point O'Woods Golf & Country Club	Benton Harbor, Michigan
1982	Rick Fehr	Point O'Woods Golf & Country Club	Benton Harbor, Michigan
1983	Billy Tuten	Point O'Woods Golf & Country Club	Benton Harbor, Michigan
1984	John Inman	Point O'Woods Golf & Country Club	Benton Harbor, Michigan
1985	Scott Verplank	Point O'Woods Golf & Country Club	Benton Harbor, Michigan
1986	Greg Parker	Point O'Woods Golf & Country Club	Benton Harbor, Michigan
1987	Hugh Royer, III	Point O'Woods Golf & Country Club	Benton Harbor, Michigan
1988	Chris DiMarco	Point O'Woods Golf & Country Club	Benton Harbor, Michigan
1989	David Sutherland	Point O'Woods Golf & Country Club	Benton Harbor, Michigan
1990	Craig Kanada	Point O'Woods Golf & Country Club	Benton Harbor, Michigan
1991	Phil Mickelson	Point O'Woods Golf & Country Club	Benton Harbor, Michigan
1992	Justin Leonard	Point O'Woods Golf & Country Club	Benton Harbor, Michigan
1993	Justin Leonard	Point O'Woods Golf & Country Club	Benton Harbor, Michigan
1994	Tiger Woods	Point O'Woods Golf & Country Club	Benton Harbor, Michigan
1995	Patrick Lee	Point O'Woods Golf & Country Club	Benton Harbor, Michigan
1996	Joel Kribel	Point O'Woods Golf & Country Club	Benton Harbor, Michigan

1997	Danny Green	Point O'Woods Golf & Country Club	Benton Harbor, Michigan
1998	Michael Henderson	Point O'Woods Golf & Country Club	Benton Harbor, Michigan
1999	Steve Scott	Point O'Woods Golf & Country Club	Benton Harbor, Michigan
2000	Michael Kirk	Point O'Woods Golf & Country Club	Benton Harbor, Michigan
2001	Bubba Dickerson	Point O'Woods Golf & Country Club	Benton Harbor, Michigan
2002	John Klauk	Point O'Woods Golf & Country Club	Benton Harbor, Michigan
2003	Chris Botsford	Point O'Woods Golf & Country Club	Benton Harbor, Michigan
2004	Ryan Moore	Point O'Woods Golf & Country Club	Benton Harbor, Michigan
2005	Jamie Lovemark	Point O'Woods Golf & Country Club	Benton Harbor, Michigan
2006	Bronson LaCassie	Point O'Woods Golf & Country Club	Benton Harbor, Michigan
2007	Jhared Hack	Point O'Woods Golf & Country Club	Benton Harbor, Michigan
2008	Danny Lee	Point O'Woods Golf & Country Club	Benton Harbor, Michigan
2009	John Hahn	Conway Farms Golf Club	Lake Forest, Illinois

NCAA Men's Division I Championship

Year	Individual Champion	College	Team Champion	Venue/Host	Location
1897	Louis Bayard Jr.	Princeton	Yale	Ardsley Country Club	Ardsley-on-Hudson, New York
1898 Fall	James Curtis	Harvard	Yale	Ardsley Country Club	Ardsley-on-Hudson, New York

1898 Spring	John Reid Jr.	Yale	Harvard	Ardsley Country Club	Ardsley-on-Hudson, New York
1899	Percy Pyne	Princeton	Harvard	Ardsley Country Club	Ardsley-on-Hudson, New York
1901	Halstead Lindsley	Harvard	Harvard	Atlantic City Country Club	Northfield, New Jersey
1902 Fall	Chandler Egan	Harvard	Harvard	Morris County Golf Club	Morristown, New Jersey
1902 Spring	Charles Hitchcock Jr.	Yale	Yale	Garden City Golf Club	Garden City, New York
1903	F. O. Reinhart	Princeton	Harvard	Garden City Golf Club	Garden City, New York
1904	A. L. White	Harvard	Harvard	Myopia Hunt Club	South Hamilton, Massachusetts
1905	Robert Abbott	Yale	Yale	Garden City Golf Club	Garden City, New York
1906	W. E. Clow Jr.	Yale	Yale	Garden City Golf Club	Garden City, New York
1907	Ellis Knowles	Yale	Yale	Nassau Country Club	Glen Cove, New York
1908	H. H. Wilder	Harvard	Yale	Brae Burn Country Club	West Newton, Massachusetts

1909	Albert Seckel	Princeton	Yale	Apawamis Club	Rye, New York
1910	Robert Hunter	Yale	Yale	Essex County Club	Manchester-by-the-Sea, Massachusetts
1911	George Stanley	Yale	Yale	Baltusrol Golf Club	Springfield, New Jersey
1912	F. C. Davison	Harvard	Yale	Ekwanok Country Club	Manchester, Vermont
1913	Nathaniel Wheeler	Yale	Yale	Huntingdon Valley Country Club	Huntingdon Valley, Pennsylvania
1914	Edward Allis	Harvard	Princeton	Garden City Golf Club	Garden City, New York
1915	Francis Blossom	Yale	Yale	Greenwich Country Club	Greenwich, Connecticut
1916	J. W. Hubbell	Harvard	Princeton	Oakmont Country Club	Oakmont, Pennsylvania
1919	A. L. Walker Jr.	Columbia	Princeton	Merion Golf Club	Ardmore, Pennsylvania
1920	Jess Sweetser	Yale	Princeton	Nassau Country Club	Glen Cove, New York
1921	Simpson Dean	Princeton	Dartmouth	Greenwich Country Club	Greenwich, Connecticut

1922	Pollack Boyd	Dartmouth	Princeton	Garden City Golf Club	Garden City, New York
1923	Dexter Cummings	Yale	Princeton	Siwanoy Country Club	Eastchester, New York
1924	Dexter Cummings	Yale	Yale	Greenwich Country Club	Greenwich, Connecticut
1925	Fred Lamprecht	Tulane	Yale	Montclair Golf Club	West Orange, New Jersey
1926	Fred Lamprecht	Tulane	Yale	Merion Golf Club	Ardmore, Pennsylvania
1927	Watts Gunn	Georgia Tech	Princeton	Garden City Golf Club	Garden City, New York
1928	Maurice McCarthy	Georgetown	Princeton	Apawamis Club	Rye, New York
1929	Tom Aycock	Yale	Princeton	Hollywood Country Club	Deal, New Jersey
1930	George Dunlap	Princeton	Princeton	Oakmont Country Club	Oakmont, Pennsylvania
1931	George Dunlap	Princeton	Yale	Olympia Fields Country Club	Olympia Fields, Illinois
1932	John Fischer	Michigan	Yale	Homestead Resort, Cascades Course	Hot Springs, Virginia

1933	Walter Emery	Oklahoma	Yale	Country Club of Buffalo	Williamsville, New York
1934	Charles Yates	Georgia Tech	Michigan	Country Club of Cleveland	Cleveland, Ohio
1935	Ed White	Texas	Michigan	Congressional Country Club	Bethesda, Maryland
1936	Chuck Kocsis	Michigan	Yale	North Shore Country Club	Glenview, Illinois
1937	Fred Haas	LSU	Princeton	Oakmont Country Club	Oakmont, Pennsylvania
1938	John Burke	Georgetown	Stanford	Louisville Country Club	Louisville, Kentucky
1939	Vincent D'Antoni	Tulane	Stanford	Wakonda Club	Des Moines, Iowa
1940	Dixon Brooke	Virginia	Princeton / LSU (tie)	Ekwanok Country Club	Manchester, Vermont
1941	Earl Stewart	LSU	Stanford	Ohio State Univ. GC, Scarlet Course	Columbus, Ohio
1942	Frank "Sandy" Tatum	Stanford	LSU / Stanford (tie)	Notre Dame Golf Course	South Bend, Indiana
1943	Wally Ulrich	Carleton	Yale	Olympia Fields Country Club	Olympia Fields, Illinois

1944	Louis Lick	Minnesota	Notre Dame	Inverness Club	Toledo, Ohio
1945	John Lorms	Ohio State	Ohio State	Ohio State Univ. GC, Scarlet Course	Columbus, Ohio
1946	George Hamer	Georgia	Stanford	Springdale Golf Course	Princeton, New Jersey
1947	Dave Barclay	Michigan	LSU	University of Michigan Golf Course	Ann Arbor, Michigan
1948	Bob Harris	San Jose State	San Jose State	Stanford Golf Course	Stanford, California
1949	Harvie Ward	North Carolina	North Texas State	Iowa State College Golf Course	Ames, Iowa
1950	Fred Wampler	Purdue	North Texas State	University of New Mexico Golf Course	Albuquerque, New Mexico
1951	Tom Nieporte	Ohio State	North Texas State	Ohio State Univ. GC, Scarlet Course	Columbus, Ohio
1952	Jim Vickers	Oklahoma	North Texas State	Purdue Course	Lafayette, Indiana
1953	Earl Moeller	Oklahoma State	Stanford	Broadmoor Golf Club	Seattle, Washington

1954	Hillman Robbins	Memphis	Southern Methodist	Brae Burn Country Club	Houston, Texas
1955	Joe Campbell	Purdue	LSU	Holston Hills Country Club	Knoxville, Tennessee
1956	Rick Jones	Ohio State	Houston	Ohio State Univ. GC, Scarlet Course	Columbus, Ohio
1957	Rex Baxter Jr.	Houston	Houston	Broadmoor Golf Club	Seattle, Washington
1958	Phil Rodgers	Houston	Houston	Taconic Golf Club	Williamstown, Massachusetts
1959	Dick Crawford	Houston	Houston	Eugene Country Club	Eugene, Oregon
1960	Dick Crawford	Houston	Houston	Broadmoor Golf Club	Seattle, Washington
1961	Jack Nicklaus	Ohio State	Purdue	South Course at Purdue University	Lafayette, Indiana
1962	Kermit Zarley	Houston	Houston	Duke University Golf Course	Durham, North Carolina
1963	R. H. Sikes	Arkansas	Oklahoma State	Wichita Country Club	Wichita, Kansas
1964	Terry Small	San Jose State	Houston	Broadmoor Golf Club	Seattle, Washington

1965	Marty Fleckman	Houston	Houston	Holston Hills Country Club	Knoxville, Tennessee
1966	Bob Murphy	Florida	Houston	Stanford Golf Course	Stanford, California
1967	Hale Irwin	Colorado	Houston	Shawnee Inn and Golf Resort	Shawnee-on-Delaware, Pennsylvania
1968	Grier Jones	Oklahoma State	Florida	New Mexico State University Golf Course	Las Cruces, New Mexico
1969	Bob Clark	Cal State, Los Angeles	Houston	Broadmoor Golf Club	Seattle, Washington
1970	John Mahaffey	Houston	Houston	Ohio State University GC, Scarlet Course	Columbus, Ohio
1971	Ben Crenshaw	Texas	Texas	Tucson National Golf Club	Tucson, Arizona
1972	Ben Crensaw/ TomKite (tie)	Texas (both)	Texas	Cape Coral Country Club	Cape Coral, Florida
1973	Ben Crenshaw	Texas	Florida	Stillwater Country Club	Stillwater, Oklahoma

1974	Curtis Strange	Wake Forest	Wake Forest	Carlton Oaks Country Club	Santee, California
1975	Jay Haas	Wake Forest	Wake Forest	Ohio State University GC, Scarlet Course	Columbus, Ohio
1976	Scott Simpson	Southern California	Oklahoma State	University of New Mexico Golf Course	Albuquerque, New Mexico
1977	Scott Simpson	Southern California	Houston	Seven Oaks Golf Club	Hamilton, New York
1978	David Edwards	Oklahoma State	Oklahoma State	Eugene Country Club	Eugene, Oregon
1979	Gary Hallberg	Wake Forest	Ohio State	Bermuda Run Country Club	Advance, North Carolina
1980	Jay Don Blake	Utah State	Oklahoma State	Ohio State University GC, Scarlet Course	Columbus, Ohio
1981	Ron Commans	Southern California	Brigham Young	Stanford Golf Course	Stanford, California
1982	Billy Ray Brown	Houston	Houston	Pinehurst Resort, No. 2 Course	Pinehurst, North Carolina
1983	Jim Carter	Arizona State	Oklahoma State	San Joaquin Country Club	Fresno, California

1984	John Inman	North Carolina	Houston	Bear Creek Golf World	Houston, Texas
1985	Clark Burroughs	Ohio State	Houston	University of Florida Golf Course	Gainesville, Florida
1986	Scott Verplank	Oklahoma State	Wake Forest	Bermuda Run Country Club	Advance, North Carolina
1987	Brian Watts	Oklahoma State	Oklahoma State	Ohio State University GC, Scarlet Course	Columbus, Ohio
1988	E. J. Pfister	Oklahoma State	UCLA	North Ranch Country Club	Westlake Village, California
1989	Phil Mickelson	Arizona State	Oklahoma	Stillwater Country Club	Stillwater, Oklahoma
1990	Phil Mickelson	Arizona State	Arizona State	University of Florida Golf Course	Gainesville, Florida
1991	Warren Schutte	UNLV	Oklahoma State	Poppy Hills Golf Course	Pebble Beach, California
1992	Phil Mickelson	Arizona State	Arizona	University of New Mexico Golf Course	Albuquerque, New Mexico

1993	Todd Demsey	Arizona State	Florida	Univ. of Kentucky Club, Big Blue Course	Lexington, Kentucky
1994	Justin Leonard	Texas	Stanford	Stonebridge Ranch Country Club	McKinney, Texas
1995	Chip Spratlin	Auburn	Oklahoma State	Ohio State University GC, Scarlet Course	Columbus, Ohio
1996	Tiger Woods	Stanford	Arizona State	The Honors Course	Ooltewah, Tennessee
1997	Charles Warren	Clemson	Pepperdine	Conway Farms Golf Club	Lake Forest, Illinois
1998	James McLean	Minnesota	UNLV	University of New Mexico Golf Course	Albuquerque, New Mexico
1999	Luke Donald	Northwestern	Georgia	Hazeltine National Golf Club	Chaska, Minnesota
2000	Charles Howell III	Oklahoma State	Oklahoma State	Grand National Golf Club, Lake Course	Opelika, Alabama

2001	Nick Gilliam	Florida	Florida	Duke University Golf Course	Durham, North Carolina
2002	Troy Matteson	Georgia Tech	Minnesota	Ohio State University GC, Scarlet Course	Columbus, Ohio
2003	Alejandro Cañizares	Arizona State	Clemson	Karsten Creek Golf Club	Stillwater, Oklahoma
2004	Ryan Moore	UNLV	California	Homestead Resort, Cascades Course	Hot Springs, Virginia
2005	James Lepp	Washington	Georgia	Caves Valley Golf Club	Owings Mills, Maryland
2006	Jonathan Moore	Oklahoma State	Oklahoma State	Sunriver Resort, Meadows Course	Sunriver, Oregon
2007	Jamie Lovemark	Southern California	Stanford	Golden Horseshoe Golf Course	Williamsburg, Virginia
2008	Kevin Chappell	UCLA	UCLA	Birck Boilermaker GC, Kampen Course	West Lafayette, Indiana

2009	Matt Hill	North Carolina State	Texas A&M	Inverness Club	Toledo, Ohio

North and South Amateur

1901	George Dutton	Pinehurst Resort, No. 2 Course	Pinehurst, North Carolina
1902	Charles Cory	Pinehurst Resort, No. 2 Course	Pinehurst, North Carolina
1903	T. Sterling Beckwith	Pinehurst Resort, No. 2 Course	Pinehurst, North Carolina
1904	Walter Travis	Pinehurst Resort, No. 2 Course	Pinehurst, North Carolina
1905	Dr. L. Lee Harban	Pinehurst Resort, No. 2 Course	Pinehurst, North Carolina
1906	Warren Wood	Pinehurst Resort, No. 2 Course	Pinehurst, North Carolina
1907	Allen Lard	Pinehurst Resort, No. 2 Course	Pinehurst, North Carolina
1908	Allen Lard	Pinehurst Resort, No. 2 Course	Pinehurst, North Carolina
1909	James Standish Jr.	Pinehurst Resort, No. 2 Course	Pinehurst, North Carolina
1910	Walter Travis	Pinehurst Resort, No. 2 Course	Pinehurst, North Carolina
1911	Chick Evans	Pinehurst Resort, No. 2 Course	Pinehurst, North Carolina
1912	Walter Travis	Pinehurst Resort, No. 2 Course	Pinehurst, North Carolina
1913	Henry Topping	Pinehurst Resort, No. 2 Course	Pinehurst, North Carolina
1914	Reginald Worthington	Pinehurst Resort, No. 2 Course	Pinehurst, North Carolina
1915	Fillmore Robeson	Pinehurst Resort, No. 2 Course	Pinehurst, North Carolina
1916	Philip Carter	Pinehurst Resort, No. 2 Course	Pinehurst, North Carolina
1917	Norman Maxwell	Pinehurst Resort, No. 2 Course	Pinehurst, North Carolina

1918	Irving Robeson	Pinehurst Resort, No. 2 Course	Pinehurst, North Carolina
1919	Edward Beall	Pinehurst Resort, No. 2 Course	Pinehurst, North Carolina
1920	Francis Ouimet	Pinehurst Resort, No. 2 Course	Pinehurst, North Carolina
1921	B. P. Merriman	Pinehurst Resort, No. 2 Course	Pinehurst, North Carolina
1922	Henry Topping	Pinehurst Resort, No. 2 Course	Pinehurst, North Carolina
1923	Frank Newton	Pinehurst Resort, No. 2 Course	Pinehurst, North Carolina
1924	Fred Knight	Pinehurst Resort, No. 2 Course	Pinehurst, North Carolina
1925	Arthur Yates	Pinehurst Resort, No. 2 Course	Pinehurst, North Carolina
1926	Page Hufty	Pinehurst Resort, No. 2 Course	Pinehurst, North Carolina
1927	George Voigt	Pinehurst Resort, No. 2 Course	Pinehurst, North Carolina
1928	George Voigt	Pinehurst Resort, No. 2 Course	Pinehurst, North Carolina
1929	George Voigt	Pinehurst Resort, No. 2 Course	Pinehurst, North Carolina
1930	Gene Homans	Pinehurst Resort, No. 2 Course	Pinehurst, North Carolina
1931	George Dunlap Jr.	Pinehurst Resort, No. 2 Course	Pinehurst, North Carolina
1932	M. Pierpont Warner	Pinehurst Resort, No. 2 Course	Pinehurst, North Carolina
1933	George Dunlap Jr.	Pinehurst Resort, No. 2 Course	Pinehurst, North Carolina
1934	George Dunlap Jr.	Pinehurst Resort, No. 2 Course	Pinehurst, North Carolina
1935	George Dunlap Jr.	Pinehurst Resort, No. 2 Course	Pinehurst, North Carolina
1936	George Dunlap Jr.	Pinehurst Resort, No. 2 Course	Pinehurst, North Carolina
1937	Robert Dunkelberger	Pinehurst Resort, No. 2 Course	Pinehurst, North Carolina
1938	Frank Strafaci	Pinehurst Resort, No. 2 Course	Pinehurst, North Carolina
1939	Frank Strafaci	Pinehurst Resort, No. 2 Course	Pinehurst, North Carolina
1940	George Dunlap Jr.	Pinehurst Resort, No. 2 Course	Pinehurst, North Carolina

1941	S. M. Alexander Jr.	Pinehurst Resort, No. 2 Course	Pinehurst, North Carolina
1942	George Dunlap Jr.	Pinehurst Resort, No. 2 Course	Pinehurst, North Carolina
1943	Harry Offutt	Pinehurst Resort, No. 2 Course	Pinehurst, North Carolina
1944	Mal Galletta	Pinehurst Resort, No. 2 Course	Pinehurst, North Carolina
1945	Ed Furgol	Pinehurst Resort, No. 2 Course	Pinehurst, North Carolina
1946	Frank Stranahan	Pinehurst Resort, No. 2 Course	Pinehurst, North Carolina
1947	Charles Dudley	Pinehurst Resort, No. 2 Course	Pinehurst, North Carolina
1948	Harvie Ward Jr.	Pinehurst Resort, No. 2 Course	Pinehurst, North Carolina
1949	Frank Stranahan	Pinehurst Resort, No. 2 Course	Pinehurst, North Carolina
1950	Bill Campbell	Pinehurst Resort, No. 2 Course	Pinehurst, North Carolina
1951	Hobart Manley Jr.	Pinehurst Resort, No. 2 Course	Pinehurst, North Carolina
1952	Frank Stranahan	Pinehurst Resort, No. 2 Course	Pinehurst, North Carolina
1953	Bill Campbell	Pinehurst Resort, No. 2 Course	Pinehurst, North Carolina
1954	Billy Joe Patton	Pinehurst Resort, No. 2 Course	Pinehurst, North Carolina
1955	Don Bisplinghoff	Pinehurst Resort, No. 2 Course	Pinehurst, North Carolina
1956	Hillman Robbins Jr.	Pinehurst Resort, No. 2 Course	Pinehurst, North Carolina
1957	Bill Campbell	Pinehurst Resort, No. 2 Course	Pinehurst, North Carolina
1958	Dick Chapman	Pinehurst Resort, No. 2 Course	Pinehurst, North Carolina
1959	Jack Nicklaus	Pinehurst Resort, No. 2 Course	Pinehurst, North Carolina
1960	Charles Smith	Pinehurst Resort, No. 2 Course	Pinehurst, North Carolina
1961	Bill Hyndman	Pinehurst Resort, No. 2 Course	Pinehurst, North Carolina
1962	Billy Joe Patton	Pinehurst Resort, No. 2 Course	Pinehurst, North Carolina
1963	Billy Joe Patton	Pinehurst Resort, No. 2 Course	Pinehurst, North Carolina

1964	Dale Morey	Pinehurst Resort, No. 2 Course	Pinehurst, North Carolina
1965	Tom Draper	Pinehurst Resort, No. 2 Course	Pinehurst, North Carolina
1966	Ward Wettlaufer	Pinehurst Resort, No. 2 Course	Pinehurst, North Carolina
1967	Bill Campbell	Pinehurst Resort, No. 2 Course	Pinehurst, North Carolina
1968	Jack Lewis Jr.	Pinehurst Resort, No. 2 Course	Pinehurst, North Carolina
1969	Joe Inman Jr.	Pinehurst Resort, No. 2 Course	Pinehurst, North Carolina
1970	Gary Cowan	Pinehurst Resort, No. 2 Course	Pinehurst, North Carolina
1971	Eddie Pearce	Pinehurst Resort, No. 2 Course	Pinehurst, North Carolina
1972	Danny Edwards	Pinehurst Resort, No. 2 Course	Pinehurst, North Carolina
1973	Mike Ford	Pinehurst Resort, No. 2 Course	Pinehurst, North Carolina
1974	George Burns II	Pinehurst Resort, No. 2 Course	Pinehurst, North Carolina
1975	Curtis Strange	Pinehurst Resort, No. 2 Course	Pinehurst, North Carolina
1976	Curtis Strange	Pinehurst Resort, No. 2 Course	Pinehurst, North Carolina
1977	Gary Hallberg	Pinehurst Resort, No. 2 Course	Pinehurst, North Carolina
1978	Gary Hallberg	Pinehurst Resort, No. 2 Course	Pinehurst, North Carolina
1979	John McGough	Pinehurst Resort, No. 2 Course	Pinehurst, North Carolina
1980	Hal Sutton	Pinehurst Resort, No. 2 Course	Pinehurst, North Carolina
1981	Corey Pavin	Pinehurst Resort, No. 2 Course	Pinehurst, North Carolina
1982	Keith Clearwater	Pinehurst Resort, No. 2 Course	Pinehurst, North Carolina
1983	Bryan Sullivan	Pinehurst Resort, No. 2 Course	Pinehurst, North Carolina
1984	Davis Love III	Pinehurst Resort, No. 2 Course	Pinehurst, North Carolina
1985	Jack Nicklaus II	Pinehurst Resort, No. 2 Course	Pinehurst, North Carolina
1986	Billy Andrade	Pinehurst Resort, No. 2 Course	Pinehurst, North Carolina

1987	Robert Goettlicher	Pinehurst Resort, No. 2 Course	Pinehurst, North Carolina
1988	Ulysses Grisette	Pinehurst Resort, No. 2 Course	Pinehurst, North Carolina
1989	Lee Porter	Pinehurst Resort, No. 2 Course	Pinehurst, North Carolina
1990	Thomas Scherrer	Pinehurst Resort, No. 2 Course	Pinehurst, North Carolina
1991	David Eger	Pinehurst Resort, No. 2 Course	Pinehurst, North Carolina
1992	Duane Bock	Pinehurst Resort, No. 2 Course	Pinehurst, North Carolina
1993	Kelly Mitchum	Pinehurst Resort, No. 2 Course	Pinehurst, North Carolina
1994	Mark Slawter	Pinehurst Resort, No. 2 Course	Pinehurst, North Carolina
1995	Paul Simson	Pinehurst Resort, No. 2 Course	Pinehurst, North Carolina
1996	Paul Simson	Pinehurst Resort, No. 2 Course	Pinehurst, North Carolina
1997	Jake Kransteuber	Pinehurst Resort, No. 2 Course	Pinehurst, North Carolina
1998	Tim Jackson	Pinehurst Resort, No. 2 Course	Pinehurst, North Carolina
1999	James Driscoll	Pinehurst Resort, No. 2 Course	Pinehurst, North Carolina
2000	David Eger	Pinehurst Resort, No. 2 Course	Pinehurst, North Carolina
2001	Michael Sims	Pinehurst Resort, No. 2 Course	Pinehurst, North Carolina
2002	Eric Jorgensen	Pinehurst Resort, No. 2 Course	Pinehurst, North Carolina
2003	Chris Stroud	Pinehurst Resort, No. 2 Course	Pinehurst, North Carolina
2004	Martin Ureta	Pinehurst Resort, No. 2 Course	Pinehurst, North Carolina
2005	Sean Moore	Pinehurst Resort, No. 2 Course	Pinehurst, North Carolina
2006	Brady Schnell	Pinehurst Resort, No. 2 Course	Pinehurst, North Carolina
2007	Phillip Mollica	Pinehurst Resort, No. 2 Course	Pinehurst, North Carolina
2008	Matt Savage	Pinehurst Resort, No. 2 Course	Pinehurst, North Carolina
2009	David Chung	Pinehurst Resort, No. 2 Course	Pinehurst, North Carolina

Trans-Mississippi Amateur

1901	John Stuart	Kansas City Country Club	Mission Hills, Kansas
1902	R. R. Kimball	Omaha Country Club	Omaha, Nebraska
1903	John Maxwell	Waveland Park Golf Club	Des Moines, Iowa
1904	H. P. Bend	The Minikahda Club	Minneapolis, Minnesota
1905	Warren Dickinson	Glen Echo Country Club	St. Louis, Missouri
1906	C. T. Jaffray	Omaha Field Club	Omaha, Nebraska
1907	Sprague Abbot	Rock Island Arsenal Golf Club	Rock Island, Illinois
1908	E. H. Seaver	Evanston Golf Club	Kansas City, Missouri
1909	Harry Legg	Des Moines Golf & Country Club	Des Moines, Iowa
1910	Harry Legg	Denver Country Club	Denver, Colorado
1911	Harry Legg	Omaha Country Club	Omaha, Nebraska
1912	Harry Legg	The Minikahda Club	Minneapolis, Minnesota
1913	Stuart Stickney	Glen Echo Country Club	St. Louis, Missouri
1914	J. D. Cady	Evanston Golf Club	Kansas City, Missouri
1915	Alden Swift	Memphis Country Club	Memphis, Tennessee
1916	Harry Legg	Interlachen Country Club	Edina, Minnesota
1917	Sam Reynolds	St. Joseph Country Club	St. Joseph, Missouri
1918	G. L. Conley	Hillcrest Country Club	Kansas City, Missouri
1919	Nelson Whitney	Saint Louis Country Club	St. Louis, Missouri
1920	Robert McKee	Rock Island Arsenal Golf Club	Rock Island, Illinois
1921	George Von Elm	Denver Country Club	Denver, Colorado
1922	R. Knepper	Omaha Country Club	Omaha, Nebraska

1923	Eddie Held	The Minikahda Club	Minneapolis, Minnesota
1924	James Manion	St. Joseph Country Club	St. Joseph, Missouri
1925	Clarence Wolff	Omaha Field Club	Omaha, Nebraska
1926	Eddie Held	Algonquin Golf Club	St. Louis, Missouri
1927	Johnny Goodman	The Broadmoor Golf Club	Colorado Springs, Colorado
1928	Arthur Bartlett	Wakonda Club	Des Moines, Iowa
1929	Robert McCrary	Omaha Field Club	Omaha, Nebraska
1930	Robert McCrary	The Broadmoor Golf Club	Colorado Springs, Colorado
1931	Johnny Goodman	Golden Valley Country Club	Golden Valley, Minnesota
1932	Gus Moreland	Oklahoma City Golf & Country Club	Oklahoma City, Oklahoma
1933	Gus Moreland	The Broadmoor Golf Club	Colorado Springs, Colorado
1934	Leland Hamman	Brook Hollow Golf Club	Dallas, Texas
1935	Johnny Goodman	Wakonda Club	Des Moines, Iowa
1936	John Dawson	Wichita Country Club	Wichita, Kansas
1937	Don Schumacher	Cherry Hills Country Club	Cherry Hills Village, Colorado
1938	Vene Savage	The Country Club of Lincoln	Lincoln, Nebraska
1939	Chick Harbert	The Broadmoor Golf Club	Colorado Springs, Colorado
1940	Art Doering	Southern Hills Country Club	Tulsa, Oklahoma
1941	Frank Stranahan	Sunset Country Club	St. Louis, Missouri
1942	John Kraft	Blue Hills Country Club	Kansas City, Missouri
1946	Skee Riegel	Denver Country Club	Denver, Colorado
1947	Charlie Coe	Wichita Country Club	Wichita, Kansas
1948	Skee Riegel	Mission Hills Country Club	Mission Hills, Kansas

1949	Charlie Coe	The Broadmoor Golf Club	Colorado Springs, Colorado
1950	Jim English	Happy Hollow Golf Club	Omaha, Nebraska
1951	L. M. Crannel Jr.	Brook Hollow Golf Club	Dallas, Texas
1952	Charlie Coe	Lakewood Country Club	Denver, Colorado
1953	Joe Conrad	Kansas City Country Club	Mission Hills, Kansas
1954	James Jackson	Cherry Hills Country Club	Cherry Hills Village, Colorado
1955	James Jackson	Wakonda Club	Des Moines, Iowa
1956	Charlie Coe	Oklahoma City Golf & Country Club	Oklahoma City, Oklahoma
1957	Rex Baxter Jr.	Brook Hollow Golf Club	Dallas, Texas
1958	Jack Nicklaus	Prairie Dunes Country Club	Hutchinson, Kansas
1959	Jack Nicklaus	Woodhill Country Club	Wayzata, Minnesota
1960	Deane Beman	Wichita Country Club	Wichita, Kansas
1961	Herb Durham	Twin Hills Golf & Country Club	Oklahoma City, Oklahoma
1962	Bob Ryan	Old Warson Country Club	St. Louis, Missouri
1963	George Archer	Phoenix Country Club	Phoenix, Arizona
1964	Wright Garrett	The Broadmoor Golf Club	Colorado Springs, Colorado
1965	George Boutell	Kansas City Country Club	Mission Hills, Kansas
1966	Jim Wiechers	Edina Country Club	Edina, Minnesota
1967	Hal Greenwood	San Antonio Country Club	San Antonio, Texas
1968	Bill Hyndman	Southern Hills Country Club	Tulsa, Oklahoma
1969	Allen Miller	Cherry Hills Country Club	Cherry Hills Village, Colorado
1970	Allen Miller	Oklahoma City Golf & Country Club	Oklahoma City, Oklahoma
1971	Allen Miller	Spyglass Hill	Pebble Beach, California

1972	Ben Crenshaw	Brook Hollow Golf Club	Dallas, Texas
1973	Gary Koch	Prairie Dunes Country Club	Hutchinson, Kansas
1974	Tom Jones	Cedar Ridge Country Club	Tulsa, Oklahoma
1975	Tim Wilson	Kansas City Country Club	Mission Hills, Kansas
1976	Doug Clarke	Spyglass Hill	Pebble Beach, California
1977	John Fought	Midland Country Club	Midland, Texas
1978	Bob Tway	Brook Hollow Golf Club	Dallas, Texas
1979	Mark Brooks	Hardscrabble Country Club	Fort Smith, Arkansas
1980	Raymond Barr	Denver Country Club	Denver, Colorado
1981	Robert Wrenn	The Minikahda Club	Minneapolis, Minnesota
1982	John Sherman	Oklahoma City Golf & Country Club	Oklahoma City, Oklahoma
1983	Greg Chapman	Kansas City Country Club	Mission Hills, Kansas
1984	John Pigg	Hills of Lakeway	Austin, Texas
1985	Bob Estes	Hardscrabble Country Club	Fort Smith, Arkansas
1986	Brian Watts	Crown Colony Country Club	Lufkin, Texas
1987	Ron Richard	Prairie Dunes Country Club	Hutchinson, Kansas
1988	Tom Merry	Woodhill Country Club	Wayzata, Minnesota
1989	Ron Richard	La Jolla Country Club	La Jolla, California
1990	Bobby Godwin	Oklahoma City Golf & Country Club	Oklahoma City, Oklahoma
1991	Mike McClung	Lakeside Golf Club	Toluca Lake, California
1992	Randy Sonnier	Wichita Country Club	Wichita, Kansas
1993	David Ojala	Kansas City Country Club	Mission Hills, Kansas
1994	Sandy Adelman	The Minikahda Club	Minneapolis, Minnesota

1995	Ed Gibstein	The Farms Golf Club	Rancho Santa Fe, California
1996	John Grace	Prairie Dunes Country Club	Hutchinson, Kansas
1997	Johnny Stevens	Brook Hollow Golf Club	Dallas, Texas
1998	Dan Dunkelberg	Cherry Hills Country Club	Cherry Hills Village, Colorado
1999	Mike Podolak	Oklahoma City Golf & Country Club	Oklahoma City, Oklahoma
2000	Mike McCoy	White Bear Yacht Club	White Bear Lake, Minnesota
2001	Chip Stewart	Kansas City Country Club	Mission Hills, Kansas
2002	John Goode	Barton Creek Resort & Club, Foothills Course	Austin, Texas
2003	Bob Kearney	Flint Hills National Golf Club	Andover, Kansas
2004	Scott McGihon	La Jolla Country Club	La Jolla, California
2005	David Bartman	Prairie Dunes Country Club	Hutchinson, Kansas
2006	Robert Funk	Brook Hollow Golf Club	Dallas, Texas
2007	Trent Brown	The Minikahda Club	Minneapolis, Minnesota
2008	Mike McCoy	Wakonda Club	Des Moines, Iowa
2009	Chris Kessler	Flint Hills National Golf Club	Andover, Kansas

Sunnehanna Amateur

1954	Don Cherry	Sunnehanna Country Club	Johnstown, Pennsylvania
1955	Hillman Robbins Jr.	Sunnehanna Country Club	Johnstown, Pennsylvania
1956	Gene Dahlbender	Sunnehanna Country Club	Johnstown, Pennsylvania
1957	Joe Campbell	Sunnehanna Country Club	Johnstown, Pennsylvania
1958	Bill Hyndman	Sunnehanna Country Club	Johnstown, Pennsylvania
1959	Tommy Aaron	Sunnehanna Country Club	Johnstown, Pennsylvania
1960	Gene Dahlbender	Sunnehanna Country Club	Johnstown, Pennsylvania
1961	Dick Siderowf	Sunnehanna Country Club	Johnstown, Pennsylvania
1962	Ed Updegraff	Sunnehanna Country Club	Johnstown, Pennsylvania
1963	Roger McManus	Sunnehanna Country Club	Johnstown, Pennsylvania
1964	Gary Cowan	Sunnehanna Country Club	Johnstown, Pennsylvania
1965	Bobby Greenwood	Sunnehanna Country Club	Johnstown, Pennsylvania
1966	Jack Lewis Jr.	Sunnehanna Country Club	Johnstown, Pennsylvania
1967	Bill Hyndman	Sunnehanna Country Club	Johnstown, Pennsylvania
1968	Bobby Greenwood	Sunnehanna Country Club	Johnstown, Pennsylvania
1969	Leonard Thompson	Sunnehanna Country Club	Johnstown, Pennsylvania
1970	Howard Twitty	Sunnehanna Country Club	Johnstown, Pennsylvania
1971	Bob Zender	Sunnehanna Country Club	Johnstown, Pennsylvania

1972	Mark Hayes	Sunnehanna Country Club	Johnstown, Pennsylvania
1973	Ben Crenshaw	Sunnehanna Country Club	Johnstown, Pennsylvania
1974	Dave Strawn	Sunnehanna Country Club	Johnstown, Pennsylvania
1975	Jamie Gonzales	Sunnehanna Country Club	Johnstown, Pennsylvania
1976	Jay Sigel	Sunnehanna Country Club	Johnstown, Pennsylvania
1977	John Cook	Sunnehanna Country Club	Johnstown, Pennsylvania
1978	Jay Sigel	Sunnehanna Country Club	Johnstown, Pennsylvania
1979	John Cook	Sunnehanna Country Club	Johnstown, Pennsylvania
1980	Bobby Clampett	Sunnehanna Country Club	Johnstown, Pennsylvania
1981	Jodie Mudd	Sunnehanna Country Club	Johnstown, Pennsylvania
1982	Brad Faxon	Sunnehanna Country Club	Johnstown, Pennsylvania
1983	Dillard Pruitt	Sunnehanna Country Club	Johnstown, Pennsylvania
1984	Scott Verplank	Sunnehanna Country Club	Johnstown, Pennsylvania
1985	Scott Verplank	Sunnehanna Country Club	Johnstown, Pennsylvania
1986	Billy Andrade	Sunnehanna Country Club	Johnstown, Pennsylvania
1987	Greg Lesher	Sunnehanna Country Club	Johnstown, Pennsylvania
1988	Jay Sigel	Sunnehanna Country Club	Johnstown, Pennsylvania
1989	Allen Doyle	Sunnehanna Country Club	Johnstown, Pennsylvania
1990	Allen Doyle	Sunnehanna Country Club	Johnstown, Pennsylvania

1991	Paul Claxton	Sunnehanna Country Club	Johnstown, Pennsylvania
1992	Allen Doyle	Sunnehanna Country Club	Johnstown, Pennsylvania
1993	Jaxon Brigman	Sunnehanna Country Club	Johnstown, Pennsylvania
1994	Allen Doyle	Sunnehanna Country Club	Johnstown, Pennsylvania
1995	John Harris	Sunnehanna Country Club	Johnstown, Pennsylvania
1996	Jeff Thomas	Sunnehanna Country Club	Johnstown, Pennsylvania
1997	Duke Delcher	Sunnehanna Country Club	Johnstown, Pennsylvania
1998	Steve Sheehan	Sunnehanna Country Club	Johnstown, Pennsylvania
1999	Ed Loar	Sunnehanna Country Club	Johnstown, Pennsylvania
2000	Ed Loar	Sunnehanna Country Club	Johnstown, Pennsylvania
2001	Lucas Glover	Sunnehanna Country Club	Johnstown, Pennsylvania
2002	Dillard Pruitt	Sunnehanna Country Club	Johnstown, Pennsylvania
2003	Matt Hendrix	Sunnehanna Country Club	Johnstown, Pennsylvania
2004	Jack Ferguson	Sunnehanna Country Club	Johnstown, Pennsylvania
2005	Michael Sims	Sunnehanna Country Club	Johnstown, Pennsylvania
2006	Webb Simpson	Sunnehanna Country Club	Johnstown, Pennsylvania
2007	Ricky Fowler	Sunnehanna Country Club	Johnstown, Pennsylvania
2008	Ricky Fowler	Sunnehanna Country Club	Johnstown, Pennsylvania
2009	Kevin Foley	Sunnehanna Country Club	Johnstown, Pennsylvania

Porter Cup

1959	John Konsek	Niagara Falls Country Club	Lewiston, New York
1960	Ward Wettlaufer	Niagara Falls Country Club	Lewiston, New York
1961	John Konsek	Niagara Falls Country Club	Lewiston, New York
1962	Ed Tutwiler	Niagara Falls Country Club	Lewiston, New York
1963	Bill Harvey	Niagara Falls Country Club	Lewiston, New York
1964	Deane Beman	Niagara Falls Country Club	Lewiston, New York
1965	Ward Wettlaufer	Niagara Falls Country Club	Lewiston, New York
1966	Bob E. Smith	Niagara Falls Country Club	Lewiston, New York
1967	Bob E. Smith	Niagara Falls Country Club	Lewiston, New York
1968	Randy Wolff	Niagara Falls Country Club	Lewiston, New York
1969	Gary Cowan	Niagara Falls Country Club	Lewiston, New York
1970	Howard Twitty	Niagara Falls Country Club	Lewiston, New York
1971	Ronnie Quinn	Niagara Falls Country Club	Lewiston, New York
1972	Ben Crenshaw	Niagara Falls Country Club	Lewiston, New York
1973	Vinny Giles	Niagara Falls Country Club	Lewiston, New York
1974	George Burns II	Niagara Falls Country Club	Lewiston, New York
1975	Jay Sigel	Niagara Falls Country Club	Lewiston, New York
1976	Scott Simpson	Niagara Falls Country Club	Lewiston, New York

1977	Vance Heafner	Niagara Falls Country Club	Lewiston, New York
1978	Bobby Clampett	Niagara Falls Country Club	Lewiston, New York
1979	John Cook	Niagara Falls Country Club	Lewiston, New York
1980	Tony DeLuca	Niagara Falls Country Club	Lewiston, New York
1981	Jay Sigel	Niagara Falls Country Club	Lewiston, New York
1982	Nathaniel Crosby	Niagara Falls Country Club	Lewiston, New York
1983	Scott Verplank	Niagara Falls Country Club	Lewiston, New York
1984	Danny Mijovic	Niagara Falls Country Club	Lewiston, New York
1985	Scott Verplank	Niagara Falls Country Club	Lewiston, New York
1986	Nolan Henke	Niagara Falls Country Club	Lewiston, New York
1987	Jay Sigel	Niagara Falls Country Club	Lewiston, New York
1988	Tony Mollica	Niagara Falls Country Club	Lewiston, New York
1989	Robert Gamez	Niagara Falls Country Club	Lewiston, New York
1990	Phil Mickelson	Niagara Falls Country Club	Lewiston, New York
1991	Gary Nicklaus	Niagara Falls Country Club	Lewiston, New York
1992	David Duval	Niagara Falls Country Club	Lewiston, New York
1993	Joey Gullion	Niagara Falls Country Club	Lewiston, New York
1994	Allen Doyle	Niagara Falls Country Club	Lewiston, New York

1995	Ryuji Imada	Niagara Falls Country Club	Lewiston, New York
1996	Joey Snyder III	Niagara Falls Country Club	Lewiston, New York
1997	John Harris	Niagara Falls Country Club	Lewiston, New York
1998	Gene Elliott	Niagara Falls Country Club	Lewiston, New York
1999	Hunter Haas	Niagara Falls Country Club	Lewiston, New York
2000	Christopher Wisler	Niagara Falls Country Club	Lewiston, New York
2001	Nick Cassini	Niagara Falls Country Club	Lewiston, New York
2002	Simon Nash	Niagara Falls Country Club	Lewiston, New York
2003	Casey Wittenberg	Niagara Falls Country Club	Lewiston, New York
2004	Spencer Levin	Niagara Falls Country Club	Lewiston, New York
2005	Pablo Martin-Benavides	Niagara Falls Country Club	Lewiston, New York
2006	Han Seung-Su	Niagara Falls Country Club	Lewiston, New York
2007	Brian Harman	Niagara Falls Country Club	Lewiston, New York
2008	Adam Mitchell	Niagara Falls Country Club	Lewiston, New York
2009	Brendan Gielow	Niagara Falls Country Club	Lewiston, New York

APPENDIX 7. WOMEN'S MAJOR AMATEUR CHAMPIONS

British Ladies' Amateur

Year	Champion	Country	Club	Location
1893	Lady Margaret Scott	England	Royal Lytham and St. Annes Golf Club	Lytham and St. Annes, Lancashire, England
1894	Lady Margaret Scott	England	Littlestone Golf Club	Littlestone-on-Sea, Kent, England
1895	Lady Margaret Scott	England	Royal Portrush Golf Club	Portrush, County Antrim, Northern Ireland
1896	Amy Pascoe	England	Royal Liverpool Golf Club	Hoylake, England
1897	Edith Orr	Scotland	Gullane Golf Club	Gullane, East Lothian, Scotland
1898	Lena Thomson	England	Great Yarmouth and Caister Golf Club	Caister-on-Sea, Great Yarmouth, Norfolk, England
1899	May Hezlet	Ireland	Royal County Down Golf Club	Newcastle, County Down, Northern Ireland
1900	Rhona Adair	Ireland	Royal North Devon Golf Club	Bideford, Devon, England
1901	Molly Graham	Scotland	Aberdovey Golf Club	Aberdovey, Gwynedd, Wales
1902	May Hezlet	Ireland	Royal Cinque Ports Golf Club	Deal, Kent, England

1903	Rhona Adair	Ireland	Royal Portrush Golf Club	Portrush, County Antrim, Northern Ireland
1904	Lottie Dod	England	Royal Troon Golf Club	Troon, South Ayrshire, Scotland
1905	Bertha Thompson	England	Royal Cromer Golf Club	Cromer-Overstrand, Norfolk, England
1906	Alice Kennion	England	Burnham and Berrow Golf Club	Somerset, England
1907	May Hezlet	Ireland	Royal County Down Golf Club	Newcastle, County Down, Northern Ireland
1908	Maud Titterton	Scotland	St. Andrews Links, Old Course	St. Andrews, Fife, Scotland
1909	Dorothy Campbell	Scotland	Royal Birkdale Golf Club	Southport, Merseyside, England
1910	Elsie Grant Suttie	Scotland	Royal North Devon Golf Club	Bideford, Devon, England
1911	Dorothy Campbell	Scotland	Royal Portrush Golf Club	Portrush, County Antrim, Northern Ireland
1912	Gladys Ravenscroft	England	Turnberry, Ailsa Course	Turnberry, South Ayrshire, Scotland
1913	Muriel Dodd	England	Royal Lytham and St. Annes Golf Club	Lytham and St. Annes, Lancashire, England
1914	Cecil Leitch	England	Hunstanton Golf Club	Hunstanton, Norfolk, England

1920	Cecil Leitch	England	Royal County Down Golf Club	Newcastle, County Down, Northern Ireland
1921	Cecil Leitch	England	Turnberry, Ailsa Course	Turnberry, South Ayrshire, Scotland
1922	Joyce Wethered	England	Royal St. George's Golf Club	Sandwich, Kent, England
1923	Doris Chambers	England	Burnham and Berrow Golf Club	Somerset, England
1924	Joyce Wethered	England	Royal Portrush Golf Club	Portrush, County Antrim, Northern Ireland
1925	Joyce Wethered	England	Royal Troon Golf Club	Troon, South Ayrshire, Scotland
1926	Cecil Leitch	England	Royal St. David's Golf Club	Harlech, Gwynedd, Wales
1927	Simone Thion de la Chaume	France	Royal County Down Golf Club	Newcastle, County Down, Northern Ireland
1928	Nanette le Blan	France	Hunstanton Golf Club	Hunstanton, Norfolk, England
1929	Joyce Wethered	England	St. Andrews Links, Old Course	St. Andrews, Fife, Scotland
1930	Diana Fishwick	England	Formby Golf Club	Merseyside, England
1931	Enid Wilson	England	Portmarnock Golf Club	Portmarnock, Fingal, Ireland
1932	Enid Wilson	England	Saunton Golf Club	Braunton, North Devon, England

1933	Enid Wilson	England	Gleneagles Resort	Auchterard, Perth and Kinross, Scotland
1934	Helen Holm	Scotland	Royal Porthcawl Golf Club	Porthcawl, South Wales, Wales
1935	Wanda Morgan	England	Royal County Down Golf Club	Newcastle, County Down, Northern Ireland
1936	Pamela Barton	England	Southport and Ainsdale Golf Club	Southport, Lancashire, England
1937	Jessie Anderson	Scotland	Turnberry, Ailsa Course	Turnberry, South Ayrshire, Scotland
1938	Helen Holm	Scotland	Burnham and Berrow Golf Club	Somerset, England
1939	Pamela Barton	England	Royal Portrush Golf Club	Portrush, County Antrim, Northern Ireland
1946	Jean Hetherington	England	Hunstanton Golf Club	Hunstanton, Norfolk, England
1947	Babe Zaharias	United States	Gullane Golf Club	Gullane, East Lothian, Scotland
1948	Louise Suggs	United States	Royal Lytham and St. Annes Golf Club	Lytham and St. Annes, Lancashire, England
1949	Frances Stephens	England	Royal St. David's Golf Club	Harlech, Gwynedd, Wales
1950	Vicomtesse de St Sauveur	France	Royal County Down Golf Club	Newcastle, County Down, Northern Ireland

1951	Catherine MacCann	Ireland	Broadstone Golf Club	Dorset, England
1952	Moira Paterson	Scotland	Royal Troon Golf Club	Troon, South Ayrshire, Scotland
1953	Marlene Stewart	Canada	Royal Porthcawl Golf Club	Porthcawl, South Wales, Wales
1954	Frances Stephens	England	Ganton Golf Club	Ganton, North Yorkshire, England
1955	Jessie Valentine	Scotland	Royal Portrush Golf Club	Portrush, County Antrim, Northern Ireland
1956	Wiffi Smith	United States	Sunningdale Golf Club	London, Greater London, England
1957	Philomena Garvey	Ireland	Gleneagles Resort	Auchterard, Perth and Kinross, Scotland
1958	Jessie Valentine	Scotland	Hunstanton Golf Club	Hunstanton, Norfolk, England
1959	Elizabeth Price	England	Royal Ascot Golf Club	Ascot, Berkshire, England
1960	Barbara McIntire	United States	Royal St. David's Golf Club	Harlech, Gwynedd, Wales
1961	Marley Spearman	England	Carnoustie Golf Links	Carnoustie, Angus, Scotland
1962	Marley Spearman	England	Royal Birkdale Golf Club	Southport, Merseyside, England
1963	Brigitte Varangot	France	Royal County Down Golf Club	Newcastle, County Down, Northern Ireland

1964	Carol Sorenson	United States	Royal St. George's Golf Club	Sandwich, Kent, England
1965	Brigitte Varangot	France	St. Andrews Links, Old Course	St. Andrews, Fife, Scotland
1966	Elizabeth Chadwick	Wales	Ganton Golf Club	Ganton, North Yorkshire, England
1967	Elizabeth Chadwick	Wales	Royal St. David's Golf Club	Harlech, Gwynedd, Wales
1968	Brigitte Varangot	France	Walton Heath Golf Club	Walton-on-the-Hill, Surrey, England
1969	Catherine Lacoste	France	Royal Portrush Golf Club	Portrush, County Antrim, Northern Ireland
1970	Dinah Oxley	England	Gullane Golf Club	Gullane, East Lothian, Scotland
1971	Mickey Walker	England	Alwoodley Golf Club	Leeds, Yorkshire, England
1972	Mickey Walker	England	Hunstanton Golf Club	Hunstanton, Norfolk, England
1973	Ann Irvin	England	Carnoustie Golf Links	Carnoustie, Angus, Scotland
1974	Carol Semple	United States	Royal Porthcawl Golf Club	Porthcawl, South Wales, Wales
1975	Nancy Roth Syms	United States	St. Andrews Links, Old Course	St. Andrews, Fife, Scotland
1976	Cathy Panton	Scotland	Silloth on Solway Golf Club	Silloth, Wigton, Cumbria, England

1977	Angela Uzielli	England	Hillside Golf Club	Southport, England
1978	Edwina Kennedy	Australia	Notts Golf Club	Ashfield, Nottinghamshire, England
1979	Maureen Madill	Northern Ireland	Nairn Golf Club	Nairn, Highlands, Scotland
1980	Anne Quast	United States	Woodhall Spa Golf Club	Woodhall Spa, Lincolnshire, England
1981	Belle Robertson	Scotland	Conwy Golf Club	Caernarvonshire, Wales
1982	Kitrina Douglas	England	Walton Heath Golf Club	Walton-on-the-Hill, Surrey, England
1983	Jill Thornhill	England	Silloth on Solway Golf Club	Silloth, Wigton, Cumbria, England
1984	Jody Rosenthal	United States	Royal Troon Golf Club	Troon, South Ayrshire, Scotland
1985	Lillian Behan	Ireland	Ganton Golf Club	Ganton, North Yorkshire, England
1986	Marnie McGuire	New Zealand	West Sussex Golf Club	Pulborough, West Sussex, England
1987	Janet Collingham	England	Royal St. David's Golf Club	Harlech, Gwynedd, Wales
1988	Joanne Furby	England	Royal Cinque Ports Golf Club	Deal, Kent, England
1989	Helen Dobson	England	Royal Liverpool Golf Club	Hoylake, England

1990	Julie Wade Hall	England	Dunbar Golf Club	Dunbar, East Lothian, Scotland
1991	Valerie Michaud	France	Pannal Golf Club	Harrogate, North Yorkshire, England
1992	Pernille Pedersen	Denmark	Saunton Golf Club	Braunton, North Devon, England
1993	Catriona Lambert	Scotland	Royal Lytham and St. Annes Golf Club	Lytham and St. Annes, Lancashire, England
1994	Emma Duggleby	England	Newport Golf Club	Newport, Wales
1995	Julie Wade Hall	England	Royal Portrush Golf Club	Portrush, County Antrim, Northern Ireland
1996	Kelli Kuehne	United States	Royal Liverpool Golf Club	Hoylake, England
1997	Alison Rose	Scotland	Cruden Bay Golf Club	Cruden Bay, Scotland
1998	Kim Rostron	England	Little Aston Golf Club	Streetly, Sutton Coldfield, England
1999	Marine Monnet	France	Royal Birkdale Golf Club	Southport, Merseyside, England
2000	Rebecca Hudson	England	Royal Birkdale Golf Club	Southport, Merseyside, England
2001	Marta Prieto	Spain	Ladybank Golf Club	Ladybank, Fife, Scotland
2002	Rebecca Hudson	England	Ashburnham Golf Club	Burry Point, Dyfed, Wales
2003	Elisa Serramia	Spain	Lindrick Golf Club	Worksop, Nottinghamshire, England

2004	Louise Stahle	Sweden	Gullane Golf Club	Gullane, East Lothian, Scotland
2005	Louise Stahle	Sweden	Littlestone Golf Club	Littlestone-on-Sea, Kent, England
2006	Belen Mozo	Spain	Royal County Down Golf Club	Newcastle, County Down, Northern Ireland
2007	Carlota Ciganda	Spain	Alwoodley Golf Club	Leeds, Yorkshire, England
2008	Anna Nordqvist	Sweden	North Berwick Golf Club, West Links	North Berwick, East Lotian, Scotland
2009	Azahara Muñoz	Spain	Royal St. David's Golf Club	Harlech, Gwynedd, Wales

U.S. Women's Amateur

1895	Lucy Barnes Brown	United States	Meadow Brook Club	Old Westbury, New York
1896	Beatrix Hoyt	United States	Morris County Golf Club	Morristown, New Jersey
1897	Beatrix Hoyt	United States	Essex County Club	Manchester-by-the-Sea, Massachusetts
1898	Beatrix Hoyt	United States	Ardsley Country Club	Ardsley-on-Hudson, New York
1899	Ruth Underhill	United States	Philadelphia Country Club, Bala Course	Gladwyne, Pennsylvania

1900	Frances Griscom	United States	Shinnecock Hills Golf Club	Southampton, New York
1901	Genevieve Hecker	United States	Baltusrol Golf Club	Springfield, New Jersey
1902	Genevieve Hecker	United States	The Country Club	Brookline, Massachusetts
1903	Bessie Anthony	United States	Chicago Golf Club	Wheaton, Illinois
1904	Georgianna Bishop	United States	Merion Golf Club	Ardmore, Pennsylvania
1905	Pauline Mackay	United States	Morris County Golf Club	Morristown, New Jersey
1906	Harriot Curtis	United States	Brae Burn Country Club	West Newton, Massachusetts
1907	Margaret Curtis	United States	Midlothian Country Club	Midlothian, Illinois
1908	Katherine Harley	United States	Chevy Chase Club	Chevy Chase, Maryland
1909	Dorothy Campbell	Scotland	Merion Golf Club	Ardmore, Pennsylvania
1910	Dorothy Campbell	Scotland	Homewood Country Club	Flossmoor, Illinois
1911	Margaret Curtis	United States	Baltusrol Golf Club	Springfield, New Jersey

1912	Margaret Curtis	United States	Essex County Club	Manchester-by-the-Sea, Massachusetts
1913	Gladys Ravenscroft	England	Wilmington Country Club	Wilmington, Delaware
1914	Katherine Harley	United States	Nassau Country Club	Glen Cove, New York
1915	Florence Vanderbeck	United States	Onwentsia Club	Lake Forest, Illinois
1916	Alexa Stirling	United States	Belmont Springs Country Club	Belmont, Massachusetts
1919	Alexa Stirling	United States	Shawnee Country Club	Topeka, Kansas
1920	Alexa Stirling	United States	Mayfield Country Club	Lyndhurst, Ohio
1921	Marion Hollins	United States	Hollywood Country Club	Deal, New Jersey
1922	Glenna Collett	United States	Greenbrier, Old White Course	White Sulphur Springs, West Virginia
1923	Edith Cummings	United States	Westchester Country Club	Rye, New York
1924	Dorothy Campbell	Scotland	Rhode Island Country Club	West Barrington, Rhode Island
1925	Glenna Collett	United States	St. Louis Country Club	St. Louis, Missouri
1926	Helen Stetson	United States	Merion Golf Club, East Course	Ardmore, Pennsylvania

1927	Miriam Burns Horn	United States	Cherry Valley Club	Garden City, New York
1928	Glenna Collett	United States	Homestead	Hot Springs, Virginia
1929	Glenna Collett	United States	Oakland Hills Country Club	Bloomfield Hills, Michigan
1930	Glenna Collett	United States	Los Angeles Country Club, North Course	Los Angeles, California
1931	Helen Hicks	United States	Country Club of Buffalo	Williamsville, New York
1932	Virginia Van Wie	United States	Salem Country Club	Peabody, Massachusetts
1933	Virginia Van Wie	United States	Exmoor Country Club	Highland Park, Illinois
1934	Virginia Van Wie	United States	Whitemarsh Valley Country Club	Whitemarsh Township, Pennsylvania
1935	Glenna Collett Vare	United States	Interlachen Country Club	Edina, Minnesota
1936	Pamela Barton	England	Canoe Brook Country Club	Summit, New Jersey
1937	Estelle Lawson Page	United States	Memphis Country Club	Memphis, Tennessee
1938	Patty Berg	United States	Westmoreland Country Club	Wilmette, Illinois

1939	Betty Jameson	United States	Wee Burn Country Club	Darien, Connecticut
1940	Betty Jameson	United States	Pebble Beach Golf Links	Pebble Beach, California
1941	Betty Hicks Newell	United States	The Country Club	Brookline, Massachusetts
1946	Babe Zaharias	United States	Southern Hills Country Club	Tulsa, Oklahoma
1947	Louise Suggs	United States	Franklin Hills Country Club	Franklin, Michigan
1948	Grace Lenczyk	United States	Pebble Beach Golf Links	Pebble Beach, California
1949	Dorothy Germain Porter	United States	Merion Golf Club, East Course	Ardmore, Pennsylvania
1950	Beverly Hanson	United States	East Lake Golf Club	Atlanta, Georgia
1951	Dorothy Kirby	United States	Town & Country Club	St. Paul, Minnesota
1952	Jackie Pung	United States	Waverley Country Club	Portland, Oregon
1953	Mary Lena Faulk	United States	Rhode Island Country Club	West Barrington, Rhode Island
1954	Barbara Romack	United States	Allegheny Country Club	Sewickley, Pennsylvania

1955	Patricia Ann Lesser	United States	Myers Park Country Club	Charlotte, North Carolina
1956	Marlene Stewart	Canada	Meridian Hills Country Club	Indianapolis, Indiana
1957	JoAnne Gunderson	United States	Del Paso Country Club	Sacramento, California
1958	Anne Quast	United States	Wee Burn Country Club	Darien, Connecticut
1959	Barbara McIntire	United States	Congressional Country Club	Bethesda, Maryland
1960	JoAnne Gunderson	United States	Tulsa Country Club	Tulsa, Oklahoma
1961	Anne Quast	United States	Tacoma Country & Golf Club	Lakewood, Washington
1962	JoAnne Gunderson	United States	Country Club of Rochester	Rochester, New York
1963	Anne Quast	United States	Taconic Golf Club	Williams College, Williamstown, Massachusetts
1964	Barbara McIntire	United States	Prairie Dunes Country Club	Hutchinson, Kansas
1965	Jean Ashley	United States	Lakewood Country Club	New Orleans, Louisiana
1966	JoAnne Gunderson	United States	Sewickley Heights Golf Club	Sewickley, Pennsylvania

1967	Mary Lou Dill	United States	Annandale Country Club	Madison, Mississippi
1968	JoAnne Gunderson	United States	Birmingham Country Club	Birmingham, Michigan
1969	Catherine Lacoste	France	Las Colinas Country Club	Dallas, Texas
1970	Martha Wilkinson	United States	Wee Burn Country Club	Darien, Connecticut
1971	Laura Baugh	United States	Atlanta Country Club	Marietta, Georgia
1972	Mary Budke	United States	St. Louis Country Club	St. Louis, Missouri
1973	Carol Semple	United States	Montclair Golf Club	West Orange, New Jersey
1974	Cynthia Hill	United States	Broadmoor Golf Club	Seattle, Washington
1975	Beth Daniel	United States	Brae Burn Country Club	West Newton, Massachusetts
1976	Donna Horton	United States	Del Paso Country Club	Sacramento, California
1977	Beth Daniel	United States	Cincinnati Country Club	Cincinnati, Ohio
1978	Cathy Sherk	Canada	Sunnybrook Golf Club	Plymouth Meeting, Pennsylvania
1979	Carolyn Hill	United States	Memphis Country Club	Memphis, Tennessee

1980	Juli Inkster	United States	Prairie Dunes Country Club	Hutchinson, Kansas
1981	Juli Inkster	United States	Waverley Country Club	Portland, Oregon
1982	Juli Inkster	United States	Broadmoor Golf Club, East Course	Colorado Springs, Colorado
1983	Joanne Pacillo	United States	Canoe Brook Country Club, North Course	Summit, New Jersey
1984	Deb Richard	United States	Broadmoor Golf Club	Seattle, Washington
1985	Michiko Hattori	Japan	Fox Chapel Golf Club	Pittsburgh, Pennsylvania
1986	Kay Cockerill	United States	Pasatiempo Golf Club	Santa Cruz, California
1987	Kay Cockerill	United States	Rhode Island Country Club	West Barrington, Rhode Island
1988	Pearl Sinn	United States	Minikahda Club	Minneapolis, Minnesota
1989	Vicki Goetze	United States	Pinehurst Resort, No. 2 Course	Pinehurst, North Carolina
1990	Pat Hurst	United States	Canoe Brook Country Club, North Course	Summit, New Jersey
1991	Amy Fruhwirth	United States	Prairie Dunes Country Club	Hutchinson, Kansas

1992	Vicki Goetze	United States	Kemper Lakes Golf Club	Long Grove, Illinois
1993	Jill McGill	United States	San Diego Country Club	Chula Vista, California
1994	Wendy Ward	United States	Homestead, Cascades Course	Hot Springs, Virginia
1995	Kelli Kuehne	United States	The Country Club	Brookline, Massachusetts
1996	Kelli Kuehne	United States	Firethorn Golf Club	Lincoln, Nebraska
1997	Silvia Cavalleri	Italy	Brae Burn Country Club	West Newton, Massachusetts
1998	Grace Park	Korea (South)	Barton Hills Country Club	Ann Arbor, Michigan
1999	Dorothy Delasin	United States	Biltmore Forest Country Club	Asheville, North Carolina
2000	Marcy Newton	United States	Waverley Country Club	Portland, Oregon
2001	Meredith Duncan	United States	Flint Hills National Golf Club	Andover, Kansas
2002	Becky Lucidi	United States	Sleepy Hollow Country Club	Scarborough, New York
2003	Virada Nirapathpongporn	Thailand	Philadelphia Country Club	Gladwyne, Pennsylvania

2004	Jane Park	United States	Kahkwa Club	Erie, Pennsylvania
2005	Morgan Pressel	United States	Ansley Golf Club, Settindown Creek Course	Atlanta, Georgia
2006	Kimberly Kim	United States	Pumpkin Ridge Golf Club	North Plains, Oregon
2007	Maria José Uribe	Colombia	Crooked Stick Golf Club	Carmel, Indiana
2008	Amanda Blumenherst	United States	Eugene Country Club	Eugene, Oregon
2009	Jennifer Song	United States / Korea	Old Warson Country Club	St. Louis, Missouri

Canadian Women's Amateur

1901	L. Young	Canada	Royal Montréal Golf Club	Île Bizard, Québec
1902	M. Thomson	Canada	Toronto Golf Club	Toronto, Ontario
1903	F. Harvey	Canada	Royal Montréal Golf Club	Île Bizard, Québec
1904	F. Harvey	Canada	Toronto Golf Club	Toronto, Ontario
1905	M. Thomson	Canada	Royal Montréal Golf Club	Île Bizard, Québec
1906	M. Thomson	Canada	Toronto Golf Club	Toronto, Ontario
1907	M. Thomson	Canada	Royal Ottawa Golf Club	Gatineau, Québec
1908	M. Thomson	Canada	Lambton Golf Club	Toronto, Ontario

1909	V. H. Anderson	Canada	Royal Montréal Golf Club	Île Bizard, Québec
1910	Dorothy Campbell	Canada	Toronto Golf Club	Toronto, Ontario
1911	Dorothy Campbell	Canada	Royal Ottawa Golf Club	Gatineau, Québec
1912	Dorothy Campbell	Canada	Rosedale Golf Club	Toronto, Ontario
1913	M. Dodd	Canada	Royal Montréal Golf Club	Île Bizard, Québec
1919	Ada Mackenzie	Canada	Beaconsfield Golf Club	Pointe-Claire, Québec
1920	Alexa Stirling	United States	Hamilton Golf Club	Hamilton, Ontario
1921	Cecil Leitch	England	Rivermead Golf Club	Ottawa, Ontario
1922	Mrs. William Gavin	Canada	Toronto Golf Club	Toronto, Ontario
1923	Glenna Collett	United States	Mt. Bruno Golf Club	Mt. Bruno, Québec
1924	Glenna Collett	United States	Hamilton Golf Club	Hamilton, Ontario
1925	Ada Mackenzie	Canada	Royal Ottawa Golf Club	Gatineau, Québec
1926	Ada MacKenzie	Canada	Elmhurst Golf Club	Winnipeg, Manitoba
1927	Helen Payson	United States	Lambton Golf Club	Toronto, Ontario
1928	Virgina Wilson	United States	Beaconsfield Golf Club	Pointe-Claire, Québec
1929	Helen Hicks	United States	Hamilton Golf Club	Hamilton, Ontario

1930	Maureen Orcutt	United States	Le Club Laval-sur-le-Lac	Laval-sur-le-Lac, Québec
1931	Maureen Orcutt	United States	Rosedale Golf Club	Toronto, Ontario
1932	Margery Kirkham	Canada	Kanawaki Golf Club	Kahnawake, Québec
1933	Ada Mackenzie	Canada	Pine Ridge Golf Club	Winnipeg, Manitoba
1934	Alexa Stirling Fraser	United States	Toronto Golf Club	Toronto, Ontario
1935	Ada Mackenzie	Canada	Jericho Country Club	Vancouver, British Columbia
1936	Mrs. A. B. Darling	Canada	Royal Montréal Golf Club	Île Bizard, Québec
1937	Mrs. John Rogers	Canada	St. Charles Country Club	Winnipeg, Manitoba
1938	Mrs. F. J. Mulqueen	Canada	Royal Ottawa Golf Club	Gatineau, Québec
1947	Grace Lenczyk	United States	Toronto Golf Club	Toronto, Ontario
1948	Grace Lenczyk	United States	Riverside Golf & Country Club	East Riverside, New Brunswick
1949	Grace DeMoss	United States	Capilano Golf & Country Club	Vancouver, British Columbia
1950	Dorothy Keilty	United States	St. Charles Country Club	Winnipeg, Manitoba
1951	Marlene Stewart	Canada	Le Club Laval-sur-le-Lac	Laval-sur-le-Lac, Québec

1952	Edean Anderson	United States	Mayfair Golf & Country Club	Edmonton, Alberta
1953	Barbara Romack	United States	London Hunt & Country Club	London, Ontario
1954	Marlene Stewart	Canada	Brightwood Golf & Country Club	Dartmouth, Nova Scotia
1955	Marlene Stewart	Canada	Royal Colwood Golf Club	Victoria, British Columbia
1956	Marlene Stewart	Canada	Niakwa Country Club	Winnipeg, Manitoba
1957	Betty Stanhope	Canada	The Royal Montréal Golf Club	Dorval, Québec
1958	Marlene Stewart-Streit	Canada	The Saskatoon Golf & Country Club	Saskatoon, Saskatchewan
1959	Marlene Stewart-Streit	Canada	St. George's Golf & Country Club	Islington, Ontario
1960	Judy Darling	Canada	Riverside Golf & Country Club	East Riverside, New Brunswick
1961	Judy Darling	Canada	Point Grey Golf & Country Club	Vancouver, British Columbia
1962	Gayle Hitchens	Canada	Glendale Golf & Country Club	St. Charles, Manitoba
1963	Marlene Stewart-Streit	Canada	Royal Ottawa Golf Club	Gatineau, Québec
1964	Margaret Masters	Canada	Calgary Golf & Country Club	Calgary, Alberta

1965	Jocelyn Bourassa	Canada	Westmount Golf & Country Club	Montréal, Québec
1966	Helene Gagnon	Canada	Ashburn Golf Club	Halifax, Nova Scotia
1967	Bridget Jackson	Canada	Riverside Country Club	Saskatoon, Saskatchewan
1968	Marlene Stewart-Streit	Canada	Kanawaki Golf Club	Cauaghnawaga, Québec
1969	Marlene Stewart-Streit	Canada	Moncton Golf & Country Club	Moncton, New Brunswick
1970	Mrs. J. D. Moore	Canada	Oakdale Golf & Country Club	Downsview, Ontario
1971	Jocelyn Bourassa	Canada	Capilano Golf & Country Club	Vancouver, British Columbia
1972	Marlene Stewart-Streit	Canada	Niakwa Country Club	Winnipeg, Manitoba
1973	Marlene Stewart-Streit	Canada	Belvedere Golf & Country Club	Charlottetown, Prince Edward Island
1974	Debbie Massey	United States	Edmonton Country Club	Edmonton, Alberta
1975	Debbie Massey	United States	Oakfield Country Club	Grand Lake, Nova Scotia
1976	Debbie Massey	United States	Cooke Municipal Golf Club	Prince Albert, Saskatchewan
1977	Cathy Sherk	Canada	Hillsdale Golf & Country Club	Boisbriand, Québec

1978	Cathy Sherk	Canada	Mactaquac Provincial Park Golf Club	Fredericton, New Brunswick
1979	Stacey West	Canada	Bally Haly Golf & Country Club	St. John's, Newfoundland
1980	Edwina Kennedy	Australia	London Hunt & Country Club	London, Ontario
1981	Jane Lock	Australia	St. Charles Country Club	Winnipeg, Manitoba
1982	Cindy Pleger	United States	Brudenell Golf Resort	Cardigan, Prince Edward Island
1983	Dawn Coe	United States	Victoria Golf Club	Victoria, British Columbia
1984	Kimberly Williams	Canada	Willow Park Golf & Country Club	Calgary, Alberta
1985	Kimberly Williams	Canada	Ashburn Golf Club	Armdale, Nova Scotia
1986	Marilyn O'Connor	Canada	Riverside Golf & Country Club	Saskatoon, Saskatchewan
1987	Tracy Kerdyk	United States	Kanawaki Golf Club	Kahnawake, Québec
1988	Michiko Hattori	United States	Shaughnessy Golf & Country Club	Vancouver, British Columbia
1989	Cheryll Damphouse	Canada	Bally Haly Golf & Country Club	St. John's, Newfoundland

1990	Sarah Lebrun	United States	Sunningdale Country Club	London, Ontario
1991	Adele Morre	United States	Glendale Golf & Country Club	Winnipeg, Manitoba
1992	Marie-Josee Rouleau	Canada	Moncton Golf & Country Club	Moncton, New Brunswick
1993	Mary-Ann Lapointe	Canada	Mayfair Golf & Country Club	Edmonton, Alberta
1994	Aileen Robertson	Canada	Mill River Golf Club	O'Leary, Prince Edward Island
1995	Tracy Lipp	Canada	Club de Golf de Beloeil	Beloeil, Québec
1996	Mary-Ann Lapointe	Canada	Normandie Golf Club	St. Louis, Missouri
1997	Anna-Jane Eathorne	Canada	Rivershore Golf Club	Kamloops, British Columbia
1998	Kareen Qually	Canada	Mississaugua Golf & Country Club	Mississauga, Ontario
1999	Mary Ann Lapointe	Canada	Elbow Springs Golf Club	Calgary, Alberta
2000	Jan Dowling	Canada	Admiral's Green Golf Club	St. John's, Newfoundland
2001	Lisa Meldrum	Canada	Niakwa Country Club	Winnipeg, Manitoba
2002	Lisa Meldrum	Canada	Ken-Wo Country Club	New Minas, Nova Scotia
2003	Lisa Meldrum	Canada	Blainvillier Golf Club	Blainville, Québec
2004	Mary-Ann Lapointe	Canada	Cooke Municipal Golf Club	Prince Albert, Saskatchewan

2005	Laura Matthews	Canada	St. Andrews Links, Old Course	St. Andrews, Fife, Scotland
2006	Jessica Potter	Canada	Moncton Golf & Country Club	Moncton, New Brunswick
2007	Stephanie Sherlock	Canada	Granite Golf Club	Stouffville, Ontario
2008	Stacey Keating	Australia	Elmhurst Golf & Country Club	Winnipeg, Manitoba
2009	Jennifer Kirby	Canada	Royal Oaks Golf Links	Moncton, New Brunswick

U.S. Collegiate Division I Championship

Division for Girls and Women's Sports (DGWS, 1941–1972), Association of Intercollegiate Athletics for Women (AIAW, 1973–1982), NCAA (1982–2009)

Year	Class	Individual Champion	College	Team Champion	Venue / Host	Location
1941	DGWS	Eleanor Dudley	Alabama	—	—	
1946	DGWS	Phyllis Otto	Northwestern	—	—	
1947	DGWS	Shirley Spock	Michigan State	—	—	
1948	DGWS	Grace Lenczyk	Stetson	—	—	
1949	DGWS	Marilyn Smith	Kansas	—	—	

1950	DGWS	Betty Rowland	Rollins	—	—	
1951	DGWS	Barbara Browning	Wellesley	—	—	
1952	DGWS	Mary Ann Villego	Ohio State	—	—	
1953	DGWS	Patricia Ann Lesser	Seattle	—	—	
1954	DGWS	Nancy Reed	Peabody	—	—	
1955	DGWS	Jackie Yates	Redlands	—	—	
1956	DGWS	Marlene Stewart	Rollins	—	—	
1957	DGWS	Marian Bailey	Northwestern	—	—	
1958	DGWS	Carole Pushing	Carleton	—	—	
1959	DGWS	Judy Eller	Miami (Florida)	—	—	
1960	DGWS	JoAnn Gunderson	Arizona State	—	—	
1961	DGWS	Judy Hoeffner	Washington	—	—	
1962	DGWS	Carol Sorenson	Arizona State	—	—	
1963	DGWS	Claudia Lindor	Western Washington State	—	—	
1964	DGWS	Patti Snook	Valparaiso	—	—	
1965	DGWS	Roberta Albers	Miami (Florida)	—	University of Florida Golf Course	Gainesville, Florida
1966	DGWS	Joyce Kazmierski	Michigan State	—	—	
1967	DGWS	Martha Wilkinson	Cal State, Fullerton	—	—	

1968	DGWS	Gail Sykes	Odessa	—	—	
1969	DGWS	Jane Bastanchury	Arizona State	—	—	
1970	DGWS	Cathy Vaughan	Arizona State	—	—	
1971	DGWS	Shelly Hamlin	Stanford	—	—	
1972	DGWS	Ann Laughlin	Miami (Florida)	—	—	
1973	AIAW	Bonnie Lauer	Michigan State	UNC, Greensboro	—	
1974	AIAW	Mary Budke	Oregon State	Rollins	—	
1975	AIAW	Barbara Barrow / Debbie Simourian	San Diego State / Wheaton	Arizona State	—	
1976	AIAW	Nancy Lopez	Tulsa	Furman	—	
1977	AIAW	Cathy Morse	Miami (Florida)	Miami (Florida)	—	
1978	AIAW	Debbie Petrizzi	Texas	Miami (Florida)	—	
1979	AIAW	Kyle O'Brien	Southern Methodist	Southern Methodist	—	
1980	AIAW	Patty Sheehan	San Jose State	Tulsa	—	
1981	AIAW	Terri Moody	Georgia	Florida State	University of Georgia Golf Course	Athens, Georgia
1982	AIAW	Kathy Baker	Tulsa	Tulsa	—	
1982	NCAA	Kathy Baker	Tulsa	Tulsa	Stanford Golf Course	Stanford, California

1983	NCAA	Penny Hammel	Miami (Florida)	Texas Christian	University of Georgia Golf Course	Athens, Georgia
1984	NCAA	Cindy Schreyer	Georgia	Miami (Florida)	University of Georgia Golf Course	Athens, Georgia
1985	NCAA	Danielle Ammaccapane	Arizona State	Florida	Amherst Golf Course	Amherst, Massachusetts
1986	NCAA	Page Dunlap	Florida	Florida	Ohio State University, Scarlet Course	Columbus, Ohio
1987	NCAA	Caroline Keggi	New Mexico	San Jose State	University of New Mexico Golf Course	Albuquerque, New Mexico
1988	NCAA	Melissa McNamara	Tulsa	Tulsa (vacated)	New Mexico State University Golf Course	Las Cruces, New Mexico
1989	NCAA	Pat Hurst	San Jose State	San Jose State	Stanford Golf Course	Stanford, California

1990	NCAA	Susan Slaughter	Arizona	Arizona State	University Club	Blythewood, South Carolina
1991	NCAA	Annika Sörenstam	Arizona	UCLA	Ohio State University, Scarlet Course	Columbus, Ohio
1992	NCAA	Vicki Goetze	Georgia	San Jose State	Arizona State University, Karsten Golf Course	Tempe, Arizona
1993	NCAA	Charlotta Sörenstam	Texas	Arizona State	University of Georgia Golf Course	Athens, Georgia
1994	NCAA	Emilee Klein	Arizona State	Arizona State	Eugene Country Club	Eugene, Oregon
1995	NCAA	Kristel Mourgue D'Algue	Arizona State	Arizona State	Country Club of Landfall, Pete Dye Course	Wilmington, North Carolina
1996	NCAA	Marisa Baena	Arizona	Arizona	Bel Air Country Club	Los Angeles, California

1997	NCAA	Heather Bowie	Texas	Arizona State	Ohio State University, Scarlet Course	Columbus, Ohio
1998	NCAA	Jennifer Rosales	Southern California	Arizona State	University Ridge Golf Course	Fitchburg, Wisconsin
1999	NCAA	Grace Park	Arizona State	Duke	Tulsa Country Club	Tulsa, Oklahoma
2000	NCAA	Jenna Daniels	Arizona	Arizona	Sunriver Resort, Meadows Course	Sunriver, Oregon
2001	NCAA	Candy Hannemann	Duke	Georgia	Victoria Hills Golf Club	DeLand, Florida
2002	NCAA	Virada Nirapathpongporn	Duke	Duke	Washington National Golf Club	Auburn, Washington
2003	NCAA	Mikaela Parmlid	Southern California	Southern California	Birck Boilermaker GC, Kampen Course	West Lafayette, Indiana

2004	NCAA	Sarah Huarte	UC-Berkeley	UCLA	Grand National Golf Course, Lake Course	Opelika, Alabama
2005	NCAA	Anna Grzebian	Duke	Duke	Sunriver Resort, Meadows Course	Sunriver, Oregon
2006	NCAA	Dewi Schreefel	Southern California	Duke	Ohio State University, Scarlet Course	Columbus, Ohio
2007	NCAA	Stacy Lewis	Arkansas	Duke	LPGA International Legends Course	Daytona Beach, Florida
2008	NCAA	Azahara Muñoz	Arizona State	Southern California	University of New Mexico Golf Course	Albuquerque, New Mexico
2009	NCAA	Maria Hernandez	Purdue	Arizona State	Caves Valley Golf Club	Owings Mills, Maryland

Eastern Amateur

Year	Winner	Club	Location
1906	Fanny Osgood	Nassau Country Club	Glen Cove, New York
1907	Mary Adams	Atlantic City Country Club	Northfield, New Jersey
1908	Fanny Osgood	Oakley Country Club	Watertown, Massachusetts
1909	Mary Adams	Baltusrol Golf Club	Springfield, New Jersey
1910	Fanny Osgood	Huntingdon Valley Country Club	Huntingdon Valley, Pennsylvania
1911	R. H. Barlow	Brae Burn Country Club	West Newton, Massachusetts
1912	R. H. Barlow	Philadelphia Cricket Club, St. Martin's Course	Philadelphia, Pennsylvania
1913	R. H. Barlow	Brae Burn Country Club	West Newton, Massachusetts
1914	H. A. Jackson	Greenwich Country Club	Greenwich, Connecticut
1915	Florence Vanderbeck	Merion Golf Club, East Course	Ardmore, Pennsylvania
1916	William Gavin	Essex County Club	Manchester-by-the-Sea, Massachusetts
1919	R. H. Barlow	Apawamis Club	Rye, New York
1920	R. H. Barlow	Philadelphia Cricket Club, St. Martin's Course	Philadelphia, Pennsylvania
1921	Florence Vanderbeck	The Country Club	Brookline, Massachusetts
1922	Glenna Collett	Westchester Country Club	Rye, New York
1923	Glenna Collett	Whitemarsh Valley Country Club	Whitemarsh Township, Pennsylvania
1924	Glenna Collett	Brae Burn Country Club	West Newton, Massachusetts
1925	Maureen Orcutt	Greenwich Country Club	Greenwich, Connecticut
1926	G. Henry Stetson	Philmont Country Club	Huntingdon Valley, Pennsylvania
1927	Glenna Collett	Belmont Springs Country Club	Belmont, Massachusetts

1928	Maureen Orcutt	Montclair Golf Club	West Orange, New Jersey
1929	Maureen Orcutt	Aronimink Golf Club	Newtown Square, Pennsylvania
1930	Francis Williams	The Country Club	Brookline, Massachusetts
1931	Helen Hicks	Engineers Country Club	Roslyn Harbor, New York
1932	Glenna Collett Vare	Merion Golf Club, East Course	Ardmore, Pennsylvania
1933	Charlotte Glutting	Brae Burn Country Club	West Newton, Massachusetts
1934	Maureen Orcutt	Wee Burn Country Club	Darien, Connecticut
1935	Glenna Collett Vare	Huntingdon Valley Country Club	Huntingdon Valley, Pennsylvania
1936	Edith Quier	Winchester Country Club	Winchester, Massachusetts
1937	Charlotte Glutting	Plainfield Country Club	Edison, New Jersey
1938	Maureen Orcutt	Philadelphia Country Club	Gladwyne, Pennsylvania
1939	Warren Beard	Charles River Country Club	Newton, Massachusetts
1940	Grace Amory	Baltimore Country Club, Five Farms, East Course	Timonium, Maryland
1941	Marion McNaughton	Westchester Country Club	Rye, New York
1946	Laddie Irwin	Aronimink Golf Club	Newtown Square, Pennsylvania
1947	Maureen Orcutt	Brae Burn Country Club	West Newton, Massachusetts
1948	Pat O'Sullivan	North Hills Country Club	Manhasset, New York
1949	Maureen Orcutt	Philmont Country Club	Huntingdon Valley, Pennsylvania
1950	Peggy Kirk	Belmont Country Club	Belmont, Massachusetts
1951	Pat O'Sullivan	Montclair Golf Club	West Orange, New Jersey
1952	Helen Sigel	Philadelphia Country Club	Gladwyne, Pennsylvania
1953	Mary Ann Downey	Congressional Country Club	Bethesda, Maryland

1954	Mae Murray Jones	Wethersfield Country Club	Wethersfield, Connecticut
1955	Mary Ann Downey	Farmington Country Club	Farmington, Connecticut
1956	Norman Woolworth	Nassau Country Club	Glen Cove, New York
1957	Joanne Goodwin	Agawam Hunt Club	Agawam, Rhode Island
1958	Mary Patton-Janssen	Allegheny Country Club	Sewickley, Pennsylvania
1959	Edward McAuliffe	Baltimore Country Club, Five Farms, East Course	Timonium, Maryland
1960	Philip Cudone	Tedesco Country Club	Marblehead, Massachusetts
1961	Marjorie Burns	Century Country Club	Purchase, New York
1962	Helen Sigel Wilson	Merion Golf Club, East Course	Ardmore, Pennsylvania
1963	Phyllis "Tish" Preuss	Pleasant Valley Country Club	Sutton, Massachusetts
1964	Nancy Roth	Wee Burn Country Club	Darien, Connecticut
1965	Nancy Roth	Hollywood Country Club	Deal, New Jersey
1966	Nancy Roth Syms	Philmont Country Club	Huntingdon Valley, Pennsylvania
1967	Phyllis "Tish" Preuss	Allegheny Country Club	Sewickley, Pennsylvania
1968	Joanne Carner	Rhode Island Country Club	West Barrington, Rhode Island
1969	Mark Porter	Gulph Mills Golf Club	King of Prussia, Pennsylvania
1970	Delancy Smith	Round Hill Club	Greenwich, Connecticut
1971	Delancy Smith	Wellesley Country Club	Wellesley, Massachusetts
1972	Paul Dye Jr.	Country Club of North Carolina	Southern Pines, North Carolina
1973	Delancy Smith	Fox Chapel Golf Club	Pittsburgh, Pennsylvania

1974	Delancy Smith	Country Club of South Carolina	Florence, South Carolina
1975	Debbie Massey	Atlantic City Country Club	Northfield, New Jersey
1976	Judy Oliver	Monroe Country Club	Monroe, New York
1977	Noreen Uihlein	Mid Pines Inn and Golf Club	Southern Pines, North Carolina
1978	Julie Green	Hillendale Country Club	Phoenix, Maryland
1979	Kathy Baker	Ridgewood Country Club	Paramus, New Jersey
1980	Patti Rizzo	Savannah Inn Country Club	Savannah, Georgia
1981	Mary Hafeman	Mid Pines Inn and Golf Club	Southern Pines, North Carolina
1982	Kathy Baker	Sewickley Heights Golf Club	Sewickley, Pennsylvania
1983	Mary Anne Widman	Seabrook Island Resort	Seabrook Island, South Carolina
1984	Tina Tombs	Rhode Island Country Club	West Barrington, Rhode Island
1985	Kimberly Williams	Prince Georges Golf and Country Club	Landover, Maryland
1986	Nancy Porter	Gulph Mills Golf Club	King of Prussia, Pennsylvania
1987	Christian Barrett	Birdwood Golf Club	Charlottesville, Virginia
1988	Katie Peterson	Mid Pines Inn and Golf Club	Southern Pines, North Carolina
1989	Katie Peterson	Long Point Club	Amelia Island, Florida
1990	Carolyn McKenzie	Leatherstocking Golf Club	Cooperstown, New York
1991	Robin Weiss	Charles River Country Club	Newton, Massachusetts
1992	Arantxa Sison	Hermitage Country Club	Richmond, Virginia
1993	Stephanie Sparks	Merion Golf Club, East Course	Ardmore, Pennsylvania
1994	Stephanie Neill	Atlanta Athletic Club	Atlanta, Georgia
1995	Tiffany Faucette	Dedham Country & Polo Club	Dedham, Massachusetts
1996	Laura Philo	Country Club of Rochester	Rochester, New York

1997	Jenny Chuasiriporn	Kingsmill Resort & Golf Club	Williamsburg, Virginia
1998	Jenny Chuasiriporn	Army Navy Country Club	Fairfax, Virginia
1999	Krissie Register	Shannopin Country Club	Pittsburgh, Pennsylvania
2000	Beth Bauer	The Country Club of Whispering Pines	Whispering Pines, North Carolina
2001	Courtney Swaim	Yeamans Hall Club	Charleston, South Carolina
2002	Virada Nirapathpongporn	Country Club of York	Pennsylvania
2003	Anne Fraser	The Members Club at St. James Plantation	Southport, North Carolina
2004	Ashley Hoagland	Bayville Golf Club	Virginia Beach, Virginia
2005	Morgan Olds	Charles River Country Club	Newton, Massachusetts
2006	Leah Wigger	Gulph Mills Golf Club	King of Prussia, Pennsylvania
2007	Natalie Sheary	Independence Golf Club	Richmond, Virginia
2008	Laura Crawford	Wake Forest Golf & Country Club	Wake Forest, North Carolina
2009	Isabelle Lendl	IMG Academies Golf & Country Club	Sarasota, Florida

North and South Women's Amateur

1903	Myra Paterson	Pinehurst Resort, No. 2 Course	Pinehurst, North Carolina
1904	Myra Paterson	Pinehurst Resort, No. 2 Course	Pinehurst, North Carolina
1905	Mary Dutton	Pinehurst Resort, No. 2 Course	Pinehurst, North Carolina
1906	Myra Paterson	Pinehurst Resort, No. 2 Course	Pinehurst, North Carolina
1907	Molly Adams	Pinehurst Resort, No. 2 Course	Pinehurst, North Carolina
1908	Julia Mix	Pinehurst Resort, No. 2 Course	Pinehurst, North Carolina

1909	Mary Fownes	Pinehurst Resort, No. 2 Course	Pinehurst, North Carolina
1910	Florence Vanderbeck	Pinehurst Resort, No. 2 Course	Pinehurst, North Carolina
1911	Louise Elkins	Pinehurst Resort, No. 2 Course	Pinehurst, North Carolina
1912	Mrs. J. Raymond Price	Pinehurst Resort, No. 2 Course	Pinehurst, North Carolina
1913	Lillian Hyde	Pinehurst Resort, No. 2 Course	Pinehurst, North Carolina
1914	Florence Harvey	Pinehurst Resort, No. 2 Course	Pinehurst, North Carolina
1915	Nonna Barlow	Pinehurst Resort, No. 2 Course	Pinehurst, North Carolina
1916	Nonna Barlow	Pinehurst Resort, No. 2 Course	Pinehurst, North Carolina
1917	Elaine Rosenthall	Pinehurst Resort, No. 2 Course	Pinehurst, North Carolina
1918	Dorothy Campbell	Pinehurst Resort, No. 2 Course	Pinehurst, North Carolina
1919	Nonna Barlow	Pinehurst Resort, No. 2 Course	Pinehurst, North Carolina
1920	Dorothy Campbell	Pinehurst Resort, No. 2 Course	Pinehurst, North Carolina
1921	Dorothy Campbell	Pinehurst Resort, No. 2 Course	Pinehurst, North Carolina
1922	Glenna Collett	Pinehurst Resort, No. 2 Course	Pinehurst, North Carolina
1923	Glenna Collett	Pinehurst Resort, No. 2 Course	Pinehurst, North Carolina
1924	Glenna Collett	Pinehurst Resort, No. 2 Course	Pinehurst, North Carolina
1925	Mrs. Melville Jones	Pinehurst Resort, No. 2 Course	Pinehurst, North Carolina
1926	Louise Fordyce	Pinehurst Resort, No. 2 Course	Pinehurst, North Carolina
1927	Glenna Collett	Pinehurst Resort, No. 2 Course	Pinehurst, North Carolina
1928	Opal Hill	Pinehurst Resort, No. 2 Course	Pinehurst, North Carolina
1929	Glenna Collett	Pinehurst Resort, No. 2 Course	Pinehurst, North Carolina
1930	Glenna Collett	Pinehurst Resort, No. 2 Course	Pinehurst, North Carolina
1931	Maureen Orcutt	Pinehurst Resort, No. 2 Course	Pinehurst, North Carolina

1932	Maureen Orcutt	Pinehurst Resort, No. 2 Course	Pinehurst, North Carolina
1933	Maureen Orcutt	Pinehurst Resort, No. 2 Course	Pinehurst, North Carolina
1934	Charlotte Glutting	Pinehurst Resort, No. 2 Course	Pinehurst, North Carolina
1935	Estelle Lawson	Pinehurst Resort, No. 2 Course	Pinehurst, North Carolina
1936	Deborah Verry	Pinehurst Resort, No. 2 Course	Pinehurst, North Carolina
1937	Estelle Lawson Page	Pinehurst Resort, No. 2 Course	Pinehurst, North Carolina
1938	Jane Cothran	Pinehurst Resort, No. 2 Course	Pinehurst, North Carolina
1939	Estelle Lawson Page	Pinehurst Resort, No. 2 Course	Pinehurst, North Carolina
1940	Estelle Lawson Page	Pinehurst Resort, No. 2 Course	Pinehurst, North Carolina
1941	Estelle Lawson Page	Pinehurst Resort, No. 2 Course	Pinehurst, North Carolina
1942	Louise Suggs	Pinehurst Resort, No. 2 Course	Pinehurst, North Carolina
1943	Dorothy Kirby	Pinehurst Resort, No. 2 Course	Pinehurst, North Carolina
1944	Estelle Lawson Page	Pinehurst Resort, No. 2 Course	Pinehurst, North Carolina
1945	Estelle Lawson Page	Pinehurst Resort, No. 2 Course	Pinehurst, North Carolina
1946	Louise Suggs	Pinehurst Resort, No. 2 Course	Pinehurst, North Carolina
1947	Babe Zaharias	Pinehurst Resort, No. 2 Course	Pinehurst, North Carolina
1948	Louise Suggs	Pinehurst Resort, No. 2 Course	Pinehurst, North Carolina
1949	Peggy Kirk	Pinehurst Resort, No. 2 Course	Pinehurst, North Carolina
1950	Pat O'Sullivan	Pinehurst Resort, No. 2 Course	Pinehurst, North Carolina
1951	Pat O'Sullivan	Pinehurst Resort, No. 2 Course	Pinehurst, North Carolina
1952	Barbara Romack	Pinehurst Resort, No. 2 Course	Pinehurst, North Carolina
1953	Pat O'Sullivan	Pinehurst Resort, No. 2 Course	Pinehurst, North Carolina
1954	Joyce Ziske	Pinehurst Resort, No. 2 Course	Pinehurst, North Carolina

1955	Wiffi Smith	Pinehurst Resort, No. 2 Course	Pinehurst, North Carolina
1956	Marlene Stewart	Pinehurst Resort, No. 2 Course	Pinehurst, North Carolina
1957	Barbara McIntire	Pinehurst Resort, No. 2 Course	Pinehurst, North Carolina
1958	Carolyn Cudone	Pinehurst Resort, No. 2 Course	Pinehurst, North Carolina
1959	Ann Casey Johnstone	Pinehurst Resort, No. 2 Course	Pinehurst, North Carolina
1960	Barbara McIntire	Pinehurst Resort, No. 2 Course	Pinehurst, North Carolina
1961	Barbara McIntire	Pinehurst Resort, No. 2 Course	Pinehurst, North Carolina
1962	Clifford Ann Creed	Pinehurst Resort, No. 2 Course	Pinehurst, North Carolina
1963	Nancy Roth	Pinehurst Resort, No. 2 Course	Pinehurst, North Carolina
1964	Phyllis "Tish" Preuss	Pinehurst Resort, No. 2 Course	Pinehurst, North Carolina
1965	Barbara McIntire	Pinehurst Resort, No. 2 Course	Pinehurst, North Carolina
1966	Nancy Roth Syms	Pinehurst Resort, No. 2 Course	Pinehurst, North Carolina
1967	Phyllis "Tish" Preuss	Pinehurst Resort, No. 2 Course	Pinehurst, North Carolina
1968	Alice Dye	Pinehurst Resort, No. 2 Course	Pinehurst, North Carolina
1969	Barbara McIntire	Pinehurst Resort, No. 2 Course	Pinehurst, North Carolina
1970	Hollis Stacy	Pinehurst Resort, No. 2 Course	Pinehurst, North Carolina
1971	Barbara McIntire	Pinehurst Resort, No. 2 Course	Pinehurst, North Carolina
1972	Jane Bastanchury-Booth	Pinehurst Resort, No. 2 Course	Pinehurst, North Carolina
1973	Beth Barry	Pinehurst Resort, No. 2 Course	Pinehurst, North Carolina
1974	Marlene Stewart	Pinehurst Resort, No. 2 Course	Pinehurst, North Carolina
1975	Cynthia Hill	Pinehurst Resort, No. 2 Course	Pinehurst, North Carolina
1976	Carol Semple	Pinehurst Resort, No. 2 Course	Pinehurst, North Carolina
1977	Marcia Dolan	Pinehurst Resort, No. 2 Course	Pinehurst, North Carolina

1978	Cathy Sherk	Pinehurst Resort, No. 2 Course	Pinehurst, North Carolina
1979	Julie Gumlia	Pinehurst Resort, No. 2 Course	Pinehurst, North Carolina
1980	Charlotte Montgomery	Pinehurst Resort, No. 2 Course	Pinehurst, North Carolina
1981	Patti Rizzo	Pinehurst Resort, No. 2 Course	Pinehurst, North Carolina
1982	Anne Quast	Pinehurst Resort, No. 2 Course	Pinehurst, North Carolina
1983	Anne Quast	Pinehurst Resort, No. 2 Course	Pinehurst, North Carolina
1984	Susan Pager	Pinehurst Resort, No. 2 Course	Pinehurst, North Carolina
1985	Lee Ann Hammack	Pinehurst Resort, No. 2 Course	Pinehurst, North Carolina
1986	Leslie Shannon	Pinehurst Resort, No. 2 Course	Pinehurst, North Carolina
1987	Carol Semple Thompson	Pinehurst Resort, No. 2 Course	Pinehurst, North Carolina
1988	Donna Andrews	Pinehurst Resort, No. 2 Course	Pinehurst, North Carolina
1989	Page Marsh	Pinehurst Resort, No. 2 Course	Pinehurst, North Carolina
1990	Brandie Burton	Pinehurst Resort, No. 2 Course	Pinehurst, North Carolina
1991	Kelly Robbins	Pinehurst Resort, No. 2 Course	Pinehurst, North Carolina
1992	Stephanie Sparks	Pinehurst Resort, No. 2 Course	Pinehurst, North Carolina
1993	Emilee Klein	Pinehurst Resort, No. 2 Course	Pinehurst, North Carolina
1994	Stephanie Neill	Pinehurst Resort, No. 2 Course	Pinehurst, North Carolina
1995	Laura Philo	Pinehurst Resort, No. 2 Course	Pinehurst, North Carolina
1996	Kristen Samp	Pinehurst Resort, No. 2 Course	Pinehurst, North Carolina
1997	Kerry Postillon	Pinehurst Resort, No. 2 Course	Pinehurst, North Carolina
1998	Beth Bauer	Pinehurst Resort, No. 2 Course	Pinehurst, North Carolina
1999	Beth Bauer	Pinehurst Resort, No. 2 Course	Pinehurst, North Carolina
2000	Candy Hannemann	Pinehurst Resort, No. 2 Course	Pinehurst, North Carolina

2001	Meredith Duncan	Pinehurst Resort, No. 2 Course	Pinehurst, North Carolina
2002	May Wood	Pinehurst Resort, No. 2 Course	Pinehurst, North Carolina
2003	Britney Lang	Pinehurst Resort, No. 2 Course	Pinehurst, North Carolina
2004	Morgan Pressel	Pinehurst Resort, No. 2 Course	Pinehurst, North Carolina
2005	Yani Tseng	Pinehurst Resort, No. 2 Course	Pinehurst, North Carolina
2006	Jenny Suh	Pinehurst Resort, No. 2 Course	Pinehurst, North Carolina
2007	Alison Walshe	Pinehurst Resort, No. 2 Course	Pinehurst, North Carolina
2008	Kristie Smith	Pinehurst Resort, No. 2 Course	Pinehurst, North Carolina
2009	Amelia Lewis	Pinehurst Resort, No. 2 Course	Pinehurst, North Carolina

Women's Trans-National Amateur

1927	Mrs. M. Burns Horn	United States	Blue Hills Country Club	Kansas City, Missouri
1928	Mrs. O. S. Hill	United States	Minikahda Country Club	Minneapolis, Minnesota
1929	Mrs. O. S. Hill	United States	Denver Country Club	Denver, Colorado
1930	Mrs. Hulbert Clarke	United States	Tulsa Country Club	Tulsa, Oklahoma
1931	Mrs. O. S. Hill	United States	St. Louis Country Club	St. Louis, Missouri

1932	Mrs. J. W. Beyer	United States	Country Club.of Hot Springs	Hot Springs, Arkansas
1933	Phyllis Buchanan	United States	Wakonda Country Club	Des Moines, Iowa
1934	Mrs. O. S. Hill	United States	Blue Hills Country Club	Kansas City, Missouri
1935	Marion Miley	United States	Omaha Field Club	Omaha, Nebraska
1936	Marion Miley	United States	Denver Country Club	Denver, Colorado
1937	Betty Jameson	United States	San Antonio Country Club	San Antonio, Texas
1938	Patty Berg	United States	Oakhurst Country Club	Tulsa, Oklahoma
1939	Patty Berg	United States	The Country Club	Minneapolis, Minnesota
1940	Betty Jameson	United States	Glen Echo Country Club	St. Louis, Missouri
1941	Mrs. Russell C. Mann	United States	River Oaks Country Club	Houston, Texas
1946	Babe Zaharias	United States	Denver Country Club	Denver, Colorado

1947	Polly Riley	United States	Metairie Country Club	New Orleans, Louisiana
1948	Polly Riley	United States	Peninsula Golf and Country Club	San Mateo, California
1949	Betsy Rawls	United States	Country Club of Lincoln	Lincoln, Nebraska
1950	Marjorie Lindsay	United States	Lake Wood Country Club	Dallas, Texas
1951	Mary Downey	United States	Quincy Country Club	Quincy, Illinois
1952	Mrs. Lyle Bowman	United States	Arizona Country Club	Phoenix, Arizona
1953	Edean Anderson	United States	Arizona Country Club	Phoenix, Arizona
1954	Vonnie Colby	United States	Glen Arven Country Club	Thomasville, Georgia
1955	Polly Riley	United States	Twin Hills Country Club	Oklahoma City, Oklahoma
1956	Wiffi Smith	United States	Monterey Peninsula Country Club	Pebble Beach, California
1957	Mrs. James Ferrie	United States	Desert Inn Country Club	Las Vegas, Nevada

1958	Marjorie Lindsay	United States	Hickory Hills Country Club	Springfield, Missouri
1959	Ann Johnstone	United States	Country Club of Hot Springs	Hot Springs, Arkansas
1960	Sandra Haynie	United States	Ken Wood Country Club	Cincinnati, Ohio
1961	JoAnne Gunderson	United States	Eugene Country Club	Eugene, Oregon
1962	Jeannie Thompson	United States	Wichita Country Club	Wichita, Kansas
1963	Judy Bell	United States	Pinehurst Country Club	Denver, Colorado
1964	Carol Sorenson	United States	Arizona Country Club	Phoenix, Arizona
1965	Sharon Miller	United States	Dubuque Golf and Country Club	Dubuque, Iowa
1966	Roberta Albers	United States	Hardscrabble Country Club	Fort Smith, Arkansas
1967	Jane Bastanchury	United States	Rochester Golf and Country Club	Rochester, Minnesota
1968	Carol Jo Skala	United States	Battle Creek Country Club	Battle Creek, Michigan

1969	Jane Bastanchury	United States	Midland Country Club	Midland, Texas
1970	Martha Wilkinson	United States	Manor Country Club	Rockville, Maryland
1971	Jane Bastanchury	United States	San Diego Country Club	Chula Vista, California
1972	Michele Walker	England	Omaha Country Club	Omaha, Nebraska
1973	Liana Zambresky	United States	Mt. Snow Country Club	Mt. Snow, Vermont
1974	Barbara Barrow	United States	Eugene Country Club	Eugene, Oregon
1975	Beverley Davis	United States	Oaks Country Club	Tulsa, Oklahoma
1976	Nancy Lopez	United States	Mission Viejo Country Club	Mission Viejo, California
1977	Catherine Reynolds	United States	Mid Pines Club	Southern Pines, North Carolina
1978	Nancy Roth Syms	United States	Wolferts Roost Country Club	Albany, New York
1979	Brenda Goldsmith	United States	Diamond Head Yacht and Country Club	Bay St. Louis, Mississippi
1980	Patrice Rizzo	United States	Country Club of Lincoln	Lincoln, Nebraska

1981	Amy Benz	United States	The Ranch Country Club	Denver, Colorado
1982	Cindy Figg	United States	Fairway Oaks Golf Club	Abilene, Texas
1983	Sherri Steinhauer	United States	Mid Pines Club	Southern Pines, North Carolina
1984	Claire Waite	England	Torresdale-Frankford Country Club	Philadelphia, Pennsylvania
1985	Leslie Shannon	United States	Wintergreen Resort	Wintergreen, Virginia
1986	Carol Semple Thompson	United States	Del Rio Country Club	Modesto, California
1987	Pearl Sinn	United States	Crestview Country Club	Wichita, Kansas
1988	Nanci Bowen	United States	Oneida Golf and Riding Club	Green Bay, Wisconsin
1989	Karen Noble	United States	Columbia Country Club	Columbia, South Carolina
1990	Cathy Mockett	United States	Tiger Point Golf and Country Club	Gulf Breeze, Florida
1991	Vicki Goetze	United States	Hickory Hills Country Club	Springfield, Missouri

1992	Debbie Parks	United States	Pinewild Country Club	Pinehurst, North Carolina
1993	Carol Semple Thompson	United States	Shannopin Country Club	Pittsburgh, Pennsylvania
1994	Ellen Port	United States	Del Rio Country Club	Modesto, California
1995	Anne-Marie Knight	Australia	Golf Club Of Tennessee	Kingston Springs, Tennessee
1996	Jenny Lee	United States	Portage Country Club	Akron, Ohio
1997	Rebekah Owens	United States	Houndslake Country Club	Aiken, South Carolina
1998	Grace Park	Korea	San Joaquin Country Club	Fresno, California
1999	Kellee Booth	United States	Oak Tree Country Club	Edmond, Oklahoma
2000	Celeste Troche	Paraguay	Houndslake Country Club	Aiken, South Carolina
2001	Virada Nirapathpongporn	United States	Fargo Country Club	Fargo, North Dakota
2002	Courtney Wood	United States	Firethorn Country Club	Lincoln, Nebraska
2003	Kailin Downs	United States	Twin Warriors Golf Club	Santa Ana Pueblo, New Mexico
2004	Brittany Lang	United States	Glenmore Country Club	Keswick, Virginia

2005	Paige Mackenzie	United States	Mid Pines Club	Southern Pines, North Carolina
2006	Susannah Aboff	United States	Stonewall, The Old Course	Elverson, Pennsylvania
2007	Laura Kueny	United States	Persimmon Ridge Golf Club	Louisville, Kentucky
2008	Ashley Freeman	United States	Bent Tree Country Club	Dallas, Texas
2009	Julia Boland	Australia	Tennessee National Golf Club	Loudon, Tennessee

Women's Western Amateur

1901	Bessie Anthony	Onwentsia Club	Lake Forest, Illinois
1902	Bessie Anthony	Onwentsia Club	Lake Forest, Illinois
1903	Bessie Anthony	Exmoor Country Club	Highland Park, Illinois
1904	Frances Everett	Glen View Club	Golf, Illinois
1905	Mrs. C. L. Dering	Homewood Country Club	Flossmoor, Illinois
1906	Mrs. C. L. Dering	Exmoor Country Club	Highland Park, Illinois
1907	Lillian French	Midlothian Country Club	Midlothian, Illinois
1908	Mrs. W. France Anderson	St. Louis Country Club	St. Louis, Missouri
1909	Vida Llewellyn	Homewood Country Club	Flossmoor, Illinois
1910	Mrs. Thurston Harris	Skokie Country Club	Glencoe, Illinois
1911	Caroline Painter	Midlothian Country Club	Midlothian, Illinois

1912	Caroline Painter	Hinsdale Golf Club	Hinsdale, Illinois
1913	Myra Helmer	Memphis Country Club	Memphis, Tennessee
1914	Mrs. H. D. Hammond	Hinsdale Golf Club	Hinsdale, Illinois
1915	Elaine V. Rosenthal	Midlothian Country Club	Midlothian, Illinois
1916	Mrs. F. C. Letts Jr.	Kent Country Club	Grand Rapids, Michigan
1917	Mrs. F. C. Letts Jr.	Flossmoor Country Club	Flossmoor, Illinois
1918	Elaine Rosenthal	Indian Hill Club	Winnetka, Illinois
1919	Mrs. Perry Fiske	Detroit Golf Club	Detroit, Michigan
1920	Mrs. F. C. Letts Jr.	Oak Park Country Club	Oak Park, Illinois
1921	Mrs. Melville Jones	Westmoreland Country Club	Wilmette, Illinois
1922	Mrs. David Gaut	Glen Echo Country Club	St. Louis, Missouri
1923	Miriam Burns	Exmoor Country Club	Highland Park, Illinois
1924	Edith Cummings	Onwentsia Club	Lake Forest, Illinois
1925	Mrs. S. L. Reinhardt	White Bear Yacht Club	White Bear, Minnesota
1926	Dorothy Page	Olympia Fields Country Club	Olympia Fields, Illinois
1927	Mrs. Harry Pressler	Lake Geneva Country Club	Lake Geneva, Wisconsin
1928	Mrs. Harry Pressler	Indian Hill Club	Winnetka, Illinois
1929	Mrs. O. S. Hill	Mayfield Country Club	South Euclid, Ohio
1930	Mrs. G. W. Tyson	Hillcrest Country Club	Kansas City, Missouri
1931	Mrs. O. S. Hill	Exmoor Country Club	Highland Park, Illinois
1932	Mrs. O. S. Hill	Country Club of Peoria	Peoria, Illinois
1933	Lucille Robinson	Oak Park Country Club	Oak Park, Illinois
1934	Mrs. L. D. Cheney	Los Angeles Country Club	Los Angeles, California

1935	Marion Miley	Westwood Country Club	Lakewood, Ohio
1936	Dorothy Traung	South Bend Country Club	South Bend, Indiana
1937	Marion Miley	Town & Country Club	St. Paul, Minnesota
1938	Patty Berg	Olympia Fields Country Club	Olympia Fields, Illinois
1939	Edith Estabrooks	Oakland Hills Country Club	Birmingham, Michigan
1940	Betty Jameson	Seattle Golf Club	Seattle, Washington
1941	Mrs. Russell Mann	Exmoor Country Club	Highland Park, Illinois
1942	Betty Jameson	Sunset Ridge Country Club	Northbrook, Illinois
1943	Dorothy Germain	Evanston Golf Club	Skokie, Illinois
1944	Dorothy Germain	Onwentsia Club	Lake Forest, Illinois
1945	Phyllis Otto	Knollwood Club	Lake Forest, Illinois
1946	Louise Suggs	The Country Club	Cleveland, Ohio
1947	Louise Suggs	Evanston Golf Club	Skokie, Illinois
1948	Dot Kielty	Olympic Club	San Francisco, California
1949	Helen Sigel	Westmoreland Country Club	Wilmette, Illinois
1950	Polly Riley	Exmoor Country Club	Highland Park, Illinois
1951	Marjorie Lindsay	Plum Hollow Golf Club	Detroit, Michigan
1952	Polly Riley	Los Angeles Country Club	Los Angeles, California
1953	Claire Doran	The Camargo Club	Cincinnati, Ohio
1954	Claire Doran	Broadmoor Country Club	Indianapolis, Indiana
1955	Patricia Ann Lesser	Olympia Fields Country Club	Olympia Fields, Illinois
1956	Anne Quast	Guyan Golf & Country Club	Huntington, West Virginia
1957	Meriam Bailey	Omaha Country Club	Omaha, Nebraska

1958	Barbara McIntire	Oak Park Country Club	Oak Park, Illinois
1959	JoAnne Gunderson	Exmoor Country Club	Highland Park, Illinois
1960	Ann Casey Johnston	Mission Hills Country Club	Kansas City, Missouri
1961	Anne Quast Sander	Annandale Golf Club	Pasadena, California
1962	Carol Sorenson	South Bend Country Club	South Bend, Indiana
1963	Barbara McIntire	Broadmoor Country Club	Colorado Springs, Colorado
1964	Barbara Fay White	Oak Park Country Club	Oak Park, Illinois
1965	Barbara Fay White	Wayzata Country Club	Wayzata, Minnesota
1966	Peggy Conley	Barrington Hills Country Club	Barrington, Illinois
1967	Mrs. Mark Potter	Bellefonte Country Club	Ashland, Kentucky
1968	Catherine Lacoste	Broadmoor Country Club	Colorado Springs, Colorado
1969	Jane Bastanchury	Oak Park Country Club	Oak Park, Illinois
1970	Jane Bastanchury	Rockford Country Club	Rockford, Illinois
1971	Beth Barry	Flossmoor Country Club	Flossmoor, Illinois
1972	Debbie Massey	Blue Hills Country Club	Kansas City, Missouri
1973	Katie Falk	Maple Bluff Country Club	Madison, Wisconsin
1974	Lancy Smith	Country Club of Indianapolis	Indianapolis, Indiana
1975	Debbie Massey	Tanglewood Golf Club	Clemmons, North Carolina
1976	Nancy Lopez	Country Club of Colorado	Colorado Springs, Colorado
1977	Lauren Howe	Flossmoor Country Club	Flossmoor, Illinois
1978	Beth Daniel	Fox Chapel Golf Club	Pittsburgh, Pennsylvania
1979	Mary Hafeman	Maple Bluff Country Club	Madison, Wisconsin
1980	Kathy Baker	Shaker Heights Country Club	Shaker Heights, Ohio

1981	Amy Benz	Moss Creek, Devils Elbow South	Hilton Head Island, South Carolina
1982	Lisa Stanley	Waterwood National	Huntsville, Texas
1983	Tammy Welborn	Industry Hills Golf Club	City of Industry, California
1984	Joanne Pacillo	New Haven Country Club	Hamden, Connecticut
1985	Kathleen McCarthy	Travis Pointe Country Club	Ann Arbor, Michigan
1986	Leslie Shannon	Flossmoor Country Club	Flossmoor, Illinois
1987	Kathleen McCarthy	Nashville Golf & Athletic Club	Brentwood, Tennessee
1988	Anne Quast Sander	Evanston Golf Club	Skokie, Illinois
1989	Katie Peterson	Landfall Club	Wilmington, North Carolina
1990	Patricia Cornett Iker	Champions Golf Club	Nicholasville, Kentucky
1991	Sarah LeBrun Ingram	Firethorn Golf Club	Lincoln, Nebraska
1992	Moira Dunn	South Bend Country Club	South Bend, Indiana
1993	Stephanie Sparks	Wynlakes Golf & Country Club	Montgomery, Alabama
1994	Stephanie Neill	Barrington Hall Golf Club	Macon, Georgia
1995	Cristie Kerr	The Links at Northfork	Ramsey, Minnesota
1996	Mary Burkhardt Shields	Fox Run Golf Club	Eureka, Missouri
1997	Stephanie Keever	Glenmore Country Club	Keswick, Virginia
1998	Grace Park	Heritage Club	Mason, Ohio
1999	Kellee Booth	The Hawthorns Golf and Country Club	Fisher, Indiana
2000	Meredith Duncan	Flossmoor Country Club	Flossmoor, Illinois
2001	Meredith Duncan	Exmoor Country Club	Highland Park, Illinois
2002	Janice Olivencia	Fincastle Country Club	Bluefield, Virginia

2003	Brittany Lang	Stone Creek Golf Club	Urbana, Illinois
2004	Sophia Sheridan	Maple Bluff Country Club	Madison, Wisconsin
2005	Jennifer Hong	Birck Boilermaker Kampen Course (Purdue)	West Lafayette, Indiana
2006	Stacy Lewis	Fincastle Country Club	Bluefield, Virginia
2007	Mallory Blackwelder	Stone Creek Golf Club	Urbana, Illinois
2008	Jennie Arsenault	Canongate at SummerGrove Golf Club	Newnan, Georgia
2009	Taylore Karle	Shawnee Country Club	Lima, Ohio

APPENDIX 8. OTHER USGA CHAMPIONS

U.S. Junior Amateur

1948	Dean Lind	University of Michigan Golf Course	Ann Arbor, Michigan
1949	Gay Brewer	Congressional Country Club	Bethesda, Maryland
1950	Mason Rudolph	Denver Country Club	Denver, Colorado
1951	Tommy Jacobs	University of Illinois Golf Course	Champaign, Illinois
1952	Don Bisplinghoff	Yale University Golf Course	New Haven, Connecticut
1953	Rex Baxter Jr.	Southern Hills Country Club	Tulsa, Oklahoma
1954	Foster Bradley Jr.	Los Angeles Country Club, North Course	Los Angeles, California
1955	Billy "Cotton" Dunn	Purdue University, South Golf Course	West Lafayette, Indiana
1956	Harlan Stevenson	Taconic Golf Club	Williams College, Williamstown, Massachusetts
1957	Larry Beck	Manor Country Club	Rockville, Maryland
1958	Gordon Baker	University of Minnesota Golf Course	St. Paul, Minnesota
1959	Larry Lee	Stanford University Golf Course	Palo Alto, California
1960	William Tindall	Milburn Golf & Country Club	Overland Park, Kansas
1961	Charles McDowell	Cornell University Golf Course	Ithaca, New York
1962	Jim Wiechers	Lochmoor Club	Grosse Pointe Woods, Michigan
1963	Gregg McHatton	Florence Country Club	Florence, South Carolina

1964	John Miller	Eugene Country Club	Eugene, Oregon
1965	Jim Masserio	Wilmington Country Club, South Course	Wilmington, Delaware
1966	Gary Sanders	California Country Club	Whittier, California
1967	John Crooks	Twin Hills Golf & Country Club	Oklahoma City, Oklahoma
1968	Eddie Pearce	The Country Club	Brookline, Massachusetts
1969	Aly Trompas	Spokane Country Club	Spokane, Washington
1970	Gary Koch	Athens Country Club	Athens, Georgia
1971	Mike Brannan	Manor Country Club	Rockville, Maryland
1972	Bob Byman	Brookhaven Country Club	Dallas, Texas
1973	Jack Renner	Singing Hills Golf & Country Club	El Cajon, California
1974	David Nevatt	Brooklawn Country Club	Bridgeport, Connecticut
1975	Brett Mullin	Richland Country Club	Nashville, Tennessee
1976	Madden Hatcher III	Hiwan Golf Club	Evergreen, Colorado
1977	Willie Wood	Ohio State University Golf Club, Scarlet Course	Columbus, Ohio
1978	Donald Hurter	Wilmington Country Club, South Course	Wilmington, Delaware
1979	Jack Larkin	Moss Creek Golf Club	Hilton Head Island, South Carolina
1980	Eric Johnson	Pine Lake Country Club	Orchard Lake, Michigan
1981	Scott Erickson	Sunnyside Country Club	Fresno, California
1982	Rick Marik	Crooked Stick Golf Club	Carmel, Indiana
1983	Tim Straub	Saucon Valley Country Club, Old Course	Bethlehem, Pennsylvania

1984	Doug Martin	Wayzata Country Club	Wayzata, Minnesota
1985	Charles Rymer	Brookfield Country Club	Clarence, New York
1986	Brian Montgomery	Muirfield Village Golf Club	Dublin, Ohio
1987	Brett Quigley	Singletree Golf Club	Edwards, Colorado
1988	Jason Widener	Yale University Golf Course	New Haven, Connecticut
1989	David Duval	Singing Hills Golf & Country Club	El Cajon, California
1990	Mathew Todd	Lake Merced Golf & Country Club	Daly City, California
1991	Tiger Woods	Bay Hill Club	Orlando, Florida
1992	Tiger Woods	Wollaston Golf Club	Milton, Massachusetts
1993	Tiger Woods	Waverley Country Club	Portland, Oregon
1994	Terry Noe	Echo Lake Country Club	Westfield, New Jersey
1995	D. Scott Hailes	Fargo Country Club	Fargo, North Dakota
1996	Shane McMenamy	Forest Highlands Golf Club	Flagstaff, Arizona
1997	Jason Allred	Aronimink Golf Club	Newtown Square, Pennsylvania
1998	James Oh	Conway Farms Golf Club	Lake Forest, Illinois
1999	Hunter Mahan	Country Club of York	York, Pennsylvania
2000	Matthew Rosenfeld	Pumpkin Ridge Golf Club, Ghost Creek Course	North Plains, Oregon
2001	Henry Liaw	Oak Hills Country Club	San Antonio, Texas
2002	Charlie Beljan	Atlanta Athletic Club, Highlands Course	Duluth, Georgia
2003	Brian Harman	Columbia Country Club	Chevy Chase, Maryland
2004	Sihwan Kim	The Olympic Club	San Francisco, California

2005	Kevin Tway	Longmeadow Country Club	Longmeadow, Massachusetts
2006	Philip Francis	Rancho Santa Fe Golf Club	Rancho Santa Fe, California
2007	Cory Whitsett	Boone Valley Golf Club	Augusta, Missouri
2008	Cameron Peck	Shoal Creek Country Club	Shoal Creek, Alabama
2009	Jordan Spieth	Trump National Golf Club	Bedminster, New Jersey

U.S. Girls' Junior Amateur

1949	Marlene Bauer	Philadelphia Country Club, Bala Course	Gladwyne, Pennsylvania
1950	Patricia Ann Lesser	Wanakah Country Club	Hamburg, New York
1951	Arlene Brooks	Onwentsia Club	Lake Forest, Illinois
1952	Mickey Wright	Monterey Peninsula Country Club, Dunes Course	Pebble Beach, California
1953	Mildred Meyerson	The Country Club	Brookline, Massachusetts
1954	Margaret Smith	Gulph Mills Golf Club	King of Prussia, Pennsylvania
1955	Carole Jo Kabler	Florence Country Club	Florence, South Carolina
1956	JoAnne Gunderson	Heather Downs Country Club	Toledo, Ohio
1957	Judy Eller	Lakewood Country Club	Denver, Colorado
1958	Judy Eller	Greenwich Country Club	Greenwich, Connecticut
1959	Judy Rand	Manor Country Club	Rockville, Maryland
1960	Carol Sorenson	The Oaks Country Club	Tulsa, Oklahoma
1961	Mary Lowell	Broadmoor Golf Club	Seattle, Washington
1962	Mary Lou Daniel	Country Club of Buffalo	Williamsville, New York

1963	Janis Ferraris	Wolfert's Roost Country Club	Albany, New York
1964	Peggy Conley	Leavenworth Country Club	Leavenworth, Kansas
1965	Gail Sykes	Hiwan Golf Club	Evergreen, Colorado
1966	Claudia Mayhew	Longue Vue Club	Verona, Pennsylvania
1967	Elizabeth Story	Hacienda Golf Club	La Habra, California
1968	Margaret Harmon	Flint Golf Club	Flint, Michigan
1969	Hollis Stacy	Brookhaven Country Club, Championship Course	Dallas, Texas
1970	Hollis Stacy	Apawamis Club	Rye, New York
1971	Hollis Stacy	Augusta Country Club	Augusta, Georgia
1972	Nancy Lopez	Jefferson City Country Club	Jefferson City, Missouri
1973	Amy Alcott	Somerset Hills Country Club	Bernardsville, New Jersey
1974	Nancy Lopez	Columbia-Edgewater Country Club	Portland, Oregon
1975	Dayna Benson	Dedham Country & Polo Club	Dedham, Massachusetts
1976	Pilar Dorado	Del Rio Golf & Country Club	Modesto, California
1977	Althea Tome	Guyan Golf & Country Club	Huntington, West Virginia
1978	Lori Castillo	Wilmington Country Club, North Course	Wilmington, Delaware
1979	Penny Hammel	Pleasant Valley Country Club	Little Rock, Arkansas
1980	Laurie Rinker	Crestview Country Club, North Course	Wichita, Kansas
1981	Kay Cornelius	Illahe Hills Country Club	Salem, Oregon
1982	Heather Farr	Greeley Country Club	Greeley, Colorado
1983	Kim Saiki	Somerset Hills Country Club	Bernardsville, New Jersey
1984	Cathy Mockett	Mill Creek Country Club	Bothell, Washington

1985	Dana Lofland	St. Clair Country Club	Pittsburgh, Pennsylvania
1986	Pat Hurst	Peach Tree Golf & Country Club	Marysville, California
1987	Michelle McGann	The Orchards Golf Club	South Hadley, Massachusetts
1988	Jamille Jose	Golden Valley Country Club	Golden Valley, Minnesota
1989	Brandie Burton	Pine Needles Lodge & Golf Club	Southern Pines, North Carolina
1990	Sandrine Mendiburu	Manasquan River Golf Club	Brielle, New Jersey
1991	Emilee Klein	Crestview Country Club	Wichita, Kansas
1992	Jamie Koizumi	Meridian Hills Country Club	Indianapolis, Indiana
1993	Kellee Booth	Mesa Verde Country Club	Costa Mesa, California
1994	Kelli Kuehne	Meadow Lark Country Club	Great Falls, Montana
1995	Marcy Newton	Longmeadow Country Club	Longmeadow, Massachusetts
1996	Dorothy Delasin	Westward Ho Country Club	Sioux Falls, South Dakota
1997	Beth Bauer	Legends Club of Tennessee, Ironwood Course	Franklin, Tennessee
1998	Leigh Anne Hardin	Merion Golf Club, East Course	Ardmore, Pennsylvania
1999	Aree Wongluekiet	Green Spring Valley Hunt Club	Owings Mills, Maryland
2000	Lisa Ferrero	Pumpkin Ridge Golf Club	North Plains, Oregon
2001	Nicole Perrot	Indian Hills Country Club	Mission Hills, Kansas
2002	Park In-Bee	Echo Lake Country Club	Westfield, New Jersey
2003	Sukjin-Lee Wuesthoff	Brooklawn Country Club	Fairfield, Connecticut
2004	Julieta Granada	Mira Vista Golf Club	Fort Worth, Texas
2005	Kim In-Kyung	BanBury Golf Club	Eagle, Idaho
2006	Jenny Shin	Carmel Country Club	Charlotte, North Carolina

2007	Kristen Park	Tacoma Country & Golf Club	Lakewood, Washington
2008	Alexis Thompson	Hartford Golf Club	West Hartford, Connecticut
2009	Amy Anderson	Trump National Golf Club	Bedminster, New Jersey

U.S. Senior Open

1980	Roberto De Vicenzo	Argentina	Winged Foot Golf Club, East Course	Mamaroneck, New York
1981	Arnold Palmer	United States	Oakland Hills Country Club, South Course	Bloomfield Hills, Michigan
1982	Miller Barber	United States	Portland Golf Club	Portland, Oregon
1983	Billy Casper	United States	Hazeltine National Golf Club	Chaska, Minnesota
1984	Miller Barber	United States	Oak Hill Country Club, East Course	Rochester, New York
1985	Miller Barber	United States	Edgewood Tahoe Golf Course	Stateline, Nevada
1986	Dale Douglass	United States	Scioto Country Club	Columbus, Ohio
1987	Gary Player	South Africa	Brooklawn Country Club	Fairfield, Connecticut
1988	Gary Player	South Africa	Medinah Country Club, Course No. 3	Medinah, Illinois

1989	Orville Moody	United States	Laurel Valley Golf Club	Ligonier, Pennsylvania
1990	Lee Trevino	United States	Ridgewood Country Club	Paramus, New Jersey
1991	Jack Nicklaus	United States	Oakland Hills Country Club, South Course	Bloomfield Hills, Michigan
1992	Larry Laoretti	United States	Saucon Valley Country Club, Old Course	Bethlehem, Pennsylvania
1993	Jack Nicklaus	United States	Cherry Hills Country Club	Cherry Hills Village, Colorado
1994	Simon Hobday	South Africa	Pinehurst Resort, No. 2 Course	Pinehurst, North Carolina
1995	Tom Weiskopf	United States	Congressional Country Club	Bethesda, Maryland
1996	Dave Stockton	United States	Canterbury Golf Club	Beachwood, Ohio
1997	Graham Marsh	Australia	Olympia Fields Country Club, North Course	Olympia Fields, Illinois
1998	Hale Irwin	United States	Riviera Country Club	Pacific Palisades, California
1999	Dave Eichelberger	United States	Des Moines Golf and Country Club	Des Moines, Iowa

2000	Hale Irwin	United States	Saucon Valley Country Club, Old Course	Bethlehem, Pennsylvania
2001	Bruce Fleisher	United States	Salem Country Club	Peabody, Massachusetts
2002	Don Pooley	United States	Caves Valley Golf Club	Owings Mills, Maryland
2003	Bruce Lietzke	United States	Inverness Club	Toledo, Ohio
2004	Peter Jacobsen	United States	Bellerive Country Club	St. Louis, Missouri
2005	Allen Doyle	United States	NCR Country Club, South Course	Kettering, Ohio
2006	Allen Doyle	United States	Prairie Dunes Country Club	Hutchinson, Kansas
2007	Brad Bryant	United States	Whistling Straits, Straits Course	Kohler, Wisconsin
2008	Eduardo Romero	Argentina	Broadmoor Golf Club, East Course	Colorado Springs, Colorado
2009	Fred Funk	United States	Crooked Stick Golf Club	Carmel, Indiana

U.S. Senior Amateur

1955	J. Wood Platt	Belle Meade Country Club	Nashville, Tennessee
1956	Fred Wright	Somerset Country Club	Mendota Heights, Minnesota
1957	J. Clark Espie	Ridgewood Country Club	Paramus, New Jersey
1958	Thomas Robbins	Monterey Peninsula Country Club, Dunes Course	Pebble Beach, California
1959	J. Clark Espie	Memphis Country Club	Memphis, Tennessee
1960	Michael Cestone	Oyster Harbors Club	Osterville, Massachusetts
1961	Dexter Daniels	Southern Hills Country Club	Tulsa, Oklahoma
1962	Merrill Carlsmith	Evanston Golf Club	Kansas City, Missouri
1963	Merrill Carlsmith	Sea Island Golf Club, Seaside Course	St. Simons Island, Georgia
1964	William Higgins	Waverley Country Club	Portland, Oregon
1965	Robert Kiersky	Fox Chapel Golf Club	Pittsburgh, Pennsylvania
1966	Dexter Daniels	Tucson National Golf Club	Tucson, Arizona
1967	Ray Palmer	Shinnecock Hills Golf Club	Southampton, New York
1968	Curtis Person Sr.	Atlanta Country Club	Marietta, Georgia
1969	Curtis Person Sr.	Wichita Country Club	Wichita, Kansas
1970	Gene Andrews	California Golf Club of San Francisco	San Francisco, California
1971	Tom Draper	Sunnybrook Golf Club	Plymouth Meeting, Pennsylvania
1972	Lewis Oehmig	Sharon Golf Club	Sharon Center, Ohio
1973	Bill Hyndman	Onwentsia Club	Lake Forest, Illinois
1974	Dale Morey	Harbour Town Golf Links	Hilton Head Island, South Carolina

1975	William Colm	Carmel Valley Golf & Country Club	Carmel Valley, California
1976	Lewis Oehmig	Cherry Hills Country Club	Cherry Hills Village, Colorado
1977	Dale Morey	Salem Country Club	Peabody, Massachusetts
1978	Keith Compton	Pine Tree Golf Club	Boynton Beach, Florida
1979	Bill Campbell	Chicago Golf Club	Wheaton, Illinois
1980	Bill Campbell	The Homestead, Cascades Course	Hot Springs, Virginia
1981	Ed Updegraff	Seattle Golf Club	Seattle, Washington
1982	Alton Duhon	Tucson Country Club	Tucson, Arizona
1983	Bill Hyndman	Crooked Stick Golf Club	Carmel, Indiana
1984	Robert Rawlins	Birmingham Country Club	Birmingham, Michigan
1985	Lewis Oehmig	Wild Dunes Beach & Racquet Club	Isle of Palms, South Carolina
1986	R. S. Williams	Interlachen Country Club	Edina, Minnesota
1987	John Richardson	Saucon Valley Country Club, Old Course	Bethlehem, Pennsylvania
1988	Clarence Moore	Milwaukee Country Club	River Hills, Wisconsin
1989	R. S. Williams	Lochinvar Golf Club	Houston, Texas
1990	Jackie Cummings	Desert Forest Golf Club	Carefree, Arizona
1991	Bill Bosshard	Crystal Downs Country Club	Frankfort, Michigan
1992	Clarence Moore	The Loxahatchee Club	Jupiter, Florida
1993	Joe Ungvary	Farmington Country Club	Farmington, Connecticut
1994	O. Gordon Brewer Jr.	The Champions Golf Club	Houston, Texas
1995	James Stahl Jr.	Prairie Dunes Country Club	Hutchinson, Kansas
1996	O. Gordon Brewer Jr.	Taconic Golf Club	Williams College, Williamstown, Massachusetts

1997	Cliff Cunningham	Atlantic Golf Club	Bridgehampton, New York
1998	Bill Shean Jr.	Skokie Country Club	Glencoe, Illinois
1999	Bill Ploeger	Portland Golf Club	Portland, Oregon
2000	Bill Shean Jr.	Charlotte Country Club	Charlotte, North Carolina
2001	Kemp Richardson	Norwood Hills Country Club	St. Louis, Missouri
2002	Greg Reynolds	Timuquana Country Club	Jacksonville, Florida
2003	Kemp Richardson	The Virginian Golf Club	Bristol, Virginia
2004	Mark Bemowski	Bel-Air Country Club	Los Angeles, California
2005	Mike Rice	The Farm Golf Club	Rocky Face, Georgia
2006	Mike Bell	Victoria National Golf Club	Newburgh, Indiana
2007	Stan Lee	Flint Hills National Golf Club	Andover, Kansas
2008	Buddy Marucci	Shady Oaks Country Club	Fort Worth, Texas
2009	Vinny Giles	The Beverly Country Club	Chicago, Illinois

U.S. Senior Women's Amateur

1962	Maureen Orcutt	Manufacturers' Golf & Country Club	Oreland, Pennsylvania
1963	Marion Choat	Country Club of Florida	Delray Beach, Florida
1964	Loma Smith	Del Paso Country Club	Sacramento, California
1965	Loma Smith	Exmoor Country Club	Highland Park, Illinois
1966	Maureen Orcutt	Lakewood Country Club	New Orleans, Louisiana
1967	Marge Mason	Atlantic City Country Club	Northfield, New Jersey
1968	Carolyn Cudone	Monterey Peninsula Country Club, Dunes Course	Pebble Beach, California

1969	Carolyn Cudone	Ridglea Country Club	Fort Worth, Texas
1970	Carolyn Cudone	Coral Ridge Country Club	Fort Lauderdale, Florida
1971	Carolyn Cudone	Sea Island Golf Club, Seaside Course	St. Simons Island, Georgia
1972	Carolyn Cudone	Manufacturers' Golf & Country Club	Oreland, Pennsylvania
1973	Gwen Hibbs	San Marcos Country Club	Chandler, Arizona
1974	Justine Cushing	Lakewood Golf Club	Point Clear, Alabama
1975	Alberta Bower	Rhode Island Country Club	West Barrington, Rhode Island
1976	Cecile Maclaurin	Monterey Peninsula Country Club, Dunes Course	Pebble Beach, California
1977	Dorothy Porter	Dunes Golf and Beach Club	Myrtle Beach, South Carolina
1978	Alice Dye	Rancho Bernardo Golf Club	San Diego, California
1979	Alice Dye	Hardscrabble Country Club	Fort Smith, Arkansas
1980	Dorothy Porter	Sea Island Golf Club, Seaside Course	St. Simons Island, Georgia
1981	Dorothy Porter	Spring Lake Golf Club	Spring Lake, New Jersey
1982	Edean Ihlanfeldt	Kissing Camels Golf Club	Colorado Springs, Colorado
1983	Dorothy Porter	Gulph Mills Golf Club	King of Prussia, Pennsylvania
1984	Constance Guthrie	Tacoma Country & Golf Club	Lakewood, Washington
1985	Marlene Stewart Streit	Sheraton Savannah Resort and Country Club	Savannah, Georgia
1986	Constance Guthrie	Lakewood Golf Club	Point Clear, Alabama
1987	Anne Sander	Manufacturers' Golf & Country Club	Oreland, Pennsylvania
1988	Lois Hodge	Sea Island Golf Club, Seaside Course	St. Simons Island, Georgia
1989	Anne Sander	Tournament Players Course	The Woodlands, Texas

1990	Anne Sander	Del Rio Golf & Country Club	Modesto, California
1991	Phyllis "Tish" Preuss	Pine Needles Lodge & Golf Club	Southern Pines, North Carolina
1992	Rosemary Thompson	Tucson Country Club	Tucson, Arizona
1993	Anne Sander	Preakness Hills Country Club	Wayne, New Jersey
1994	Marlene Stewart Streit	Sea Island Golf Club, Seaside Course	St. Simons Island, Georgia
1995	Jean Smith	Somerset Country Club	Mendota Heights, Minnesota
1996	Gayle Borthwick	Broadmoor Golf Club	Seattle, Washington
1997	Nancy Fitzgerald	Yeamans Hall Club	Charleston, South Carolina
1998	Gayle Borthwick	Golden Horseshoe Golf Club, Green Course	Williamsburg, Virginia
1999	Carol Semple Thompson	Desert Mountain Club, Cochise Course	Scottsdale, Arizona
2000	Carol Semple Thompson	Sea Island Golf Club, Seaside Course	St. Simons Island, Georgia
2001	Carol Semple Thompson	Allegheny Country Club	Sewickley, Pennsylvania
2002	Carol Semple Thompson	Mid Pines Inn and Golf Club	Southern Pines, North Carolina
2003	Marlene Stewart Streit	Barton Creek Resort & Club, Foothills Course	Austin, Texas
2004	Carolyn Creekmore	Pasatiempo Golf Club	Santa Cruz, California
2005	Diane Lang	The Apawamis Club	Rye, New York
2006	Diane Lang	Sea Island Golf Club, Seaside Course	St. Simons Island, Georgia
2007	Anna Schultz	Sunriver Resort, Meadow Course	Sunriver, Oregon
2008	Diane Lang	Tulsa Country Club	Tulsa, Oklahoma
2009	Sherry Herman	The Homestead, Cascades Course	Hot Springs, Virginia

U.S. Mid-Amateur

1981	Jim Holtgrieve	Bellerive Country Club	St. Louis, Missouri
1982	William Hoffer	Knollwood Club	Lake Forest, Illinois
1983	Jay Sigel	Cherry Hills Country Club	Cherry Hills Village, Colorado
1984	Michael Podolak	Atlanta Athletic Club, Highlands Course	Duluth, Georgia
1985	Jay Sigel	The Vintage Club, Mountain Course	Indian Wells, California
1986	Bill Loeffler	Annandale Country Club	Madison, Mississippi
1987	Jay Sigel	Brook Hollow Golf Club	Dallas, Texas
1988	David Eger	Prairie Dunes Country Club	Hutchinson, Kansas
1989	James Taylor	Crooked Stick Golf Club	Carmel, Indiana
1990	Jim Stuart	Troon Golf & Country Club	Scottsdale, Arizona
1991	Jim Stuart	Long Cove Club	Hilton Head Island, South Carolina
1992	Danny Yates	Detroit Golf Club, North Course	Detroit, Michigan
1993	Jeff Thomas	Eugene Country Club	Eugene, Oregon
1994	Tim Jackson	Hazeltine National Golf Club	Chaska, Minnesota
1995	Jerry Courville Jr.	Caves Valley Golf Club	Owings Mills, Maryland
1996	John "Spider" Miller	Hartford Golf Club	West Hartford, Connecticut
1997	Ken Bakst	Dallas Athletic Club, Blue Course	Mesquite, Texas
1998	John "Spider" Miller	NCR Country Club, South Course	Kettering, Ohio
1999	Danny Green	Old Warson Country Club	St. Louis, Missouri
2000	Greg Puga	The Homestead, Cascades Course	Hot Springs, Virginia
2001	Tim Jackson	San Joaquin Country Club	Fresno, California
2002	George Zahringer	The Stanwich Club	Greenwich, Connecticut

2003	Nathan Smith	Wilmington Country Club, South Course	Wilmington, Delaware
2004	Austin Eaton III	Sea Island Golf Club, Seaside Course	St. Simons Island, Georgia
2005	Kevin Marsh	The Honors Course	Chattanooga, Tennessee
2006	Dave Womack	Forest Highlands Golf Club, Canyon Course	Flagstaff, Arizona
2007	Trip Kuehne	Bandon Dunes Golf Resort	Bandon, Oregon
2008	Steve Wilson	Milwaukee Country Club	River Hills, Wisconsin
2009	Nathan Smith	Kiawah Island Golf Resort, Ocean Course	Kiawah Island, South Carolina

U.S. Women's Mid-Amateur

1987	Cindy Scholefield	Southern Hills Country Club	Tulsa, Oklahoma
1988	Martha Lang	Amelia Island Plantation	Amelia Island, Florida
1989	Robin Weiss	The Hills Of Lakeway Golf Club	Lakeway, Texas
1990	Carol Semple Thompson	Allegheny Country Club	Sewickley, Pennsylvania
1991	Sarah Lebrun Ingram	Desert Highlands Golf Club	Scottsdale, Arizona
1992	Marion Maney-Mcinerney	Old Marsh Golf Club	Palm Beach Gardens, Florida
1993	Sarah Lebrun Ingram	Rochester G. & Country Club	Rochester, Minnesota
1994	Sarah Lebrun Ingram	Tacoma Country & Golf Club	Lakewood, Washington
1995	Ellen Port	Essex County Club	Manchester-by-the-Sea, Massachusetts
1996	Ellen Port	Mission Hills Country Club, Dinah Shore Course	Rancho Mirage, California
1997	Carol Semple Thompson	Atlantic City Country Club	Northfield, New Jersey

1998	Virginia Derby Grimes	Champions Golf Club, Cypress Creek Course	Houston, Texas
1999	Alissa Herron	Cherokee Town & Country Club	Atlanta, Georgia
2000	Ellen Port	Big Canyon Country Club	Newport Beach, California
2001	Laura Shanahan	Fox Run Golf Club	Eureka, Missouri
2002	Kathy Hartwiger	Eugene Country Club	Eugene, Oregon
2003	Amber Marsh	Long Cove Club	Hilton Head Island, South Carolina
2004	Corey Weworski	Holston Hills Country Club	Knoxville, Tennessee
2005	Mary-Ann Lapointe	Shadow Hawk Golf Club	Richmond, Texas
2006	Meghan Bolger	Old Waverly Golf Club	West Point, Mississippi
2007	Meghan Bolger	Desert Forest Golf Club	Carefree, Arizona
2008	Joan Higgins	Barton Hills Country Club	Ann Arbor, Michigan
2009	Martha Stacy-Leach	Golden Hills Golf and Turf Club	Ocala, Florida

U.S. Public Amateur (Publinx)

1922	Edmund Held	Ottawa Park	Toledo, Ohio
1923	Richard Walsh	East Potomac Park	Washington, DC
1924	Joseph Coble	Community Country Club	Dayton, Ohio
1925	Raymond McAuliffe	Salisbury Country Club	Garden City, New York
1926	Lester Bolstad	Grover Cleveland Park	Buffalo, New York
1927	Carl Kauffmann	Ridgewood Golf Links	Cleveland, Ohio
1928	Carl Kauffmann	Cobb's Creek	Philadelphia, Pennsylvania

1929	Carl Kauffmann	Forest Park	St. Louis, Missouri
1930	Robert Wingate	Municipal Links	Jacksonville, Florida
1931	Charles Ferrera	Keller Golf Course	Saint Paul, Minnesota
1932	R. L. Miller	Shawnee Golf Club	Louisville, Kentucky
1933	Charles Ferrera	Eastmoreland Golf Club	Portland, Oregon
1934	David Mitchell	South Park Allegheny County Links	Pittsburgh, Pennsylvania
1935	Frank Strafaci	Coffin Course	Indianapolis, Indiana
1936	B. Patrick Abbott	Bethpage State Park, Black Course	Farmingdale, New York
1937	Bruce McCormick	Harding Park Course	San Francisco, California
1938	Al Leach	Highland Park Municipal Golf Course	Cleveland, Ohio
1939	Andrew Szwedko	Mt. Pleasant Park Golf Course	Baltimore, Maryland
1940	Robert Clark	Rackham Golf Course	Detroit, Michigan
1941	William Welch Jr.	Indian Canyon Golf Course	Spokane, Washington
1946	Smiley Quick	Wellshire Golf Course	Denver, Colorado
1947	Wilfred Crossley	Meadowbrook Golf Course	Minneapolis, Minnesota
1948	Michael Ferentz	North Fulton Park Golf Course	Atlanta, Georgia
1949	Kenneth Towns	Rancho Golf Course	Los Angeles, California
1950	Stanley Bielat	Seneca Golf Course	Louisville, Kentucky
1951	Dave Stanley	Brown Deer Park Golf Course	Milwaukee, Wisconsin
1952	Omer Bogan	Miami Country Club	Miami, Florida
1953	Ted Richards Jr.	West Seattle Golf Course	Seattle, Washington
1954	Gene Andrews	Cedar Crest Golf Course	Dallas, Texas
1955	Sam Kocsis	Coffin Municipal Golf Course	Indianapolis, Indiana

1956	James Buxbaum	Harding Park Golf Course	San Francisco, California
1957	Don Essig III	Hershey Park Golf Club	Hershey, Pennsylvania
1958	Dan Sikes	Silver Lake Golf Club	Orland Park, Illinois
1959	William Wright	Wellshire Golf Course	Denver, Colorado
1960	Verne Callison	Ala Wai Golf Course	Honolulu, Hawaii
1961	R. H. Sikes	Rackham Golf Course	Detroit, Michigan
1962	R. H. Sikes	Sheridan Park Golf Course	Tonawanda, New York
1963	Robert Lunn	Haggin Oaks Municipal Golf Course	Sacramento, California
1964	William McDonald	Francis A. Gross Golf Course	Minneapolis, Minnesota
1965	Arne Dokka	North Park Golf Course	Pittsburgh, Pennsylvania
1966	Lamont Kaser	Brown Deer Park Golf Course	Milwaukee, Wisconsin
1967	Verne Callison	Jefferson Park Golf Course	Seattle, Washington
1968	Gene Towry	Tenison Memorial Municipal Golf Course	Dallas, Texas
1969	John Jackson Jr.	Downing Golf Course	Erie, Pennsylvania
1970	Robert Risch	Cog Hill Golf & Country Club, #4	Lemont, Illinois
1971	Fred Haney	Papago Golf Course	Phoenix, Arizona
1972	Bob Allard	Coffin Municipal Golf Course	Indianapolis, Indiana
1973	Stan Stopa	Flanders Valley Golf Course	Flanders, New Jersey
1974	Charles Barenaba Jr.	Brookside Golf Club, #1 Course	Pasadena, California
1975	Randy Barenaba	Wailua Golf Course	Lihue, Kauai, Hawaii
1976	Eddie Mudd	Bunker Hills Golf Course	Coon Rapids, Minnesota
1977	Jerry Vidovic	Brown Deer Park Golf Course	Milwaukee, Wisconsin
1978	Dean Prince	Bangor Municipal Golf Course	Bangor, Maine

1979	Dennis Walsh	West Delta Golf Course	Portland, Oregon
1980	Jodie Mudd	Edgewood Tahoe Golf Course	Stateline, Nevada
1981	Jodie Mudd	Bear Creek Golf World, Masters Course	Houston, Texas
1982	Billy Tuten	Eagle Creek Golf Course	Indianapolis, Indiana
1983	Billy Tuten	Hominy Hill Golf Course	Colts Neck, New Jersey
1984	Bill Malley	Indian Canyon Golf Course	Spokane, Washington
1985	Jim Sorenson	Wailua Golf Course	Lihue, Kauai, Hawaii
1986	Bill Mayfair	Tanglewood Park, Championship Course	Clemmons, North Carolina
1987	Kevin Johnson	Glenview Golf Club	Cincinnati, Ohio
1988	Ralph Howe III	Jackson Hole Golf & Tennis Club	Jackson, Wyoming
1989	Tim Hobby	Cog Hill Golf & Country Club, #4	Lemont, Illinois
1990	Michael Combs	Eastmoreland Golf Club	Portland, Oregon
1991	David Berganio Jr.	Otter Creek Golf Club	Columbus, Indiana
1992	Warren Schutte	Edinburgh Course	Brooklyn Park, Minnesota
1993	David Berganio Jr.	Riverside Dunes Golf Club	Brighton, Colorado
1994	Guy Yamamoto	Eagle Bend Golf Course	Bigfork, Montana
1995	Chris Wollmann	Stow Acres Country Club, North Course	Stow, Massachusetts
1996	Tim Hogarth	Wailua Golf Course	Lihue, Kauai, Hawaii
1997	Tim Clark	Kearney Hill Golf Links	Lexington, Kentucky
1998	Trevor Immelman	Torrey Pines Golf Course, South Course	La Jolla, California
1999	Hunter Haas	Spencer T. Olin Community Golf Course	Alton, Illinois
2000	D. J. Trahan	Heron Lakes, Great Blue	Portland, Oregon
2001	Chez Reavie	Pecan Valley Golf Club	San Antonio, Texas

2002	Ryan Moore	The Orchards Golf Club	Washington, Michigan
2003	Brandt Snedeker	Blue Heron Pines Golf Club, East Course	Galloway, New Jersey
2004	Ryan Moore	Rush Creek Golf Club	Maple Grove, Minnesota
2005	Clay Ogden	Shaker Run Golf Club	Lebanon, Ohio
2006	Casey Watabu	Gold Mountain Golf Club, Olympic Course	Bremerton, Washington
2007	Colt Knost	Cantigny Golf	Wheaton, Illinois
2008	Jack Newman	Murphy Creek Golf Course	Aurora, Colorado
2009	Brad Benjamin	Jimmie Austin/University of Oklahoma Golf Course	Norman, Oklahoma

U.S. Women's Public Amateur (Publinx)

1977	Kelly Fuiks	Yahara Hills Golf Course, East Course	Madison, Wisconsin
1978	Kelly Fuiks	Myrtlewood Golf Course, Palmetto Course	Myrtle Beach, South Carolina
1979	Lori Castillo	Braemar Golf Course	Edina, Massachusetts
1980	Lori Castillo	Center Square Golf Club	Worcester, Pennsylvania
1981	Mary Enright	Emerald Valley Golf Course	Creswell, Oregon
1982	Nancy Taylor	Alvamar Golf Club	Lawrence, Kansas
1983	Kelli Antolock	Ala Wai Golf Course	Honolulu, Hawaii
1984	Heather Farr	Meadowbrook Golf Course	Minneapolis, Minnesota
1985	Danielle Ammaccapane	Flanders Valley Golf Course	Flanders, New Jersey
1986	Cindy Schreyer	SentryWorld Golf Course	Stevens Point, Wisconsin
1987	Tracy Kerdyk	Cog Hill Golf & Country Club, #4	Lemont, Illinois

1988	Pearl Sinn	Page Belcher Golf Course	Tulsa, Oklahoma
1989	Pearl Sinn	Indian Canyon Golf Course	Spokane, Washington
1990	Cathy Mockett	Hyland Hills Golf Course	Westminster, Colorado
1991	Tracy Hanson	Birdwood Golf Course	Charlottesville, Virginia
1992	Amy Fruhwirth	Haggin Oaks Municipal Golf Course	Sacramento, California
1993	Connie Masterson	Jackson Hole Golf & Tennis Club	Jackson, Wyoming
1994	Jill McGill	Tam O'Shanter Golf Course, Hills Course	Niles, Illinois
1995	Jo Jo Robertson	Hominy Hill Golf Course	Colts Neck, New Jersey
1996	Heather Graff	Spencer T. Olin Community Golf Course	Alton, Illinois
1997	Jo Jo Robertson	Center Square Golf Club	Worcester, Pennsylvania
1998	Amy Spooner	Kapalua Resort, Bay Course	Kapalua, Maui, Hawaii
1999	Jody Niemann	Santa Ana Golf Club	Santa Ana, California
2000	Catherine Cartwright	Legacy Golf Links	Aberdeen, North Carolina
2001	Candie Kung	Kemper Lakes Golf Course	Long Grove, Illinois
2002	Annie Thurman	Sunriver Resort, Meadow Course	Sunriver, Oregon
2003	Michelle Wie	Ocean Hammock Golf Club	Palm Coast, Florida
2004	Yani Tseng	Golden Horseshoe Golf Club, Green Course	Williamsburg, Virginia
2005	Lee Eun-Jung	Swope Memorial Golf Course	Kansas City, Missouri
2006	Tiffany Joh	Walking Stick Golf Course	Pueblo, Colorado
2007	Mina Harigae	Kearney Hill Golf Links	Lexington, Kentucky
2008	Tiffany Joh	Erin Hills Golf Course	Erin, Wisconsin
2009	Jennifer Song	Red Tail Golf Club	Lakewood, Illinois

APPENDIX 9. OTHER INTERNATIONAL CHAMPIONS

WGC Accenture Match Play

1999	Jeff Maggert	United States	La Costa Resort and Spa	Carlsbad, California
2000	Darren Clarke	Northern Ireland	La Costa Resort and Spa	Carlsbad, California
2001	Steve Stricker	United States	Metropolitan Golf Club	Victoria, Australia
2002	Kevin Sutherland	United States	La Costa Resort and Spa	Carlsbad, California
2003	Tiger Woods	United States	La Costa Resort and Spa	Carlsbad, California
2004	Tiger Woods	United States	La Costa Resort and Spa	Carlsbad, California
2005	David Toms	United States	La Costa Resort and Spa	Carlsbad, California
2006	Geoff Ogilvy	Australia	La Costa Resort and Spa	Carlsbad, California
2007	Henrik Stenson	Sweden	The Gallery Golf Club	Marana, Arizona
2008	Tiger Woods	United States	The Gallery Golf Club	Marana, Arizona
2009	Geoff Ogilvy	Australia	Ritz-Carlton Golf Club	Marana, Arizona

WGC CA Championship

1999	Tiger Woods	United States	Valderrama Golf Club	Sotogrande, Andalusia, Spain

2000	Mike Weir	Canada	Valderrama Golf Club	Sotogrande, Andalusia, Spain
2002	Tiger Woods	United States	Mount Juliet Conrad	Ireland
2003	Tiger Woods	United States	Capital City Club	Atlanta, Georgia
2004	Ernie Els	South Africa	Mount Juliet Conrad	Ireland
2005	Tiger Woods	United States	Harding Park Golf Club	San Francisco, California
2006	Tiger Woods	United States	The Grove	Hertfordshire, England
2007	Tiger Woods	United States	Doral Golf Resort & Spa	Miami, Florida
2008	Geoff Ogilvy	Australia	Doral Golf Resort & Spa	Miami, Florida
2009	Phil Mickelson	United States	Doral Golf Resort & Spa	Miami, Florida

WGC Bridgestone Invitational

1999	Tiger Woods	United States	Firestone Country Club	Akron, Ohio
2000	Tiger Woods	United States	Firestone Country Club	Akron, Ohio
2001	Tiger Woods	United States	Firestone Country Club	Akron, Ohio
2002	Craig Parry	Australia	Firestone Country Club	Akron, Ohio

2003	Darren Clarke	Northern Ireland	Firestone Country Club	Akron, Ohio
2004	Stewart Cink	United States	Firestone Country Club	Akron, Ohio
2005	Tiger Woods	United States	Firestone Country Club	Akron, Ohio
2006	Tiger Woods	United States	Firestone Country Club	Akron, Ohio
2007	Tiger Woods	United States	Firestone Country Club	Akron, Ohio
2008	Vijay Singh	Fiji	Firestone Country Club	Akron, Ohio
2009	Tiger Woods	United States	Firestone Country Club	Akron, Ohio

British Senior Open

1987	Neil Coles	England	Turnberry, Ailsa Course	Turnberry, South Ayrshire, Scotland
1988	Gary Player	South Africa	Turnberry, Ailsa Course	Turnberry, South Ayrshire, Scotland
1989	Bob Charles	New Zealand	Turnberry, Ailsa Course	Turnberry, South Ayrshire, Scotland

1990	Gary Player	South Africa	Turnberry, Ailsa Course	Turnberry, South Ayrshire, Scotland
1991	Bobby Verwey	South Africa	Royal Lytham & St. Annes Golf Club	Lytham and St. Annes, Lancashire, England
1992	John Fourie	South Africa	Royal Lytham & St. Annes Golf Club	Lytham and St. Annes, Lancashire, England
1993	Bob Charles	New Zealand	Royal Lytham & St. Annes Golf Club	Lytham and St. Annes, Lancashire, England
1994	Tom Wargo	United States	Royal Lytham & St. Annes Golf Club	Lytham and St. Annes, Lancashire, England
1995	Brian Barnes	Scotland	Royal Portrush Golf Club	Portrush, County Antrim, Northern Ireland
1996	Brian Barnes	Scotland	Royal Portrush Golf Club	Portrush, County Antrim, Northern Ireland
1997	Gary Player	South Africa	Royal Portrush Golf Club	Portrush, County Antrim, Northern Ireland

1998	Brian Huggett	Wales	Royal Portrush Golf Club	Portrush, County Antrim, Northern Ireland
1999	Christy O'Connor Jr.	Ireland	Royal Portrush Golf Club	Portrush, County Antrim, Northern Ireland
2000	Christy O'Connor Jr.	Ireland	Royal County Down Golf Club	Newcastle, County Down, Northern Ireland
2001	Ian Stanley	Australia	Royal County Down Golf Club	Newcastle, County Down, Northern Ireland
2002	Noboru Sugai	Japan	Royal County Down Golf Club	Newcastle, County Down, Northern Ireland
2003	Tom Watson	United States	Turnberry, Ailsa Course	Turnberry, South Ayrshire, Scotland
2004	Pete Oakley	United States	Royal Portrush Golf Club	Portrush, County Antrim, Northern Ireland
2005	Tom Watson	United States	Royal Aberdeen Golf Club	Aberdeen, Scotland

2006	Loren Roberts	United States	Turnberry, Ailsa Course	Turnberry, South Ayrshire, Scotland
2007	Tom Watson	United States	Muirfield Links	Gullane, East Lothian, Scotland
2008	Bruce Vaughan	United States	Royal Troon Golf Club	Troon, South Ayrshire, Scotland
2009	Loren Roberts	United States	Sunningdale Golf Club	London, Greater London, England

British Boys' Amateur

1921	A. D. D. Mathieson	Royal Ascot Golf Club	Ascot, Berkshire, England
1922	H. S. Mitchell	Royal Ascot Golf Club	Ascot, Berkshire, England
1923	A. D. D. Mathieson	Dunbar Golf Club	Dunbar, East Lothian, Scotland
1924	R. W. Peattie	Coombe Hill Golf Club	Kingston-on-Thames, Surrey, England
1925	R. W. Peattie	Royal Burgess Golfing Society	Barnton, Edinburgh, Scotland
1926	E. A. McRuvie	Coombe Hill Golf Club	Kingston-on-Thames, Surrey, England
1927	E. W. Fiddian	Royal Burgess Golfing Society	Barnton, Edinburgh, Scotland
1928	S. Scheftel	Formby Golf Club	Merseyside, England
1929	J. Lindsay	Royal Burgess Golfing Society	Barnton, Edinburgh, Scotland
1930	J. Lindsay	Fulwell Golf Club	Hampton, Middlesex, England

1931	H. Thomson	Glasgow Golf Club	Killermont, Glasgow, Scotland
1932	I. S. MacDonald	Royal Lytham & St. Annes Golf Club	Lytham and St. Annes, Lancashire, England
1933	P. B. Lucas	Carnoustie Golf Links	Carnoustie, Angus, Scotland
1934	R. S. Burles	Moortown Golf Club	Leeds, Yorkshire, England
1935	J. D. A. Langley	Royal Aberdeen Golf Club	Aberdeen, Scotland
1936	J. Bruen	Royal Birkdale Golf Club	Southport, Merseyside, England
1937	I. M. Roberts	Bruntsfield Links	Edinburgh, Scotland
1938	W. Smeaton	Moortown Golf Club	Leeds, Yorkshire, England
1939	S. B. Williamson	Carnoustie Golf Links	Carnoustie, Angus, Scotland
1946	A. F. D. MacGregor	Bruntsfield Links	Edinburgh, Scotland
1947	J. Armour	Royal Liverpool Golf Club	Hoylake, England
1948	J. D. Pritchett	Kilmarnock, Barassie Golf Club	Troon, Ayrshire, Scotland
1949	H. MacAnespie	St. Andrews Links, Old Course	St. Andrews, Fife, Scotland
1950	J. Glover	Royal Lytham & St. Annes Golf Club	Lytham and St. Annes, Lancashire, England
1951	N. Dunn	Prestwick Golf Club	Prestwick, South Ayrshire, Scotland
1952	Michael Bonallack	Formby Golf Club	Merseyside, England
1953	A. E. Shepperson	Dunbar Golf Club	Dunbar, East Lothian, Scotland

1954	A. F. Bussell	Royal Liverpool Golf Club	Hoylake, England
1955	S. C. Wilson	Kilmarnock, Barassie Golf Club	Troon, Ayrshire, Scotland
1956	J. F. Ferguson	Sunningdale Golf Club	London, Greater London, England
1957	D. Ball	Carnoustie Golf Links	Carnoustie, Angus, Scotland
1958	R. Braddon	Moortown Golf Club	Leeds, Yorkshire, England
1959	A. R. Murphy	Pollok Golf Club	Glasgow, Scotland
1960	P. Cros	Olton Golf Club	Solihull, West Midlands, England
1961	F. S. Morris	Dalmahoy Country Club	Edinburgh, Scotland
1962	P. M. Townsend	Royal Mid-Surrey Golf Club	Richmond, Surrey, England
1963	A. H. C. Soutar	Prestwick Golf Club	Prestwick, South Ayrshire, Scotland
1964	P. M. Townsend	Formby Golf Club	Merseyside, England
1965	G. R. Milne	Gullane Golf Club	Gullane, East Lothian, Scotland
1966	A. Phillips	Moortown Golf Club	Leeds, Yorkshire, England
1967	Peter Tupling	Western Gailes Golf Club	Ayrshire, Scotland
1968	S. C. Evans	St. Annes Old Links Golf Club	St. Annes on Sea, Lancashire, England
1969	M. Foster	Dunbar Golf Club	Dunbar, East Lothian, Scotland
1970	I. D. Gradwell	Hillside Golf Club	Southport, England
1971	H. Clark	Kilmarnock, Barassie Golf Club	Troon, Ayrshire, Scotland

1972	G. Harvey	Moortown Golf Club	Leeds, Yorkshire, England
1973	D. M. Robertson	Blairgowrie Golf Club	Perth, Perthshire, Scotland
1974	T. R. Shannon	Royal Liverpool Golf Club	Hoylake, England
1975	B. Marchbank	Bruntsfield Links	Edinburgh, Scotland
1976	M. Mouland	Sunningdale Golf Club	London, Greater London, England
1977	I. Ford	Downfield Golf Club	Dundee, Scotland
1978	S. Keppler	Seaton Carew Golf Club	Hartlepool, County Durham, England
1979	Ronan Rafferty	Kilmarnock, Barassie Golf Club	Troon, Ayrshire, Scotland
1980	D. Muscroft	Formby Golf Club	Merseyside, England
1981	J. Lopez	Gullane Golf Club	Gullane, East Lothian, Scotland
1982	M. Grieve	Burnham & Berrow Golf Club	Somerset, England
1983	José María Olazábal	Glenbervie Golf Club	Falkirk, Scotland
1984	L. Vannet	Royal Porthcawl Golf Club	Porthcawl, South Wales, Wales
1985	J. Cook	Royal Burgess Golfing Society	Barnton, Edinburgh, Scotland
1986	L. Walker	Seaton Carew Golf Club	Hartlepool, County Durham, England
1987	C. O'Carroll	Kilmarnock, Barassie Golf Club	Troon, Ayrshire, Scotland
1988	S. Pardoe	Formby Golf Club	Merseyside, England
1989	C. Watts	Nairn Golf Club	Nairn, Highlands, Scotland

1990	M. Welch	Hunstanton Golf Club	Hunstanton, Norfolk, England
1991	F. Valera	Montrose Golf Links	Montrose, Angus, Scotland
1992	L. Westerberg	Royal Mid-Surrey Golf Club	Richmond, Surrey, England
1993	D. Howell	Glenbervie Golf Club	Falkirk, Scotland
1994	C. Smith	Little Aston Golf Club	Streetly, Sutton Coldfield, England
1995	S. Young	Dunbar Golf Club	Dunbar, East Lothian, Scotland
1996	K. Ferrie	Littlestone Golf Club	Littlestone-on-Sea, Kent, England
1997	Sergio García	Saunton Golf Club	Braunton, North Devon, England
1998	S. O'Hara	Ladybank Golf Club	Ladybank, Fife, Scotland
1999	A. Gutiérrez	Royal St. David's Golf Club	Harlech, Gwynedd, Wales
2000	D. Inglis	Hillside Golf Club	Southport, England
2001	P. Martin	Ganton Golf Club	Ganton, North Yorkshire, England
2002	M. Pilling	Carnoustie Golf Links	Carnoustie, Angus, Scotland
2003	R. Davies	Royal Liverpool Golf Club	Hoylake, England
2004	J. Findlay	Conwy Golf Club	Caernarvonshire, Wales
2005	B. Neumann	Hunstanton Golf Club	Hunstanton, Norfolk, England
2006	M. Nixon	Royal Aberdeen Golf Club	Aberdeen, Scotland
2007	E. Cuartero	Royal Porthcawl Golf Club	Porthcawl, South Wales, Wales
2008	P. Figueiredo	Little Aston Golf Club	Streetly, Sutton Coldfield, England

APPENDIX 10. PROFESSIONAL TOUR AWARDS

PGA Tour Awards

Vardon Trophy—Lowest Scoring Average

1937	Harry Cooper	United States	500 points
1938	Sam Snead	United States	520 points
1939	Byron Nelson	United States	473 points
1940	Ben Hogan	United States	423 points
1941	Ben Hogan	United States	494 points
1947	Jimmy Demaret	United States	69.90
1948	Ben Hogan	United States	69.30
1949	Sam Snead	United States	69.37
1950	Sam Snead	United States	69.23
1951	Lloyd Mangrum	United States	70.05
1952	Jack Burke Jr.	United States	70.54
1953	Lloyd Mangrum	United States	70.22
1954	E. J. "Dutch" Harrison	United States	70.41
1955	Sam Snead	United States	69.86
1956	Cary Middlecoff	United States	70.35
1957	Dow Finsterwald	United States	70.30
1958	Bob Rosburg	United States	70.11
1959	Art Wall Jr.	United States	70.35
1960	Billy Casper	United States	69.95
1961	Arnold Palmer	United States	69.85
1962	Arnold Palmer	United States	70.27
1963	Billy Casper	United States	70.58
1964	Arnold Palmer	United States	70.01
1965	Billy Casper	United States	70.85
1966	Billy Casper	United States	70.27
1967	Arnold Palmer	United States	70.18
1968	Billy Casper	United States	69.82
1969	Dave Hill	United States	70.34
1970	Lee Trevino	United States	70.64
1971	Lee Trevino	United States	70.27
1972	Lee Trevino	United States	70.89
1973	Bruce Crampton	Australia	70.57

1974	Lee Trevino	United States	70.53
1975	Bruce Crampton	Australia	70.57
1976	Don January	United States	70.56
1977	Tom Watson	United States	70.32
1978	Tom Watson	United States	70.16
1979	Tom Watson	United States	70.27
1980	Lee Trevino	United States	69.73
1981	Tom Kite	United States	69.80
1982	Tom Kite	United States	70.21
1983	Ray Floyd	United States	70.61
1984	Calvin Peete	United States	70.56
1985	Don Pooley	United States	70.36
1986	Scott Hoch	United States	70.08
1987	Dan Pohl	United States	70.25
1988	Chip Beck	United States	69.46
1989	Greg Norman	Australia	69.49
1990	Greg Norman	Australia	69.10
1991	Fred Couples	United States	69.59
1992	Fred Couples	United States	69.38
1993	Nick Price	Zimbabwe	69.11
1994	Greg Norman	Australia	68.81
1995	Steve Elkington	Australia	69.92
1996	Tom Lehman	United States	69.32
1997	Nick Price	Zimbabwe	68.98
1998	David Duval	United States	69.13
1999	Tiger Woods	United States	68.43
2000	Tiger Woods	United States	67.79
2001	Tiger Woods	United States	68.81
2002	Tiger Woods	United States	68.56
2003	Tiger Woods	United States	68.41
2004	Vijay Singh	Fiji	68.84
2005	Tiger Woods	United States	68.66
2006	Jim Furyk	United States	68.86
2007	Tiger Woods	United States	67.79
2008	Sergio García	Spain	69.12
2009	Tiger Woods	United States	68.05

Byron Nelson Trophy—Lowest Adjusted Scoring Average

1980	Lee Trevino	United States	69.73
1981	Tom Kite	United States	69.80
1982	Tom Kite	United States	70.21
1983	Ray Floyd	United States	70.61
1984	Calvin Peete	United States	70.56
1985	Don Pooley	United States	70.36
1986	Scott Hoch	United States	70.08
1987	David Frost	South Africa	70.09
1988	Greg Norman	Australia	69.38
1989	Payne Stewart	United States	69.49
1990	Greg Norman	Australia	69.10
1991	Fred Couples	United States	69.38
1992	Fred Couples	United States	69.38
1993	Greg Norman	Australia	68.90
1994	Greg Norman	Australia	68.81
1995	Greg Norman	Australia	69.06
1996	Tom Lehman	United States	69.32
1997	Nick Price	Zimbabwe	68.98
1998	David Duval	United States	69.13
1999	Tiger Woods	United States	68.43
2000	Tiger Woods	United States	67.79
2001	Tiger Woods	United States	68.81
2002	Tiger Woods	United States	68.56
2003	Tiger Woods	United States	68.41
2004	Vijay Singh	Fiji	68.84
2005	Tiger Woods	United States	68.66
2006	Tiger Woods	United States	68.11
2007	Tiger Woods	United States	67.79
2008	Sergio García	Spain	69.12
2009	Tiger Woods	United States	68.05

Leading Money Winners

1934	Paul Runyan	United States	$6,767
1935	Johnny Revolta	United States	$9,543

1936	Horton Smith	United States	$7,682
1937	Harry Cooper	United States	$14,139
1938	Sam Snead	United States	$19,534
1939	Henry Picard	United States	$10,303
1940	Ben Hogan	United States	$10,655
1941	Ben Hogan	United States	$18,358
1942	Ben Hogan	United States	$13,143
1944	Byron Nelson	United States	$37,968
1945	Byron Nelson	United States	$63,336
1946	Ben Hogan	United States	$42,556
1947	Jimmy Demaret	United States	$27,937
1948	Ben Hogan	United States	$32,112
1949	Sam Snead	United States	$31,594
1950	Sam Snead	United States	$35,759
1951	Lloyd Mangrum	United States	$26,089
1952	Julius Boros	United States	$37,033
1953	Lew Worsham	United States	$34,002
1954	Bob Toski	United States	$65,820
1955	Julius Boros	United States	$63,122
1956	Ted Kroll	United States	$72,836
1957	Dick Mayer	United States	$65,835
1958	Arnold Palmer	United States	$42,608
1959	Art Wall Jr.	United States	$53,168
1960	Arnold Palmer	United States	$75,263
1961	Gary Player	South Africa	$64,540
1962	Arnold Palmer	United States	$81,448
1963	Arnold Palmer	United States	$128,230
1964	Jack Nicklaus	United States	$113,285
1965	Jack Nicklaus	United States	$140,752
1966	Billy Casper	United States	$121,945
1967	Jack Nicklaus	United States	$188,998
1968	Billy Casper	United States	$205,169
1969	Frank Beard	United States	$164,707
1970	Lee Trevino	United States	$157,037
1971	Jack Nicklaus	United States	$244,491
1972	Jack Nicklaus	United States	$320,542

1973	Jack Nicklaus	United States	$308,362
1974	Johnny Miller	United States	$353,022
1975	Jack Nicklaus	United States	$298,149
1976	Jack Nicklaus	United States	$266,439
1977	Tom Watson	United States	$310,653
1978	Tom Watson	United States	$362,429
1979	Tom Watson	United States	$462,636
1980	Tom Watson	United States	$530,808
1981	Tom Kite	United States	$375,699
1982	Craig Stadler	United States	$446,462
1983	Hal Sutton	United States	$426,668
1984	Tom Watson	United States	$476,260
1985	Curtis Strange	United States	$542,321
1986	Greg Norman	Australia	$653,296
1987	Curtis Strange	United States	$925,941
1988	Curtis Strange	United States	$1,147,644
1989	Tom Kite	United States	$1,395,278
1990	Greg Norman	Australia	$1,165,477
1991	Corey Pavin	United States	$979,430
1992	Fred Couples	United States	$1,344,188
1993	Nick Price	Zimbabwe	$1,478,557
1994	Nick Price	Zimbabwe	$1,499,927
1995	Greg Norman	Australia	$1,654,959
1996	Tom Lehman	United States	$1,780,159
1997	Tiger Woods	United States	$2,066,833
1998	David Duval	United States	$2,591,031
1999	Tiger Woods	United States	$6,616,585
2000	Tiger Woods	United States	$9,188,321
2001	Tiger Woods	United States	$5,687,777
2002	Tiger Woods	United States	$6,912,625
2003	Vijay Singh	Fiji	$7,573,907
2004	Vijay Singh	Fiji	$10,905,166
2005	Tiger Woods	United States	$10,628,024
2006	Tiger Woods	United States	$9,941,563
2007	Tiger Woods	United States	$10,867,052
2008	Vijay Singh	Fiji	$6,601,094
2009	Tiger Woods	United States	$10,508,163

Arnold Palmer Trophy—Most Wins for Year

1922	Walter Hagen	United States	4
1923	Walter Hagen / Joe Kirkwood Sr.	United States / United States	5
1924	Walter Hagen	United States	5
1925	Leo Diegel	United States	5
1926	Bill Mehlhorn / MacDonald Smith	United States / United States	5
1927	Johnny Farrell	United States	7
1928	Bill Mehlhorn	United States	7
1929	Horton Smith	United States	8
1930	Gene Sarazen	United States	8
1931	Wiffy Cox	United States	4
1932	Gene Sarazen	United States	4
1933	Paul Runyan	United States	9
1934	Paul Runyan	United States	7
1935	Henry Picard / Johnny Revolta	United States / United States	5
1936	Ralph Guldahl / Jimmy Hines / Henry Picard	United States / United States / United States	3
1937	Harry Cooper	United States	8
1938	Sam Snead	United States	8
1939	Henry Picard	United States	8
1940	Jimmy Demaret	United States	6
1941	Sam Snead	United States	7
1942	Ben Hogan	United States	6
1944	Byron Nelson	United States	8
1945	Byron Nelson	United States	18
1946	Ben Hogan	United States	13
1947	Ben Hogan	United States	7
1948	Ben Hogan	United States	10
1949	Cary Middlecoff	United States	7
1950	Sam Snead	United States	11
1951	Cary Middlecoff	United States	6
1952	Jack Burke Jr. / Sam Snead	United States / United States	5

1953	Ben Hogan	United States	5
1954	Bob Toski	United States	4
1955	Cary Middlecoff	United States	6
1956	Mike Souchak	United States	4
1957	Arnold Palmer	United States	4
1958	Ken Venturi	United States	4
1959	Gene Littler	United States	5
1960	Arnold Palmer	United States	8
1961	Arnold Palmer	United States	6
1962	Arnold Palmer	United States	8
1963	Arnold Palmer	United States	7
1964	Tony Lema	United States	5
1965	Jack Nicklaus	United States	5
1966	Billy Casper	United States	4
1967	Jack Nicklaus	United States	5
1968	Billy Casper	United States	6
1969	Four players tied	United States	3
1970	Billy Casper	United States	4
1971	Lee Trevino	United States	6
1972	Jack Nicklaus	United States	7
1973	Jack Nicklaus	United States	7
1974	Johnny Miller	United States	8
1975	Jack Nicklaus	United States	5
1976	Ben Crenshaw / Hubert Green	United States / United States	3
1977	Tom Watson	United States	5
1978	Tom Watson	United States	5
1979	Tom Watson	United States	5
1980	Tom Watson	United States	7
1981	Bill Rogers	United States	4
1982	Craig Stadler / Tom Watson / Calvin Peete	United States / United States / United States	4
1983	Eight players tied	United States	2
1984	Tom Watson / Denis Watson	United States / South Africa	3
1985	Curtis Strange / Lanny Wadkins	United States / United States	3

1986	Bob Tway	United States	4
1987	Paul Azinger; Curtis Strange	United States / United States	3
1988	Curtis Strange	United States	4
1989	Tom Kite / Steve Jones	United States / United States	3
1990	Wayne Levi	United States	4
1991	Eight players tied	United States	2
1992	John Cook / Fred Couples / Davis Love, III	United States / United States / United States	3
1993	Nick Price	Zimbabwe	4
1994	Nick Price	Zimbabwe	6
1995	Lee Janzen / Greg Norman	United States / Australia	3
1996	Phil Mickelson	United States	4
1997	Tiger Woods	United States	4
1998	David Duval	United States	4
1999	Tiger Woods	United States	8
2000	Tiger Woods	United States	9
2001	Tiger Woods	United States	5
2002	Tiger Woods	United States	5
2003	Tiger Woods	United States	5
2004	Vijay Singh	Fiji	9
2005	Tiger Woods	United States	6
2006	Tiger Woods	United States	8
2007	Tiger Woods	United States	7
2008	Tiger Woods	United States	4
2009	Tiger Woods	United States	6

PGA of America Player of the Year

1948	Ben Hogan	United States
1949	Sam Snead	United States
1950	Ben Hogan	United States
1951	Ben Hogan	United States
1952	Julius Boros	United States

1953	Ben Hogan	United States
1954	Ed Furgol	United States
1955	Doug Ford	United States
1956	Jack Burke Jr.	United States
1957	Dick Mayer	United States
1958	Dow Finsterwald	United States
1959	Art Wall Jr.	United States
1960	Arnold Palmer	United States
1961	Jerry Barber	United States
1962	Arnold Palmer	United States
1963	Julius Boros	United States
1964	Ken Venturi	United States
1965	Dave Marr	United States
1966	Billy Casper	United States
1967	Jack Nicklaus	United States
1968		No award
1969	Orville Moody	United States
1970	Billy Casper	United States
1971	Lee Trevino	United States
1972	Jack Nicklaus	United States
1973	Jack Nicklaus	United States
1974	Johnny Miller	United States
1975	Jack Nicklaus	United States
1976	Jack Nicklaus	United States
1977	Tom Watson	United States
1978	Tom Watson	United States
1979	Tom Watson	United States
1980	Tom Watson	United States
1981	Bill Rogers	United States
1982	Tom Watson	United States
1983	Hal Sutton	United States
1984	Tom Watson	United States
1985	Lanny Wadkins	United States
1986	Bob Tway	United States
1987	Paul Azinger	United States
1988	Curtis Strange	United States

1989	Tom Kite	United States
1990	Nick Faldo	England
1991	Corey Pavin	United States
1992	Fred Couples	United States
1993	Nick Price	Zimbabwe
1994	Nick Price	Zimbabwe
1995	Greg Norman	Australia
1996	Tom Lehman	United States
1997	Tiger Woods	United States
1998	Mark O'Meara	United States
1999	Tiger Woods	United States
2000	Tiger Woods	United States
2001	Tiger Woods	United States
2002	Tiger Woods	United States
2003	Tiger Woods	United States
2004	Vijay Singh	Fiji
2005	Tiger Woods	United States
2006	Tiger Woods	United States
2007	Tiger Woods	United States
2008	Pádraig Harrington	Ireland
2009	Tiger Woods	United States

PGA Tour Player of the Year

1990	Wayne Levi	United States
1991	Fred Couples	United States
1992	Fred Couples	United States
1993	Nick Price	Zimbabwe
1994	Nick Price	Zimbabwe
1995	Greg Norman	Australia
1996	Tom Lehman	United States
1997	Tiger Woods	United States
1998	Mark O'Meara	United States
1999	Tiger Woods	United States
2000	Tiger Woods	United States
2001	Tiger Woods	United States

2002	Tiger Woods	United States
2003	Tiger Woods	United States
2004	Vijay Singh	Fiji
2005	Tiger Woods	United States
2006	Tiger Woods	United States
2007	Tiger Woods	United States
2008	Pádraig Harrington	Ireland
2009	Tiger Woods	United States

Rookie of the Year

1990	Robert Gamez	United States
1991	John Daly	United States
1992	Mark Carnevale	United States
1993	Vijay Singh	Fiji
1994	Ernie Els	South Africa
1995	Woody Austin	United States
1996	Tiger Woods	United States
1997	Stewart Cink	United States
1998	Steve Flesch	United States
1999	Carlos Franco	Paraguay
2000	Michael Clark II	United States
2001	Charles Howell III	United States
2002	Jonathan Byrd	United States
2003	Ben Curtis	United States
2004	Todd Hamilton	United States
2005	Sean O'Hair	United States
2006	Trevor Immelman	South Africa
2007	Brandt Snedeker	United States
2008	Andrés Romero	Argentina
2009	Tiger Woods	United States

Comeback Player of the Year

1991	Bruce Fleisher / D. A. Weibring	United States / United States
1992	John Cook	United States

1993	Howard Twitty	United States
1994	Hal Sutton	United States
1995	Bob Tway	United States
1996	Steve Jones	United States
1997	Bill Glasson	United States
1998	Scott Verplank	United States
1999	Steve Pate	United States
2000	Paul Azinger	United States
2001	Joe Durant	United States
2002	Gene Sauers	United States
2003	Peter Jacobsen	United States
2004	John Daly	United States
2005	Jay Haas	United States
2006	Steve Stricker	United States
2007	Steve Stricker	United States
2008	Dudley Hart	United States
2009	Not awarded	

European PGA Tour Awards

Order of Merit Winner

1971	Peter Oosterhuis	England	£9,270
1972	Peter Oosterhuis	England	£18,525
1973	Peter Oosterhuis	England	£17,455
1974	Peter Oosterhuis	England	£32,127
1975	Dale Hayes	South Africa	£20,508
1976	Seve Ballesteros	Spain	£39,504
1977	Seve Ballesteros	Spain	£46,436
1978	Seve Ballesteros	Spain	£54,348
1979	Sandy Lyle	Scotland	£49,233
1980	Sandy Lyle	Scotland	£66,060
1981	Bernhard Langer	West Germany	£81,036
1982	Greg Norman	Australia	£66,406
1983	Nick Faldo	England	£119,416
1984	Bernhard Langer	West Germany	£139,344
1985	Sandy Lyle	Scotland	£162,553

1986	Seve Ballesteros	Spain	£242,209
1987	Ian Woosnam	Wales	£253,717
1988	Seve Ballesteros	Spain	£451,560
1989	Ronan Rafferty	Northern Ireland	£400,311
1990	Ian Woosnam	Wales	£574,166
1991	Seve Ballesteros	Spain	£545,354
1992	Nick Faldo	England	£708,522
1993	Colin Montgomerie	Scotland	£613,683
1994	Colin Montgomerie	Scotland	£762,720
1995	Colin Montgomerie	Scotland	£835,051
1996	Colin Montgomerie	Scotland	£875,146
1997	Colin Montgomerie	Scotland	£798,948
1998	Colin Montgomerie	Scotland	£993,077
1999	Colin Montgomerie	Scotland	€1,822,880
2000	Lee Westwood	England	€3,125,147
2001	Retief Goosen	South Africa	€2,862,806
2002	Retief Goosen	South Africa	€2,360,128
2003	Ernie Els	South Africa	€2,975,374
2004	Ernie Els	South Africa	€4,061,905
2005	Colin Montgomerie	Scotland	€2,794,223
2006	Pádraig Harrington	Ireland	€2,489,337
2007	Justin Rose	England	€2,944,945
2008	Robert Karlsson	Sweden	€2,732,748
2009	Lee Westwood	England	€4,237,762

LPGA Tour Awards

Player of the Year

1966	Kathy Whitworth	United States
1967	Kathy Whitworth	United States
1968	Kathy Whitworth	United States
1969	Kathy Whitworth	United States
1970	Sandra Haynie	United States
1971	Kathy Whitworth	United States
1972	Kathy Whitworth	United States
1973	Kathy Whitworth	United States

1974	JoAnne Carner	United States
1975	Sandra Palmer	United States
1976	Judy Rankin	United States
1977	Judy Rankin	United States
1978	Nancy Lopez	United States
1979	Nancy Lopez	United States
1980	Beth Daniel	United States
1981	JoAnne Carner	United States
1982	JoAnne Carner	United States
1983	Patty Sheehan	United States
1984	Betsy King	United States
1985	Nancy Lopez	United States
1986	Pat Bradley	United States
1987	Ayako Okamoto	Japan
1988	Nancy Lopez	United States
1989	Betsy King	United States
1990	Beth Daniel	United States
1991	Pat Bradley	United States
1992	Dottie Mochrie	United States
1993	Betsy King	United States
1994	Beth Daniel	United States
1995	Annika Sörenstam	Sweden
1996	Laura Davies	England
1997	Annika Sörenstam	Sweden
1998	Annika Sörenstam	Sweden
1999	Karrie Webb	Australia
2000	Karrie Webb	Australia
2001	Annika Sörenstam	Sweden
2002	Annika Sörenstam	Sweden
2003	Annika Sörenstam	Sweden
2004	Annika Sörenstam	Sweden
2005	Annika Sörenstam	Sweden
2006	Lorena Ochoa	Mexico
2007	Lorena Ochoa	Mexico
2008	Lorena Ochoa	Mexico
2009	Lorena Ochoa	Mexico

Vare Trophy—Lowest Scoring Average

1953	Patty Berg	United States
1954	Babe Zaharias	United States
1955	Patty Berg	United States
1956	Patty Berg	United States
1957	Louise Suggs	United States
1958	Beverly Hanson	United States
1959	Betsy Rawls	United States
1960	Mickey Wright	United States
1961	Mickey Wright	United States
1962	Mickey Wright	United States
1963	Mickey Wright	United States
1964	Mickey Wright	United States
1965	Kathy Whitworth	United States
1966	Kathy Whitworth	United States
1967	Kathy Whitworth	United States
1968	Carol Mann	United States
1969	Kathy Whitworth	United States
1970	Amy Alcott	United States
1971	Kathy Whitworth	United States
1972	Kathy Whitworth	United States
1973	Judy Rankin	United States
1974	JoAnne Carner	United States
1975	JoAnne Carner	United States
1976	Judy Rankin	United States
1977	Judy Rankin	United States
1978	Nancy Lopez	United States
1979	Nancy Lopez	United States
1980	Amy Alcott	United States
1981	JoAnne Carner	United States
1982	JoAnne Carner	United States
1983	JoAnne Carner	United States
1984	Patty Sheehan	United States
1985	Nancy Lopez	United States
1986	Pat Bradley	United States
1987	Betsy King	United States

1988	Colleen Walker	United States
1989	Beth Daniel	United States
1990	Beth Daniel	United States
1991	Pat Bradley	United States
1992	Dottie Mochrie	United States
1993	Betsy King	United States
1994	Beth Daniel	United States
1995	Annika Sörenstam	Sweden
1996	Annika Sörenstam	Sweden
1997	Karrie Webb	Australia
1998	Annika Sörenstam	Sweden
1999	Karrie Webb	Australia
2000	Karrie Webb	Australia
2001	Annika Sörenstam	Sweden
2002	Annika Sörenstam	Sweden
2003	Pak Se-Ri	Korea (South)
2004	Grace Park	Korea (South)
2005	Annika Sörenstam	Sweden
2006	Lorena Ochoa	Mexico
2007	Lorena Ochoa	Mexico
2008	Lorena Ochoa	Mexico
2009	Lorena Ochoa	Mexico

Rookie of the Year

1962	Mary Mills	United States
1963	Clifford Ann Creed	United States
1964	Susie Maxwell-Berning	United States
1965	Margie Masters	United States
1966	Jan Ferraris	United States
1967	Sharron Moran	United States
1968	Sandra Post	Canada
1969	Jane Blalock	United States
1970	JoAnne Carner	United States
1971	Sally Little	South Africa
1972	Jocelyne Bourassa	Canada
1973	Laura Baugh	United States

1974	Jan Stephenson	Australia
1975	Amy Alcott	United States
1976	Bonnie Lauer	United States
1977	Debbie Massey	United States
1978	Nancy Lopez	United States
1979	Beth Daniel	United States
1980	Myra Blackwelder	United States
1981	Patty Sheehan	United States
1982	Patti Rizzo	United States
1983	Stephanie Farwig	United States
1984	Juli Inkster	United States
1985	Penny Hammel	United States
1986	Jody Rosenthal	United States
1987	Tammie Green	United States
1988	Liselotte Neumann	Sweden
1989	Pamela Wright	Scotland
1990	Hiromi Kobayashi	Japan
1991	Brandie Burton	United States
1992	Helen Alfredsson	Sweden
1993	Suzanne Strudwick	England
1994	Annika Sörenstam	Sweden
1995	Pat Hurst	United States
1996	Karrie Webb	Australia
1997	Lisa Hackney	England
1998	Pak Se-Ri	Korea (South)
1999	Mi Hyun Kim	Korea (South)
2000	Dorothy Delasin	United States / Philippines
2001	Han Hee-Won	Korea (South)
2002	Beth Bauer	United States
2003	Lorena Ochoa	Mexico
2004	Ahn Shi-Hyun	Korea (South)
2005	Paula Creamer	United States
2006	Lee Seon-Hwa	Korea (South)
2007	Angela Park	Brazil
2008	Yani Tseng	Chinese Taipei
2009	Shin Ji-Yai	Korea (South)

Leading Money Winner

1950	Babe Zaharias	United States	$14,800
1951	Babe Zaharias	United States	$15,087
1952	Betsy Rawls	United States	$14,505
1953	Louise Suggs	United States	$19,816
1954	Patty Berg	United States	$16,011
1955	Patty Berg	United States	$16,492
1956	Marlene Bauer Hagge	United States	$20,235
1957	Patty Berg	United States	$16,272
1958	Beverly Hanson	United States	$12,639
1959	Betsy Rawls	United States	$26,774
1960	Louise Suggs	United States	$16,892
1961	Mickey Wright	United States	$22,236
1962	Mickey Wright	United States	$21,641
1963	Mickey Wright	United States	$31,269
1964	Mickey Wright	United States	$29,800
1965	Kathy Whitworth	United States	$28,658
1966	Kathy Whitworth	United States	$33,517
1967	Kathy Whitworth	United States	$32,937
1968	Kathy Whitworth	United States	$48,379
1969	Carol Mann	United States	$49,152
1970	Kathy Whitworth	United States	$30,235
1971	Kathy Whitworth	United States	$41,181
1972	Kathy Whitworth	United States	$65,063
1973	Kathy Whitworth	United States	$82,864
1974	JoAnne Carner	United States	$87,094
1975	Sandra Palmer	United States	$76,374
1976	Judy Rankin	United States	$150,734
1977	Judy Rankin	United States	$122,890
1978	Nancy Lopez	United States	$189,814
1979	Nancy Lopez	United States	$197,489
1980	Beth Daniel	United States	$231,000
1981	Beth Daniel	United States	$206,998
1982	JoAnne Carner	United States	$310,400
1983	JoAnne Carner	United States	$291,404
1984	Betsy King	United States	$266,771

1985	Nancy Lopez	United States	$416,472
1986	Pat Bradley	United States	$492,021
1987	Ayako Okamoto	Japan	$466,034
1988	Sherri Turner	United States	$350,851
1989	Betsy King	United States	$654,132
1990	Beth Daniel	United States	$863,578
1991	Pat Bradley	United States	$763,118
1992	Dottie Mochrie	United States	$693,335
1993	Betsy King	United States	$595,992
1994	Laura Davies	England	$687,201
1995	Annika Sörenstam	Sweden	$666,533
1996	Karrie Webb	Australia	$1,002,000
1997	Annika Sörenstam	Sweden	$1,236,789
1998	Annika Sörenstam	Sweden	$1,092,748
1999	Karrie Webb	Australia	$1,591,959
2000	Karrie Webb	Australia	$1,876,853
2001	Annika Sörenstam	Sweden	$2,105,868
2002	Annika Sörenstam	Sweden	$2,863,904
2003	Annika Sörenstam	Sweden	$2,029,506
2004	Annika Sörenstam	Sweden	$2,544,707
2005	Annika Sörenstam	Sweden	$2,588,240
2006	Lorena Ochoa	Mexico	$2,592,872
2007	Lorena Ochoa	Mexico	$4,364,994
2008	Lorena Ochoa	Mexico	$2,754,660
2009	Shin Ji-Yai	Korea (South)	$1,807,334

Most Wins for the Year

1950	Babe Zaharias	United States	6
1951	Babe Zaharias	United States	7
1952	Betsy Rawls / Louise Suggs	United States / United States	6
1953	Louise Suggs	United States	8
1954	Louise Suggs / Babe Zaharias	United States / United States	5
1955	Patty Berg	United States	6

1956	Marlene Bauer Hagge	United States / United States	8
1957	Betsy Rawls / Patty Berg	United States / United States	5
1958	Mickey Wright	United States	5
1959	Betsy Rawls	United States	10
1960	Mickey Wright	United States	6
1961	Mickey Wright	United States	10
1962	Mickey Wright	United States	10
1963	Mickey Wright	United States	13
1964	Mickey Wright	United States	11
1965	Kathy Whitworth	United States	8
1966	Kathy Whitworth	United States	9
1967	Kathy Whitworth	United States	8
1968	Carol Mann / Kathy Whitworth	United States / United States	10
1969	Carol Mann	United States	8
1970	Shirley Englehorn	United States	4
1971	Kathy Whitworth	United States	5
1972	Kathy Whitworth / Jane Blalock	United States / United States	5
1973	Kathy Whitworth	United States	7
1974	JoAnne Carner / Sandra Haynie	United States / United States	6
1975	Carol Mann / Sandra Haynie	United States / United States	4
1976	Judy Rankin	United States	6
1977	Judy Rankin / Debbie Austin	United States / United States	5
1978	Nancy Lopez	United States	9
1979	Nancy Lopez	United States	8
1980	Donna Caponi / JoAnne Carner	United States / United States	5
1981	Donna Caponi	United States	5
1982	JoAnne Carner / Beth Daniel	United States / United States	5

1983	Pat Bradley / Patty Sheehan	United States / United States	4
1984	Patty Sheehan / Amy Alcott	United States / United States	4
1985	Nancy Lopez	United States	5
1986	Pat Bradley	United States	5
1987	Jane Geddes	United States	5
1988	Five players tied		3
1989	Betsy King	United States	6
1990	Beth Daniel	United States	7
1991	Pat Bradley / Meg Mallon	United States / United States	4
1992	Dottie Mochrie	United States	4
1993	Brandie Burton	United States	3
1994	Beth Daniel	United States	4
1995	Annika Sörenstam	Sweden	3
1996	Laura Davies / Dottie Pepper / Karrie Webb	England / United States / Australia	4
1997	Annika Sörenstam	Sweden	6
1998	Annika Sörenstam / Pak Se-Ri	Sweden / Korea (South)	4
1999	Karrie Webb	Australia	6
2000	Karrie Webb	Australia	7
2001	Annika Sörenstam	Sweden	8
2002	Annika Sörenstam	Sweden	11
2003	Annika Sörenstam	Sweden	6
2004	Annika Sörenstam	Sweden	8
2005	Annika Sörenstam	Sweden	10
2006	Lorena Ochoa	Mexico	6
2007	Lorena Ochoa	Mexico	8
2008	Lorena Ochoa	Mexico	7
2009	Lorena Ochoa / Shin Ji-Yai	Mexico / Korea (South)	3

PGA Developmental Tour Awards

Ben Hogan Tour (1990–1992), Nike Tour (1993–1999), Buy.com Tour (2000–2002), Nationwide Tour (2003–2009)

Leading Money Winners

1990	Jeff Maggert	United States	$108,644
1991	Tom Lehman	United States	$141,934
1992	John Flannery	United States	$164,115
1993	Sean Murphy	United States	$166,293
1994	Chris Perry	United States	$167,148
1995	Jerry Kelly	United States	$188,878
1996	Stewart Cink	United States	$251,699
1997	Chris Smith	United States	$225,201
1998	Bob Burns	United States	$178,664
1999	Carl Paulson	United States	$223,051
2000	Spike McRoy	United States	$300,638
2001	Chad Campbell	United States	$394,552
2002	Patrick Moore	United States	$381,965
2003	Zach Johnson	United States	$494,882
2004	Jimmy Walker	United States	$371,346
2005	Troy Matteson	United States	$495,009
2006	Ken Duke	United States	$382,443
2007	Richard Johnson	Wales	$445,421
2008	Matt Bettencourt	United States	$447,863
2009	Michael Sim	Australia	$644,142

Player of the Year

1990	Jeff Maggert	United States
1991	Tom Lehman	United States
1992	John Flannery	United States
1993	Sean Murphy	United States
1994	Chris Perry	United States
1995	Jerry Kelly	United States
1996	Stewart Cink	United States
1997	Chris Smith	United States
1998	Bob Burns	United States

1999	Carl Paulson	United States
2000	Spike McRoy	United States
2001	Chad Campbell	United States
2002	Patrick Moore	United States
2003	Zach Johnson	United States
2004	Jimmy Walker	United States
2005	Jason Gore	United States
2006	Ken Duke	United States
2007	Nick Flanagan	Australia
2008	Brendon de Jonge	Zimbabwe
2009	Michael Sim	Australia

Ladies European Tour Awards

Order of Merit Winner

1979	Catherine Panton-Lewis	Scotland	£4,965
1980	Muriel Thomson	Scotland	£8,008
1981	Jenny Lee Smith	England	£13,518
1982	Jenny Lee Smith	England	£12,551
1983	Muriel Thomson	Scotland	£9,225
1984	Dale Reid	Scotland	£28,239
1985	Laura Davies	England	£21,735
1986	Laura Davies	England	£37,500
1987	Dale Reid	Scotland	£53,815
1988	Marie-Laure de Lorenzi	France	£109,360
1989	Marie-Laure de Lorenzi	France	£77,534
1990	Trish Johnson	England	£83,043
1991	Corinne Dibnah	Australia	£89,058
1992	Laura Davies	England	£66,333
1993	Karen Lunn	Australia	£81,266
1994	Liselotte Neumann	Sweden	£102,750
1995	Annika Sörenstam	Sweden	£130,324
1996	Laura Davies	England	£110,880
1997	Alison Nicholas	England	£94,590
1998	Helen Alfredsson	Sweden	£125,975
1999	Laura Davies	England	£204,522

2000	Sophie Gustafson	Sweden	8,777 pts
2001	Raquel Carriedo	Spain	10,661 pts
2002	Paula Marti	Spain	6,589 pts
2003	Sophie Gustafson	Sweden	917.95 pts
2004	Laura Davies	England	777.26 pts
2005	Iben Tinning	Denmark	€204,672
2006	Laura Davies	England	€471,727
2007	Sophie Gustafson	Sweden	€222,081
2008	Gwladys Nocera	France	€391,840
2009	Sophie Gustafson	Sweden	€281,315

Player of the Year

1995	Annika Sörenstam	Sweden
1996	Laura Davies	England
1997	Alison Nicholas	England
1998	Sophie Gustafson	Sweden
1999	Laura Davies	England
2000	Sophie Gustafson	Sweden
2001	Raquel Carriedo	Spain
2002	Annika Sörenstam	Sweden
2003	Sophie Gustafson	Sweden
2004	Stéphanie Arricau	France
2005	Iben Tinning	Denmark
2006	Gwladys Nocera	France
2007	Bettina Hauert	Germany
2008	Gwladys Nocera	France
2009	Catriona Matthew	Scotland

Rookie of the Year

1984	Kitrina Douglas	England
1985	Laura Davies	England
1986	Patricia Gonzalez	Spain
1987	Trish Johnson	England
1988	Laurette Maritz	South Africa
1989	Helen Alfredsson	Sweden

1990	Pearl Sinn	Korea (South)
1991	Helen Wadsworth	Wales
1992	Sandrine Mendiburu	France
1993	Annika Sörenstam	Sweden
1994	Tracy Hanson	United States
1995	Karrie Webb	Australia
1996	Anne-Marie Knight	Australia
1997	Anna Berg	Sweden
1998	Laura Philo	United States
1999	Elaine Ratcliffe	England
2000	Giulia Sergas	Italy
2001	Suzann Pettersen	Norway
2002	Kirsty Taylor	England
2003	Rebecca Stevenson	Australia
2004	Minea Blomqvist	Finland
2005	Elisa Serramia	Spain
2006	Nikki Garrett	Australia
2007	Louise Stahle	Sweden
2008	Melissa Reid	England
2009	Anna Nordquist	Sweden

Lowest Scoring Average

1983	Beverly Huke	England	74.98
1984	Dale Reid	Scotland	73.01
1986	Laura Davies	England	72.09
1987	Dale Reid	Scotland	72.70
1988	Marie-Laure de Lorenzi	France	72.30
1989	Marie-Laure de Lorenzi	France	70.84
1990	Trish Johnson	England	70.64
1991	Alison Nicholas	England	71.71
1992	Laura Davies	England	70.35
1993	Laura Davies	England	71.63
1994	Liselotte Neumann	Sweden	69.56
1995	Annika Sörenstam	Sweden	69.75
1996	Marie-Laure de Lorenzi	France	71.39
1997	Marie-Laure de Lorenzi	France	72.20

1998	Laura Davies	England	71.96
1999	Laura Davies	England	70.50
2000	Sophie Gustafson	Sweden	71.21
2001	Catriona Matthew	Scotland	70.08
2002	Sophie Gustafson	Sweden	70.59
2003	Sophie Gustafson	Sweden	69.93
2004	Laura Davies	England	70.31
2005	Laura Davies	England	70.35
2006	Annika Sörenstam	Sweden	68.33
2007	Sophie Gustafson	Sweden	70.96
2008	Suzann Pettersen	Norway	68.60
2003	Sophie Gustafson	Sweden	69.93
2004	Laura Davies	England	70.31
2005	Laura Davies	England	70.35
2006	Annika Sörenstam	Sweden	68.33
2007	Sophie Gustafson	Sweden	70.96
2008	Suzann Pettersen	Norway	68.60
2009	Catriona Matthew	Scotland	70.83

APPENDIX 11. OTHER AWARDS

Bob Jones Award

1955	Francis Ouimet	United States
1956	Bill Campbell	United States
1957	Babe Zaharias	United States
1958	Margaret Curtis	United States
1959	Findlay Douglas	United States
1960	Chick Evans	United States
1961	Joe Carr	Ireland
1962	Horton Smith	United States
1963	Patty Berg	United States
1964	Charlie Coe	United States
1965	Glenna Collett Vare	United States
1966	Gary Player	South Africa
1967	Richard Tufts	United States
1968	Bob Dickson	United States
1969	Gerald Micklem	England
1970	Roberto De Vicenzo	Argentina
1971	Arnold Palmer	United States
1972	Michael Bonallack	England
1973	Gene Littler	United States
1974	Byron Nelson	United States
1975	Jack Nicklaus	United States
1976	Ben Hogan	United States
1977	Joe Dey	United States
1978	Bing Crosby / Bob Hope	United States
1979	Tom Kite	United States
1980	Charles Yates	United States
1981	JoAnne Carner	United States
1982	Billy Joe Patton	United States
1983	Maureen Ruttle Garrett	United States
1984	Jay Sigel	United States
1985	Fuzzy Zoeller	United States
1986	Jess Sweetser	United States
1987	Tom Watson	United States

1988	Isaac Grainger	United States
1989	Chi Chi Rodriguez	United States
1990	Peggy Kirk Bell	United States
1991	Ben Crenshaw	United States
1992	Gene Sarazen	United States
1993	P. J. Boatwright Jr.	United States
1994	Lewis Oehmig	United States
1995	Herbert Warren Wind	United States
1996	Betsy Rawls	United States
1997	Fred Brand Jr.	United States
1998	Nancy Lopez	United States
1999	Ed Updegraff	United States
2000	Barbara McIntire	United States
2001	Tom Cousins	United States
2002	Judy Rankin	United States
2003	Carol Semple Thompson	United States
2004	Jack Burke Jr.	United States
2005	Nick Price	Zimbabwe
2006	Jay Haas	United States
2007	Louise Suggs	United States
2008	George H. W. Bush	United States
2009	O. Gordon Brewer Jr.	United States
2010	Mickey Wright	United States

Ben Hogan (College) Award

1990	Kevin Wentworth	Oklahoma State University
1991	Brian Bridges	Kent State University
1992	Jon Lindquist	Gustavus Adolphus College
1993	Marten Olander	University of Alabama
1994	William Blackman	University of New Mexico
1995	Trip Kuehne	Oklahoma State University
1996	Mark Wilson	University of North Carolina
1997	Jeff Fahrenbruch	University of Texas
1998	Jamie Broce	Ball State University
1999	Steve Friesen	University of Nebraska
2000	Chris James	University of Oklahoma

2001	Wil Collins	University of New Mexico
2002	D. J. Trahan	Clemson University
2003	Ricky Barnes	University of Arizona
2003	Hunter Mahan	Oklahoma State University
2004	Bill Haas	Wake Forest University
2005	Ryan Moore	University of Nevada-Las Vegas
2006	Matt Every	University of Florida
2007	Chris Kirk	University of Georgia
2008	Rickie Fowler	Oklahoma State University
2009	Kyle Stanley	Clemson University

William D. Richardson Award

1948	Robert Hudson	United States
1949	Scotty Fessenden	United States
1950	Bing Crosby	United States
1951	Richard Tufts	United States
1952	Chick Evans	United States
1953	Bob Hope	United States
1954	Babe Zaharias	United States
1955	Dwight D. Eisenhower	United States
1956	George S. May	United States
1957	Francis Ouimet	United States
1958	Bob Jones	United States
1959	Patty Berg	United States
1960	Fred Corcoran	United States
1961	Joe Dey	United States
1962	Walter Hagen	United States
1963	Joe Graffis / Herb Graffis	United States / United States
1964	Clifford Roberts	United States
1965	Gene Sarazen	United States
1966	Robert Harlow	United States
1967	Max Elbin	United States
1968	Charles Bartlett	United States
1969	Arnold Palmer	United States
1970	Roberto De Vicenzo	Argentina
1971	Lincoln Werden	United States

1972	Leo Fraser	United States
1973	Ben Hogan	United States
1974	Byron Nelson	United States
1975	Gary Player	South Africa
1976	Herbert Warren Wind	United States
1977	Mark Cox	United States
1978	Jack Nicklaus	United States
1979	Jim Gaquin	United States
1980	Jack Tuthill	United States
1981	Robert Trent Jones Sr.	United States
1982	Chi Chi Rodriguez	Puerto Rico
1983	Bill Campbell	United States
1984	Sam Snead	United States
1985	Lee Trevino	United States
1986	Kathy Whitworth	United States
1987	Frank Hannigan	United States
1988	Roger Barry	United States
1989	Ben Crenshaw	United States
1990	P. J. Boatwright Jr.	United States
1991	Tom Watson	United States
1992	Deane Beman	United States
1993	Harvey Penick	United States
1994	Peggy Kirk Bell	United States
1995	Joseph Jemsek	United States
1996	Bob Green	United States
1997	Peter Dobereiner	England
1998	Dick Taylor	United States
1999	Judy Rankin	United States
2000	Nancy Lopez	United States
2001	Karsten Solheim	United States
2002	Judy Bell	United States
2003	Dave Anderson	United States
2004	Mark McCormack	United States
2005	Dan Jenkins	United States
2006	Frank “Sandy” Tatum	United States
2007	The Harmon Family	United States

2008	Louise Suggs	United States
2009	Furman Bisher	United States

Ben Hogan Award (Golf Writers' Association of America)

1954	Babe Zaharias	United States
1955	Ed Furgol	United States
1956	Dwight D. Eisenhower	United States
1957	Clint Russell	United States
1958	Dale Bourisseau	United States
1959	Charley Boswell	United States
1960	Skip Alexander	United States
1961	Horton Smith	United States
1962	Jimmy Nichols	United States
1963	Bobby Nichols	United States
1964	Bob Morgan	United States
1965	Ernest Jones	United States
1966	Ken Venturi	United States
1967	Warren Pease	United States
1968	Shirley Englehorn	United States
1969	Curtis Person Sr.	United States
1970	Joe Lazaro	United States
1971	Larry Hinson	United States
1972	Ruth Jessen	United States
1973	Gene Littler	United States
1974	Gay Brewer	United States
1975	Patty Berg	United States
1976	Paul Hahn	United States
1977	Des Sullivan	United States
1978	Dennis Walters	United States
1979	John Mahaffey	United States
1980	Lee Trevino	United States
1981	Kathy Linney	United States
1982	Al Geiberger	United States
1983	Calvin Peete	United States
1984	Jay Sigel	United States

1985	Rod Funseth	United States
1986	Fuzzy Zoeller	United States
1987	Charles Owens	United States
1988	Pat Browne	United States
1989	Sally Little	South Africa / United States
1990	Linda Craft	United States
1991	Pat Bradley	United States
1992	Jim Nelford	United States
1993	Shelley Hamlin	United States
1994	Jim Ferree	United States
1995	Paul Azinger	United States
1996	Bob Murphy	United States
1997	Steve Jones	United States
1998	Terry-Jo Myers	United States
1999	Casey Martin	United States
2000	José María Olazábal	Spain
2001	Robert Allenby	Australia
2002	Scott Verplank	United States
2003	Jeff Julian	United States
2004	Bruce Edwards	United States
2005	Hubert Green	United States
2006	Bart Bryant	United States
2007	Judy Rankin	United States
2008	Denis Watson	Zimbabwe
2009	Erik Compton	United States

PGA of America Awards Professional of the Year

1955	Bill Gordon	Tam O'Shanter Country Club, Chicago, Illinois
1956	Harry Shepard	Mark Twain Community Golf Club, Elmira, New York
1957	Dugan Aycock	Lexington Country Club, Lexington, North Carolina
1958	Harry Pezzullo	Mission Hills Golf Club, Northbrook, Illinois

1959	Eddie Duino	San Jose Country Club, San Jose, California
1960	Warren Orlick	Tam O'Shanter Country Club, Orchard Lake, Michigan
1961	Don Padgett	Green Hills Country Club, Selma, Indiana
1962	Tom Lo Presti	Haggin Oaks Golf Club, Sacramento, California
1963	Bruce Herd	Flossmoor Country Club, Flossmoor, Illinois
1964	Lyle Wehrman	Merced Golf & Country Club, Merced, California
1965	Hubby Habjan	Onwentsia Club, Lake Forest, Illinois
1966	Bill Strausbaugh Jr.	Turf Valley Country Club, Ellicott City, Maryland
1967	Ernie Vossler	Quail Creek Country Club, Oklahoma City, Oklahoma
1968	Hardy Loudermilk	Oak Hills Country Club, San Antonio, Texas
1969	A. Highboard Smith	Arnold Center Country Club, Tullahoma, Tennessee
1969	Wally Mund	Midland Hills Country Club, St. Paul, Minnesota
1970	Grady Shumate	Tanglewood Golf Club, Clemmons, North Carolina
1971	Ross Collins	Dallas Athletic Club, Dallas, Texas
1972	Howard Morrette	Twin Lakes Country Club, Kent, Ohio
1973	Warren Smith	Cherry Hills Country Club, Englewood, Colorado
1974	Paul Harney	Paul Harney's Golf Club, Hatchville, Massachusetts
1975	Walker Inman Jr.	Scioto Country Club, Columbus, Ohio
1976	Ron Letellier	Cold Spring Harbor, New York
1977	Don Soper	Royal Oak Golf Club, Royal Oak, Michigan
1978	Walter Lowell	Canton Public Golf Club, Canton, Connecticut

1979	Gary Ellis	Pittsburgh Field Club, Pittsburgh, Pennsylvania
1980	Stan Thirsk	Kansas City Country Club, Shawnee Mission, Kan
1981	John Gerring	Atlanta Country Club, Marietta, Georgia
1982	Bob Popp	Omaha Country Club, Omaha, Nebraska
1983	Ken Lindsay	Colonial Country Club, Jackson, Mississippi
1984	Jerry Mowlds	Columbia-Edgewater Country Club, Portland, Oregon
1985	Jerry Cozby	Hillcrest Country Club, Bartlesville, Oklahoma
1986	David Ogilvie	Flossmoor Country Club, Flossmoor, Illinois
1987	Bob Ford	Oakmont Country Club, Oakmont, Pennsylvania
1988	Hank Majewski	Wakefield Valley Golf Club, Westminister, Maryland
1989	Tom Addis III	Singing Hills Country Club, El Cajon, California
1990	Jim Albus	Piping Rock Club, Locust Valley, New York
1991	Joe Jemsek	Cog Hill Golf & Country Club, Lemont, Illinois
1992	Marty Kavanaugh II	Hamilton County Park District, Cincinnati, Ohio
1993	Don Kotnik	Toledo Country Club, Toledo, Ohio
1994	Dick Murphy	Peachtree Golf Club, Atlanta, Georgia
1995	David Price	Bent Tree Country Club, Dallas, Texas
1996	Randall Smith	Royal Oaks Country Club, Dallas, Texas
1997	Tom Sargent	Mesa Verde Country Club, Costa Mesa, California
1998	Ken Morton Sr.	Haggin Oaks Golf Complex, Sacramento, California

1999	Ed Hoard	Athens Country Club, Athens, Georgia
2000	Charles "Vic" Kline	Indian Tree Golf Club, Arvada, Colorado
2001	Tony Morosco	Weston Country Club, Weston, Mass
2002	Jock Olson	Interlachen Country Club, Edina, Minnesota
2003	Jim Brotherton Jr.	Old Overton Golf Club, Vestavia Hills, Alabama
2004	Craig Harmon	Oak Hill Country Club, Rochester, New York
2005	Bill Eschenbrenner	Lone Star Golf Club, El Paso, Texas
2006	Jim Manthis	University of Minnesota Les Bolstad Golf Course, Coon Rapids, Minnesota
2007	Brent Krause	Wynlakes Golf & Country Club, Montgomery, Alabama
2008	Jim Antkiewicz	The Club at Nevillewood, Nevillewood, Pennsylvania
2009	Jack Barber	Meridian Hills Country Club, Indianapolis, Indiana

Bill Strausbaugh Award

1979	Dale Mead	Del Rio Country Club, Modesto, California
1980	Mal McMullen	Kokomo Country Club, Kokomo, Indiana
1981	William Heald	Riverside Golf Club, North Riverside, Illinois
1982	Robert Smith	Wolferts Roost Country Club, Albany, New York
1983	Patrick Rielly	Annandale Golf Club, Pasadena, California
1984	Bill Eschenbrenner	El Paso Country Club, El Paso, Texas
1985	Roger Van Dyke	Flint Golf Club, Flint, Michigan
1986	Richard Churilla	Wheeling Country Club, Wheeling, West Virginia

1987	Richard Walker	Morris Park Country Club, South Bend, Indiana
1988	Earl Maurer	Onondaga Golf & Country Club, Fayetteville, New York
1989	Marty Kavanaugh II	Hamilton County Park District, Cincinnati, Ohio
1990	Ron Hoetmer	Overlake Golf & Country Club, Medina, Washington
1991	Michael Burke	Pass Christian Isles Golf Club, Pass Christian Isles, Mississippi
1992	William Munguia	Plantation Golf Club, Olive Branch, Mississippi
1993	John Poole	Chester Valley Golf Club, Malvern, Pennsylvania
1994	Kurt Sokolowski	Pinebrook Country Club, Weston, Massachusetts
1995	Ed Ibarguen	Duke University Golf Club, Durham, North Carolina
1996	William Mitchell	Innis Arden Golf Club, Old Grenwich, Connecticut
1997	Doug Ritter	Meadia Heights Country Club, Lancaster, Pennsylvania
1998	Tom Tetrault	Fall River Country Club, Fall River, Massachusetts
1999	William Heald	Riverside Golf Club, Riverside, Illinois
2000	Glenn Brown	Westwood Country Club, Vienna, Virginia
2001	Gary Reynolds	Hartford Golf Club, Hartford, Connecticut
2002	Jerry Hogge	Methodist College, Fayetteville, North Carolina
2003	Steve Napoli	Wannamoisett Golf Club, Rumford, Rhode Island
2004	Paul Reinking	Kankakee Country Club, Kankakee, Illinois

2005	Tom Nieporte	Winged Foot Golf Club, Mamaroneck, New York
2006	Michael Harmon	Secession Golf Course, Beaufort, South Carolina
2007	Michael Doctor	Skaneateles Country Club, Skaneateles, New York
2008	Clayton Cole	Cherry Hills Country Club, Cherry Hills Village, Colorado
2009	Dennis Satyshur	Cave's Valley Country Club, Owings Mills, Maryland

Horton Smith Award

1965	Emil Beck	Black River Country Club, Port Huron, Michigan
1966	Gene Mason	Columbia-Edgewater Country Club, Portland, Oregon
1967	Donald Fischesser	Evansville Country Club, Evansville, Indiana
1968	R. William Clarke	Hillendale Country Club, Phoenix, Maryland
1969	Paul Hahn	Country Club of Miami, Miami, Florida
1970	Joe Walser	Oklahoma City Country Club, Oklahoma City, Oklahoma
1971	Irvin Schloss	Dunedin, Florida
1972	John Budd	New Port Richey, Florida
1973	George Aulbach	Pecan Valley Country Club, San Antonio, Texas
1974	Bill Hardy	Chevy Chase Club, Chevy Chase, Maryland
1975	John Henrich	Elma Meadows Golf Club, Elma, New York
1976	Jim Bailey	Adams Park Golf Course, Brighton, Colorado
1977	Paul Runyan	Green Gables Country Club, Denver, Colorado

1978	Andy Nusbaum	Siwanoy Country Club, Bronxville, New York
1979	Howard Smith	Riverside Golf Club, Diamond Bar, California
1980	Dale Mead	Del Rio Golf & Country Club, Modesto, California
1981	Tom Addis III	Singing Hills Country Club, El Cajon, California
1982	Kent Cayce	Evansville Country Club, Evansville, Indiana
1983	Bill Strausbaugh Jr.	Columbia Country Club, Chevy Chase, Maryland
1984	Don Essig III	The Hoosier Links, New Palestine, Indiana
1985	Larry Startzel	Country Club of Lansing, Lansing,, Michigan
1986	Mark Darnell	West Lake Country Club, Augusta, Georgia
1987	Ken Lindsay	Colonial Country Club, Jackson, Mississippi
1988	Guy Wimberly	Arroyo Del Oso Golf Club, Albuquerque, New Mexico
1989	Verne Perry	Cedars Golf Club, Brush Prairie, Washington
1990	Mike Hebron	Smithtown Landing Country Club, St. James, New York
1991	Joe Terry	Gulf Shores Golf Club, Gulf Shores, Alabama
1992	Conrad Rehling	Univ. of Alabama Golf Club, Tuscaloosa, Alabama
1993	Rick Burton	Alamance Country Club, Burlington, North Carolina
1994	Bill Eschenbrenner	El Paso Country Club, El Paso, Texas
1995	Ken Morton Sr.	Haggin Oaks Golf Club, Sacramento, California

1996	Ed Hoard	Athens Country Club, Athens, Georgia
1997	Warren "Stoney" Brown	Crane Creek Country Club, Boise, Idaho
1998	Ed Ibarguen	Duke University Golf Club, Durham, North Carolina
1999	Coleman Plecker	Manor Country Club, Rockville, Maryland
2000	David Normand Jr.	Indian Hills Golf Club, Murfreesboro, Tennessee
2001	Paul Bergen	The Legends Club of Tennessee, Franklin, Tennessee
2002	Brent Krause	Wynlakes Golf & Country Club, Montgomery, Alabama
2003	Ray Cutright	Idle Hour Golf Club, Macon, Georgia
2004	Ralph Bernhisel	Phoenix Country Club, Phoenix, Arizona
2005	Warren Bottke	Abacoa Golf Club, Jupiter, Florida
2006	Tom Tatnall	Tatnall Association Golf Course, Ridgeland, Mississippi
2007	Thomas Carpus	Kennett Square Golf & Country Club, Kennett Square, Pennsylvania
2008	Mark Wilson	Watermark Country Club, Grand Rapids, Michigan
2009	Derek Hardy	Talega Country Club, Santa Ana, California

LPGA Teaching Division Awards Professional of the Year

1980	Nancy Gammon	United States
1981	Peggy Kirk Bell	United States
1982	Nell Frewin	United States
1983	Lorraine Klippel	United States
1984	Mary Dagraedt	United States
1985	Bobbie Stewart	United States

1986	Margo Walden	United States
1987	Becky Sauers	United States
1988	Kathy Murphy	United States
1989	Pat Lange	United States
1990	Chris Burkhart	United States
1991	Paula Wagasky	United States
1992	Lorraine Klippel	United States
1993	Sue Fiscoe	United States
1994	Nancy Bunton	United States
1995	Pam Phipps	United States
1996	Marion Walker	United States
1997	Kathy Wake	United States
1998	Jane Broderick	United States
1999	Sandra Eriksson	United States
2000	Cathy Jo Johnson	United States
2001	Nancy Henderson	United States
2002	Debbie O'Connell	United States
2003	Dawne Kortgaard / Lisa Masters	United States / United States
2004	Holly Juergens	United States
2005	Susan Roll	United States
2006	Janet Phillips	United States
2007	J. Kristy Vik	United States
2008	Donna White	United States
2009	Linda Nevatt	United States

Coach of the Year

1981	Mary Dagraedt	Miami-Dade Community College, Miami, Florida
1982	Ann Casey Johnstone	Stephens College, Columbia, Missouri
1983	Barbara Smith	Longwood College, Farmville, Virginia
1984	Patricia Weis	University of Texas, Austin, Texas
1985	Diane Thomason	University of Iowa, Iowa City, Iowa

1986	Linda Vollstedt	Arizona State University, Tempe, Arizona
1987	Mary Beth Nienhaus	Appleton West High School, Appleton, Wisconsin
1988	Jackie Steinmann	University of California, Los Angeles (UCLA), Los Angeles, California
1989	Barbara Smith	Longwood College, Farmville, Virginia
1990	Cathy Bright	University of Southern California, Los Angeles, California
1991	Carol Ludvigson	University of Oklahoma, Norman, Oklahoma
1992	Iris Schneider	Rollins College, Winter Park, Florida
1993	Linda Vollstedt	Arizona State University, Tempe, Arizona
1994	Sarah Hindi	University of New Mexico, Albuquerque, New Mexico
1995	Mary Beth McGirr	University of North Carolina, Greensboro (UNC-G), Greensboro, North Carolina
1996	Beans Kelly	University of Georgia, Athens, Georgia
1997	Debby King	University of Memphis, Memphis, Tennessee
1998	Jackie Booth	University of New Mexico, Albuquerque, New Mexico
1999	Kathleen Teichert	University of Michigan, Ann Arbor, Michigan
2000	Nancy Lewis	San Jose State University, San Jose, California
2001	Dianne Dailey	Wake Forest University, Winston-Salem, North Carolina
2002	Jackie Booth	University of New Mexico, Albuquerque, New Mexico
2003	Nancy McDaniel	University of California, Berkeley, California

2004	Sally Austin	University of North Carolina, Chapel Hill, North Carolina
2005	Shelly Haywood	University of Arizona, Tuscon, Arizona
2006	Janet Bolle-Carl	University of Cincinnati, Cincinnati, Ohio
2007	Maria Lopez	Embry Riddle Aeronautical University, Daytona Beach, Florida
2008	Michelle Melia	Fairleigh Dickinson University, Teaneck, New Jersey
2009	Kelley Hester	University of Georgia, Athens, Georgia

Teacher of the Year

1958	Helen Dettweiler	United States
1959	Shirley Spork	United States
1960	Barbara Rotvig	United States
1961	Peggy Kirk Bell	United States
1962	Ellen Griffin	United States
1963	Vonnie Colby	United States
1964	Sally Doyle	United States
1965	Goldie Bateson	United States
1966	Ann Casey Johnstone	United States
1967	Jackie Pung	United States
1968	Gloria Fecht	United States
1969	JoAnne Winter	United States
1970	Gloria Armstrong	United States
1971	Jeanette Rector	United States
1972	Lee Spencer	United States
1973	Penny Zavichas	United States
1974	Mary Dagraedt	United States
1975	Carol Johnson	United States
1976	Marge Burns	United States
1977	Dr. DeDe Owens	United States
1978	Shirley Englehorn	United States
1979	Bobbie Ripley	United States

1980	Betty Dodd	United States
1981	Jane Read	United States
1982	Barbara Romack	United States
1983	Rina Ritson	United States
1984	Shirley Spork	United States
1985	Annette Thompson	United States
1986	Barbara Crawford-O'Brien	United States
1987	Linda Craft	United States
1988	Judy Whitehouse	United States
1989	Sharon Miller	United States
1990	Dana Rader	United States
1991	Dr. Betsy Clark	United States
1992	Lynn Marriott	United States
1993	Dr. DeDe Owens	United States
1994	Jane Frost	United States
1995	Kay McMahon	United States
1996	Gale Peterson	United States
1997	Diane McHeffey	United States
1998	Carol Preisinger	United States
1999	Amy Fox	United States
2000	Nancy Quarcelino	United States
2001	Kathy Murphy	United States
2002	Krista Dunton	United States
2003	Nancy Bender	United States
2004	Rosey Bartlett	United States
2005	Marie Claire De Bartoli	United States
2006	Cheryl Anderson	United States
2007	Teresa Zamboni	United States
2008	Karen Palacios-Jansen	United States
2009	Rita Reasons	United States

Ellen Griffin Rolex Award

1989	Peggy Kirk Bell	United States
1990	Linda Craft	United States
1991	Shirley Englehorn	United States
1992	Harvey Penick	United States

1993	Goldie Bateson	United States
1994	Carol Clark Johnson	United States
1995	Joanne Winter	United States
1996	Ann Casey Johnstone	United States
1997	Dr. DeDe Owens	United States
1998	Shirley Spork	United States
1999	Betty Hicks	United States
2000	Dr. Gary Wiren	United States
2001	Penny Zavichas	United States
2002	Annette Thompson	United States
2003	Dr. Barbara Smith	United States
2004	Marge Burns	United States
2005	Pat Lange	United States
2006	Donna White	United States
2007	Betsy Cullen	United States
2008	Lynn Marriott	United States
2009	Kay McMahon	United States

USGA Presidents

1894–1896	Theodore A. Havemeyer	Newport Golf Club	Newport, Rhode Island
1897–1898	Laurence Curtis	The Country Club	Brookline, Massachusetts
1899–1900	W. B. Thomas	The Country Club	Brookline, Massachusetts
1901–1902	R. H. Robertson	Shinnecock Hills Golf Club	Southampton, New York
1903–1904	G. Herbert Windeler	The Country Club	Brookline, Massachusetts
1905–1906	Ransom H. Thomas	Morris County Golf Club	Convent Station, New Jersey
1907–1908	Daniel Chauncey	Garden City Golf Club	Garden City, New York
1909–1910	Herbert Jaques	The Country Club	Brookline, Massachusetts

1911–1912	Silas H. Strawn	Glen View Club	Golf, Illinois
1913–1914	Robert C. Watson	National Golf Links of America	Southampton, New York
1915–1916	Frank L. Woodward	Denver Country Club	Denver, Colorado
1917	Howard W. Perrin	Merion Cricket Club	Haverford, Pennsylvania
1918–1919	Frederick S. Wheeler	Apawamis Club	Rye, New York
1920	George H. Walker	National Golf Links of America	Southampton, New York
1921	Howard F. Whitney	Nassau Country Club	Glen Cove, New York
1922–1923	J. Frederick Byers	Allegheny Country Club	Sewickley, Pennsylvania
1924–1925	Wynant D. Vanderpool	Morris County Golf Club	Convent Station, New Jersey
1926–1927	William C. Fownes Jr.	Oakmont Country Club	Oakmont, Pennsylvania
1928	Melvin A. Traylor	Glen View Club	Golf, Illinois
1929–1930	Findlay S. Douglas	Apawamis Club	Rye, New York
1931–1932	Herbert H. Ramsay	National Golf Links of America	Southampton, New York
1933–1934	Herbert Jaques	The Country Club	Brookline, Massachusetts
1935	Prescott S. Bush	Round Hill Club	Greenwich, Connecticut
1936–1937	John G. Jackson	Deepdale Golf Club	Great Neck, New York
1938–1939	Archibald M. Reid	St. Andrew's Golf Club	Hastings-on-Hudson, New York

1940–1941	Harold W. Pierce	The Country Club	Brookline, Massachusetts
1942–1943	George W. Blossom Jr.	Onwentsia Club	Lake Forest, Illinois
1944–1945	Morton G. Bogue	Deepdale Golf Club	Great Neck, New York
1946–1947	Charles W. Littlefield	Montclair Golf Club	Montclair, New Jersey
1948–1949	Fielding Wallace	Augusta National Golf Club	Augusta, Georgia
1950–1951	James D. Standish Jr.	Country Club of Detroit	Gross Pointe Farms, Michigan
1952–1953	Totton P. Heffelfinger	Minikahda Club	Minneapolis, Minnesota
1954–1955	Isaac B. Grainger	Montclair Golf Club	Montclair, New Jersey
1956–1957	Richard S. Tufts	Pinehurst Country Club	Pinehurst, North Carolina
1958–1959	John D. Ames	Onwentsia Club	Lake Forest, Illinois
1960–1961	John G. Clock	Virginia Country Club	Long Beach, California
1962–1963	John M. Winters Jr.	Southern Hills Country Club	Tulsa, Oklahoma
1964–1965	Clarence W. Benedict	Winged Foot Golf Club	Mamaroneck, New York
1966–1967	William Ward Foshay	Round Hill Club	Greenwich, Connecticut
1968–1969	Hord W. Hardin	Bellerive Country Club	Creve Coeur, Missouri
1970–1971	Philip H. Strubing	Sunnybrook Golf Club	Plymouth Meeting, Pennsylvania
1972–1973	Lynford Lardner Jr.	Milwaukee Country Club,	Milwaukee, Wisconsin

1974–1975	Harton S. Semple	Sewickley Heights Golf Club	Sewickley, Pennsylvania
1976–1977	Harry W. Easterly Jr.	Country Club of Virginia	Richmond, Virginia
1978–1979	Frank D. Tatum Jr.	San Francisco Golf Club	San Francisco, California
1980–1981	Will F. Nicholson Jr.	Denver Country Club	Denver, Colorado
1982–1983	William C. Campbell	Guyan Golf & Country Club	Huntington, West Virginia
1984–1985	James R. Hand	Sleepy Hollow Country Club	Scarborough-on-Hudson, New York
1986–1987	William J. Williams Jr.	Siwanoy Country Club	Bronxville, New York
1988–1989	William C. Battle	Farmington Country Club	Charlottesville, Virginia
1990–1991	C. Grant Spaeth	San Francisco Golf Club	San Francisco, California
1992–1993	Stuart F. Bloch	Wheeling Country Club	Wheeling, West Virginia
1994–1995	Reg Murphy	Caves Valley Golf Club	Owings Mills, Maryland
1996–1997	Judy Bell	Broadmoor Golf Club	Colorado Springs, Colo.
1998–1999	F. Morgan Taylor Jr.	Seminole Golf Club	Juno Beach, Florida
2000–2001	Trey Holland	Meridian Hills Country Club	Indianapolis, Indiana
2002–2003	Reed K. Mackenzie	Hazeltine National Golf Club	Chaska, Minnesota
2004–2005	Fred S. Ridley	Old Memorial Golf Club	Tampa, Florida
2006–2007	Walter Driver Jr.	Peachtree Golf Club	Atlanta, Georgia

2008–2009	James F. Vernon	Lakeside Golf Club	Burbank, California
2010	James B. Hyler Jr.	Old Chatham Golf Club	Durham, North Carolina

Captains of the Royal and Ancient

Year	Date of Induction	Captain
1754	14 May 1754	William Landale
1755	1 October 1755	Thomas Boswall
1756	6 October 1756	Alexander Duncan
1758	10 May 1758	Hugh Fraser
1759	9 May 1759	Sir James Carnegie
1761	11 September 1761	Alexander Duncan
1762	22 September 1762	Hugh Fraser
1763	15 October 1763	Sir Henry Seton
1764	3 October 1764	William St. Clair
1765	2 October 1765	The Honourable Francis Charteris
1766	24 October 1766	William St. Clair
1767	3 September 1767	James Durham
1768	22 September 1768	William St. Clair
1769	5 October 1769	Dr. George Forrest
1770	11 October 1770	Henry Bethune
1771	3 October 1771	Ninian Imrie
1772	29 October 1772	James Morrison
1773	7 October 1773	Patrick Rigg
1774	6 October 1774	John Hay
1775	4 October 1775	The Earl of Balcarres
1776	2 October 1776	Roger Ayton
1777	8 October 1777	John Balfour
1778	7 October 1778	Walter Boswell
1779	6 October 1779	James Morrison
1780	4 October 1780	James Durham
1781	3 October 1781	Alexander Duncan
1782	2 October 1782	The Earl of Balcarres
1783	8 October 1783	Major William Morrison
1784	6 October 1784	Robert Low

1785	5 October 1785	Captain John Cheape
1786	4 October 1786	Colonel John Thomson
1787	3 October 1787	James Cheape
1788	8 October 1788	Captain James Dalrymple
1789	7 October 1789	Captain William Nairne
1790	6 October 1790	Patrick Rigg
1791	5 October 1791	Alexander Duncan
1792	3 October 1792	The Earl of Crawford
1793	2 October 1793	John Patullo
1794	8 October 1794	Captain Alexander Aytone
1795	7 October 1795	Alexander Anderson
1796	5 October 1796	James Morrison
1797	4 October 1797	Thomas Erskine
1798	3 October 1798	Methven Erskine
1799	2 October 1799	John Dalyell
1800	1 October 1800	Robert Patullo
1801	7 October 1801	George Cheape
1802	6 October 1802	Hugh Cleghorn
1803	5 October 1803	George Paterson
1804	3 October 1804	John Anstruther Thomson
1805	2 October 1805	Colonel David Dewar
1806	1 October 1806	William Dalgleish
1807	7 October 1807	General George Moncrieff
1808	5 October 1808	Alexander Guthrie
1809	4 October 1809	James Home Rigg
1810	3 October 1810	John Maitland
1811	2 October 1811	Thomas Bruce
1812	7 October 1812	Robert Gillespie Smyth
1813	6 October 1813	General James Durham
1814	5 October 1814	George Cheape
1815	11 October 1815	John Makgill
1816	2 October 1816	Sir John Anstruther
1817	1 October 1817	David Moncrieff
1818	30 September 1818	John Murray
1819	22 September 1819	Robert Bruce
1820	11 October 1820	David, Earl of Leven & Melville

1821	26 September 1821	Colonel Alexander Bethune
1822	9 October 1822	Alexander Binny
1823	29 October 1823	John Whyte Melville
1824	13 October 1824	Lieutenant-Colonel James Lindesay
1825	14 September 1825	Sir Ralph Anstruther
1826	11 October 1826	Charles Maitland Christie
1827	17 October 1827	Captain James Cheape
1828	29 October 1828	John Dalyell
1829	30 September 1829	Sir David Erskine
1830	22 September 1830	Francis Balfour
1831	21 September 1831	James Stuart Oliphant
1832	10 October 1832	Charles Halkett Craigie
1833	25 September 1833	Major Robert Anstruther
1834	24 September 1834	Lieutenant-General Sir John Oswald
1835	16 September 1835	Major John Murray Bleshes
1836	12 October 1836	Major John Murray Belshes
1837	20 September 1837	Captain George Moncrieff
1838	3 October 1838	Onesiphorous Tyndall Bruce
1839	9 October 1839	John Grant
1840	7 October 1840	Henry Stewart
1841	13 October 1841	David Gilliespie
1842	12 October 1842	John Balfour
1843	18 October 1843	Sir David Baird
1844	2 October 1844	Sir Thomas Moncrieffe
1845	8 October 1845	George Makgill
1846	14 October 1846	Robert Lindsay
1847	20 October 1847	Frederick L. S. Wedderburn
1848	18 October 1848	James Wolfe Murray
1849	24 October 1849	James T. Oswald
1850	16 October 1850	James O. Fairlie
1851	15 October 1851	George Whyte Melville
1852	20 October 1852	Edward James Jackson
1853	12 October 1853	Earl of Eglinton and Winton
1854	18 October 1854	James Hay Erskine Wemyss
1855	17 October 1855	Lord Loughborough
1856	22 October 1856	Sir Hugh Lyon Playfair

1857	30 September 1857	Robert Cathcart
1858	29 September 1858	John Anstruther Thomson
1859	28 September 1859	Sir David Baird
1860	3 October 1860	Sir Thomas Erskine
1861	2 October 1861	George Dempster
1862	1 October 1862	Earl of Dalhousie
1863	30 September 1863	HRH The Prince of Wales
1864	28 September 1864	Viscount Dupplin
1865	27 September 1865	Lieutenant-General Sir John Low
1866	3 October 1866	Sir Robert Anstruther
1867	2 October 1867	Sir John Trotter Bethune
1868	7 October 1868	Sir Coutts Lindsay
1869	29 September 1869	Alexander Bethune
1870	28 September 1870	Robert Hay
1871	27 September 1871	John Blackwood
1872	2 October 1872	Alexander Kinloch
1873	1 October 1873	William Baille Skene
1874	30 September 1874	William Patrick Adam
1875	29 September 1875	The Honourable Charles Carnegie
1876	27 September 1876	HRH Prince Leopold
1877	26 September 1877	John Inglis
1878	25 September 1878	The Honourable George Waldegrave Leslie
1879	24 September 1879	Earl of Elgin and Kincardine
1880	29 September 1880	Earl of Glasgow
1881	28 September 1881	Captain Randle Jackson
1882	27 September 1882	The Honourable Robert Preston Bruce
1884	24 September 1884	George Glennie
1885	30 September 1885	Earl of Aberdeen
1886	29 September 1886	Captain Daniel Shaw Stewart
1887	28 September 1887	John Hay Athole Macdonald
1888	26 September 1888	Captain George Clerk Cheape
1889	25 September 1889	Sir Robert Anstruther Dalyell
1890	24 September 1890	John Henry Baxter
1891	30 September 1891	Sir Ralph Anstruther
1892	28 September 1892	Andrew Graham Murray

1893	27 September 1893	James Ogilvy R. Fairlie
1894	26 September 1894	The Right Honourable Arthur James Balfour, MP
1895	25 September 1895	John Oswald
1896	30 September 1896	James George Baird Hay
1897	29 September 1897	Henry S. Wedderburn
1898	28 September 1898	William John Mure
1899	27 September 1899	The Honourable Thomas Cochrane
1900	26 September 1900	Lord Justice General Blair Balfour
1901	25 September 1901	Walter T. J. S. Steuart Fothringham
1902	24 September 1902	Sir John Gilmour
1903	30 September 1903	Sir Robert Finlay
1904	28 September 1904	Ralph Dalyell
1905	27 September 1905	Colonel David Alexander Kinloch
1906	26 September 1906	Leslie Balfour Melville
1907	25 September 1907	The Right Honourable Earl of Stair
1908	30 September 1908	Horace G. Hutchinson
1909	29 September 1909	The Right Honourable Lord Kinross
1910	28 September 1910	Samuel Mure Fergusson
1911	27 September 1911	Sir Ludovic James Grant
1912	25 September 1912	Walter Edwin Fairlie
1913	24 September 1913	Henry William Forster
1919	24 September 1919	Lieutenant-Colonel Henry Alexander Bethune
1920	29 September 1920	Field Marshal Earl Haig
1921	28 September 1921	Robert Tuite Boothby
1922	27 September 1922	HRH The Prince of Wales
1923	25 September 1923	Colonel Sir Alexander Sprot
1924	24 September 1924	James Younger
1925	30 September 1925	Edward B. H. Blackwell
1926	29 September 1926	Lieutenant-Colonel Sir John Gilmour
1927	28 September 1927	James T. Inglis
1928	26 September 1928	Angus V. Hambro
1929	25 September 1929	Colonel Philip G. M. Skene
1930	24 September 1930	HRH The Duke of York
1931	30 September 1931	John William Beaumont Pease

1932	28 September 1932	Earl of Lindsay
1933	27 September 1933	Sir Ernley R. H. Blackwell
1934	26 September 1934	Bernard Darwin
1935	25 September 1935	William Norman Boase
1936	30 September 1936	Sir John Simon
1937	29 September 1937	HRH The Duke of Kent
1938	28 September 1938	Colonel Henry Holmes Sutherland
1946	25 September 1946	Roger Henry Wethered
1947	17 September 1947	Lord Teviot of Burghclere
1948	22 September 1948	Cyril James Hastings Tolley
1949	21 September 1949	Lord Balfour of Burleigh
1950	20 September 1950	Sir George Cunningham
1951	19 September 1951	Francis DeSales Ouimet
1952	17 September 1952	Lord Brabazon of Tara
1953	16 September 1953	Lieutenant-Colonel John Inglis
1954	22 September 1954	Viscount Bruce of Melbourne
1955	21 September 1955	Sir Charles Glen McAndrew
1956	19 September 1956	Dr. Harold Gardiner-Hill
1957	18 September 1957	John Beaumont Beck
1958	17 September 1958	Lord of Henryton Morton
1959	16 September 1959	Henry Hutchison Turcan
1960	21 September 1960	Lord Cohen
1961	20 September 1961	William Tweddell
1962	19 September 1962	Sir William Giles Newsom Walker
1963	18 September 1963	Thomas Francis Blackwell
1964	16 September 1964	George Alec Hill
1965	22 September 1965	James Lockhart Mitchell
1966	21 September 1966	John Geoffrey Blackwell
1967	20 September 1967	Major Thomas Steuart Fothringham
1968	6 May 1968	Gerald Hugh Micklem
1969	17 September 1969	The Right Honourable William Stephen Ian Whitelaw
1970	17 September 1970	George William Mackie
1971	23 September 1971	Alan Darlington Cave
1972	21 September 1972	Sir Iain Maxwell Stewart
1973	20 September 1973	Donald Neil Vaughan Smith

1974	19 September 1974	Sir John Carmichael
1975	18 September 1975	Joseph Charles Dey
1976	23 September 1976	Thomas Cockayne Harvey
1977	22 September 1977	Wilbur Montgomery Muirhead
1978	21 September 1978	Major David A. Blair
1979	20 September 1979	James Stewart Lawson
1980	18 September 1980	Walter Ronald Alexander
1981	17 September 1981	Sir James Hugh, KCVO CBE TD Neill
1982	23 September 1982	Peter Farquhar Gardiner-Hill
1983	22 September 1983	John George Salvesen
1984	20 September 1984	John Edward Behrend
1985	19 September 1985	Hector Colin Maclaine
1986	18 September 1986	Sir Robin Cater
1987	17 September 1987	William Cammack Campbell
1988	22 September 1988	Alexander Sinclair
1989	21 September 1989	Michael Francis Attenborough
1990	20 September 1990	Dr. David Max Marsh
1991	19 September 1991	Joseph B. Carr
1992	17 September 1992	The Honourable John Martin Lindesay-Bethune
1993	23 September 1993	Hugh, The Right Honourable Lord Griffiths, MC
1994	22 September 1994	Gordon Boyd Buchanan Jeffrey
1995	21 September 1995	Ivan Henry McCaw
1996	19 September 1996	Thomas Harvey Douglas
1997	18 September 1997	Dr. Alexander MacKechnie Mathewson, MD, ChB, MRCGP, DL
1998	17 September 1998	John Charles Beharrell
1999	16 September 1999	Sir Michael F. Bonallack, OBE
2000	21 September 2000	William John Uzielli
2001	20 September 2001	Graeme Maxwell Simmers, CBE
2002	19 September 2002	John Whitmore
2003	18 September 2003	HRH The Duke of York, KG, KCVO, ADC
2004	23 September 2004	Arthur Richard Cole-Hamilton, CBE
2005	22 September 2005	The Right Honourable Sir Thomas K. N. Z. M Gault

2006	21 September 2006	Michael Stanley Randle Lunt
2007	20 September 2007	David James Harrison
2008	18 September 2008	Hamish Martin Johnson Ritchie
2009	24 September 2009	Colin Murray Brown

Donald Ross Award (American Society of Golf Course Architects)

1976	Robert Trent Jones	ASGCA, Founding Member of ASGCA
1977	Herbert Warren Wind	Golf Digest Columnist, Author
1978	Herb and Joe Graffis	Founders, National Golf Foundation
1979	Joe Dey	Former Executive Director of the USGA
1980	Gerald Micklem	Former Captain, Royal and Ancient
1981	James Rhodes	Governor of Ohio
1982	Geoffrey Cornish	ASGCA Golf Course Architect, Historian Fellow
1983	Al Radko Former	Director, USGA Green Section
1984	Dinah Shore	Sponsor of Women's Golf Tournaments
1985	Peter Dobereiner	London Observer Columnist, Author
1986	Deane Beman	PGA Tour Commissioner
1987	Charles Price	Golf Writer, Author
1988	Frank Hannigan	USGA Executive Director
1989	Dick Taylor	Editor, Golf World Magazine
1990	John Zoller	Former Executive Director, Northern California Golf Association
1991	Michael Bonallack	Secretary, Royal and Ancient
1992	Paul Fullmer	ASGCA Executive Secretary
1993	Brent Wadsworth	Golf Course Builder
1994	James Watson	Agronomist
1995	Pete Dye	ASGCA Fellow Golf Course Architect
1996	Ron Whitten	Golf Writer
1997	Gene Sarazen	Professional Golfer
1998	Judy Bell	President, USGA
1999	Arnold Palmer	ASGCA Professional Golfer Fellow

2000	Jaime Ortiz-Patiño	Owner / President, Valderrama Golf Club
2001	Jack Nicklaus	ASGCA Professional Golfer, Golf Course Architect
2002	Byron Nelson	Professional Golfer
2003	Bill Campbell	President, USGA; Captain, Royal & Ancient
2004	Thomas Cousins	Philanthropist, Urban Golf Developer
2005	John Singleton	Irrigation Pioneer
2006	Jim Awtrey	CEO, PGA of America
2007	Dr. Michael Hurdzan	Golf Course Architect, ASGCA
2008	George Peper	Golf Writer and Publisher
2009	Ron Dodson	Sustainable Golf Advocate

Golf Writers Trophy (British Golf Writers' Association)

1951	Max Faulkner
1952	Elizabeth Price
1953	Joe Carr
1954	Frances Stephens
1955	Ladies' Golf Union Junior Team (B. Bostock, captain)
1956	John Beharrell
1957	Dai Rees
1958	Harry Bradshaw
1959	Eric Brown
1960	Sir Stuart Goodwin
1961	Cdr. R. C. T. Roe
1962	Marley Spearman
1963	Michael Lunt
1964	Eisenhower Trophy Team (Joe Carr, captain)
1965	Gerald Micklem
1966	Ronnie Shade
1967	John Panton
1968	Michael Bonallack
1969	Tony Jacklin
1970	Tony Jacklin
1971	Walker Cup Team (Michael Bonallack, captain)
1972	Mickey Walker

1973	Peter Oosterhuis
1974	Peter Oosterhuis
1975	The Golf Foundation
1976	Eisenhower Trophy Team (S. Saddler, captain)
1977	Christy O'Connor Sr.
1978	Peter McEvoy
1979	Seve Ballesteros
1980	Sandy Lyle
1981	Bernhard Langer
1982	Gordon Brand Jr.
1983	Nick Faldo
1984	Seve Ballesteros
1985	Ryder Cup Team (Tony Jacklin, captain)
1986	Curtis Cup Team (Diane Bailey, captain)
1987	Ryder Cup Team (Tony Jacklin, captain)
1988	Sandy Lyle
1989	Walker Cup Team (Geoffrey Marks, captain)
1990	Nick Faldo
1991	Seve Ballesteros
1992	Solheim Cup Team (Mickey Walker, captain)
1993	Bernhard Langer
1994	Laura Davies
1995	Ryder Cup Team (Bernard Gallacher, captain)
1996	Colin Montgomerie
1997	Alison Nicholas
1998	Lee Westwood
1999	Sergio Garcia
2000	Lee Westwood
2001	Walker Cup Team (Peter McEvoy, captain)
2002	Ryder Cup Team (Sam Torrance, captain)
2003	Annika Sörenstam
2004	Ryder Cup Team (Bernhard Langer, captain)
2005	Annika Sörenstam
2006	Ryder Cup Team (Ian Woosnam, captain)
2007	Pádraig Harrington
2008	Pádraig Harrington
2009	Lee Westwood

Bibliography

It has been said that the volume of literature on any sport is inversely proportional to the size of the ball. Thus golf, with the smallest ball of any major ball game, has engendered a huge amount of literature. So much, in fact, that this bibliography needs to be separated into sections based on topics, which we have done below. This should not be considered an exhaustive list, although it is relatively comprehensive and certainly a good start for the interested reader. Those desiring a more complete bibliography of golf are referred to *The Game of Golf and the Printed Word: 1566–2005*, written by Richard Donovan and Rand Jerris, published by Castalio Press (Endicott, N.Y., 2006).

CONTENTS

History of Golf 726
Play of the Game 739
The Players 747
Competitions 766
Courses and Clubs 774
Golf and Country Club Histories 784
The Art of the Game 791
General Reference 792
Magazines 793
Websites 794
Research Libraries and Information Sources 795

HISTORY OF GOLF

General History

Alliss, Peter, ed. *Golf: A Way of Life*. London: Stanley Paul, 1987.

Astor, Gerald. *The PGA World Golf Hall of Fame Book*. New York: Simon and Schuster, 1991.

Barkow, Al, et al. *20th Century Golf Chronicle*. Lincolnwood, Ill.: Publications International, revised, 1998.

Barrett, Ted. *Golf: A History*. London: Carlton Books, 2005.

Browning, Robert H. K. *A History of Golf: The Royal and Ancient Game*. London: J. M. Dent, 1955.

Clark, Robert. *Golf: A Royal and Ancient Game*. Edinburgh: R. & R. Clark, 1875.

Concannon, Dale. *Golf, the Early Days: The Royal and Ancient Game from its Origins to 1939*. North Vancouver: Cavendish Books, 1995.

———. *Spitfire on the Fairways: And Other Unexpected Hazards of Golf in Wartime*. London: Arum Press, 2003.

Cook, Kevin, ed. *Sports Illustrated—The Golf Book*. New York: Sports Illustrated Books/Time, 2009.

Cotton, Henry. *Golf: A Pictorial History*. Glasgow: Collins, 1975.

———. *A History of Golf Illustrated*. Philadelphia, Pa.: J. B. Lippincott, 1975.

———. *The Picture Story of the Golf Game*. Manchester, England: World Distributors, 1965.

Dobereiner, Peter. *The Glorious World of Golf*. London: Hamlyn, 1973.

Elliott, Alan, and John Allen May. *The Golf Monthly Illustrated History of Golf*. London: Hamlyn, 1990.

Elliott, Bill. *The Sporting Life: Golf*. Devon, England: David & Charles, 1998.

Flannery, Michael, and Richard Leech. *Golf through the Ages: 600 Years of Golfing Art*. Fairfield, La.: Golf Links Press, 2004.

Gibson, Nevin. *A Pictorial History of Golf*. New York: A. S. Barnes, 2nd ed. rev., 1974.

Golf Digest. *Golf's Greatest Players, Courses and Voices: 50 Years of the Best*. New York: Golf Digest, 2000.

Green, Robert. *Golf: An Illustrated History of the Game*. London: Willow, 1987.

Grimsley, Will. *Golf: Its History, People and Events*. Englewood Cliffs, N.J.: Prentice Hall, 1966.

Hilton, Harold, and Garden G. Smith. *The Royal and Ancient Game of Golf*. London: Golf Illustrated, 1912.

Hutchinson, Horace Gordon. *Golf: The Badminton Library*. London: Longmans, Green, multiple editions, 1890–1911.

——. *The Book of Golf and Golfers*. London: Longmans, Green, 2nd ed. rev., 1899.

——. *Fifty Years of Golf*. London: Country Life, 1919.

Ishikawa, Hiroyuki. *A History of Golf*. Tokyo: MCR Company, 2001 (text in Japanese).

McGrath, Charles, and David McCormick. *The Ultimate Golf Book: A History and Celebration of the World's Greatest Game*. Boston: Houghton Mifflin, 2002.

Menzies, Gordon, ed. *The World of Golf*. London: BBC, 1982.

Peper, George. *Story of Golf*. New York: T.V. Books, 1999.

Platts, Mitchell. *Illustrated History of Golf*. New York: Gramercy Books, rev. ed., 2000.

Price, Charles. *The World of Golf: A Panorama of Six Centuries of the Game's History*. New York: Random House, 1962.

Scott, Tom. *The Story of Golf: From Its Origins to the Present Day*. London: Arthur Baker, 1972.

Sidorsky, Robert. *Golf 365 Days: A History*. New York: Harry N. Abrams, 2008.

Stanley, Louis T. *A History of Golf*. London: Weidenfeld and Nicolson, 1991.

Stirk, David. *Golf, History and Tradition 1500–1945*. Ludlow, England: Excellent Press, 1998.

Strege, John. *When War Played Through: Golf During WWII*. New York: Gotham Books, 2005.

Valerien, Harry. *Golf: Faszination Eines Weltsports*. Munich: Sudwest Verlag, 1989.

Wethered, Joyce, Roger Wethered, et al. *The Game of Golf: The Lonsdale Library*. London: Seeley Service, 1931.

Origins of the Game

Geddes, Olive M. *A Swing through Time: Golf in Scotland 1457–1743*. 2nd ed. Edinburgh: The National Library of Scotland, rev., 2007.

Hamilton, David. *Golf—Scotland's Game*. Kilmacolm, Scotland: The Partick Press, 1998.

Hawtree, Fred W. *Triple Bauge: Promenades in Medieval Golf*. Oxford, England: Cambuc Archives, 1996.

Johnston, Alastair J. *The Clapcott Papers*. Edinburgh: Privately printed, 1985.

Johnston, Alastair J., and James F. Johnston. *The Chronicles of Golf: 1457–1857*. Cleveland, Ohio: Alaistair J. Johnston, 1993.

Nijs, Geert, and Sara Nijs. *Choule: The Non-Royal But Most Ancient Game of Crosse*. Bourgogne, France: Privately printed, 2008.

Nolan, James. *Of Golf and Dukes and Princes: Early Golf in France*. Worcestershire, England: Grant Books, 1982.

Temmerman, Jacques. *Golf & Kolf: Seven Centuries of History*. Belgium: Martial & Snoeck, 1993.

Van Hengel, Steven J. H. *Early Golf*. 3rd ed. Vaduz, Liechtenstein: Strengholt, rev., 1990.

History of Golf in Africa

——. *Golfing in Southern Africa*. Cape Town: South African Golf, 1958.

Fall, Robert Geoffrey. *History of Golf at the Cape: In Which Is Also Treated the Origin of the Game of Golf, Golf Stories and a Register of S.A Clubs*. Cape Town: Argus, 1918.

Hooper, Richard W., ed. *The Game of Golf in East Africa*. Nairobi: W. Boyd, 1953.

O'Donnell, Paddy. *South Africa's Wonderful World of Golf*. Pretoria: Don Nelson, 1973.

Ward, Barry, and Tom McArthur. *Hassan II Trophy Silver Jubilee 1971–1996, Including a Moroccan Golfing Adventure*. Glasgow: Marrakesh Express, 1996.

History of Golf in Australasia

Australia

Creagh, John, editor. *Golden Years of Australian Golf*. Sydney: K. G. Murray, 1977.

Daley, Paul, and D. Scarletti. *The Sandbelt: Melbourne's Golfing Heaven*. Baronia, Australia: Plus Four Publishing, 2001.

De Groot, Colin, and Jim Webster. *Pro Golf, Out of the Rough: The Illustrated History of Professional Golf in Australia*. Cattai, Australia: Professional Golfers' Association of Australia, 1991.

Harding, Karen, ed. *Women's Golf Victoria: Celebrating 100 Years of Women's Golf*. Victoria, Australia: Harding Media Services, 2006.

Innes, David J. *The Story of Golf in New South Wales 1851–1987*. Darlinghurst, Australia: New South Wales Golf Association, 1988.

Mansfield, Garry. *A History of Golf in Victoria*. Elsternwick, Australia: Victorian Golf Association, 1987.

McLaren, Muir, ed. *The Australian Golfer's Handbook*. Various editions. Sydney, Australia: Langside Publishing, 1957–1980.

Perry, Phyllis. *From Green to Gold: The First Fifty Years of the Australian Ladies Golf Union*. 2nd ed. Australia: Australian Ladies Golf Union, rev., 1976.

Pollard, Jack. *Australian Golf: The Game and the Players*. North Ryde, Australia: Collins, 1990.

Richter, Bruce S. *Fifty Years and More: History of Brisbane District Golf Association, 1929–2000*. Brisbane: Brisbane District Golf Association, 2000.

———. *Links with the Past: History of the Queensland Golf Union 1914–1998*. Queensland, Australia: Privately printed, 1998.

Riddell, Gervase Carre. *Evolution of Golf in Victoria*. Victoria, Australia: Privately printed, 1982.

Saunders, Pauline. *Golfers to the Fore: Heritage and Records of South Australian Golf Clubs*. Adelaide: South Australian Ladies' Golf Union, 1988.

Scarth, John, ed. *The History of Golf in Australia*. Mollymook Beach, Australia: Privately printed, 2008.

Smith, Terry. *Australian Golf: The First 100 Years*. Sydney: Lester-Townsend, 1988.

———. *The Champions and the Courses They Played: Celebrating the Centenary of the Australian Open*. Sydney: Australian Golf Union, 2004.

———. *The Complete Book of Australian Golf*. 3rd ed. Sydney: ABC Enterprises, rev., 1988.

Soutar, Daniel C. *The Australian Golfer*. 2nd ed. Melbourne: E. W. Cole, rev., 1908.

Tressider, Phil. *Great Days of Australian Golf*. Bellevue Hill, Australia: Ironbark Press, 1990.

Wade, Colin A. *Golf Course Histories of the Lower South East of South Australia 1902–1995*. Naracoorte, Australia: Privately printed, 1995.

India

Wadhwaney, K. R. *The Romance of the Indian Open, 1964–2003*. New Delhi: Siddharth Publications, 2003.

Japan

Ito, Cho. "Golf in Japan." In *Transactions and Proceedings of the Japan Society* 24:55–62. London, 1927.

Japan Golf Association. *Japan Golf Association: 70 Year History*. Tokyo: Japan Golf Association, 1992 (text in Japanese).

Settsu, Mowa. *The History of Golf in Japan: 60 Years*. Tokyo: Baseball Magazine Company, 1977 (text in Japanese).

New Zealand

Hornabrook, John. *Golden Years of New Zealand Golf.* Christchurch: Whitcombe & Tombs, 1967.

Kelly, G. M. *Golf in New Zealand: A Centennial History*. Wellington: The New Zealand Golf Association, 1971.

History of Golf in Europe

Van Hengel, Stephen J. H., et al. *Colf, Kolf, Golf: Van Middeleeuws Volksspel Tot Moderne Sport*. Zutphen, Netherlands: Uitgeverij Terra, 1982.

Austria

Arnoldner, Christian. *Golf, the Royal and Ancient Game: Geschichte des Golfsports in Osterreich und den ehemalingen Kronlandern von 1901 bis zur Gegenwart*. Vienna: Christian Brandstatter, 2007.

Denmark

Dreyer, Frederik. *Golf i Denmark 1898–1945*. Copenhagen: Danish Golf Union, n.d.

France

Bocquet, Alain R. *Le Golf: Des Origines à Nos Jours*. Paris: Editions Hervas, 1988.

Jeanneau, Georges. *Le Golf en France: Quelques siècles d'histoire*. Saint-Laurent, France: Atlantica, 1999.

LaFaurie, Andre-Jean. *Le Golf, son histoire de 1304 à nos jours*. Paris: Jacques Grancher, 1988.

Nolan, James. *Of Golf and Dukes and Princes: Early Golf in France*. Droitwich, England: Grant Books, 1982.

Germany

Quanz, Dietrich, editor. *100 Jahre Golf in Deutschland*. Germany: Deutscher Golf Verband, 2007.

Great Britain

Cousins, Geoffrey. *Golf in Britain*. London: Routledge and Kegan Paul, 1975.
Darwin, Bernard. *Golf Between Two Wars*. London: Chatto and Windus, 1944.
Darwin, Bernard, et al. *A History of Golf in Britain*. London: Cassell, 1952.
Forgan, Robert. *The Golfer's Handbook, Including History of the Game, Hints to Beginners, the Feats of Champion Golfers, Lists of Leading Clubs and Their Office-Bearers, etc*. Cupar, Scotland: John Innes, 1881.
Foster, Harry. *Links along the Line: The Story of the Development of Golf between Liverpool and Southport*. Birkdale, England: The Birkdale and Ainsdale Historical Research Society, 1996.
Harris, Robert. *Sixty Years of Golf*. London: Batchworth, 1953.
Hopkins, John. *Golf in Wales: The Centenary 1895–1995*. Cwmbran, Wales: The Welsh Golfing Union, 1994.
Moran, Frank. *Golfer's Gallery*. 2nd ed. Edinburgh: Oliver and Boyd, rev., 1949.
Morrison, J. S. F. *Around Golf*. London: Arthur Baker, 1939.
Nalder, Ian. *Golf and the Railway Connection: A Selective History of the Impact of the Railways on Golf in England, Wales, and Ireland*. Dalkeith, Scotland: Scottish Cultural Press, 2003.
Stanley, Louis T. *History of Golf*. London: Weidenfeld and Nicolson, 1991.

Ireland

Gibson, William H. *Early Irish Golf: The First Courses, Clubs and Pioneers*. Naas, Ireland: Oak Leaf, 1988.
Gilleece, Dermot, and John Redmond. *Irish Ladies' Golf Union 1893–1993: An Illustrated Centenary History*. Dublin: Privately printed, 1993.
Menton, William A. *The Golfing Union of Ireland 1891–1991*. Dublin: Gill and Macmillan, 1991.
O'Donoghue, Shane. *Legends in Their Spare Time*. Dublin: Primary ABC, 2007.
Redmond, John. *The Book of Irish Golf*. Dublin: Gill and Macmillan, 1997.

Scotland

Campbell, Malcolm. *The Scottish Golf Book*. Chicago, Ill.: Sports Publishing, 1999.
Chambers, Robert. *A Few Rambling Remarks on Golf, with the Rules as Laid Down by the Royal and Ancient Golf Club of St. Andrews*. Edinburgh: W. and R. Chambers, 1862.

Coull, William W., et al. *Golf in Montrose*. 2nd ed. Montrose, Scotland: Privately printed, rev., 2004.

Cundell, James. *Rules of the Thistle Golf Club: With Some Historical Notices Relative to the Progress of the Game of Golf in Scotland*. Edinburgh: Privately printed, 1824.

Dalrymple, W., ed. *Golfer's Guide to the Game and Greens of Scotland* (later published as *Golfer's Guide for the United Kingdom*). Edinburgh: W. H. White, 1894.

Kerr, John. *The Golf Book of East Lothian*. Edinburgh: Privately printed, 1896.

McKinlay, S. L. *Scottish Golf and Golfers: A Collection of Weekly Golf Columns from the Glasgow Herald 1956–1980*. Stamford, Conn.: Ailsa, 1992.

McPherson, J. Gordon. *Golf and Golfers: Past and Present*. Edinburgh: William Blackwood, 1891.

Miller, T. D. *Famous Scottish Links and Other Golfing Papers*. Edinburgh: R. and R. Clark, 1911.

Musselburgh Golf Club. *Laws of the Musselburgh Golf Club, with Some Notices Respecting the Game*. Musselburgh, Scotland: Privately printed, 1829.

Peter, H. Thomas. *Reminiscences of Golf and Golfers*. Edinburgh: James Thin, 1890.

Sinclair, Graham. *A History of Golf Clubs in Fife*. Fife, Scotland: Fife Golfing Association, 1988.

Wentworth, James, ed. *Scottish Ladies' Golfing Association: A Centenary Celebration*. Glasgow: Scotland Ladies Golfing Association, 2006.

St. Andrews

Balfour, James. *Reminiscences of Golf on St. Andrews Links*. Edinburgh: David Douglas, 1887.

Bennett, Andrew. *The Book of St. Andrews Links: Containing Plan of Golf Course, Description of the Greens, Rules of the Game, Bye-Laws of the Links, Regulations for Starting, Golfing Rhymes, etc*. St. Andrews and Edinburgh, Scotland: J. and G. Innes and J. Menzies, 1898.

Gummer, Scott. *The Seventh at St. Andrews: How Scotsman David McLay Kidd and His Ragtag Band Built the First New Course on Golf's Holy Soil in Nearly a Century*. New York: Gotham Books, 2007.

Jarrett, T. G. *St. Andrews Golf Links: The First 600 years*. Edinburgh: Mainstream Publishing, 1995.

Mackie, Keith. *Golf at St. Andrews*. Gretna, La.: Pelican, 1995.

Olman, John M., and Morton W. Olman. *St. Andrews and Golf.* Cincinnati, Ohio: Market Street Press, 1995.

Robertson, James K. *St. Andrews: Home of Golf.* 3rd ed. St. Andrews, Scotland: Citizen Office, revised by Tom Jarrett, 1984.

Stanley, Louis T. *St. Andrews.* Topsfield, Mass.: Salem House, 1986.

Sweden

Thermaenius, Pehr. *Golf in Sweden.* Sweden: Swedish Society of Golf Historians, 2009.

Tisell, Gunnar. *Golfhandboken.* Stockholm: P. A. Norstedt and Soeners Foerlag, 1953.

History of Golf in North America

Canada

Barclay, James. *Canada's Professional Golfers: The Scottish Invasion, 1881–1933, an Illustrated History and Annotated Register.* Toronto: Golf Historical Society of Canada, 1997.

——. *Golf in Canada: A History.* Toronto: McClelland and Stewart, 1992.

Boyle, Mickey. *Ninety Years of Golf: An Illustrated History of Golf in Saskatchewan.* Regina, Canada: Saskatchewan Golf Association, 1987.

Costello, Ralph. *The Story of New Brunswick Golf Association: The First Fifty Years.* Fredericton, Canada: New Ireland Press, 1987.

Gordon, John. *The Grand Old Game: A Century of Golf in Canada, pour le plaisir du jeu un siècle de golf au Canada.* Toronto: Warwick Publishing, 1995.

——. *The Great Golf Courses of Canada.* 3rd ed. Willowdale, Canada: Firefly, rev., 1999.

Hackett, J. Alan. *Manitoba Links: A Kaleidoscopic History of Golf.* Winnipeg, Canada: Gold Quill Publishing, 1998.

Hewson, Karen, ed. *The Open Golf Championship of Canada 1904–2004: A Century of Champions.* Toronto: Key Porter Books, 2004.

Jackson, Barney, ed. *History of the Canadian Open at Glen Abbey.* Toronto: Privately printed, 1984.

Kavanaugh, L. V. *The History of Golf in Canada.* Toronto: Fitzhenry and Whiteside, 1973.

Olson, Arv. *Backspin: 100 years of Golf in British Columbia.* Vancouver, Canada: Privately printed, 1992.

Witteveen, Gordon. *Keeping the Green in Canada*. Markham, Ontario, Canada: Stewart Publishing, 2008.

Mexico

Vargas, Celestino Perez, and Federico Chao. *100 Anos de Golf en Mexico*. Mexico City: Mexican Golf Federation, 1999.
Wright, Harry. *A Short History of Golf in Mexico and the Mexico City Country Club*. New York: Privately printed, 1938.

Puerto Rico

Monge, Jaime. *History of Golf in Puerto Rico*. Puerto Rico: Privately printed, 2004.

United States of America

Barkow, Al. *Gettin' to the Dance Floor: An Oral History of American Golf*. New York: Atheneum, 1986.
———. *The Golden Era of Golf: How America Rose to Dominate the Old Scots Game*. New York: St. Martin's Press, 2000.
Burgess, Charles D. *Golf Links: Chay Burgess, Francis Ouimet, and the Bringing of Golf to America*. Cambridge, Mass.: Rounder Books, 2005.
Eubanks, Steve. *At the Turn: How Two Electrifying Years Changed Golf Forever*. New York: Crown Publishers, 2001.
Frost, Mark. *The Greatest Game Ever Played: Harry Vardon, Francis Ouimet, and the Birth of Modern Golf*. New York: Hyperion, 2002.
———. *The Match: The Day the Game of Golf Changed Forever*. New York: Hyperion, 2007.
Kirsch, George. *Golf in America*. Urbana: University of Illinois Press, 2009.
Labbance, Bob, and Brian Siplo. *The Vardon Invasion: Harry's Triumphant 1900 American Tour*. Ann Arbor, Mich.: Sports Media Group, 2008.
Laney, Al. *Following the Leaders*. Stamford, Conn.: Ailsa, 1991.
Lee, James P. *Golf in America*. New York: Dodd, Mead, 1895.
Lowe, Stephen R. *Sir Walter and Mr. Jones: Walter Hagen, Bobby Jones, and the Rise of American Golf*. Chelsea, Mich.: Sleeping Bear Press, 2000.
Martin, Harry Brownlaw. *Fifty Years of American Golf*. New York: Dodd, Mead, 1936.
Mayo, James M. *The American Country Club: Its Origins and Development*. New Brunswick, N.J.: Rutgers University Press, 1998.

Moss, Richard J. *Golf and the American Country Club*. Urbana: University of Illinois Press, 2001.

O'Connor, Ian. *Arnie and Jack: Palmer, Nicklaus and Golf's Greatest Rivalry*. New York: Houghton Mifflin, 2008.

Peper, George. *Golf in America: The First One Hundred Years*. In collaboration with Robin Macmillan and James A. Frank. New York: Harry N. Abrams, 1988.

Roden, Lincoln, III. *Golf's Golden Age 1945–1954: From Nelson to Hogan to Palmer*. Huntingdon Valley, Pa.: Reed Drabick, 1996.

Sampson, Curt. *The Eternal Summer: Palmer, Nicklaus, and Hogan in 1960, Golf's Eternal Year*. Dallas, Tex.: Taylor Publishing, 1992.

Sounes, Howard. *The Wicked Game: Arnold Palmer, Jack Nicklaus, Tiger Woods and the Story of Modern Golf*. New York: William Morrow, 2004.

U.S. Golf Association. *Golf: The Greatest Game*. New York: HarperCollins, 1994.

Wind, Herbert Warren. *The Story of American Golf: Its Champions and Its Championships*. 3rd ed. New York: Knopf, rev., 1975.

Local and Regional Histories

Brown, George E., III. *100 Years of Minnesota Golf*. Edina, Minn.: Minnesota Golf Association, 2001.

Byrdy, Stan. *Augusta and Aiken in Golf's Golden Age*. Charleston, S.C.: Arcadia, 2002.

Cronin, Tim. *A Century of Golf: Western Golf Association 1899–1999*. Chelsea, Mich.: Sleeping Bear Press, 1998.

Ducibella, Jim. *Par Excellence: A Celebration of Golf in Virginia*. Champaign, Ill.: Sports Publishing, 2000.

Elliott, Mal. *100 Years of Kansas Golf*. Wichita, Kan.: Elfco, 1996.

Elston, Bill. *Golf History of Spokane, WA: A 101 Year Tradition*. Marceline, Mo.: Walsworth Publishing Company, 1999.

Finegan, James W. *A Centennial Tribute to Golf in Philadelphia: The Champions and Championships, the Clubs and the Courses*. Philadelphia, Pa.: Golf Association of Philadelphia, 1996.

Finley, Thomas Alton. *Golf in the Upstate Since 1895 (South Carolina)*. Greenville, S.C.: Olde Sport Publishing, 1999.

Godevarica, Tom. *Chicago Golf: The First 100 years*. Chicago, Ill.: Eagle Communications Group, 1991.

Haas, Gene. *Playing Through: A History of the Wisconsin State Golf Association 1901–2001*. Brookfield, Wisc.: Wisconsin State Golf Association, 2001.

Healey, James. *Golfing Before the Arch: A History of St. Louis Golf*. St. Louis, Mo.: Privately printed, 1987.

Hopkins, Kenneth Lowell. *Cleveland Area Golf*. Chicago, Ill.: Arcadia Publishing, 2004.

Indiana Golf Association. *Celebrating a Century of Golf in Indiana*. Franklin, Ind.: Indiana Golf Association, 2000.

Krakauer, Kenneth. *When Golf Came to Kansas City*. Kansas City, Mo.: Adler's, 1986.

Larrabee, Gary. *The Green and Gold Coast: The History of Golf on Boston's North Shore 1893–2001*. Beverly, Mass., 2001.

Lemon, Del. *The Story of Golf in Oklahoma*. Norman: University of Oklahoma Press, 2001.

Lonnstrom, Douglas A. *History of Golf in New York's Capital Region*. Slingerlands, N.Y.: CML Press, 1998.

Mahoney, Jack. *The Golf History of New England*. 2nd ed. Weston, Mass.: Privately printed, rev., 1995.

Matson, Bruce H. *Golf in the Commonwealth: A History of the VSGA and the Royal and Ancient Game in Virginia*. Virginia Beach, Va.: The Donning Company, 2004.

McCarthy, Moira. *On the Greens of Massachusetts: The Story of the Women's Golf Association of Massachusetts 1900–2000*. Norton, Mass.: Women's Golf Association of Massachusetts, 2001.

Moorhead, Richard, and Nick Wynne. *Golf in Florida 1886–1950*. Charleston, S.C.: Arcadia Publishing, 2008.

Pace, Lee. *Golf in the Carolinas: The Carolinas Golf Association 1909–2009*. West End, N.C.: Carolinas Golf Association, 2008.

Pearce, Gene. *The History of Golf in Tennessee: 1894–2001*. Franklin, Tenn.: Hillsboro Press, 2002.

———. *Southern Golf Association: The First Hundred Years*. Birmingham, Ala.: Privately printed, 2004.

Price, Charles, and George C. Rogers Jr. *The Carolina Lowcountry: Birthplace of American Golf 1786*. Hilton Head Island, S.C.: Sea Pines, 1980.

Quirin, William L. *America's Linksland: A Century of Long Island Golf*. Chelsea, Mich.: Sleeping Bear Press, 2002.

———. *Golf Clubs of the MGA: A Centennial History of Golf in the New York Metropolitan Area*. New York: Golf Magazine Properties, 1997.

Reaves, Randolph P. *The History of Golf in Alabama: A Century of Memories*. Montgomery, Ala.: Publications for Professionals, 1988.

Sampson, Curt. *Centennial—Texas Golf Association 100 Years*. Dallas, Tex.: Brown Books, 2006.

Sandler, Rob. *Legends of Hawaii Golf: The First Century*. Honolulu: Exclusively Hawaii Publishing, 2003.

Sheehan, Larry, et al. *A Commonwealth of Golfers: 1903–2003*. Norton, Mass.: Massachusetts Golf Association, 2003.

Sheelley, Jeff. *Championships and Friendships: The First 100 Years of the Pacific Northwest Golf Association*. Seattle, Wash.: Pacific Northwest Golf Association, 1999.

Stricklin, Art. *Links, Lore and Legends: The Story of Texas Golf*. Lanham, Md.: Taylor Trade Publishing, 2005.

Thomas, Robert D. *A 100 Year History of the Southern California Golf Association*. Los Angeles, Calif.: Southern California Golf Association, 1998.

West, Norrie. *100 Years of Golf in San Diego County*. San Diego, Calif.: Privately printed, 1987.

Western Pennsylvania Golf Association. *A Century of Golf in Western Pennsylvania*. Pittsburgh, Pa.: Western Pennsylvania Golf Association, 1998.

Women's Metropolitan Golf Association. *The Women's Metropolitan Golf Association: Celebrating 100 Years, 1899–1999*. Franklin, Va.: Q Publishing, 1999.

Zuckerman, Joel. *Golf in the Lowcountry: An Extraordinary Journey through Hilton Head Island and Savannah*. Hilton Head Island, S.C.: Saron Press, 2003.

Golf and the American Presidency

Campbell, Shepherd, and Peter Landau. *Presidential Lies: The Illustrated History of White House Golf*. New York: Macmillan, 1996.

Van Natta, Don, Jr. *First Off the Tee: Presidential Hackers, Duffers and Cheaters from Taft to Bush*. New York: Public Affairs, 2003.

History of African American Golf

Dawkins, Marvin P., and Graham C. Kinloch. *African American Golfers during the Jim Crow Era*. Westport, Conn.: Praeger, 2000.

Johnson, M. Mikell. *The African American Woman Golfer: Her Legacy*. Westport, Conn.: Praeger, 2008.

McDaniel, Pete. *Uneven Lies: The Heroic Story of African Americans in Golf*. Greenwich, Conn.: The American Golfer, 2000.

Robinson, Lenwood, Jr. *Skins and Grins: The Plight of the Black American Golfer*. Evanston, Ill.: Chicago Spectrum Press, 1997.

Sinette, Calvin. *Forbidden Fairways: African Americans and the Game of Golf*. Chelsea, Mich.: Sleeping Bear Press, 1998.

History of Women's Golf

Chambers, Marcia. *The Unplayable Lie: The Untold Story of Women and Discrimination in Golf*. Trumbull, Connecticut, and New York: N.Y.T Special Services, 1995.

Cossey, Rosalynde. *Golfing Ladies: Five Centuries of Golf in Great Britain and Ireland*. London: Orbis, 1984.

Crane, Malcolm. *The Story of Ladies' Golf*. London: Stanley Paul, 1991.

Crosset, Todd W. *Outsiders in the Clubhouse: The World of Women's Professional Golf*. Albany: State University of New York Press, 1995.

Glenn, Rhonda. *The Illustrated History of Women's Golf*. Dallas, Tex.: Taylor Publishing, 1991.

Hezlet, May (Mrs. M. E. L. Ross). *Ladies Golf*. London: Hutchinson, 1904.

Hudson, David L., Jr. *Women in Golf: The Players, the History, and the Future of the Sport*. Westport, Conn.: Praeger, 2008.

Johnson, M. Mikell. *The African American Woman Golfer: Her Legacy*. Westport, Conn.: Praeger, 2008.

Leonard, Terri. *In the Women's Clubhouse: The Greatest Women Golfers in Their Own Words*. Chicago, Ill.: Contemporary Books, 2000.

Macdonald, Robert S., and Herbert Warren Wind, eds. *The Great Women Golfers*. 2nd ed. Stamford, Conn.: The Classics of Golf, rev., 1994.

Mair, Lewine. *The Dunlop Lady Golfer's Companion*. Lavenham, Suffolk: Eastland Press, 1980.

———. *One Hundred Years of Women's Golf*. Edinburgh: Mainstream Publishing/Ladies Golf Union, 1992.

Nickerson, Elinor. *Golf: A Women's History*. Jefferson, N.C.: McFarland, 1987.

Vaughan, Roger. *Golf, the Woman's Game*. New York: Stewart, Tabori and Chang, 2001.

Wilson, Enid. *A Century of Women Golfers*. London: Country Life, 1961.

History of Junior Golf

Cook, Kevin. *Driven: Teen Phenoms, Mad Parents, Swing Science and the Future of Golf*. New York: Gotham Books, 2008.

Echikson, William. *Shooting for Tiger: How Golf's Obsessed New Generation Is Transforming a Country Club Sport*. Philadelphia, Pa.: Public Affairs (Perseus Books Group), 2009.

PLAY OF THE GAME

The Rules of Golf

The Rules of Golf are jointly written by the game's governing bodies—the U.S. Golf Association, for the United States of America, its territories and possessions, and Mexico; and the Royal & Ancient Golf Club of St. Andrews, for the rest of the world. The USGA and R&A have each published the *Rules of Golf* on a regular basis—originally on an annual basis, but biennially from 2004 to the present. In addition to the *Rules of Golf* book proper, the USGA and R&A also publish *Decisions of the Rules of Golf* on a biennial basis.

History of the Rules

Chapman, Kenneth. *The Rules of the Green: A History of the Rules of Golf.* Chicago, Ill.: Triumph Books, 1997.

Clapcott, C. B. *The Rules of the Ten Oldest Golf Clubs from 1754–1848: Together with the Rules of the Royal & Ancient Golf Club of St. Andrews for the Years 1858, 1877, 1888.* Edinburgh: Golf Monthly, 1935.

Cousins, Geoffrey. *Golfers at Law.* London: Stanley Paul, 1958.

Glover, John. *Golf: A Celebration of 100 Years of the Rules Of Play.* London: Macmillan, 1997.

Honourable Company of Edinburgh Golfers. *Laws to Be Observed by the Members of the Golfing Company in Playing Golf.* Edinburgh: Privately printed, 1775.

Understanding and Interpreting the Rules

Chapman, Hay. *Law of the Links: Rules, Principles and Etiquette of Golf.* San Francisco: Privately printed, 1922.

Dey, Joseph C., et al. *Golf Rules in Pictures.* New York and Far Hills, N.J.: U.S. Golf Association, various dates.

Dobereiner, Peter. *Golf Rules Explained.* 10th ed. Revised and updated by Bill Elliott. London: David and Charles, 2000.

Francis, Richard Standish. *Golf: Its Rules and Decisions.* 2nd ed. New York: Macmillan, rev., 1939.

Gould, David. *Golf Rules Illustrated.* New York: Callaway Editions, 2000.

Kuhn, Jeffrey S., and Bryan A. Garner. *The Rules of Golf in Plain English.* Chicago: University of Chicago Press, 2004.

Newell, Steve. *The Golf Rules Problem Solver*. London: Chrysalis Books Group, 2005.

Palmer, Arnold. *Playing by the Rules: All the Rules of the Game, Complete with Memorable Rulings from Golf's Rich History*. New York: Pocket Books, 2002.

Rutter, Haydn. *The Illustrated Golf Rules Dictionary*. Revised edition. Chicago, Ill.: Triumph Books, 2000.

Tufts, Richard S. *The Principles behind the Rules of Golf*. 2nd ed. Pinehurst, N.C.: Privately printed, rev., 1961.

U.S. Golf Association. *A Guide to the Rules on Clubs and Balls*. Far Hills, N.J.: U.S. Golf Association, 2002.

U.S. Golf Association and Gary A. Galyean. *Golf Rules Illustrated*. Revised edition. London: Hamlyn, 2008.

Watson, Tom. *The Rules of Golf*. 4th ed. In collaboration with Frank Hannigan. New York: Times Books, rev., 1996.

Etiquette

Bailey, Bill. *Golf Etiquette 101: Your Guide to Proper Behavior on the Course and in the Clubhouse*. 2nd edition. Rocklin, Calif.: Prima Publishing, 1998.

Campbell, Malcolm. *The DK Pocket Guide to Golf Etiquette: A Guide to Rules and Behavior*. New York: DK Publishing, 1997.

Companiotte, John. *Golf Rules and Etiquette Simplified: What You Need to Know to Walk the Links Like a Pro*. New York: McGraw-Hill, 2006.

Corbett, Jim. *The Pocket Idiot's Guide to Golf Rules and Etiquette*. New York: Alpha Books, 2007.

Gould, David. *Golfer's Code: A Guide to a Proper and Civilized Golf Game*. New York: Fairchild Publications, 1993.

Post, Peter. *Playing Through: A Guide to the Unwritten Rules of Golf*. New York: HarperCollins, 2008.

Puett, Barbara, and Jim Apfelbaum. *Golf Etiquette*. Revised edition. New York: St. Martin's Press, 2003.

The R&A. *The Etiquette of Golf, Explained by Padraig Harrington*. St. Andrews, Scotland: The R&A, 2009.

Steinbreder, John. *Golf Rules and Etiquette for Dummies*. New York: Hungry Minds, 2001.

U.S. Golf Association. *The Spirit of the Game: An Etiquette Program*. Far Hills, N.J.: U.S. Golf Association, various dates.

Handicapping

History of Handicapping

Clapcott, C. B. *The History of Handicapping*. United States: Privately printed, 1924.

The History of the Standard Scratch Score and Handicapping Scheme. Hawick, Scotland: The British Golf Union's Joint Advisory Council, 1951.

Knuth, Dean. *The History of Handicapping*. Far Hills, N.J.: U.S. Golf Association, 2004.

Handicapping Systems (Historic)

Calkins, Leighton. *A System for Club Handicapping*. New York: Arthur Pottow, 1905.

Callaway, Lionel. *New and Improved System of Simplified Handicapping for Golfers*. Fort Lauderdale, Fla.: Privately printed, 1952.

Chicago District Golf Association. *Method of Rating Golf Courses and Official Handicap System of the CDGA*. Chicago, Ill.: Chicago District Golf Association, 1940.

Ladies' Golf Union. *The L.G.U. System of Handicapping*. United Kingdom: Ladies' Golf Union, 1895.

Royal Canadian Golf Association. *National Golf Handicap and Course Rating System*. Toronto: Royal Canadian Golf Association, 1967.

The Schemes for Standard Scratch Scores and Uniform Handicapping. London: Golf Union's Joint Advisory Committee of the British Isles, 1926 (also later editions with variant titles).

The Standard Scratch Score and Handicapping System Revised by the Council of National Golf Unions. Nottingham, England: Council of National Golf Unions, 1978.

U.S. Golf Association. *Calkins System of Calculating Handicaps*. New York: U.S. Golf Association, 1927.

Handicapping Systems (Current)

U.S. Golf Association. *The USGA Handicap System: With the USGA Course Rating System and USGA Handicap Decisions*. Far Hills, N.J.: U.S. Golf Association, 2008.

Golf Instruction

Golf instruction accounts for the greatest number of titles in the game's library. It is unnecessary to enumerate all of these titles. Rather, the selection of titles presented here follows two principles: works that represent major milestones in the teaching of the game (e.g., the first instructional book, the first book on the psychology of the game, the first instructional book for women, important teaching methods and methodologies, etc.); and books that were written by significant players, which often contain considerable autobiographical content, and thus can be of significant historical interest.

Landmark Titles

Aultman, Dick. *The Methods of Golf's Masters*. In collaboration with Ken Bowden. New York: Coward, McCann and Geoghegan, 1975.

——. *The Square-to-Square Golf Swing*. Norwalk, Conn.: Golf Digest, 1970.

Ballard, Jimmy. *How to Perfect Your Golf Swing*. Norwalk, Conn.: Golf Digest, 1981.

Beldam, George W. *Great Golfers: Their Methods at a Glance*. London: Macmillan, 1904.

Blake, Mindy. *The Golf Swing of the Future*. London: Souvenir Press, 1972.

Boomer, Percy. *On Learning Golf*. London: John Lane, 1942.

Cochran, Alastair, and John Stobbs. *The Search for the Perfect Swing*. London: Heinemann, 1968.

Dante, James, and Leo Diegel. *The Nine Bad Shots of Golf and What to Do about Them*. New York: Whittlesey House, 1947.

Dunn, John Duncan. *Natural Golf*. New York: G. P. Putnam's Sons, 1931.

Dunn, Seymour. *Golf Fundamentals: Orthodoxy of Style*. Lake Placid, N.Y.: Privately printed, 1922.

Farnie, Henry Brougham [A Keen Hand, pseud.]. *The Golfer's Manual: Being an Historical and Descriptive Account of the National Game of Scotland*. Cupar, Scotland: Whitehead and Orr, 1857.

Grout, Jack, and Dick Aultman. *Let Me Teach You Golf as I Taught Jack Nicklaus*. New York: Atheneum, 1975.

Haultain, Arnold. *The Mystery of Golf*. Boston: Houghton Mifflin, 1908.

Hebron, Michael. *Building and Improving Your Golf Mind, Golf Body, Golf Swing*. Smithtown, N.Y.: Smithtown Country Club, 1993.

Hecker, Genevieve (Mrs. Charles T. Stout). *Golf for Women*. New York: Baker and Taylor, 1904.

Jacobs, John. *50 Greatest Golf Lessons of the Century: Private Sessions with the Golf Greats*. In collaboration with Steve Newell. London: CollinsWillow, 1999.

——. *50 Years of Golfing Wisdom*. In collaboration with Steve Newell. London: CollinsWillow, 2005.

——. *Golf Doctor: Diagnosis, Explanation and Correction of Golfing Faults*. In collaboration with Dick Aultman. London: Stanley Paul, 1979.

——. *Practical Golf*. In collaboration with Ken Bowden. New York: Quadrangle, 1972.

Jones, Ernest, and David Eisenburg. *Swing the Clubhead*. New York: Dodd, Mead, 1952.

Jones, Ernest, and Innis Brown. *Swinging into Golf*. New York: Whittelesey House, 1937.

Kelley, Homer. *The Golfing Machine: The Star System of Golf*. Seattle, Wash.: Star System, 1969.

Leadbetter, David. *The Golf Swing*. In collaboration with John Huggan. London: CollinsWillow, 1990.

Low, George. *The Master of Putting*. In collaboration with Al Barkow. New York: Atheneum, 1983.

Low, John Laing. *Concerning Golf*. London: Hodder and Stoughton, 1903.

McLean, Jim. *The Eight-Step Swing: A Revolutionary Golf Technique by a Pro Coach*. New York: HarperCollins, 1994.

Morley, David C. *The Missing Links: Golf and the Mind*. In collaboration with Ken Bowden. New York: Atheneum, 1976.

Morrison, Alex. *A New Way to Better Golf*. New York: Simon and Schuster, 1932.

Pelz, Dave. *Dave Pelz's Putting Bible*. In collaboration with James A. Frank. New York: Doubleday, 2000.

Penick, Harvey. *Harvey Penick's Little Red Book: Lessons and Teachings from a Lifetime of Golf*. In collaboration with Bud Shrake. New York: Simon and Schuster, 1992.

Wethered, Roger, and Joyce Wethered. *Golf from Two Sides*. London: Longmans, Green, 1922.

Whigham, H. J. *How to Play Golf*. Chicago, Ill.: Herbert S. Stone, 1897.

Instructional Books by Significant Players

Armour, Tommy. *A Round of Golf with Tommy Armour*. New York: Simon and Schuster, 1959.

——. *How to Play Your Best Golf All the Time*. New York, Simon and Schuster, 1953.

Ballesteros, Seve. *Trouble Shooting*. In collaboration with Robert Green. New York: Broadway, 1996.

Barnes, James M. *Picture Analysis of Golf Strokes*. Philadelphia, Pa.: Lippincott, 1919.

Berg, Patty. *Golf Illustrated*. New York: A. S. Barnes, 1950.
Boros, Julius. *Swing Easy, Hit Hard*. New York: Harper and Row, 1965.
Braid, James. *Advanced Golf, or, Hints and Instructions for Progressive Players*. London: Methuen, 1908.
Casper, Billy. *My Million Dollar Shots*. New York: Grosset and Dunlap, 1970.
Charles, Bob. *Left-Handed Golf*. In collaboration with Roger P. Ganem. Englewood Cliffs, N.J.: Prentice-Hall, 1965.
Els, Ernie. *The Complete Short Game*. In collaboration with Steve Newell. New York: Broadway Books, 1998.
———. *How to Build a Classic Golf Swing*. New York: HarperCollins, 1996.
Faldo, Nick. *A Swing for Life*. In collaboration with Richard Simmons. London: Weidenfeld and Nicholson, 1995.
Floyd, Raymond. *The Elements of Scoring*. In collaboration with Jaime Diaz. New York: Simon and Schuster, 1998.
Hogan, Ben. *Five Lessons: The Modern Fundamentals of Golf*. In collaboration with Herbert Warren Wind. New York: A. S. Barnes, 1957.
———. *Power Golf*. New York: A. S. Barnes, 1948.
Jones, Robert Tyre, Jr. *Bobby Jones on Golf*. Garden City, N.Y.: Doubleday, 1966.
Middlecoff, Cary. *The Golf Swing*. Englewood Cliffs, N.J.: Prentice-Hall, 1974.
Miller, Johnny. *Pure Golf*. In collaboration with Dale Shankland. New York: Doubleday, 1976.
Nelson, Byron. *Shape Your Swing the Modern Way*. In collaboration with Larry Dennis. Norwalk, Conn.: Golf Digest, 1976.
———. *Winning Golf*. New York: A. S. Barnes, 1946.
Nicklaus, Jack. *Golf My Way*. In collaboration with Ken Bowden. New York: Simon and Schuster, 1974.
Norman, Greg. *Shark Attack: Greg Norman's Guide to Aggressive Golf*. Melbourne: Macmillan, 1987.
Palmer, Arnold. *Go for Broke: My Philosophy of Winning Golf*. In collaboration with William Barry Furlong. New York: Simon and Schuster, 1973.
Park, William. *The Game of Golf*. London: Longmans, Green, 1896.
Player, Gary. *Bunker Play*. In collaboration with Mike Wade. New York: Broadway Books, 1996.
Ray, Edward. *Inland Golf*. London: Werner Laurie, 1913.
Simpson, Walter Grindley. *The Art of Golf*. Edinburgh: David Douglas, 1887.
Snead, Sam. *Natural Golf*. New York: A. S. Barnes, 1953.
Sorenstam, Annika. *Golf Annika's Way*. In collaboration with the editors of *Golf Magazine*. New York: Gotham Books, 2004.
Travis, Walter J. *Practical Golf*. 3rd ed. New York: Harper's, rev., 1909.

Vardon, Harry. *The Complete Golfer*. London: Methuen, 1905.

Venturi, Ken. *The Venturi Analysis*. In collaboration with Al Barkow. New York: Atheneum, 1981.

Watson, Tom. *Getting Up and Down: How to Save Strokes from Forty Yards In*. In collaboration with Nick Seitz. New York: Random House, 1983.

Woods, Tiger. *How I Play Golf*. In collaboration with the editors of *Golf Digest*. New York: Warner Books, 2001.

Wright, Mickey. *Play Golf the Wright Way*. Garden City, N.Y.: Doubleday, 1962.

Zaharias, Mildred Didrikson. *Championship Golf*. New York: A. S. Barnes, 1948.

Golfers with Disabilities

Drane, Dan, and Martin Block. *Accessible Golf: Making It a Game for All*. Champaign, Ill.: Human Kinetics, 2006.

Jones, Greg, and Mike Towle. *Golf and ADA: A Winning Twosome*. Fort Worth, Tex: The Summit Group, 1993.

National Golf Foundation. *Accommodating Disabled Golfers*. 2nd ed. Jupiter, Fla.: National Golf Foundation, 1998.

Owens, DeDe. *Teaching Golf to Special Populations*. West Point, N.Y.: Leisure Press, 1984.

Thrower, Henry. *Proposed Design Guidelines for New and Existing Golf Facilities under the Americans with Disabilities Act*. Palm Beach Gardens, Fla.: PGA of America, 1994.

U.S. Golf Association. *A Modification of the Rules of Golf for Golfers with Disabilities*. Far Hills, N.J., various dates.

Golf Equipment

History

Henderson, Ian T., and David I. Stirk. *Golf in the Making*. 2nd ed. Crawley, England: Henderson and Stirk, rev., 1982.

Golf Clubs—History of Club Making

Ellis, Jeffrey B. *The Clubmaker's Art: Antique Golf Clubs and Their History*. 2nd ed. Oak Harbour, Wash.: Zephyr Productions, rev., 2007.

———. *The Golf Club: 400 Years of the Good, the Beautiful and the Creative*. Oak Harbour, Wash.: Zephyr Productions, 2000.

Georgiady, Peter. *Compendium of British Club Makers*. 2nd ed. Greensboro, N.C.: Airlie Hall Press, rev., 1997

———. *North American Club Makers*. Greensboro, N.C.: Airlie Hall Press, 1998.

Liberman, Noah. *The Flat Stick: The History, Romance and Heartbreak of the Putter*. New York: HarperCollins, 2006.

Overturf, Rich. *Thanks Ely!: How Ely Callaway and the Big Bertha Revolutionized Golf*. Victoria, Canada: Trafford Publishing, 2006.

Seagle, Janet. *The Club Makers*. 5th ed. Far Hills, N.J.: U.S. Golf Association, rev., 1989.

Stirk, David. *Golf: The Great Clubmakers*. London: H. F. and G. Witherby, 1992.

Clubfitting and Clubmaking

Darrell Survey. *The Darrell Survey: Golf Equipment Almanac*. Los Angeles: Darrell Survey, 2000–present.

Jackson, Jeff. *The Modern Guide to Golf Clubmaking: The Principle, and Techniques of Building Golf Clubs from Component Parts*. Newark, Ohio: Dynacraft Golf Products, 1994.

Jackson, Jeff, and Jeff Summitt. *Total Clubfitting in the 21st Century: A Complete Program for Fitting Golf Equipment*. Newark, Ohio: Dynacraft, 2001.

Maltby, Ralph. *Golf Club Design, Fitting, Alternations and Repair*. 4th ed. Newark, Ohio: Ralph Maltby Enterprises, rev., 1995.

Paul, Carl. *Golf Clubmaking and Repair*. Austin, Tex.: Paul Associates, 1984.

Sheets, Jeff. *The Perfect Fit: Fitting Today's Golf Equipment to Today's Golfer*. Round Rock, Tex.: Sheets Publishing, 2008.

Wichern, Eric. *The Truth about Graphite Golf Shafts: Everything a Golfer Should Know about Graphite-Shafted Golf Clubs*. Lenexa, Kan.: A&E Publishing, 1994.

Wishon, Tom W. *The Modern Guide to Clubmaking: The Principles and Techniques of Building Golf Clubs from Component Parts*. Newark, Ohio: Dynacraft, 1987.

———. *The Modern Guide to Shaft Fitting: Featuring the Dynacraft Shaft Fitting Index*. Newark, Ohio: Dynacraft, 1992.

———. *The Right Sticks: Equipment Myths That Could Wreck Your Golf Game*. Ann Arbor, Mich.: Sports Media Group, 2008.

———. *The Search for the Perfect Golf Club*. In collaboration with Tom Grunder. Ann Arbor, Mich.: Sports Media Group, 2005.

Golf Balls

Hamilton, David. *Precious Gum: The Story of the Gutta Ball*. Kilmacolm, Scotland: The Partick Press, 2004.
Machat, Udo, and Larry Dennis. *The Golf Ball*. Oakland, Calif.: Sports Images, 2000.
Martin, John Stuart. *The Curious History of the Golf Ball: Mankind's Most Fascinating Sphere*. New York: Horizon Press, 1968.
McGimpsey, Kevin W. *The Story of the Golf Ball*. London: Kevin W. McGimpsey, 2003.

Other Equipment

Valenta, Irwin R. *The Singular History of the Golf Tee*. Greensboro, N.C.: Privately printed, 1995.

The Science of Golf

Jorgensen, Theodore P. *The Physics of Golf*. 2nd ed. New York: Springer Verlag, rev., 1999.
Wesson, John. *The Science of Golf*. Oxford, England: Oxford University Press, 2009.
World Scientific Congress of Golf. *Golf and Science I-IV: Proceedings of the World Scientific Congress of Golf*. Various publishers, 1990–2002.
Zumerchik, John. *Newton on the Tee: A Good Walk through the Science of Golf*. New York: Simon and Schuster, 2002.

THE PLAYERS

Collective Biographies

Alliss, Peter. *The Who's Who of Golf*. In collaboration with Michael Hobbs. London: Orbis, 1983.
Darsie, Darsie L. *My Greatest Day in Golf*. New York: A. S. Barnes, 1950.
Dobereiner, Peter. *The Lord's Taverners Fifty Greatest Golfers: The Fifty Greatest Post-War Golfers from around the World*. London: Kingswood/Quixote, 1985.
Elliott, Len, and Barbara Kelly. *Who's Who in Golf*. New Rochelle, N.Y.: Arlington House, 1976.

Emery, David. *Who's Who in International Golf*. London: Sphere Books, 1983.

Gilchrist, Roger E., and Mark Emerson. *Gilchrist's Who's Who in Golf*. Alexander, N.C.: Alexander Books, 2001.

Jerris, Rand. *Golf's Golden Age: Robert T. Jones Jr. and the Legendary Players of the 10s, 20s, and 30s*. Washington, D.C.: National Geographic, 2005.

Laidlaw, Renton. *Golfing Heroes: All Time Greats Past and Present*. London: Century Benham, 1989.

Leach, Henry, ed. *Great Golfers in the Making*. London: Methuen, 1907.

Mackintosh, David, ed. *Golf's Greatest Eighteen: Today's Top Golf Writers Debate and Rank the Sport's Greatest Champions*. Chicago, Ill.: Contemporary Books, 2003.

Macwilliam, Rob. *Who's Who in Golf*. London: Hamlyn, 2001.

McCord, Robert. *The Golf 100: Ranking the Greatest Players of All Time*. 2nd ed. New York: Citadel Press, rev., 2004.

McCullough, Bob. *My Greatest Day in Golf: The Legends of Golf Recount Their Greatest Moments*. New York: St. Martin's Press, 2001.

Morrison, Ian. *100 Greatest Golfers*. London: Bison Books, 1988.

———. *Who's Who in Golf*. London: Hamlyn, 1988.

Tait, Alistair. *Golf: The Legends of the Game*. 2nd ed. Buffalo, N.Y.: Firefly Books, rev., 2003.

Wexler, Daniel. *The Book of Golfers: a Biographical History of the Royal & Ancient Game*. Ann Arbor, Mich.: Sports Media Group, 2005.

Individual Biographies and Autobiographies

Amy Alcott

Alcott, Amy. *The Leaderboard: Conversations on Golf and Life*. In collaboration with Don Wade. New York: Atria Books, 2009.

Peter Alliss

Alliss, Peter. *Alliss through the Looking Glass: My World of Golf*. London: Cassell, 1963.

———. *Peter Alliss: An Autobiography*. Glasgow: Fontana/Collins, 1982.

Paul Azinger

Azinger, Paul, and Ken Abraham. *Zinger: A Champion's Story of Determination, Courage and Charging Back*. New York: HarperCollins, 1995.

A. J. Balfour

Balfour, Arthur James, Earl of. *Chapters of Autobiography*. London: Cassell, 1930.

John Ball

Behrend, John. *John Ball of Hoylake*. Droitwich, England: Grant Books, 1989.

Severiano Ballesteros

Ballesteros, Severiano, and Dudley Doust. *Seve: The Young Champion*. London: Hodder and Stoughton, 1982.

Cannon, David. *Severiano Ballesteros*. London: Kingswood Press, 1986.

Green, Robert. *Seve: Golf's Flawed Genius*. London: Robson Books, 2006.

St. John, Lauren. *Seve: Ryder Cup Hero*. Nashville, Tenn.: Rutledge Hill Press, 1997.

Laura Baugh

Baugh, Laura, and Steve Eubanks. *Out of the Rough: An Intimate Portrait of Laura Baugh and Her Sobering Journey*. Nashville, Tenn.: Rutledge Hill Press, 1999.

Frank Beard

Beard, Frank. *Pro: Frank Beard on the Golf Tour*. Edited by Dick Schaap. New York: World, 1970.

Beard, Frank, and John Garrity. *Making the Turn: A Year inside the PGA Senior Tour*. New York: Macmillan, 1992.

Judy Bell

Bell, Judy. *Breaking the Mold: The Journey of the Only Woman President of the United States Golf Association*. In collaboration with Rhonda Glenn. Chelsea, Mich.: Sleeping Bear Press, 2002.

Ted Blackwell

Moreton, John F. *Like Jehu He Drove Furiously*. United Kingdom: Black Pear Press, 2007.

Jane Blalock

Blalock, Jane, and Dwayne Netland. *The Guts to Win*. Norwalk, Conn.: Golf Digest, 1977.

Tommy Bolt

Bolt, Tommy. *The Hole Truth: Inside Big-Time, Big-Money Golf*. In collaboration with Jimmy Mann. Philadelphia: Lippincott, 1971.

Charley Boswell

Boswell, Charley, and Curt Anders. *Now I See*. New York: Meredith Press, 1969.

Harry Bradshaw

Gilleece, Dermot. *The Brad: The Life and Times of Harry Bradshaw*. Ireland: Privately printed, 1988.

James Braid

Darwin, Bernard. *James Braid*. London: Hodder and Stoughton, 1952.

MacAlindin, Bob. *James Braid Champion Golfer*. Droitwich, England: Grant Books, 2003.

Michael Campbell

Gray, Russell. *Michael Campbell: Rookie on Tour*. Auckland, New Zealand: Hodder Moa Beckett, 1996.

Joe Carr

Gilleece, Dermot. *Breaking 80: The Life and Times of Joe Carr*. Dublin: Poolberg Press, 2002.

Billy Casper

Peery, Paul D. *Billy Casper: Winner*. Englewood Cliffs, N.J.: Prentice-Hall, 1967.

Neil Coles

Coles, Neil. *Neil Coles on Golf*. London: Stanley Paul, 1965.

Fred Corcoran

Corcoran, Fred, and Bud Harvey. *Unplayable Lies: The Story of Sport's Most Successful Impresario*. New York: Duell, Sloan and Pearce, 1965.

Henry Cotton

Cotton, Henry. *My Golfing Album*. London: Country Life, 1959.
Dobereiner, Peter. *Maestro: The Life of Sir Henry Cotton*. London: Hodder and Stoughton, 1992.

Fred Couples

Bissell, Kathlene. *Fred Couples: Golf's Reluctant Superstar*. Lincolnwood, Ill.: Contemporary Books, 1999.

Ben Crenshaw

Crenshaw, Ben. *A Feel for the Game*. In collaboration with Melanie Hauser. New York: Doubleday, 2001.

Harriot and Margaret Curtis

Halsted, Isabella. *The Aunts*. Manchester, Mass.: Sharksmouth Press, 1992.

John Daly

Daly, John. *My Life In and Out of the Rough*. In collaboration with Glen Waggoner. New York: HarperCollins, 2006.
Newsham, Gavin. *John Daly: Letting the Big Dog Eat*. London: Virgin Books, 2003.
Wartman, William. *John Daly: Wild Thing*. New York: HarperPaperbacks, 1996.

Bernard Darwin

Darwin, Bernard. *Life Is Sweet, Brother*. London: Collins, 1940.

———. *The World That Fred Made: An Autobiography*. London: Chatto and Windus, 1955.

Laura Davies

Davies, Laura, and Lewine Mair. *Laura Davies Naturally*. London: Bloomsbury Publishing, 1996.

Jimmy Demaret

Companiotte, John. *Jimmy Demaret: The Swing's the Thing*. Ann Arbor, Mich.: Clock Tower Press, 2004.

Dwight D. Eisenhower

Lewis, Catherine. *Don't Ask Me What I Shot: How Eisenhower's Love of Golf Helped Shape 1950s America*. New York: McGraw-Hill, 2007.

Palmer, Norman, and William V. Levy. *Five Star Golf*. New York: Duell, Sloan and Pearce, 1964.

Sowell, David. *Eisenhower and Golf: A President at Play*. Jefferson, N.C.: McFarland, 2007.

Chick Evans

Evans, Charles, Jr. *Chick Evans' Golf Book: The Story of the Sporting Battles of the Greatest of All Amateur Golfers*. Chicago, Ill.: Thos. W. Wilson, 1921.

Nick Faldo

Concannon, Dale. *Driven: The Definitive Biography of Nick Faldo*. London: Virgin Books, 2001.

Faldo, Nick. *Faldo: In Search of Perfection*. In collaboration with Bruce Critchley. London: George Weidenfeld and Nicholson, 1994.

———. *The Rough with the Smooth: Breaking into Professional Golf*. In collaboration with Mitchell Platts. London: Stanley Paul, 1980.

Hopkins, John. *Nick Faldo in Perspective*. London: George Allen and Unwin, 1985.

Jack Fleck

Fleck, Jack. *The Jack Fleck Story: The Legacy of the Playoff of the Century and the Greatest Upset in Sports History*. United States: JC Publishing, 2002.

W. C. Fownes

Stewart, John W. *William Clark Fownes, Jr.: The Man, the Golfer, the Leader*. Lutherville, Md.: MacKenzie Investment Corporation, 2003.

Althea Gibson

Gibson, Althea. *So Much to Live For*. New York: G. P. Putnam's Sons, 1968.

Johnny Goodman

Blaine, Michael. *The King of Swings: Johnny Goodman, the Last Amateur to Beat the Pros at Their Own Game*. New York: Houghton Mifflin, 2006.

Herb Graffis

Warters, Jim. *The Brothers Graffis: A Retrospective in Memory of Herb and Joe Graffis*. Jupiter, Fla.: National Golf Foundation, 1992.

Walter Hagen

Clavin, Tom. *Sir Walter: Walter Hagen and the Invention of Professional Golf*. New York: Simon and Schuster, 2005.

Hagen, Walter. *The Walter Hagen Story*. In collaboration with Margaret Seaton Heck. New York: Simon and Schuster, 1956.

Dutch Harrison

Leighton, Beach. *Mr. Dutch: The Arkansas Traveler*. Champaign, Ill.: Sagamore Publishing, 1991.

Claude "Butch" Harmon

Harmon, Claude "Butch," Jr. *The Pro: Lessons from My Father about Golf and Life*. New York: Crown Publishers, 2006.

Betty Hicks

Hicks, Betty. *My Life from Fairway to Airway*. New York: iUniverse, 2006.

Harold Hilton

Garcia, John L. B. *Harold Hilton: His Golfing Life and Times*. Droitwich, England: Grant Books, 1992.
Hilton, Harold. *My Golfing Reminiscences*. London: James Nisbet, 1907.

Ben Hogan

Davis, Martin, ed. *Ben Hogan: The Man behind the Mystique*. Greenwich, Conn.: The American Golfer, 2002.
———. *The Hogan Mystique: Classic Photographs of the Great Ben Hogan by Jules Alexander*. Greenwich, Conn.: The American Golfer, 1994.
Demaret, Jimmy. *My Partner, Ben Hogan*. New York: McGraw Hill, 1954.
Dodson, James. *Ben Hogan: An American Life*. New York: Doubleday, 2004.
Sampson, Curt. *Hogan*. Nashville, Tenn.: Rutledge Hill Press, 1996.

Marion Hollins

Outerbridge, David E. *Champion in a Man's World: The Biography of Marion Hollins*. Chelsea, Mich.: Sleeping Bear Press, 1998.

Bob Hope

Hope, Bob, and Dwayne Netland. *Bob Hope's Confessions of a Hooker: My Lifelong Love Affair with Golf*. Garden City, N.Y.: Doubleday, 1985.

Tony Jacklin

Jacklin, Tony. *Jacklin: The Champion's Own Story*. London: Hodder and Stoughton, 1970.
———. *Tony Jacklin: The First Forty Years*. In collaboration with Renton Laidlaw. London: Queen Anne Press, 1985.
Kahn, Liz. *Tony Jacklin: The Price of Success*. London: Hamlyn, 1979.

Peter Jacobsen

Jacobsen, Peter, and Jack Sheehan. *Buried Lies: True Tales and Tall Stories from the PGA Tour*. New York: G. P. Putnam's Sons, 1993.

Robert T. Jones Jr.

Davis, Martin, ed. *The Greatest of Them All: The Legend of Bobby Jones.* Greenwich, Conn.: The American Golfer, 1996.

Frost, Mark. *The Grand Slam: Bobby Jones, America, and the Story of Golf.* New York: Hyperion, 2004.

Jones, Robert Tyre, Jr. *Golf Is My Game*. Garden City, N.Y.: Doubleday, 1960.

Jones, Robert Tyre, Jr., and O. B. Keeler. *Down the Fairway: The Golf Life and Play of Robert T. Jones Jr*. New York: Minton, Balch, 1927.

Keeler, O. B. *The Boy's Life of Bobby Jones*. New York: Harpers, 1931.

Lewis, Catherine M. *Bobby Jones and the Quest for the Grand Slam*. Chicago, Ill.: Triumph Books, 2005.

———. *Considerable Passions: Golf, the Masters, and the Legacy of Bobby Jones*. Chicago, Ill.: Triumph Books, 2000.

Matthews, Sidney L. *Bobby Jones Extra*. Tallahassee, Fla.: IQ Press, 2004.

———. *Bobby: The Life and Times of Bobby Jones*. Ann Arbor, Mich.: Sports Media Group, 2005.

———. *The History of Bobby Jones' Clubs*. Tallahassee, Fla.: Impregnable Quadrilateral Press, 1992.

———. *Life and Times of Bobby Jones*. Chelsea, Mich.: Sleeping Bear Press, 1995.

Miller, Richard. *Triumphant Journey: The Saga of Bobby Jones and the Grand Slam of Golf.* New York: Holt, Rinehart and Winston, 1980.

Rapoport, Ron. *The Immortal Bobby: Bobby Jones and the Golden Age of Golf.* Hoboken, N.J.: John Wiley, 2005.

Rice, Grantland. *The Bobby Jones Story: From the Writings of O. B. Keeler*. Atlanta, Ga.: Tupper and Love, 1953.

O. B. Keeler

Keeler, O. B. *The Autobiography of an Average Golfer*. New York: Greenberg, 1925.

Peggy Kirk Bell

Bell, Peggy Kirk. *The Gift of Golf, My Life with a Wonderful Game*. In collaboration with Lee Pace. Southern Pines, N.C.: Pine Needles Lodge and Golf Club/The Pilot, 2001.

Tom Kite

Kite, Tom, and Mickey Herskowitz. *A Fairway to Heaven: My Lessons from Harvey Penick on Golf and Life*. New York: William Morrow, 1997.

Catherine Lacoste

Jeanneau, Georges. *1967—Catherine Lacoste remporte l'U.S. Open*. Levallois-Perrot, France: French Golf Federation, 2007.

Bernhard Langer

Langer, Bernhard. *Bernhard Langer: My Autobiography*. In collaboration with Stuart Weir. London: Hodder and Stoughton, 2002.

———. *While the Iron Is Hot: An Autobiography*. In collaboration with Bill Elliott. London: Stanley Paul, 1988.

Joe Lazaro

Lazaro, Joe. *The Right Touch: Blind Golf Champion*. Weston, Mass.: John Mahoney, 1978.

Cecil Leitch

Leitch, Cecil. *Golf*. London: Thorton Butterworth, 1922.

Tony Lema

Lema, Tony. *Golfer's Gold: An Inside View of the Pro Tour*. In collaboration with Gwilym S. Brown. Boston: Little, Brown, 1964.

Gene Littler

Littler, Gene, and Jack Tobin. *The Real Score*. Waco, Tex.: Ward Books, 1976.

Bobby Locke

Locke, Bobby. *Bobby Locke on Golf*. London: Country Life, 1953.

Norval, Ronald. *King of the Links: The Story of Bobby Locke*. Cape Town, South Africa: Maskew Miller, 1951.

Henry Longhurst

Longhurst, Henry. *My Life and Soft Times*. London: Cassell, 1971.

Nancy Lopez

Lopez, Nancy. *The Education of a Woman Golfer*. In collaboration with Peter Schwed. New York: Simon and Schuster, 1979.

Sandy Lyle

Lyle, Sandy. *To the Fairway Born: Sandy Lyle, the Autobiography*. London: Headline Publishing, 2006.

Stewart Maiden

Matthew, Sidney. *Kiltie the Kingmaker: The Ten Lost Lessons of Bobby Jones's Teacher Stewart Maiden*. Ann Arbor, Mich.: Sports Media Group, 2004.

Casey Martin

Cunneff, Tom. *Walk a Mile in My Shoes: The Casey Martin Story*. Nashville, Tenn.: Rutledge Hill Press, 1998.

Arnaud Massy

Jeanneau, Georges, and Nicolas Jeanneau. *La victoire d'Arnaud Massy au British Open, 1907*. Levallois-Perrot, France: French Golf Federation, 2007.

Gary McCord

McCord, Gary. *Just a Range Ball in a Box of Titleists: On and off the Tour with Gary McCord*. New York: G. P. Putnam's Sons, 1997.

Phil Mickelson

Mickelson, Phil. *One Magical Sunday: But Winning Isn't Everything*. In collaboration with Donald T. Phillips. New York: Warner Books, 2005.

Colin Montgomerie

Montgomerie, Colin, and Lewine Mair. *The Real Monty: The Autobiography of Colin Montgomerie*. London: Orion Books, 2002.

Old and Young Tom Morris

Cook, Kevin. *Tommy's Honor: The Story of Old Tom Morris and Young Tom Morris, Golf's Founding Father and Son*. New York: Gotham Books, 2007.

Joy, David. *The Scrapbook of Old Tom Morris*. Chelsea, Mich.: Sleeping Bear Press, 2001.

Malcolm, David, and Peter E. Crabtree. *Tom Morris of St. Andrews: The Colossus of Golf 1821–1908*. Ballater, Scotland: Glengarden Press, 1908.

Tulloch, W. W. *The Life of Old Tom Morris, with Glimpses of St. Andrews and Its Golfing Celebrities*. London: T. Werner Laurie, 1908.

Byron Nelson

Companiotte, John. *Byron Nelson: The Most Remarkable Year in the History of Golf*. Chicago, Ill.: Triumph Books, 2006.

Davis, Martin. *Byron Nelson: The Story of Golf's Finest Gentleman and the Greatest Winning Streak in History*. Greenwich, Conn.: The American Golfer, 1997.

Nelson, Byron. *Byron Nelson: The Little Black Book, the Personal Diary of Golf Legend Byron Nelson 1935–1947*. Arlington, Tex.: Summit Publishing, 1992.

——. *How I Played the Game*. Dallas, Tex.: Taylor Publishing, 1993.

Jack Nicklaus

Davis, Martin. *Jack Nicklaus: Simply the Best*. Greenwich, Conn.: The American Golfer, 2007.

Nicklaus, Jack. *Golf and Life*. In collaboration with John Tickell. New York: St. Martin's Press, 2003.

——. *The Greatest Game of All: My Life in Golf*. In collaboration with Herbert Warren Wind. New York: Simon and Schuster, 1969.

——. *Jack Nicklaus: Memories and Memorabilia from Golf's Golden Bear*. In collaboration with Dave Shedloski. New York: Stewart, Tabori and Chang, 2007.

——. *Jack Nicklaus: My Story*. In collaboration with Ken Bowden. New York: Simon and Schuster, 1997.

Shaw, Mark. *Nicklaus*. Dallas, Tex.: Taylor Publishing, 1997.

Shedloski, David S. *Golden Twilight: Jack Nicklaus in His Final Championship Season*. Chelsea, Mich.: Sleeping Bear Press, 2001.

Greg Norman

Norman, Greg. *Greg Norman: My Story*. In collaboration with Don Lawrence. Sydney, Australia: Aurora Press, 1983.

——. *The Way of the Shark: Lessons on Golf, Business and Life*. In collaboration with Donald T. Phillips. New York: Atria Books, 2006.

St. John, Lauren. *Shark: The Biography of Greg Norman*. Nashville, Tenn.: Rutledge Hill Press, 1998.

Tressider, Phil. *The Shark Bites Back*. Chippendale, Australia: Pan Macmillan, 1993.

Vigeland, Carl. *Stalking the Shark: Pressure and Passion on the Pro Golf Tour*. New York: W. W. Norton, 1996.

Moe Norman

O'Connor, Tim. *The Feeling of Greatness: The Moe Norman Story*. Indianapolis, Ind.: Masters Press, 1995.

Sauerwein, Stan. *Moe Norman: The Canadian Golfing Legend with the Perfect Swing*. Canmore, Canada: Altitude Publishing, 2004.

Andy North

North, Andy, and Burton Rocks. *The Long and Short of It*. New York: St. Martin's Press, 2002.

Christy O'Connor

O'Connor, Christy, and John Redmond. *Christy O'Connor: His Autobiography as Told to John Redmond*. Dublin: Gill and Macmillan, 1985.

Smith, Seamus. *"Himself": Christy O'Connor*. Dublin: Colorman, 1995.

Francis Ouimet

Ouimet, Francis. *A Game of Golf: A Book of Reminiscences*. Boston: Houghton Mifflin, 1932.

Se Ri Pak

Stewart, Mark. *Se Ri Pak: Drive to Win*. Brookfield, Conn.: The Millbrook Press, 2000.

Wakamatsu, Tad, and Katuzo Suetake. *Se Ri*. Japan: Take Shobo, 1999.

Arnold Palmer

Bisher, Furman. *The Birth of a Legend: Arnold Palmer's Golden Year 1960*. Englewood Cliffs, N.J.: Prentice-Hall, 1972.
Dodson, James. *A Golfer's Life: Arnold Palmer*. New York: Ballantine Books, 1999.
Guest, Larry. *Arnie: Inside the Legend*. Orlando, Fla.: Tribune Publishing, 1993.
Hauser, Thomas. *Arnold Palmer: A Personal Journey*. San Francisco: Collins Publishers, 1994.
McCormack, Mark H. *Arnie: The Evolution of a Legend*. New York: Simon and Schuster, 1967.
Palmer, Arnold. *Arnold Palmer: Memories, Stories, and Memorabilia from a Life on and off the Course*. New York: Stewart, Tabori and Chang, 2004.

Willie Park Sr. and Willie Park Jr.

Adams, John. *The Parks of Musselburgh: Golfers, Architects, Clubmakers*. Droitwich, England: Grant Books, 1991.
Stephen, Walter. *Willie Park Junior: The Man Who Took Golf to the World*. Edinburgh: Luath Press, 2005.

Gary Player

Player, Gary. *Gary Player World Golfer*. In collaboration with Floyd Thatcher. London: Pelham, 1975.
———. *Grand Slam Golf*. London: Cassell, 1966.
———. *To Be the Best: Reflections of a Champion*. In collaboration with Michael McDonnell. London: Sidgwick and Jackson, 1991.

Ted Ray

Ray, Ted. *Golf: My Slice of Life*. London: W. H. Allen, 1972.

Dai Rees

Rees, Dai. *Golf Today*. London: Arthur Barker, 1962.
Rees, Dai, and John Ballantine. *Thirty Years of Championship Golf*. London: Stanley Paul, 1968.

Allan Robertson

Adamson, Alastair Beaton. *Allan Robertson, Golfer: His Life and Times*. Worcestershire, England: Grant Books, 1985.

Doug Sanders

Sanders, Doug. *Come Swing with Me: My Life on and off the Tour*. In collaboration with Larry Sheehan. Garden City, N.Y.: Doubleday, 1974.

Gene Sarazen

Olman, John M. *The Squire: The Legendary Golfing Life of Gene Sarazen*. Cincinnati, Ohio: Olman Industries, 1986.

Sarazen, Gene. *Thirty Years of Championship Golf: The Life and Times of Gene Sarazen*. In collaboration with Herbert Warren Wind. New York: Prentice-Hall, 1950.

Sewsunker Papwa Sewgolum

Nicholson, Christopher. *Papwa Sewgolum: From Pariah to Legend*. Johannesburg, South Africa: Wits University Press, 2005.

Patty Sheehan

Sheehan, Patty, and Betty Hicks. *Patty Sheehan on Golf*. Dallas: Taylor Publishing, 1996.

Dinah Shore

Kort, Michele. *Dinah: Three Decades of Sex, Golf, and Rock and Roll*. Los Angeles: Out Traveler Books, 2005.

Charlie Sifford

Sifford, Charlie. *Just Let Me Play: The Story of Charlie Sifford, the First Black PGA Golfer*. In collaboration with James Gullo. New York: British American Publishing, 1992.

Horton Smith

Smith, Horton, and Marian Benton. *The Velvet Touch*. New York: A. S. Barnes, 1961.

Sam Snead

Barkow, Al. *Sam: The One and Only Sam Snead*. Ann Arbor, Mich.: Sports Media Group, 2005.

Snead, Sam. *The Education of a Golfer*. In collaboration with Al Stump. New York: Simon and Schuster, 1962.

——. *Slammin' Sam*. In collaboration with George Mendoza. New York: Donald J. Fine, 1986.

Karsten Solheim

Sumner, Tracy. *Karsten's Way: The Life Changing Story of Karsten Solheim, Pioneer in Golf Club Design and the Founder of Ping*. Chicago, Ill.: Northfield Publishing, 2000.

Payne Stewart

Chastain, Bill. *Payne at Pinehurst: The Greatest U.S. Open Ever*. New York: Thomas Dunne Books, 2004.

Guest, Larry. *The Payne Stewart Story*. Kansas City, Mo.: Andrews McMeel, 2001.

Stewart, Tracy. *Payne Stewart: The Authorized Biography*. In collaboration with Ken Abraham. Nashville, Tenn.: Broadman and Holman, 2000.

Alexa Stirling

Barclay, James A. *The Golfer and the Carpenter: The Life, Letters and Diaries of Alexa Stirling Fraser*. Toronto: Privately printed, 2001.

F. G. Tait

Low, John L. *F. G. Tait: A Record*. London: James Nisbet, 1900.

J. H. Taylor

Begbie, Harold. *J. H. Taylor, or, the Inside of a Week*. London: Mills and Boon, 1925.

Taylor, J. H. *Golf: My Life's Work*. London: Jonathan Cape, 1943.

Alvin Clarence "Titanic" Thompson

Stowers, Carlton. *The Unsinkable Titanic Thompson*. Burnet, Tex.: Eakin Press, 1982.

Peter Thomson

Mitchell, Peter. *The Complete Golfer: Peter Thomson*. Port Melbourne, Australia: Lothian Publishing, 1991.

Jerry Travers

Travers, Jerome D., and James J. Crowell. *The Fifth Estate: Thirty Years of Golf*. New York: Knopf, 1926.

Walter J. Travis

Labbance, Bob. *The Old Man: The Biography of Walter J. Travis*. Chelsea, Mich.: Sleeping Bear Press, 2000.

Lee Trevino

Trevino, Lee. *The Snake in the Sandtrap (and Other Adventures on the Tour)*. New York: Holt, Rinehart and Winston, 1985.

———. *They Call Me Super Mex*. In collaboration with Sam Blair. New York: Random House, 1982.

Harry Vardon

Howell, Audrey. *Harry Vardon: The Revealing Story of a Champion Golfer*. London: Stanley Paul, 1991.

Vardon, Harry. *My Golfing Life*. London: Hutchinson, 1933.

Glenna Collett Vare

Collett, Glenna. *Ladies in the Rough*. In collaboration with James M. Neville. New York: Knopf, 1928.

Ken Venturi

Venturi, Ken. *Comeback: The Ken Venturi Story*. In collaboration with Oscar Fraley. New York: Duell, Sloan and Pearce, 1966.

Norman Von Nida

Von Nida, Norman, and Ben Robertson. *The Von: Stories and Suggestions from Australian Golf's Little Master*. St. Lucia, Australia: University of Queensland Press, 1999.

Von Nida, Norman, and Muir Maclaren. *Golf Is My Business*. London: Frederick Muller, 1956.

Karrie Webb

Happell, Charles. *Karrie Webb*. Melbourne: Legend Books, 2002.

Tresidder, Phil. *Karrie Webb: The Making of Golf's Tigress*. Sydney: Pan Macmillan, 2000.

Mike Weir

Rubenstein, Lorne. *Mike Weir: The Road to the Masters*. Toronto: McClelland and Stewart, 2003.

Weir, Mike. *On Course with Mike Weir: Insights and Instruction from a Left-Hander on the PGA Tour*. In collaboration with Tim Campbell and Scott Morrison. Toronto: McGraw-Hill Ryerson, 2001.

Joyce Wethered

Tinkler, Basil Ashton. *Joyce Wethered: The Great Lady of Golf*. Stroud, England: Tempus, 2004.

Wethered, Joyce. *Golfing Memories and Methods*. London: Hutchinson, 1933.

Kathy Whitworth

Whitworth, Kathy. *Kathy Whitworth's Little Book of Golf Wisdom*. In collaboration with Jay Golden. New York: Skyhorse Publishing, 2007.

Michelle Wie

Adelson, Eric. *The Sure Thing: The Making and Unmaking of Golf's Phenom Michelle Wie*. New York: ESPN Books/Ballantine Books, 2009.

Mario, Jennifer. *Michelle Wie: The Making of a Champion*. New York: St. Martin's Griffin, 2006.

Craig Wood

Martin, J. Peter. *Craig Wood, The Blond Bomber: Native Son of Lake Placid*. Lake Placid, N.Y.: Adirondack Golf, 2002.

Tiger Woods

Callahan, Tom. *In Search of Tiger Woods: A Journey through Golf with Tiger Woods*. New York: Crown, 2003.

Feinstein, John. *The First Coming. Tiger Woods: Master or Martyr*. New York: The Library of Contemporary Thought, 1998.

Kupelian, Vartan. *Stalking the Tiger: A Writer's Diary*. Chelsea, Mich.: Sleeping Bear Press, 1997.

Mahony, Jeff, ed. *Tiger Woods 2001: The Year of the Tiger*. Middletown, Conn.: CheckerBee Publishing, 2001.

Rosaforte, Tim. *Raising the Bar: The Championship Years of Tiger Woods*. New York: St. Martin's Press, 2000.

———. *Tiger Woods: The Making of a Champion*. 2nd ed. New York: St. Martin's Press, rev., 1997.

Sampson, Curt. *Chasing Tiger*. New York: Atria Books, 2002.

Smiley, Bob. *Following the Roar: Trailing Tiger for All 604 Holes of His Most Spectacular Season*. New York: HarperCollins, 2008.

Sprayregen, Gerald, and William Hallberg. *The Soul of Tiger Woods*. New York: Gramercy Books, 1998.

Stafford, Ian. *In Search of the Tiger*. London: Ebury Press, 2003.

Strege, John. *Tiger: A Biography of Tiger Woods*. New York: Broadway Books, 1997.

Woods, Earl. *Training a Tiger: A Father's Guide to Raising a Winner in Both Golf and Life*. In collaboration with Pete McDaniel. New York: HarperCollins, 1997.

Ian Woosnam

Woosnam, Ian. *Woosie: My Autobiography*. London: CollinsWillow, 2002.

Babe Didrikson Zaharias

Cayleff, Susan. *Babe: The Life and Legend of Babe Didrikson Zaharias*. Urbana: University of Illinois Press, 1995.

Zaharias, Mildred Didrikson, and Harry Paxton. *This Life I've Led: My Autobiography*. New York: A. S. Barnes, 1956.

Caddies

History of Caddies

Clayton, Ward. *Men on the Bag: The Caddies of Augusta National*. Ann Arbor, Mich.: Sports Media Group, 2004.

Graves, Charles, and Henry Longhurst. *Candid Caddies*. London: Duckworth, 1935.

Jordan, G. Gunby. *Caddies*. In collaboration with Don Wade. Columbus, Ga.: Green Island Press, 1987.

Mackenzie, Richard. *A Wee Nip at the 19th Hole: A History of the St. Andrews Caddie*. Chelsea, Mich.: Sleeping Bear Press, 1997.

Stewart, Jerry. *Pebble Beach: Golf and the Forgotten Men*. Ann Arbor, Mich.: Sports Media Group, 2005.

Stirk, David. *Carry Your Bag, Sir*. London: H. F. and G. Witherby, 1989.

Caddie Autobiographies

Argea, Angelo. *The Bear and I: The Story of the World's Most Famous Caddie*. In collaboration with Jolee Edmonston. New York: Atheneum, 1979.

Bamberger, Michael. *The Green Road Home: A Caddie's Journal of Life on the Pro Golf Tour*. Chicago, Ill.: Contemporary, 1986.

Carrick, Michael, and Steve Duno. *Caddie Sense: Revelations of a PGA Tour Caddie on Playing the Game Of Golf*. New York: Thomas Dunne Books, 2000.

Donegan, Lawrence. *Four-Iron in the Soul*. London: Viking, 1997.

Hargreaves, Ernest. *Caddie in the Golden Age: My Years with Walter Hagen and Henry Cotton*. London: Partridge Press, 1993.

Reilly, Rick. *Who's Your Caddy? Looping for the Great, Near Great, and Reprobates of Golf*. New York: Doubleday, 2003.

COMPETITIONS

History of Professional Tours

Cousins, Geoffrey. *Lords of the Links: The Story of Professional Golf*. London: Hutchinson Benson, 1977.

History of the PGA of America

Graffis, Herb. *The PGA: The Official History of the Professional Golfers' Association of America*. New York: Crowell, 1975.

History of the PGA Tour

Barkow, Al. *Golf's Golden Grind: The History of the Tour*. New York: Harcourt Brace Jovanovich, 1974.

——. *The History of the PGA Tour*. New York: Doubleday, 1989.

D'Antonio, Michael. *Tin Cup Dreams: A Long Shot Makes It on the PGA Tour*. New York: Hyperion, 2000.

Durrance, Dick, II, and John Yow. *The PGA Tour: A Look behind the Scenes*. Kansas City, Mo.: Andrews McMeel, 2003.

Feinstein, John. *A Good Walk Spoiled: Days and Nights on the PGA Tour*. Boston: Little, Brown, 1995.

——. *Tales from Q School: Inside Golf's Fifth Major*. New York: Little, Brown and Company, 2007.

Gleason, Dan. *The Great, the Grand, and the Also-Ran: Rabbits and Champions on the Pro Golf Tour*. New York: Random House, 1976.

Gould, David. *Q School Confidential: Inside Golf's Cruelest Tournament*. New York: St. Martin's Press, 1999.

Keane, Christopher. *The Tour*. New York: Stein and Day, 1974.

Lewis, Chris. *The Scorecard Always Lies: A Year behind the Scenes on the PGA Tour*. New York: Free Press, 2007.

Nash, Bruce, et al. *The Hole Truth: Inside the Ropes of the PGA Tour*. Kansas City, Mo.: Andrews McMeel, 1992.

Shipnuck, Alan. *Bud, Sweat, and Tees: A Walk on the Wild Side of the PGA Tour*. New York: Simon and Schuster, 2001.

Strege, John. *Tournament Week: Inside the Ropes and behind the Scenes on the PGA Tour*. New York: HarperCollins, 2000.

Yow, John. *The PGA Tour: A Look behind the Scenes, Photographs by Dick Durrance II*. Kansas City, Mo.: Andrews McMeel, 2003.

History of Individual PGA Tour Events

Fowler, Vance. *MCI Classic: The Heritage of Golf: A Tournament Retrospective*. Hilton Head Island, S.C.: The Heritage Classic Foundation, 1995.

Greenspan, Glenn. *The Players Championship: A Historical Perspective 1974–1988*. Jacksonville, Fla.: PGA Tour, 1988.

Griffin, Keith, ed. *50 Years of Great Golf: 50th Anniversary of the Canon Greater Hartford Open*. Hartford, Conn.: Hometown Marketing, 2001.

Herbst, Dave. *Classic Memories: A 20 Year Retrospective of the Golf Classic at Walt Disney World Resort, 1971–1990*. Lake Buena Vista, Fla.: Walt Disney Company, 1991.

Mullins, Richard. *The Phoenix Open: A 50 Year History*. Phoenix, Ariz.: The Thunderbirds, 1984.

Netland, Dwayne. *The Crosby: Greatest Show in Golf*. New York: Doubleday, 1975.

Roberson, Dennis. *Colonial, the Tournament: 60 years of Greatness*. Dallas, Tex.: Panache Partners, 2006.

Seifert, Martin, ed. *Los Angeles Open 50th Anniversary*. Los Angeles: Privately printed, 1976.

Wade, Don, and Martin Davis. *The Players Championship: 25th Anniversary: 1974–1998*. Greenwich, Conn.: The American Golfer, 1988.

History of the Senior PGA Tour

Shaw, Mark. *Diamonds in the Rough: Championship Golf on the Senior PGA Tour*. New York: Ballantine Books, 1998.

History of British PGA

Holt, Richard, et al. *The Professional Golfers' Association 1901–2001: One Hundred Years of Service to Golf*. Droitwich, England: Grant Books, 2002.

Jackson, Alan E. *The British Professional Golfers 1887–1930, a Register*. Droitwich, England: Grant Books, 1994.

History of European PGA Tour

Lewis, Peter N. *The Dawn of Professional Golf: The Genesis of the European Tour 1894–1914*. New Ridley, England: Hobbs and McEwan, 1995.

St. John, Lauren. *Shooting at Clouds: Inside the European PGA Tour*. Edinburgh: Mainstream Publishing, 1991.

Major Championships

Brenner, Morgan G. *The Majors of Golf: Complete Records of the Open, the U.S. Open, the PGA Championship and the Masters, 1860–2008*. Jefferson, N.C.: McFarland, 2009.

Evans, Alun. *The Golf Majors: Records and Yearbook*. 4th ed. Cheltenham, England: Sports Books, rev., 2005.

Feinstein, John. *The Majors: In Pursuit of Golf's Holy Grail*. Boston: Little, Brown, 1999.

Peper, George. *Grand Slam Golf: Courses of the Masters, the U.S. Open, the British Open, the PGA Championship*. New York: Harry N. Abrams, 1991.

Williams, Michael. *Grand Slam: Golf's Major Championships*. London: Hamlyn, 1988.

Open Championship (British Open)

Alliss, Peter. *The Open: The British Open Championships since the War*. In collaboration with Michael Hobbs. London: Collins, 1984.

Burnet, Bobby. *The St. Andrews Opens*. Edinburgh: Sportprint, 1990.

Colville, George M. *Five Open Champions and the Musselburgh Golf Story*. Musselburgh, Scotland: Colville Books, 1980.

Corcoran, Michael. *Duel in the Sun: Tom Watson and Jack Nicklaus in the Battle of Turnberry*. New York: Simon and Schuster, 2000.

Cousins, Geoffrey, and Tom Scott. *A Century of Opens*. London: Frederick Muller, 1971.

Dabell, Norman. *One Hand on the Claret Jug: How They Nearly Won the Open*. Edinburgh: Mainstream Publishing, 2006.

———. *Winning the Open: The Caddies' Stories*. 2nd ed. Edinburgh: Mainstream Publishing, 2001.

Fay, Michael J. *Golf as It Was in the Beginning: The Legendary British Open Courses*. New York: Universe Publishing, 2002.

Hobbs, Michael. *Great Opens: Historic British and American Championships 1913–1975*. London: David and Charles, 1976.

———. *The Open 1960–1990*. Westone, England: Pipkin Press, 1991.

Mortimer, Charles G., and Fred Pignon. *The Story of the Open Golf Championship: 1860–1950*. London: Jarrolds, 1952.

Murray, Francis. *The British Open: A History of Golf's Greatest Championship*. Chicago, Ill.: Contemporary Books, 2000.

Norwood, Bev, ed. *The Open Championship*. London: various publishers, 1985–2009.

Sampson, Curt. *Royal and Ancient: Blood, Sweat, and Fear at the British Open*. New York: Villard, 2000.

Samuel, John. *The Guardian History of the Open Championship*. London: Fourth Estate, 1992.

Scott, Tom. *A Century of Golf 1860–1960*. England: Masius and Fergusson, 1960.

Masters Tournament

Bisher, Furman. *The Masters: Augusta Revisited, an Intimate View*. Birmingham, Ala.: Oxmoor House, 1976.

Christian, Frank. *Augusta National and the Masters: A Photographer's Scrapbook*. 2nd ed. In collaboration with Cal Brown. Chelsea, Mich.: Sleeping Bear Press, 2004.

Eubanks, Steve. *Augusta: Home of the Masters Tournament*. Nashville, Tenn.: Rutledge Hill Press, 1997.

Green, Ron. *Shouting at Amen Corner: Dispatches from the Masters, the World's Greatest Golf Tournament*. Champaign, Ill.: Sports Publishing, 1999.

The Masters. (various authors). Augusta, Ga.: Augusta National Golf Club, 1978–present (official annual).

Owens, David. *The Making of the Masters: Clifford Roberts, Augusta National, and Golf's Most Prestigious Tournament*. New York: Simon and Schuster, 1999.

Price, Charles. *A Golf Story: Bobby Jones, Augusta National and the Masters Tournament*. New York: Atheneum, 1986.

Rider, Steve. *Europe at the Masters*. Thrupp, England: Green Umbrella Publishing, 2006.

Sampson, Curt. *The Lost Masters: Grace and Disgrace in '68*. New York: Atria Books, 2005.

———. *The Masters: Golf, Money and Power in Augusta*. New York: Villard, 1998.

Schaap, Dick. *The Masters: The Winning of a Golf Classic*. New York: Random House, 1970.

Shipnuck, Alan. *The Battle of Augusta National: Hootie, Martha and the Masters of the Universe*. New York: Simon and Schuster, 2004.

Sowell, David. *The Masters: A Hole-By-Hole History of America's Golf Classic*. 2nd ed. Dulles, Va.: Potomac Books, rev., 2007.

Taylor, Dawson. *The Masters: Golf's Most Prestigious Tradition*. 4th ed. Chicago, Ill.: Contemporary Books, rev., 1986.

PGA Championship

Companiotte, John, and Catherine Lewis. *The PGA Championship: The Season's Final Major*. Ann Arbor, Mich.: Clock Tower Press, 2004.

Peper, George, ed. *The PGA Championship 1916–1984*. Palm Beach Gardens, Fla.: PGA of America, 1985.

PGA Championships Annual. (various authors). Cleveland, Ohio: IMG, 1995 to present.

United States Open

Barrett, David. *Golf Courses of the U.S. Open*. New York: Abrams, 2007.

Brown, Scott. *The Major: 7 Days at Golf's Greatest Championship*. Chelsea, Mich.: Sleeping Bear Press, 2000.

Delery, John, and Angus G. Garber III. *100 Years of the U.S. Open: A Century of Excellence*. 4th ed. New York: MetroBooks, rev., 2000.

Feinstein, John. *Open: Inside the Ropes at Bethpage Black*. Boston: Little, Brown, 2003.

Graubart, Julian I. *Golf's Greatest Championship: The 1960 U.S. Open*. New York: Donald I. Fine Books, 1997.

Johnson, Sal. *The Official U.S. Open Almanac*. Dallas, Tex.: Taylor Publishing, 1995.

Mediate, Rocco, and John Feinstein. *Are You Kidding Me?: The Story of Rocco Mediate's Extraordinary Battle with Tiger Woods at the U.S. Open*. New York: Little, Brown, 2009.

Schapp, Dick. *Massacre at Winged Foot: The U.S. Open, Minute by Minute*. New York: Random House, 1974.

Sommers, Robert. *The U.S. Open: Golf's Ultimate Challenge*. 2nd ed. New York: Oxford University Press, rev., 1996.

Steinbreder, John. *Golf Courses of the U.S. Open*. Dallas, Tex.: Taylor Publishing, 1996.

Strege, John. *Tiptoeing through Hell: Playing the U.S. Open on Golf's Most Treacherous Courses*. New York: HarperCollins, 2002.

U.S. Open Official Annual. (various authors). Cleveland, Ohio: IMG, 1985–2009.

Ryder Cup

Browne, P. J. *Reading the Green: The Inside Line on the Irish in the Ryder Cup*. Dublin: Currach Press, 2008.

Bubka, Bob, and Tom Clavin. *The Ryder Cup: Golf's Greatest Event*. New York: Crown Publishers, 1999.

Clarke, Darren. *Complete Illustrated History of the Ryder Cup: Golf's Greatest Drama*. Chicago, Ill.: Triumph Books, 2006.

———. *Heroes All: My Ryder Cup Story*. London: Hodder and Stoughton, 2006.

Concannon, Dale. *The Ryder Cup: Seven Decades of Golfing Glory, Drama and Controversy*. London: Arum Press, 2001.

Critchley, Bruce. *The Captain's Challenge: Winning the Ryder Cup*. Cambridge, England: Icon Books, 2008.

Dabell, Norman. *How We Won the Ryder Cup: The Caddies' Stories*. 3rd ed. Edinburgh: Mainstream Publishing, 2003.

Feherty, David. *David Feherty's Totally Subjective History of the Ryder Cup*. In collaboration with James A. Frank. New York: Rugged Land, 2004.

Fry, Peter. *Samuel Ryder: The Man behind the Ryder Cup*. Coveway, England: Wright Press, 2000.

Gallacher, Bernard. *Captain at Kiawah*. In collaboration with Renton Laidlaw. London: Chapmans, 1991.

Hobbs, Michael. *The Ryder Cup: The Illustrated History*. Droitwich, England: Grant Books, 1989.

Jarman, Colin M. *The Ryder Cup: The Definitive History of Playing Golf for Pride and Country*. Chicago, Ill.: Contemporary Books, 1999.

Knight, Matthew. *The "Times" Ryder Cup: A Complete Photographic Record from the 1920s to the Present Day*. London: Times Books, 2006.

Rosaforte, Tim. *Heartbreak Hill: The Anatomy of a Ryder Cup*. New York: St. Martin's Press, 1996.

Stafford, Ian. *Easy Ryder: Europe's Magnificent K Club Triumph*. Edinburgh: Mainstream Publishing, 2006.

Trevillion, Paul. *Dead Heat: The '69 Ryder Cup Classic*. London: Stanley Paul, 1969.

Williams, Michael. *The Official History of the Ryder Cup: 1927–1989*. London: Stanley Paul, 1989.

Important Amateur Events

Behrend, John. *The Amateur: The Story of the Amateur Golf Championship 1885–1995*. Droitwich, England: Grant Books, 1995.

Sheehan, Colin, ed. *The Amateur Championship: The History and Personal Recollections of Its Champions*. Pearl River, N.Y.: The Classics of Golf, 2006.

Simmonds, Gordon C. *The Walker Cup 1922–2003: Golf's Finest Tournament*. 2nd ed. Droitwich, England: Grant Books, rev., 2004.

Yerger III, John. *The Story of Sunnehanna Country Club and the Sunnehanna Amateur*. Johnstown, Pa.: Privately printed, 2004.

Olympic Golf

Jeanneau, Georges. *Golf and the Olympic Games*. In collaboration with Nicolas Jeanneau. Levalloi-Perret, France: Federation Française de Golf, 2003.

History of the LPGA

Burnett, Jim. *Tee Times: On the Road with the Ladies Professional Golf Tour*. New York: Scribners, 1997.

Darden, Dee. *Inside the Ropes: Life on the LPGA Tour as Seen through the Lens of Photographer and Caddy*. Cincinnati, Ohio: Fairway Publications, 1994.

Kahn, Liz. *The LPGA: The Unauthorized Version, the History of the Ladies' Professional Golf Association*. Menlo Park, Calif.: Group Fore Productions, 1996.

Sanson, Nanette S., ed. *Champions of Women's Golf: Celebrating Fifty Years of the LPGA*. Naples, Fla.: Quail Mark Books, 2000.

Reference Annuals

American Annual Golf Guide and Year Book. New York: Angus, 1916–1931.

Balsillie, Robert Ness, ed. *Fraser's Golf Directory and Year Book*. Montreal, Canada: Fraser, 1923–1937.

Bauchope, C. Robertson, and David Scott Duncan, eds. *The Golfing Annual*. London: Horace Cox, 1888–1910.

Clougher, T. R. *Golf Clubs of the Empire*. London: Clougher, 1927–1932.

Crawley, Leonard. *Playfair Golf Annual*. London: Playfair Books, 1950–1954.

Dalrymple, W. *Golfer's Guide to the Game and Greens of Scotland* (published later as *Golfer's Guide for the United Kingdom;* and *Golfer's Guide Annual*). Edinburgh: W. H. White, 1894–1899.

Edmund, Nick, ed. *Following the Fairways*. London: Kensington West Productions, 1986–2001.

——. *Heineken World of Golf*. London: Stanley Paul, 1993–1995.

Frischknecht, Dean W. *American College Golf Guide*. Hillsboro, Oreg.: Dean W. Frischknecht Publishing, 1989–2003.

Gambatese, Joseph, ed. *The Golf Guide*. Belleair Bluff, Fla.: Snibbe Publications, 1963–1989.

Golf Digest Almanac. Norwalk, Conn.: Golf Digest, 1984–1989.

Golf World Magazine. *Piccadilly World of Golf*. London: Wayland Publishers, 1972–1976.

Golfer's Handbook (published later as *The Royal & Ancient Golfer's Handbook*). Edinburgh: The Golf Agency, 1899–2009.

Guide Plumon. *The Continental Golf Year Book (Annuaire des Golfes de France et du Continent)*. Paris: Guides Plumon, 1927–1950.

Ladies Golf Union Annual (published later as *The Ladies Golf Union Year Book* and *The Lady Golfer's Handbook)*. Various locations: various publishers, 1893–present.

Low, John L., et al., eds. *Nisbet's Golf Year Book*. London: James Nisbet, 1905–1914.

McCormack, Mark H. *The World of Professional Golf* (and various titles). Various locations: various publishers, 1967–2009.

McLean, Terry, et al., *The DB Golf Annual*. Auckland, New Zealand: MOA, 1974–1980.

Ostermann, H. T. *Golf in Europe*. Mannheim, Germany: Editions Golfing Europe, 1961–1982.

Richardson, William D., et al. *Barnes' Official Golf Guide*. New York: A. S. Barnes, 1947–1949.

Richardson, William D., and Lincoln Werden. *Annual Golf Review*. New York: Golfer's Year Book, 1931–1934.

———. *The Golfer's Yearbook*. New York: Golfer's Year Book, 1930–1933.

Simms, George. *John Player Golf Yearbook*. London: Queen Anne Press, 1973–1976.

———. *The World of Golf*. London: Macdonald and Jane's, 1977–1980.

Spalding's Official Golf Guide. New York: American Sports Publishing, 1895–1932.

Stanley, Louis T., ed. *Pelham Golf Year*. London: Pelham Books, 1981–1982.

Van Tassel Sutphen, W. G., and Josiah Newman, eds. *Harper's Official Golf Guide*. New York: Harper and Brothers and The Grafton Press, 1900–1902.

Annuals, Media Guides, and Yearbooks

In addition to the publications detailed above, the best sources for tournament and championship records are the various annual media guides and yearbooks issued by the major golf associations. It would be unwieldy to list the bibliographic details for each of these publications. However, researchers interested in pursuing such records can find extensive collections of these publications in all major golf libraries. Annuals, media guides, and yearbooks have been issued by Champions Tour (formerly as Senior PGA Tour), LPGA, Masters, Nationwide Tour (formerly Nike Tour), PGA European Tour, PGA of America, PGA Tour, USGA, WPGA (Europe), and others.

COURSES AND CLUBS

Golf Course Design and Construction

Bauer, Aleck. *Hazards: Those Essential Elements in a Golf Course Without Which the Game Would Be Dull and Uninteresting*. Chicago, Ill.: Toby Rubovits, 1913.

Bendelow, Tom. *Golf Courses by the American Park Builders*. Chicago, Ill.: American Park Builders, 1926.

Bengyfield, William H. *Specifications for a Method of Putting Green Construction*. Far Hills, N.J.: U.S. Golf Association, 1989.

Colt, Harry S., and Charles H. Alison. *Some Essays on Golf Course Architecture*. London: Country Life and George Newnes, 1920.

Cory, Gregory L., et al. *Golf Course Development in Residential Communities*. Washington, D.C.: Urban Land Institute, 2001.

Crockford, Claude. *The Complete Golf Course: Turf and Design*. Mt. Eliza, Australia: Thomson Wolveridge and Associates, 1993.

Daley, Paul. *Favorite Holes by Design: The Architects' Choice*. Glen Waverly, Australia: Full Swing Golf Publishing, 2004.

———. *Golf Architecture: A Worldwide Perspective*. Volumes 1–4. Glen Waverly, Australia: Full Swing Golf Publishing, 2002–2009.

———. *Links Golf: The Inside Story*. South Yarra, Australia: Hardie Grant Books, 2000.

Davis, William B., et al. *The Sand Putting Green: Construction and Management*. Oakland, Calif.: Division of Agriculture and Natural Resources, University of California, 1990.

Doak, Tom. *The Anatomy of a Golf Course*. New York: Lyons and Burford, 1992.

Douglas, Nigel B. *Golf Course Design: Modern Day Issues and Experiences*. Hertford, England: Authors Online, 2004.

Golf Course Superintendents Association of America. *Golf Greens: History, Theory, Construction and Maintenance*. 3rd ed. Lawrence, Kans.: Golf Course Superintendents Association of America, rev., 1996.

Graves, Robert Muir, and Geoffrey S. Cornish. *Classic Golf Hole Design: Using the Greatest Holes as Inspiration for Modern Courses*. New York: John Wiley and Sons, 2002.

Hawtree, Fred W. *The Golf Course: Planning, Design, Construction and Maintenance*. London: E. and F. N. Spon, 1983.

Hummel, Norman W., Jr., and Michael Hurdzan. *Golf Greens: History, Theory, Construction and Maintenance*. Lawrence, Kans.: Golf Course Superintendents Association of America, 2001.

Hunter, Robert. *The Links*. New York: Scribners, 1926.

Hurdzan, Michael. J. *Building a Practical Golf Facility: A Step-By-Step Guide to Realizing a Dream*. Chicago, Ill.: American Society of Golf Course Architects, 2003.

———. *Golf Course Architecture: Evolutions in Design, Construction, and Restoration Technology*. 2nd ed. Hoboken, N.J.: John Wiley, rev., 2006.

———. *Golf Greens: History, Design, and Construction*. Hoboken, N.J.: John Wiley, 2004.

Hutchinson, Horace Gordon, ed. *Golf Greens and Greenkeeping*. London: Country Life, 1906.

Jones, Robert Trent, Jr. *Golf by Design: How to Lower Your Score by Reading the Features of a Course*. Boston: Little, Brown, 1993.

———. *Golf Course Architecture*. New York: Thompson and Jones, 1938.

Kato, Shunsuke. *What Makes a Good Golf Course Good*. Tokyo: Kato International Design, 1990.

Klein, Bradley S. *Rough Meditations*. 2nd ed. Hoboken, N.J.: John Wiley, rev., 2006.

MacKenzie, Alister J. *Golf Course Architecture: Economy in Course Construction and Green Keeping*. London: Simpkin, Marshall, Hamilton, Kent, 1920.

———. *The Spirit of St. Andrews*. Chelsea, Mich.: Sleeping Bear Press, 1995.

Muirhead, Desmond, and Guy L. Rando. *Golf Course Development and Real Estate*. Washington, D.C.: The Urban Land Institute, 1994.

Price, Robert. *Scotland's Golf Courses*. 2nd ed. Aberdeen, Scotland: Aberdeen University Press, rev., 2002.

Richardson, Forrest L. *Routing the Golf Course: The Art and Science That Forms the Golf Journey*. Hoboken, N.J.: John Wiley , 2002.

Richardson, Forrest L., and Mark K. Fine. *Bunkers, Pits and Other Hazards: A Guide to Design, Maintenance and Preservation of Golf's Essential Elements*. Hoboken, N.J.: John Wiley, 2006.

Riddell, Gervase Carre. *Golf Architecture in Australia: Its Design and Construction*. Swan Hill, Australia: Privately printed, 1972.

Strawn, John. *Driving the Green: The Making of a Golf Course*. New York: HarperCollins, 1991.

Sutton, Martin A. F., ed. *Golf Course Design, Construction and Upkeep*. 2nd ed. London: Simpkin Marshall, rev., 1950.

Sutton, Martin H. F., ed. *The Book of the Links: A Symposium on Golf*. London: W. H. Smith, 1912.

Thomas, George C., Jr. *Golf Architecture in America: Its Strategy and Construction*. Los Angeles: Times-Mirror Press, 1927.

Tillinghast, A. W. *Planning a Golf Course*. Philadelphia, Pa.: Privately printed, 1917.

Wethered, H. N., and T. Simpson. *The Architectural Side of Golf*. London: Longmans, Green, 1929.

History of Golf Course Design

Cornish, Geoffrey S. *Eighteen Stakes on a Sunday Afternoon: A Chronicle of Golf Course Architecture in North America*. Droitwich, England: Grant Books, 2002.

Cornish, Geoffrey, and Michael J. Hurdzan. *Golf Course Design: An Annotated Bibliography with Highlights of Its History and Resources*. Droitwich, England: Grant Books, 2006.

Cornish, Geoffrey S., and Ronald W. Whitten. *The Architects of Golf: A Survey of Golf Course Design from Its Beginnings to the Present, with an Encyclopedic Listing of Golf Course Architects and Their Courses*. New York: HarperCollins, 1993.

Hawtree, Fred W. *Aspects of Golf Course Architecture 1899–1924*. Droitwich, England: Grant Books, 1998.

Shackelford, Geoff. *The Art of Golf Design*. Chelsea, Mich.: Sleeping Bear Press, 2001.

———. *The Golden Age of Golf Design*. Chelsea, Mich.: Sleeping Bear Press, 1999.

———. *Grounds for Golf: The History and Fundamentals of Golf Course Design*. New York: Thomas Dunne, 2003.

———. *Masters of the Links*. Chelsea, Mich.: Sleeping Bear Press, 1997.

Shiels, Michael Patrick, and the American Society of Golf Course Architects. *Secrets of the Great Golf Course Architects*. New York: Skyhorse Publishing, 2008.

Wexler, Daniel. *Lost Links: Forgotten Treasures of Golf's Golden Age*. Chelsea, Mich.: Clock Tower Press, 2003.

———. *The Missing Links: America's Greatest Lost Golf Courses and Holes*. Chelsea, Mich.: Sleeping Bear Press, 2000.

Golf Course Architects

Tom Bendelow

Bendelow, Stuart W. *Thomas "Tom" Bendelow: The Johnny Appleseed of American Golf*. Savannah, Ga.: Williams and Company, 2006.

James Braid

Moreton, John. *The Golf Courses of James Braid*. Droitwich, England: Grant Books, 1996.

Moreton, John, and Ian Cumming. *James Braid: Golf Course Designer*. United Kingdom: Black Bear Press, 2007.

H. S. Colt

Hawtree, Fred W. *Colt and Co., Golf Course Architects: A Biographical Study of Henry Shapland Colt 1869–1951 with His Partners C. H. Allison, J. S. F. Morrison and Dr. A. Mackenzie*. Woodstock, England: Cambuc Archive, 1991.

Pete Dye

Dye, Pete. *Bury Me in a Pot Bunker: Golf through the Eyes of the Game's Most Challenging Course Designer*. In collaboration with Mark Shaw. Reading, Mass.: Addison-Wesley, 1994.

Zuckerman, Joel. *Pete Dye Golf Courses: Fifty Years of Visionary Design*. New York: Harry N. Abrams, 2008.

Tom Fazio

Fazio, Tom. *Golf Course Designs*. In collaboration with Cal Brown. New York: Harry N. Abrams, 2000.

Robert Trent Jones Jr.

Kirk, John, and Timothy Jacobs. *The Golf Courses of Robert Trent Jones Jr.* New York: Gallery, 1988.

Robert Trent Jones Sr.

Jones, Robert Trent. *Golf's Magnificent Challenge*. In collaboration with Larry Dennis. New York: McGraw-Hill, 1988.

Charles Blair Macdonald

Bahto, George. *The Evangelist of Golf: The Story of Charles Blair Macdonald*. Chelsea, Mich.: Clock Tower Press, 2002.

Macdonald, Charles Blair. *Scotland's Gift, Golf: Reminiscences 1872–1927*. New York: Scribners, 1928.

Alister MacKenzie

Byrdy, Stan. *Alister Mackenzie's Masterpiece: Augusta National Golf Club*. Ann Arbor, Mich.: Sports Media, 2005.

Doak, Tom, et al. *The Life and Work of Dr. Alister MacKenzie*. Chelsea, Mich.: Sleeping Bear Press, 2001.

Shackelford, Geoff. *Alister Mackenzie's Cypress Point Club*. Chelsea, Mich.: Sleeping Bear Press, 2000.

Perry Maxwell

Clouser, Christopher. *The Midwest Associate: The Life and Works of Perry Duke Maxwell*. Victoria, Canada: Trafford Publishing, 2006.

Tom Morris Sr.

Kroeger, Robert. *The Golf Courses of Old Tom Morris*. Cincinnati, Ohio: Heritage Communications, 1995.

Jack Nicklaus

Jacobs, Timothy. *The Golf Courses of Jack Nicklaus*. London: Bison Books, 1989.

Nicklaus, Jack. *Nicklaus by Design: Golf Course Strategy and Architecture*. In collaboration with Chris Millard. New York: Harry N. Abrams, 2002.

Donald Ross

Dunn, Paul, and P. J. Dunn. *Great Donald Ross Golf Courses You Can Play*. Lanham, Md.: Derrydale, 2001.

Fay, Michael J. *Golf As It Was Meant to Be Played: A Celebration of Donald Ross's Vision of the Game*. New York: Universe Publishing, 2000.

Klein, Bradley S. *Discovering Donald Ross: The Architect and His Golf*. Chelsea, Mich.: Sleeping Bear Press, 2001.

Ross, Donald. *Golf Has Never Failed Me: The Lost Commentaries of Legendary Golf Architect Donald J. Ross*. Chelsea, Mich. Sleeping Bear Press, 1996.

George C. Thomas Jr.

Shackelford, Geoff. *The Captain: George C. Thomas, Jr. and His Golf Architecture*. Chelsea, Mich.: Sleeping Bear Press, 1996.

Stanley Thompson

Barclay, James. *The Toronto Terror*. Chelsea, Mich.: Sleeping Bear Press, 2000.

Bell, Mike. *The Golf Courses of Stanley Thompson: Celebrating Canada's Historic Masterpieces*. Toronto: Photoscape, 2007.

A. W. Tillinghast

Tillinghast, A. W. *The Course Beautiful: A Collection of Articles and Photographs on Golf Course Design*. Springfield, N.J.: Tree Wolf Productions, 1996.

———. *Gleanings from the Wayside: My Recollections as a Golf Architect*. Springfield, N.J.: Tree Wolf Productions, 2001.

———. *Reminiscences of the Links: A Treasury Of Essays and Vintage Photographs on Scottish and Early American Golf*. Springfield, N.J.: Tree Wolf Productions, 1998.

Young, Phillip. *Tillinghast: Creator of Golf Courses*. Pearl River, N.Y.: Future Classics of Golf, 2005.

Golf Course Maintenance

Beard, James B. *Turfgrass Management for Golf Courses*. 2nd ed. Chelsea, Mich.: Ann Arbor Press; Far Hills, N.J.: U.S. Golf Association, rev., 2002.

Beard, James B, et. al. *Turfgrass Bibliography from 1672 to 1972*. Ann Arbor: Michigan State University Press, 1977.

Labbance, Bob, and Gordon Witteveen. *Keepers of the Green: A History of Golf Course Management*. Chelsea, Mich.: Ann Arbor Press and Golf Course Superintendents Association of America, 2002.

Lees, Peter. *Care of the Green*. New York: C. B. Wilcox, 1918.

McCarty, L. B. *Best Golf Course Management Practices*. 2nd ed. Upper Saddle River, N.J.: Pearson Education, rev., 2005.

Golf Courses Worldwide

Allen, Peter. *Famous Fairways: A Look at the World of Championship Courses*. London: Stanley Paul, 1968.

Bonallack, Sir Michael, and Steve Smyers. *Golf Courses: Fairways of the World*. New York: Rizzoli International, 2006.

Cronan, Jan, ed. *Golf Travel by Design: How You Can Play the World's Best Golf Courses by the Sport's Top Architects*. Guilford, Conn.: Globe Pequot Press, 2003.

Davis, William H. *The World's Best Golf*. Trumbull, Conn., and New York: Golf Digest/Pocket Books, 1991.

Diaz, Jaime, et al. *Hallowed Ground: Golf's Greatest Places*. Shelton, Conn.: The Greenwich Workshop Press, 1999.

Doak, Tom. *The Confidential Guide to Golf Courses*. 3rd ed. Chelsea, Mich.: Sleeping Bear Press, rev., 1996.

Golob, Fulvio, and Giulia Muttoni. *Golf Around the World: The Great Game and Its Most Spectacular Courses*. Vercelli, Italy: White Star Publishers, 2008.

Green, Robert, and Brian Morgan. *Classic Holes of Golf: A Grand Tour of the World's Most Challenging, Historic and Beautiful Golf Holes*. New York: Prentice Hall Press, 1989.

Hutchinson, Horace Gordon, et al. *Famous Golf Links*. London: Longmans, Green, 1891.

Leach, Henry. *The Happy Golfer*. London: Macmillan, 1914.

Longhurst, Henry. *Round in Sixty-Eight*. London: Werner Laurie, 1953.

McCallen, Brian. *Golf Resorts of the World: The Best Places to Stay and Play*. New York: Harry N. Abrams, 1993.

Morgan, Brian. *A World Portrait of Golf*. London: Arum Press, 1988.

Oliver, Darius. *Planet Golf: The Definitive Reference to Great Golf Courses outside the United States of America*. New York: Abrams, 2007.

Peper, George. *The 500 World's Greatest Golf Holes*. In collaboration with the editors of *Golf Magazine*. New York: Artisan, 2000.

Rawlinson, Mark, ed. *World Atlas of Golf: The Greatest Courses and How They Are Played*. London: Hamlyn, 2008.

Golf Courses in Africa

McLean, Stuart. *South African Golf Courses: A Portrait of the Best*. Cape Town, South Africa: Struik, 1993.

Quick, Tina L., et al. *Rhinos in the Rough: A Golfer's Guide to Kenya*. Nairobi: Kenway Productions, 1993.

Winter, Grant. *Guide to Southern African Golf Courses*. Cape Town, South Africa: Struik, 1986.

Golf Courses in Australasia

Clark, Liz. *Birdies, Bogeys and Kiwis: Golfing around New Zealand*. Sidney, Canada: Wild West Coast Publishing, 2008.

Clarke, Alan, and Neil Ffrench-Blake, eds. *South East Asia Golf Guide*. Brackley, England: Priory, 1995.

Hyde, Tom. *100 Essential New Zealand Golf Holes*. Wellington: Awa Press, 2008.

Morris, John, and Leonard Cobb. *Great Golf Holes of New Zealand*. Auckland: Morris/Cobb Publishers, 1971.

Moyer, Robin, and Trevor Ball. *The Great Golf Courses of China*. Hong Kong: Pacific Empire International, 2006.

Oliver, Darius. *Australia's Finest Golf Courses*. Sydney: New Holland, 2003.
Ramsey, Tom. *Discover Australia's Golf Courses*. Melbourne: Dent, 1987.
———. *Great Australian Golf Courses*. Sydney: Weldon Publishing, 1990.
Thomson, Peter. *Peter Thomson's Classic Golf Holes of Australia*. Melbourne: Lothian Publishing, 1988.

Golf Courses in Europe

Dobereiner, Peter. *Golf Courses of the European PGA Tour*. In collaboration with Gordon Richardson. London: Aurum Press, 1992.
Hutchinson, Horace Gordon. *The Golfing Pilgrim: On Many Links*. London: Methuen, 1898.

France

Bessey, Jean-Francois. *Golf: France's Most Beautiful Courses*. France: Editions Terre D Images, 1999.

United Kingdom

Allen, Peter. *Play the Best Courses: Great Golf in the British Isles*. London: Stanley Paul, 1973.
———. *The Sunley Book of Royal Golf*. London: Stanley Paul, 1988.
Darwin, Bernard. *The Golf Courses of the British Isles*. London: Duckworth, 1910.
De St. Jorre, John. *Legendary Golf Clubs of Scotland, England, Wales and Ireland*. Wellington, Fla.: Edgeworth Editions, 1998.
Dickinson, Patric. *A Round of Golf Courses*. London: Evans Brothers, 1951.
Finegan, James W. *All Courses Great and Small: A Golfer's Pilgrimage to England and Wales*. New York: Simon and Schuster, 2003.
———. *Where Golf Is Great: The Finest Courses of Scotland and Ireland*. New York: Artisan, 2006.
Harvey, Geoff, and Vanessa Strowger. *Britain's 100 Extraordinary Golf Holes*. London: Aesculus Press, 2006.
Hutchinson, Horace Gordon. *British Golf Links: A Short Account of the Leading Golf Links of the United Kingdom*. London: J. S. Virtue, 1897.
Price, Mike Berners. *The Centurions of Golf: 100 English Courses Celebrating 100 Years of Golf*. Little Gaddesden, England: Radial Sports Publishing, 2006.
Staddon, Jackie, and Hilary Weston. *The Golf Tour Great Britain and Ireland: The Essential Guide to 43 Major Courses*. Basingstoke, England: AA Publishing, 2007.

Steel, Donald. *Classic Golf Links of Great Britain and Ireland*. London: Chapmans, 1992.

Worley, David. *Journey through the Links*. London: Aurum Press, 2007.

Ireland

Coyne, Tom. *A Course Called Ireland: A Long Walk in Search of a Country, a Pint, and the Next Tee*. New York: Gotham Books, 2009.

De St. Jorre, John. *Legendary Golf Links of Ireland*. Wellington, Fla.: Edgeworth Editions, 2006.

Finegan, James W. *Emerald Fairways and Foam-Flecked Seas: A Golfer's Pilgrimage to the Courses of Ireland*. New York: Simon and Schuster, 1996.

Lambrecht, Lawrence Casey. *Emerald Gems: The Links of Ireland*. Westerly, R.I.: Lambrecht Photography, 2002.

Phinney, Richard, and Scott Whitley. *Links of Heaven: A Complete Guide to Golf Journeys in Ireland*. Ottawa: Baltray Books, 1996.

Redmond, John. *Great Golf Courses of Ireland*. Dublin: Gill and Macmillan, 1999.

Zingg, Paul J. *An Emerald Odyssey: In Search of the Gods of Golf and Ireland*. Wilton, Ireland: The Collins Press, 2008.

Scotland

Bamberger, Michael. *To the Linksland: A Golfing Adventure*. New York: Viking, 1992.

Finegan, James W. *Blasted Heaths and Blessed Greens: A Golfer's Pilgrimage to the Courses of Scotland*. New York: Simon and Schuster, 1996.

Lyle, Sandy. *The Championship Courses of Scotland*. In collaboration with Bob Ferrier. Kingswood, England: Windmill, 1982.

McGuire, Brenda, and John McGuire. *Golf by the Water's Edge: Scotland's Seaside Links*. New York: Abbeville Press, 1997.

Peper, George. *Two Years in St. Andrews: At Home on the 18th Hole*. New York: Simon and Schuster, 2006.

Rubenstein, Lorne. *A Season in Dornoch: Golf and Life in the Scottish Highlands*. New York: Simon and Schuster, 2001.

Golf Courses in the United States

De St. Jorre, John. *Legendary Golf Clubs of the American East*. Wellington, Fla.: Edgeworth Editions, 2003.

Jenkins, Dan. *Sports Illustrated's the Best 18 Golf Holes in America*. New York: Delacorte, 1966.

Klein, Bradley S., and Golfweek Magazine. *A Walk in the Park: Golfweek's Guide to America's Best Classic and Modern Golf Courses*. Champaign, Ill.: Sports Publishing, 2004.

McCallen, Brian. *Golf Magazine's Top 100 Courses You Can Play*. New York: Harry N. Abrams, 1999.

Miller, Richard. *America's Greatest Golfing Resorts*. Indianapolis, Ind: Bobbs-Merrill, 1977.

Peper, George. *Golf Courses of the PGA Tour*. 3rd ed. New York: Harry N. Abrams, rev., 2004.

Pioppi, Anthony. *To the Nines*. Ann Arbor, Mich.: Sports Media Group, 2006.

Seelig, Pat. *Historic Golf Courses of America*. Dallas, Tex.: Taylor Publishing, 1994.

Stachura, Mike. *Classic American Courses: Golf's Enduring Designs, from Pot Bunkers to Island Greens*. United States: Carlton Books, 2003.

Golf Courses in South America

Golf Courses & Links de Argentina. 2nd ed. Buenos Aires: Versraeten Editores, rev., 2003.

GOLF AND COUNTRY CLUB HISTORIES

In recent years, it has become customary for golf and country clubs to publish history books to commemorate significant anniversaries—25th, 50th, 75th, and, particularly, centennial celebrations. These books typically contain information about the founding of the clubs, the design and construction of the golf courses, important competitions at the clubs, and significant club members. As such, these books are important sources of historical information for scholars and researchers. To date, more than 2,500 club histories have been published, and the number increases significantly each year. Thus, the following list is far from comprehensive, comprising, instead, books that have been published by the most prestigious clubs around the world. The list is arranged alphabetically by continent and country, then, alphabetically by club name within each country.

Clubs in Africa

(Royal Durban) Kerr, W. M. *The History of Royal Durban Golf Club*. Durban, South Africa: Privately printed, 1992.

Clubs in Australasia

Australia

(Kingston Heath) Williams, Stewart H. *The Test of Time: The History of Kingston Heath Golf Club*. South Melbourne: Macmillan Company, 1981.
(New South Wales) Armstrong, Geoff. *Golf at La Perouse: New South Wales Golf Club*. Alexandria, Australia: FPC Magazines, 2003.
(Royal Melbourne) Johnson, Joseph. *The Royal Melbourne Golf Club: A Centenary History*. Melbourne: Royal Melbourne Golf Club, 1991.

India

(Royal Calcutta) Suirita, Pearson. *The Royal Calcutta Golf Club: 1829–1979*. Calcutta: Royal Calcutta Golf Club, 1979.

Japan

(Hirono) Akiyama, Masakuni. *Hirono Golf Club*. Osaka: Interstate Well Golf Company, 1992 (text in Japanese).
(Tokyo) Tokyo Golf Club. *Tokyo Golf Club: 75 Year History*. Tokyo: Privately printed, 1988 (text in Japanese).

Clubs in Europe

England

(Royal Birkdale) Johnson, A. J. D. *The History of Royal Birkdale Golf Club*. Ascot, England: Springwood Books, 1988.
(Royal Liverpool) Behrend, John, and John Graham. *Golf at Hoylake: A Royal Liverpool Golf Club Anthology*. Droitwich, England: Grant Books, 1990.
(Royal Liverpool) Pinnington, Joe. *Mighty Winds . . . Mighty Champions: The Official History of the Royal Liverpool Golf Club*. Wirral, England: Guy Woodland, 2006.
(Royal Lytham and St. Annes) Nickson, E. A. *The Lytham Century and Beyond: A History of Royal Lytham and St Anne's Golf Club 1886–2000*. Lytham St. Annes, England: Privately printed, 2000.
(Royal St. Georges) Furber, F. R. *A Course for Heroes: A History of Royal St. George's Golf Club*. Sandwich, England: Privately printed, 1996.
(Sunningdale) Royds, Nicholas, ed. *The Sunningdale Centenary: 1900–2000*. Sunningdale, England: Privately printed, 2000.

(Sunningdale) Whitfield, John. *Sunningdale Golf Club: 1900–2000*. Sunningdale, England: Privately printed, 2000.

(Walton Heath) Pilley, Phil. *Heather and Heaven: Walton Heath Golf Club 1903–2003*. Tadworth, England: Privately printed, 2003.

(Wenthworth) Laidlaw, Renton, ed. *Wentworth: A Host of Happy Memories*. Virginia Water, England: Wentworth Club, 1993.

France

(Morfontaine) Dulout, Jean E. *Chronique 1930–1999: Au revoir Morfontaine*. Chantilly, France: Horarius and Cie, 2000.

Ireland

(Ballybunion) Redmond, John. *Ballybunion Golf Club: An Illustrated Centenary History 1893–1993*. Ballybunion, Ireland: Privately printed, 1993.

(Lahinch) Glynn, Enda. *A Century of Golf at Lahinch: 1892–1992*. Lahinch, Ireland: Privately printed, 1991.

(Royal County Down) Latham, Richard A. *The Evolution of the Links at the Royal County Down Golf Club*. Little Gaddesden, England: Radial Sports Publishing, 2006.

(Royal County Down) McCaw, Harry, and Brum Henderson. *Royal County Down Golf Club: The First Century*. Newcastle, Ireland: Privately printed, 1988.

(Royal Portrush) Bamford, J. L. (Ian). *Royal Portrush Golf Club: A History, 1888–1988*. Portrush, Ireland: Privately printed, 1988.

Scotland

(Carnoustie) Ford, Donald. *The Carnoustie Story*. Scotland: Donald Ford Images, 2006.

(Carnoustie) Goodale, Richard. *Experience Carnoustie Golf Links*. Stokesley, England: Personal Navigation Systems, 2007.

(Muirfield) Mair, Norman. *Muirfield, Home of the Honourable Company, 1774–1994*. Edinburgh: Mainstream Publishing, 1994.

(Muirfield) Pottinger, George. *Muirfield and the Honourable Company*. Edinburgh: Scottish Academic Press, 1972.

(Old Course, St. Andrews) Goodale, Richard. *Experience the Old Course, St. Andrews Links*. Stokesley, England: Personal Navigation Systems, 2006.

(Old Course, St. Andrews) Macpherson, Scott. *St. Andrews, The Evolution of the Old Course: The Impact on Golf of Time, Tradition and Technology*. Christchurch, New Zealand: Hazard Press, 2007.

(Old Course, St. Andrews) Muirhead, Desmond, and Tip Anderson. *How to Play the Old Course*. Newport Beach, Calif.: Newport Press, 2000.

(Prestwick) Smail, David Cameron, ed. *Prestwick Golf Club, Birthplace of the Open: The Club, the Members and the Championships 1851–1989*. Prestwick, Scotland: Privately printed, 1989.

(R&A) Behrend, John, and Peter N. Lewis. *Challenges & Champions: The Royal & Ancient Golf Club 1754–1883*. Vol. 1. St. Andrews, Scotland: The Royal & Ancient Golf Club of St. Andrews, 1998.

(R&A) Behrend, John, et al. *Champions and Guardians: The Royal & Ancient Golf Club 1884–1939*. Vol. 2. St. Andrews, Scotland: The Royal & Ancient Golf Club of St. Andrews, 2000.

(R&A) Everard, Henry Sterling Crawford. *A History of the Royal and Ancient Golf Club, St. Andrews from 1754–1900*. Edinburgh: William Blackwood, 1907.

(R&A) Lewis, Peter N., et al. *Art and Architecture of the Royal and Ancient Golf Club*. St. Andrews, Scotland: The Royal & Ancient Golf Club of St. Andrews, 1997.

(R&A) Salmond, J. G. *The Story of the R&A: Being the History of the First Two Hundred Years of the Royal and Ancient Golf Club of St. Andrews*. London: Macmillan, 1956.

(R&A) Steel, Donald, and Peter N. Lewis. *Traditions and Change: The Royal & Ancient Golf Club 1939–2004*. Vol. 3. St. Andrews, Scotland: The Royal & Ancient Golf Club of St. Andrews, 2004.

(Royal Dornoch) Macleod, John. *A History of the Royal Dornoch Golf Club 1897–1999*. Elgin, Scotland: Moravian, 2000.

(Royal Musselburgh) Ironside, Robert, and Harry Douglas. *Royal Musselburgh Golf Club: 1774–1999*. Prestonpans, Scotland: Royal Musselburgh Golf Club, 2000.

(Royal Troon) Crampsey, R. A. *The Breezy Links O'Troon: A History of Royal Troon Golf Club*. Troon, Scotland: Privately printed, 2001.

(Turnberry) Boyd, Jack, et al. *The Bonnie Links of Turnberry*. Turnberry, Scotland: Privately printed, 2004.

Spain

(Valderrama) Ortiz-Patino, Jaime. *Valderrama: The First Ten Years 1985–1995, The Making of Spain's Ryder Cup Course*. London: Privately printed, 1995.

(Valderrama) Ortiz-Patino, Jaime. *Valderrama: The Ryder Cup Years 1992–1997*. London: Privately printed, 1999.

Sweden

(Falsterbo) Bachmann, Rolk, et al. *Falsterbo Golfklubb 75 Aar: 1909–1984*. Falsterbo, Sweden: Falsterbo Golfklubb, 1984.

Clubs in North America

Canada

(Banff Springs) Hart, E. J. *Banff Springs Golf: A Heritage of the Royal and Ancient Game in the Canadian Rockies*. Banff, Canada: EJH Literary Enterprises, 1999.

(Hamilton) King, Leslie J. *One Hundred Years of Golf: The Hamilton Golf and Country Club 1894–1994*. Hamilton, Canada: Privately printed, 1993.

(Royal Montreal) Campbell, Duncan C., et al. *The Royal Montreal Golf Club: 1873–2000*. Montreal, Canada: Privately printed, 2001.

(St. George's G&CC) Barclay, James A. *St. George's Golf and Country Club's 75th Anniversary: 1929–2004*. Etobicoke, Canada: Privately printed, 2004.

United States

(Augusta National) Roberts, Clifford. *The Story of Augusta National Golf Club*. Garden City, N.Y.: Doubleday, 1976.

(Baltusrol) Trebus, Robert S., and Richard C. Wolffe Jr. *Baltusrol, 100 Years: The Centennial History of Baltusrol Golf Club*. Springfield, N.J.: Privately printed, 1995.

(Bandon Dunes) Goodwin, Stephen. *Dream Golf: The Making of Bandon Dunes*. Chapel Hills, N.C.: Algonquin Books, 2006.

(Bethpage Black) Jones, Rees, and John Paul Newport. *Bethpage Black Course Field Notes*. New York: T&L Golf, 2002.

(Bethpage Black) Young, Philip. *Golf for the People: Bethpage and the Black*. Bloomington, Ind.: 1st Books Library, 2002.

(Chicago) Goodner, Ross, and Ben Crenshaw. *Chicago Golf Club 1892–1992*. Wheaton, Ill.: Privately printed, 1991.

(Colonial) Pate, Russ. *The Legacy Continues: A 50-Year History of Colonial Country Club*. Fort Worth, Tex.: Privately printed, 1986.

(The Country Club, Brookline) De St. Jorre, John. *The Story of Golf at the Country Club*. Brookline, Mass.: Privately printed, 2009.

(Cypress Point) Lapham, Roger D., Jr. *The History of Cypress Point Club*. Pebble Beach, Calif.: Privately printed, 1996.

(Medinah) Cronin, Tim. *The Spirit of Medinah: 75 Years of Fellowship and Championships*. Medinah, Ill.: Privately printed, 2001.

(Merion) Tolhurst, Desmond, and Gary A. Galyean. *Golf at Merion*. Ardmore, Pa.: Privately printed, 2005.

(Oakland Hills) Perry, Bryon. *75 Years at Oakland Hills: A Jubilee Celebration*. Warren, Mich.: Perry and White, 1991.

(Oakmont) Parascenzo, Marino. *Oakmont 100 Years*. Oakmont, Pa.: Privately printed, 2003.

(Olympic) Skuse, Dick, ed. *The Olympic Club of San Francisco: 1860–1960*. San Francisco: Privately printed, 1960.

(Pebble Beach) Hotelling, Neal. *Pebble Beach Golf Links: The Official History*. Chelsea, Mich.: Sleeping Bear Press, 1999.

(Pebble Beach) March, Ray, and the editors of Golf Digest. *A Paradise Called Pebble Beach*. Trumbull, Conn.: Golf Digest, 1992.

(Pinehurst) Mandell, Richard. *Pinehurst, Home of American Golf: The Evolution of a Legend*. Pinehurst, N.C.: T. Eliot Press, 2007.

(Pinehurst) Pace, Lee. *The Spirit of Pinehurst*. Village of Pinehurst, N.C.: Pinehurst, 2004.

(Pine Valley) Finegan, James W. *Pine Valley Golf Club: A Unique Haven of the Game*. Clementon, N.J.: Privately printed, 2000.

(Prairie Dunes) Elliott, Mal. *Perry Maxwell's Prairie Dunes*. Chelsea, Mich.: Sleeping Bear Press, 2002.

(Riviera) Shackelford, Geoff. *The Riviera Country Club: A Definitive History*. Pacific Palisades, Calif.: Riviera Country Club, 1995.

(St. Andrew's) Martin, Harry Brownlaw, and A. B. Halliday. *St. Andrew's Golf Club, 1888–1938*. Hastings-on-Hudson, N.Y.: Privately printed, 1938.

(St. Andrew's) Tolhurst, Desmond. *St. Andrew's Golf Club: The Birth Place of American Golf*. Rye, N.Y.: Karjan Publishing, 1989.

(Seminole) Dodson, James. *The Story of Seminole*. June Beach, Fla.: Seminole Golf Club, 2007.

(Shinnecock Hills) Goodner, Ross. *The 75 Year History of Shinnecock Hills Golf Club*. Southampton, N.Y.: Privately printed, 1966.

(Shinnecock Hills) Peper, George. *Shinnecock Hills Golf Club 1891–1991*. Southampton, N.Y.: Privately printed, 1991.

(Southern Hills) Klappenbach, Ernie. *Southern Hills Country Club: A Fifty-Seven Year History 1935–1992*. Vol. 1–2. Tulsa, Okla.: Privately printed, 1992.

(TPC at Sawgrass) Dettlaff, Billy, ed. *A Storyteller's Guide: The Players and TPC Sawgrass*. Jacksonville, Fla.: PGA Tour, 2007.

(Winged Foot) Smith, Douglas Larue. *Winged Foot Story II: The Golf, the People, the Friendly Trees*. 2nd ed. Mamaroneck, N.Y.: Privately printed, rev., 1994.

Golf Clubhouses

Diedrich, Richard. *The 19th Hole: Architecture of the Golf Clubhouse*. Mulgrave, Australia: Images Publishing Group, 2008.

McKinney, Robert W. *The Clubhouse: A Brief History of the Golf Clubhouse with Accompanying Notes on Design Issues*. Houston, Tex.: M and R Press, 1997.

Wendehack, Clifford Charles. *Golf and Country Clubs: A Survey of the Requirements of Planning, Construction and Equipment of the Modern Club House*. New York: William Helburn, 1929.

Municipal Golf Courses

American Institute of Park Executives. *Public Golf*. Chicago, Ill.: American Institute of Park Executives, n.d.

Amick, William. *Planning the Municipal Golf Course*. Chicago, Ill.: American Society of Golf Course Architects, n.d.

Colt, H. S., and C. H. Alison. *Municipal Golf Courses*. East Hendred, England: Privately printed, n.d.

Cook, Walter L., and Roy Holland. *Public Golf Courses: A Guide to Their Development and Operation*. Wheeling, W.Va.: American Institute of Park Executives, 1964.

Fitzpatrick, F. Stuart. *Municipal Golf Courses*. Washington, D.C.: Chamber of Commerce of the U.S. Civic Development Department, 1930.

National Golf Foundation. *Golf Course Operations and Maintenance Survey Report: Municipal Edition*. Jupiter, Fla.: National Golf Foundation, 1993.

———. *Guidelines of Planning and Developing a Public Golf Course*. Jupiter, Fla.: National Golf Foundation, n.d.

———. *Municipal Golf Facilities: A Growth Industry*. 2nd ed. Jupiter, Fla.: National Golf Foundation, 1999.

Public Links Section (USGA). *Municipal and Public Golf Courses in the United States, with Statistical Information*. New York: U.S. Golf Association, various dates.

Rainmaker Golf Development. *Issues in Municipal Golf Development*. Columbia, Md.: Privately printed, 2005.

THE ART OF THE GAME

Golf Art

Darwin, Bernard. *A Golfer's Gallery by Old Masters*. London: Country Life, 1927.

Henderson, Ian T., and David I Stirk. *Shortspoon—Major F. P. Hopkins 1830–1913, Golfing Artist and Journalist*. Crawley, England: Henderson and Stirk, 1984.

Hobbs, Michael. *Golf: A Visual History*. London: Brian Trodd, 1991.

Langton, Harry. *Thomas Hodge: The Golf Artist of St. Andrews*. London: Sports Design International, 2000.

Lewis, Peter N., and Angela D. Howe. *The Golfers: The Story behind the Painting*. Edinburgh: The Trustees of the National Galleries of Scotland, 2004.

Pilley, Phil, ed. *Golfing Art*. London: Stanley Paul, 1988.

Golf Literature

Hamilton, David. *The Thorn Tree Clique: A New Analysis of Mathieson's Poem "The Goff."* Kilmacolm, Scotland: The Partick Press, 2001.

Mathison, Thomas. *"The Goff": A Heroi-Comical Poem in Three Cantos*. Edinburgh: Privately printed, 1743.

Murphy, Michael. *Golf in the Kingdom*. New York: Viking Press, 1972.

Updike, John. *Golf Dreams: Writings on Golf*. New York: Alfred A. Knopf, 1996.

Wind, Herbert Warren. *An Introduction to the Literature of Golf*. New York: Ailsa, 1996.

Wodehouse, P. G. *The Golf Omnibus*. London: Barrie and Jenkins, 1973 (Contains selections from *Divots*, 1927; *Golf Without Tears*, 1924; *The Clicking of Cuthbert*, 1922; and *The Heart of a Goof*, 1926).

Anthologies of Noted Authors

Boswell, Thomas. *Strokes of Genius*. Garden City, N.Y.: Doubleday, 1987.

Bowden, Ken. *Teeing Off: Players, Techniques, Characters, Experiences and Reflections from a Lifetime inside Golf*. Chicago, Ill.: Triumph Books, 2008.

Cooke, Alistair. *Golf: The Marvelous Mania*. New York: Arcade Publishing, 2008.

Darwin, Bernard. *Bernard Darwin on Golf*. Guilford, Conn.: Lyons, 2003.

Dobereiner, Peter. *For the Love of Golf*. London: Stanley Paul, 1981.

Garrity, John. *Tiger 2.0 . . . and Other Great Stories from the World of Golf*. New York: Sports Illustrated Books, 2008.

Jenkins, Dan. *The Dogged Victims of Inexorable Fate*. Boston: Little, Brown, 1970.

———. *Fairways and Greens*. New York: Doubleday, 1994.

———. *Jenkins at the Majors: Sixty Years of the World's Best Golf Writing*. New York: Doubleday, 2009.

Longhurst, Henry. *The Essential Henry Longhurst*. London: Willow, 1988.

Price, Charles. *Golfer-at-Large*. New York: Antheneum, 1982.

Rubenstein, Lorne. *This Round's On Me: Lorne Rubenstein on Golf*. Toronto: McClelland and Stewart, 2009.

Stanley, Louis T. *Fresh Fairways*. London: Methuen, 1949.

———. *Green Fairways*. London: Methuen, 1947.

Tait, Alastair. *Broken Fairways*. United Kingdom: Dolman Scott, 2008.

Ward-Thomas, Pat. *The Long Green Fairway*. London: Hodder and Stoughton, 1966.

Wind, Herbert Warren. *The Complete Golfer*. New York: Simon and Schuster, 1954.

———. *Following Through: Herbert Warren Wind on Golf*. New York: Ticknor and Fields, 1985.

GENERAL REFERENCE

Barrett, Ted. *The Complete Encyclopedia of Golf*. Chicago, Ill.: Triumph Books, 2005.

Billian, Douglas C. *Golf Book of Records*. Atlanta, Ga.: Billian Publishing, 1989.

Bortstein, Larry. *Who's Who in Golf*. N.p.: Bert Randolph Sugar, 1972.

Campbell, Malcolm. *The New Encyclopedia of Golf*. 3rd ed. New York: Dorling Kindersley, 2001.

Corcoran, Michael. *The Golf Dictionary: A Guide to the Language and Lingo of the Game*. Dallas, Tex.: Taylor Publishing, 1997.

Cox, Gregg M. *Do You Speak Golf? International Golfer's Language Guide*. Vancouver, Wash.: Pandemic International, 1991.

Davies, Peter. *The Historical Dictionary of Golfing Terms: From 1500 to the Present*. New York: Michael Kesend, 1992.

Donovan, Richard E., and Rand Jerris. *The Game of Golf and the Printed Word, 1566–2005:A Bibliography of Golf Literature in the English Language*. Endicott, N.Y.: Castalio Press, 2006.

Evans, Webster. *Encyclopedia of Golf*. 3rd ed. London: Robert Hale, rev., 1980.

Gibson, Nevin. *The Encyclopedia of Golf: With the Official All-Time Records*. 2nd ed. New York: A. S. Barnes, rev., 1964.

Golf Magazine. *Golf Magazine's Encyclopedia of Golf*. 4th ed. New York: HarperCollins, rev., 1993.

Lawrenson, Derek. *The Complete Encyclopedia of Golf*. London: Carlton, 1999.

Marrandette, David G. *Golf Playoffs: A Sourcebook of Major Championships Men's and Women's Amateur and Professional Playoffs, 1876–1990*. Jefferson, N.C.: McFarland, 1991.

Morrison, Ian. *The Hamlyn Encyclopedia of Golf*. Twickenham, England: Hamlyn, 1986.

Murdoch, Joseph S. F. *The Library of Golf 1743–1966: A Bibliography of Golf Books*. Detroit, Mich.: Gale Research, 1968.

Murdoch, Joseph S. F., and Janet Seagle. *Golf: A Guide to Information Sources*. Detroit, Mich.: Gale Research, 1979.

Plumridge, Chris. *The Illustrated Encyclopedia of World Golf*. New York: Exeter Books, 1988.

Ryde, Peter, ed. *Royal and Ancient Championship Records 1860–1980*. St. Andrews, Scotland: The Royal and Ancient Golf Club of St. Andrews, 1981.

Scharff, Robert, and the editors of Golf Magazine. *Golf Magazine's Encyclopedia of Golf*. 2nd ed. New York: Harper and Row, rev., 1973.

Steel, Donald, and Peter Ryde. *The Encyclopedia of Golf*. New York: Viking Press, 1975.

Summers, David, ed. *The Golf Book: The Players, the Gear, the Strokes, the Courses, the Championships*. New York: DK Publishing, 2008.

Swales, Andrew. *The Guinness Book of Golf Facts and Feats*. Enfield, England: Guinness Publishing, 1996.

U.S. Golf Association. *Record Book of the USGA Championships*. New York and Far Hills, N.J.: U.S. Golf Association, various years.

Wexler, Daniel. *The Golfer's Library: A Reader's Guide to Three Centuries of Golf Literature*. Ann Arbor, Mich.: Sports Media Group, 2004.

MAGAZINES

From the late 19th century to the present, more than 800 golf periodicals in more than 20 languages have been published around the world. Many of these appeared only briefly, but others enjoyed long publication histories, some of which continue today. Due to the often brief existence of these periodicals, complete and accurate publication records are not available for the great majority of these titles. Yet, they are important sources of information for anyone conducting research on the game. The largest public collections of golf periodicals are maintained by the USGA Museum, Library of Congress, and British Library. The USGA Museum, for example, holds complete runs or individual issues of more than 750 different titles. Researchers wishing to pursue these materials can consult the online catalogs for these institutions.

British Library: catalogue.bl.uk/
Library of Congress: catalog.loc.gov/
USGA Museum: www.usgamuseum.com/researchers/usga_library/

WEBSITES

Amateurgolf.com: www.amateurgolf.com
American Junior Golf Association: www.ajga.org
American Society of Golf Course Architects: www.asgca.org
Asian Tour: www.asiantour.com
Australian PGA Tour: www.pgatour.com.au
British Open: www.opengolf.com
Club Managers Association of America: www.cmaa.org
English Golf Union: www.englishgolfunion.org
European Golf Association: www.ega-golf.ch
European Institute of Golf Course Architects: www.eigca.org
European Tour: www.europeantour.com
The First Tee: www.thefirsttee.org
Futures Golf Tour: www.futurestour.com
The Golf Channel: www.thegolfchannel.com
Golf Course Builders Association of America: www.gcbaa.org
Golf Course Superintendents Association of America: www.gcsaa.org
Golf Range Association of America: www.golfrange.org
Golf 20/20: www.golf2020.com
Golf Union of Ireland: www.gui.ie
International Association of Golf Administrators: www.iaga.org
Japanese Tour: www.jgto.org
Juniorlinks: www.juniorlinks.com
Ladies European Tour: www.ladieseuropeantour.com
Ladies Golf Union: wwwluga.org
LPGA: www.lpga.com
The Masters: www.masters.com
National Golf Course Owners Association: www.ngcoa.org
National Golf Foundation: www.ngf.org

PGA of America: www.pga.com
PGA of Europe: www.pgae.com
PGA Tour: www.pgatour.com
Ping American College Golf Guide: www.collegegolf.com
Professional Caddies Association: www.pcaworldwide.com
Professional Clubmakers' Society: www.proclubmakers.org
Professional Golf Teachers Association of America: www.pgtaa.com
The R&A Ltd.: www.randa.org
Royal Canadian Golf Association: www.rcga.org
Ryder Cup: www.rydercup.com
Scottish Golf Union: www.scottishgolfunion.org
South Africa Tour: www.sunshinetour.com
Tiger Woods Foundation: www.twfound.org
U.S. Golf Association: www.usga.org
U.S. Open Championship: www.usopen.com
World Golf Foundation: www.worldgolffoundation.org
Other important sites for current golf news and information include: ESPN .com, Golf.com, GolfDigest.com, Golfweek.com and SI.com.

RESEARCH LIBRARIES AND INFORMATION SOURCES

British Golf Museum, St. Andrews, Scotland
Canadian Golf Hall of Fame and Museum, Oakville, Ontario, Canada
Herbert Warren Wind Papers, Yale University Libraries, New Haven, Connecticut
LA 84 Foundation, Los Angeles, California
Library of Congress, Washington, District of Columbia
Michigan State University Turfgrass Information Center, East Lansing, Michigan
National Golf Foundation, Jupiter, Florida
National Library of Scotland, Edinburgh, Scotland
New York Public Library, New York, New York
PGA Historical Center, Port St. Lucie, Florida
Tufts Archives, Village of Pinehurst, North Carolina
University of St. Andrews Library, St. Andrews, Scotland
USGA Museum, Far Hills, New Jersey

About the Authors

Bill Mallon, M.D., is an orthopedic surgeon who is in his second career. In his first career, he played for four years (1976–1979) on the U.S. PGA Tour. During his golf career, he won more than 40 tournaments, both as an amateur and as a professional. In addition to his medical career, he has written extensively on sports history, notably on the Olympics. He is the author of a series of books on the earliest Olympic Games (1896–1920) and is a founding member and former president of the International Society of Olympic Historians. For his contributions to the Olympic movement, he received the Olympic Order in Silver in 2001. He has coauthored three editions of the *Historical Dictionary of the Olympic Movement*. He has written several medical books and articles related to golf. Since 2008, he has served as the editor in chief of the *Journal of Shoulder and Elbow Surgery*.

Rand Jerris has been the director of the USGA Museum in Far Hills, New Jersey, since 2002. He has served as director of communications for the USGA since 2009. He holds a Ph.D. in art and archaeology from Princeton University, where his dissertation research focused on the architecture and decoration of early medieval churches in the Swiss, Austrian, and Italian Alps. He is the author of *Golf's Golden Age: Robert T. Jones Jr. and the Legendary Players of the '10s, '20s, and '30s* and coauthor, with Richard E. Donovan, of *The Game of Golf and the Printed Word: 1566–2005*. He has contributed numerous articles on golf history and art history to a variety of popular magazines and academic journals. He served two years on the board of the International Sports Heritage Association. For his contributions to golf history, he received the Joseph Murdoch Medal from the British Golf Collectors Society in 2007.